Merriam-Webster's Vocabulary Builder

Second Edition

Mary Wood Cornog

Merriam-Webster, Incorporated
Springfield, Massachusetts

A GENUINE MERRIAM-WEBSTER

The name *Webster* alone is no guarantee of excellence. It is used by a number of publishers and may serve mainly to mislead an unwary buyer.

Merriam-Webster™ is the name you should look for when you consider the purchase of dictionaries or other fine reference books. It carries the reputation of a company that has been publishing since 1831 and is your assurance of quality and authority.

INTRODUCTION
to the Second Edition

Merriam-Webster's Vocabulary Builder is designed to achieve two goals: (1) to add a large number of words to your permanent working vocabulary, and (2) to teach the most useful of the classical word-building roots to help you continue expanding your vocabulary in the future.

To achieve these goals, *Merriam-Webster's Vocabulary Builder* employs an original approach that takes into account how people learn and remember. Some vocabulary builders simply present their words in alphabetical order; some provide little or no discussion of the words and how to use them; and a few even fail to show the kinds of sentences in which the words usually appear. But memorizing a series of random and unrelated things can be difficult and time-consuming. The fact is that we tend to remember words easily and naturally when they appear in some meaningful context, when they've been shown to be useful and therefore worth remembering, and when they've been properly explained to us. Knowing precisely how to use a word is just as important as knowing what it means.

Greek and Latin have been the sources of most of the words in the English language (the third principal source being the family of Germanic languages). All these words were added to the language long after the fall of the Roman empire, and more continue to be added to this day, with most new words—especially those in the sciences—still making use of Greek and Latin roots. A knowledge of Greek and Latin roots will not only help you remember the meanings of the words in this book but will help you guess at the meanings of new words that you run into elsewhere. Remember what a root means and you'll have at least a fighting chance of understanding a word in which it appears.

The roots in this book are only a fraction of those that exist, but they include almost all the roots that have produced the largest number of common English words. All these roots (sometimes called *stems*) formed parts of Greek and Latin words. Some are shown in more than one form (for example, CRAC/CRAT), which means that they changed form in the original language, just as *buy* and *bought* are forms of the same English word.

Each of the more than 250 roots in this book is followed by four words based on the root. Each group of eight words (two roots) is followed by two quizzes. Every fifth group of words is a special eight-word section which may contain words based on classical mythology or history, words borrowed directly from Greek or Latin, or other special categories of terms. Each set of 40 words makes up a unit. Thus, the 30 units in the book discuss in detail a total of 1,200 words. In addition, the brief paragraphs discussing each word include in italics many words closely related to the main words. So mastering a single word (for example, *compel*) can increase your vocabulary by several words (in this case, *compelling*, *compulsion*, and *compulsive*).

The words presented here aren't all on the same level of difficulty—some are quite simple and some are truly challenging—but the great majority are words that could be encountered on the SAT and similar standardized tests. Most of them are in the vocabularies of well-educated Americans, including professionals such as scientists, lawyers, professors, and doctors. Even the words you feel familiar with may only have a place in your *recognition* vocabulary—that is, the words you recognize when you see or hear them but don't actually use in your own speech and writing.

Each main word is followed by its most common pronunciation. Any pronunciation symbols unfamiliar to you can be learned easily by referring to the Pronunciation Symbols table on page vii.

The definition comes next. We've tried to provide only the most common senses or meanings of each word, in simple and straightforward language, and no more than two definitions of any word are given. (A more complete range of definitions can be found in a college dictionary such as *Merriam-Webster's Collegiate Dictionary*.)

An example sentence marked with a bullet (•) follows the definition. This sentence by itself can indicate a great deal about the word, including the kind of sentence in which it often appears. It can also serve as a memory aid; when you meet the word in the future, you may recall the example sentence more easily than the definition.

An explanatory paragraph rounds out each entry. The paragraph may do a number of things: It may tell you what else you need to know in order to use the word intelligently and correctly, when the definition and example sentence aren't enough. It may tell you more about the word's roots and its history. It may discuss additional meanings or provide additional example sentences. It may demonstrate the use of closely related words. And it may provide an informative or entertaining glimpse into a subject related to the word. The intention is to make you as comfortable as possible with each word in turn and to enable you to start using it immediately, without fear of embarrassment.

The quizzes following each eight-word group, along with the review quizzes at the end of each unit, will test your memory. Many of them ask you to fill in a blank in a sentence. Others require you to identify *synonyms* (words with the same or very similar meaning) or *antonyms* (words with the opposite meaning). Perhaps most difficult are the *analogies*, which ask that you choose the word that will make the relationship between the last two words the same as the relationship between the first two. Thus, you may be asked to complete the analogy "calculate : count :: expend : _____" (which can be read as "*Calculate* is to *count* as *expend* is to _____") by choosing one of four words: *stretch*, *speculate*, *pay*, and *explode*. Since *calculate* and *count* are nearly synonyms, you will choose a near synonym for *expend,* so the correct answer is *pay.*

Studies have shown that the only way a new word will remain alive in your vocabulary is if it's regularly reinforced through use and through reading. Learn the word here and look and listen for it elsewhere; you'll probably find yourself running into it frequently, just as when you've bought a new car you soon realize how many other people own the same model.

Carry this book in your shoulder bag or leave it on your night table. Whenever you find yourself with a few minutes to spare, open it to the beginning of a brief root group. (There's no real need to read the units in any particular order, since each unit is entirely self-contained. However, studying the book straight through from the beginning will ensure that you make maximum use of it.) Pick a single word or a four-word group or an eight-word section; study it, test yourself, and then try making up new sentences for each word. Be sure to pronounce every new word aloud at least once, along with its definition.

Start using the words immediately. As soon as you feel confident with a word, start trying to work it into your writing wherever appropriate—your papers and reports, your diary and your poetry. An old saying goes, "Use it three times and it's yours." That may be, but don't stop at three. Make the words part of your *working* vocabulary, the words that you can not only recognize when you see or hear them but that you can comfortably call on whenever you need them. Astonish your friends, amaze your relatives, astound *yourself* (while trying not to be too much of a show-off)—and have fun!

———————

Acknowledgments: The first edition of this book, written by Mary Wood Cornog, also benefited from the contributions of numerous members of the Merriam-Webster staff, including Michael G. Belanger, Brett P. Palmer, Stephen J. Perrault, and Mark A. Stevens. This new edition was edited by Mark A. Stevens, with assistance from C. Roger Davis and with the support and encouragement of Merriam-Webster's president and publisher, John M. Morse.

PRONUNCIATION SYMBOLS

ə — banana, collide, abut

ˈə, ˌə — humdrum, abut

ᵊ — immediately preceding \l\, \n\, \m\, \ŋ\, as in battle, mitten, eaten, and sometimes open \ˈō-pᵊm\, lock and key \-ᵊŋ-\

ər — further, merger, bird

a — mat, map, mad, gag, snap, patch

ā — . day, fade, date, aorta, drape, cape

ä — bother, cot

är — car, heart, bazaar, bizarre

aù — now, loud, out

b — baby, rib

ch — chin, nature \ˈnā-chər\

d — did, adder

e — bet, bed, peck

er — bare, fair, wear, millionaire

ē — easy, mealy

f — fifty, cuff

g — go, big, gift

h — hat, ahead

i — tip, banish, active

ir — near, deer, mere, pier

ī — site, side, buy, tripe

j — job, gem, edge, join, judge

k — kin, cook, ache

l — lily, pool

m — murmur, dim, nymph

n — no, own

ⁿ — indicates that a preceding vowel or diphthong is pronounced with the nasal passages open, as in French *un bon vin blanc* \œⁿ-bōⁿ-vaⁿ-bläⁿ\

ŋ — sing \ˈsiŋ\, singer \ˈsiŋ-ər\, finger \ˈfiŋ-gər\, ink \ˈiŋk\

ō — bone, know, beau

ò — saw, all, gnaw, caught

òi — coin, destroy

òr — boar, port, door, shore

p — pepper, lip

r — red, rarity

s — source, less

sh — as in shy, mission, machine, special

t — tie, attack, late, later, latter

th — as in thin, ether

th — then, either, this

ü — rule, youth, union \ˈyün-yən\, few \ˈfyü\

ù — pull, wood, book

ùr — boor, tour, insure

v — vivid, give

w — we, away

y — yard, young, cue \ˈkyü\, mute\ ˈmyüt\, union \ˈyün-yən\

z — zone, raise

zh — as in vision, azure \ˈa-zhər\

\ — backslash used in pairs to mark the beginning and end of a transcription: \ˈpen\

ˈ — mark preceding a syllable with primary (strongest) stress: \ˈpen-mən-ˌship\

ˌ — mark preceding a syllable with secondary (medium) stress: \ˈpen-mən-ˌship\

- — mark of syllable division

UNIT

1

BENE is Latin for "well." A *benefit* is a good result or effect. Something *beneficial* produces good results or effects. The Latin root can be heard in other languages as well: "Good!" or "Fine!" in Spanish is "Bueno!"; in French, it's "Bon!"; and in Italian, just say "Bene!"

---

benediction \ˌbe-nə-ˈdik-shən\ A prayer that asks for God's blessing, especially a prayer that concludes a worship service.

• The moment the bishop had finished his benediction, she squeezed quickly out of her row and darted out the cathedral's side entrance.

In *benediction*, the *bene* root is joined by another Latin root, *dictio*, "speaking" (see DICT, p. 272), so the word's meaning becomes something like "well-wishing." Perhaps the best-known benediction is the so-called Aaronic Benediction from the Bible, which begins, "May the Lord bless you and keep you." An important section of the Catholic Mass was traditionally known as the *Benedictus*, after its first word (meaning "blessed"). It was St. *Benedict* who organized the first Christian monasteries; many Christians have been baptized Benedict in his honor, and 16 popes have taken it as their papal name.

benefactor \ˈbe-nə-ˌfak-tər\ Someone who helps another person or group, especially by giving money.

- An anonymous benefactor had given $15 million to establish an ecological institute at the university.

A benefactor may be involved in almost any field. One may endow a scholarship fund; another may give money to expand a library; still another may leave a generous sum to a hospital in her will. The famous *benefactions* of John D. Rockefeller included the gifts that established the University of Chicago, the Rockefeller Foundation, and Rockefeller University. Many benefactors have reported that giving away their money turned out to be the most rewarding thing they ever did.

beneficiary \ˌbe-nə-ˈfi-shē-ˌer-ē\ A person or organization that benefits or is expected to benefit from something, especially one that receives money or property when someone dies.

- Living in a trailer in near-poverty, she received word in the mail that her father had died, naming her as the sole beneficiary of his life-insurance policy.

Beneficiary is often used in connection with life insurance, but it shows up in many other contexts as well. A college may be the beneficiary of a private donation. Your uncle's will may make a church his sole beneficiary, in which case all his money and property will go to it when he dies. A "third-party beneficiary" of a contract is a person (often a child) who the people signing the contract (which is usually an insurance policy or an employee-benefit plan) want to benefit from it. In a more general way, a small business may be a beneficiary of changes to the tax code, or a restaurant may be the beneficiary when the one across the street closes down and its whole lunch crowd starts coming in.

benevolence \bə-ˈnev-ləns\ Kindness, generosity.

- In those financially desperate years, the young couple was saved only by the benevolence of her elderly great-uncle.

Part of *benevolence* comes from the Latin root meaning "wish." The novels of Charles Dickens often include a *benevolent* figure who rescues the main characters at some point—Mr. Brownlow in *Oliver Twist*, Abel Magwitch in *David Copperfield*, Mr. Jarndyce in Bleak House, Ebenezer Scrooge in *A Christmas Carol*. To be benevolent, it helps to have money, but it's not necessary; kind assistance of a non-financial sort may turn out to be lifesaving benevolence as well.

AM comes from the Latin *amare*, "to love." The Roman god of love was known by two different names, Cupid and *Amor. Amiable* means "friendly or good-natured," and *amigo* is Spanish for "friend."

amicable \ˈa-mi-kə-bəl\ Friendly, peaceful.

- Their relations with their in-laws were generally amicable, despite some bickering during the holidays.

Amicable often describes relations between two groups, or especially two nations—for example, the United States and Canada, which are proud of sharing the longest unguarded border in the world. So we often speak of an amicable meeting or an amicable settlement. When *amicable* describes more personal relations, it may indicate a rather formal friendliness. But it's always nice when two friends who've been quarreling manage to have an amicable conversation and to say amicable good-byes at the end.

enamored \i-ˈna-mərd\ Charmed or fascinated; inflamed with love.

- Rebecca quickly became enamored of the town's rustic surroundings, its slow pace, and its eccentric characters.

Computer hackers are always enamored of their new programs and games. Millions of readers have found themselves enamored with Jane Austen's novels. And Romeo and Juliet were, of course, utterly enamored of each other. But we also often use the word in negative contexts: A friend at work may complain that she's not enamored of the new boss, and when you start talking about how you're not enamored with the neighbors it may be time to move. (Note that both *of* and *with* are commonly used after *enamored*.)

amorous \ˈa-mə-rəs\ Having or showing strong feelings of attraction or love.

- It turned out that the amorous Congressman had gotten his girlfriend a good job and was paying for her apartment.

A couple smooching on a park bench could be called amorous, or a young married couple who are always hugging and kissing. But the word is often used a bit sarcastically, as when a tabloid newspaper gets hold of some scandalous photos and calls the participants "the amorous pair." In such cases, we may be encouraged to think the attraction is more physical than emotional.

paramour \\'per-ə-ˌmùr\ A lover, often secret, not allowed by law or custom.

• He had been coming to the house for two years before her brothers realized that he was actually the paramour of their shy and withdrawn sister.

Paramour came to English from French (a language based on Latin), though the modern French don't use the word. Since *par amour* meant "through love," it implies a relationship based solely on love, often physical love, rather than on social custom or ceremony. So today it tends to refer to the lover of a married man or woman, but may be used for any lover who isn't obeying the social rules.

Quizzes

A. Choose the closest synonym:

1. beneficiary   a. benefit b. prayer c. recipient
       d. contributor
2. amorous   a. friendly b. sympathetic c. loving d. kind
3. benediction   a. blessing b. gift c. saint d. favor
4. amicable   a. difficult b. friendly c. curious d. lazy
5. enamored   a. strengthened b. engaged c. fond d. free
6. benefactor   a. supporter b. priest c. donation
       d. kindness
7. paramour   a. lover b. husband c. heaven d. affection
8. benevolence   a. value b. kindness c. luck d. approval

B. Complete the analogy:

1. charming : enchanting :: amorous : _____
       a. sublime b. pleasant c. likeable d. passionate
2. greeting : farewell :: benediction : _____
       a. motto b. speech c. curse d. saying
3. lender : borrower :: benefactor : _____
       a. giver b. beneficiary c. participant d. partner
4. gentle : tender :: enamored : _____
       a. lively b. charmed c. cozy d. enraged
5. liking : appreciation :: benevolence : _____
       a. opinion b. sentimentality c. interest d. generosity

---

6. frozen : boiling :: amicable : _____
    a. calm b. comfortable c. shy d. unfriendly
7. patient : doctor :: beneficiary : _____
    a. tycoon b. investor c. lover d. benefactor
8. friend : companion :: paramour : _____
    a. lover b. theater c. mother d. wife

BELL comes from the Latin word meaning "war." *Bellona* was the little-known Roman goddess of war; her husband, Mars, was the god of war.

---

antebellum \ˌan-ti-ˈbe-ləm\ Existing before a war, especially before the American Civil War (1861–65).

• When World War I was over, the French nobility found it impossible to return to their extravagant antebellum way of life.

Even countries that win a war often end up worse off than they had been before, and the losers almost always do. So *antebellum* often summons up images of ease, elegance, and entertainment that disappeared in the postwar years. In the American South, the antebellum way of life depended on a social structure, based on slavery, that collapsed after the Civil War; Margaret Mitchell's *Gone with the Wind* shows the nostalgia and bitterness felt by wealthy Southerners after the war more than the relief and anticipation experienced by those released from slavery. In Europe, World War I shattered the grand life of the upper classes, even in victorious France and Britain, and changed society hugely in the space of just four years.

bellicose \ˈbe-li-ˌkōs\ Warlike, aggressive, quarrelsome.

• The more bellicose party always got elected whenever there was tension along the border and the public believed that military action would lead to security.

Since *bellicose* describes an attitude that hopes for actual war, the word is generally applied to nations and their leaders. In the 20th century, it was commonly used to describe such figures as Germany's Kaiser Wilhelm, Italy's Benito Mussolini, and Japan's General Tojo, leaders who believed their countries had everything to gain by starting wars. The international relations of a nation with a bellicose foreign policy tend to be stormy and difficult, and *bellicosity* usually makes the rest of the world very uneasy.

belligerence \bə-'li-jə-rəns\ Aggressiveness, combativeness.

- The belligerence in Turner's voice told them that the warning was a serious threat.

Unlike *bellicose* and *bellicosity*, the word *belligerence* can be used at every level from the personal to the global. The belligerence of Marlon Brando's performances as the violent Stanley Kowalski in *A Streetcar Named Desire* electrified the country in the 1940s and '50s. At the same time, *belligerent* speeches by leaders of the Soviet Union and the United States throughout the Cold War were keeping the world on edge. *Belligerent* is even a noun; the terrible war in the Congo in recent years, for example, has involved seven nations as belligerents.

rebellion \ri-'bel-yən\ Open defiance and opposition, sometimes armed, to a person or thing in authority.

- A student rebellion that afternoon in Room 13 resulted in the new substitute teacher racing out of the building in tears.

Plenty of teenagers *rebel* against their parents in all kinds of ways. But a rebellion usually involves a group. Armed rebellions are usually put down by a country's armed forces, or at least kept from expanding beyond a small area. The American War of Independence was first viewed by the British as a minor rebellion that would soon run its course, but this particular rebellion led to a full-fledged revolution—that is, the overthrow of a government. Rebellion, armed or otherwise, has often alerted those in power that those they control are very unhappy.

PAC is related to the Latin words for "agree" and "peace." The *Pacific Ocean*—that is, the "Peaceful Ocean"—was named by Ferdinand Magellan because it seemed so calm after he had sailed through the storms near Cape Horn. (Magellan obviously had never witnessed a Pacific typhoon.)

pacify \'pa-sə-ˌfī\ (1) To soothe anger or agitation. (2) To subdue by armed action.

- It took the police hours to pacify the angry demonstrators.

Someone stirred up by a strong emotion can usually be pacified by some kind words and the removal of its causes. Unhappy babies are often given a rubber *pacifier* for sucking to make them stop crying. During the Vietnam War, *pacification* of an area meant using armed force to drive out the enemy, which might be followed by bringing the local people over to our side by building schools and providing social services. But an army can often bring "peace" by pure force, without soothing anyone's emotions.

pacifist \\'pa-sə-fist\\ A person opposed to war or violence, especially someone who refuses to bear arms or to fight, on moral or religious grounds.

• Her grandfather had fought in the Marines in World War II, but in his later years he had become almost a pacifist, opposing every war for one reason or another.

The Quakers and the Jehovah's Witnesses are *pacifist* religious groups, and Henry David Thoreau and Martin Luther King are probably the most famous American pacifists. Like these groups and individuals, pacifists haven't always met with sympathy or understanding. Refusing to fight ever, for any reason, calls for strong faith in one's own moral or religious convictions, since *pacifism* during wartime has often gotten people persecuted and even thrown in prison.

pact \\'pakt\\ An agreement between two or more people or groups; a treaty or formal agreement between nations to deal with a problem or to resolve a dispute.

• The girls made a pact never to reveal what had happened on that terrifying night in the abandoned house.

Pact has "peace" at its root because a pact often ends a period of unfriendly relations. The word is generally used in the field of international relations, where diplomats may speak of an "arms pact," a "trade pact," or a "fishing-rights pact." But it may also be used for any solemn agreement or promise between two people; after all, whenever two parties shake hands on a deal, they're not about to go to war with each other.

pace \\'pā-sē\\ Contrary to the opinion of.

• She had only three husbands, *pace* some Hollywood historians who claim she had as many as six.

This word looks like another that is much more familiar, but notice how it's pronounced. It is used only by intellectuals, and often printed in italics so that the reader doesn't mistake it for the other word. Writers use it when correcting an opinion that many people believe; for example, "The costs of the program, *pace* some commentators, will not be significant." So what does *pace* have to do with peace? Because it says "Peace to them (that is, to the people I'm mentioning)—I don't want to start an argument; I just want to correct the facts."

Quizzes

A. Match the word on the left to the correct definition on the right:

1.	antebellum	a.	quarrelsome
2.	*pace*	b.	solemn agreement
3.	rebellion	c.	to make peaceful
4.	pacify	d.	before the war
5.	pacifist	e.	aggressiveness
6.	belligerence	f.	opposition to authority
7.	pact	g.	contrary to the opinion of
8.	bellicose	h.	one who opposes war

B. Fill in each blank with the correct letter:

a.	antebellum	e.	rebellion
b.	pacifist	f.	bellicose
c.	pact	g.	pacify
d.	*pace*	h.	belligerence

1. The native _____ began at midnight, when a gang of youths massacred the Newton family and set the house afire.
2. The grand _____ mansion has hardly been altered since it was built in 1841.
3. The Senate Republicans, outraged by their treatment, were in a _____ mood.
4. _____ some of the younger scholars, no good evidence has been found that Japan was involved in the incident.
5. The cease-fire _____ that had been reached with such effort was shattered by the news of the slaughter.

---

6. Their relations during the divorce proceedings had been mostly friendly, so his _____ in the judge's chambers surprised her.
7. The world watched in amazement as the gentle _____ Gandhi won India its independence with almost no bloodshed.
8. Her soft lullabies could always _____ the unhappy infant.

CRIM comes from the Latin words for "fault or crime" or "accusation." It's obvious where the root shows up most commonly in English. A *crime* is an act forbidden by the government, which the government itself will punish you for, and for which you may be branded a *criminal*. A crime is usually more serious than a *tort* (see TORT, p. 488), a "civil wrong" for which the wronged person must himself sue if he wants to get repaid in some way.

---

criminology \ˌkri-mə-ˈnä-lə-jē\ The study of crime, criminals, law enforcement, and punishment.

• His growing interest in criminology led him to become a probation officer.

Criminology includes the study of all aspects of crime and law enforcement—criminal psychology, the social setting of crime, prohibition and prevention, investigation and detection, capture and punishment. Thus, many of the people involved—legislators, social workers, probation officers, judges, etc.—could possibly be considered *criminologists,* though the word usually refers only to scholars and researchers.

decriminalize \dē-ˈkri-mə-nə-ˌlīz\ To remove or reduce the criminal status of.

• An angry debate over decriminalizing doctor-assisted suicide raged all day in the statehouse.

Decriminalization of various "victimless crimes"—crimes that don't directly harm others, such as private gambling and drug-taking—has been recommended by conservatives as well as liberals, who often claim that it would ease the burden on the legal system, decrease the amount of money flowing to criminals, and increase personal liberty. Decriminalization is not the same as legalization; decriminalization may still call for a small fine (like a traffic ticket), and may apply only to use or possession of something, leaving the actual sale of goods or services illegal.

incriminate \in-'kri-mə-ˌnāt\ To show evidence of involvement in a crime or a fault.

• The muddy tracks leading to and from the cookie jar were enough to incriminate them.

Testimony may incriminate a suspect by placing him at the scene of a crime, and *incriminating* evidence is the kind that strongly links him to it. But the word doesn't always refer to an actual crime. We can say, for instance, that a virus has been incriminated as the cause of a type of cancer, or that video games have been incriminated in the decline in study skills among young people.

recrimination \rē-ˌkri-mə-'nā-shən\ (1) An accusation in answer to an accusation made against oneself. (2) The making of such an accusation.

• Their failure to find help led to endless and pointless recriminations over responsibility for the accident.

Defending oneself from a verbal attack by means of a counter-attack is as natural as physical self-defense. So a disaster often brings recriminations among those connected with it, and divorces and child-custody battles usually involve recriminations between husband and wife. An actual crime isn't generally involved, but it may be; when two suspects start exchanging angry recriminations after they've been picked up, it often leads to one of them turning against the other in court.

PROB comes from the Latin words for "prove or proof" and "honesty or integrity." A *probe*, whether it's a little object for testing electrical circuits or a spacecraft headed for Mars, is basically something that's looking for evidence or proof. And *probable* originally described something that wasn't certain but might be "provable."

---

approbation \ˌa-prə-'bā-shən\ A formal or official act of approving; praise, usually given with pleasure or enthusiasm.

- The senate signaled its approbation of the new plan by voting for it unanimously.

Approbation is a noun form of *approve*, but approbation is usually stronger than mere *approval*. An official commendation for bravery is an example of approbation; getting reelected to office by a wide margin indicates public approbation; and the social approbation received by a star quarterback in high school usually makes all the pain worthwhile.

probate \'prō-ˌbāt\ The process of proving in court that the will of someone who has died is valid, and of administering the estate of a dead person.

- When her father died, she thought she would be able to avoid probate, but she wasn't that lucky.

Ever since people have written wills, those wills have had to be proven genuine by a judge. Without a probate process, greedy acquaintances or relatives could write up a fake will stating that all the person's wealth belonged to them. To establish a will as genuine, it must generally be witnessed and stamped by someone officially licensed to do so (though wills have sometimes been approved even when they were just written on a piece of scrap paper, with no witnesses). Today we use *probate* more broadly to mean everything that's handled in *probate court*, a special court that oversees the handling of estates (the money and property left when someone dies), making sure that everyone eventually receives what is properly theirs.

probity \'prō-bə-tē\ Absolute honesty and uprightness.

- Her unquestioned probity helped win her the respect of her fellow judges.

Probity is a quality the public generally hopes for in its elected officials but doesn't always get. Bankers, for example, have traditionally been careful to project an air of probity, even though banking scandals and bailouts have made this harder than ever. An aura of probity surrounds such public figures as Warren Buffett and Bill Moyers, men to whom many Americans would entrust their children and their finances.

reprobate \'re-prə-ˌbāt\ A person of thoroughly bad character.

- His wife finally left him, claiming he was a reprobate who would disappear for weeks at a time, gambling and drinking away all his money.

The related verb of *reprobate* is *reprove*, which originally, as the opposite of *approve*, meant "to condemn." Thus, a reprobate, as the word was used in Biblical translations, was someone condemned to hell. But for many years *reprobate* has been said in a tone of joshing affection, usually to describe someone of doubtful morals but good humor. Shakespeare's great character Falstaff—a lazy, lying, boastful, sponging drunkard—is the model of a reprobate, but still everyone's favorite Shakespeare character.

Quizzes

A. Indicate whether the following pairs of words have the same or different meanings:

1. decriminalize / tolerate   same ___ / different ___
2. probity / fraud   same ___ / different ___
3. criminology / murder   same ___ / different ___
4. incriminate / acquit   same ___ / different ___
5. probate / trial   same ___ / different ___
6. recrimination / faultfinding   same ___ / different ___
7. reprobate / scoundrel   same ___ / different ___
8. approbation / criticism   same ___ / different ___

B. Match the definition on the left to the correct word on the right:

1. utter honesty   a. approbation
2. approval   b. reprobate
3. rascal   c. recrimination
4. legal process for wills d. criminology
5. study of illegal behavior e. probity
6. accuse   f. probate
7. reduce penalty for   g. decriminalize
8. counterattack   h. incriminate

GRAV comes from the Latin word meaning "heavy, weighty, serious." *Gravity* is, of course, what makes things heavy, and without it there wouldn't be any life on earth, since nothing would stay *on* earth at all. This doesn't stop us from yelling in outrage when the familiar laws of gravity cause something to drop to the floor and break.

grave \\'grāv\\ (1) Requiring serious thought or concern. (2) Serious and formal in appearance or manner.

• We realized that the situation was grave and that the slightest incident could spark all-out war.

Gravity has a familiar physical meaning but also a nonphysical meaning—basically "seriousness." Thus, something *grave* possesses gravity. You can refer to the gravity of a person's manner, though public figures today seem to have a lot less gravity than they used to have. Or you can talk about a grave situation, as in the example sentence. But even though Shakespeare makes a pun on *grave* when a dying character talks about being buried the next day ("Ask for me tomorrow and you shall find me a grave man"), the word meaning "hole for burying a body" isn't actually related.

gravitas \\'gra-və-ˌtäs\\ Great or very dignified seriousness.

• The head of the committee never failed to carry herself with the gravitas she felt was appropriate to her office.

This word comes to us straight from Latin. Among the Romans, gravitas was thought to be essential to the character and functions of any adult (male) in authority. Even the head of a household or a low-level official would strive for this important quality. We use *gravitas* today to identify the same solemn dignity in men and women, but it seems to come easier in those who are over 60, slow-moving—and a bit overweight.

gravitate \\'gra-və-ˌtāt\\ To move or be drawn toward something, especially by natural tendency or as if by an invisible force.

• On hot evenings, the town's social life gravitated toward the lakefront, where you could stroll the long piers eating ice cream or dance at the old Casino.

To gravitate is to respond, almost unconsciously, to a force that works like *gravity* to draw things steadily to it as if by their own weight. Thus, young people gravitate toward a role model, moths gravitate to a flame, a conversation might gravitate toward politics, and everyone at a party often gravitates to the bar.

aggravate \\'a-grə-ˌvāt\ (1) To make (an injury, problem, etc.) more serious or severe. (2) To annoy or bother.

• She went back to the soccer team before the knee was completely healed, which naturally aggravated the injury.

Since the *grav-* root means basically "weighty or serious," the original meaning of *aggravate* was "to make more serious." A bad relationship with your parents can be aggravated by marrying someone who nobody likes, for example, or a touchy trade relationship between two countries can be aggravated by their inability to agree on climate-change issues. Depression can be aggravated by insomnia—and insomnia can be aggravated by depression. But when most people use *aggravate* today, they employ its "annoy" sense, as in "What really aggravates my dad is having to listen to that TV all day long."

LEV comes from the Latin adjective *levis,* meaning "light," and the verb *levare,* meaning "to raise or lighten." So a *lever* is a bar used to lift something, by means of *leverage.* And *levitation* is the magician's trick in which a body seems to rise into the air by itself.

---

alleviate \ə-'lē-vē-ˌāt\ To lighten, lessen, or relieve, especially physical or mental suffering.

• Cold compresses alleviated the pain of the physical injury, but only time could alleviate the effect of the insult.

Physical pain or emotional anguish, or a water shortage or traffic congestion, can all be alleviated by providing the appropriate remedy. But some pain or anguish or shortage or congestion will remain: to alleviate is not to cure.

elevation \ˌe-lə-'vā-shən\ (1) The height of a place. (2) The act or result of lifting or raising someone or something.

• Her doctor is concerned about the elevation of her blood pressure since her last visit.

When you're hiking, you may be interested in knowing the highest elevation you'll be reaching. Psychologists use the term "mood elevation" to mean improvement in a patient's depression, and some leg ailments require elevation of the limb, usually so that it's higher than the heart for part of each day. *Elevation* can also mean "promotion"; thus, a vice president may be *elevated* to president, or a captain may be elevated to admiral.

cantilever \\'kan-tə-ˌlē-vər\ A long piece of wood, metal, etc., that sticks out from a wall to support something above it.

• The house's deck, supported by cantilevers, jutted out dramatically over the rocky slope, and looking over the edge made him dizzy.

Cantilevers hold up a surface or room without themselves being supported at their outer end. Many outdoor balconies are *cantilevered*, and theater balconies may be as well. A cantilevered bridge may have a huge span (as long as 1,800 feet) built out on either side of a single large foundation pier. Architects sometimes use cantilevered construction to produce dramatic effects; Frank Lloyd Wright's "Fallingwater" house, which extends out over a rocky river, is a famous example. But the Grand Canyon's "Skywalk" has become perhaps the best-known piece of cantilevered construction in America.

levity \\'le-və-tē\ Lack of appropriate seriousness.

• The Puritan elders tried to ban levity of all sorts from the community's meetings, but found it increasingly difficult to control the younger generation.

Levity originally was thought to be a physical force exactly like gravity but pulling in the opposite direction, like the helium in a balloon. As recently as the 19th century, scientists were still arguing about its existence. Today *levity* refers only to lightness in manner. To stern believers of some religious faiths, levity is often regarded as almost sinful. But the word, like its synonym *frivolity*, now has an old-fashioned ring to it and is usually used only half-seriously.

Quizzes

A. Fill in each blank with the correct letter:

a. grave   e. alleviate
b. gravitate   f. cantilever
c. gravitas   g. levity
d. aggravate   h. elevation

1. Even the smallest motion would _____ the pain in his shoulder.
2. She hesitated to step onto the balcony, which was supported by a single _____.
3. At their father's funeral they showed the same solemn _____ at which they had often laughed during his lifetime.
4. To relieve the swelling, the doctor recommended _____ of her legs several times a day.
5. Attracted magically by the music, all animals and natural objects would _____ toward the sound of Orpheus's lyre.
6. With the two armies moving toward the border, they knew the situation was _____.
7. The neighboring nations organized an airlift of supplies to _____ the suffering caused by the drought.
8. The board meeting ended in an unusual mood of _____ when a man in a gorilla suit burst in.

B. Match the word on the left to the correct definition on the right:

1. levity   a. solemn dignity
2. gravitas   b. relieve
3. grave   c. raising
4. alleviate   d. support beam
5. elevation   e. move toward as if drawn
6. aggravate   f. lack of seriousness
7. cantilever   g. serious
8. gravitate   h. worsen

Words from Mythology and History

cicerone \ˌsi-sə-ˈrō-nē\ A guide, especially one who takes tourists to museums, monuments, or architectural sites and explains what is being seen.

• On Crete they sought out a highly recommended cicerone, hoping to receive the best possible introduction to the noteworthy historical sites.

The Roman statesman and orator Cicero was renowned for his elegant style and great knowledge (and occasional long-windedness). So 18th-century Italians seem to have given the name *cicerone* to the guides who would show well-educated foreigners around the great cultural sites of the ancient Roman empire—guides who sought to be as eloquent and informed as Cicero in explaining the world in which he lived.

hector \ˈhek-tər\ To bully or harass by bluster or personal pressure.

• He would swagger around the apartment entrance with his friends and hector the terrified inhabitants going in and out.

In Homer's great *Iliad,* Hector was the leader of the Trojan forces, and the very model of nobility and honor. In the Greek war against Troy, he killed several great warriors before being slain by Achilles. His name began to take on its current meaning only after gangs of bullying young rowdies, many of them armed soldiers recently released from service following the end of the English Civil War, began terrorizing the residents of late-17th-century London. The gangs took such names as the Roysters, the Blades, the Bucks, and the Bloods, but the best-known of them was called the Hectors. The names Blades and Hectors may have seemed appropriate because, like Hector and Achilles, they often fought with swords.

hedonism \ˈhē-də-ˌni-zəm\ An attitude or way of life based on the idea that pleasure or happiness should be the chief goal.

• In her new spirit of hedonism, she went out for a massage, picked up champagne and chocolate truffles, and made a date that evening with an old boyfriend.

Derived from the Greek word for "pleasure," hedonism over the ages has provided the basis for several philosophies. The ancient

Epicureans and the 19th-century Utilitarians both taught and pursued *hedonistic* principles. But although we generally use the word today when talking about immediate pleasures for the senses, philosophers who talk about hedonism are usually talking about quiet pleasures that aren't pursued in a selfish way.

nestor \\ˈnes-ˌtȯr\\ A senior figure or leader in one's field.

• The guest of honor was a nestor among journalists, and after dinner he shared some of his wisdom with the audience.

Nestor was another character from the *Iliad,* the eldest of the Greek leaders in the Trojan War. A great warrior as a young man, he was now noted for his wisdom and his talkativeness, both of which increased as he aged. These days, a nestor is not necessarily long-winded, but merely wise and generous with his advice.

spartan \\ˈspär-tən\\ Marked by simplicity, avoidance of luxury, and often strict self-discipline or self-denial.

• When he was single, he had lived a spartan life in a tiny, undecorated apartment with one chair, a table, and a bed.

In ancient times, the Greek city-state of Sparta had a reputation for the severe and highly disciplined way of life it enforced among its citizens, so as to keep them ready for war at any time. Physical training was required for both men and women. A boy would begin his military training at 7 and would live in army barracks for much of his life, even after he was married. Today, when a cargo ship or a remote beach resort offers "spartan accommodations," some tourists jump at the chance for a refreshing change from the luxuries they've been used to—and no one worries that they'll be forced out of bed at dawn to participate in war games.

stentorian \\sten-ˈtȯr-ē-ən\\ Extremely loud, often with especially deep richness of sound.

• Even without a microphone, his stentorian voice was clearly audible in the last rows of the auditorium.

Stentor, like Hector, was a warrior in the *Iliad,* but on the Greek side. His unusually powerful voice (Homer calls him "brazen-voiced"—that is, with a voice like a brass instrument) made him the natural choice for delivering announcements and proclamations to the assembled Greek army, in an era when there was no way of artificially increasing the volume of a voice.

stoic \\'stō-ik\ Seemingly indifferent to pleasure or pain.

- She bore the pain of her broken leg with such stoic patience that most of us had no idea she was suffering.

The *Stoics* were members of a philosophical movement that first appeared in ancient Greece and lasted well into the Roman era. *Stoicism* taught that humans should seek to free themselves from joy, grief, and passions of all kinds in order to attain wisdom; its teachings thus have much in common with Buddhism. The great Stoics include the statesman Cicero, the playwright Seneca, and the emperor Marcus Aurelius, whose *Meditations* is the most famous book of Stoic philosophy. Today we admire the kind of stoicism that enables some people (who may never have even heard of Marcus Aurelius) to endure both mental and physical pain without complaint.

sybaritic \\,si-bə-'ri-tik\ Marked by a luxurious or sensual way of life.

- When I knew them they were living a sybaritic existence—hopping from resort to resort, each more splendid than the last—but a year later the money ran out.

The ancient city of Sybaris (near modern Terranova di Sibari), founded by the Greeks on the toe of Italy's "boot," was famous for the wealth and luxury of its citizens in the 6th century B.C. But the *Sybarites'* wealth made them overconfident, and when they went to war with a nearby city, they were defeated by a much smaller army. After the victory, their enemies diverted the course of the river running through Sybaris so that it destroyed the whole city forever.

Quiz

Choose the closest definition:

1. hedonism   a. preference for males   b. habit of gift-giving   c. tendency to conceal feelings   d. love of pleasure

2. hector   a. encourage b. harass c. deceive d. swear
3. cicerone   a. guide b. cartoon character c. orator
        d. lawyer
4. spartan   a. cheap b. Greek c. severe d. luxurious
5. nestor   a. journalist b. long-winded elder c. domestic
        hen d. judge
6. stoic   a. pleasure-seeking b. bullying c. repressed
        d. unaffected by pain
7. sybaritic   a. pleasure-seeking b. free of luxury
        c. sisterly d. ice-cold
8. stentorian   a. obnoxious b. muffled c. loud d. dictated

Review Quizzes

A. Fill in each blank with the correct letter:

a. bellicose   h. benevolence
b. stentorian   i. incriminate
c. *pace*   j. gravitate
d. sybaritic   k. hector
e. grave   l. enamored
f. alleviate   m. stoic
g. belligerence   n. pacify

1. Her grandfather had a _____ manner, moved slowly,
    and never laughed.
2. The mood at the resort was _____, and the drinking
    and dancing continued long into the night.
3. To rattle the other team, they usually _____ them
    constantly.
4. The judge was known for issuing all his rulings in a
    _____ voice.
5. He wouldn't even have a place to live if it weren't for
    the _____ of his wealthy godfather.
6. Thoroughly _____ of the splendid Victorian house,
    they began to plan their move.
7. She attempted to _____ his anxiety by convincing him
    he wasn't to blame.
8. Whenever she entered a bar alone, the lonely men would
    always _____ toward her.

9. Their refusal to cease work on nuclear weapons was seen as a _____ act by the neighboring countries.

10. _____ my many critics, I have never had reason to change my views on the subject.

11. Unable to calm the growing crowd, he finally ordered the police to _____ the area by force.

12. Whenever her boyfriend saw anyone looking at her, his _____ was alarming.

13. He bore all his financial losses with the same _____ calm.

14. Who would have guessed that it would take the killer's own daughter to _____ him.

B. Choose the closest definition:

1. hedonism   a. fear of heights   b. hatred of crowds   c. liking for children   d. love of pleasure

2. levity   a. lightness   b. policy   c. leverage   d. literacy

3. aggravate   a. lessen   b. decorate   c. intensify   d. lighten

4. reprobate   a. researcher   b. commissioner   c. scoundrel   d. reformer

5. bellicose   a. fun-loving   b. warlike   c. impatient   d. jolly

6. decriminalize   a. discriminate   b. legalize   c. legislate   d. decree

7. antebellum   a. preventive   b. unlikely   c. impossible   d. prewar

8. benediction   a. slogan   b. prayer   c. greeting   d. expression

9. pact   a. bundle   b. form   c. agreement   d. presentation

10. amicable   a. technical   b. sensitive   c. friendly   d. scenic

11. criminology   a. crime history   b. crime book   c. crime study   d. crime story

12. approbation   a. approval   b. resolution   c. reputation   d. substitution

C. Match the definition on the left to the correct word on the right:

1. secret lover   a. elevation

2. estate process   b. gravitas

3. accusation   c. probate

4. integrity   d. probity

5. gift receiver
6. giver
7. peace lover
8. promotion
9. dignity
10. revolt

e. recrimination
f. paramour
g. benefactor
h. beneficiary
i. rebellion
j. pacifist

UNIT

2

MANIA in Latin means "madness," and the meaning passed over into English unchanged. Our word *mania* can mean a mental illness, or at least an excessive enthusiasm. We might call someone a *maniac* who was wild, violent, and mentally ill—or maybe just really enthusiastic about something. Too much caffeine might make you a bit *manic*. But the intense mood swings once known as *manic-depressive illness* are now usually called *bipolar disorder* instead.

---

kleptomania \ˌklep-tə-ˈmā-nē-ə\ A mental illness in which a person has a strong desire to steal things.

• Kleptomania leads its sufferers to steal items of little value that they don't need anyway.

Klepto- comes from the Greek word *kleptein*, "to steal." Even though kleptomania is often the butt of jokes, it's actually a serious mental illness, often associated with mood disorders, anxiety disorders, eating disorders, and substance abuse. Kleptomaniacs tend to be depressed, and many live lives of secret shame because they're afraid to seek treatment.

dipsomaniac \ˌdip-sə-ˈmā-nē-ˌak\ A person with an extreme and uncontrollable desire for alcohol.

• She didn't like the word *alcoholic* being applied to her, and liked *dipsomaniac* even less.

Dipsomaniac comes from the Greek noun *dipsa,* "thirst," but thirst usually has nothing to do with it. Some experts distinguish between an alcoholic and a dipsomaniac, reserving *dipsomaniac* for someone involved in frequent episodes of binge drinking and blackouts. In any case, there are plenty of less respectful words for a person of similar habits: *sot, lush, wino, souse, boozer, guzzler, tippler, tosspot, drunkard, boozehound*—the list goes on and on and on.

megalomaniac \ˌme-gə-lō-ˈmā-nē-ˌak\ A mental disorder marked by feelings of great personal power and importance.

* When the governor started calling for arming his National Guard with nuclear weapons, the voters finally realized they had elected a megalomaniac.

Since the Greek root *megalo-* means "large," someone who is *megalomaniacal* has a mental disorder marked by feelings of personal grandeur. *Megalomania* has probably afflicted many rulers throughout history: The Roman emperor Caligula insisted that he be worshipped as a living god. Joseph Stalin suffered from the paranoia that often accompanies megalomania, and had thousands of his countrymen executed as a result. J.-B. Bokassa, dictator of a small and extremely poor African nation, proclaimed himself emperor of the country he renamed the Central African Empire. And even democratically elected leaders have often acquired huge egos as a result of public acclaim. But *megalomaniac* is generally thrown around as an insult and rarely refers to real mental illness.

egomaniac \ˌē-gō-ˈmā-nē-ˌak\ Someone who is extremely self-centered and ignores the problems and concerns of others.

* He's a completely unimpressive person, but that doesn't keep him from being an egomaniac.

Ego is Latin for "I," and in English *ego* usually means "sense of self-worth." Most people's egos stay at a healthy level, but some become exaggerated. Egomaniacs may display a grandiose sense of self-importance, with fantasies about their own brilliance or beauty, intense envy of others, a lack of sympathy, and a need to be adored or feared. But, like *megalomaniac,* the word *egomaniac* is thrown around by lots of people who don't mean much more by it than *blowhard* or *know-it-all.*

PSYCH comes from the Greek word *psyche*, meaning "breath, life, soul." *Psychology* is the science of mind and behavior, and a *psychologist* treats or studies the mental problems of individuals and groups. *Psychiatry* is a branch of medicine that deals with mental and emotional disorders, and a *psychiatrist* (like any other doctor) may prescribe drugs to treat them.

psyche \\ˈsī-kē\ Soul, personality, mind.

• Analysts are constantly trying to understand the nation's psyche and why the U.S. often behaves so differently from other countries.

Sometime back in the 16th century, we borrowed the word *psyche* directly from Greek into English. In Greek mythology, Psyche was a beautiful princess who fell in love with Eros (Cupid), god of love, and went through terrible trials before being allowed to marry him. The story is often understood to be about the soul redeeming itself through love. (To the Greeks, *psyche* also meant "butterfly," which suggests how they imagined the soul.) In English, *psyche* often sounds less spiritual than *soul*, less intellectual than *mind*, and more private than *personality*.

psychedelic \ˌsī-kə-ˈde-lik\ (1) Of or relating to a drug (such as LSD) that produces abnormal and often extreme mental effects such as hallucinations. (2) Imitating the effects of psychedelic drugs.

• In her only psychedelic experience, back in 1970, she had watched with horror as the walls began crawling with bizarrely colored creatures.

The most famous—or notorious—of the psychedelic drugs is LSD, a compound that can be obtained from various mushrooms and other fungi but is usually created in the lab. The other well-known *psychedelics* are psilocybin (likewise obtained from fungi) and mescaline (obtained from peyote cactus). How psychedelics produce their effects is still fairly mysterious, partly because research ceased for almost 20 years because of their reputation, but scientists are determined to find the answers and much research is now under way. Psychedelics are now used to treat anxiety in patients with cancer, and are being tested in the treatment of such serious conditions as severe depression, alcoholism, and drug addiction.

psychosomatic \\,sī-kō-sə-ˈma-tik\\ Caused by mental or emotional problems rather than by physical illness.

- Her doctor assumed her stomach problems were psychosomatic but gave her some harmless medication anyway.

Since the Greek word *soma* means "body," *psychosomatic* suggests the link between mind and body. Since one's mental state may have an important effect on one's physical state, research on new medicines always involves giving some patients in the experiment a placebo (fake medicine), and some who receive the sugar pills will seem to improve. You may hear someone say of someone else's symptoms, "Oh, it's probably just psychosomatic," implying that the physical pain or illness is imaginary—maybe just an attempt to get sympathy—and that the person could will it away if he or she wanted to. But this can be harsh and unfair, since, whatever the cause is, the pain is usually real.

psychotherapist \\,sī-kō-ˈther-ə-pist\\ One who treats mental or emotional disorder or related bodily ills by psychological means.

- He's getting medication from a psychiatrist, but it's his sessions with the psychotherapist that he really values.

Many psychologists offer psychological counseling, and psychological counseling can usually be called *psychotherapy*, so many psychologists can be called psychotherapists. The most intense form of psychotherapy, called *psychoanalysis*, usually requires several visits a week. A competing type of therapy known as *behavior therapy* focuses on changing a person's behavior (often some individual habit such as stuttering, tics, or phobias) without looking very deeply into his or her mental state.

Quizzes

A. Fill in each blank with the correct letter:

a. psychedelic
b. kleptomania
c. psyche
d. egomaniac

e. megalomaniac
f. psychosomatic
g. dipsomaniac
h. psychotherapist

1. Her boss was an _____ who always needed someone around telling him how brilliant he was.
2. Testing _____ drugs on cancer patients was difficult because of their unpredictable mental effects.
3. By now the dictator had begun to strike some observers as a possibly dangerous _____.
4. His fear of AIDS was so intense that he'd been developing _____ symptoms, which his doctor hardly bothered to check out anymore.
5. After finding several of her missing things in the other closet, she began wondering if her roommate was an ordinary thief or actually suffering from _____.
6. They'd only been together two weeks, but already she suspected there was a lot hidden in the depths of her boyfriend's _____.
7. A medical report from 1910 had identified her great-grandfather as a _____, and ten years later his alcoholism would kill him.
8. He hated the thought of drugs but knew he needed someone to talk to, so his brother recommended a local _____.

B. Match each word on the left to the best definition on the right:

1. psyche
2. egomaniac
3. psychotherapist
4. psychosomatic
5. dipsomaniac
6. megalomaniac
7. kleptomania
8. psychedelic

a. alcoholic
b. caused by the mind
c. person deluded by thoughts of grandeur
d. producing hallucinations
e. compulsive thieving
f. mind
g. extremely self-centered person
h. "talk" doctor

CEPT comes from the Latin verb meaning "take, seize." *Capture,* which is what a *captor* has done to a *captive,* has the same meaning. *Captivate* once meant literally "capture," but now means only to capture mentally through charm or appeal. But in some other English words this root produces, such as those below, its meaning is harder to find.

reception \ri-ˈsep-shən\ (1) The act of receiving. (2) A social gathering where guests are formally welcomed.

• Although the reception of her plan by the board of directors was enthusiastic, it was months before anything was done about it.

Reception is the noun form of *receive*. So at a formal reception, guests are received or welcomed or "taken in." A bad TV reception means the signal isn't being received well. When a new novel receives good reviews, we say it has met with a good critical reception. If it gets a poor reception, on the other hand, that's the same as saying that it wasn't *well-received*.

intercept \ˌin-tər-ˈsept\ To stop, seize, or interrupt (something or someone) before arrival.

• The explosives had been intercepted by police just before being loaded onto the jet.

Since the prefix *inter* means "between" (see INTER, p. 653), it's not hard to see how *intercept* was created. Arms shipments coming to a country are sometimes intercepted, but such *interceptions* can sometimes be understood as acts of war. In football, soccer, and basketball, players try to intercept the ball as it's being passed by the other team. In years gone by, letters and documents being carried between officers or officials were sometimes intercepted when the carrier was caught; today, when these communications are generally electronic, an intercepted e-mail isn't actually stopped, but simply read secretly by a third party.

perceptible \pər-ˈsep-tə-bəl\ Noticeable or able to be felt by the senses.

• Her change in attitude toward him was barely perceptible, and he couldn't be sure he wasn't just imagining it.

Perceptible includes the prefix *per-*, meaning "through," so the word refers to whatever can be taken in through the senses. A *perceptive* person picks up minor changes, small clues, or hints and shades of meaning that others can't *perceive*, so one person's *perception*—a tiny sound, a slight change in the weather, a different tone of voice— often won't be perceptible to another.

susceptible \sə-ˈsep-tə-bəl\ (1) Open to some influence; responsive. (2) Able to be submitted to an action or process.

- She impressed everyone immediately with her intelligence, so they're now highly susceptible to her influence and usually go along with anything she proposes.

With its prefix *sus-,* "up," *susceptible* refers to something or someone that "takes up" or absorbs like a sponge. A sickly child may be susceptible to colds, and an unlucky adult may be susceptible to back problems. A lonely elderly person may be susceptible to what a con man tells him or her on the phone. And students are usually susceptible to the teaching of an imaginative professor—that is, likely to enjoy and learn from it.

FIN comes from the Latin word for "end" or "boundary." *Final* describes last things, and a *finale* or a *finish* is an ending. (And at the end of a French film, you may just see the word "Fin.") But its meaning is harder to trace in some of the other English words derived from it.

---

confine \kən-ˈfīn\ (1) To keep (someone or something) within limits. (2) To hold (someone) in a location.

- He had heard the bad news from the CEO, but when he spoke to his employees he confined his remarks to a few hints that sales had slipped.

Confine means basically to keep someone or something within borders. Artist Frida Kahlo taught herself to paint when she was confined to bed after a serious bus accident. A person under "house arrest" is confined to his or her house by the government. The discussion at a meeting may be confined to a single topic. A town may keep industrial development confined to one area by means of zoning. And when potholes are being repaired, traffic on a two-way road may be confined to a single lane.

definitive \di-ˈfi-nə-tiv\ (1) Authoritative and final. (2) Specifying perfectly or precisely.

- The team's brilliant research provided a definitive description of the virus and its strange mutation patterns.

Something definitive is complete and final. A definitive example is the perfect example. A definitive answer is usually a strong yes or no. A definitive biography contains everything we'll ever need to know about someone. Ella Fitzgerald's famous 1950s recordings of

American songs have even been called definitive—but no one ever wanted them to be the last.

finite \ˈfī-ˌnīt\ Having definite limits.

• Her ambitions were infinite, but her wealth was finite.

It has come as a shock to many of us to realize that resources such as oil—and the atmosphere's ability to absorb greenhouse gases—are finite rather than unlimited. The debate continues as to whether the universe is finite or *infinite* and, if it's finite, how to think about what lies beyond it. Religion has always concerned itself with the question of the finite (that is, human life on earth) versus the infinite (God, eternity, and infinity). But *finite* is mostly used in scientific writing, often with the meaning "definitely measurable."

infinitesimal \ˌin-ˌfi-nə-ˈte-sə-məl\ Extremely or immeasurably small.

• Looking more closely at the research data, he now saw an odd pattern of changes so infinitesimal that they hadn't been noticed before.

Just as *infinite* describes something immeasurable ("without limit"), *infinitesimal* describes something endlessly small. When Antonie van Leeuwenhoek invented the microscope in the 17th century, he was able to see organisms that had been thought too *infinitesimally* small to exist. But today's electron microscope allows us to see infinitesimal aspects of matter that even Leeuwenhoek could not have imagined.

Quizzes

A. Fill in each blank with the correct letter:

a. confine   e. finite
b. susceptible   f. intercept
c. definitive   g. infinitesimal
d. reception   h. perceptible

1. By the fall there had been a _____ change in the mood of the students.

2. An _____ speck of dust on the lens can keep a CD player from functioning.
3. They waited weeks to hear about the board's _____ of their proposal.
4. Let's _____ this discussion to just the first part of the proposal.
5. Small children are often _____ to nightmares after hearing ghost stories in the dark.
6. He was at the post office the next morning, hoping to _____ the foolish letter he had sent yesterday.
7. We have a _____ number of choices, in fact maybe only three or four.
8. This may be the best book on the subject so far, but I wouldn't call it _____.

B. Match the word on the left to the correct definition on the right:

1. confine   a. noticeable
2. susceptible   b. ultimate
3. definitive   c. seize
4. reception   d. easily influenced
5. finite   e. tiny
6. intercept   f. limit
7. infinitesimal   g. receiving
8. perceptible   h. limited

JECT comes from *jacere*, the Latin verb meaning "throw" or "hurl." To *reject* something is to throw (or push) it back; to *eject* something is to throw (or drive) it out; and to *inject* something is to throw (or squirt) it into something else.

---

interject \ˌin-tər-ˈjekt\ To interrupt a conversation with a comment or remark.

• His anger was growing as he listened to the conversation, and every so often he would interject a crude comment.

According to its Latin roots, *interject* ought to mean literally "throw between." For most of the word's history, however, the only things that have been interjected have been comments dropped suddenly into a conversation. *Interjections* are often humorous, and sometimes even insulting, and the best interjections are so quick that the conversation isn't even interrupted.

conjecture \kən-'jek-chər\ To guess.

* He was last heard of in Bogotá, and they conjectured that he had met his end in the Andes at the hands of the guerrillas.

Formed with the prefix *con-*, "together," *conjecture* means literally "to throw together"—that is, to produce a theory by putting together a number of facts. So, for example, Columbus conjectured from his calculations that he would reach Asia if he sailed westward, and his later *conjecture* that there was a "Northwest Passage" by sea from the Atlantic to the Pacific over the North American continent was proved correct centuries later.

projection \prə-'jek-shən\ An estimate of what might happen in the future based on what is happening now.

* The president has been hearing different deficit projections all week from the members of his economic team.

Projection has various meanings, but what they all have in common is that something is sent out or forward. A movie is *projected* onto a screen; a skilled actress projects her voice out into a large theater without seeming to shout; and something sticking out from a wall can be called a projection. But the meaning we focus on here is the one used by businesses and governments. Most projections of this kind are estimates of a company's sales or profits—or of the finances of a town, state, or country—sometime in the future.

trajectory \trə-'jek-tə-rē\ The curved path that an object makes in space, or that a thrown object follows as it rises and falls to earth.

* Considering the likely range, trajectory, and accuracy of a bullet fired from a cheap handgun at 100 yards, the murder seemed incredible.

Formed with part of the prefix *trans-*, "across," *trajectory* means a "hurling across." By calculating the effect of gravity and other forces, the trajectory of an object launched into space at a known speed can be computed precisely. Missiles stand a chance of hitting their target only if their trajectory has been plotted accurately. The word is used most often in physics and engineering, but not always; we can also say, for example, that the trajectory of a whole life may be set in a person's youth, or that a new book traces the long trajectory of the French empire.

TRACT comes from *trahere,* the Latin verb meaning "drag or draw." Something *attractive* draws us toward it. Something *distracting* pulls your attention away. And when you *extract* something from behind the sofa, you drag it out.

---

traction \\'trak-shən\ The friction that allows a moving thing to move over a surface without slipping.

- The spinning wheels were getting no traction on the ice, and we began to slip backward down the hill.

A *tractor* is something that pulls something else. We usually use the word for a piece of farm machinery, but it's also the name of the part of a big truck that includes the engine and the cab. Tractors get terrific traction, because of their powerful engines and the deep ridges on their huge wheels. A cross-country skier needs traction to kick herself forward, but doesn't want it to slow her down when she's gliding, so the bottom of the skis may have a "fish-scale" surface that permits both of these at the same time.

retract \ri-'trakt\ (1) To pull back (something) into something larger. (2) To take back (something said or written).

- She was forced to retract her comment about her opponent after it was condemned in the press.

The prefix *re-* ("back") gives *retract* the meaning of "draw back." Just as a cat retracts its claws into its paws when they aren't being used, a public figure may issue a *retraction* in order to say that he or she no longer wants to say something that has just been said. But it's sometimes hard to know what a retraction means: Was the original statement an error or an outright lie? Sometimes a politician even has to retract something that everyone actually assumes is the truth. Thousands of citizens were forced to publicly *retract* their "wrong" ideas by the Soviet government in the 1930s, though few of them had actually changed their minds. Someone wrongly accused may demand a retraction from his accuser—though today it seems more likely that he'll just go ahead and sue.

protracted \prō-'trak-təd\ Drawn out, continued, or extended.

• No one was looking forward to a protracted struggle for custody of the baby.

With its prefix *pro-*, "forward," *protracted* usually applies to something drawn out forward in time. A protracted strike may cripple a company; a protracted rainy spell may rot the roots of vegetables; and a protracted lawsuit occasionally outlives the parties involved. Before the invention of the polio vaccines, polio's many victims had no choice but to suffer a protracted illness and its aftereffects.

intractable \ˌin-'trak-tə-bəl\ Not easily handled, led, taught, or controlled.

• Corruption in the army was the country's intractable problem, and for many years all foreign aid had ended up in the colonels' pockets.

Intractable simply means "untreatable," and even comes from the same root. The word may describe both people and conditions. A cancer patient may suffer intractable pain that doctors are unable to treat. An intractable alcoholic goes back to the bottle immediately after "drying out." Homelessness, though it hardly existed thirty years ago, is now sometimes regarded as an intractable problem.

Quizzes

A. Choose the odd word:

1. conjecture   a. suppose   b. assume   c. guess   d. know
2. protracted   a. lengthened   b. continued   c. circular
        d. extended
3. projection   a. survey   b. forecast   c. report   d. history
4. traction   a. grip   b. drive   c. pulling force   d. steering
5. trajectory   a. curve   b. path   c. arc   d. target
6. retract   a. unsay   b. withdraw   c. force   d. take back
7. interject   a. insert   b. grab   c. add   d. stick in
8. intractable   a. unbelievable   b. uncontrollable
        c. stubborn   d. difficult

B. Match each definition on the left to the correct word on the right:

1.	pulling force	a.	protracted
2.	assume	b.	interject
3.	expectation	c.	trajectory
4.	difficult	d.	traction
5.	unsay	e.	conjecture
6.	drawn out	f.	intractable
7.	curved path	g.	retract
8.	interrupt with	h.	projection

DUC/DUCT, from the Latin verb *ducere*, "to lead," shows up regularly in English. *Duke* means basically "leader." The Italian dictator Mussolini was known simply as *Il Duce*, "the leader." But such words as *produce* and *reduce* also contain the root, even though their meanings show it less clearly.

---

conducive \kən-ˈdü-siv\ Tending to promote, encourage, or assist; helpful.

• She found the atmosphere in the quiet café conducive to study and even to creative thinking.

Something conducive "leads to" a desirable result. A cozy living room may be conducive to relaxed conversation, just as a boardroom may be conducive to more intense discussions. Particular tax policies are often conducive to savings and investment, whereas others are conducive to consumer spending. Notice that *conducive* is almost always followed by *to*.

deduction \dē-ˈdək-shən\ (1) Subtraction. (2) The reaching of a conclusion by reasoning.

• Foretelling the future by deduction based on a political or economic theory has proved to be extremely difficult.

To *deduct* is simply to subtract. A tax deduction is a subtraction from your taxable income allowed by the government for certain expenses, which will result in your paying lower taxes. Your insurance *deductible* is the amount of a medical bill that the insurance company makes you subtract before it starts to pay—in other words, the amount that will come out of your own pocket. But *deduction* also means "reasoning," and particularly reasoning based on general principles to produce specific findings. Mathematical reasoning is almost always deduction, for instance, since it is based on general rules. But when Dr. Watson exclaims "Brilliant deduction, my dear Holmes!" he simply means "brilliant reasoning," since Sherlock Holmes's solutions are based on specific details he has noticed rather than on general principles.

induce \in-ˈdüs\ (1) Persuade, influence. (2) Bring about.

* To induce him to make the call we had to promise we wouldn't do it again.

Inducing is usually gentle persuasion; you may, for instance, induce a friend to go to a concert, or induce a child to stop crying. An *inducement* is something that might lure you to do something, though inducements are occasionally a bit menacing, like the Godfather's offer that you can't refuse. *Induce* also sometimes means "produce"; thus, doctors must at times induce labor in a pregnant woman. Notice that *induct* and *induction* are somewhat different from *induce* and *inducement*, though they come from the identical roots.

seduction \si-ˈdək-shən\ (1) Temptation to sin, especially temptation to sexual intercourse. (2) Attraction or charm.

* The company began its campaign of seduction of the smaller firm by inviting its top management to a series of weekends at expensive resorts.

Seduction, with its prefix *se-*, "aside," means basically "lead aside or astray." In Hawthorne's novel *The Scarlet Letter*, Hester Prynne is forced to wear a large scarlet A, for "adulteress," after it is revealed that she's been *seduced* by the Reverend Dimmesdale. Seduction also takes less physical forms. Advertisements constantly try to seduce us (often using sex as a temptation) into buying products we hadn't even known existed.

SEQU comes from the Latin verb *sequi*, meaning "to follow." A *sequel* follows the original novel, film, or television show.

---

sequential \si-ˈkwen-shəl\ (1) Arranged in order or in a series. (2) Following in a series.

- In writing the history of the revolution, his challenge was to put all the events of those fateful days in proper sequential order.

Things in *sequence,* or regular order, are arranged *sequentially.* Most novels and films move sequentially, but some use techniques such as flashbacks that interrupt the movement forward in time. Sequential courses in college must follow each other in the proper order, just like sequential tasks or steps.

subsequent \\'səb-si-kwənt\\ Following in time, order, or place; later.

- Through all her subsequent love affairs, she never stopped thinking about the man who got away.

The prefix *sub-* normally means "below," and the *sub-* in *subsequent* seems to imply that everything after the first is somehow inferior. As the definition states, *subsequent* can refer to time ("All our subsequent attempts to contact her failed"), order ("The subsequent houses on the list looked even worse"), or place ("The subsequent villages on the river heading east become steadily more primitive"). But *subsequently*, as in "I subsequently learned the real story," simply means "later."

consequential \\ˌkän-sə-'kwen-shəl\\ (1) Resulting. (2) Important.

- None of our discussions thus far has been very consequential; next week's meeting will be the important one.

Something consequential follows or comes along with something else. The "resulting" meaning of *consequential* is usually seen in legal writing. For example, "consequential losses" are losses that supposedly resulted from some improper behavior, about which the lawyer's client is suing. But normally *consequential* means "significant" or "important," and it's especially used for events that will produce large *consequences*, or results.

non sequitur \\'nän-'se-kwə-tər\\ A statement that does not follow logically from anything previously said.

- Rattled by the question, his mind went blank, and he blurted out a non sequitur that fetched a few laughs from members of the audience.

Non sequitur is actually a complete sentence in Latin, meaning "It does not follow"—that is, something said or written doesn't logically follow what came before it. It was Aristotle who identified the non sequitur as one of the basic fallacies of logic—that is, one of the ways in which a person's reasoning may go wrong. For Aristotle, the non sequitur is usually a conclusion that doesn't actually result from the reasoning and evidence presented. Sometime when you're listening to politicians answering questions, see how many non sequiturs you can spot.

Quizzes

A. Match the definition on the left to the correct word on the right:

1.	out-of-place statement	a.	deduction
2.	persuade	b.	non sequitur
3.	temptation	c.	induce
4.	subtraction	d.	subsequent
5.	helpful	e.	seduction
6.	ordered	f.	consequential
7.	following	g.	conducive
8.	significant	h.	sequential

B. Fill in each blank with the correct letter:

a.	conducive	e.	consequential
b.	deduction	f.	subsequent
c.	induce	g.	non sequitur
d.	seduction	h.	sequential

1. The detectives insisted on a detailed and _____ account of the evening's events.

2. She fended off all his clumsy attempts at _____.

3. Conditions on the noisy hallway were not at all _____ to sleep.

4. There were a few arguments that first day, but all the _____ meetings went smoothly.

5. He sometimes thought that missing that plane had been the most _____ event of his life.

6. They arrived at the correct conclusion by simple _____.

7. He's hopeless at conversation, since practically everything he says is a _____.
8. He had tried to _____ sleep by all his usual methods, with no success.

Words from Mythology

Apollonian \ˌa-pə-ˈlō-nē-ən\ Harmonious, ordered, rational, calm.

• After a century of Romantic emotion, some composers adopted a more Apollonian style, producing clearly patterned pieces that avoided extremes of all kinds.

In Greek mythology, Apollo was the god of the sun, light, prophecy, and music, and the most revered of all the gods. Partly because of the writings of Nietzsche, we now often think of Apollo (in contrast to the god Dionysus) as a model of calm reason, and we may call anything with those qualities *Apollonian*. This isn't the whole story about Apollo, however; he had a terrible temper and could be viciously cruel when he felt like it.

bacchanalian \ˌba-kə-ˈnāl-yən\ Frenzied, orgiastic.

• The bacchanalian partying on graduation night resulted in three wrecked cars, two lawsuits by unamused parents, and more new experiences than most of the participants could remember the next day.

The Roman god of drama, wine, and ecstasy, Bacchus was the focus of a widespread celebration, the *Bacchanalia*. The festivities were originally secret, and only initiated members could participate. There was wine in abundance, and participants were expected to cut loose from normal restraints and give in to all sorts of wild desires. Eventually the Bacchanalia became more public and uncontrolled, finally getting so out of hand that in 186 B.C. the Roman authorities had it banned. Much the same bacchanalian spirit fills tropical carnivals every year, including New Orleans' Mardi Gras.

delphic \ˈdel-fik\ Unclear, ambiguous, or confusing.

- All she could get from the strange old woman were a few delphic comments that left her more confused than ever about the missing documents.

Delphi in Greece was the site of a temple to Apollo at which there resided an oracle, a woman through whom Apollo would speak, foretelling the future. The Greeks consulted the oracle frequently on matters both private and public. The prophecies were given in difficult poetry that had to be interpreted by priests, and even the interpretations could be hard to understand. When Croesus, king of Lydia, asked what would happen if he attacked the Persians, the oracle announced that he would destroy a great empire; what she didn't say was that the empire destroyed would be his own. Modern-day descendants of the oracle include some political commentators, who utter words of delphic complexity every week.

Dionysian \ˌdī-ə-ˈni-zhē-ən\ Frenzied, delirious.

- Only in the tropics did such festivals become truly Dionysian, he said, which was why he was booking his flight to Rio.

Dionysus was the Greek forerunner of Bacchus. He was the inventor of wine, which he gave to the human race. For that gift and for all the wild behavior that it led to, Dionysus became immensely popular, and he appears in a great many myths. He is often shown holding a wine goblet, with his hair full of vine leaves, and attended by a band of goat-footed satyrs and wild female spirits called maenads. In the 19th century, scholars such as Nietzsche claimed that the ancient world could be understood as a continuing conflict between the attitudes represented by Apollo (see *Apollonian* above) and Dionysus—that is, between order and disorder, between moderation and excess, between the controlled and the ecstatic.

jovial \ˈjō-vē-əl\ Jolly, good-natured.

- Their grandfather was as jovial and sociable as their grandmother was quiet and withdrawn.

Jove, or Jupiter, was the Roman counterpart of the Greek's Zeus, and like Zeus was regarded as chief among the gods. When the Romans were naming the planets, they gave the name Jupiter to the one that, as they may have already known, was the largest of all (though only the second-brightest to the naked eye). When the practice of astrology reached the Roman empire from the East, astrologers declared that those "born under Jupiter" were destined to be merry and generous, and many centuries later this would result in the words *jovial* and *joviality*.

mercurial \mər-'kyùr-ē-əl\ Having rapid and unpredictable changes of mood.

- His mother's always mercurial temper became even more unpredictable, to the point where the slightest thing would trigger a violent fit.

The god Mercury, with his winged cap and sandals, was the very symbol of speed, and the planet Mercury was named for him by the Romans because it is the fastest-moving of the planets. His name was also given to the liquid silver metal that skitters around on a surface so quickly and unpredictably. And the word *mercurial* seems to have come from the metal, rather than directly from the god (or an astrologer's view of the planet's influence). Mercurial people are usually bright but impulsive and changeable (and sometimes a bit unstable).

Olympian \ō-'lim-pē-ən\ Lofty, superior, and detached.

- Now 77, he moved slowly and spoke to the younger lawyers in Olympian tones, but his college friends could remember when he was a brash, crazy risk-taker.

The Greek gods lived high atop Mt. Olympus, which allowed them to watch what went on in the human realm below and intervene as they saw fit. They insisted on being properly worshipped by humans, but otherwise tended to treat the affairs of these weak and short-lived creatures almost like a sport. So *Olympian* describes someone who seems "lofty" and "above it all," as if surveying a scene in which other people appear the size of ants. The Olympic Games were first celebrated in the 8th century B.C., at the religious site called Olympia (far from Mt. Olympus), and *Olympian* today actually most often refers to Olympic athletes.

venereal \və-'nir-ē-əl\ Having to do with sexual intercourse or diseases transmitted by it.

- In the 19th century syphilis especially was often fatal, and venereal diseases killed some of the greatest figures of the time.

Venus was the Roman goddess of love, the equivalent of the Greek Aphrodite. Since she governed all aspects of love and desire, a word derived from her name was given to the diseases acquired through sexual contact. Most of these venereal diseases have been around for many centuries, but only in the 20th century did doctors devise tests to identify them or medicines to cure them. Today the official term is *sexually transmitted disease,* or STD; but even this name turns out to be ambiguous, since some of these diseases can be contracted in other ways as well.

Quiz

Choose the correct synonym and the correct antonym:

1. Dionysian   a. frenzied b. angry c. calm d. fatal
2. apollonian   a. fruity b. irrational c. single
     d. harmonious
3. mercurial   a. stable b. changeable c. sociable
     d. depressed
4. jovial   a. youthful b. mean-spirited c. merry
     d. magical
5. olympian   a. involved b. lame c. detached d. everyday
6. venereal   a. sensual b. intellectual c. diseased
     d. arthritic
7. bacchanalian   a. restrained b. dynamic c. frenzied
     d. forthright
8. delphic   a. clear b. dark c. stormy d. ambiguous

Review Quizzes

A.   Choose the closest definition:

1. reprobate   a. prosecution b. scoundrel c. trial
     d. refund
2. intercept   a. throw b. seize c. arrest d. close
3. confine   a. erect b. restrict c. ignore d. lock out
4. deduction   a. addition b. flirtation c. total
     d. reasoning
5. subsequent   a. unimportant b. early c. first d. later

6. sequential a. important b. noticeable
   c. in order d. distant
7. non sequitur a. distrust b. refusal c. odd statement
   d. denial
8. conjecture a. ask b. state c. guess d. exclaim
9. perceptible a. noticeable b. capable c. readable
   d. thinkable
10. finite a. vast b. finished c. nearby d. limited

B. Match the definition on the left to the correct word on the right:

1. guess   a. olympian
2. soul   b. perceptible
3. lengthy   c. conjecture
4. godlike   d. definitive
5. ordered   e. protracted
6. clear-cut   f. psyche
7. noticeable   g. susceptible
8. sensitive   h. jovial
9. significant   i. sequential
10. jolly   j. consequential

C. Fill in each blank with the correct letter:

a. mercurial   f. seduction
b. induce   g. bacchanalian
c. intractable   h. traction
d. amicable   i. retract
e. interject   j. trajectory

1. The public isn't aware of the company's _____ of Congress through its huge contributions over many years.
2. The truck was getting almost no _____ on the snowy road.
3. The prison situation is _____, and likely to get worse.
4. He tried to _____ his statement the next day, but the damage had been done.
5. Surprisingly, her first and second husbands actually have a completely _____ relationship.
6. The argument had gotten fierce, but he somehow managed to _____ a remark about how they were both wrong.

7. The disappointing _____ of his career often puzzled his friends.
8. She again told her family that nothing could _____ her to marry him.
9. By 2:00 a.m. the party was a scene of _____ frenzy.
10. Her only excuse for her behavior was her well-known _____ temper.

UNIT

3

AMBI means "on both sides" or "around"; *ambi-* comes from Latin. Most of us are either right-handed or left-handed, but *ambidextrous* people can use their right and left hand equally well.

---

ambiguous \am-'bi-gyủ-wəs\ (1) Doubtful or uncertain especially from being obscure or indistinct. (2) Unclear in meaning because of being understandable in more than one way.

• Successful politicians are good at giving ambiguous answers to questions on difficult issues.

Ambiguous comes from the Latin verb *ambigere,* "to be undecided." When we say someone's eyes are an ambiguous color, we mean we cannot decide which color they are—blue or green? The *ambiguity* of the Mona Lisa's smile makes us wonder what she's thinking about. An ambiguous order is one that can be taken in at least two ways; on the other hand, the order "Shut up!" may be rude but at least it's *unambiguous.*

ambient \'am-bē-ənt\ Existing or present on all sides.

• The ambient lighting in the restaurant was low, and there was a bright candle at each table.

Ambient light is the light that fills an area or surrounds something that's being viewed, like a television screen or a painting. Scientists sometimes refer to the ambient temperature, the temperature of the surrounding air. "Ambient music" is the term used today for "atmospheric" background music usually intended for relaxation or meditation. The candlelit restaurant in the example sentence is probably trying for a romantic *ambience,* or "atmosphere."

ambivalent \am-'bi-və-lənt\ (1) Holding opposite feelings and attitudes at the same time toward someone or something. (2) Continually wavering between opposites or alternative courses of action.

• He was ambivalent about the trip: he badly wanted to travel but hated to miss the summer activities at home.

Ambivalent is a fairly new word, less than a hundred years old, and, not surprisingly, it was first used by psychologists. Since being ambivalent means simply having mixed feelings about some question or issue, some of us spend most of our lives in a state of *ambivalence.* We might feel ambivalence about accepting a high-paying job that requires us to work long hours, about lending money to someone we like but don't know well—or about ordering a Tutti-Frutti Chocolate Banana Sundae El Supremo after we've been starving on a strict diet for weeks.

ambit \'am-bət\ The range or limit covered by something (such as a law).

• The treatment of farm animals generally falls outside the ambit of animal-cruelty laws in the U.S.

Ambit is a rather formal term, often used by lawyers, as in, "With this new legislation, tobacco now falls within the ambit of FDA regulation." It almost always refers to something abstract rather than an actual physical range. So, for example, an immigrant might live completely within the ambit of her immigrant community until she started college, where she might find herself in a much broader social ambit. Most of the Latin American colonies were established by Spain, but in the 19th century, as the U.S. became stronger and Spain became weaker, they began to enter the ambit of U.S. power.

EPI is a Greek prefix that may mean various things, but usually "on, over" or "attached to." So an earthquake's *epicenter* is the ground right over the center of the quake. And your *epidermis* is the outer layer of your skin, on top of the inner *dermis.*

epilogue \\'e-pə-ˌlòg\ The final section after the main part of a book or play.

• Her editor told her the book really needed an epilogue, to tell where each member of the family is today.

From its Greek roots, *epilogue* means basically "words attached (at the end)." An epilogue often somehow wraps up a story's action, as in the one for a famous Shakespeare play that ends, "For never was a story of more woe / Than this of Juliet and her Romeo." In nonfiction books, we now often use the term *afterword* instead of *epilogue*, just as we now generally use *foreword* instead of *prologue* (see LOG, p. 203). Movies also often have a kind of epilogue—maybe a scene after the exciting climax when the surviving lovers meet in a café to talk about their future. The epilogue of a musical composition, after all the drama is over, is called the *coda* (Italian for "tail").

epiphyte \\'e-pi-ˌfīt\ A plant that obtains its nutrients from the air and the rain and usually grows on another plant for support.

• The strangler fig begins life as an epiphyte on a tree branch, drops its tendrils to take root in the ground around the trunk, and slowly covers and strangles the tree to death.

Epiphytic plants are sometimes known as "air plants" because they seemingly survive on thin air. They rely on their host plants merely for physical support, not nourishment. Tropical epiphytes include orchids, ferns, and members of the pineapple family. To a newcomer in the tropical rain forest, the first sight of a great tree with large epiphytes hanging from every level can be eerie and astonishing. Familiar epiphytes of the temperate zone include lichens, mosses, and algae, which may grow on rocks or water without touching the soil.

epitaph \\'e-pi-ˌtaf\ An inscription on a grave or tomb in memory of the one buried there.

• The great architect Christopher Wren designed London's majestic St. Paul's Cathedral, the site of his tomb and epitaph: "Si monumentum requiris, circumspice" ("If you seek my monument, look around you").

Epitaph includes the root from the Greek word *taphos*, "tomb" or "funeral." Traditionally, *epitaph* refers to a tombstone inscription, but it can also refer to brief memorial statements that resemble such inscriptions. One of the most famous is Henry Lee's epitaph for George Washington: "First in war, first in peace, and first in the hearts of his countrymen."

epithet \\'e-pi-ˌthet\\ (1) A descriptive word or phrase occurring with or in place of the name of a person or thing. (2) An insulting or demeaning word or phrase.

• King Richard I of England earned the epithet "Lionhearted," while his brother, King John, was given the epithet "Lackland."

From its Greek roots, *epithet* would mean something "put on," or added. Sometimes the added name follows a given name, as in Erik the Red or Billy the Kid. In other cases, the epithet precedes the personal name, as in Mahatma ("Great-souled") Gandhi. In still others, it's used in place of the actual name, as in El Greco ("The Greek") or El Cid ("The Lord"). In its other common meaning, an *epithet* is a mocking or insulting name (like "Lackland" in the example sentence). When enemies are said to be "hurling epithets" at each other, it means they're exchanging angry insults.

Quizzes

A. Fill in each blank with the correct letter:

a. ambiguous   e. epithet
b. epiphyte   f. ambivalent
c. ambient   g. epilogue
d. epitaph   h. ambit

1. An _____ seems to live on air and water alone.
2. When the _____ light is low, photographers use a flash.
3. She felt _____ about the invitation, and couldn't decide whether to accept or decline.
4. Is any _____ inscribed on Grant's Tomb?
5. Andrew Jackson's _____, describing his lean toughness, was "Old Hickory."
6. Lord Raglan's _____ order confused the commander of the Light Brigade and led to its disastrous charge.
7. Her visit in the spring was a kind of _____ to our relationship, which had really ended two months earlier.

8. The subject really falls within the _____ of economics rather than sociology.

B. Match each word on the left with its correct definition on the right:

1. ambivalent
2. epithet
3. ambit
4. epiphyte
5. ambiguous
6. epitaph
7. ambient
8. epilogue

a. having more than one meaning
b. surrounding
c. wavering
d. grave inscription
e. range
f. descriptive nickname
g. ending
h. non-parasitic plant growing on another

HYP/HYPO is a Greek prefix meaning "below, under." Many *hypo-* words are medical. A *hypodermic* needle injects medication under the skin. *Hypotension*, or low blood pressure, can be just as unhealthy as the better-known *hypertension*, or high blood pressure.

---

hypochondriac \\ˌhī-pō-ˈkän-drē-ˌak\\ A person overly concerned with his or her own health who often suffers from delusions of physical disease.

• Hercule Poirot, the detective hero of the Agatha Christie mysteries, is a notorious hypochondriac, always trying to protect himself from drafts.

One disease a hypochondriac really does suffer from is *hypochondria*, the anxiety and depression that come from worrying too much about one's own health. Even though it's easy to joke about hypochondriacs, hypochondria is no joking matter for the sufferer. Somewhat surprisingly, the second part of *hypochondria* derives from *chondros*, the Greek word for "cartilage." The cartilage in question is that of the sternum, or breastbone. From ancient times, doctors believed that certain internal organs or regions were the seat of various diseases, both physical and mental, and the area under the breastbone was thought to be the source of hypochondria.

hypoglycemia \ˌhī-pō-glī-'sē-mē-ə\ Abnormal decrease of sugar in the blood.

- She had been controlling her hypoglycemia through diet and vitamins, but she now realized she needed to add daily exercise as well.

The root *glyk-* means "sweet" in Greek, so *glyc* shows up in the names of various terms referring to a sugar as a chemical ingredient, such as *glycerine* and *monoglyceride*. People with diabetes have difficulty controlling the sugar in their blood. Too little can be dangerous; its early symptoms may be as minor as nervousness, shaking, and sweating, but it can lead to seizures and unconsciousness. Luckily, it can be taken care of easily by eating or drinking something high in carbohydrates. Its opposite, *hyperglycemia* (see HYPER, p. 457), is the main symptom of diabetes, and usually requires an injection of insulin, which the sufferer usually gives himself. Today many people—though not doctors—use *hypoglycemia* to mean a completely different condition, with some of the same milder symptoms, that doesn't involve low blood sugar.

hypothermia \ˌhī-pō-'thər-mē-ə\ Subnormal temperature of the body.

- By the time rescuers were able to pull the boy from the pond's icy waters, hypothermia had reached a life-threatening stage.

Hypothermia, which usually results from submersion in icy water or prolonged exposure to cold, may constitute a grave medical emergency. It begins to be a concern when body temperature dips below 95°F, and the pulse, breathing, and blood pressure start to decline. Below 90°, the point at which the normal reaction of shivering ceases, emergency treatment is called for.

hypothetical \ˌhī-pə-'the-tə-kəl\ (1) Involving an assumption made for the sake of argument or for further study or investigation. (2) Imagined for purposes of example.

- The candidate refused to say what she would do if faced with a hypothetical military crisis.

The noun *hypothesis* comes straight from the Greek word meaning "foundation" or "base"—that is something "put under" something else. So a hypothesis is something you assume to be true in order that you can use it as the base or basis for a line of reasoning—and any such assumption can be called hypothetical. So, for example, the theory that the dinosaurs became extinct because of a giant meteor that struck the earth near the Yucatán Peninsula involves the hypothesis that such a collision would have had such terrible effects on the earth's climate that the great reptiles would have been doomed. Once a hypothesis has been thoroughly studied and researched without being proved wrong, it generally comes to be called a *theory* instead.

THERM/THERMO comes from the Greek word meaning "warm." A *thermometer* measures the amount of warmth in a body, the air, or an oven. A *thermostat* makes sure the temperature stays at the same level. And it's easy to see why the German manufacturers of a vacuum-insulated bottle back in 1904 gave it the name Thermos.

---

thermal \\'thər-məl\\ (1) Of, relating to, or caused by heat. (2) Designed to insulate in order to retain body heat.

• A special weave called thermal weave traps insulating air in little pockets to increase the warmth of long underwear and blankets.

In days gone by, much of the male population of the northern states in the cold months would wear a garment of thermal underwear covering the entire body, called a union suit. Union suits kept sodbusters, cowboys, and townsfolk alike not only warm but also itchy and a little on the smelly side (back when bathing once a week was considered the height of cleanliness). Thermal imaging is photography that captures "heat pictures"—rather than ordinary light pictures—of objects. And thermal pollution occurs when industrial water use ends up warming a river in a damaging way. Small-plane pilots use *thermal* as a noun for a warm updraft, often over a plowed field or desert, that lifts their wings, just as it enables hawks to soar upward without moving their wings.

thermodynamics \\ˌthər-mō-dī-'na-miks\\ Physics that deals with the mechanical actions or relations of heat.

• With his college major in electrical engineering, he assumed it would be an easy step to a graduate-school concentration in thermodynamics.

Thermodynamics (see DYNAM, p. 389) is based on the fact that all forms of energy, including heat and mechanical energy, are basically the same. Thus, it deals with the ways in which one form of energy is converted into another, when one of the forms is heat. The study of thermodynamics dates from before the invention of the first practical steam engine—an engine that uses steam to produce physical power—in the 18th century. Today most of the world's electrical power is actually produced by steam engines, and the principal use of thermodynamics is in power production.

thermonuclear \‚thər-mō-¹nü-klē-ər\ Of or relating to the changes in the nucleus of atoms with low atomic weight, such as hydrogen, that require a very high temperature to begin.

* In the 1950s and '60s, anxious American families built thousands of underground "fallout shelters" to protect themselves from the radiation of a thermonuclear blast.

Nuclear is the adjective for *nucleus*, the main central part of an atom. The original nuclear explosives, detonated in 1945, were so-called *fission* bombs, since they relied on the fission, or splitting, of the nuclei of uranium atoms. But an even greater source of destructive power lay in nuclear *fusion*, the forcing together of atomic nuclei. The light and heat given off by stars such as the sun come from a sustained fusion—or thermonuclear—reaction deep within it. On earth, such thermonuclear reactions were used to develop the hydrogen bomb, a bomb based on a fusion reaction that merged hydrogen atoms to become helium atoms. The thermonuclear era, which began in 1952, produced bombs hundreds of times more powerful than those exploded at the end of World War II. Why the *thermo-* in *thermonuclear*? Because great heat is required to trigger the fusion process, and the trigger used is actually a fission bomb.

British thermal unit The quantity of heat required to raise the temperature of one pound of water one degree Fahrenheit at a specified temperature.

* Wood-stove manufacturers compete with each other in their claims of how many British thermal units of heat output their stoves can produce.

Despite its name, the British thermal unit, or BTU, may be more widely used in North America than in Britain. Air conditioners, furnaces, and stoves are generally rated by BTUs. (Though "BTUs" is often short for "BTUs per hour"; in air-conditioner ratings, for instance, "BTUs" really means "BTUs of cooling capacity per hour.") Fuels such as natural gas and propane are also compared using BTUs. The BTU first appeared in 1876 and isn't part of the metric system—the metric unit of energy is the much smaller *joule*—so it isn't much used by scientists, but its practicality keeps it popular for consumer goods and fuels. A better-known heat unit is the *calorie*; a BTU is equal to about 252 calories. (Since the familiar food calorie is actually a *kilocalorie*, a BTU equals only about a quarter of a food calorie.)

Quizzes

A. Choose the closest definition:

1. hypothermia   a. excitability b. subnormal temperature c. external temperature d. warmth
2. thermodynamics   a. science of motion b. nuclear science c. science of explosives d. science of heat energy
3. hypoglycemia   a. extreme heat b. low blood sugar c. low energy d. high blood pressure
4. thermal   a. boiling b. heat-related c. scorching d. cooked
5. hypothetical   a. typical b. substandard c. sympathetic d. assumed
6. hypochondriac   a. person with imaginary visions b. person with heart congestion c. person with imaginary ailments d. person with imaginary relatives
7. British thermal unit   a. unit of electricity b. heat unit c. ocean current unit d. altitude unit
8. thermonuclear   a. nuclear reaction requiring high heat b. chemical reaction requiring a vacuum c. biological reaction producing bright light d. nuclear reaction based on distance from the sun

B. Indicate whether the following pairs of words have the same or different meanings:

1. British thermal unit / calorie   same ___ / different ___
2. hypochondriac / wise man   same ___ / different ___
3. thermal / insulating   same ___ / different ___
4. thermonuclear / destructive   same ___ / different ___

5.	hypoglycemia / high blood sugar	same ___ / different ___
6.	hypothetical / supposed	same ___ / different ___
7.	thermodynamics / explosives	same ___ / different ___
8.	hypothermia / low blood sugar	same ___ / different ___

POLY comes from *polys,* the Greek word for "many." A *polytech-nic* institute offers instruction in many technical fields. *Polygamy* is marriage in which one has many spouses, or at least more than the legal limit of one. And *polysyllabic* words are words of many syllables—of which there are quite a few in this book.

---

polyp \\'pä-ləp\\ (1) A sea invertebrate that has a mouth opening at one end surrounded by stinging tentacles. (2) A growth projecting from a mucous membrane, as on the colon or vocal cords.

• She had had a polyp removed from her throat, and for two weeks afterward she could only whisper.

This term comes from *polypous,* a Greek word for "octopus," which meant literally "many-footed." To the untrained eye, the inverte-brate known as the polyp may likewise appear to be many-footed, though it never walks anywhere since its "feet" are tentacles, used for stinging tiny organisms which the polyp then devours. The types of tumor known as polyps got their name because some seem to be attached to the surface by branching "foot"-like roots, even though most do not. Polyps of the nose or vocal cords are usually only inconvenient, causing breathing difficulty or hoarseness, and can be removed easily; however, polyps in the intestines can sometimes turn cancerous.

polyglot \\'pä-lē-ˌglät\\ (1) One who can speak or write several languages. (2) Having or using several languages.

• As trade between countries increases, there is more need for polyglots who can act as negotiators.

Polyglot contains the root *glot,* meaning "language." It is used both as a noun and as an adjective. Thus, we could say that an international airport is bound to be *polyglot,* with people from all over the world speaking their native languages. One of history's more interesting

Unit 3 55

polyglots was the Holy Roman Emperor Charles V, who claimed that he addressed his horse only in German, conversed with women in Italian and with men in French, but reserved Spanish (his original language) for his talks with God.

polymer \'pä-lə-mər\ A chemical compound formed by a reaction in which two or more molecules combine to form larger molecules with repeating structural units.

• Nylon, a polymer commercially introduced in 1938, can be spun and woven into fabrics or cast as tough, elastic blocks.

There are many natural polymers, including shellac, cellulose, and rubber. But synthetic polymers only came into being around 1870 with Celluloid, known especially for its use in photographic film. After many decades of development, the *polymeric* compounds now include *polypropylene,* used in milk crates, luggage, and hinges; *polyurethane,* used in paints, adhesives, molded items, rubbers, and foams; and *polyvinyl chloride* (PVC), used to make pipes that won't rust. And let's not forget *polyester,* which gave us a lot of uncool clothing in the 1970s but whose strength and resistance to corrosion have ensured that it remains an extremely useful material for all kinds of goods.

polygraph \'pä-lē-ˌgraf\ An instrument for recording changes in several bodily functions (such as blood pressure and rate of breathing) at the same time; lie detector.

• My brother-in-law is completely law-abiding, but he's such a nervous type that he's failed two polygraph tests at job interviews.

With its *graph-* root (see GRAPH, p. 277), *polygraph* indicates that it writes out several different results. A polygraph's output consists of a set of squiggly lines on a computer screen, each indicating one function being tested. The functions most commonly measured are blood pressure, breathing rate, pulse, and perspiration, all of which tend to increase when you lie. Polygraphs have been in use since 1924, and have gotten more sensitive over the years, though many experts still believe that they're unreliable and that a prepared liar can fool the machine. They're used not only for law enforcement but perhaps more often by employers—often the police department itself!—who don't want to hire someone who has broken the law in the past but won't admit to it.

PRIM comes from *primus,* the Latin word for "first." Something *primary* is first in time, rank, or importance. Something *primitive* is in its first stage of development. And something *primeval* had its origin in the first period of world or human history.

primal \\'prī-məl\\ Basic or primitive.

• There was always a primal pleasure in listening to the rain beat on the roof at night and dropping off to sleep in front of the fire.

Primal generally describes something powerful and almost instinctual. So when we speak of the primal innocence of youth or the primal intensity of someone's devotion, we're suggesting that the emotions or conditions being described are basic to our animal nature. Sitting around a campfire may feel like a primal experience, in which we share the emotions of our cave-dwelling ancestors. Intense fear of snakes or spiders may have primal roots, owing to the poison that some species carry. In "primal scream" therapy, popular in the 1970s, patients relive painful childhood experiences and express their frustration and anger through uncontrolled screaming and even violence.

primer \\'pri-mər\\ (1) A small book for teaching children to read. (2) A small introductory book on a subject.

• She announced that she'd be passing out a primer on mutual funds at the end of the talk.

Primers were once a standard part of every child's education. The first primer printed in North America, *The New England Primer* (ca. 1690), was typical; it contained many quotations from the Bible and many moral lessons, and the text was accompanied by numerous woodcut illustrations. We no longer use the word in early education, but it's widely used in everyday speech. Notice how *primer* is pronounced; don't mix it up with the kind of paint that's pronounced with a long *i* sound.

primate \\'prī-ˌmāt\\ Any member of the group of animals that includes human beings, apes, and monkeys.

• Dr. Leakey sent three young women to work with individual primates: Jane Goodall with the chimpanzees, Dian Fossey with the gorillas, and Birute Galdakis with the orangutans.

It was the great biologist Carolus Linnaeus who gave the primates their name, to indicate that animals of this order were the most advanced of all. Linnaeus listed human beings with the apes a hundred years before Charles Darwin would publish his famous work on evolution. When people told him that our close relationship to the apes and monkeys was impossible because it disagreed with the Bible, he responded that, from the biological evidence, he simply couldn't come to a different conclusion. Among the mammals, the primates are distinguished by their large brains, weak sense of smell, lack of claws, long pregnancies, and long childhoods, among other things. Along with the apes and monkey, the Primate order includes such interesting animals as the lemurs, tarsiers, galagos, and lorises.

primordial \prī-ˈmȯr-dē-əl\ (1) First created or developed. (2) Existing in or from the very beginning.

• Many astronomers think the universe is continuing to evolve from a primordial cloud of gas.

Primordial can be traced back to the Latin word *primordium,* or "origin," and applies to something that is only the starting point in a course of development or progression. A primordial landscape is one that bears no sign of human use, and a primordial cell is the first formed and least specialized in a line of cells. The substance out of which the earth was formed and from which all life evolved is commonly called "the primordial ooze" or "the primordial soup"— even by scientists.

Quizzes

A. Fill in each blank with the correct letter:

a. primer	e. polyp
b. polyglot	f. primordial
c. primate	g. polymer
d. polygraph	h. primal

1. The only language instruction the child had ever gotten was from a basic _____, but he was already reading at the fifth-grade level.

2. Rubber is a natural _____ that remains the preferred material for many uses.
3. The asteroids in our solar system may be remnants of a _____ cloud of dust.
4. She had never passed a _____ test, since apparently her heart rate always shot up when she was asked a question.
5. All the _____ species look after their children for much longer than almost any other mammals.
6. Having gone to school in four countries as a child, she was already a fluent _____.
7. They were charmed by the _____ innocence of the little village.
8. The medical tests had revealed a suspicious-looking _____ on his stomach.

B. Indicate whether the following pairs have the same or different meanings:

1. polyp / oyster   same ___ / different ___
2. primate / ape-family member   same ___ / different ___
3. polymer / molecule with
       repeating units   same ___ / different ___
4. primer / firstborn   same ___ / different ___
5. polyglot / speaking many
       languages   same ___ / different ___
6. primal / highest   same ___ / different ___
7. polygraph / lie detector   same ___ / different ___
8. primordial / primitive   same ___ / different ___

HOM/HOMO comes from *homos,* the Greek word for "same," which in English words may also mean "similar." A *homograph* is a word spelled like another word but different in meaning or pronunciation, and a *homosexual* is a person who favors others of the same sex. (This root has nothing to do with the Latin *homo,* meaning "person," as in *Homo sapiens,* the French *homme,* and the Spanish *hombre*.)

homonym \\'hä-mə-ˌnim\\ One of two or more words pronounced and/or spelled alike but different in meaning.

• The *pool* of "a pool of water" and the *pool* of "a game of pool" are homonyms.

Homonym can be troublesome because it may refer to three distinct classes of words. Homonyms may be words with identical pronunciations but different spellings and meanings, such as *to, too,* and *two*. Or they may be words with both identical pronunciations and identical spellings but different meanings, such as *quail* (the bird) and *quail* (to cringe). Finally, they may be words that are spelled alike but are different in pronunciation and meaning, such as the *bow* of a ship and *bow* that shoots arrows. The first and second types are sometimes called *homophones*, and the second and third types are sometimes called *homographs*—which makes naming the second type a bit confusing. Some language scholars prefer to limit *homonym* to the third type.

homogeneous \\ˌhō-mə-'jē-nē-əs\\ (1) Of the same or a similar kind. (2) Of uniform structure or composition throughout.

• Though she was raised in a small town, she found the city more interesting because its population was less homogeneous.

A slab of rock is homogeneous if it consists of the same material throughout, like granite or marble. A neighborhood might be called homogeneous if all the people in it are similar, having pretty much the same background, education, and outlook. *Homogeneity* is fine in a rock, though some people find it a little boring in a neighborhood (while others find it comforting). Note that many people spell this word *homogenous*, and pronounce it that way too.

homologous \\hō-'mä-lə-gəs\\ Developing from the same or a similar part of a remote ancestor.

• Arms and wings are homologous structures that reveal the ancient relationship between birds and four-legged animals.

In his famous discussion of the panda's thumb, Stephen Jay Gould carefully explains how this thumb is not homologous to the human thumb. Although the two digits are used in much the same way (the panda's thumb is essential for stripping bamboo of its tasty leaves, the staple of the panda's diet), the panda's thumb developed from a bone in its wrist and is an addition to the five "fingers" of its paw. The tiny stirrup and anvil bones of our inner ear, however, do seem to be homologous with the bones that allow a garter snake to swallow a frog whole.

homogenize \hō-ˈmä-jə-ˌnīz\ (1) To treat (milk) so that the fat is mixed throughout instead of floating on top. (2) To change (something) so that its parts are the same or similar.

• By now the suburb had gotten so homogenized that he couldn't tell the families on his street apart.

Homogenized milk has been around so long—about a hundred years—that many Americans have never seen milk with the cream on top, and probably think cream separation only happens in expensive yogurt. But *homogenize* was being used before anyone succeeded in getting milk and cream to mix. People who use the word often dislike the idea that everything is becoming the same, whether it's radio shows that are no longer produced locally or schools that rely too much on standardized testing.

DIS comes from Latin, where it means "apart." In English, its meanings have increased to include "opposite" or "not" (as in *distaste, disagreeable*), "deprive of" (*disinfect*), or "exclude or expel from" (*disbar*). The original meaning can still be seen in a word like *dissipate*, which means "to break up and scatter."

---

dissuade \di-ˈswād\ To convince (someone) not to do something.

• The thought of the danger he might be facing on the journey makes her uneasy, and she's trying to dissuade him from going.

Dissuade is the opposite of *persuade*, though it's a less common word. The dissuading may be done by a person or by something else: A bad weather forecast may dissuade a fisherman from going out to sea that day, but a warning on a cigarette pack almost never dissuades a real smoker from having his or her next cigarette.

disorient \dis-ˈȯr-ē-ˌent\ To cause to be confused or lost.

• By now the hikers were completely disoriented, and darkness was falling fast.

The Orient is the East (just as the Occident is the West). The verb *orient* comes from the traditional practice of building Christian churches so that the altar is at the building's easterly end—in other words, "orienting" the church. One reason for this practice is that the Book of Matthew says, "As the lightning comes from the East . . . so also will the Son of Man"—that is, just like the sun in the morning, Jesus in his Second Coming will appear in the East. *Orienteering* is participating in a cross-country race in which each person uses a map and compass to navigate the course. *Orient* comes from the word meaning "to rise" (like the sun), and still today it's easy for a hiker to become disoriented when an overcast sky hides the sun.

discredit \dis-ˈkre-dət\ (1) To cause (someone or something) to seem dishonest or untrue. (2) To damage the reputation of (someone).

- His book had been thoroughly discredited by scholars, and his reputation was badly damaged.

Since one meaning of *credit* is "trust," *discredit* means basically "destroy one's trust." A scientific study may be discredited if it turns out it was secretly written up by someone paid by a drug company. An autobiography may be discredited if someone discovers that the best parts came out of a novel. A lawyer may try to discredit testimony in a trial by revealing that the witness just got out of the slammer. Many political campaigns rely on discrediting one's opponents; desperate politicians have learned that, if they can claim that someone attacking them has been completely discredited, it might work even if it isn't true.

dislodge \dis-ˈläj\ To force out of a place, especially a place of rest, hiding, or defense.

- Senators are attempting to dislodge the bill from the committee, where the chairman has failed to act on it for five months.

A *lodge* is usually a kind of rooming house or hotel, and the verb *lodge* often means staying or sleeping in such a place. Thus, *dislodge* means removing a person or thing from where it's been staying. So, for instance, you might use a toothpick to dislodge a seed from between your teeth, police might use tear gas to dislodge a sniper from his hiding place, and a slate tile dislodged from a roof could be dangerous to someone hanging out on the street below.

Quizzes

A. Choose the closest definition:

1. dislodge   a. drink slowly b. scatter c. make pale
   d. remove
2. homonym   a. word meaning the same as another
   b. word spelled and sounded the same as another
   c. one with same name as another d. one who loves
   another of the same sex
3. discredit   a. cancel a bank card b. show to be
   untrue   c. dissolve d. lower one's grade
4. homogeneous   a. self-loving b. unusually brilliant
   c. having many parts d. consistent throughout
5. dissuade   a. remove b. break up c. advise against
   d. sweep away
6. homologous   a. of different length b. of similar size
   c. of different stages d. of similar origin
7. disorient   a. confuse b. disagree c. take away d. hide
8. homogenize   a. treat as the same b. explain
   thoroughly c. speak the same language d. mix
   thoroughly

**B. Match the definition on the left to the correct word
on the right:**

1. word spelled like another	a.	disorient
2. pry loose	b.	homogenize
3. having a consistent texture	c.	dissuade
4. perplex	d.	homonym
5. evolutionarily related	e.	discredit
6. damage a reputation	f.	homologous
7. make the same throughout	g.	dislodge
8. convince otherwise	h.	homogeneous

Latin Borrowings

ad hoc \\'ad-'häk\\ Formed or used for a particular purpose or for
immediate needs.

- The faculty formed an ad hoc committee to deal with the question
  of First Amendment rights on campus.

Ad hoc literally means "for this" in Latin, and in English this almost always means "for this specific purpose." Issues that come up in the course of a project often require immediate, ad hoc solutions. An ad hoc investigating committee is authorized to look into a matter of limited scope. An ad hoc ruling by an athletic council is intended to settle a particular case, and is not meant to serve as a model for later rulings. If an organization deals with too many things on an ad hoc basis, it may mean someone hasn't been doing enough planning.

ad hominem \\'ad-'hä-mə-nem\\ Marked by an attack on an opponent's character rather than by an answer to the arguments made or the issues raised.

• Presidential campaigns have often relied on ad hominem attacks rather than serious discussion of important issues.

Ad hominem in Latin means "to the man"—that is, "against the other person." The term comes from the field of rhetoric (the art of speaking and writing). If you have a weak argument, one easy way to defend yourself has always been to attack your opponent verbally in a personal way. Since such attacks require neither truth nor logic to be effective, their popularity has never waned.

alter ego \\'ȯl-tər-'ē-gō\\ (1) A trusted friend or personal representative. (2) The opposite side of a personality.

• The White House chief of staff is a political alter ego, who knows, or should know, who and what the President considers most important.

In Latin, *alter ego* literally means "second I." An alter ego can be thought of as a person's clone or second self. A professional alter ego might be a trusted aide who knows exactly what the boss wants done. A personal alter ego might be a close friend who is almost like a twin. *Alter ego* can also refer to the second, hidden side of one's own self. In Robert Louis Stevenson's classic *The Strange Case of Doctor Jekyll and Mr. Hyde,* Dr. Jekyll is a good-hearted, honorable man; but after taking a potion, his alter ego, the loathsome and diabolical Mr. Hyde, takes over his personality.

de facto \\dē-'fak-tō\\ Being such in practice or effect, although not formally recognized; actual.

• Although there was never a general declaration of war, the two countries were at war in a de facto sense for almost a decade.

Literally meaning "from the fact," *de facto* in English can be applied to anything that has the substance of something without its formal name. A de facto government is one that operates with all of the power of a regular government but without official recognition. De facto segregation isn't the result of laws, but can be just as real and deep-rooted as legally enforced segregation. The de facto leader of a group is just the one who all the rest seem to follow. (Compare *de jure*, p. 398.)

quid pro quo \ˌkwid-ˌprō-ˈkwō\ Something given or received for something else.

• He did something very nice for me years ago, so getting him that job was really a quid pro quo.

In Latin, *quid pro quo* means literally "something for something." Originally, the phrase was used to mean the substitution of an inferior medicine for a good one. Today it often doesn't suggest anything negative; for most people, it just means "a favor for a favor." But in politics the phrase is often used when, for example, a wealthy corporation gives a lot of money to a candidate and expects to get a big favor in return. In such cases, some of us may prefer to describe the money as a *bribe* and the quid pro quo as a *payoff*.

ex post facto \ˌeks-ˌpōst-ˈfak-tō\ Done, made, or formulated after the fact.

• When Carl tells us his "reasons" for why he behaved badly, they're nothing but ex post facto excuses for impulsive behavior.

Ex post facto is Latin for "from a thing done afterward." Approval for a project that's given ex post facto—after the project already has been begun or completed—may just have been given in order to save face. An ex post facto law is one that declares someone's action to be criminal only after it was committed—a procedure forbidden by our Constitution.

modus operandi \ˈmō-dəs-ˌä-pə-ˈran-ˌdī\ A usual way of doing something.

• A criminal who commits repeated crimes can often be identified by his modus operandi.

Modus operandi is Latin for "method of operating." The term is often associated with police work, and it's a favorite of mystery writers. In speech and dialogue, it's often abbreviated to "m.o." (as in "We're beginning to get a handle on the killer's m.o., but we can't go public with it yet"). But it's not only used in criminal contexts. So a frequent gambler who likes to play the horses may have a particular modus operandi for picking winners. And the familiar modus operandi of a cutthroat retailer may be to undersell competitors, drive them out of business, and then raise prices afterwards.

modus vivendi \\'mō-dəs-vi-'ven-dē\\ (1) A practical compromise or arrangement that is acceptable to all concerned. (2) A way of life.

• During the budget crisis, the Democratic governor and the Republican legislature established a good working modus vivendi.

Modus vivendi literally means "manner of living" in Latin, and it sometimes has that meaning in English as well. Usually, though, a modus vivendi is a working arrangement that disputing parties can live with, at least until a more permanent solution can be found. Typically, a modus vivendi is an arrangement that ignores differences and difficulties. So, for example, two people going through a bitter divorce may be able to arrive at a modus vivendi that allows them to at least maintain an appearance of civility and dignity.

Quiz

Choose the closest definition:

1. alter ego   a. church structure b. bad conscience
   c. intimate friend d. self-love
2. modus vivendi   a. pie with ice cream
   b. compromise c. stalemate d. immoral conduct
3. ad hoc   a. for this purpose b. permanent
   c. long-range d. for many reasons
4. ex post facto   a. in anticipation b. sooner or later
   c. coming after d. someday
5. ad hominem   a. based on personalities b. based on
   logic c. based on issues d. based on sexual preference
6. modus operandi   a. procedure b. way of moving
   c. crime d. arrest

7. de facto   a. in transit   b. in effect   c. in debt
     d. in theory
8. quid pro quo   a. proven truth   b. philosophical
     question   c. mystery   d. something given in return

Review Quizzes

A. Complete the analogy:

1. anxious : calm :: ambivalent : _____
     a. neutral   b. certain   c. funloving   d. jittery
2. prologue : beginning :: epilogue : _____
     a. start   b. end   c. book   d. drama
3. past : previous :: ex post facto : _____
     a. beforehand   b. afterward   c. during   d. actually
4. local : here :: ambient : _____
     a. there   b. somewhere   c. nowhere   d. everywhere
5. rodent : woodchuck :: primate : _____
     a. zoology   b. mammal   c. antelope   d. baboon
6. support : assist :: dissuade : _____
     a. distrust   b. convince   c. soothe   d. discourage
7. personal : impersonal :: ad hominem : _____
     a. to the time   b. to the issue   c. to the end   d. to the
     maximum
8. floral : flowers :: thermal : _____
     a. weight   b. pressure   c. terms   d. heat

B. Fill in each blank with the correct letter:

a. ad hoc	i. dissuade
b. ambivalent	j. modus vivendi
c. modus operandi	k. primer
d. epithet	l. alter ego
e. thermonuclear	m. polyglot
f. quid pro quo	n. hypochondriac
g. polymer	o. ambit
h. homogeneous	

1. A real _____, she could speak four languages and read
three others.

2. The independent-minded teenager and her overprotective parents struggled to arrive at a _____ that both sides could accept.

3. The usual _____ for the songwriters was for one to write the lyrics first and then for the other to compose the music.

4. She is such a close friend that she seems like my _____.

5. The Congressman's vote was seen as a _____ for the insurance industry's campaign contributions.

6. She's the only person who could possibly _____ him from proceeding with this foolish plan.

7. Much thought has gone into the designing of _____ power plants that run on nuclear fusion.

8. The development of the first synthetic _____ for use as fabric revolutionized the garment industry.

9. "Gray-eyed" is the standard _____ used to describe the goddess Athena.

10. She had written a little _____ on volunteering, which she was now expanding into a full-length book.

11. Jessica was _____ about going to the party: it sounded exciting, but she wouldn't know any of the other guests.

12. In her middle age she became a thorough _____, always convinced she was suffering from some new disease.

13. You should blend all ingredients thoroughly to produce a _____ mixture.

14. An _____ committee was named to come up with ideas for redecorating the waiting room.

15. He reminded the audience that particle physics didn't really fall within the _____ of his expertise.

C. Indicate whether the following pairs have the same or different meanings:

1. de facto / actually   same ___ / different ___
2. hypothermia / heatstroke   same ___ / different ___
3. primordial / existing from
     the beginning   same ___ / different ___
4. ambient / atmospheric   same ___ / different ___
5. polyphonic / religious   same ___ / different ___
6. primal / first   same ___ / different ___

7. ambiguous / unclear   same ___ / different ___
8. modus operandi / way of life   same ___ / different ___
9. homologous / blended   same ___ / different ___
10. discredit / mislead   same ___ / different ___
11. thermal / soil-related   same ___ / different ___
12. epiphyte / parasite   same ___ / different ___
13. quid pro quo / synonym   same ___ / different ___
14. epitaph / grave inscription   same ___ / different ___
15. dislodge / deflate   same ___ / different ___

UNIT

4

VOR comes from the Latin verb *vorare,* "to eat," and the ending *-ivorous* shows up in words that refer to eaters of certain kinds of food. *Frugivorous* (for "fruit-eating"), *granivorous* (for "grain-eating"), and *graminivorous* (for "grass-eating") aren't too rare, but you won't run across *phytosuccivorous* ("plant-sap-eating") every day.

---

carnivorous \kär-ˈni-və-rəs\ Meat-eating or flesh-eating.

• He'd gotten tired of his vegetarian guinea pigs and decided he preferred carnivorous pets such as ferrets.

The order of mammals that Linnaeus named the Carnivora includes such families as the dogs, the bears, the raccoons, the weasels, the hyenas, the cats, and the seals. Most *carnivores* eat only meat in the wild, but some have varied diets; some bears, for instance, normally eat far more vegetation than meat. Carnivores have powerful jaws and complex teeth, and most are highly intelligent. Humans, like their ape cousins, are basically *omnivores* (see p. 344).

herbivorous \hər-ˈbi-və-rəs\ Plant-eating.

• In spite of their frightening appearance, marine iguanas are peaceable herbivorous animals that feed mostly on seaweed.

Many herbivorous animals, such as rabbits, deer, sheep, and cows, are noted for their gentle and passive ways. But such behavior is not universal among *herbivores*. Rhinoceroses and elephants, for instance, are capable of inflicting serious damage if threatened, and among dinosaurs, the herbivorous Diplodocus had a thick tail that could be used as a lethal weapon against attacking carnivores. Herbivorous humans are usually called *vegetarians*.

insectivorous \ˌin-ˌsek-ˈtiv-rəs\ Feeding on insects.

• Their rather odd 12-year-old son kept insectivorous plants in his bedroom and fed them live flies.

A wide variety of animals could be called *insectivores*—most of the birds, for example, as well as the spiders. Of the amphibians, frogs and many lizards are largely insectivorous. Even some fish get much of their food from insects. The order of mammals called Insectivora contains the shrews, moles, and hedgehogs, though bats and anteaters are also insectivores. Many insects are themselves insectivores; the dragonfly, for instance, is a swift insectivorous terror that lives up to its name. But it's the insectivorous plants that tend to fascinate us; of the over 600 species, the best known are the Venus flytrap (which snaps shut on its prey), the pitcher plants (which drown insects in a tiny pool of water), and the sundews (which capture insects with their sticky surfaces).

voracious \və-ˈrā-shəs\ Having a huge appetite.

• One of the hardest parts of dieting is watching skinny people with voracious appetites consume large amounts of food without gaining weight.

Voracious can be applied to people, animals, and even things, and doesn't always refer to consuming food. Thus, teenagers are voracious eaters; you may become a voracious reader on vacation; and Americans have long been voracious consumers. The most voracious bats may eat three-quarters of their weight in insects in a single night. Some countries have a voracious appetite for oil. Voracious corporations keep "swallowing" other companies through mergers.

CARN comes from a Latin word meaning "flesh" or "meat." *Carnation* originally meant "the color of flesh," which was once the only color of the flower we call the carnation. In Christian countries, Lent is the period when the faithful traditionally give up something they love, often meat. The days leading up to Lent are known as the *carnival* season, from the Italian *carnelevare*, later shortened to *carnevale*, which meant "removal of meat"—though during carnival, of course, people indulge in just about everything, and the removal of meat only comes later.

carnage \\\'kär-nij\\ Great destruction of life (as in a battle); slaughter.

- Countries around the world appealed to all sides of the conflict to stop the carnage of the war in Bosnia.

This word was taken over straight from French (a Latin-based language), and has mostly referred to large-scale killing in wartime. But *carnage* needn't refer only to slaughter on the battlefield. With tens of thousands of people dying each year in automobile accidents, it's appropriate to speak of carnage on the nation's highways. And those concerned about the effects of the violence we see constantly on TV and movie screens may refer to that as carnage as well.

carnal \\\'kär-nəl\\ Having to do with bodily pleasures.

- The news stories about students on Spring Break tend to focus on the carnal pleasures associated with the annual ritual.

In Christianity in past centuries, *carnal* was often used as the opposite of *spiritual,* describing what are sometimes called "the pleasures of the flesh." Thus, gluttony—the consumption of excessive food and drink—was a deadly carnal sin, whereas the holiest monks and hermits might eat hardly anything and never touch wine. Today *carnal* has a somewhat old-fashioned sound; when we use it, we generally mean simply "sexual."

incarnate \\in-\'kär-nət\\ Given bodily or actual form; especially, having human body.

- For the rest of his life, he would regard his childhood nanny as goodness incarnate.

Incarnate often has a religious ring to it, since for centuries it has been used in the Christian church, which regards Jesus as the *incarnation* of God—that is, as God made human. Surprisingly, neither word appears in Bible translations; instead, the Latin word *incarnatus* appears in the Christian creeds (basic statements of belief) and the Catholic Mass. Regardless, *incarnate* soon began to be used with various nouns: "the devil incarnate," "evil incarnate," etc. Notice that *incarnate* is one of the rare adjectives that usually, but not always, follows its noun. *Incarnate* is also a verb, though with a slightly different pronunciation: "This report simply incarnates the prejudices of its authors," "For her followers, she incarnates the virtue of selflessness," etc.

reincarnation \ˌrē-ˌin-ˌkär-ˈnā-shən\ (1) Rebirth in new bodies or forms of life. (2) Someone who has been born again with a new body after death.

• Even as a child he struck everyone as a reincarnation of his grandfather, not in his features but in his manner and personality.

It's easy to make fun of people who claim to be the reincarnation of Cleopatra or Napoleon, but they don't come from a culture that takes reincarnation seriously. In Hindu belief, a person must pass through a series of reincarnations—some of which may be as insects or fish— before fully realizing that the bodily pleasures are shallow and that only spiritual life is truly valuable; only then do the reincarnations cease. For Hindus, an "old soul" is a person who seems unusually wise from early in life, and whose wisdom must have come from passing through many reincarnations.

Quizzes

A. Indicate whether the following pairs have the same or different meanings:

1. carnage / slaughter   same ___ / different ___
2. insectivorous / buglike   same ___ / different ___
3. reincarnation / rebirth   same ___ / different ___
4. voracious / extremely hungry   same ___ / different ___
5. carnal / spiritual   same ___ / different ___
6. herbivorous / vegetarian   same ___ / different ___
7. incarnate / holy   same ___ / different ___
8. carnivorous / meat-eating   same ___ / different ___

B. Fill in each blank with the correct letter:

a. reincarnation   e. voracious
b. insectivorous   f. herbivorous
c. carnage   g. carnal
d. carnivorous   h. incarnate

1. Sheep, cattle, and antelope are _____; unlike dogs and cats, they show no interest in meat.
2. The school tried to shield students from _____ temptations.
3. The smallest mammal is the bumblebee bat, an _____ creature about the size of a dime.

4. Today he speaks of his former stepfather as evil _____, and his mother doesn't argue with him.

5. From the variety of books on his shelves, we could tell he was a _____ reader.

6. Even the ambulance drivers were horrified by the _____ of the accident.

7. As a child she loved to watch them throw meat to the _____ ones, especially the lions and tigers.

8. The current Dalai Lama is said to be the 13th _____ of the first one, who lived in the 15th century.

CRED comes from *credere,* the Latin verb meaning "to believe" or "to entrust." We have a good *credit* rating when institutions trust in our ability to repay a loan, and we carry *credentials* so that others will believe that we are who we say we are.

---

credence \\'krē-dəns\\ Mental acceptance of something as true or real; belief.

• He scoffed and said no one still gives any credence to the story of the Loch Ness monster.

Credence is close in meaning to *belief,* but there are differences. Unlike *belief, credence* is seldom used in connection with faith in a religion or philosophy. Instead *credence* is often used in reference to reports, rumors, and opinions. And, unlike *belief,* it tends to be used with the words *give, lack, lend,* and *gain.* So a new piece of evidence may lend credence to the alibi of a criminal suspect. Claims that a political candidate can become the next President gain credence only after the candidate wins a few primaries. And although stories about Elvis sightings persist, they lack credence for most people.

credible \\'kre-də-bəl\\ (1) Able to be believed; reasonable to trust or believe. (2) Good enough to be effective.

• Because of her past criminal record, the defense lawyers knew she wouldn't be a credible witness.

Credible evidence is evidence that's likely to be believed. A credible plan is one that might actually work, and a credible excuse is one your parents might actually believe. And just as *credible* means "believable," the noun *credibility* means "believability." (But we no longer use *incredible* to mean the literal opposite of *credible*, just as we no longer use *unbelievable* as the literal opposite of *believable*.) Since *cred* is short for *credibility*, "street cred" is the kind of credibility among tough young people that you can only get by proving yourself on the mean streets of the inner city.

credulity \kri-ˈdü-lə-tē\ Readiness and willingness to believe on the basis of little evidence.

• Thrillers and action movies only succeed if they don't strain our credulity too much.

A particularly far-fetched story may be said to strain credulity, stretch credulity, put demands on our credulity, or make claims on our credulity. Credulity is a quality of innocent children (of all ages) and isn't always a bad thing; it must have been pure credulity that enabled Chicago White Sox and Philadelphia Phillies fans to wait so long for a World Series victory ("This is the year they're going to take it!"), which probably made life bearable for them. The related adjective is *credulous*. F. Scott Fitzgerald once defined advertising as "making dubious promises to a credulous public."

credo \ˈkrē-ˌdō\ (1) A statement of the basic beliefs of a religious faith. (2) A set of guiding principles or beliefs.

• She claims she made her money on Wall Street just by following the old credo "Buy low, sell high."

Credo comes straight from the Latin word meaning "I believe," and is the first word of many religious credos, or *creeds*, such as the Apostles' Creed and the Nicene Creed. But the word can be applied to any guiding principle or set of principles. Of course, you may choose a different credo when you're 52 than when you're 19. But here is the credo of the writer H. L. Mencken, written after he had lived quite a few years: "I believe that it is better to tell the truth than to lie. I believe that it is better to be free than to be a slave. And I believe that it is better to know than to be ignorant."

FID comes from *fides,* the Latin word for "faith" or "trust." *Fidelity* is another word for "faithfulness." *Confidence* is having faith in someone or something. An *infidel* is someone who lacks a particular kind of religious faith. And the once-popular dog's name *Fido* is Latin for "I trust."

affidavit \ˌa-fə-ˈdā-vət\ A sworn statement made in writing.

- The whole family had signed affidavits stating that they believed the will to be valid.

In Latin, *affidavit* means "he (she) has sworn an oath," and an affidavit is always a sworn written document. If it contains a lie, the person making it may be prosecuted. Affidavits are often used in court when it isn't possible for someone to appear in person. Police officers must usually file an affidavit with a judge to get a search warrant. Affidavits (unlike similar signed statements called *depositions*) are usually made without an opposing lawyer being present and able to ask questions.

diffident \ˈdi-fə-dənt\ Lacking confidence; timid, cautious.

- He always found it a struggle to get his most diffident students to speak in front of the class.

Diffident means lacking faith in oneself—in other words, the opposite of *confident*. Distrust in your abilities or opinions usually makes you hesitate to speak or act. Patients who feel diffident around their doctors, for example, don't dare ask them many questions. A helpful friend tries to instill confidence in place of *diffidence*.

fiduciary \fi-ˈdü-shē-ˌer-ē\ (1) Having to do with a confidence or trust. (2) Held in trust for another.

- Pension-fund managers have a fiduciary responsibility to invest the pension's funds for the sole benefit of those who will receive the pensions.

A fiduciary relationship is one in which one person places faith in another. Stockbrokers and real-estate agents have fiduciary duties to their clients, which means they must act in their clients' best financial interests. Members of a company's board of directors have a fiduciary responsibility to protect the financial interests of the company's shareholders. There are legal requirements for those with fiduciary responsibility, and they can be sued for breach of fiduciary duty if they fail.

perfidy \ˈpər-fə-dē\ Faithlessness, disloyalty, or treachery.

- While working for the CIA he was lured into becoming a double agent, and it seems he paid a high price for his perfidy.

The *perfidious* Benedict Arnold plotted with the British to surrender West Point to them during the American Revolution—an act that made his name a synonym for *traitor*. In recent years, the perfidy of the double agents Aldrich Ames (of the CIA) and Robert Hanssen (of the FBI) has become notorious.

Quizzes

A. Fill in each blank with the correct letter:

a. perfidy   e. credo
b. credible   f. affidavit
c. diffident   g. fiduciary
d. credulity   h. credence

1. She gave little _____ to his story about his deranged girlfriend and the kitchen knife.

2. Their account of the burglary didn't strike investigators as _____, and the insurance company refused to pay.

3. For her own best friend to take up with her former husband was _____ that could never be forgiven.

4. He's so _____ that you'd never believe he gives talks in front of international organizations.

5. The family trust had been so badly mismanaged that it appeared there had been a violation of _____ responsibility.

6. The company's odd but charming _____ was "Don't be evil."

7. The _____ stated that no oral agreement had ever been made.

8. Her _____ is enormous; no story in the supermarket tabloids is too far-fetched for her.

B. Match the definition on the left to the correct word on the right:

1. bad faith   a. perfidy
2. timid   b. credible
3. acceptance   c. diffident
4. trust-based   d. credulity
5. sworn document   e. credo
6. believable   f. affidavit

7.	principles	g.	fiduciary
8.	trustfulness	h.	credence

CURR/CURS comes from *currere*, the Latin verb meaning "to run." Although words based on this root don't tend to suggest speed, the sense of movement remains. *Current*, for instance, refers to running water in a stream or river, or electrons running through a wire, and an *excursion* is a trip from one place to another.

concurrent \kən-'kər-ənt\ Happening or operating at the same time.

• The killer was sentenced to serve three concurrent life terms in prison.

Things that are concurrent usually not only happen at the same time but also are similar to each other. So, for example, multitasking computers are capable of performing concurrent tasks. When we take more than one medication at a time, we run the risks involved with concurrent drug use. And at any multiplex theater several movies are running *concurrently*.

cursory \'kər-sə-rē\ Hastily and often carelessly done.

• Having spent the weekend going to parties, she had only given the chapter a cursory reading before class on Monday.

Unlike the other words in this section, *cursory* always implies speed. But it also stresses a lack of attention to detail. Cursory observations are generally shallow or superficial because of their speed. And when citizens complain about a cursory police investigation of a crime, they're distressed by its lack of thoroughness, not its speed.

discursive \dis-'kər-siv\ Passing from one topic to another.

• Some days he allowed himself to write long discursive essays in his diary instead of his usual simple reporting of the day's events.

The Latin verb *discurrere* meant "to run about," and from this word we get our word *discursive*, which often means rambling about over a wide range of topics. A discursive writing style generally isn't encouraged by writing teachers. But some of the great 19th-century writers, such as Charles Lamb and Thomas de Quincey, show that the discursive essay, especially when gracefully written and somewhat personal in tone, can be a pleasure to read. And the man often called the inventor of the essay, the great Michel de Montaigne, might touch on dozens of different topics in the course of a long discursive essay.

precursor \ˈprē-ˌkər-sər\ One that goes before and indicates the coming of another.

• Scientists are trying to identify special geological activity that may be a precursor to an earthquake, which will help them predict the quake's size, time, and location.

With its prefix *pre-*, meaning "before," a precursor is literally a "forerunner," and in fact *forerunner* first appeared as the translation of the Latin *praecursor*. But the two words function a little differently today. A forerunner may simply come before another thing, but a precursor generally paves the way for something. So, for example, the Office of Strategic Services in World War II was the immediate precursor of today's Central Intelligence Agency, while the blues music of the 1930s and 1940s was only one of the precursors of the rock and roll of today.

PED comes from the Latin word for "foot." A *pedal* is pushed by the foot; a *pedicure* is a treatment of the feet, toes, and toenails; and a *pedestal* is what a statue stands on—in a sense, its foot.

---

quadruped \ˈkwä-drə-ˌped\ An animal having four feet.

• She always tells her friends that their farm has five kinds of quadrupeds: sheep, goats, cows, horses, and pigs.

The quadrupeds include almost all the mammals. (Among the exceptions are whales, bats, and humans.) The Greek equivalent of this Latin word is *tetrapod*. However, the two are not identical, since the tetrapod classification includes *bipeds* such as birds, in which two of the limbs are no longer used for walking. Insects all have six legs, of course, and in the sea there are eight-legged *octopods* (including the octopus). But there are no animals of any kind with an odd number of legs.

pedigree \\'pe-də-₁grē\ The line of ancestors of a person or animal.

- She talks a lot about her pedigree, but never mentions that a couple of her uncles spent time in prison.

What does someone's ancestry have to do with feet? Because someone once thought that a family tree, or genealogical chart, resembled a crane's foot (in French, *pied de grue*), even though cranes' feet only have four talons or claws, no more than any other bird, while a family tree may have hundreds of branches. The word *pedigree* is usually used for purebred animals—cats, racehorses, and dogs, as well as livestock such as cows and sheep. Some people continue to believe that "purity" in human family trees is a good thing as well, though most of us find the idea a little creepy.

impediment \im-'pe-də-mənt\ Something that interferes with movement or progress.

- Her poorly developed verbal ability was the most serious impediment to her advancement.

Impediment comes from a Latin verb that meant "to interfere with" or "to get in the way of progress," as if by tripping up the feet of someone walking. In English, *impediment* still suggests an obstruction or obstacle along a path; for example, a lack of adequate roads and bridges would be called an impediment to economic development. Impediments usually get in the way of something we want. So we may speak of an impediment to communication, marriage, or progress—but something that slows the progress of aging, disease, or decay is rarely called an impediment.

pedestrian \pə-'des-trē-ən\ Commonplace, ordinary, or unimaginative.

- While politicians endlessly discussed the great issues facing Russia, the Russians worried about such pedestrian concerns as finding enough food, shelter, and clothing.

Most of us know *pedestrian* as a noun meaning someone who travels on foot. But the adjective sense of *pedestrian* as defined here is actually its original meaning. To be pedestrian was to be drab or dull, as if plodding along on foot rather than speeding on horseback or by coach. *Pedestrian* is often used to describe a colorless or lifeless writing style, but it can also describe politicians, public tastes, personal qualities, or possessions. In comparison with the elaborate stage shows put on by today's rock artists, for instance, most of the stage presentations of 1960s rock stars seem pedestrian.

Quizzes

A. Fill in each blank with the correct letter:

a. concurrent   e. cursory
b. pedigree   f. impediment
c. precursor   g. discursive
d. pedestrian   h. quadruped

1. The warm days in March were a _____ to spring floods that were sure to come.
2. His rather snobbish grandmother only seemed to be concerned about his fiancée's _____.
3. After only a _____ look at the new car, he knew he had to have it.
4. The presence of her little sister was a definite _____ to her romantic plans for the evening.
5. She came to enjoy the _____ style of the older, rambling essays.
6. From his fleeting glimpse, all he could tell was that it was a small brown _____ that could move very fast.
7. Convention-goers had to decide which of the _____ meetings to attend.
8. His sister's trips to Borneo made his vacations at the seashore seem _____.

B. Match the definition on the left to the correct word on the right:

1. simultaneous   a. impediment
2. obstacle   b. precursor
3. four-footed animal   c. quadruped
4. forerunner   d. discursive
5. hasty   e. pedestrian
6. ancestry   f. pedigree
7. rambling   g. cursory
8. ordinary   h. concurrent

FLECT comes from *flectere,* the Latin verb meaning "to bend." The root sometimes takes the form *flex-.* Things that are *flexible* can be bent, and when you *flex* a muscle, you're usually bending a limb—which, as a trainer at the gym will tell you, requires the use of *flexor* muscles.

---

deflect \di-ˈflekt\ To turn aside, especially from a straight or fixed course.

• The stealth technology used on bombers and fighter jets works by deflecting radar energy, making them "invisible."

Use of the physical meaning of *deflect* is common. Thus, a soccer goalie's save might involve deflecting the ball rather than catching it, and workers wear eye shields to deflect tiny particles flying out of machines. But the nonphysical meaning may be even more common. A Hollywood actress might deflect criticism about her personal life by giving lavishly to charity, for example, and we've all tried to change the subject to deflect a question we really didn't want to answer.

reflective \ri-ˈflekt\ (1) Capable of reflecting light, images, or sound waves. (2) Thoughtful.

• He likes action movies and going out drinking with friends, but when you get to know him you realize he's basically reflective and serious.

Reflective people are people who *reflect* on things—that is, look back at things that have been done or said in order to think calmly and quietly about them. Most reflective people would agree with Socrates that (as he told the jury that would soon sentence him to death) "The unexamined life is not worth living." Reflective people tend to be a bit philosophical and intellectual. But almost everyone has reflective moods; gazing into a fireplace or a campfire seems to do it to almost everyone.

genuflect \ˈjen-yù-ˌflekt\ To kneel on one knee and then rise as an act of respect.

• At religious shrines in China, pilgrims may not only genuflect but actually lie down flat on the ground.

Genuflection, which contains the root *genu-*, "knee," has long been a mark of respect and obedience. King Arthur's Knights of the Round Table genuflected not only when he knighted them but whenever they greeted him formally, and this custom remains in countries today that are still ruled by royalty. In some churches, each worshipper is expected to genuflect whenever entering or leaving a pew on the central aisle.

inflection \in-ˈflek-shən\ (1) A change in the pitch, tone, or loudness of the voice. (2) The change in form of a word showing its case, gender, number, person, tense, mood, voice, or comparison.

• She couldn't understand her grandfather's words, but she knew from his inflection that he was asking a question.

Changing the pitch, tone, or loudness of our words are ways we communicate meaning in speech, though not on the printed page. A rising inflection at the end of a sentence generally indicates a question, and a falling inflection indicates a statement, for example. Another way of *inflecting* words is by adding endings: *-s* to make a noun plural, *-ed* to put a verb in the past tense, *-er* to form the comparative form of an adjective, and so on.

POST comes from a Latin word meaning "after" or "behind." A *postscript* (or PS) is a note that comes after an otherwise completed letter, usually as an afterthought. *Postpartum* refers to the period following childbirth, with any related events and complications. To *postdate* a check is to give it a date after the day it was written.

---

posterior \pō-ˈstir-ē-ər\ Situated toward or on the back; rear.

• In a human *posterior* and *dorsal* can both refer to the back, but in a fish *posterior* refers to the tail area.

Posterior comes from the Latin word *posterus,* meaning "coming after." *Posterior* is often used as a technical term in biology and medicine to refer to the back side of things, and is the opposite of *anterior,* which refers to the front side. For example, as more people took up running as a sport, doctors began to see an increase in stress fractures along the posterior as well as the anterior surface of the lower leg bones. In some technical fields, *posterior* may mean "later." When used as a noun, *posterior* simply means "buttocks."

posthumous \\ˈpäs-chə-məs\\ (1) Published after the death of the author. (2) Following or happening after one's death.

- Though Van Gogh scarcely sold a single painting during his lifetime, he rose to posthumous fame as one of the world's great artists.

Posthumous fame is fame that comes a little late. In fact, its original meaning in English is "born after the death of the father." Bill Clinton was the posthumous son of a father who died in an automobile accident. The word is now mostly used of artistic works that appear after the death of the artist, or the changing reputation of a dead artist. Such posthumous works as Herman Melville's *Billy Budd*, the diary of Anne Frank, and almost all the poetry of Emily Dickinson have become legendary, and in each case they had a major influence on the writer's reputation.

postmodern \\ˌpōst-ˈmä-dərn\\ Having to do with a movement in architecture, art, or literature that is a reaction against modernism and that reintroduces traditional elements and techniques in odd contexts as well as elements from popular culture.

- The postmodern AT&T building in New York, with the "Chippendale" top that reminds viewers of an antique dresser, aroused a storm of criticism.

With its prefix *post-*, *postmodern* describes a movement that has reacted against modernism. Modernism, dating from around the start of the 20th century, represented a sharp break from 19th-century styles. But in the 1970s architects began to be dissatisfied with the stark simplicity of most modern architecture and began including in their mostly modern designs such traditional elements as columns, arches, and keystones and sometimes startling color contrasts such as might have come from advertising and pop culture. In art and literature, as in architecture, *postmodernism* often seems to be making fun of tradition, especially by denying that there's any real distinction between serious and popular art or writing. Wherever it has shown up, postmodernism has been greeted with a mixture of approval, disapproval, and sometimes amusement.

postmortem \\ˌpōst-ˈmȯr-təm\\ (1) Occurring after death. (2) Following the event.

- In their postmortem discussion of the election, the reporters tried to explain how the polls and predictions could have been so completely wrong.

Post mortem is Latin for "after death." In English, *postmortem* refers to an examination, investigation, or process that takes place after death. A postmortem examination of a body (often simply called a *postmortem*) is often needed to determine the time and cause of death; the stiffening called rigor mortis is one postmortem change that doctors look at to determine when death occurred. Today we've come to use *postmortem* to refer to any examination or discussion that takes place after an event.

Quizzes

A. Choose the closest definition:

1. posthumous   a. before the event b. born prematurely c. occurring after death d. early in development
2. reflective   a. merry b. thoughtful c. glowing d. gloomy
3. posterior   a. on the front b. on the back c. underneath d. on top
4. deflect   a. fold over b. kneel c. turn aside d. protect
5. postmodern   a. ultramodern b. traditional c. contemporary d. mixing styles
6. inflection   a. style in art b. change in pitch c. muscle d. part to the rear
7. genuflect   a. kneel b. flex a muscle c. fold back d. change one's tone of voice
8. postmortem   a. after the event b. before the event c. caused by the event d. causing the event

B. Complete the analogy:

1. postscript : letter :: postmortem : _____
   a. examination b. death c. body d. morgue
2. clever : dull :: reflective : _____
   a. lazy b. educated c. calm d. empty-headed
3. prenatal : before birth :: posthumous : _____
   a. after birth b. before life c. after death d. famous

4. reflect : mirror :: deflect : _____
   a. shield b. laser c. metal d. spear
5. accent : syllable :: inflection : _____
   a. note b. hint c. turn d. word
6. wave : friendship :: genuflect : _____
   a. salute b. knee c. power d. obedience
7. exterior : interior :: posterior : _____
   a. frontal b. behind c. beside d. above
8. hip-hop : music :: postmodern : _____
   a. tradition b. design c. style d. architecture

Words from Mythology

calypso \kə-ˈlip-sō\ A folk song or style of singing of West Indian origin that has a lively rhythm and words that are often made up by the singer.

- If you take a Caribbean vacation in December, you end up listening to a lot of Christmas carols played to a calypso beat.

In Homer's *Odyssey,* the nymph Calypso detains Odysseus for seven years on his way home from the Trojan War, using all her wiles to hold him on her lush island. For many people, the calypso music of the West Indian islands, which was eventually brought to America by singers such as the Andrews Sisters and later Harry Belafonte, has some of the same captivating power as the nymph, though the lyrics that are often improvised to the melodies tend to make fun of local people and happenings. The original name for these songs, however, actually seems to be based on a similar-sounding African word, for which, early in the 20th century, someone began substituting this name from Greek mythology.

odyssey \ˈä-də-sē\ (1) A long, wandering journey full of trials and adventures. (2) A spiritual journey or quest.

- Their six-month camping trip around the country was an odyssey they would always remember.

Odysseus, the hero of Homer's *Odyssey,* spends 20 years traveling home from the Trojan War. He has astonishing adventures and learns a great deal about himself and the world; he even descends to the underworld to talk to the dead. Thus, an odyssey is any long, complicated journey, often a quest for a goal, and may be a spiritual or psychological journey as well as an actual voyage.

palladium \pə-ˈlā-dē-əm\ A precious, silver-white metal related to platinum that is used in electrical contacts and as an alloy with gold to form white gold.

• Most wedding rings today are simple bands of gold, platinum, or palladium.

Pallas Athena was one of the poetical names given to the Greek goddess Athena (although it's no longer clear what Pallas was supposed to mean), and the original palladium was a statue of Athena that was believed to have the power to protect the ancient city of Troy. When an asteroid belt was discovered between Mars and Jupiter, most of the asteroids were named after figures in Greek mythology, and one of the first to be discovered was named Pallas in 1803. In the same year, scientists isolated a new silvery metal element, which they named *palladium* in honor of the recently discovered asteroid.

Penelope \pə-ˈne-lə-pē\ A modest domestic wife.

• Critics of Hillary Rodham Clinton in the 1990s would perhaps have preferred her to be a Penelope, quietly tending the White House and staying out of politics.

In the *Odyssey*, Penelope waits 20 long years for her husband Odysseus to return from Troy. During that time, she must raise their son and fend off the attentions of numerous rough suitors. She preserves herself for a long time by saying she cannot remarry until she has finished weaving a funeral shroud for her aging father-in-law; however, what she weaves each day she secretly unravels each night. A Penelope thus appears to be the perfect, patient, faithful wife (and may be using her clever intelligence to keep herself that way).

procrustean \prō-ˈkrəs-tē-ən\ Ruthlessly disregarding individual differences or special circumstances.

• The school's procrustean approach seemed to assume that all children learned in the same way and at the same rate.

In the Greek tale of the hero Theseus, Procrustes was a bandit who ambushed travelers and, after robbing them, made them lie on an iron bed. To make sure they "fit" this bed, he would cut off the parts that hung off the ends or stretch the body if it was too short; either way, the unlucky traveler always died. When he made the mistake of confronting Theseus, Procrustes was made to "fit" his own bed. Something procrustean takes no account of individual differences but cruelly and mercilessly makes everything the same.

protean \\'prō-tē-ən\\ (1) Displaying great versatility or variety. (2) Able to take on many different forms or natures.

• A protean athlete, he left college with offers from the professional leagues to play baseball, football, and basketball.

As the story is told in the *Odyssey*, at the end of the Trojan War the sea god Proteus revealed to King Menelaus of Sparta how to get home from Troy with his unfaithful wife, the beautiful Helen of Troy. Before Proteus would give up the information, though, Menelaus had to capture him—no mean feat, since Proteus had the ability to change into any natural shape he chose. The word *protean* came to describe this ability to change into many different shapes or to play many different roles in quick succession.

sibyl \\'si-bəl\\ A female prophet or fortune-teller.

• The villagers told him about an aged woman who lived alone in a hut on a nearby mountain, a sibyl who knew the future and would prophesy under the right conditions.

Ancient writers refer to the existence of various women in such countries as Babylonia, Greece, Italy, and Egypt, through whom the gods regularly spoke. These sibyls were easy to confuse with the oracles, women who were likewise mouthpieces of the gods, at such sites as Apollo's temple at Delphi. The most famous sibyl was the Sibyl of Cumae in Italy, a withered crone who lived in a cave. Her prophecies were collected into twelve books, three of which survived to be consulted by the Romans in times of national emergencies. She is one of the five sibyls memorably depicted by Michelangelo on the ceiling of the Sistine Chapel.

siren \\'sī-rən\\ A woman who tempts men with bewitching sweetness.

• Reporters treated her like a sex symbol, but she lacked the graceful presence and air of mystery of a real siren.

The sirens were a group of partly human female creatures that lured sailors onto destructive rocks with their singing. Odysseus and his

men encountered the sirens on their long journey home from Troy.
The only way to sail by them safely was to make oneself deaf to
their enchanting song, so Odysseus packed the men's ears with wax,
while he himself, ever curious, kept his ears open but had himself
tied to the mast to keep from flinging himself into the water or
steering his ship toward sure destruction in his desire to see them.
A siren today is a sinister but almost irresistible woman. A *siren
song*, however, may be any appeal that lures a person to act against
his or her better judgment.

Quiz

Fill in each blank with the correct letter:

a.	odyssey	e.	sibyl
b.	calypso	f.	procrustean
c.	Penelope	g.	siren
d.	palladium	h.	protean

1. They danced and sang to the rhythm of the _____
   music long into the night.
2. While he was away on maneuvers, his wife stayed
   loyally at home like a true _____.
3. Critics condemn modern education as _____, forcing
   all students into narrow and limited modes of
   thinking.
4. On their four-month _____ they visited most of the
   major cities of Asia.
5. The wedding rings were white gold, a mixture of gold
   and _____.
6. She won her reputation as the office _____ after her
   third successful prediction of who would get married
   next.
7. Actors like Robin Williams seem _____ in their ability
   to assume different characters.
8. She was a _____ of the screen in the 1920s, luring
   men to their doom in movie after movie.

Review Quizzes

A. Choose the closest definition:

1. carnage   a. meat b. slaughter c. flesh d. battle
2. precursor   a. shadow b. forerunner c. follower d. oath
3. diffident   a. angry b. different c. aggressive d. shy
4. pedestrian   a. useless b. footlike c. unusual d. boring
5. credence   a. creation b. belief c. doubt d. destruction
6. credible   a. believable b. acceptable
   c. praiseworthy d. remarkable
7. pedigree   a. wealth b. education c. breeding d. purity
8. impediment   a. help b. obstacle c. footpath
   d. obligation
9. voracious   a. vast b. hungry c. fierce d. unsatisfied
10. protean   a. meaty b. powerful c. changeable
    d. professional

B. Indicate whether the following pairs of words have the same or different meanings:

1. procrustean / merciful   same __ / different __
2. credulity / distrust   same __ / different __
3. concurrent / simultaneous   same __ / different __
4. cursory / hurried   same __ / different __
5. odyssey / journey   same __ / different __
6. deflect / absorb   same __ / different __
7. perfidy / disloyalty   same __ / different __
8. posterior / front   same __ / different __
9. siren / temptress   same __ / different __
10. herbivorous / plant-eating   same __ / different __

C. Complete the analogy:

1. fiduciary : trust-based :: carnivorous : _____
   a. vegetarian b. meat-eating c. greedy d. hungry
2. cursory : brief :: carnal : _____
   a. musical b. festive c. deadly d. sexual
3. genuflect : kneel :: affidavit : _____
   a. financial affairs b. courtroom testimony c. legal advice d. sworn statement
4. insectivorous : insects :: herbivorous : _____
   a. plants b. herbs c. grains d. flowers

5. carnage : bloodbath :: Penelope : _____
   a. wife b. mother c. daughter d. siren
6. ambivalent : uncertain :: pedestrian : _____
   a. slow b. colorful c. unexciting d. explosive
7. credence : trust :: discursive : _____
   a. fast b. slow-moving c. wide-ranging
   d. all-knowing
8. procrustean : inflexible :: inflection : _____
   a. way of life b. tone of voice c. financial affairs
   d. part of speech

UNIT

5

MAL comes from a Latin word meaning "bad." A *malady* is a bad condition—a disease or illness—of the body or mind. *Malpractice* is bad medical practice. *Malodorous* things smell bad. And a *malefactor* is someone guilty of bad deeds.

---

malevolent \mə-ˈle-və-lənt\ Having or showing intense ill will or hatred.

• Captain Ahab sees Moby Dick not simply as a whale but as a powerfully malevolent foe.

Malevolence runs deep. Malevolent enemies have bitter and lasting feelings of ill will. Malevolent racism and bigotry can erupt in acts of violence against innocent people. Malevolence can also show itself in hurtful words, and can sometimes be seen in something as small as an angry look or gesture.

malicious \mə-ˈli-shəs\ Desiring to cause pain, injury, or distress to another.

• The boys didn't take the apples with any malicious intent; they were just hungry and didn't know any better.

Malicious and *malevolent* are close in meaning, since both refer to ill will that desires to see someone else suffer. But while *malevolent* suggests deep and lasting dislike, *malicious* usually means petty and spiteful. Malicious gossipers are often simply envious of a neighbor's good fortune. Vandals may take malicious pleasure in destroying and defacing property but usually don't truly hate the owners. *Malice* is an important legal concept, which has to be proved in order to convict someone of certain crimes such as first-degree murder.

malign \mə-'līn\ To make harsh and often false or misleading statements about.

• Captain Bligh of the *Bounty* may be one of the most unjustly maligned figures in British naval history.

Malign is related to verbs like *defame, slander,* and *libel.* The person or group being maligned is the victim of false or misleading statements, even if the *maligner* isn't necessarily guilty of deliberate lying. Someone or something that's frequently criticized is often said to be "much maligned," which suggests that the criticism isn't entirely fair or deserved. *Malign* is also an adjective, and writers often refer to a person's malign influence. The very similar *malignant,* which used to be a common synonym of *malign,* today tends to describe dangerous medical conditions, especially cancerous tumors.

malnourished \ˌmal-'nər-isht\ Badly or poorly nourished.

• When they finally found the children in the locked cabin, they were pale and malnourished but unharmed.

Malnourished people can be found in all types of societies. Famine and poverty are only two of the common causes of *malnutrition.* In wealthier societies, malnutrition is often the result of poor eating habits. Any diet that fails to provide the nutrients needed for health and growth can lead to malnutrition, and some malnourished people are actually fat.

CATA comes from the Greek *kata,* one of whose meanings was "down." A *catalogue* is a list of items put down on paper, and a *catapult* is a weapon for hurling missiles down on one's enemies.

cataclysm \'ka-tə-ˌkli-zəm\ (1) A violent and massive change of the earth's surface. (2) A momentous event that results in great upheaval and often destruction.

• World War I was a great cataclysm in modern history, marking the end of the old European social and political order.

The *-clysm* part of *cataclysm* comes from the Greek word meaning "to wash," so *cataclysm*'s original meaning was "flood, deluge," and especially Noah's Flood itself. A cataclysm causes great and lasting changes. An earthquake or other natural disaster that changes the landscape is one kind of cataclysm, but a violent political revolution may also be a *cataclysmic* event. Many cataclysms could instead be called *catastrophes*.

catacomb \ˈka-tə-ˌkōm\ An underground cemetery of connecting passageways with recesses for tombs.

- The early Christian catacombs of Rome provide a striking glimpse into the ancient past for modern-day visitors.

About forty Christian catacombs have been found near the roads that once led into Rome. After the decline of the Roman empire these cemeteries were forgotten, not to be rediscovered until 1578. *Catacomb* has come to refer to different kinds of underground chambers and passageways. The catacombs of Paris are abandoned stone quarries that were not used for burials until 1787. The catacombs built by a monastery in Palermo, Sicily, for its deceased members later began accepting bodies from outside the monastery; today you may wander through looking at hundreds of mummified corpses propped against the catacomb walls, dressed in tattered clothes that were once fashionable.

catalyst \ˈka-tə-list\ (1) A substance that speeds up a chemical reaction or lets it take place under different conditions. (2) Someone or something that brings about or speeds significant change or action.

- The assassination of Archduke Ferdinand in Sarajevo in 1914 turned out to be the catalyst for World War I.

Chemical catalysts are substances that, in very small amounts, can bring about important chemical changes in large quantities of material. The *catalytic* converter in your car's exhaust system, for instance, uses tiny amounts of platinum to swiftly convert the engine's dangerous gases to carbon dioxide and water vapor. And it's easy to see how the meaning of *catalyst* could broaden to include nonchemical situations. We can now say, for example, that the Great Depression served as the catalyst for such important social reforms as Social Security.

catatonic \ˌka-tə-ˈtä-nik\ (1) Relating to or suffering from a form of schizophrenia. (2) Showing an unusual lack of movement, activity, or expression.

• After an hour, extreme boredom had produced a catatonic stupor in those of the audience who were still awake.

Catatonia is primarily a form of the terrible mental disease known as schizophrenia, though it may show up in patients with a variety of other mental conditions. A common symptom is extreme muscular rigidity; catatonic patients may be "frozen" for hours or even days in a single position. Its causes remain mysterious. Serious though the condition is, most nondoctors use *catatonic* humorously to describe people who seem incapable of moving or changing expression.

Quizzes

A. Choose the closest definition:

1. malevolent   a. wishing evil b. wishing well
      c. blowing violently d. badly done
2. cataclysm   a. loud applause b. feline behavior
      c. disaster d. inspiration
3. malign   a. speak well of b. speak to c. speak ill of
      d. speak of repeatedly
4. catacomb   a. underground road b. underground
      cemetery c. underground spring d. underground
      treasure
5. malicious   a. vague b. explosive c. confusing d. mean
6. catatonic   a. refreshing b. slow c. motionless
      d. boring
7. malnourished   a. fed frequently b. fed poorly
      c. fed excessively d. fed occasionally
8. catalyst   a. literary agent b. insurance agent
      c. cleaning agent d. agent of change

**B. Indicate whether the following pairs of words have
the same or different meanings:**

1. catacomb / catastrophe   same __ / different __
2. malnourished / overfed   same __ / different __
3. cataclysm / disaster   same __ / different __

4.	malign / slander	same __ / different __
5.	catatonic / paralyzed	same __ / different __
6.	catalyst / cemetery	same __ / different __
7.	malicious / nasty	same __ / different __
8.	malevolent / pleasant	same __ / different __

PROT/PROTO comes from Greek and has the basic meaning "first in time" or "first formed." *Protozoa* are one-celled animals, such as amoebas and paramecia, that are among the most basic members of the biological kingdom. A *proton* is an elementary particle that, along with neutrons, can be found in all atomic nuclei. A *protoplanet* is a whirling mass of gas and dust that astronomers believe may someday become a planet.

protagonist \prō-'ta-gə-nist\ The main character in a literary work.

• Macbeth is the ruthlessly ambitious protagonist of Shakespeare's play, but it is his wife who pulls the strings.

Struggle, or conflict, is central to drama. The protagonist or hero of a play, novel, or film is involved in a struggle of some kind, either against someone or something else or even against his or her own emotions. So the hero is the "first struggler," which is the literal meaning of the Greek word *prōtagōnistēs*. A character who opposes the hero is the *antagonist,* from a Greek verb that means literally "to struggle against."

protocol \'prō-tə-ˌkȯl\ (1) A code of diplomatic or military rules of behavior. (2) A set of rules for the formatting of data in an electronic communications system.

• The guests at the governor's dinner were introduced and seated according to the strict protocol governing such occasions.

The basic meaning of *proto-* is a little harder to follow in this word. *Protocol* comes from a Greek word for the first sheet of a papyrus roll. In English, *protocol* originally meant "a first draft or record," and later specifically the first draft of a diplomatic document, such as a treaty. The "diplomatic" connection led eventually to its current meaning of "rules of behavior." Someone wearing Bermuda shorts and sandals to a state dinner at the White House would not be acting "according to protocol," and royal protocol forbids touching the queen of England except to shake her hand. But *protocol* is also now used for other sets of rules, such as those for doing a scientific experiment or for handling computer data.

protoplasm \\'prō-tō-ˌpla-zəm\ The substance that makes up the living parts of cells.

• A mixture of organic and inorganic substances, such as protein and water, protoplasm is regarded as the physical basis of life.

After the word *protoplasm* was coined in the mid-19th century for the jellylike material that is the main substance of a cell, it began to be used widely, especially by scientists and others who imagined that the first life-forms must have arisen out of a great seething *protoplasmic* soup. Since protoplasm includes all the cell's living material, inside and outside the nucleus, it is a less useful scientific word today than more precise terms such as *cytoplasm*, which refers only to the living material outside the nucleus. But many remain fascinated by the image of that soup bubbling away as the lightning flashes and the volcanoes erupt.

prototype \\'prō-tō-ˌtīp\ (1) An original model on which something is patterned. (2) A first, full-scale, usually working version of a new type or design.

• There was great excitement when, after years of top-secret development, the prototype of the new Stealth bomber first took to the skies.

A prototype is someone or something that serves as a model or inspiration. A successful fund-raising campaign can serve as a prototype for future campaigns, for example, and the legendary Robin Hood is the *prototypical* honorable outlaw, the inspiration for countless other romantic heroes. But the term is perhaps most widely used in the world of technology; every new "concept car," for example, starts off as a unique prototype.

ANTE is Latin for "before" or "in front of." *Antediluvian,* which describes something very old or outdated, literally means "before the flood"—that is, Noah's Flood. And *antebellum* literally means "before the war," usually the American Civil War.

antechamber \\'an-ti-ˌchām-bər\ An outer room that leads to another and is often used as a waiting room.

• The antechamber to the lawyer's office was both elegant and comfortable, designed to inspire trust and confidence.

One expects to find an antechamber outside the private chambers of a Supreme Court Justice or leading into the great hall of a medieval castle. In the private end of the castle the lord's or lady's bedchamber would have its own antechamber, which served as a dressing room and sitting room, but could also house bodyguards if the castle came under siege. *Anteroom* is a less formal synonym, one that's often applied to the waiting rooms of professional offices today.

antedate \\'an-ti-ˌdāt\ (1) To date something (such as a check) with a date earlier than that of actual writing. (2) To precede in time.

• Nantucket Island has hundreds of beautifully preserved houses that antedate the Civil War.

Dinosaurs antedated the first human beings by almost 65 million years, though this stubborn fact never used to stop cartoonists and screenwriters from having the two species inhabit the same story line. Dictionary editors are constantly noticing how the oral use of a word may antedate its first appearance in print by a number of years. Antedating a check or a contract isn't illegal unless it's done for the purpose of fraud (the same is true of its opposite, *postdating*).

antecedent \ˌan-tə-'sē-dᵊnt\ (1) A word or phrase that is referred to by a pronoun that follows it. (2) An event or cause coming before something.

• As I remember, she said "My uncle is taking my father, and he's staying overnight," but I'm not sure what the antecedent of "he" was.

A basic principle of clear writing is to keep your antecedents clear. Pronouns are often used in order not to repeat a noun (so instead of saying "Sheila turns 22 tomorrow, and Sheila is having a party," we replace the second "Sheila" with "she"). But sloppy writers sometimes leave their antecedents unclear (for instance, "Sheila helps Kathleen out, but she doesn't appreciate it," where it isn't clear who "she" is). Watch out for this possible problem when using not just *he* and *she* but also *they, them, it, this,* and *that*. And keep in mind that *antecedent* isn't just a grammar term. You may talk about the antecedents of heart disease (such as bad eating habits), the antecedents of World War II (such as the unwise Treaty of Versailles), and even your own antecedents (your mother, grandfather, etc.).

anterior \an-ˈtir-ē-ər\ (1) Located before or toward the front or head. (2) Coming before in time or development.

• When she moved up to join the first-class passengers in the plane's anterior section, she was delighted to recognize the governor in the next seat.

Anterior generally appears in either medical or scholarly contexts. Anatomy books refer to the anterior lobe of the brain, the anterior cerebral artery, the anterior facial vein, etc. Scholar and lawyers may use *anterior* to mean "earlier in time or order." For example, supporters of states' rights point out that the individual states enjoyed certain rights anterior to their joining the union. And prenuptial agreements are designed to protect the assets that one or both parties acquired anterior to the marriage.

Quizzes

A. Fill in each blank with the correct letter:

a. antedate   e. prototype
b. protoplasm   f. antecedent
c. anterior   g. protocol
d. protagonist   h. antechamber

1. The _____ of *The Wizard of Oz* is a Kansas farm girl named Dorothy.
2. According to official _____, the Ambassador from England ranks higher than the Canadian Consul.
3. A butterfly's antennae are located on the most _____ part of its body.
4. There under the microscope we saw the cell's _____ in all its amazing complexity.
5. She was tempted to _____ the letter to make it seem that she had not forgotten to write it but only to mail it.
6. The engineers have promised to have the _____ of the new sedan finished by March.

7. Please step into the judge's _____; she'll be with you in a few minutes.

8. The British would say "The company are proud of their record," since they treat "the company" as a plural _____.

B. Match the definition on the left to the correct word on the right:

1.	to date before	a.	protocol
2.	cell contents	b.	antechamber
3.	what comes before	c.	protagonist
4.	rules of behavior	d.	antecedent
5.	toward the front	e.	protoplasm
6.	model	f.	antedate
7.	waiting room	g.	prototype
8.	hero or heroine	h.	anterior

ORTHO comes from *orthos*, the Greek word for "straight," "right," or "true." *Orthotics* is a branch of therapy that straightens out your stance or posture by providing artificial support for weak joints or muscles. And *orthograde* animals, such as human beings, walk with their bodies in a "straight" or vertical position.

---

orthodontics \ˌȯr-thə-ˈdän-tiks\ A branch of dentistry that deals with the treatment and correction of crooked teeth and other irregularities.

• A specialty in orthodontics would require three more years of study after completing her dentistry degree.

Orthodontics has been practiced since ancient times, but the elaborate techniques familiar to us today were introduced only in recent decades. Braces, retainers, and headgear are used to fix such conditions as crowding of the teeth and overbites. According to a 1939 text, "Speech defects, psychiatric disturbances, personality changes, . . . all are correctable through *orthodontic* measures," though many adolescents, having endured the embarrassment of rubber bands breaking and even of entangling their braces while kissing, might disagree.

orthodox \\'òr-thə-ˌdäks\ (1) Holding established beliefs, especially in religion. (2) Conforming to established rules or traditions; conventional.

• The O'Briens remain orthodox Catholics, faithfully observing the time-honored rituals of their church.

An orthodox religious belief or interpretation is one handed down by a church's founders or leaders. When capitalized, as in *Orthodox Judaism*, *Orthodox* refers to a branch within a larger religious organization that claims to honor the religion's original or traditional beliefs. The steadfast holding of established beliefs that is seen in religious *orthodoxy* is apparent also in other kinds of orthodox behavior. Orthodox medical treatment, for example, follows the established practices of mainstream medicine. *Unorthodox* thinking is known in business language as "thinking outside the box."

orthopedics \ˌòr-thə-'pē-diks\ The correction or prevention of deformities of the skeleton.

• For surgery to correct the child's spinal curvature, they were referred to the hospital's orthopedics section.

Just as an orthodontist corrects crookedness in the teeth, an *orthopedist* corrects crookedness in the skeleton. *Orthopedics* is formed in part from the Greek word for "child," and many *orthopedic* patients are in fact children. But adults also often have need of orthopedic therapy, as when suffering from a joint disease like arthritis or when recovering from a broken arm or leg.

orthography \òr-'thä-grə-fē\ The spelling of words, especially spelling according to standard usage.

• Even such eloquent writers as George Washington and Thomas Jefferson were deficient in the skill of orthography.

Even as recently as the 19th century, the orthography of the English language was still unsettled. Not until spelling books like Noah Webster's and textbooks like "McGuffey's Readers" came along did uniform spelling become established in the U.S. Before that, there was much *orthographic* variation, even among the more educated. The many people who still have problems with spelling can take heart from Mark Twain, who once remarked, "I don't give a damn for a man that can spell a word only one way."

RECT comes from the Latin word *rectus,* which means "straight" or "right." To *correct* something is to make it right. A *rectangle* is a four-sided figure with straight parallel sides. *Rectus,* short for Latin *rectus musculus,* may refer to any of several straight muscles, such as those of the abdomen.

rectitude \\'rek-tə-ˌtüd\\ Moral integrity.

• The school superintendent was stern and not terribly popular, but no one questioned her moral rectitude.

We associate straightness with honesty, so if we suspect someone is lying we might ask if they're being "straight" with us, and we might call a lawbreaker *crooked* or label him a *crook. Rectitude* may sound a little old-fashioned today, but the virtue it represents never really goes out of style.

rectify \\'rek-tə-ˌfī\\ To set right; remedy.

• The college is moving to rectify this unfortunate situation before anyone else gets hurt.

We rectify something by straightening it out or making it right. We might rectify an injustice by seeing to it that a wrongly accused person is cleared. An error in a financial record can be rectified by replacing an incorrect number with a correct one. If the error is in our tax return, the Internal Revenue Service will be happy to rectify it for us; we might then have to rectify the impression that we were trying to cheat on our taxes.

rectilinear \\ˌrek-tə-'li-nē-ər\\ (1) Moving in or forming a straight line. (2) Having many straight lines.

• After admiring Frank Lloyd Wright's rectilinear buildings for years, the public was astonished by the giant spiral of the Guggenheim Museum.

Rectilinear patterns or constructions are those in which straight lines are strikingly obvious. In geometry, *rectilinear* usually means "perpendicular"; thus, a rectilinear polygon is a many-sided shape whose angles are all right angles (the footprints of most houses, with their extensions and garages, are good examples). But *rectilinear* is particularly used in physics. Rectilinear motion is motion in which the speed remains constant and the path is a straight line; and rectilinear rays, such as light rays, travel in a straight line.

directive \də-'rek-tiv\ Something that guides or directs; especially, a general instruction from a high-level body or official.

• At the very beginning of the administration, the cabinet secretary had sent out a directive to all border-patrol personnel.

As the definition states, a directive *directs*. A directive from a school principal might provide guidance about handling holiday celebrations in class. A directive from the Vatican might specify new wording for the Mass in various languages. Even the European Union issues directives to its member countries, which they often ignore.

Quizzes

A. Choose the closest definition:

1. orthodox   a. straight b. pier c. conventional
   d. waterfowl
2. rectify   a. redo b. make right c. modify
   d. make longer
3. orthopedics   a. foot surgery b. children's medicine
   c. medical dictionaries d. treatment of skeletal defects
4. directive   a. leader b. sign c. order d. straightener
5. orthography   a. correct color b. correct map c. correct
   direction d. correct spelling
6. rectitude   a. roughness b. integrity c. certainty
   d. sameness
7. orthodontics   a. dentistry for children b. dentistry for
   gums c. dentistry for crooked teeth d. dentistry for
   everyone
8. rectilinear   a. employing straight lines b. employing
   curved lines c. employing 45° angles d. employing
   circles

B. Indicate whether the following pairs have the same or different meanings:

1. orthodox / crucial   same ___ / different ___
2. rectitude / honesty   same ___ / different ___

3.	orthopedics / broken bones	same ___ / different ___
4.	directive / question	same ___ / different ___
5.	orthography / architecture	same ___ / different ___
6.	rectilinear / straight	same ___ / different ___
7.	orthodontics / fixing of crooked teeth	same ___ / different ___
8.	rectify / damage	same ___ / different ___

EU comes from the Greek word for "well"; in English words it can also mean "good" or "true." A veterinarian who performs *euthanasia* is providing a very sick or hopelessly injured animal a "good" or easy death.

eugenic \yü-'je-nik\ Relating to or fitted for the production of good offspring through controlled breeding.

• Eugenic techniques have been part of sheep breeding for many years.

The word *eugenic*, like the name *Eugene*, includes the Greek root meaning "born" (see GEN, p. 409). Breeders of farm animals have long used eugenic methods to produce horses that run faster, for example, or pigs that provide more meat. Through *eugenics*, Holstein cows have become one of the world's highest producers of milk. But eugenics also has a dark side. The idea of human eugenics was taken up enthusiastically by the Nazis in the 20th century, with terrible consequences.

euphemism \'yü-fə-ˌmi-zəm\ An agreeable or inoffensive word or expression that is substituted for one that may offend or disgust.

• The Victorians, uncomfortable with the physical side of human existence, had euphemisms for most bodily functions.

The use of euphemisms is an ancient part of the English language, and perhaps of all languages, and all of us use them. *Golly* and *gosh* started out as euphemisms for *God,* and *darn* is a familiar euphemism for *damn. Shoot, shucks,* and *sugar* are all *euphemistic* substitutes for a well-known vulgar word. *Pass away* for *die, mis-*

speak for *lie*, *downsize* for *fire*, *senior citizen* for *old person*—the list goes on and on.

euphoria \yù-'fŏr-ē-ə\ A strong feeling of well-being or happiness.

- Swept up in the euphoria of a Super Bowl victory, the whole city seemed to have poured out into the streets.

Euphoria is the feeling of an intense (and usually temporary) "high." Doctors use the word for the kind of abnormal or inappropriate high spirits that might be caused by a drug or by mental illness, but euphoria is usually natural and appropriate. When we win enough money in the lottery to buy several small Pacific islands, or even just when the home team wins the championship, we have good reason to feel *euphoric*.

eulogy \'yù-lə-jē\ (1) A formal speech or writing especially in honor of a dead person. (2) High praise.

- The book was a fond eulogy to the 1950s, when Americans had joined social organizations of all kinds.

With its *-logy* ending (see LOG, p. 203), *eulogy* means literally something like "good speech." We are told to speak only good of the dead, but a *eulogist* actually makes a speech in the dead person's honor—often often instead for someone living, who might actually be there in the audience. The most famous eulogies include Lincoln's Gettysburg Address and Pericles' funeral oration for the Athenian warriors; but these are only two of the many great eulogies, which continue to be delivered not only at funerals and memorial services but at retirement parties, anniversary parties, and birthday parties.

DYS comes from Greek, where it means "bad" or "difficult." So *dysphagia* is difficult swallowing, and *dyspnea* is difficult or labored breathing. *Dysphasia* is an inability to use and understand language because of injury to or disease of the brain. *Dys-* is sometimes close in meaning to *dis-* (see DIS, p. 60), but try not to confuse the two.

---

dystopia \dis-'tō-pē-ə\ An imaginary place where people lead dehumanized and often fearful lives.

- For a 10-year-old British boy, boarding school could be a grim dystopia, with no comforts, harsh punishments, and constant bullying.

Dystopia was created from Utopia, the name of an ideal country imagined by Sir Thomas More in 1516. For More, the suffix *-topia* meant "place" (see TOP, p. 338), and *u-* (from the Greek root *ou*) meant "no," but also perhaps "good" (see EU, p. 103). In other words, More's Utopia was too good to be true. It's probably no accident that *dystopia* was first used around 1950, soon after George Orwell published his famous novel *Nineteen Eighty-Four* and 16 years after Aldous Huxley published *Brave New World*. These two are still the most famous of the 20th century's many depressingly *dystopian* novels. And what about all those bleak futuristic films: *Blade Runner, Brazil, The Matrix,* and the rest? What does it mean when no one will paint a picture of a happy future?

dyslexia \dis-ˈlek-sē-ə\ A disturbance or interference with the ability to read or to use language.

- She managed to deal with her dyslexia through careful tutoring all throughout elementary school.

Dyslexia is a neurological disorder that usually affects people of average or superior intelligence. *Dyslexic* individuals have an impaired ability to recognize and process words and letters. Dyslexia usually shows itself in the tendency to read and write words and letters in reversed order; sometimes similar reversals occur in the person's speech. Dyslexia has been shown to be treatable through patient instruction in proper reading techniques.

dyspeptic \dis-ˈpep-tik\ (1) Relating to or suffering from indigestion. (2) Having an irritable temperament; ill-humored.

- For decades the dyspeptic columnist served as the newspaper's—and the city's—resident grouch.

Dyspepsia comes from the Greek word for "bad digestion." Interestingly, the Greek verb *pessein* can mean either "to cook" or "to digest"; bad cooking has been responsible for a lot of dyspepsia. Dyspepsia can be caused by many diseases, but dyspeptic individuals are often the victims of their own habits and appetites. Worry, overeating, inadequate chewing, and excessive smoking and drinking can all bring on dyspepsia. Today we generally use *dyspeptic* to mean "irritable"—that is, in the kind of mood that could be produced by bad digestion.

dysplasia \dis-ˈplā-zhə\ Abnormal development of cells or organs, or an abnormal structure resulting from such growth.

• The infant was born with minor hip dysplasia, which was fixed by a routine operation.

Of the dozens of medical terms that begin with the *dys-* prefix, *dysplasia* (with the suffix *-plasia*, meaning "development") is one of the more common, though not many nondoctors know it. Structural dysplasias are usually something you're born with; they often involve the hip or the kidneys. But cell dysplasia is often associated with cancer. And a *dysplastic* mole—a mole that changes shape in an odd way—is always something to be concerned about.

Quizzes

A. Fill in each blank with the correct letter:

a. euphemism   e. dyslexia
b. dysplasia   f. euphoria
c. eulogy   g. dystopia
d. dyspeptic   h. eugenic

1. There is many a _____ for the word *die*, and many more for the word *drunk*.
2. The novel paints a picture of a _____ in which the effects of climate change have wrecked the social order.
3. Her _____ for her longtime friend was the most moving part of the ceremony.
4. Because his _____ was discovered early, he was able to receive the special reading instruction he needed.
5. The end of the war was marked by widespread _____ and celebration.
6. Ebenezer Scrooge, in *A Christmas Carol*, is a thoroughly _____ character.
7. Though the dog is the product of generations of _____ breeding, she is high-strung and has terrible eyesight.
8. The tests had detected some suspicious cell _____, but her doctors told her not to worry since it was at a very early stage.

B. **Match the word on the left to the correct definition on the right:**

1. dysplasia
2. euphemism
3. dyslexia
4. eugenic
5. dystopia
6. euphoria
7. dyspeptic
8. eulogy

a. nightmarish society
b. crabby
c. abnormal growth
d. speech of praise
e. polite term
f. reading disorder
g. promoting superior offspring
h. great happiness

Latin Borrowings

a fortiori \ˌä-ˌfȯr-tē-ˈȯr-ē\ All the more certainly.

• If drug users are going to be subject to mandatory sentences, then, a fortiori, drug dealers should be subject to them also.

A fortiori in Latin literally means "from the stronger (argument)." The term is used when drawing a conclusion that's even more obvious or convincing than the one just drawn. Thus, if teaching English grammar to native speakers is difficult, then, a fortiori, teaching English grammar to nonnative speakers will be even more challenging.

a posteriori \ˌä-ˌpōs-tir-ē-ˈȯr-ē\ Relating to or derived by reasoning from known or observed facts.

• Most Presidents will come to the a posteriori conclusion that a booming economy is entirely due to their own economic policies.

A posteriori, Latin for "from the latter," is a term from logic, which usually refers to reasoning that works backward from an effect to its causes. This kind of reasoning can sometimes lead to false conclusions. The fact that sunrise follows the crowing of a rooster, for example, doesn't necessarily mean that the rooster's crowing caused the sun to rise.

a priori \ˌä-prē-ˈȯr-ē\ Relating to or derived by reasoning from self-evident propositions.

- Her colleagues rejected the a priori argument because it rested on assumptions they felt weren't necessarily true.

A priori, Latin for "from the former," is traditionally contrasted with *a posteriori* (see above). The term usually describes lines of reasoning or arguments that proceed from the general to the particular, or from causes to effects. Whereas a posteriori knowledge is knowledge based solely on experience or personal observation, a priori knowledge is knowledge that comes from the power of reasoning based on self-evident truths. So, for example, "Every mother has had a child" is an a priori statement, since it shows simple logical reasoning and isn't a statement of fact about a specific case (such as "This woman is the mother of five children") that the speaker knew about from experience.

bona fide \\'bō-nə-ˌfīd\\ (1) Made in good faith, without deceit. (2) Authentic or genuine.

- According to the broker, they've made a bona fide offer to buy the property.

Bona fide means "in good faith" in Latin. When applied to business deals and the like, it stresses the absence of fraud or deception. A bona fide sale of securities is an entirely aboveboard transaction. Outside of business and law, *bona fide* implies mere sincerity and earnestness. A bona fide promise is one that the person has every intention of keeping. A bona fide proposal of marriage is one made by a suitor who isn't kidding around. *Bona fide* also has the noun form *bona fides*; when someone asks about someone else's *bona fides*, it usually means evidence of their qualifications or achievements.

carpe diem \\'kär-pā-'dē-ˌem\\ Enjoy the pleasures or opportunities of the moment without concern about the future.

- When he learned the phrase "Carpe diem" in high-school Latin class, he knew he'd found the motto he would live by for the rest of his life.

Carpe diem, a phrase that comes from the Roman poet Horace, means literally "Pluck the day," though it's usually translated as "Seize the day." A free translation might be "Enjoy yourself while you have the chance." For some people, *Carpe diem* serves as the closest thing to a philosophy of life as they'll ever have.

caveat emptor \\'ka-vē-ˌät-'emp-tər\\ Let the buyer beware.

- The best rule to keep in mind when buying anything from a pushcart is: "Caveat emptor."

"Without a warranty, the buyer must take the risk" is the basic meaning of the phrase *caveat emptor.* In the days when buying and selling was carried on in the local marketplace, the rule was a practical one. Buyer and seller knew each other and were on equal footing. The nature of modern commerce and technology placed the buyer at a disadvantage, however, so a stack of regulations have been written by federal, state, and local agencies to protect the consumer against dangerous or defective products, fraudulent practices, and the like. But the principle that a buyer needs a warranty if he is to avoid risk remains an important legal concept. Note that a *caveat* is a small warning or explanation intended to avoid misinterpretation.

corpus delicti \\ˈkȯr-pəs-di-ˈlik-ˌtī\\ (1) The substantial and basic fact or facts necessary to prove that a crime has been committed. (2) The material substance, such as the murdered body, on which a crime has been committed.

- The police believed they had solved the crime, but couldn't prove their case without the corpus delicti.

Corpus delicti literally means "body of the crime" in Latin. In its original sense, the body in question refers not to a corpse but to the body of essential facts that, taken together, prove that a crime has been committed. In popular usage, *corpus delicti* also refers to the actual physical object upon which a crime has been committed. In a case of arson, it would be a ruined building; in a murder case, the victim's corpse.

curriculum vitae \\kə-ˈri-kyù-ləm-ˈvē-ˌtī\\ A short summary of one's career and qualifications, typically prepared by an applicant for a position; résumé.

- The job advertisement asked for an up-to-date curriculum vitae and three recommendations.

The Latin phrase *curriculum vitae,* often abbreviated CV, literally means "the course of one's life." The term is usually used for applications for jobs in the sciences and medicine and for teaching positions in colleges and universities. A shorter term is simply *vita*, meaning "life." In other fields, *résumé* is more commonly used in the U.S.; in England, however, *curriculum vitae* is the usual term for any job application.

Quiz

Fill in each blank with the correct letter:

a. a priori   e. carpe diem
b. curriculum vitae f. a fortiori
c. caveat emptor   g. corpus delicti
d. a posteriori   h. bona fide

1. To ensure that all reservations are _____, the cruise line requires a nonrefundable deposit.
2. If Britain can't afford a space program, then _____ neither can a much poorer country like India.
3. The philosopher published his own _____ proof of the existence of God.
4. Their motto is " _____," and the two of them have more fun than anyone else I know.
5. She sent out a _____ full of impressive educational and professional credentials.
6. All of the elements were available to establish the _____ of the defendant's crime.
7. This art critic takes the _____ position that if Pablo Picasso painted it, it's a masterpiece of modern art.
8. When you go out to buy a used car, the best advice, warranty or no warranty, is still " _____."

Review Quizzes

A. Complete the analogy:

1. antagonist : villain :: protagonist : _____
    a. maiden b. wizard c. knight d. hero
2. radical : rebellious :: orthodox : _____
    a. routine b. conventional c. sane d. typical
3. fake : fraudulent :: bona fide : _____
    a. copied b. certain c. authentic d. desirable
4. slang : vulgar :: euphemism : _____
    a. habitual b. polite c. dirty d. dumb

5. identify : name :: rectify : _____
     a. make over b. make new c. make right d. make up
6. better : inferior :: anterior : _____
     a. before b. beside c. above d. behind
7. warranty : guarantee :: caveat emptor : _____
     a. explanation b. warning c. endorsement d. contract
8. jovial : merry :: dyspeptic : _____
     a. grumpy b. sleepy c. dopey d. happy
9. lively : sluggish :: catatonic : _____
     a. active b. petrified c. feline d. tired
10. benevolent : wicked :: malevolent : _____
     a. evil b. silly c. noisy d. kindly

B. Fill in each blank with the correct letter:

a. antechamber	i. curriculum vitae
b. a posteriori	j. catacomb
c. euphoria	k. dysplasia
d. malign	l. eugenic
e. a fortiori	m. malnourished
f. orthography	n. protoplasm
g. prototype	o. orthodontics
h. directive	

1. Before car makers produce a new model, they always build and test a _____.
2. Her short stories are her main qualification for the job, but the college needs her _____ as well.
3. They were shown into an elegant _____ where they awaited their audience with the king.
4. After graduation from dental school, Kyle took a postgraduate course in _____.
5. That yappy little dog makes the _____ assumption that he's what keeps me from breaking into the house.
6. The jellylike substance in cells is called _____.
7. These abused and _____ children can't be expected to pay attention in class.
8. In poor countries, hip _____ is rarely fixed in the early years.
9. They felt such _____ that they almost wept with joy.
10. Since they earned high honors for achieving a 3.7 average, _____ we should do so for getting a 3.8.

11. He argues that _____ is more important than ever, since the success of your Web searches depends on your spelling.

12. It is common for boxers to _____ each other in crude terms before a big match.

13. Their department had received a _____ that morning regarding flexibility in the work schedule.

14. When they went to Rome, they made sure to visit at least one underground _____.

15. _____ experimentation has produced a new breed of sheep with thick, fast-growing wool.

C. Indicate whether the following pairs have the same or different meanings:

1. corpus delicti / basic evidence   same ___ / different ___
2. rectify / straighten   same ___ / different ___
3. malicious / mean   same ___ / different ___
4. protocol / rules of behavior   same ___ / different ___
5. a priori / determined later   same ___ / different ___
6. dyslexia / speech patterns   same ___ / different ___
7. cataclysm / religious teachings   same ___ / different ___
8. antedate / occur before   same ___ / different ___
9. orthopedics / shoe repair   same ___ / different ___
10. rectilinear / curvy   same ___ / different ___
11. orthodox / Christian   same ___ / different ___
12. carpe diem / look ahead   same ___ / different ___
13. prototype / model   same ___ / different ___
14. catalyst / distributor   same ___ / different ___
15. rectitude / stubbornness   same ___ / different ___

UNIT

6

EQU comes from the Latin word *aequus*, meaning "equal." To *equalize* means to make things equal. Things that are *equivalent* have the same value, use, or meaning. All three sides of an *equilateral* triangle are of the same length. And an *equation* (for instance, 21 + 47 = 68) is a statement that two mathematical expressions are equal.

equable \\'e-kwə-bəl\\ (1) Tending to remain calm. (2) Free from harsh changes or extreme variation.

• Her friends thought it odd that such an equable woman had married a man so moody and unpredictable.

Equable usually describes either climate or personality. The word seems to be used less today than in decades past, maybe because the personality type is less admired than it used to be. A steady, calm, equable personality may not produce much excitement but usually makes for a good worker and a good parent, and maybe even a longer life. In the words of the poet Robert Service: "Avoid extremes: be moderate / In saving and in spending. / An equable and easy gait / Will win an easy ending."

adequacy \\'a-di-kwə-sē\\ Being equal to some need or requirement.

• Environmentalists doubt the adequacy of these regulations to protect the wilderness areas.

When we question the adequacy of health-care coverage, or parking facilities, or school funding, we're asking if they are *equal* to our need. The adjective *adequate* means "enough" or "acceptable"—though in sentences like "His performance was adequate," it really means "no better than acceptable."

equilibrium \\ˌē-kwə-ˈli-brē-əm\\ (1) A state in which opposing forces are balanced so that one is not stronger or greater than the other. (2) A state of emotional balance or calmness.

• The news had come as a shock, and it took him several minutes to recover his equilibrium.

Equilibrium contains a root from the Latin *libra*, meaning "weight" or "balance." As a constellation, zodiac symbol, and astrological sign, Libra is usually pictured as a set of balance scales, often held by the blindfolded goddess of justice, which symbolizes fairness, equality, and justice. *Equilibrium* has special meanings in biology, chemistry, physics, and economics, but in all of them it refers to the balance of competing influences.

equinox \\ˈē-kwə-ˌnäks\\ A day when day and night are the same length.

• She and her friends got together for an equinox party twice a year to celebrate the arrival of the fall and the spring.

If you know that *nox* means "night" in Latin, it's not hard to remember the meaning of *equinox*. There are two equinoxes in the year: the spring equinox, around March 21, and the fall equinox, around September 23. The equinoxes are contrasted with the *solstices*, when the sun is farthest north and south of the equator. The summer solstice occurs around June 22 (the longest day of the year), the winter solstice around December 22 (the shortest day).

QUIS is derived from the Latin verb meaning "to seek or obtain." The roots *quer, quir,* and *ques* are derived from the same Latin verb and give us words such as *inquiry* and *question.*

inquisition \\ˌin-kwə-ˈzi-shən\\ A questioning or examining that is often harsh or severe.

• The President's first choice for the job turned him down, fearing the Senate hearings would turn into an inquisition into her past.

While an *inquiry* can be almost any search for truth, the related word *inquisition* suggests a long, thorough investigation that involves extensive and harsh questioning. Though the two words originally had about the same meaning, today *inquisition* tends to remind us of the Spanish Inquisition, an ongoing trial conducted by church-appointed *inquisitors* that began in the Middle Ages and sought out nonbelievers, Jews, and Muslims, thousands of whom were sentenced to torture and to burning at the stake.

perquisite \\'pər-kwə-zət\\ (1) A privilege or profit that is provided in addition to one's base salary. (2) Something claimed as an exclusive possession or right.

• A new car, a big house, and yearly trips to Europe were among the perquisites that made the presidency of Wyndam College such an attractive position.

Though the Latin source of *perquisite* originally meant "something insistently asked for," the "ask" meaning has mostly vanished from the English word. A perquisite, often called simply a *perk,* is instead something of value that the holder of a particular job or position is entitled to, usually without even asking. The President of the United States, for instance, enjoys as perquisites the use of Camp David and Air Force One. Perhaps because perquisites are usually available to only a small number of people, the word sometimes refers to non-job-related privileges that are claimed as exclusive rights.

acquisitive \\ə-'kwi-zə-tiv\\ Eager to acquire; greedy.

• With each year the couple became more madly acquisitive, buying jewelry, a huge yacht, and two country estates.

Unlike most tribal peoples and the populations of some older countries, we Americans live in an acquisitive society, a society devoted to getting and spending. And America often makes successfully acquisitive people into heroes; even Ebenezer Scrooge, that model of miserly greed and *acquisitiveness,* was once defended by a White House chief of staff. An acquisitive nation may seek to *acquire* other territories by force. But mental *acquisition* of specialized knowledge or skills—or new vocabulary!—doesn't deprive others of the same information.

requisition \\ˌre-kwə-'zi-shən\\ A demand or request (such as for supplies) made with proper authority.

• The teachers had grown impatient with having to submit a requisition for even routine classroom supplies.

Requisition was originally a noun but is now probably more common as a verb. So we either can speak of sending our office's purchasing department a requisition for computers, or of *requisitioning* more computers from the department. The word has an official sound to it. However, one of Hollywood's bittersweet love stories begins when Omar Sharif, playing a World War II freedom fighter, says to Ingrid Bergman, who is the owner of a stately old yellow Rolls Royce, "I've come to requisition your car."

Quizzes

A. Indicate whether the following pairs of terms have the same or different meanings:

1. equilibrium / weight   same ___ / different ___
2. inquisition /curiosity   same ___ / different ___
3. equable / steady   same ___ / different ___
4. perquisite / salary   same ___ / different ___
5. equinox /May Day   same ___ / different ___
6. acquisitive / greedy   same ___ / different ___
7. requisition / requirement   same ___ / different ___
8. adequacy / surplus   same ___ / different ___

B. Fill in each blank with the correct letter:

a. equinox   e. adequacy
b. requisition   f. acquisitive
c. equilibrium   g. equable
d. perquisite   h. inquisition

1. They're a quiet, pleasant couple, with very _____ temperaments.
2. You couldn't even get a pencil unless you filled out a _____.
3. In a healthy economy, supply and demand are in a state of approximate _____.
4. Daylight saving time begins in March, shortly before the _____ and the arrival of spring.
5. There was more than enough water, but he worried about the _____ of their food supplies.
6. The whole family was _____ by nature, and there were bitter legal battles over the will.

7. His status as newcomer did carry the special _____ of being able to ask a lot of questions.
8. Louisa feared an _____ into her background and previous involvements.

PLE/PLEN comes from a Latin word meaning "to fill." It can be seen in the words *plenty*, meaning basically "filled," and *complete*, meaning "thoroughly filled."

---

plenary \\'plē-nə-rē\\ (1) Including all who have a right to attend. (2) Complete in all ways.

• For the convention's plenary session, five thousand members gathered to hear a star speaker.

Plenary often shows up in writing referring to the "plenary power" held by a government, and is particularly used for powers mentioned in a constitution. For example, under the U.S. Constitution, the Congress has plenary power to wage war, which means that no one else—not the courts, not the states, not the president—has any power whatsoever to second-guess Congress about warmaking. But in recent years, that hasn't stopped some presidents from starting conflicts that looked a lot like wars to most people. At a conference, the plenary sessions (unlike the various smaller "presentations," "workshops," "forums," and "seminars" that otherwise fill the day) try to bring everyone together in the same room.

complement \\'käm-plə-mənt\\ (1) Something that fills up or makes perfect; the amount needed to make something complete. (2) A counterpart.

• On the committee, the two young people provided an energetic complement to the older members.

A complement fills out or balances something. We think of salt as the complement of pepper (maybe mostly because of their colors), and the right necktie is a perfect complement to a good suit. *Complement* can also mean "the full quantity, number, or amount"; thus, a ship's complement of officers and crew is the whole force necessary for full operation. *Complement* is actually most common as a verb; we may say, for example, that a bright blue scarf *complements* a cream-colored outfit beautifully. Don't confuse *complement* with *compliment*, which means an expression of respect or affection.

deplete \di-'plēt\ To reduce in amount by using up.

* Years of farming on the same small plot of land had left the soil depleted of minerals.

The *de-* prefix often means "do the opposite of," so *deplete* means the opposite of "fill." Thus, for example, a kitchen's food supplies can be rapidly depleted by hungry teenagers. But *deplete* often suggests something more serious. Desertions can deplete an army; layoffs can deplete an office staff; and too much time in bed can rapidly deplete your muscular strength.

replete \ri-'plēt\ Fully or abundantly filled or supplied.

* The professor's autobiography was replete with scandalous anecdotes about campus life in the 1950s.

Replete implies that something is filled almost to capacity. Autumn landscapes in New England are replete with colorful foliage. Supermarket tabloids are always replete with details of stars' lives, whether real or imaginary. And a professor may complain that most of the papers she received were replete with errors in grammar and punctuation.

METR/METER comes to us from Greek by way of Latin; in both languages it refers to "measure." A *thermometer* measures heat; a *perimeter* is the measure around something; and things that are *isometric* are equal in measure.

---

metric \'me-trik\ (1) Relating to or based on the metric system. (2) Relating to or arranged in meter.

* Americans have resisted using the metric system for years, but are now slowly getting accustomed to a few of the metric units.

The metric system was invented in France in the years following the French Revolution, and a version of it is now used in most of the world to measure distance, weight, and volume. Basic metric units include the *kilogram* (the basic unit of weight), the *liter* (the basic unit of volume), and of course the *meter* (the basic unit of length—see below). *Metric*—or more often *metrical*—can also refer to the basic underlying rhythm of songs and poetry. So while the scientists' measurements are usually metric, the poets' are usually metrical.

meter \\'mē-tər\\ (1) The basic metric unit of length, equal to about 39.37 inches. (2) A systematic rhythm in poetry or music.

- The basic meter of the piece was 3/4, but its rhythms were so complicated that the 3/4 was sometimes hard to hear.

Meter is a metric measurement slightly longer than a yard; thus, a 100-meter dash might take you a second longer than a 100-yard dash. But the word has a different sense in music, where people aren't separated by whether they use the metric system. For a musician, the meter is the regular background rhythm, expressed by the "time signature" written at the beginning of a piece or section: 2/2, 2/4, 3/8, 4/4, 6/8, etc. Within a meter, you can create rhythms that range from the simple to the complex. So, for example, "America the Beautiful" is in 4/4 meter (or "4/4 time"), but so are most of the rhythmically complex songs written by Paul Simon, Burt Bacharach, or Stevie Wonder. In ordinary conversation, though, most people use "rhythm" to include meter and everything that's built on top of it. In poetry, meter has much the same meaning; however, poetic meters aren't named with numbers but instead with traditional Greek and Latin terms such as *iambic* and *dactylic*.

odometer \\ō-'dä-mə-tər\\ An instrument used to measure distance traveled.

- Jennifer watched the odometer to see how far she would have to drive to her new job.

Odometer includes the root from the Greek word *hodos,* meaning "road" or "trip." An odometer shares space on your dashboard with a speedometer, a tachometer, and maybe a "tripmeter." The odometer is what crooked car salesmen tamper with when they want to reduce the mileage a car registers as having traveled. One of life's little pleasures is watching the odometer as all the numbers change at the same time.

tachometer \\ta-'kä-mə-tər\\ A device used to measure speed of rotation.

- Even though one purpose of a tachometer is to help drivers keep their engine speeds down, some of us occasionally try to see how high we can make the needle go.

A tachometer is literally a "speed-measurer," since the Greek root *tach-* means "speed." This is clear in the names of the *tachyon,* a particle of matter that travels faster than the speed of light (if it actually exists, it's so fast that it's impossible to see with any instrument), and *tachycardia,* a medical condition in which the heart races uncontrollably. Since the speed that an auto tachometer measures is speed of rotation of the crankshaft, the numbers it reports are revolutions per minute, or rpm's.

Quizzes

A. **Match the word on the left to the correct definition on the right:**

1.	meter	a.	drain
2.	tachometer	b.	brimming
3.	metric	c.	counterpart
4.	replete	d.	beat pattern
5.	odometer	e.	distance measurer
6.	deplete	f.	rotation meter
7.	plenary	g.	general
8.	complement	h.	relating to a measuring system

B. **Choose the closest definition:**

1. deplete   a. straighten out b. draw down c. fold
      d. abandon
2. replete   a. refold b. repeat c. abundantly provided
      d. fully clothed
3. odometer   a. intelligence measurer b. heart-rate
      measurer c. height measurer d. mile measurer
4. tachometer   a. rpm measurer b. sharpness measurer
      c. fatigue measurer d. size measurer
5. complement   a. praise b. number required
      c. abundance d. usual dress
6. metric   a. relating to poetic rhythm b. relating to ocean
      depth c. relating to books d. relating to particles of
      matter
7. plenary   a. for hours b. for life c. for officials
      d. for everyone
8. meter   a. weight b. rhythm c. speed d. force

AUD, from the Latin verb *audire,* is the root that has to do with hearing. What is *audible* can be heard. An *audience* is a group of listeners, sometimes seated in an *auditorium.* And *audio* today can mean almost anything that has to do with sound.

auditor \ˈȯ-də-tər\ A person who formally examines and verifies financial accounts.

• It seems impossible that so many banks could have gotten into so much trouble if their auditors had been doing their jobs.

The *auditing* of a company's financial records by independent examiners on a regular basis is necessary to prevent "cooking the books," and thus to keep the company honest. We don't normally think of auditors as listening, since looking at and adding up numbers is their basic line of work, but auditors do have to listen to people's explanations, and perhaps that's the historical link. Hearing is more obviously part of another meaning of *audit,* the kind that college students do when they sit in on a class without taking exams or receiving an official grade.

auditory \ˈȯ-də-ˌtȯr-ē\ (1) Perceived or experienced through hearing. (2) Of or relating to the sense or organs of hearing.

• With the "surround-sound" systems in most theaters, going to a movie is now an auditory experience as much as a visual one.

Auditory is close in meaning to *acoustic* and *acoustical,* but *auditory* usually refers more to hearing than to sound. For instance, many dogs have great auditory (not acoustic) powers, and the *auditory nerve* lets us hear by connecting the inner ear to the brain. *Acoustic* and *acoustical* instead refer especially to instruments and the conditions under which sound can be heard; so architects concern themselves with the acoustic properties of an auditorium, and instrument makers with those of a clarinet or piano.

audition \ȯ-ˈdi-shən\ A trial performance to evaluate a performer's skills.

• Auditions for Broadway shows attract so many hopeful unknown performers that everyone in the business calls them "cattle calls."

Most stars are discovered at auditions, where a number of candidates read the same part and the director chooses. Lana Turner famously skipped the audition process and was instead discovered by an agent sipping a soda in a Sunset Boulevard café at age 16. *Audition* can also be a verb; so, for example, after Miss Turner gained her stardom, actors had to audition to be her leading man. But when musicians audition for a job in an orchestra, it's usually behind a screen so that the judges won't even know their sex and therefore can't do anything but listen.

inaudible \i-ˈnȯ-də-bəl\ Not heard or capable of being heard.

- The coach spoke to her in a low voice that was inaudible to the rest of the gymnastics team.

With its negative prefix *in-*, *inaudible* means the opposite of *audible*. What's clearly audible to you may be inaudible to your elderly grandfather. Modern spy technology can turn inaudible conversations into audible ones with the use of high-powered directional microphones, so if you think you're being spied on, make sure there's a lot of other noise around you. And if you don't want everyone around you to know you're bored, keep your sighs inaudible.

SON is the Latin root meaning "sound." *Sonata*, meaning a piece for one or two instruments, was originally an Italian verb meaning "sounded" (when singers were involved, the Italians used a different verb). And *sonorous* means full, loud, or rich in sound.

---

sonic \ˈsä-nik\ (1) Having to do with sound. (2) Having to do with the speed of sound in air (about 750 miles per hour).

- A sonic depth finder can easily determine the depth of a lake by bouncing a sound signal off the bottom.

A sonic boom is an explosive sound created by a shock wave formed at the nose of an aircraft. In 1947 a plane piloted by Chuck Yeager burst the "sound barrier" and created the first sonic boom. In the decades afterward sonic booms became a familiar sound to Americans. (Because of steps that were eventually taken, sonic booms are rarely heard anymore.) Today *sonic* is often used by ambitious rock musicians to describe their experimental sounds.

dissonant \ˈdi-sə-nənt\ (1) Clashing or discordant, especially in music. (2) Incompatible or disagreeing.

- Critics of the health-care plan pointed to its two seemingly dissonant goals: cost containment, which would try to control spending, and universal coverage, which could increase spending.

Since *dissonant* includes the negative prefix *dis-*, what is dissonant sounds or feels unresolved, unharmonic, and clashing. Early in the 20th century, composers such as Arnold Schoenberg and his students developed the use of *dissonance* in music as a style in itself. But to many listeners, the sounds in such music are still unbearable, and most continue to prefer music based on traditional tonality. *Dissonant* is now often used without referring to sound at all. *Cognitive dissonance*, for example, is what happens when you believe two different things that can't actually both be true.

resonance \\'re-zə-nəns\\ (1) A continuing or echoing of sound. (2) A richness and variety in the depth and quality of sound.

- The resonance of James Earl Jones's vocal tones in such roles as Darth Vader made his voice one of the most recognizable of its time.

Many of the finest musical instruments possess a high degree of resonance which, by producing additional vibrations and echoes of the original sound, enriches and amplifies it. Violins made by the Italian masters Stradivari and Guarneri possess a quality of resonance that later violinmakers have never precisely duplicated. And you may have noticed how a particular note will start something in a room buzzing, as one of the touching surfaces begins to *resonate* with the note. Because of that, *resonance* and *resonate*—along with the adjective *resonant*—aren't always used to describe sound. For example, you may say that a novel resonates strongly with you because the author seems to be describing your own experiences and feelings.

ultrasonic \\ˌəl-trə-'sä-nik\\ Having a frequency higher than what can be heard by the human ear.

- My grandfather's dog is always pricking up its ears at some ultrasonic signal, while he himself is so deaf he can't even hear a bird singing.

Ultrasound, or *ultrasonography*, works on the principle that sound is reflected at different speeds by tissues or substances of different densities. Ultrasound technology has been used medically since the 1940s. *Sonograms*, the pictures produced by ultrasound, can reveal heart defects, tumors, and gallstones; since low-power ultrasonic waves don't present any risks to a body, they're most often used to display fetuses during pregnancy in order to make sure they're healthy. *Ultrasonics* has many other uses, including underwater *sonar* sensing. High-power ultrasonics are so intense that they're actually used for drilling and welding.

Quizzes

A. Indicate whether the following pairs of words have the same or different meanings:

1.	dissonant / jarring	same ___ / different ___
2.	inaudible / invisible	same ___ / different ___
3.	resonance / richness	same ___ / different ___
4.	audition / tryout	same ___ / different ___
5.	ultrasonic / radical	same ___ / different ___
6.	auditor / performer	same ___ / different ___
7.	sonic / loud	same ___ / different ___
8.	auditory / hearing-related	same ___ / different ___

B. Match the word on the left to the correct definition on the right:

1.	inaudible	a.	involving sound
2.	auditory	b.	impossible to hear
3.	ultrasonic	c.	beyond the hearing range
4.	resonance	d.	a critical hearing
5.	auditor	e.	relating to hearing
6.	sonic	f.	unharmonious
7.	dissonant	g.	financial examiner
8.	audition	h.	continuing or echoing sound

ERR, from the Latin verb *errare*, means "to wander" or "to stray." The root is seen in the word *error*, meaning a wandering or straying from what is correct or true. *Erratum* (plural, *errata*) is Latin for "mistake"; so an errata page is a book page that lists mistakes found too late to correct before the book's publication.

errant \'er-ənt\ (1) Wandering or moving about aimlessly. (2) Straying outside proper bounds, or away from an accepted pattern or standard.

• Modern-day cowboys have been known to use helicopters to spot errant calves.

Errant means both "wandering" and "mistaken." A *knight-errant* was a wandering knight who went about slaying dragons or rescuing damsels in distress (at least when he was on good behavior). *Arrant* is a old-fashioned spelling of *errant*; an *arrant knave* (the phrase comes from Shakespeare) is an extremely untrustworthy individual. An errant sock might be one that's gotten lost; an errant politician might be one who's been caught cheating; and an errant cloud might be one that floats by all alone in a deep-blue sky on a summer day.

aberrant \ə-'ber-ənt\ Straying or differing from the right, normal, or natural type.

• Sullivan's increasingly aberrant behavior was leading his friends to question his mental stability.

Something aberrant has wandered away from the usual path or form. The word is generally used in a negative way; aberrant behavior, for example, may be a symptom of other problems. But the discovery of an aberrant variety of a species can be exciting news to a biologist, and identifying an aberrant gene has led the way to new treatments for diseases.

erratic \i-'ra-tik\ (1) Having no fixed course. (2) Lacking in consistency.

• In the 1993 World Series, the Phillies weren't helped by the erratic performance of their ace relief pitcher, "Wild Thing."

Erratic can refer to literal "wandering." A missile that loses its guidance system may follow an erratic path, and a river with lots of twists and bends is said to have an erratic course. *Erratic* can also mean "inconsistent" or "irregular." So a stock market that often changes direction is said to be acting *erratically;* an erratic heartbeat can be cause for concern; and if your car idles erratically it may mean that something's wrong with the spark-plug wiring.

erroneous \i-'rō-nē-əs\ Mistaken, incorrect.

• For years her parents had had an erroneous idea of her intelligence, because she didn't begin to talk until the age of six.

Erroneous basically means "containing errors," and, since most of us are constantly suffering from mistaken notions, the word is often used in front of words such as "assumption" and "idea." It's also used to describe the kind of mistaken information that can lead to erroneous theories, erroneous conclusions, and erroneous decisions.

CED comes from the Latin verb *cedere*, meaning "to proceed" or "to yield." *Proceed* itself employs the root, as does *recede*, and their related nouns *procession* and *recession* employ another form of the Latin verb.

---

cede \'sēd\ To give up, especially by treaty; yield.

• Their 88-year-old father reluctantly ceded control over his finances to two of the children this year.

Cede is often a formal term used in discussing territory and rights, but is also used less formally. So, for example, Spain ceded Puerto Rico to the U.S. in 1898, following the Spanish-American War, and the U.S. ceded control of the Panama Canal to Panama in 1999. Critics warn that we are ceding leadership in alternative-energy technology to China. Citizens of one European country or another are always worrying that their own country is ceding too much power to the European Union. A tennis player doesn't have any choice when she cedes her no. 1 ranking to a rival.

concede \kən-'sēd\ To admit grudgingly; yield.

• To his friends, Senator Beasley concedes that his reelection campaign was badly run and that he made several damaging errors.

After the votes have been counted, one candidate traditionally concedes the election to his or her opponent by giving a *concession* speech. If you're lucky, your boss will concede that she was wrong the last time she criticized you. But in the middle of an argument, we're not all so good at conceding that the other guy might have a good point.

accede \ak'-sēd\ (1) To give in to a request or demand. (2) To give approval or consent.

• This time Congress refused to accede to the demands of the president, and began cutting the funding for the war.

To accede usually means to yield, often under pressure and with some reluctance, to the needs or requests of others. Voters usually accede to a tax increase only when they're convinced it's the only real solution to a shortfall in government funding. A patient may accede to surgery only after the doctor assures him it's better than the alternatives. If you accede to your spouse's plea to watch the new reality show at 9:00, you may get to choose something better at 10:00.

precedent \\'pre-sə-dənt\\ Something done or said that may be an example or rule to guide later acts of a similar kind.

• When Judy bought Christmas presents for all her relatives one year, she claimed that it set no precedent, but it did.

A precedent is something that *precedes*, or comes before. The Supreme Court relies on precedents—that is, earlier laws or decisions that provide some example or rule to guide them in the case they're actually deciding. When hostages are being held for ransom, a government may worry about setting a bad precedent if it gives in. And a company might "break with precedent" by naming a foreigner as its president for the first time.

Quizzes

A. Complete the analogy:

1. descending : ascending :: errant : _____
   a. moving b. wandering c. fixed d. straying
2. grab : seize :: cede : _____
   a. hang on b. hand over c. hang up d. head out
3. fruitful : barren :: erroneous : _____
   a. productive b. pleasant c. targeted d. correct
4. disagree : argue :: concede : _____
   a. drive b. hover c. yield d. refuse
5. stable : constant :: erratic : _____
   a. fast b. invisible c. mistaken d. unpredictable
6. swerve : veer :: accede : _____
   a. agree b. descent c. reject d. demand

7. typical : normal :: aberrant : _____
   a. burdened   b. roving   c. odd   d. missing

8. etiquette : manners :: precedent : _____
   a. courtesy   b. tradition   c. rudeness   d. behavior

B. Fill in each blank with the correct letter:

a. aberrant   e. erratic
b. errant   f. erroneous
c. precedent   g. cede
d. concede   h. accede

1. Her low opinion of him turned out to be based on several _____ assumptions.

2. The judges could find no _____ to guide them in deciding how to deal with the case.

3. Like many malaria sufferers, she experienced _____ changes in her temperature.

4. Occasionally an _____ cow would be found on the back lawn, happily grazing on the fresh clover.

5. She's very stubborn, and in an argument she'll never _____ a single point.

6. After several incidents of disturbingly _____ behavior, his parents began taking him to a psychiatrist.

7. After lengthy negotiations, the union will probably _____ to several of the company's terms.

8. The treaty requires that both sides _____ several small tracts of land.

Words from Mythology and History

Augean stable \ò-ˈjē-ən-ˈstā-bəl\ A condition or place marked by great accumulation of filth or corruption.

- Leaders of many of the newly formed nations of Eastern Europe found that the old governments of their countries had become Augean stables that they must now clean out.

Augeus, the mythical king of Elis, kept great stables that held 3,000 oxen and had not been cleaned for thirty years when Hercules was assigned the job as one of his famous "twelve labors." This task was enormous even for someone so mighty, so Hercules shifted the course of two rivers to make them pour through the stables. *Augean* by itself has come to mean "extremely difficult or distasteful," and to "clean the Augean stable" usually means either to clear away corruption or to perform a large and unpleasant task that has long called for attention. So today we refer to "Augean tasks," "Augean labor," or even "Augean clutter." And the British firm Augean PLC is—what else?—a waste-management company.

Croesus \ˈkrē-səs\ A very rich person.

• Warren Buffett's extraordinary record of acquiring and investing made him an American Croesus.

Croesus, which tends to appear in the phrase "rich as Croesus," was the name of a king of Lydia, an ancient kingdom in what is now western Turkey, who died around 546 B.C. Lydia was probably the first country in history to use coins, and under the wealthy and powerful Croesus the first coins of pure silver and gold were produced, which may have added to the legends surrounding his wealth. But it was Croesus who the Greek lawgiver Solon was thinking about when he said "Count no man happy until his death"—and indeed Croesus was finally overthrown and may even have been burned alive.

dragon's teeth \ˈdra-gənz-ˈtēth\ Seeds of conflict.

• Many experts believed that, in invading a Middle Eastern country that hadn't attacked us, we were sowing dragon's teeth.

The Phoenician prince Cadmus once killed a dragon, and was instructed by the goddess Athena to plant its teeth in the ground. From the many teeth, there immediately sprang up an army of fierce armed men. The goddess then directed him to throw a precious stone into their midst, and they proceeded to slaughter each other until only the five greatest warriors were left; these became Cadmus's generals, with whom he constructed the great city-state of Thebes. When we "sow dragon's teeth," we're creating the conditions for future trouble.

Hades \ˈhā-dēz\ The underground home of the dead in Greek mythology.

• In a dramatic scene, he crawls up out of the ground coated in black petroleum as though emerging from Hades.

In Greek mythology, Hades is both the land of the dead and the god who rules there. Hades the god (who the Greeks also called Pluto) is the brother of Zeus and Poseidon, who rule the skies and the seas. The realm called Hades, where he rules with his wife Persephone, is the region under the earth, full of mineral wealth and fertility and home to dead souls. *Hades* today is sometimes used as a polite term for *Hell* ("It's hotter than Hades in here!").

lethargic \lə-'thär-jik\ (1) Lazily sluggish. (2) Indifferent or apathetic.

• Once again the long Sunday dinner had left most of the family feeling stuffed and lethargic.

The philosopher Plato wrote that before a dead person could leave the underworld to begin a new life, he or she had to drink from the river Lethe, whose name means "forgetfulness" in Greek, and forget all aspects of one's former life and the time spent in Hades (usually pretty awful, according to Plato). But *lethargic* and its noun *lethargy* never actually refer to forgetting; instead, they describe the weak, ghostly state of the dead spirits—so weak that they may require a drink of blood before they can even speak.

Midas touch \'mī-dəs-'təch\ The talent for making money in every venture.

• Investors are always looking for an investment adviser with the Midas touch, but after a couple of good years each adviser's brilliance usually seems to vanish.

Midas was a legendary king of Phrygia (in modern-day Turkey). In return for a good deed, he was granted one wish by the god Dionysus, and asked for the power to turn everything he touched into gold. When he discovered to his horror that his touch had turned his food and drink—and even his daughter—to gold, he begged Dionysus to take back the gift, and Dionysus agreed to do so. When "Midas touch" is used today, the moral of this tale of greed is usually ignored.

Pyrrhic victory \'pir-ik-'vik-tə-rē\ A victory won at excessive cost.

• That win turned out to be a Pyrrhic victory, since our best players sustained injuries that would sideline them for weeks.

In 279 B.C. Pyrrhus, the king of Epirus, a country in northwest Greece, defeated the Romans at the Battle of Ausculum, but lost all of his best officers and many men. He is said to have exclaimed after the battle, "One more such victory and we are lost." Pyrrhic victories are more common than we tend to think. Whenever we win an argument but in so doing manage to offend the friend we were arguing with, or whenever a country invades another country but rouses widespread opposition in surrounding countries in the process, it's probably a Pyrrhic victory that has been achieved.

stygian \\'sti-jē-ən\ Extremely dark, dank, gloomy, and forbidding.

- When the power went out in the building, the halls and stairwells were plunged in stygian darkness.

The Greek underworld of Hades was cold and dark, rather than blazing like the Christian image of Hell. The river Styx, whose name meant "hateful" in Greek, was the chief river of the underground, and the souls of the dead were ferried across its poisonous waters into Hades by the boatman Charon. The Styx was so terrible that even the gods swore by its name in their most solemn oaths. The name Stygia, borrowed from *stygian*, is used for a country in fantasy games today; but a stygian atmosphere, a stygian tunnel, stygian darkness, and so on, still describe the dreary cheerlessness of the Greek underworld.

Quiz

Choose the word that does not belong:

1. lethargic   a. lazy   b. sluggish   c. energetic
   d. indifferent
2. Croesus   a. rich   b. powerful   c. impoverished
   d. successful
3. Midas touch   a. talented   b. unsuccessful   c. rich
   d. prosperous
4. Pyrrhic victory   a. unqualified   b. costly
   c. dangerous   d. destructive
5. Augean stable   a. purity   b. corruption   c. filth
   d. Herculean
6. Hades   a. underworld   b. heaven   c. dead   d. eternity

7. dragon's teeth   a. dangerous   b. troublesome
     c. sensible   d. conflict
8. stygian   a. glamorous   b. gloomy   c. grim   d. dank

Review Quizzes

A. Match each word on the left to its *antonym* on the right:

1. cede   a.   true
2. erroneous   b.   generous
3. dissonant   c.   energetic
4. lethargic   d.   fill
5. replete   e.   imbalance
6. acquisitive   f.   typical
7. deplete   g.   acquire
8. equilibrium   h.   hearable
9. inaudible   i.   empty
10. aberrant   j.   harmonious

B. Complete the analogies:

1. allow : forbid :: cede : _____ a. take   b. agree
    c. soothe   d. permit
2. lively : energetic :: erratic : _____ a. calm
    b. changeable   c. steady   d. weary
3. complain : whine :: accede : _____ a. go over   b. give
    in   c. give out   d. go along
4. noisy : raucous :: dissonant : _____ a. musical
    b. symphonic   c. harsh   d. loud
5. amount : quantity :: complement _____ a. remainder
    b. extra   c. extension   d. minority
6. spendthrift : thrifty :: acquisitive : _____ a. wealthy
    b. uncertain   c. curious   d. unselfish

C. Fill in each blank with the correct letter:

a. auditor   f.   erratic
b. tachometer   g.   Midas touch
c. dragon's teeth   h.   accede
d. complement   i.   Pyrrhic victory
e. Croesus   j.   metric

1. My grandfather has never had any money, but his brother is rich as _____.

2. Every scientist in the world uses a version of the _____ system, but the American public has always resisted it.

3. An _____ had been going over the company's financial records all week.

4. The triumphant corporate takeover proved to be a _____, since the resulting debt crippled the corporation for years.

5. The children made only _____ progress because they kept stopping to pick flowers.

6. Some of the faculty have decided to quietly _____ to the students' request for less homework.

7. She's been sowing _____ with her mean gossip, and by now no one in the department is speaking to anyone else.

8. When the traffic gets too noisy, I have to glance at the _____ to see if the engine is racing.

9. Fresh, hot bread is the perfect _____ to any dinner.

10. Her wealthy father had always had the _____, and his money-making genius was still a mystery to her.

UNIT

7

VIS comes from a Latin verb meaning "see." *Vision* is what enables us to see, *visual* images are *visible* to our eyes, and a *visitor* is someone who comes to see something. The same verb actually gives us another root, *vid-,* as in Julius Caesar's famous statement about his military exploits, "Veni, vidi, vici" ("I came, I saw, I conquered"), and such common English words as *video.*

vista \\'vi-stə\\ (1) A distant view. (2) An extensive mental view, as over a stretch of time.

• The economic vista for the next two years looks excellent, according to a poll of business economists.

Vista is generally used today for broad sweeping views of the kind you might see from a mountaintop. But the word originally meant an avenue-like view, narrowed by a line of trees on either side. And *vista* has also long been used (like *view* and *outlook*) to mean a mental scan of the future—as if you were riding down a long grand avenue and what you could see a mile or so ahead of you was where you'd be in the very near future.

vis-à-vis \\ˌvē-zä-'vē\\ In relation to or compared with.

• Many financial reporters worry about the loss of U.S. economic strength vis-à-vis our principal trading partners.

Vis-à-vis comes from Latin by way of French, where it means literally "face-to-face." In English it was first used to mean a little horse-drawn carriage in which two people sat opposite each other. From there it acquired various other meanings, such as "dancing partner." Today it no longer refers to actual physical faces and bodies, but its modern meaning comes from the fact that things that are face-to-face can easily be compared or contrasted. So, for example, a greyhound is very tall vis-à-vis a Scottie, and the Red Sox have often fared badly vis-à-vis the Yankees.

visionary \\ˈvi-zhə-ˌner-ē\\ (1) A person with foresight and imagination. (2) A dreamer whose ideas are often impractical.

- His followers regarded him as an inspired visionary; his opponents saw him as either a con man or a lunatic.

A visionary is someone with a strong *vision* of the future. Since such visions aren't always accurate, a visionary's ideas may either work brilliantly or fail miserably. Even so, *visionary* is usually a positive word. Martin Luther King, Jr., for instance, was a visionary in his hopes and ideas for a just society. The word is also an adjective; thus, for example, we may speak of a *visionary* project, a visionary leader, a visionary painter, or a visionary company.

envisage \\in-ˈvi-zij\\ To have a mental picture of; visualize.

- A mere three weeks after they had started dating, the two were already arguing, and none of us could envisage the relationship lasting for long.

One of the imagination's most valuable uses is its ability to see something in the "mind's eye"—that is, to *visualize, envision,* or envisage something. Envisaging a possibility may be one of the chief abilities that separate human beings from the other animals. What we envisage may be physical (such as a completed piece of furniture) or nonphysical (such as finishing college). Envisaging life with a puppy might lead us down to the pound to buy one, and envisaging the sinking of an island nation may focus our minds on climate change.

SPECT comes from the Latin verb *specere,* meaning "to look at," and produces several familiar English words. *Spectacles* can be glasses that you look through; but a spectacle can also be a remarkable sight—in Roman times, perhaps a *spectacular* chariot race or a *spectacularly* bloody battle between gladiators and wild beasts, mounted for the pleasure of its *spectators.*

aspect \\'a-ˌspekt\ (1) A part of something. (2) A certain way in which something appears or may be regarded.

• Many experts believe the mental aspect of distance racing is more important than the physical aspect.

Since *aspectus* in Latin means "looked at," an aspect of something is basically the direction from which it's looked at. So we may say that travel is your favorite aspect of your job, or that eating well is one aspect of a healthy life. If you look at a stage set from the front, it looks completely different than from behind, where all the mechanisms are visible, and both aspects are important. The word can be very useful when you're analyzing something, and it's used a great deal in the writings of scholars.

prospect \\'prä-ˌspekt\ (1) The possibility that something will happen in the future. (2) An opportunity for something to happen.

• There was little prospect of a breakthrough in the negotiations before the elections.

Since the Latin prefix *pro-* often means "forward" (see PRO, p. 631), *prospect* refers to looking forward. The prospect of a recession may lead investors to pull their money out of the stock market. Graduates of a good law school usually have excellent prospects for finding employment. *Prospective* students roam campuses with their parents in the year before they plan to enter college.

perspective \pər-'spek-tiv\ (1) Point of view; the angle, direction, or standpoint from which a person looks at something. (2) The art or technique of painting or drawing a scene so that objects in it seem to have depth and distance.

• From the perspective of the lowly soldier, the war looked very different.

To the modern mind, it's hard to believe that perspective had to be "discovered," but before the 1400s paintings simply lacked accurate perspective. Instead, important people and objects were simply shown larger than less important ones; and although distant objects were sometimes shown smaller than near ones, this wasn't done in a regular and accurate way. Just as odd, many paintings didn't represent the other meaning of *perspective* either—that is, a scene might not be shown as if it were being seen from one single place. Today, *perspective* is used much like *standpoint*. Just as *standpoint* once used to mean simply the physical place where you stand but today also means the way you "see" things as a result of who you are and what you do, the same could be said about *perspective*.

prospectus \prə-'spek-təs\ A printed statement that describes something (such as a new business or a stock offering) and is sent out to people who may be interested in buying or investing.

• The prospectus for the mutual fund says nothing about how its profit forecasts were calculated.

Like *prospect*, *prospectus* looks forward. Thus, a prospectus originally outlined something that didn't yet exist, describing what it would become. This might even be a book; the great dictionary of Noah Webster, like that of Samuel Johnson, was first announced in the form of a prospectus, so that well-to-do people might actually subscribe to it—that is, pay for it in advance so that Webster would have money to live on while writing it. Soon, *prospectus* was being used to mean a description of a private school or college, intended to attract new students. Today the word very often means a description of a stock offering or mutual fund, whether new or not.

Quizzes

A. Fill in each blank with the correct letter:

a. perspective	e. envisage
b. vis-à-vis	f. aspect
c. prospectus	g. visionary
d. prospect	h. vista

1. When she considered Cleveland _____ other cities where she might have to live, she always chose Cleveland.
2. The _____ of spending an evening with such an unhappy couple was just depressing.
3. His ambitious plans for the city marked him as a true _____.
4. The most troubling _____ of the whole incident was the public reaction.
5. The _____ for the new development was full of glowing descriptions that made both of us suspicious.

6. Turning a corner, they found themselves gazing out on the broad _____ of the river valley.

7. Some judges only look at crimes like these from the _____ of the police.

8. Her therapist keeps asking her if she could _____ getting back together with her husband.

B. Match the definition on the left to the correct word on the right:

1.	compared to	a.	perspective
2.	advance description	b.	envisage
3.	prophet	c.	vis-à-vis
4.	imagine	d.	aspect
5.	standpoint	e.	prospectus
6.	outlook	f.	visionary
7.	element	g.	prospect
8.	view	h.	vista

VOC comes from the Latin words meaning "voice" and "speak." So a *vocal* ensemble is a singing group. A *vocation* was originally a "calling" from God to do religious work as a priest, monk, or nun, though today most people use the word just to mean a career. And a *vocabulary* is a set of words for speaking.

---

equivocate \i-ˈkwi-və-ˌkāt\ (1) To use ambiguous language, especially in order to deceive. (2) To avoid giving a direct answer.

- As the company directors continued to equivocate, the union prepared to return to the picket lines.

With its root *equi-*, meaning "equal," *equivocate* suggests speaking on both sides of an issue at the same time. An *equivocal* answer is one that manages not to take a stand; an *unequivocal* answer, by contrast, is strong and clear. Politicians are famous for equivocating, but *equivocation* is also typical of used-car salesmen, nervous witnesses in a courtroom, and guys whose girlfriends ask them how committed they are to a relationship.

---

irrevocable \i-ˈre-və-kə-bəl\ Impossible to call back or retract.

- She had told him she wasn't going to see him again, but he couldn't believe her decision was irrevocable.

Irrevocable has a formal sound to it and is often used in legal contexts. Irrevocable trusts are trust funds that cannot be dissolved by the people who created them (the other kind is a *revocable* trust). An irrevocable credit is an absolute obligation from a bank to provide credit to a customer. Irrevocable gifts, under U.S. tax law, are gifts that are given by one living person to another and can't be reclaimed by the giver. But the word isn't always legal; we've all had to make irrevocable decisions, decisions that commit us absolutely to something.

advocate \\'ad-və-ˌkāt\\ To speak in favor of.

- Our lawyer is advocating a suit against the state, but most of us would rather try some other approaches first.

The verb *advocate* may be followed by *for* ("advocated for better roads," "advocated for merging the two school districts") or by a noun or gerund ("advocating an increase in the military budget," "advocated closing the budget gap"). But *advocate* isn't only a verb: An *advocate* is someone who advocates for you, or argues on your side. Originally, this was often a lawyer in court, and in Britain *advocate* is still a term for "lawyer."

vociferous \\vō-'si-fə-rəs\\ Making noisy or emphatic outcries.

- Whenever the referee at these soccer games makes a questionable call, you hear vociferous protests from half the parents.

A vociferous group shouts loudly and insistently, and they're usually not too happy about something. So, for example, we often hear about vociferous critics, vociferous demands, vociferous opponents, or a vociferous minority. When a small group makes itself vociferous enough, everyone else may even start thinking it's actually a majority.

PHON is a Greek root meaning "sound," "voice," or "speech." It's probably most familiar in the form of the English suffix *-phone*, in words that begin with a Greek or Latin root as well. Thus, the *tele-* in *telephone* means "far," the *micro-* in *microphone* means "small," the *xylo-* in *xylophone* means "wood," and so on.

---

phonics \\'fä-niks\\ A method of teaching beginners to read and pronounce words by learning the characteristic sounds of letters, letter groups, and especially syllables.

• My son's school switched to phonics instruction several years ago, and reading achievement in the early grades has been improving.

In the field of beginning reading, there are two basic schools of thought in the U.S. today. One emphasizes "whole language" teaching, which relies on teaching a lot of reading; the other emphasizes phonics, teaching how letters and syllables correspond to sounds. Phonics instruction may be especially difficult in English, since English has the most difficult spelling of any Western language. Consider the various ways we create the *f* sound in *cough, photo,* and *giraffe,* or the *sh* sound in *special, issue, vicious,* and *portion,* or the *k* sound in *tack, quite,* and *shellac,* and how we pronounce the *o* in *do, core, lock,* and *bone,* or the *ea* in *lead, ocean, idea,* and *early.* Teaching phonics obviously isn't an easy job, but it's probably an important one.

phonetic \\fə-'ne-tik\\ Relating to or representing the sounds of the spoken language.

• In almost every Spanish word the pronunciation is clear from the spelling, so the phonetic part of learning Spanish isn't usually a big challenge.

The English alphabet is phonetic—that is, the letters represent sounds. The Chinese alphabet, however, isn't phonetic, since its symbols represent ideas rather than sounds. But even in English, a letter doesn't always represent the same sound; the "a" in *cat, father,* and *mate,* for example, represents three different sounds. Because of this, books about words often use specially created phonetic alphabets in which each symbol stands for a single sound in order to represent pronunciations. So in this book, *cat, father,* and *mate* would be *phonetically* represented as \\'kat, \\'fä-thər, and \\'māt.

polyphonic \\ˌpä-lē-'fä-nik\\ Referring to a style of music in which two or more melodies are sung or played against each other in harmony.

• Whenever he needed something calming, he would put on some quiet polyphonic music from the Renaissance and just let the voices waft over him.

Since *poly-* means "many" (see POLY, p. 54), polyphonic music has "many voices." In *polyphony,* each part has its own melody, and they weave together in a web that may become very dense; a famous piece by Thomas Tallis, composed around 1570, has 40 separate voice parts. Polyphony reached its height during the 16th century with Italian madrigals and the sacred music of such composers as Tallis, Palestrina, and Byrd. Usually when we speak of polyphony we're talking about music of Bach's time and earlier; but the principles remain the same today, and songwriters such as the Beatles have sometimes used polyphony as well.

cacophony \kə-ˈkä-fə-nē\ Harsh or unpleasant sound.

• In New York she was often dragged off by her boyfriend to downtown jazz concerts, where she struggled to make sense of what sounded like nothing but cacophony.

Cacophony employs the Greek prefix *caco-,* meaning "bad," but not everything we call *cacophonous* is necessarily bad. Grunge, thrash, hardcore, and goth music are unlistenable to some people and very popular to others. Open-air food markets may be marked by a cacophony of voices but also by wonderful sights and sounds. On the other hand, few people can really enjoy, for more than a few minutes, the cacophony of jackhammers, car horns, and truck engines that assaults the city pedestrian on a hot day in August.

Quizzes

A. Complete the analogy:

1. initial : beginning :: irrevocable : _____
     a. usual b. noisy c. final d. reversible
2. arithmetic : numbers :: phonics : _____
     a. letters b. notes c. meanings d. music
3. prefer : dislike :: advocate : _____
     a. oppose b. support c. assist d. boost
4. multistoried : floor :: polyphonic : _____
     a. poetry b. melody c. story d. harmony
5. reject : accept :: equivocate : _____
     a. decide b. specify c. detect d. delay
6. melodic : notes :: phonetic : _____
     a. sounds b. signs c. ideas d. pages

7. monotonous : boring :: vociferous : _____
    a. vegetarian b. angry c. favorable d. noisy
8. stillness : quiet :: cacophony : _____
    a. melodious b. dissonant c. creative d. birdlike

B. Indicate whether the following pairs have the same or different meanings:

1. advocate / describe   same ___ / different ___
2. phonetic / phonelike   same ___ / different ___
3. equivocate / refuse   same ___ / different ___
4. polyphonic / many-voiced   same ___ / different ___
5. irrevocable / unfortunate   same ___ / different ___
6. cacophony / din   same ___ / different ___
7. vociferous / calm   same ___ / different ___
8. phonics / audio   same ___ / different ___

CUR, from the Latin verb *curare*, means basically "care for." Our verb *cure* comes from this root, as do *manicure* ("care of the hands") and *pedicure* ("care of the feet").

---

curative \\'kyùr-ə-tiv\\ Having to do with curing diseases.

• As soon as the antibiotic entered his system, he imagined he could begin to feel its curative effects.

Medical researchers are finding curative substances in places that surprise them. Folklore has led to some "new" *cures* of old diseases, and natural substances never before tried have often proved effective. Quinine, which comes from a tree in the Andes, was the original drug for malaria; aspirin's main ingredient came from willow bark; and Taxol, a drug used in treating several cancers, was originally extracted from the bark of a yew tree. The curative properties of these natural drugs are today duplicated in the laboratory.

curator \\'kyùr-,ā-tər\\ Someone in charge of something where things are on exhibit, such as a collection, a museum, or a zoo.

• In recent decades, zoo curators have tried to make the animals' surroundings more and more like their natural homes.

In a good-sized art museum, each curator is generally responsible for a single department or collection: European painting, Asian sculpture, Native American art, and so on. *Curatorial* duties include acquiring new artworks, caring for and repairing objects already owned, discovering frauds and counterfeits, lending artworks to other museums, and mounting exhibitions of everything from Greek sculpture to 20th-century clothing.

procure \prō-ˈkyu̇r\ To get possession of; obtain.

- Investigators were looking into the question of how the governor had procured such a huge loan at such a favorable rate.

While *procure* has the general meaning of "obtain," it usually implies that some effort is required. It may also suggest getting something through a formal set of procedures. In many business offices, a particular person is responsible for procuring supplies, and government agencies have formal *procurement* policies. When teenagers use an older friend to procure the wrong kind of supplies for their parties, they often risk getting into trouble.

sinecure \ˈsi-nə-ˌkyu̇r\ A job or position requiring little work but usually providing some income.

- The job of Dean of Students at any college is no sinecure; the hours can be long and the work draining.

Sinecure contains the Latin word *sine*, "without," and thus means "without care." In some countries, the government in power may be free to award sinecure positions to their valued supporters; in other countries, this would be regarded as corruption. The positions occupied by British royalty are called sinecures by some people, who claim they enjoy their enormous wealth in return for nothing at all. But their many supporters point to the amount of public-service, charitable, and ceremonial work they perform, not to mention the effort they put into promoting Britain to the world.

PERI, in both Latin and Greek, means "around." A *period* is often a span of time that keeps coming around regularly, day after day or year after year. With a *periscope,* you can see around corners. *Peristalsis* is the process that moves food around the intestines; without it, digestion would grind to a halt.

---

perimeter \pə-ˈri-mə-tər\ The boundary or distance around a body or figure.

• In a medieval siege, an army would surround the perimeter of a city's high walls, denying the population any food from outside as it assaulted the walls with catapults and battering rams.

The perimeter of a prison is ringed with high walls and watchtowers, and the entire perimeter of Australia is bounded by water. In geometry, you may be asked to calculate the perimeter of various geometrical shapes. In basketball, the perimeter is the area beyond the free-throw circle; a "perimeter player" tends to stay outside that circle. Try not to confuse this word with *parameter,* which usually means a rule or limit that controls what something is or how it can be done.

periodontal \ˌper-ē-ō-ˈdän-təl\ Concerning or affecting the tissues around the teeth.

• Years of bad living had filled his teeth with cavities, but it was periodontal disease that finished them off.

In dentistry, cavities are important but they aren't the whole story; what happens to your gums is every bit as vital to your dental health. When you don't floss regularly to keep plaque from forming on your teeth and gums, the gums will slowly deteriorate. Dentists called *periodontists* specialize in the treatment of periodontal problems, and when the gums have broken down to the point where they can't hold the teeth in place a periodontist may need to provide dental implants, a costly and unpleasant process. But even a periodontist can't keep your gums healthy; that job is up to you.

peripatetic \ˌper-ə-pə-ˈte-tik\ (1) Having to do with walking. (2) Moving or traveling from place to place.

• She spent her early adult years as a peripatetic musician, traveling from one engagement to another.

The philosopher Aristotle had his school at the Lyceum gymnasium in Athens. The Lyceum may have resembled the Parthenon in being surrounded by a row of columns, or colonnade, which the Greeks would have called a *peripatoi.* Aristotle was also said to have paced slowly while teaching, and the Greek word for "pacing" was *peripatos.* And finally, *peripatos* meant simply "discussion." Whatever the source of the word, Aristotle and his followers became known as the *Peripatetics,* and the "pacing" sense led to *peripatetic*'s English meaning of traveling or moving about. Johnny Appleseed is a good example of a peripatetic soul, and peripatetic executives and salespeople today stare into their laptop computers while endlessly flying from city to city.

peripheral \pə-'ri-fə-rəl\ (1) Having to do with the outer edges, especially of the field of vision. (2) Secondary or supplemental.

• Like most good fourth-grade teachers, he had excellent peripheral vision, and the kids were convinced that he had eyes in the back of his head.

Your peripheral vision is the outer area of your field of vision, where you can still detect movement and shapes. It can be very valuable when, for instance, you're driving into Chicago at rush hour, especially when switching lanes. When people call an issue in a discussion peripheral, they mean that it's not of primary importance, and they're probably suggesting that everyone get back to the main topic. *Peripheral* is now also a noun: computer peripherals are the added components—printers, webcams, microphones, etc.—that increase a computer's capacities.

Quizzes

A. Fill in each blank with the correct letter:

a. curative   e. peripheral
b. sinecure   f. perimeter
c. procure   g. peripatetic
d. curator   h. periodontal

1. The _____ benefits of antibiotics have saved many lives.

2. _____ vision is part of what most eye doctors test in their patients.

3. What he had hoped to be an undemanding _____ turned out to be the hardest but most rewarding job of his career.

4. Because of deer, she needed to put up a fence along the _____ of the garden.

5. We asked our purchasing manager to _____ new chairs for the office.

6. In his youth he had been amazingly _____, hitchhiking thousands of miles on three continents.

7. The museum's _____ of African art narrates a guided tour of the exhibit.

8. Regular flossing can prevent most _____ disease.

B. Choose the closest definition:

1. sinecure   a. hopeful sign   b. unsuccessful search   c. careless act   d. easy job

2. curator   a. doctor   b. lawyer   c. caretaker   d. spectator

3. periodontal   a. visual   b. inside a tooth   c. around a tooth   d. wandering

4. peripatetic   a. wandering   b. unemployed   c. surrounding   d. old-fashioned

5. procure   a. say   b. obtain   c. look after   d. heal

6. curative   a. purifying   b. healing   c. saving   d. repairing

7. perimeter   a. factor   b. characteristic   c. supplement   d. boundary

8. peripheral   a. supplementary   b. around a tooth   c. wandering   d. dangerous

---

SENS comes from the Latin noun *sensus,* meaning "feeling" or "sense." *Sense* itself obviously comes straight from the Latin. A *sensation* is something you sense. And if you're *sensitive*, you feel or sense things sharply, maybe even too sharply.

---

sensor \\'sen-ˌsȯr\\ A device that detects a physical quantity (such as a movement or a beam of light) and responds by transmitting a signal.

• The outdoor lights are triggered by a motion sensor that detects changes in infrared energy given off by moving human bodies.

Sensors are used today almost everywhere. Radar guns bounce microwaves off moving cars. A burglar alarm may use a photosensor to detect when a beam of light has been broken, or may use ultrasonic sound waves that bounce off moving objects. Still other sensors may detect pressure (barometers) or chemicals (Breathalyzers and smoke detectors). Stud finders, used by carpenters to locate wooden studs under a wall, may employ magnets or radar. Wired gloves, which relay information about the position of the fingers, are used in virtual-reality environments. A cheap car alarm may be nothing but a shock sensor, in which a strong vibration will cause two metal surfaces to come together.

desensitize \dē-'sen-sə-ˌtīz\ To cause (someone or something) to react less to or be less affected by something.

- Even squeamish nursing students report becoming desensitized to the sight of blood after a few months of training.

Physical desensitizing is something that biologists have long been aware of. Basic training in the armed forces tries to desensitize new recruits to pain. We can desensitize ourselves to the summer heat by turning off the air conditioning, or become desensitized to the cold by walking barefoot in the snow. But *desensitize* is more often used when talking about negative emotions. Parents worry that their children will be desensitized to violence by playing video games. Soldiers may become desensitized to death on the battlefield. Desensitizing may be natural and desirable under some circumstances, but maybe not so good in others.

extrasensory \ˌek-strə-'sens-rē\ Not acting or occurring through any of the known senses.

- A kind of extrasensory capacity seems to tell some soldiers when danger is near.

Since *extra* means "outside, beyond" (see EXTRA, p. 163), *extrasensory* means basically "beyond the senses." Extrasensory perception, or ESP, usually includes communication between minds involving no obvious contact (*telepathy*), gaining information about something without using the normal senses (*clairvoyance*), or predicting the future (*precognition*). According to polls, about 40% of Americans believe in ESP, and many of them have had personal experiences that seem to prove its existence. When someone jumps into your mind months or years after you had last thought of him or her, and the next day you learn that the person has just died, it can be hard to convince yourself it was just coincidence. Still, scientific attempts to prove the existence of ESP have never been terribly successful.

sensuous \'sen-shủ-wəs\ (1) Highly pleasing to the senses. (2) Relating to the senses.

- Part of what audiences loved about her was the delight she took in the sensuous pleasures of well-prepared food.

Sensuous and *sensual* are close in meaning but not identical, and *sensuous* was actually coined by the poet John Milton so that he wouldn't have to use *sensual*. *Sensuous* usually implies pleasing of the senses by art or similar means; great music, for example, can be a source of sensuous delight. *Sensual,* on the other hand, usually describes gratification of the senses or physical appetites as an end in itself; thus we often think (perhaps unfairly) of wealthy Romans leading lives devoted to sensual pleasure. You can see why the Puritan Milton might have wanted another word.

SOPH come from the Greek words meaning "wise" and "wisdom." In English the root sometimes appears in words where the wisdom is of the "wise guy" variety, but in words such as *philosophy* we see it used more respectfully.

---

sophistry \'sä-fə-strē\ Cleverly deceptive reasoning or argument.

* For lawyers and politicians, the practice of sophistry from time to time is almost unavoidable.

The Sophists were a group of Greek teachers of rhetoric and philosophy, famous during the 5th century B.C., who moved from town to town offering their teaching for a fee. The Sophists originally represented a respectable school of philosophy, but some critics claimed that they tried to persuade by means of clever but misleading arguments. The philosopher Plato wrote negatively about them, and the comic dramatist Aristophanes made fun of them, showing them making ridiculously fine distinctions about word meanings. We get our modern meanings of *sophist, sophistry,* and the adjective *sophistical* mostly from the opinions of these two men.

sophisticated \sə-'fis-tə-ˌkā-təd\ (1) Having a thorough knowledge of the ways of society. (2) Highly complex or developed.

* In *Woman of the Year,* Katharine Hepburn plays a sophisticated journalist who can handle everything except Spencer Tracy.

A sophisticated argument is thorough and well-worked-out. A satellite is a sophisticated piece of technology, complex and designed to accomplish difficult tasks. A sophisticated person, such as Humphrey Bogart in *Casablanca,* knows how to get around in the world.

But *sophistication* isn't always admired. As you might guess, the word is closely related to *sophistry* (see above), and its original meanings weren't very positive, and still today many of us aren't sure we really like *sophisticates*.

sophomoric \ˌsä-fə-ˈmȯr-ik\ Overly impressed with one's own knowledge, but in fact undereducated and immature.

* We can't even listen to those sophomoric songs of his, with their attempts at profound wisdom that just demonstrate how little he knows about life.

Sophomoric seems to include the roots *soph-,* "wise," and *moros,* "fool" (seen in words such as *moron*), so the contrast between wisdom and ignorance is built right into the word. Cambridge University introduced the term *sophomore* for its second-year students in the 17th century (though it's no longer used in Britain), maybe to suggest that a sophomore has delusions of wisdom since he's no longer an ignorant freshman. In America today, *sophomore* is ambiguous since it can refer to either high school or college. But *sophomoric* should properly describe something—wit, behavior, arguments, etc.—that is at least trying to be *sophisticated*.

theosophy \thē-ˈä-sə-fē\ A set of teachings about God and the world based on mystical insight, especially teachings founded on a blend of Buddhist and Hindu beliefs.

* He had experimented with a number of faiths, starting with Buddhism and ending with a mixture of Eastern and Western thought that could best be called theosophy.

The word *theosophy*, combining roots meaning "God" and "wisdom," appeared back in the 17th century, but the well-known religious movement by that name, under the leadership of the Russian Helena Blavatsky, appeared only around 1875. Blavatsky's theosophy combined elements of Plato's philosophy with Christian, Buddhist, and Hindu thought (including reincarnation), in a way that she claimed had been divinely revealed to her. The *Theosophical* Society, founded in 1875 to promote her beliefs, still exists, as does the *Anthroposophical* Society, founded by her follower Rudolf Steiner.

Quizzes

A. Indicate whether the following pairs of words have the same or different meanings:

1. sophisticated / worldly-wise   same ___ / different ___
2. sensuous / sensitive   same ___ / different ___
3. theosophy / mythology   same ___ / different ___
4. extrasensory / extreme   same ___ / different ___
5. sophistry / wisdom   same ___ / different ___
6. desensitize / deaden   same ___ / different ___
7. sophomoric / wise   same ___ / different ___
8. sensor / scale   same ___ / different ___

B. Match the word on the left to the correct definition on the right:

1. theosophy   a. immaturely overconfident
2. extrasensory   b. detector
3. sensuous   c. doctrine of God and the world
4. sophomoric   d. pleasing to the senses
5. sophistry   e. false reasoning
6. desensitize   f. not using the senses
7. sophisticated   g. make numb
8. sensor   h. highly complex

Words from Mythology and History

Achilles' heel \ə-'ki-lēz-'hēl\ A vulnerable point.

• By now his rival for the Senate seat had discovered his Achilles' heel, the court records of the terrible divorce he had gone through ten years earlier.

When the hero Achilles was an infant, his sea-nymph mother dipped him into the river Styx to make him immortal. But since she held him by one heel, this spot did not touch the water and so remained mortal and vulnerable, and it was here that Achilles was eventually mortally wounded. Today, the tendon that stretches up the calf from the heel is called the *Achilles tendon*. But the term *Achilles' heel* isn't used in medicine; instead, it's only used with the general meaning "weak point"—for instance, to refer to a section of a country's borders that aren't militarily protected, or to a *Jeopardy* contestant's ignorance in the Sports category.

arcadia \är-'kā-dē-ə\ A region or setting of rural pleasure and peacefulness.

• The Pocono Mountains of Pennsylvania are a vacationer's arcadia.

Arcadia, a beautiful rural area in Greece, became the favorite setting for poems about ideal innocence unaffected by the passions of the larger world, beginning with the works of the Roman poet Virgil. There, shepherds play their pipes and sigh with longing for flirtatious nymphs; shepherdesses sing to their flocks; and goat-footed nature gods play in the fields and woods. Today, city dwellers who hope to retire to a country house often indulge in *arcadian* fantasies about what rural life will be like.

Cassandra \kə-'san-drə\ A person who predicts misfortune or disaster.

• They used to call him a Cassandra because he often expected the worst, but his predictions tended to come true.

Cassandra, the daughter of King Priam of Troy, was one of those beautiful young maidens with whom Apollo fell in love. He gave her the gift of prophecy in return for the promise of her sexual favors, but at the last minute she refused him. Though he could not take back his gift, he angrily pronounced that no one would ever believe her predictions; so when she prophesied the fall of her city to the Greeks and the death of its heroes, she was laughed at by the Trojans. A modern-day Cassandra goes around predicting gloom and doom—and may turn out to be right some of the time.

cyclopean \ˌsī-klə-'pē-ən\ Huge or massive.

• They're imagining a new medical center on a cyclopean scale—a vast ten-block campus with thirty high-rise buildings.

The Cyclopes of Greek mythology were huge, crude giants, each with a single eye in the middle of his forehead. Odysseus and his men had a terrible encounter with a Cyclops, and escaped utter disaster only by stabbing a burning stick into the monster's eye. The great stone walls at such ancient sites as Troy and Mycenae are called cyclopean because the stones are so massive and the construction (which uses no cement) is so expert that it was assumed that only a superhuman race such as the Cyclopes could have achieved such a feat.

draconian \drə-ˈkō-nē-ən\ Extremely severe or cruel.

• The severe punishments carried out in Saudi Arabia, including flogging for drunkenness, hand amputation for robbery, and beheading for drug trafficking, strike most of the world as draconian.

Draconian comes from the name of Draco, a leader of Athens in the 7th century B.C. who in 621 B.C. produced its first legal code. The punishments he prescribed were extraordinarily harsh; almost anyone who couldn't pay his debts became a slave, and even minor crimes were punishable by death. So severe were these penalties that it was said that the code was written in blood. In the next century, the wise leader Solon would revise all of Draco's code, retaining the death penalty only for the crime of murder.

myrmidon \ˈmər-mə-ˌdän\ A loyal follower, especially one who executes orders unquestioningly.

• To an American, these soldiers were like myrmidons, all too eager to do the Beloved Leader's bidding.

In the Trojan War, the troops of the great hero Achilles were called Myrmidons. As bloodthirsty as wolves, they were the fiercest fighters in all Greece. They were said to have come from the island of Aegina, where, after the island's entire population had been killed by a plague, it was said to have been repopulated by Zeus, by turning all the ants in a great anthill into men. Because of their insect origin, the Myrmidons were blindly loyal to Achilles, so loyal that they would die without resisting if ordered to. The Trojans would not be the last fighting force to believe that a terrifying opposing army was made up of men who were not quite human.

nemesis \ˈne-mə-səs\ A powerful, frightening opponent or rival who is usually victorious.

• During the 1970s and '80s, Japanese carmakers became the nemesis of the U.S. auto industry.

The Greek goddess Nemesis doled out rewards for noble acts and vengeance for evil ones, but it's only her vengeance that anyone remembers. According to the Greeks, Nemesis did not always punish an offender right away, but might wait as much as five generations to avenge a crime. Regardless, her cause was always just and her eventual victory was sure. But today a nemesis doesn't always dispense justice; a powerful drug lord may be the nemesis of a Mexican police chief, for instance, just as Ernst Stavro Blofeld was James Bond's nemesis in three of Ian Fleming's novels.

Trojan horse \\'trō-jən-'hȯrs\\ Someone or something that works from within to weaken or defeat.

• Researchers are working on a kind of Trojan horse that will be welcomed into the diseased cells and then destroy them from within.

After besieging the walls of Troy for ten years, the Greeks built a huge, hollow wooden horse, secretly filled it with armed warriors, and presented it to the Trojans as a gift for the goddess Athena, and the Trojans took the horse inside the city's walls. That night, the armed Greeks swarmed out and captured and burned the city. A Trojan horse is thus anything that looks innocent but, once accepted, has power to harm or destroy—for example, a computer program that seems helpful but ends up corrupting or demolishing the computer's software.

Quiz

Fill in each blank with the correct letter:

a.	myrmidon	e.	Achilles' heel
b.	draconian	f.	nemesis
c.	cyclopean	g.	Cassandra
d.	Trojan horse	h.	arcadia

1. He's nothing but a _____ of the CEO, one of those creepy aides who's always following him down the hall wearing aviator sunglasses.
2. A "balloon mortgage," in which the low rates for the first couple of years suddenly explode into something completely unaffordable, should be feared as a _____.
3. They marveled at the massive ancient _____ walls, which truly seemed to have been built by giants.

4. On weekends they would flee to their little _____ in rural New Hampshire, leaving behind the trials of the working week.

5. In eighth grade his _____ was a disagreeable girl named Rita who liked playing horrible little tricks.

6. His gloomy economic forecasts earned him a reputation as a _____.

7. Historians point to the _____ treaty terms of World War I as a major cause of World War II.

8. Believing the flattery of others and enjoying the trappings of power have often been the _____ of successful politicians.

Review Quizzes

A. **Choose the correct synonym and the correct antonym:**

1. peripheral   a. central b. logical c. sincere
   d. secondary

2. curative   a. humane b. unhealthful c. sensible
   d. healing

3. irrevocable   a. final b. undoable c. unbelievable
   d. vocal

4. perimeter   a. essence b. edge c. center d. spurt

5. nemesis   a. ally b. no one c. enemy d. bacteria

6. sophomoric   a. silly b. wise c. cacophonous
   d. collegiate

7. Achilles' heel   a. paradise b. heroism
   c. strong point d. vulnerability

8. peripatetic   a. stay-at-home b. exact c. wandering
   d. imprecise

9. vociferous   a. speechless b. steely c. sweet-
   sounding d. loud

10. visionary   a. idealist b. cinematographer
    c. conservative d. writer

11. sophisticated   a. rejected b. advanced c. worldly-
    wise d. innocent

12. equivocate   a. equalize b. dither c. decide d. enjoy

B. Choose the closest definition:

1. phonetic   a. called b. twitched c. sounded
   d. remembered
2. sophistry   a. deception b. musical composition
   c. sound reasoning d. pleasure
3. procure   a. appoint b. obtain c. decide d. lose
4. vista   a. summit b. outlook c. mountain d. avenue
5. cacophony   a. fraud b. argument c. racket d. panic
6. vis-à-vis   a. compared to b. allowed to c. rented to
   d. talked to
7. perspective   a. judgment b. self-examination
   c. standpoint d. landscape
8. peripheral   a. auxiliary b. central c. relating to the
   sun d. philosophical
9. draconian   a. clever b. massive c. disastrous d. severe
10. polyphonic   a. multi-melodic b. uniformly
    harmonic c. relatively boring d. musically varied
11. cyclopean   a. whirling b. gigantic c. rapid
    d. circular
12. envisage   a. surround b. imagine c. investigate
    d. envy
13. periodontal   a. relating to feet b. around the sun
    c. around the teeth d. around a corner
14. curator   a. caretaker b. watcher c. doctor d. purchaser
15. Cassandra   a. optimist b. economist c. pessimist
    d. oculist

C. Fill in each blank with the correct letter:

a. equivocate   f. Trojan horse
b. sensuous   g. arcadia
c. cacophony   h. theosophy
d. extrasensory   i. sinecure
e. nemesis   j. desensitize

1. The job turned out to be a _____, and no one cared if
   he played golf twice a week.
2. The huge Senate bill was a _____, filled with items
   that almost none of the senators were aware of.
3. We opened the door onto a haze of cigarette smoke and
   a _____ of music and laughter.

4. In an old book on _____ she found a philosophy very similar to the one she and her boyfriend were exploring.

5. She was sure her old _____ was plotting to get her fired.

6. After a month of barefoot running, he had managed to thoroughly _____ the soles of his feet.

7. The letter described their new Virginia farm as a kind of _____ of unspoiled nature.

8. Whenever they asked for a definite date, he would _____ and try to change the subject.

9. She lay in the bath with her eyes closed in a kind of _____ daydream.

10. Husband and wife seemed to communicate by _____ means, each always guessing what the other needed before anything was said.

UNIT

8

PORT comes from the Latin verb *portare*, meaning "to carry." Thus, something *portable* can be carried around. A *porter* carries your luggage, whether through a train station or high into the Himalayas. When we *transport* something, we have it carried from one place to another. And goods for *export* are carried away to another country.

---

portage \ˈpȯr-tij\ The carrying of boats or goods overland from one body of water to another; also, a regular route for such carrying.

• The only portage on the whole canoe route would be the one around the great waterfall on our second day.

Portage was borrowed from French back in the 15th century to mean "carrying, transporting" or "freight," and it has kept its simple "carrying" sense to the present day. But its first known use in its "carrying of boats" sense came in 1698, and the obstacle that the canoes couldn't be steered over was none other than Niagara Falls. Though canoes are much lighter today than they used to be, a long portage that includes a lot of camping gear can still test a camper's strength.

portfolio \pȯrt-ˈfō-lē-ō\ (1) A flat case for carrying documents or artworks. (2) The investments owned by a person or organization.

- In those days, a graphic artist who had recently moved to New York would just schlep his portfolio around to every magazine office in the city.

Portfolio is partly based on the Latin *folium*, meaning "leaf, sheet." A portfolio usually represents a portable showcase of your talents. Today actual portfolios are used less than they used to be by artists, since most commercial artists have a Web site dedicated to showing off their art. But *portfolio* in its other common meaning is extremely common. Not so long ago, a broker would keep each of his or her clients' investments in a separate notebook or portfolio. Today the investment portfolio, like an artist's portfolio, usually takes the form of a Web page, even though everyone still uses the same old word.

comport \kəm-ˈpȯrt\ (1) To be in agreement with. (2) To behave.

- This new evidence comports with everything we know about what happened that night.

With its prefix *com-*, "with," the Latin word *comportare* meant "to bring together." So it's easy to see how in English we could say that a college's policy comports with state law, or that a visit to your parents doesn't comport with your other weekend plans, or that your aunt and uncle won't listen to anything on TV that doesn't comport with their prejudices. The "behave" sense of the word comes through French, and its essential meaning is how a person "carries" him- or herself. So you may say, for instance, that your 17-year-old comported himself well (for once!) at the wedding reception, or that an ambassador always comports herself with dignity—that is, her *comportment* is always dignified—or that your class comported itself in a way that was a credit to the school.

deportment \di-ˈpȯrt-mənt\ Manner of conducting oneself socially.

- At social events she would constantly sneak glances at Alexandra, in quiet admiration of her elegant and graceful deportment.

We've all seen pictures of girls walking around balancing books on their heads in an effort to achieve the poise of a princess or a film star. Classes in deportment were once a standard part of a young lady's upbringing, offered in all the girls' colleges; and you can still take private deportment classes, where you'll learn about posture and body language, how to move, sit, stand, shake hands, dress, drink and eat, and much more. But deportment isn't all about refined female grace. In fact, *deport* is often used as a synonym for *comport*, but usually in a positive way; thus, people are often said to deport themselves well, confidently, with dignity, like gentlemen or ladies, and so on.

PEND comes from the Latin verb *pendere,* meaning "to hang" or "to weigh." (In the Roman era, weighing something large often required hanging it from a hook on one side of the balance scales.) We find the root in English words like *appendix,* referring to that useless and sometimes troublesome tube that hangs from the intestine, or that section at the back of some books that might contain some useful additional information.

---

pendant \\'pen-dənt\\ Something that hangs down, especially as an ornament.

• Around her neck she was wearing the antique French pendant he had given her, with its three rubies set in silver filigree.

Most pendants are purely decorative. But a pendant may also hold a picture or a lock of hair of a lover or a child. And, perhaps because they hang protectively in front of the body and near the heart, pendants have often had symbolic and magical purposes. Thus, a pendant may be a charm or amulet, or its gems or metals may be felt to have health-giving properties. In architecture, a pendant is an ornament that hangs down from a structure, but unlike a necklace pendant it's usually solid and inflexible.

append \\ə-'pend\\ To add as something extra.

• She appended to the memo a list of the specific items that the school was most in need of.

Append is a somewhat formal word. Lawyers, for example, often speak of appending items to other documents, and lawmakers frequently append small bills to big ones, hoping that everyone will be paying attention only to the main part of the big bill and won't notice. When we append a small separate section to the end of a report or a book, we call it an *appendix*. But in the early years of e-mail, the words we decided on were *attach* and *attachment*, probably because appendixes are thought of as unimportant, whereas the attachment is often the whole reason for sending an e-mail.

appendage \ə-ˈpen-dij\ (1) Something joined on to a larger or more important body or thing. (2) A secondary body part, such as an arm or a leg.

- She often complained that she felt like a mere appendage of her husband when they socialized with his business partners.

Appendix isn't the only noun that comes from *append*. Unlike *appendix*, *appendage* doesn't suggest the end of something, but simply something attached. The word is often used in biology to refer to parts of an animal's body: an insect's antennae, mouthparts, or wings, for example. The appendages of some animals will grow back after they've been removed; a salamander, for example, can regrow a finger, and the tiny sea squirt can regrow all its appendages—and even its brain.

suspend \sə-ˈspend\ (1) To stop something, or to force someone to give up some right or position, for a limited time. (2) To hang something so that it is free on all sides.

- The country has been suspended from the major trade organizations, and the effects on its economy are beginning to be felt.

When something is suspended, it is "left hanging"; it is neither in full operation nor permanently ended. *Suspense* is a state of uncertainty and maybe anxiety. When we watch a play or movie, we enjoy experiencing a "suspension of disbelief"; that is, we allow ourselves to believe we're watching reality, even though we aren't truly fooled. *Suspension* can also mean physical hanging; thus, in a suspension bridge, the roadway actually hangs from huge cables. When some substance is "in suspension," its particles are "hanging" in another substance, mixed into it but not actually dissolved, like fine sand in water, or sea spray in the air at the seashore.

Quizzes

A. Choose the closest definition:

1. pendant   a. porch   b. salary   c. flag   d. ornament
2. portfolio   a. mushroom   b. folder   c. painting
     d. carriage
3. suspend   a. study carefully   b. watch closely   c. slip
     gradually   d. stop temporarily
4. deportment   a. manner   b. section   c. departure
     d. promotion
5. append   a. close up   b. predict   c. attach   d. reconsider
6. portage   a. small dock   b. river obstacle   c. light boat
     d. short carry
7. comport   a. bend   b. behave   c. join   d. transport
8. appendage   a. hanger   b. body organ   c. limb
     d. companion

B. Fill in each blank with the correct letter:

a. portage	e. appendage
b. portfolio	f. pendant
c. deportment	g. append
d. comport	h. suspend

1. He found himself peering at her silver _____, trying to
make out the odd symbols that formed the design.
2. Their _____ consisted mostly of high-tech stocks.
3. On the organizational chart, the group appears way
down in the lower left corner, looking like a
minor _____ of the company.
4. The biggest challenge would be the half-mile _____
around the river's worst rapids.
5. This is the entire report, to which we'll _____ the
complete financial data when we submit it.
6. She never fails to impress people with her elegant _____
in the most difficult social situations.
7. Whenever his mother got wind of more bad behavior,
she would _____ his allowance for a month.
8. These figures don't _____ with the ones you showed us
yesterday.

PAN comes from a Greek word meaning "all"; as an English prefix, it can also mean "completely," "whole," or "general." A *panoramic* view is a complete view in every direction. A *pantheon* is a temple dedicated to all the gods of a religion. A *pandemic* outbreak of a disease may not affect the entire human population, but enough to produce a catastrophe.

panacea \ˌpa-nə-ˈsē-ə\ A remedy for all ills or difficulties; cure-all.

• Educational reform is sometimes viewed as the panacea for all of society's problems.

Panacea comes from a Greek word meaning "all-healing," and Panacea was the goddess of healing. In the Middle Ages and the Renaissance, alchemists who sought to concoct the "elixir of life" (which would give eternal life) and the "philosopher's stone" (which would turn ordinary metals into gold) also labored to find the panacea. But no such medicine was ever found, just as no solution to all of a society's difficulties has ever been found. Thus, *panacea* is almost always used to criticize the very idea of a total solution ("There's no panacea for the current problems plaguing Wall Street").

pandemonium \ˌpan-də-ˈmō-nē-əm\ A wild uproar or commotion.

• Pandemonium erupted in the stadium as the ball shot past the goalie into the net.

In John Milton's *Paradise Lost,* the fallen Satan has his heralds proclaim "A solemn Councel forthwith to be held / At Pandaemonium, the high Capital / Of Satan and his Peers." Milton got the name for his capital of hell, where Satan gathered together all his demons, by linking *pan* with the Latin word *daemonium,* "evil spirit." For later writers, *pandemonium* became a synonym for hell itself, since hell was then often seen as a place of constant noise and confusion, but also for any wicked and lawless place. Nowadays it's used to refer to the uproar itself rather than the place where it occurs.

pantheism \ˈpan-thē-ˌi-zəm\ A system of belief that regards God as identical with the forces and laws of the universe.

- Most of her students seemed to accept a vague kind of pantheism, without any real belief that God had ever appeared in human form.

Pantheistic ideas—and most importantly the belief that God is equal to the universe, its physical matter, and the forces that govern it—are found in the ancient books of Hinduism, in the works of many Greek philosophers, and in later works of philosophy and religion over the centuries. Much modern New Age spirituality is pantheistic. But most Christian thinkers reject pantheism because it makes God too impersonal, doesn't allow for any difference between the creation and the creator, and doesn't seem to allow for humans to make meaningful moral choices.

panoply \ˈpa-nə-plē\ (1) A magnificent or impressive array. (2) A display of all appropriate accessory items.

- The full panoply of a royal coronation was a thrilling sight for the throngs of sidewalk onlookers and the millions of television viewers.

The fully armed Greek soldier was an impressive sight, even if Greek armor never became as heavy as that of medieval knights on horseback (who couldn't possibly have marched in such outfits). *Panoplia* was the Greek word for the full suit of armor, and the English *panoply* originally likewise referred to the full suit of armor worn by a soldier or knight. Today *panoply* may refer to full ceremonial dress or lavish ceremonial decoration of any kind. And it can also refer to striking spectacle of almost any kind: the breathtaking panoply of autumn foliage, or the stirring panoply of a military parade, for example.

EXTRA is Latin for "outside" or "beyond." So anything *extraterrestrial* or *extragalactic* takes place beyond the earth or the galaxy. Something *extravagant*, such as an *extravaganza*, goes way beyond the normal. And *extra* is naturally a word itself, a shortening of *extraordinary*, "beyond the ordinary."

---

extradite \ˈek-strə-ˌdīt\ To deliver an accused criminal from one place to another where the trial will be held.

- Picked up by the Colorado police for burglary, he's being extradited to Mississippi to face trial for murder.

Extradition from one state to another is generally a straightforward process. But extradition may become more complicated when two countries are involved, even though most countries have signed treaties stating that they will send criminals to the country where they are wanted. Many countries often won't send their own citizens to another country for trial; countries that don't permit the death penalty may not agree to send a suspect back to face such a penalty; and most countries won't extradite someone accused of political crimes. When extradition seems unlikely, a country may actually kidnap someone from another country, but this is illegal and rare.

extrapolate \ik-ˈstra-pə-ˌlāt\ To extend or project facts or data into an area not known in order to make assumptions or to predict facts or trends.

- Economists predict future buying trends partly by extrapolating from current economic data.

Scientists worry about the greenhouse effect because they have extrapolated the rate of carbon-dioxide buildup and predicted that its effect on the atmosphere will become increasingly severe. On the basis of their *extrapolations,* they have urged governments and businesses to limit factory and automobile emissions. Notice that it's acceptable to speak of extrapolating existing data (to produce new data), extrapolating *from* existing data (to produce new data), or extrapolating new data (from existing data)—in other words, it isn't easy to use this word wrong.

extrovert \ˈek-strə-ˌvərt\ A person mainly concerned with things outside him- or herself; a sociable and outgoing person.

- These parties are always full of loud extroverts, and I always find myself hiding in a corner with my drink.

Extrovert (sometimes spelled *extravert*) means basically "turned outward"—that is, toward things outside oneself. The word was coined by the eminent psychologist C. G. Jung in the early 20th century. The opposite personality type, in Jung's view, was the *introvert.* Extroverts seem to be favored by societies such as ours, even though introverts seem to be on average more mentally gifted. Psychologists have said that the only personality traits that can be identified in newborn infants are shyness and lack of shyness, which are fairly close to—but not really the same as—*introversion* and *extroversion.*

extraneous \ek-'strā-nē-əs\ (1) Existing or coming from the outside. (2) Not forming an essential part; irrelevant.

• Be sure your essays are well focused, with any discussion of extraneous topics kept to a minimum.

Extraneous and *strange* both come from the same Latin word, *extraneus*, which basically meant "external" or "coming from outside." But unlike *strange*, *extraneous* is a slightly formal word, often used by scientists and social scientists. Researchers always try to eliminate extraneous factors (or "extraneous variables") from their studies. A researcher conducting a psychological test, for example, would try to make sure that the people were tested under the same conditions, and were properly divided according to gender, age, health, and so on.

Quizzes

A. Fill in each blank with the correct letter:

a. extrapolate   e. extradite
b. panoply   f. pantheism
c. extraneous   g. extrovert
d. panacea   h. pandemonium

1. From these figures, economists can _____ data that shows a steady increase in employment.
2. Being a natural _____, he took to his new career as a salesman easily.
3. The new voice-mail system comes with the usual full _____ of options.
4. _____ broke out at the news of the victory.
5. The treaty with Brazil doesn't require us to _____ a criminal who's a native-born American.
6. He's locked himself in his studio to ensure that there won't be any _____ distractions.
7. She had always believed in vitamins as a _____, but they weren't always able to fight off infections.
8. He attended the Presbyterian church, even though for many years his real beliefs had been a mixture of Buddhism and _____.

B. **Indicate whether the following pairs of terms have the same or different meanings:**

1. panacea / antibiotic   same ___ / different ___
2. pandemonium / chaos   same ___ / different ___
3. pantheism / priesthood   same ___ / different ___
4. panoply / display   same ___ / different ___
5. extrapolate / project   same ___ / different ___
6. extraneous / necessary   same ___ / different ___
7. extradite / hand over   same ___ / different ___
8. extrovert / schizophrenic   same ___ / different ___

PHOT comes from the Greek word for "light." *Photography* uses light to create an image on film or paper, and a *photocopy* is an image made by using light and tiny electrically charged ink particles.

photoelectric \ˌfō-tō-i-ˈlek-trik\ Involving an electrical effect produced by the action of light or other radiation.

• They wanted to avoid the kind of smoke detector that uses radioactive materials, so they've installed the photoelectric kind instead.

The *photoelectric effect* occurs when light (or similar radiation such as X-rays) falls on a material such as a metal plate and causes it to emit electrons. The discovery of the photoelectric effect led to important new theories about matter (and to a Nobel Prize for Albert Einstein). *Photoelectric cells,* or *photocells*, are used in burglar-alarm light detectors and garage-door openers (both employ a beam of light that is broken when something moves across it), and also to play soundtracks on movie film (where a light beam shines through the soundtrack encoded on the film and is "read" by the photocells).

photovoltaic \ˌfō-tō-väl-ˈtā-ik\ Involving the direct generation of electricity when sunlight or other radiant energy falls on the boundary between dissimilar substances (such as two different semiconductors).

• Photovoltaic technology is being applied to thin film that can produce as much energy as solar cells while using far less semi-conducting material.

The *-voltaic* part of *photovoltaic* comes from the name of Alessandro Volta, inventor of the electric battery. Thus, unlike photoelectric cells, which use electricity for certain small tasks, photovoltaic (or PV) cells actually produce electricity. Solar cells, the standard type of photovoltaic cells (often called simply *photocells*), operate without chemicals and with no moving parts to create energy directly from sunlight. Much research is now being done on creating an alternative technology—solar film, which could be stuck onto almost any surface, or possibly even sprayed on.

photon \\'fō-ˌtän\\ A tiny particle or bundle of radiant energy.

• The idea that light consists of photons is difficult until you begin to think of a ray of light as being caused by a stream of tiny particles.

It was Albert Einstein who first theorized that the energy in a light beam exists in small bits or particles, and scientists today know that light sometimes behaves like a wave (somewhat like sound or water) and sometimes like a stream of particles. The energies of photons range from high-energy gamma rays and X-rays down to low-energy infrared and radio waves, though all travel at the same speed. The amazing power of lasers is the result of a concentration of photons that have been made to travel together in order to hit their target at the same time.

photosynthesis \\ˌfō-tō-'sin-thə-sis\\ The process by which green plants use light to produce organic matter from carbon dioxide and water.

• Sagebrush survives in harsh climates because it's capable of carrying on photosynthesis at very low temperatures.

The Greek roots of *photosynthesis* combine to produce the basic meaning "to put together with the help of light." Photosynthesis is what first produced oxygen in the atmosphere billions of years ago, and it's still what keeps it there. Sunlight splits the water molecules (made of hydrogen and oxygen) held in a plant's leaves and releases the oxygen in them into the air. The leftover hydrogen combines with carbon dioxide to produce carbohydrates, which the plant uses as food—as do any animals or humans who might eat the plant.

LUC comes from the Latin noun *lux*, "light," and the verb *lucere*, "to shine or glitter." In ancient Rome, *Lucifer*, meaning "Light-bearer," was the name given to the morning star, but the name was eventually transferred by Christians to Satan. This tradition, which dates back to the period before Christ, said that Lucifer had once been among the angels but had wanted to be the great light in the sky, and for his pride had been cast out of heaven and thus became the opponent of everything good.

---

lucid \ˈlü-səd\ (1) Very clear and easy to understand. (2) Able to think clearly.

• On his last visit he had noticed that his elderly mother hadn't seemed completely lucid.

Mental *lucidity* is easy to take for granted when we're young, though alcohol, drugs, and psychological instability can confuse the mind at any age. We all hope to live to 100 with our mental abilities intact, which is entirely possible; avoiding the condition called dementia (which includes the well-known Alzheimer's disease) often involves a combination of decent genes, physical and mental activity, and a good diet. Writing *lucidly*, on the other hand, can take a lot of work at any age; you've probably had the experience of trying to read a set of instructions and wondering if the writer even grew up speaking English.

elucidate \i-ˈlü-sə-ˌdāt\ To clarify by explaining; explain.

• A good doctor should always be willing to elucidate any medical jargon he or she uses.

The basic meaning of *elucidate* is "to shed light on." So when you elucidate, you make transparent or clear something that had been murky or confusing. *Elucidation* of a complex new health-care policy may be a challenge. Elucidation of the terms of use for a credit card may be the last thing its provider wants to do. The physicist Carl Sagan had a gift for elucidating astronomical science to a large audience, his *lucid* explanations making clear how stars are born and die and how the universe may have begun.

lucubration \ˌlü-kyu̇-ˈbrā-shən\ (1) Hard and difficult study. (2) The product of such study.

- Our professor admitted that he wasn't looking forward to reading through any more of our lucubrations on novels that no one enjoyed.

Lucubration came to mean "hard study" because it originally meant study done by lamplight, and in a world without electric lights, such study was likely to be the kind of hard work that would only a dedicated student like Abe Lincoln would make a habit of. The word has a literary feel to it, and it's often used with a touch of sarcasm.

translucent \tranz-ˈlü-sənt\ Partly transparent; allowing light to pass through without permitting objects beyond to be seen clearly.

- Architects today often use industrial glass bricks in their home designs, because translucent walls admit daylight while guarding privacy.

With its prefix *trans-*, meaning "through," *translucent* describes material that light shines through without making anything on the other side clearly visible, unlike a *transparent* material. Frosted glass, often used in bathroom windows, is translucent, as is stained glass. Red wine in a crystal goblet, when held before a candle in a dark corner of a quiet restaurant, usually proves to be translucent as well.

Quizzes

A. Fill in each blank with the correct letter:

a. photovoltaic   e. photoelectric
b. lucid   f. lucubration
c. photon   g. photosynthesis
d. translucent   h. elucidate

1. A soft light filtered through the _____ white curtains separating the two rooms.
2. _____ cells on the roof capture the sun's energy, and with the small windmill nearby they produce more energy than the house needs.
3. Few of us can truly imagine that light can be reduced to a tiny packet of energy called a _____.
4. In graduate school, his lively social life was replaced with three years of intense _____.

5. A large tree with a 40-inch trunk may produce two-thirds of a pound of oxygen every day through _____.

6. His 88-year-old aunt is in a nursing home, and he never knows which days she'll be _____.

7. The alarm system depends on _____ technology that detects when someone breaks a beam of light in a doorway.

8. Whenever anyone asks the professor to _____, he just makes everything more complicated instead of less.

B. Match the definition on the left to the correct word on the right:

1.	involving the interaction of light with matter	a. lucubration
2.	production of carbohydrates	b. photoelectric
3.	clarify	c. translucent
4.	passing light but only blurred images	d. elucidate
5.	elemental particle	e. photovoltaic
6.	brightly clear	f. photosynthesis
7.	hard study	g. photon
8.	using light to generate electricity	h. lucid

MOR/MORT comes from Latin words meaning "to die" and "death." A *mortuary* is a place where dead bodies are kept until burial, and a *postmortem* examination is one conducted on a recently dead body. The Latin phrase "Memento mori" means "Remember that you must die"; so a *memento mori* is the name we give to a reminder of death; the skulls you can find carved on gravestones in old cemeteries are examples.

mortality \mȯr-ˈta-lə-tē\ (1) The quality or state of being alive and therefore certain to die. (2) The number of deaths that occur in a particular time or place.

• Mortality rates were highest among those who those who lived closest to the plant.

Young people tend to assume they will never die; but a person's sense of his or her mortality generally increases year by year, and often increases greatly after a serious accident or illness. Still, many people refuse to change behaviors that would improve their chances of living into old age. Mortality rates are calculated by government agencies, insurance companies, and medical researchers. Infant mortality rates provide a good indicator of a country's overall health; in recent years, the rates in countries like Iceland, Singapore, and Japan have been much better than in the U.S.

moribund \\'mòr-ə-bənd\\ (1) In the process of dying or approaching death. (2) Inactive or becoming outmoded.

- Church attendance in Britain has fallen in recent years, but no one would say the Anglican church is moribund.

Moribund is still sometimes used in its original literal sense of "approaching death," but it's much more often used to describe things. When the economy goes bad, we hear about moribund mills and factories and towns; the economy itself may even be called moribund. Critics may speak of the moribund state of poetry, or lament the moribund record or newspaper industry.

amortize \\'a-mər-ˌtīz\\ To pay off (something such as a mortgage) by making small payments over a period of time.

- For tax purposes, they chose to amortize most of the business's start-up costs over a three-year period.

Amortize is most common as a legal term, and many of us first come across it when we take out a mortgage or start a business. Financial officers and tax lawyers can choose how to legally amortize various types of business expenses, some of which may seem much better than others. In mortgage *amortization*, much of what you pay month by month is actually interest on the mortgage debt, especially at the beginning. So what does amortizing have to do with death? Basically, to amortize a debt means to "kill" it slowly over time.

mortify \\'mòr-tə-ˌfī\\ (1) To subdue or deaden (the body) especially by self-discipline or self-inflicted pain. (2) To embarrass greatly.

- Our 14-year-old is mortified whenever he sees us dancing, especially if any of his school friends are around.

Mortify once actually meant "put to death," but no longer. Its "deaden" sense is most familiar to us in the phrase "mortifying the flesh," which refers to a custom once followed by devout Christians, who would starve themselves, deprive themselves of every comfort, and even whip themselves in order to subdue their bodily desires and punish themselves for their sins. But the most common use of *mortify* today is the "humiliate" sense; its connection with death is still apparent when we speak of "dying of embarrassment."

TROPH comes from the Greek *trophe*, meaning "nourishment." This particular *troph-* root doesn't show up in many everyday English words (the *troph-* in words like *trophy, apostrophe,* and *catastrophe* has a different meaning), but instead tends to appear in scientific terms.

---

atrophy \\\'a-trə-fē\\ (1) Gradual loss of muscle or flesh, usually because of disease or lack of use. (2) A decline or degeneration.

• After a month in a hospital bed, my father required a round of physical therapy to deal with his muscular atrophy.

From its literal Greek roots, *atrophy* would mean basically "lack of nourishment." Although the English word doesn't usually imply any lack of food, it always refers to a wasting away. Those who have been bedridden for a period of time will notice that their muscles have *atrophied*. And muscular atrophy is a frequent result of such diseases as cancer and AIDS. We also use *atrophy* in a much more general sense. After being out of work a few years, you may find your work skills have atrophied; someone who's been living an isolated life may discover the same thing about his or her social skills; and a democracy can atrophy when its citizens cease to pay attention to how they're being governed.

hypertrophy \\hī-\'pər-trə-fē\\ (1) Excessive development of an organ or part. (2) Exaggerated growth or complexity.

• Opponents claimed that the Defense Department, after years of being given too much money by the Congress, was now suffering from hypertrophy.

When the prefix *hyper-*, "above, beyond" (see HYPER, p. 457), is joined to *-trophy*, we get the opposite of *atrophy*. An organ or part becomes *hypertrophic* when it grows so extremely that its function is affected. Muscle hypertrophy is common in men who do strength training, and is often harmless; but extreme muscle hypertrophy generally involves taking steroids, which can do great damage to the body. Hypertrophy of the heart sounds as if it might be healthy, but instead it's usually a bad sign. As the example sentence shows, *hypertrophy*, like *atrophy*, can be used in nonmedical ways as well.

dystrophy \'di-strə-fē\ Any of several disorders involving the nerves and muscles, especially muscular dystrophy.

• The most common of the muscular dystrophies affects only males, who rarely live to the age of 40.

Since the prefix *dys-* means "bad" or "difficult" (see DYS, p. 104), *dystrophy* is always a negative term. Originally it meant "a condition caused by improper nutrition," but today the term is instead used for a variety of other conditions, particularly conditions that noticeably affect the muscles. Of the many types of muscular dystrophy, the best known is Duchenne's, a terrible disease that strikes about one in 3,300 males and produces severe wasting of the muscles. However, the muscular dystrophies generally affect many other organs and systems as well. And the other dystrophies, which tend to involve the eyes or hands, don't much resemble the muscular dystrophies.

eutrophication \yü-ˌtrō-fə-'kā-shən\ The process by which a body of water becomes enriched in dissolved nutrients.

• Local naturalists are getting worried about the increasing eutrophication they've been noticing in the lake.

Eutrophication, which comes from the Greek *eutrophos*, "well-nourished" (see EU, p. 103), has become a major environmental problem. Nitrates and phosphates, especially from lawn fertilizers, run off the land into rivers and lakes, promoting the growth of algae and other plant life, which take oxygen from the water, causing the death of fish and mollusks. Cow manure, agricultural fertilizer, detergents, and human waste are often to blame as well. In the 1960s and '70s, the eutrophication of Lake Erie advanced so extremely that it became known as the "dead lake." And many areas of the oceans worldwide—some more than 20,000 square miles in extent—have become "dead zones," where almost no life of any kind exists.

Quizzes

A. Choose the closest definition:

1. mortality   a. deadliness b. danger c. disease
   d. death rate
2. hypertrophy   a. excessive growth b. low birth rate
   c. increased speed d. inadequate nutrition
3. amortize   a. bring back b. pay down c. make love
   d. die off
4. atrophy   a. expansion b. swelling c. exercise
   d. wasting
5. mortify   a. weaken b. bury c. embarrass d. kill
6. dystrophy   a. bone development b. muscular
   wasting c. nerve growth d. muscle therapy
7. moribund   a. deathlike b. unhealthy c. lethal d. dying
8. eutrophication   a. inadequate moisture b. excessive
   growth c. loss of sunlight d. healthy nourishment

B. Fill in each blank with the correct letter:

a. eutrophication   e. moribund
b. atrophy   f. mortify
c. hypertrophy   g. mortality
d. dystrophy   h. amortize

1. By the 1960s, most of the textile industry had moved
   south, and the mill town seemed _____.
2. In muscular _____, the wasting begins in the legs and
   advances to the arms.
3. Most people don't spend much time thinking about
   their _____ until they're in their thirties or forties.
4. They should be able to _____ their mortgage
   completely by the time they retire.
5. Muscular _____ as extreme as that is only possible
   with steroids.
6. Some religious sects still engage in acts designed
   to _____ the flesh.
7. By then the pond had almost entirely filled in with
   plant life, a result of the _____ caused by the factory's
   discharges.
8. In the four weeks before he has the cast taken off, his
   muscles will _____ quite a lot.

Words from Mythology and History

aeolian harp \ē-'ō-lē-ən-'härp\ A box-shaped instrument with strings that produce musical sounds when the wind blows on them.

• Poets have long been fascinated by the aeolian harp, the only instrument that produces music without a human performer.

According to the ancient Greeks, Aeolus was the king or guardian of the winds. He lived in a cave with his many, many sons and daughters, and sent forth whatever wind Zeus asked for. When Odysseus stopped there on his way home from Troy, he received a bag of winds to fill his sails. But while he was asleep, his men, thinking it contained treasure, opened the bag and released the raging winds, which blew their ships all the way back to their starting point. An aeolian harp produces enchanting harmonies when the wind passes over it. According to Homer, it was the god Hermes who invented the harp, by having the wind blow over the dried sinews attached to the shell of a dead tortoise.

cynosure \'sī-nə-ˌshür\ (1) A guide. (2) A center of attention.

• Near the club's dance floor, a young rock star was hanging out, the cynosure of a small crowd of admirers.

In Greek *kynosoura* means "dog's tail," and in Latin *Cynosura* came to mean the constellation Ursa Minor (Little Bear)—what we usually call the Little Dipper. The first star on the dog's or bear's "tail," or the dipper's "handle," is Polaris, the North Star, long used as a guide for seamen or travelers lost on a clear night, since, unlike the other stars, it always remains in the same position in the northern sky, while the other constellations (and even the rest of its own constellation) slowly revolve around it. Since *Cynosura* also came to mean the star itself, the English *cynosure* now may mean both "guide" and "center of attention."

laconic \lə-'kä-nik\ Using extremely few words.

• Action-film scripts usually seem to call for laconic leading men who avoid conversation but get the job done.

Ancient Sparta was located in the region of Greece known as Laconia, and the Greek word *lakonikos* could mean both "Laconian" and "Spartan." The disciplined and militaristic Spartans, the finest warriors of their time, were known for putting up with extreme conditions without complaint. So English writers who knew their ancient history came to use *laconic* to describe the habit of saying few words. Today we can refer not only to a laconic person but also to laconic wit, a laconic answer, or a laconic phrase—such as "Men of few words require few laws," uttered by a Spartan king.

mnemonic \ni-'mä-nik\ Having to do with the memory; assisting the memory.

• Sales-training courses recommend various mnemonic devices as a way of remembering peoples' names.

The Greek word for memory is *mnemosyne*, and Mnemosyne was the goddess of memory and the mother of the Muses. So something that helps the memory is a mnemonic aid, or simply a *mnemonic*. Such traditional mnemonic devices as "Every Good Boy Does Fine" (for the notes on the lines of a musical staff with a treble clef) or the "Thirty days hath September" rhyme help to recall simple rules or complicated series that might otherwise slip away. (For extra credit, guess what "King Henry Died Drinking Chocolate Milk" or "King Philip Could Only Find Green Socks" stands for.) Notice that the first *m* isn't pronounced, unlike in other *-mne-* words such as *amnesia* and *amnesty*.

platonic \plə-'tä-nik\ (1) Relating to the philosopher Plato or his teachings. (2) Involving a close relationship from which romance and sex are absent.

• The male and female leads in sitcoms often keep their relationship platonic for the first few seasons, but romance almost always wins out in the end.

The philosopher Plato presented his theories in a series of dramatic conversations between Socrates and other people, now called the "Platonic dialogues." Among many other important concepts, he taught that everything here on earth is a pale imitation—like a shadow—of its ideal form, and this ideal form is now often called the "platonic form." But *platonic* is probably usually seen in the phrase "platonic love." Because Socrates (through Plato) teaches that the philosophical person should turn his passion for a lover into appreciation of beauty and love of a higher power and of the universe, close but nonsexual friendship between two people who might be thought to be romantically attracted is today known as platonic love or friendship.

sapphic \\'sa-fik\ (1) Lesbian. (2) Relating to a poetic verse pattern associated with Sappho.

- The Roman poets Catullus and Horace composed wonderful love poems in sapphic verse.

The poet Sappho wrote poems of self-reflection but also of passion, some of it directed to the women attending the school she conducted on the Greek island of Lesbos around 600 B.C. Even though most of the poems survive only as fragments, they have been greatly admired for many centuries. They were written in an original rhythmical pattern, which has become known as sapphic verse. Later admirers, such as the Roman poets Catullus and Horace, honored her by adopting the sapphic meter for their own poetry. Because of Sappho, the island of Lesbos also gave its name to lesbianism, which writers often used to call sapphic love.

Socratic \sō-'kra-tik\ Having to do with the philosopher Socrates or with his teaching method, in which he systematically questioned the student in conversation in order to draw forth truths.

- She challenges her students by using the Socratic method, requiring them to think and respond constantly in every class.

Socrates lived and taught in Athens in the 5th century B.C., but left no writings behind, so all we know of him comes through the works of his disciple Plato, almost all of which claim to be accounts of Socrates' conversations with others. Today Socrates is best remembered for his method of teaching by asking increasingly difficult questions, the so-called *Socratic method.* This generally involves the use of *Socratic induction,* a way of gradually arriving at generalizations through a process of questions and answers, and *Socratic irony,* in which the teacher pretends ignorance while questioning his students skillfully to make them aware of their errors in understanding.

solecism \\'sō-lə-ˌsi-zəm\ (1) A grammatical mistake in speaking or writing. (2) A blunder in etiquette or proper behavior.

- The poor boy committed his first solecism immediately on entering by tracking mud over the Persian rug in the dining room.

In ancient Asia Minor (now Turkey), there was a city called Soloi where the inhabitants spoke Greek that was full of grammatical errors. So errors in grammar, and later also small errors in formal social behavior, came to be known (at least by intellectuals) as solecisms. The British magazine *The Economist* publishes a list of solecisms to be avoided in its prose, including the use of "try and" when you mean "try to," "hone in on" when you mean "home in on," and so forth. Social solecisms, such as mentioning how inferior the wine is to someone who turns out to be the hostess's sister, are more commonly called by a French name, *faux pas*.

Quiz

Fill in each blank with the correct letter:

a. solecism
b. sapphic
c. platonic
d. Socratic

e. cynosure
f. aeolian harp
g. mnemonic
h. laconic

1. She always learns her students' names quickly by using her own _____ devices.
2. Every so often, a breeze would spring up and the _____ in the window would emit its beautiful harmonies.
3. New Yorkers tend to think of their city as the _____ of the nation.
4. The _____ method is inappropriate for normal courtroom interrogation.
5. After encountering the fifth _____ in the report, we began to lose faith in the writer.
6. Her father-in-law was _____ in her presence but extremely talkative around his son.
7. As an experiment, he had written a poem in _____ verse, but he suspected that the rhythm was more suited to Greek.
8. The dinner was good, but saying that it approached the _____ ideal of a meal was probably too much.

Review Quizzes

A. Fill in each blank with the correct letter.

a. elucidate
b. appendage
c. solecism
d. pantheism
e. comport

f. laconic
g. moribund
h. deportment
i. mortality
j. atrophy

1. After spending four years at home, she's afraid her professional skills have begun to _____.

2. Her impressive résumé doesn't _____ well with her ignorance of some basic facts about the business.

3. He can't go to a cocktail party without committing at least one _____ and offending a couple of people.

4. Like most farmers, he's fairly _____, but when he says something it's usually worth listening to.

5. For kids their age they have excellent manners, and everyone admires their _____ around adults.

6. It was a large beetle with an odd _____ coming off the top of its head.

7. The book's introduction helps _____ how the reader can make the best use of it.

8. _____ has been a common element in religious belief in the West over many centuries.

9. The newspaper has suffered declines in both advertisements and readership over the last few years and is clearly _____.

10. The _____ rates from these kinds of cancer have been going down as new treatments have been adopted.

B. Indicate whether the following pairs of words have the same or different meanings:

1. mnemonic / ideal   same ___ / different ___
2. hypertrophy / overgrowth   same ___ / different ___
3. extrapolate / project   same ___ / different ___
4. mortify / stiffen   same ___ / different ___
5. appendage / attachment   same ___ / different ___
6. cynosure / guide   same ___ / different ___
7. extrovert / champion   same ___ / different ___
8. append / attach   same ___ / different ___

9. amortize / pay down   same ___ / different ___
10. lucid / glittering   same ___ / different ___
11. atrophy / enlarge   same ___ / different ___
12. translucent / cross-lighted same ___ / different ___
13. solecism / goof   same ___ / different ___
14. pandemonium / uproar   same ___ / different ___
15. extraneous / superb   same ___ / different ___
16. lucubration / nightmare   same ___ / different ___
17. photosynthesis / reproduction same ___ / different ___
18. panacea / remedy   same ___ / different ___
19. elucidate / charm   same ___ / different ___
20. deportment / behavior   same ___ / different ___

**C. Match the definition on the left to the correct word
   on the right:**

1. question-and-answer   a. panoply
2. elementary particle of light b. pendant
3. stop temporarily   c. sapphic
4. hanging ornament   d. comport
5. impressive display   e. translucent
6. nonsexual   f. platonic
7. behave   g. photon
8. dying   h. Socratic
9. lesbian   i. suspend
10. light-diffusing   j. moribund

UNIT

9

HER comes from the Latin verb *haerere,* meaning "to stick." Another form of the verb produces the root *hes-,* seen in such words as *adhesive,* which means basically "sticky" or "sticking," and *hesitate,* which means more or less "stuck in one place."

adherent \ad-ˈhir-ənt\ (1) Someone who follows a leader, a party, or a profession. (2) One who believes in a particular philosophy or religion.

• The general's adherents heavily outnumbered his opponents and managed to shout them down repeatedly.

Just as tape *adheres* to paper, a person may adhere to a cause, a faith, or a belief. Thus, you may be an adherent of Hinduism, an adherent of environmentalism, or an adherent of the Republican Party. A plan for cutting taxes always attracts adherents easily, regardless of what the cuts may result in.

cohere \kō-ˈhir\ To hold together firmly as parts of the same mass.

• His novels never really cohere; the chapters always seem like separate short stories.

When you finish writing a paper, you may feel that it coheres well, since it's sharply focused and all the ideas seem to support each other. When all the soldiers in an army platoon feel like buddies, the platoon has become a *cohesive* unit. In science class you may learn the difference between *cohesion* (the tendency of a chemical's molecules to stick together) and *adhesion* (the tendency of the molecules of two different substances to stick together). Water molecules tend to cohere, so water falls from the sky in drops, not as separate molecules. But water molecules also *adhere* to molecules of other substances, so raindrops will often cling to the underside of a clothesline for a while before gravity pulls them down.

incoherent \ˌin-kō-ˈhir-ənt\ (1) Unclear or difficult to understand. (2) Loosely organized or inconsistent.

• The police had found him in an abandoned warehouse, and they reported that he was dirty, hungry, and incoherent.

Incoherent is the opposite of *coherent,* and both commonly refer to words and thoughts. Just as *coherent* means well ordered and clear, *incoherent* means disordered and hard to follow. *Incoherence* in speech may result from emotional stress, especially anxiety or anger. Incoherence in writing may simply result from poor planning; a twelve-page term paper that isn't written until the night before it's due will generally suffer from incoherence.

inherent \in-ˈhir-ənt\ Part of something by nature or habit.

• A guiding belief behind our Constitution is that individuals have certain inherent rights that can't be taken away.

Inherent literally refers to something that is "stuck in" something else so firmly that they can't be separated. A plan may have an inherent flaw that will cause it to fail; a person may have inherent virtues that everyone admires. Since the flaw and the virtues can't be removed, the plan may simply have to be thrown out and the person will remain virtuous forever.

FUG comes from the Latin verb *fugere,* meaning "to flee or escape." Thus, a *refugee* flees from some threat or danger, while a *fugitive* is usually fleeing from the law.

---

centrifugal \sen-ˈtri-fyu̇-gəl\ Moving outward from a center or central focus.

• Their favorite carnival ride was the Round-up, in which centrifugal force flattened them against the outer wall of a rapidly spinning cage.

Centrifugal force is what keeps a string with a ball on the end taut when you whirl it around. A *centrifuge* is a machine that uses centrifugal force. At the end of a washing machine's cycle, it becomes a weak and simple centrifuge as it whirls the water out of your clothes. Centrifuges hundreds of thousands of times as powerful are essential to nuclear technology and drug manufacturing. Part of an astronaut's training occurs in a centrifuge that generates force equal to several times the force of gravity (about like a washing machine) to get them used to the forces they'll encounter in a real space mission.

refuge \\'re-ˌfyüj\\ Shelter or protection from danger or distress, or a place that provides shelter or protection.

• Caught in a storm by surprise, they took refuge in an abandoned barn.

The *re-* in *refuge* means basically "back" or "backward" rather than "again" (see RE, p. 635); thus, a *refugee* is someone who is "fleeing backward." *Refuge* tends to appear with certain other words: you generally "seek refuge," "take refuge," or "find refuge." Religion may be a refuge from the woes of your life; a beautiful park may be a refuge from the noise of the city; and your bedroom may be a refuge from the madness of your family.

fugue \\'fyüg\\ A musical form in which a theme is echoed and imitated by voices or instruments that enter one after another and interweave as the piece proceeds.

• For his debut on the church's new organ, the organist chose a fugue by J. S. Bach.

Bach and Handel composed many fugues for harpsichord and organ in which the various parts (or voices) seem to flee from and chase each other in an intricate dance. Each part, after it has stated the theme or melody, apparently flees from the next part, which takes up the same theme and sets off in pursuit. Simple rounds such as "Three Blind Mice" or "Row, Row, Row Your Boat" could be called fugues for children, but a true fugue can be long and extremely complex.

subterfuge \\'səb-tər-ˌfyüj\\ (1) A trick designed to help conceal, escape, or evade. (2) A deceptive trick.

• The conservatives' subterfuge of funding a liberal third-party candidate in order to take votes away from the main liberal candidate almost worked that year.

With its "flee" root, the Latin verb *subterfugere* meant "to escape or avoid." Thus, a subterfuge is a way of escaping blame, embarrassment, inconvenience—or even prison—by tricky means. The life of spies consists of an endless series of subterfuges. In the more everyday world, putting words like "heart-healthy" on junk-food packaging is a subterfuge to trick unwary shoppers. And getting a friend to call about an "emergency" in order to get out of an evening engagement is about the oldest subterfuge in the book.

Quizzes

A. Fill in each blank with the correct letter:

a. cohere
b. refuge
c. incoherent
d. fugue

e. centrifugal
f. adherent
g. subterfuge
h. inherent

1. The author tries to take on so many different subjects that the book really doesn't _____ very well.
2. All the plans for the surprise party were in place except the _____ for keeping her out of the house until 6:30.
3. She had left Scientology and was now an _____ of the Unification Church.
4. Fleeing the Nazis, he had found _____ in the barn of a wealthy family in northern Italy.
5. By the time his fever reached 105°, the boy was mumbling _____ sentences.
6. A rock tied to a string and whirled about exerts _____ force on the string.
7. Mahatma Gandhi believed goodness was _____ in humans.
8. As the last piece in the recital, she had chosen a particularly difficult _____ by Bach.

B. Choose the closest definition:

1. inherent   a. built-in b. inherited c. confused d. loyal
2. fugue   a. mathematical formula b. musical form
      c. marginal figure d. masonry foundation
3. adherent   a. sticker b. stinker c. follower d. flower
4. centrifugal   a. moving upward b. moving backward
      c. moving downward d. moving outward

5. cohere   a. control b. react c. pause d. unite
6. subterfuge   a. overhead serve b. underhanded plot
    c. powerful force d. secret supporter
7. incoherent   a. attached b. constant c. controlled
    d. confused
8. refuge   a. starting point b. hideout c. goal d. return

COSM comes from the Greek word for "order." Since the Greeks believed the universe was an orderly place, words in this group usually relate to the universe. So *cosmonaut* was the word for a space traveler from the former Soviet Union. (The roots of our own word, *astronaut*, suggest "star traveler" instead.) Oddly enough, *cosmetics* comes from the same root, since putting things in order is similar to decorating something—such as your face.

---

cosmos \\'käz-₁mōs\\ (1) The universe, especially when it is viewed as orderly and systematic. (2) Any orderly system that is complete in itself.

• The astronomer, the biologist, and the philosopher all try in their own ways to make sense of the cosmos.

Cosmos often simply means "universe." But the word is generally used to suggest an orderly or harmonious universe, as it was originally used by Pythagoras in the 6th century B.C. Thus, a religious mystic may help put us in touch with the cosmos, and so may a physicist. The same is often true of the adjective *cosmic*: Cosmic rays (really particles rather than rays) bombard us from outer space, but cosmic questions come from human attempts to find order in the universe.

cosmology \\käz-'mä-lə-jē\\ (1) A theory that describes the nature of the universe. (2) A branch of astronomy that deals with the origin and structure of the universe.

• New Age teachers propose a cosmology quite unlike the traditional Jewish, Christian, or Islamic ways of viewing the universe.

Most religions and cultures include some kind of cosmology to explain the nature of the universe. In modern astronomy, the leading cosmology is still the Big Bang theory, which claims that the universe began with a huge explosion that sent matter and energy spreading out in all directions. One reason why fans watch *Star Trek* is for the various cosmologies depicted in the show, including different conceptions of space, time, and the meaning of life.

microcosm \\'mī-krə-ˌkä-zəm\\ Something (such as a place or an event) that is seen as a small version of something much larger.

• The large hippie communes of the 1960s and '70s were microcosms of socialist systems, with most of socialism's advantages and disadvantages.

A troubled urban school can look like a microcosm of America's educational system. A company's problems may be so typical that they can represent an entire small country's economic woes "in microcosm." *Microcosm,* and especially its synonym *microcosmos,* are also sometimes used when talking about the microscopic world. The documentary film *Microcosmos* is devoted to the remarkable insect life in an ordinary meadow on a single summer's day.

cosmopolitan \\ˌkäz-mə-'pä-lə-tən\\ (1) Having international sophistication and experience. (2) Made up of persons, elements, or influences from many different parts of the world.

• New York, like most cosmopolitan cities, offers a wonderful array of restaurants featuring foods from around the world.

Since *cosmopolitan* includes the root *polit-,* from the Greek word for "citizen," someone who is cosmopolitan is a "citizen of the world." She may be able to read the morning paper in Rio de Janeiro, attend a lecture in Madrid, and assist at a refugee camp in Uganda with equal ease—and maybe all in the same week. And a city or a country that is cosmopolitan has aspects and elements that come from various countries.

SCI comes from the Latin verb *scire,* "to know" or "to understand." The root appears in such common words as *science,* which originally meant simply "knowledge," and *conscience,* meaning "moral knowledge." And to be *conscious* is to be in a state where you are able to know or understand.

---

conscientious \ˌkän-shē-ˈen-shəs\ (1) Governed by morality; scrupulous. (2) Resulting from painstaking or exact attention.

- New employees should be especially conscientious about turning in all their assignments on time.

Conscience and its adjective *conscientious* both come from a Latin verb meaning "to be aware of guilt." *Conscientious* indicates extreme care, either in observing moral laws or in performing assigned duties. A conscientious person is someone with a strong moral sense, who has feelings of guilt when he or she violates it. A conscientious worker has a sense of duty that forces him or her to do a careful job. A conscientious report shows painstaking work on the part of the writer. And a *conscientious objector* is someone who, for reasons of conscience, refuses to fight in an army.

nescience \ˈne-shəns\ Lack of knowledge or awareness: ignorance.

- About once every class period, my political-science professor would angrily denounce the nescience of the American public.

This word, which means literally "non-knowledge," is only used by intellectuals, and the same is true of its adjective, *nescient*. We all have heard the remarkable facts: 40% of us believe that humans and dinosaurs lived on earth at the same time; 49% believe that the President can ignore the Constitution; 60% can't name the three branches of government; 75% can't find Israel on a map; and so on. Is it any wonder we Americans are sometimes called nescient?

prescient \ˈpre-shənt\ Having or showing advance knowledge of what is going to happen.

- For years she had read the *Wall Street Journal* every morning, looking for prescient warnings about crashes, crises, and catastrophes on the horizon.

Being truly prescient would require supernatural powers. But well-informed people may have such good judgment as to appear prescient, and *prescient* is often used to mean "having good foresight." Some newspaper columnists may seem prescient in their predictions, but we can't help suspecting that any apparent *prescience* is usually the result of leaks from people with inside knowledge.

unconscionable \ən-'kän-shə-nə-bəl\ (1) Not guided by any moral sense; unscrupulous. (2) Shockingly excessive, unreasonable, or unfair.

- When the facts about how the cigarette industry had lied about its practices for decades finally came out, most Americans found the behavior unconscionable.

Something that can't be done in good *conscience* is unconscionable, and such acts can range from betraying a confidence to mass murder. For a five-syllable word, *unconscionable* is actually quite common. This is partly because it isn't always used very seriously; so, for example, a critic is free to call a fat new book "an unconscionable waste of trees." In law, an unconscionable contract is one that, even though it was signed by both parties, is so ridiculous that a judge will just throw it out.

Quizzes

A. Complete the analogy:

1. clever : brainy :: prescient : _____
   a. evil b. wise c. existing d. painstaking
2. village : city :: microcosm : _____
   a. flea circus b. universe c. scale model d. bacteria
3. bold : shy :: cosmopolitan : _____
   a. planetary b. naive c. unique d. nearby
4. informed : ignorant :: conscientious : _____
   a. careful b. all-seeing c. well-informed d. scientific
5. geology : earth :: cosmology : _____
   a. sophistication b. universe c. explanation d. appearance
6. data : information :: nescience : _____
   a. wisdom b. ignorance c. judgment d. learning
7. forest : trees :: cosmos : _____
   a. stars b. earth c. orbits d. universe
8. corrupt : honest :: unconscionable : _____
   a. orderly b. attractive c. universal d. moral

B. Match the definition on the right to the correct word on the left:

1. cosmopolitan   a. having foresight
2. nescience   b. universe
3. microcosm   c. lack of knowledge
4. conscientious   d. well-traveled
5. unconscionable   e. small world
6. cosmology   f. scrupulous
7. prescient   g. inexcusable
8. cosmos   h. description of the universe

JUNCT comes from the Latin verb *jungere*, meaning "to join." A *junction* is a place where roads or railways come together. A *conjunction* is a word that joins two other words or groups of words: "this *and* that," "to be *or* not to be."

---

juncture \ˈjəŋk-chər\ (1) An important point in a process or activity. (2) A place where things join: junction.

• The architect claims his design for the new Islamic Museum represents a juncture of Muslim and Western culture.

The meaning of *juncture* can be entirely physical; thus, you can speak of the juncture of the turnpike and Route 116, or the juncture of the Shenandoah and Potomac Rivers. But it more often means something nonphysical. This may be a moment in time, especially a moment when important events are "crossing" ("At this critical juncture, the President called together his top security advisers"). But *juncture* also often refers to the coming together of two or more ideas, systems, styles, or fields ("These churches seem to operate at the juncture of religion and patriotism," "Her job is at the juncture of product design and marketing," etc.).

adjunct \ˈa-ˌjəŋkt\ Something joined or added to another thing of which it is not a part.

• All technical-school students learn that classroom instruction can be a valuable adjunct to hands-on training.

With its prefix, *ad-*, meaning "to or toward," *adjunct* implies that one thing is "joined to" another. A car wash may be operated as an adjunct to a gas station. An *adjunct* professor is one who's attached to the college without being a full member of the salaried faculty. And anyone trying to expand his or her vocabulary will find that daily reading of a newspaper is a worthwhile adjunct to actual vocabulary study.

disjunction \dis-ˈjəŋk-shən\ A break, separation, or sharp difference between two things.

- By now she realized there was a serious disjunction between the accounts of his personal life that his two best friends were giving her.

A disjunction may be a mere lack of connection between two things, or a large gulf. There's often a huge disjunction between what people expect from computers and what they know about them, and the disjunction between a star's public image and her actual character may be just as big. We may speak of the disjunction between science and morality, between doing and telling, or between knowing and explaining. In recent years, *disjunction* seem to have been losing out to a newer synonym, the noun *disconnect*.

conjunct \kən-ˈjəŋkt\ Bound together; joined, united.

- Politics and religion were conjunct in 18th-century England, and the American colonists were intent on separating the two.

With its prefix *con-*, meaning "with, together," *conjunct* means basically "joined together." A rather intellectual word, it has special meanings in music (referring to a smooth melodic line that doesn't skip up or down) and astronomy (referring to two stars or planets that appear next to each other), but its more general "bound together" meaning is rarer. A *conjunction* is a word (particularly *and, or,* or *but*) that joins together words or groups of words, and an adverb that joins two clauses or sentences (such as *so, however, meanwhile, therefore,* or *also*) is called a *conjunctive adverb*—or simply a *conjunct*.

PART, from the Latin word *pars*, meaning "part," comes into English most obviously in our word *part*. An *apartment* or *compartment* is part of a larger whole. The same is usually true of a *particle*.

---

bipartite \bī-ˈpär-ˌtīt\ (1) Being in two parts. (2) Shared by two.

- The report is a bipartite document, and all the important findings are in the second section.

Usually a technical word, *bipartite* is common in medicine and biology. A bipartite patella, for example, is a split kneecap; many people are born with them. Many creatures have a bipartite life cycle, living life in two very distinct forms. As one example, the velella begins life as a creature that travels with thousands of others in the form of a kind of sailboat, blown across the ocean's surface with the wind; only later does each velella turn into a tiny jellyfish.

impartial \im-'pär-shəl\ Fair and not biased; treating or affecting all equally.

- Representatives of labor and management agreed to have the matter decided by an impartial third party.

To be "partial to" or "partial toward" someone or something is to be somewhat biased or prejudiced, which means that a person who is partial really only sees part of the whole picture. To be impartial is the opposite. The United Nations sends impartial observers to monitor elections in troubled countries. We hope judges and juries will be impartial when they hand down verdicts. But grandparents aren't expected to be impartial when describing their new grandchild.

participle \'pär-tə-ˌsi-pəl\ A word that is formed from a verb but used like an adjective.

- In the phrase "the crying child," "crying" is a present participle; in "satisfaction guaranteed," "guaranteed" is a past participle.

English verbs can take several basic forms, which we call their *principal parts*: the infinitive ("to move," "to speak," etc.), the past tense ("moved," "spoke"), the past participle ("moved," "spoken"), and the present participle ("moving," "speaking"). The participles are words that "take part" in two different word classes: that is, verb forms that can also act like adjectives ("the spoken word," "a moving experience"). A grammatical error called a *dangling participle* occurs when a sentence begins with a participle that doesn't modify the subject; in the sentence "Climbing the mountain, the cabin came in view," for example, "climbing" is a dangling participle since it doesn't modify "cabin."

partisan \'pär-tə-zən\ (1) A person who is strongly devoted to a particular cause or group. (2) A guerrilla fighter.

• Throughout his career on the Supreme Court, he had been a forthright partisan of the cause of free speech.

A partisan is someone who supports one *part* or *party*. Sometimes the support takes the form of military action, as when guerrilla fighters take on government forces. But *partisan* is actually most often used as an adjective, usually referring to support of a political party. so if you're accused of being too partisan, or of practicing partisan politics, it means you're mainly interested in boosting your own party and attacking the other one.

Quizzes

A. Choose the closest definition:

1. juncture   a. opening b. crossroads c. end
      d. combination
2. impartial   a. fair b. biased c. accurate d. opinionated
3. adjunct   a. warning b. addition c. disclosure
      d. difference
4. participle   a. verb part b. warning c. supplement
      d. guerrilla fighter
5. conjunct   a. joined b. difficult c. spread out
      d. simplified
6. bipartite   a. double-edged b. twice-married
      c. two-part d. having two parties
7. disjunction   a. prohibition b. break c. requirement
      d. intersection
8. partisan   a. judge b. teacher c. supporter d. leader

B. Indicate whether the following pairs of words have the same or different meanings:

1. impart / give   same ___ / different ___
2. conjunct / split   same ___ / different ___
3. participle / verb part   same ___ / different ___
4. impartial / supportive   same ___ / different ___
5. adjunct / supplement   same ___ / different ___
6. juncture / train station   same ___ / different ___
7. partisan / fighter   same ___ / different ___
8. disjunction / connection   same ___ / different ___

MIS comes from the Latin verb *mittere,* "to send." A *missile* is something sent speeding through the air or water. And when your class is *dismissed* at the end of the day, you're sent home.

mission \\'mi-shən\ (1) A task that someone is given to do, especially a military task. (2) A task that someone considers an important duty.

• She considers it her mission to prevent unwanted puppies and kittens from being born.

Your own *mission* in life can be anything you pursue with almost religious enthusiasm. People with a mission—whether it's stopping drunk driving, keeping the town's public areas clean, increasing local recycling, or building a community center—very often succeed in really changing things.

missionary \\'mi-shə-,ner-ē\ A person undertaking a mission, and especially a religious missionary.

• North American missionaries have been working in Central America for decades, and you can find their churches in even the most remote jungle regions.

Beginning around 1540, an order of Catholic priests known as the Jesuits began to send its members to many parts of the world to convert peoples who believed in other gods to Christianity. Wherever they went, the Catholic missionaries built central buildings for their religious work, and the buildings themselves became known as *missions*; many 17th-century missions in the American West and Southwest are now preserved as museums. Their foes, the Protestants, soon began sending out their own missionaries, and today Protestant missionaries are probably far more numerous.

emissary \\'e-mə-,ser-ē\ Someone sent out to represent another; an agent.

• Now in his 70s, he had served over many years as a presidential emissary to many troubled regions of the world.

Like *missionaries,* emissaries are sent on missions. However, emissaries are more likely to be representing governments, political leaders, and nonreligious institutions, and an emissary's mission is usually to negotiate or to gather information. So a president may send a trusted emissary to a war-torn region to discuss peace terms.

A company's CEO may send an emissary to check out another company that they may be thinking of buying. And a politician may send out an emissary to persuade a wealthy individual to become a supporter.

transmission \trans-ˈmi-shən\ (1) The act or process of sending something from one point to another, especially sending electrical signals to a radio, television, computer, etc. (2) The gears by which the power is passed from the engine to the axle in a motor vehicle.

• Even in the Middle Ages, transmission of news of a ruler's death across the Asian continent could be accomplished by sun reflectors within 24 hours.

Since *trans-* means "across" (see TRANS, p. 626), it's not hard to see the meaning of *transmission*. Disease transmission occurs when an infection passes from one living thing to another. TV signal transmission can be interrupted by tree leaves, including moving leaves and branches during a storm. Your car's transmission *transmits* the engine's power to the axle, changing the gears to keep the engine working with maximum efficiency at various speeds.

PEL comes from the Latin verb *pellere*, meaning "to move or drive." So a *propeller* moves a small airplane forward. And if you *dispel* someone's fears, you "drive them away."

---

compel \kəm-ˈpel\ (1) To force (someone) to do something. (2) To make (something) happen.

• After returning from the lecture, they felt compelled to contribute to one of the refugee relief agencies.

The prefix *com-* acts as a strengthener in this word; thus, to compel is to drive powerfully, or force. So you may feel compelled to speak to a friend about his drinking, or compelled to reveal a secret in order to prevent something from happening. A *compulsion* is usually a powerful inner urge; a *compulsive* shopper or a compulsive gambler usually can't hold onto money for long. You might not want to do something unless there's a *compelling* reason; however, a compelling film is simply one that seems serious and important.

expel \ik-'spel\ (1) To drive or force out. (2) To force to leave, usually by official action.

• For repeatedly ignoring important agreements over several years, the two countries were eventually expelled from the trade organization.

To expel is to drive out, and its usual noun is *expulsion. Expel* is similar to *eject,* but *expel* suggests pushing out while *eject* suggests throwing out. Also, ejecting may only be temporary: the player ejected from a game may be back tomorrow, but the student expelled from school is probably out forever.

impel \im-'pel\ To urge or drive forward by strong moral force.

• As the meeting wore on without any real progress being made, she felt impelled to stand and speak.

Impel is very similar in meaning to *compel,* and often a perfect synonym, though it tends to suggest even more strongly an inner drive to do something and a greater urgency to act, especially for moral reasons. But when *impel* takes its noun and adjective forms, it changes slightly. So an *impulse*—such as "impulse buying," when you suddenly see something cool and know you've got to have it— often isn't based on anything very serious. And *impulsive* behavior in general, such as blurting out something stupid on the spur of the moment, is the kind of thing you're supposed to get over when you grow up.

repel \ri-'pel\ (1) To keep (something) out or away. (2) To drive back.

• Her son, knowing how she was repelled by rats and snakes, had started keeping them in his bedroom.

Since *re-* can mean not just "again" but also "back" (see RE-, p. 635), *repel* means "drive back." *Repel* has two common adjective forms; thus, a *repellent* or *repulsive* odor may drive us into the other room. Its main noun form is *repulsion.* Magnets exhibit both attraction and repulsion, and the goal of an armed defense is the repulsion of an enemy; but we generally use *repulsion* to mean "strong dislike." In recent years, *repulse* has been increasingly used as a synonym for *repel* ("That guy repulses me").

Quizzes

A. Fill in each blank with the correct letter:

a. mission   e. expel
b. missionary   f. impel
c. emissary   g. repel
d. transmission   h. compel

1. They knew that hunger would eventually _____ the grizzly to wake up.
2. An _____ was sent to the Duke with a new offer.
3. Men like him normally _____ her, so I'm surprised that she seems interested.
4. _____ of the bacteria usually occurs through close personal contact.
5. Though the Senate can _____ a member for certain crimes, it's almost never been done.
6. The only people in the village who could speak English were a Peace Corps volunteer and a _____ at the little church.
7. Don't count on conscience to _____ most people to make the right choice under such difficult circumstances.
8. Their _____ on this occasion was to convince their elderly father to surrender his driver's license.

B. Match the definition on the left to the correct word on the right:

1. force by moral pressure   a. transmission
2. evangelist   b. compel
3. drive irresistibly   c. repel
4. disgust   d. mission
5. agent   e. expel
6. sending   f. missionary
7. drive out   g. impel
8. errand   h. emissary

Words from Mythology

arachnid \ə-'rak-ˌnid\ A member of the class Arachnida, which principally includes animals with four pairs of legs and no antennae, such as spiders, scorpions, mites, and ticks.

• His interest in arachnids began when, as a child, he would watch spiders build their gorgeous webs in the corners of the porch.

The Greek word for "spider" is *arachne*, and, according to Greek mythology, the original arachnid was a girl named Arachne. A marvelous weaver, she made the mistake of claiming she was better at her craft than the goddess Athena. In a contest between the two, she angered the goddess by weaving a remarkable tapestry showing the gods behaving badly. As punishment, Athena changed Arachne into a spider, fated to spend her life weaving. With their eight legs, arachnids are easily distinguished from the six-legged insects, on which they feed by injecting digesting juices and then sucking up the liquefied remains.

calliope \kə-'lī-ə-pē\ A musical instrument similar to an organ in which whistles are sounded by steam or compressed air.

• The town's old calliope, with its unmistakable sound, summoned them to the fair every summer.

To the ancient Greeks, the Muses were nine goddesses, each of whom was the spirit of one or more of the arts and sciences. Calliope was the Muse of heroic or epic poetry, who inspired poets to write such epics as the *Iliad* and the *Odyssey*. Since the lengthy epics were generally sung from beginning to end, she was responsible for a great deal of musical reciting. But she wouldn't necessarily have approved of having her name used for the hooting organlike instrument that was invented in America around 1855. Calliopes gave a festive air to the great showboats that floated up and down the Mississippi and Ohio Rivers giving theatrical performances; the loudest could supposedly be heard eight miles away, attracting customers from all around. Today they are mostly heard on merry-go-rounds and at circuses.

dryad \'drī-əd\ A wood nymph.

• The ancient Greeks' love of trees can be seen in their belief that every tree contained a dryad, which died when the tree was cut.

The term *dryad* comes from the Greek word for "oak tree." As the Greeks saw it, every tree (not only oaks) had a spirit. The best known of the dryads was Daphne. The beautiful daughter of a river god, she was desired by the god Apollo; as he was about to capture her, she prayed to her father to save her, and he transformed her into a laurel tree. In her honor, Apollo commanded that the poet who won the highest prize every year be crowned with a laurel wreath. The Greeks' respect for trees unfortunately failed to keep Greece's forests from shrinking greatly over the centuries, and those that remain produce little wood of good quality.

fauna \\'fȯ-nə\\ Animal life, especially the animals that live naturally in a given area or environment.

• The larger fauna of the county include coyotes, black bear, deer, moose, wild turkey, hawks, and vultures.

Faunus and Fauna were the Roman woodland god and goddess for whom animals were a particular concern. Faunus was the Roman equivalent of the Greek god Pan, and like Pan, he had goats' legs. Their goat-legged helpers, called *fauns,* were known for their love of pleasure and mischief. The fauna of a continent are often very similar across a broad east-west band; from north to south, however, they may vary greatly.

flora \\'flȯr-ə\\ Plant life, especially the flowering plants that live naturally in a specific area or environment.

• Scientists are busily identifying the flora of the Amazon rain forest before the rapid expansion of commercial interests consumes it.

Flora means "flower" in Latin, and Flora was the Roman goddess of spring and flowering plants, especially wildflowers and plants not raised for food. She was shown as a beautiful young woman in a long, flowing dress with flowers in her hair, strewing flowers over the earth. English preserves her name in such words as *floral, floret,* and *flourish.* A region's flora may range from tiny violets to towering trees. The common phrase "flora and fauna" covers just about every visible living thing.

herculean \\ˌhər-kyu̇-'lē-ən\\ (1) Extremely strong. (2) Extremely extensive, intense, or difficult.

• Accomplishing all the things he promised during the presidential campaign will be a herculean task.

The hero Hercules, son of the god Zeus by a human mother, was famous for his superhuman strength. To pacify the wrath of the god Apollo, he was forced to perform twelve enormously difficult tasks, or "labors." These ranged from descending into the underworld to bring back the terrifying dog that guarded its entrance to destroying the many-headed monster called the Hydra. Any job or task that's extremely difficult or calls for enormous strength is therefore called herculean.

Pandora's box \pan-'dȯr-əz-'bäks\ A source of many troubles.

- In a thundering speech, he predicted that, if the bill was passed, the new policy would open a Pandora's box of economic problems.

The god Prometheus stole fire from heaven to give to the human race, which originally consisted only of men. To punish humanity, the other gods created the first woman, the beautiful Pandora. As a gift, Zeus gave her a box, which she was told never to open. However, as soon as he was out of sight she took off the lid, and out swarmed all the troubles of the world, never to be recaptured. Only Hope was left in the box, stuck under the lid. Anything that looks ordinary but may produce unpredictable harmful results can thus be called a Pandora's box.

Scylla and Charybdis \'si-lə-and-kə-'rib-dəs\ Two equally dangerous alternatives.

- Doctors and patients who need to calculate the ideal dosage of the medication, knowing how it can trigger a different dangerous condition, often feel caught between Scylla and Charybdis.

The Strait of Messina is the narrow passage between the island of Sicily and the "toe" of Italy's "boot." In Greek mythology, two monsters hovered on either side of the strait. Scylla, a female monster with six snake-like heads, each with pointed teeth, barked like a dog from the rocks on the Italian side. Charybdis, on the Sicilian side, caused a whirlpool by swallowing the waters of the sea three times a day. When Odysseus attempted to sail between them, he encountered disaster on both sides. Being caught between Scylla and Charybdis is a lot like being between a rock and a hard place.

Quiz

Complete the analogy:

1. hobgoblin : imp :: dryad : _____
   a. moth b. oak tree c. nymph d. dragonfly
2. difficult : simple :: herculean : _____
   a. intense b. easy c. mammoth d. strong
3. wrath : anger :: Scylla and Charybdis : _____
   a. rage b. double peril c. ferocity d. whirlpools
4. piano : nightclub :: calliope : _____
   a. organ b. circus c. church d. steam
5. canine : dog :: flora : _____
   a. oak trees b. wood nymphs c. plants d. animals
6. reptile : snake :: arachnid : _____
   a. toad b. salamander c. bird d. scorpion
7. cabinet : china :: Pandora's box : _____
   a. pleasures b. troubles c. taxes d. music
8. cattle : livestock :: fauna : _____
   a. meadows b. flowers c. wildlife d. trees

Review Quizzes

A. Choose the correct synonym:

1. impartial   a. fair b. biased c. cautious d. undecided
2. cosmopolitan   a. bored b. intelligent
   c. inexperienced d. well-traveled
3. incoherent   a. clear b. uncertain c. confused
   d. unknown
4. mission   a. greeting b. assignment c. support
   d. departure
5. compel   a. drive b. prevent c. eject d. compare
6. inherent   a. local b. inherited c. acquired d. built-in
7. cosmos   a. chaos b. order c. universe d. beauty
8. impart   a. grant b. stick c. combine d. withhold
9. adjunct   a. addition b. neighbor c. connection
   d. acquaintance
10. repel   a. attract b. greet c. offend d. send

B. Match the definition on the right to the correct word on the left:

1. emissary
2. conscientious
3. participle
4. impel
5. dryad
6. prescient
7. Scylla and Charybdis
8. subterfuge
9. herculean
10. adjunct

a. verb part
b. cause to act
c. equal perils
d. agent
e. foresighted
f. attachment
g. careful
h. very difficult
i. trick
j. tree spirit

C. Fill in each blank with the correct letter:

a. adherent
b. centrifugal
c. conscientious
d. arachnid
e. transmission

f. flora
g. expel
h. prescient
i. disjunction
j. subterfuge

1. He's no longer really an _____ of that economic philosophy.
2. The most successful stockbrokers have the reputation of being almost eerily _____.
3. Most philosophers see no _____ between science and morality.
4. _____ force keeps roller-coaster cars from crashing to the ground.
5. _____ of electric power over long distances always involves considerable losses.
6. Unlike the spiders, the _____ we call the daddy longlegs has no waist.
7. The archerfish can _____ sudden jets of water at insects, knocking them into the lake or river.
8. She won praise for her _____ handling of details.
9. He always used to be able to get hold of Grateful Dead tickets by some kind of _____.
10. The _____ of the West Creek Valley includes at least a dozen rare species.

UNIT

10

PUT comes from the Latin verb *putare*, meaning "to think, consider, or believe." So, for example, a *reputation* is what others think of you. But when the root shows up in such words as *compute*, *dispute*, and *deputy*, its meaning is harder to trace.

---

reputed \ri-ˈpyü-təd\ Believed to be a certain way by popular opinion.

• The 15th-century prince Vlad the Impaler is reputed to have inspired the character Dracula, though in fact, evil though Vlad was, Dracula's creator only borrowed his nickname.

Reputed is used constantly today by reporters, and almost always to describe suspected criminals—"the reputed mobster," "the reputed drug kingpin," "the reputed gang leader," etc. But the word shouldn't be left to journalists; your elderly aunt may, for instance, be reputed to have made a large fortune in oil, or to have had four husbands who all died mysteriously. *Reputed* is easy to confuse with *reputable,* and they used to mean the same thing—that is, "having a good reputation"—but it's become rare to hear *reputed* used with that meaning today.

disrepute \ˌdis-ri-ˈpyüt\ Loss or lack of good reputation; disgrace.

• The family had fallen into disrepute after the conviction and imprisonment of his father and uncle.

A *reputation* can be easy to lose, and someone who is no longer respectable may eventually find he's become genuinely *disreputable*—the kind of person that almost no one wants to be seen with. Disrepute isn't only for individuals: A company may fall into disrepute as a result of news stories about its products' defects; drug scandals have brought entire sports into disrepute; and a scientific theory may fall into disrepute as a result of new discoveries.

impute \im-'pyüt\ To attribute.

- The British imputed motives of piracy to American ships trying to prevent them from interfering with American trade during the War of 1812.

Imputing something to someone (or something) usually means observing something invisible in that person (or thing). We may impute meaning to a play or novel, or to a casual remark by a friend, that was never intended. Many of us like to impute bad motives to others, while always regarding our own motives as pure. In tax law, imputed income is something that isn't actual money but might as well be—for example, the free use of a car lent to you by your employer.

putative \'pyü-tə-tiv\ Generally supposed; assumed to exist.

- To strengthen the case for the defense, a putative expert took the stand.

Putative is almost always used to express doubt or skepticism about a common belief. Thus, Tintagel Castle in Cornwall, a picturesque ruin, is the putative fortress of the medieval King Arthur. The residents of New York City are *putatively* chic, neurotic, rude, and dangerous. And cable TV is full of putative experts, who often turn out not to have much knowledge of the subjects they're talking about.

LOG, from the Greek word *logos,* meaning "word," "speech," or "reason," is found particularly in English words that end in *-logy* and *-logue.* The ending *-logy* often means "the study of"; so, for instance, *biology* is the study of life, and *anthropology* is the study of humans. And *-logue* usually indicates a type of discussion; thus, *dialogue* is conversation between two people or groups, and an *epilogue* is an author's last words on a subject. But exceptions aren't hard to find.

---

physiology \ˌfi-zē-ˈä-lə-jē\ (1) A branch of biology dealing with the processes and activities by which living things, tissues, and cells function. (2) The life processes and activities of a living thing or any of its parts.

• For students planning to go to medical school, the university's most popular major is Human Physiology.

The Latin root *physio-* generally means "physical," so human physiology deals with just about everything that keeps us alive and working, and other physiology specialties do the same for other animals and for plants. To do anything serious in the field of health, you've obviously got to know how the body's organs and cells function normally. Physiology used to be considered separately from anatomy, which focuses on the body's structures; however, it's now known that structure and function can't easily be separated in a scientific way, so "anatomy and physiology" are often spoken of in the same breath.

methodology \ˌme-thə-ˈdä-lə-jē\ A set of methods or rules followed in a science or field.

• Some researchers claimed that Dr. Keller's methodology was sloppy and had led to unreliable conclusions.

The methodology employed in an experiment is essential to its success, and bad methodology has spoiled thousands of research projects. So whenever a piece of research is published in a scientific or medical journal, the researchers always carefully describe their methodology; otherwise, other scientists couldn't possibly judge the quality of what they've done.

ideology \ˌī-dē-ˈä-lə-jē\ The set of ideas and beliefs of a group or political party.

• By the time she turned 19, she realized she no longer believed in her family's political ideology.

The root *ideo-,* as you might guess, means "idea." Ideas and theories about human behavior can always be carried too far, since such behavior is very hard to pin down. So *ideological* thinkers—people who come up with large theories about how the world works and try to explain everything (and maybe even predict the future) according to those theories—are almost always disappointed, sooner or later, to find that it doesn't really work out. A person intensely devoted to a set of political ideas or theories can be called an *ideologue*—

a translation of the French *idéologue*, a word actually coined by Napoleon as a label for those political thinkers full of ideas he had no use for.

cardiology \ˌkär-dē-ˈä-lə-jē\ The study of the heart and its action and diseases.

• After his heart attack, he actually bought himself a cardiology textbook and set about learning everything he could about his unreliable organ.

The root *card-* (closely related to *cord*—see CORD, p. 269) shows up in many heart-related words. *Cardiologists* frequently find themselves studying *cardiograms*, the charts of heart activity, made by machines called *cardiographs*. Heart attacks, and deaths caused by them, have both declined as a result of better medical emergency procedures, cholesterol-lowering drugs, and a decline in smoking. But the factors likely to actually improve heart health, such as better diets and more *cardiovascular* exercise (exercise, such as running, that improves the heart and blood vessels), haven't made any progress at all. So we should all be prepared to perform *cardiopulmonary resuscitation* (an emergency procedure done on someone whose heart has stopped, to get the heart and lungs working again).

Quizzes

A. Indicate whether the following pairs of words have the same or different meanings:

1. putative / supposed   same __ / different __
2. ideology / beliefs   same __ / different __
3. reputed / questioned   same __ / different __
4. cardiology / game theory   same __ / different __
5. disrepute / shame   same __ / different __
6. methodology / carefulness   same __ / different __
7. impute / compute   same __ / different __
8. physiology / bodybuilding   same __ / different __

B. Choose the closest definition:

1. methodology   a. endurance   b. patience   c. authority
     d. system
2. impute   a. imply   b. revise   c. attribute   d. defy

3. reputed   a. famous b. accused c. determined
   d. supposed
4. ideology   a. notion b. philosophy c. standard
   d. concept
5. putative   a. assumed b. appointed c. solved d. ignored
6. cardiology   a. ear specialty b. heart specialty c. brain
   specialty d. nerve specialty
7. disrepute   a. argument b. violence c. untruth
   d. disgrace
8. physiology   a. sports medicine b. body language
   c. study of medicine d. study of organisms

TERR comes from the Latin *terra,* "earth." A *territory* is a large
expanse of land. *Terra firma* is Latin for "firm ground" as opposed
to the swaying seas. A *terrace* is a leveled area, often one created for
farming on a sloping hill. And the French word for potato, *pomme
de terre,* means literally "apple of the earth."

parterre \pär-ˈter\ (1) A decorative garden with paths between the
beds of plants. (2) The back area of the ground floor of a theater,
often under the balcony.

• The city's park boasts a beautiful parterre with many varieties
  of roses.

Parterre comes to English by way of French, where it means "on the
ground." And in the early years of the theater, the parterre was truly
on the ground. In Shakespeare's day, an English theater's parterre
was the cheap standing-room area right in front of the stage, normally filled with rowdy spectators. The original idea of the French
parterre garden, with its carefully designed plots and walkways,
was to present an artistic pattern when seen from above—from a
balcony, a raised terrace, or the top of an outdoor staircase. English
gardeners responded with garden designs that tried to make their
viewers half-forget that they were seeing something created by
humans rather than untamed nature itself.

subterranean \ˌsəb-tə-ˈrā-nē-ən\ Underground.

• In Carlsbad Caverns National Park there is an astonishing subterranean chamber over half a mile long.

A tunnel is a subterranean road or pathway, and a subway is a subterranean railway. The subterranean vaults at Fort Knox hold billions of dollars of gold reserves. Subterranean reservoirs called *aquifers* are tapped for water; in places where the pressure on the subterranean water is great enough, a hole drilled in the ground will bring it bubbling to the surface.

terrarium \tə-ˈrer-ē-əm\ An enclosure, usually transparent, with a layer of dirt in the bottom in which plants and sometimes small animals are kept indoors.

• When no one was watching, they dropped their snake in the fifth-grade terrarium, and then waited in the hall to hear the screams.

The turtle exhibit at a zoo is often in the form of a terrarium, as are some of the exhibits at a plant conservatory. In an ant terrarium, elementary-school students watch the ants dig their network of tunnels as if no one were watching. Terrariums try to create conditions as close as possible to a natural habitat. A covered terrarium can often sustain itself for months on the moisture trapped inside. But creating a good terrarium requires careful control not only of humidity but also of temperature, as well as good ventilation; the lighting should include the full spectrum of sunlight as well as a day-night regulator.

terrestrial \tə-ˈres-trē-əl\ (1) Having to do with Earth or its inhabitants. (2) Living or growing on land instead of in water or air.

• The roadrunner, although a largely terrestrial bird, can take flight for short periods when necessary.

Everything on or having to do with Earth can be called terrestrial. Mercury, Venus, and Mars are often called the terrestrial planets, since they are rocky balls somewhat like Earth rather than great globes of gas like Jupiter, Saturn, Uranus, and Neptune. Something *extraterrestrial* comes from beyond the earth and its atmosphere; the word can be used to describe anything "out of this world," from moon rocks to meteors. Turning to the second sense of *terrestrial*, animals are often divided into the terrestrial (land-living) and the aquatic (water-living). And sometimes terrestrial animals are contrasted with *arboreal* animals, those that live in trees.

MAR, from the Latin word *mare,* meaning "sea," brings its salty tang to several English words. A *submarine* is an undersea ship. *Marine* means basically "relating to the sea," so when the Continental Marines were established back in 1775, their job was to provide on-board security on naval ships; but they immediately began to be used on land as well, and the marines have continued to operate on both land and sea ever since.

marina \mə-ˈrē-nə\ A dock or harbor where pleasure boats can be moored securely, often with facilities offering supplies or repairs.

• The coast of Florida has marinas all along it for the use of anything from flimsy sailboats to enormous yachts.

Marina comes straight from Latin, where it means simply "of the sea." At a modern marina, sailors can acquire whatever they need for their next excursion, or they can tie up their boats until the next weekend comes along. Some even imitate John D. MacDonald's famous detective hero Travis McGee, who lives on his boat in Miami and rarely leaves the marina.

aquamarine \ˌä-kwə-mə-ˈrēn\ (1) A transparent blue or blue-green gem. (2) A pale blue or greenish blue that is the color of clear seawater in sunlight.

• Many of the houses on the Italian Riviera are painted aquamarine to match the Mediterranean.

Aqua marina is Latin for "seawater," so when a lovely blue-green form of the semiprecious gem known as beryl was given an English name several centuries ago, *aquamarine* seemed appropriate. Aquamarine is the ideal color that most of us carry around in our heads when we imagine the waters that lap the shores of the Greek and Caribbean islands on a sunny day. But even the Mediterranean and the Caribbean can take on lots of other colors depending on weather conditions.

mariner \ˈmer-ə-nər\ A seaman or sailor.

• When he signed on as a mariner, the young Ishmael never suspected that the ship would be pursuing a great white whale.

In Coleridge's *Rime of the Ancient Mariner,* an old seaman tells of how, by shooting a friendly albatross, he had brought storms and disaster to his ship, and how as punishment his shipmates hung the great seabird around the mariner's neck and made him wear it until it rotted. The word *mariner* has occasionally been used to mean simply "explorer," as in the famous Mariner spaceflights in the 1960s and '70s, the first to fly close to Mars, Venus, and Mercury.

maritime \\'mer-ə-ˌtīm\\ (1) Bordering on or having to do with the sea. (2) Having to do with navigation or commerce on the sea.

- As a result of the ocean, Canada's Maritime Provinces—New Brunswick, Nova Scotia, and Prince Edward Island—have a late spring but a mild winter.

The maritime countries of Portugal and England produced many seafaring explorers during the 16th and 17th centuries, many of whom sailed under the flags of other countries. Sailing for the Spanish, Ferdinand Magellan captained the ship that was the first to circle the world, charting many new maritime routes as it went. Henry Hudson, funded by the Dutch, sailed up what we call today the Hudson River, claiming the maritime area that now includes New York City for the Netherlands.

Quizzes

A. Complete the analogy:

1. crepe : pancake :: parterre : _____
   a. balcony   b. planet   c. garden   d. parachute
2. motel : motorist :: marina : _____
   a. dock   b. pier   c. sailor   d. boat
3. aquarium : water :: terrarium : _____
   a. plants   b. turtles   c. rocks   d. earth
4. urban : city :: maritime : _____
   a. beach   b. dock   c. sea   d. harbor
5. aquatic : water :: terrestrial : _____
   a. sea   b. land   c. forest   d. mountain
6. pink : red :: aquamarine : _____
   a. blue   b. watery   c. turquoise   d. yellow
7. submarine : underwater :: subterranean : _____
   a. blue   b. belowground   c. hollow   d. rumbling
8. logger : lumberjack :: mariner : _____
   a. doctor   b. lawyer   c. chief   d. sailor

B. Match the definition on the left to the correct word on the right:

1. theater area
2. blue-green gem
3. under the ground
4. near the sea
5. contained habitat
6. seaman
7. small harbor
8. earthly

a. mariner
b. terrestrial
c. marina
d. terrarium
e. maritime
f. parterre
g. subterranean
h. aquamarine

PATH comes from the Greek word *pathos*, which means "feeling" or "suffering." So a *pathetic* sight moves us to pity, and a *sympathetic* friend "feels with" you when you yourself are suffering.

---

pathos \ˈpā-ˌthäs\ (1) An element in life or drama that produces sympathetic pity. (2) An emotion of sympathetic pity.

• The pathos of the blind child beggars she had seen in India could still keep her awake at night.

Pathos comes directly from Greek. According to Aristotle, the persuasive power of public speaking relies on three elements: the speaker's authority, the logic of the speech, and the speech's pathos. Aristotle claims that pathos is the appeal to the audience's sense of right and wrong, and that it is this (unlike authority and logic) that moves the audience's emotions. Today we usually speak of pathos as an element in fiction, film, drama, music, or even painting, or the real-life pathos of a situation or personality. Since *pathos* is closely related to *pathetic*, it's not surprising that, like *pathetic*, *pathos* may occasionally be used a bit sarcastically.

apathetic \ˌa-pə-ˈthe-tik\ (1) Showing or feeling little or no emotion. (2) Having no interest.

• His apathetic response to the victory bewildered his friends.

Apathy, or lack of emotion, is central to Albert Camus's famous novel *The Stranger,* in which the main character's indifference toward almost everything, including his mother's death, results in his imprisonment. We feel little *sympathy* for him, and may even feel *antipathy,* or dislike. The American voter is often called apathetic; of all the industrial democracies, only in America does half the adult population fail to vote in major elections. As you can see, *apathetic* isn't the opposite of *pathetic,* even though the *a-* that it begins with means "not" or "without."

empathy \\'em-pə-thē\ The feeling of, or the ability to feel, the emotions and sensations of another.

* Her maternal empathy was so strong that she often seemed to be living her son's life emotionally.

In the 19th century, Charles Dickens counted on producing an *empathetic* response in his readers strong enough to make them buy the next newspaper installment of each novel. Today, when reading a novel such as *A Tale of Two Cities,* only the most hard-hearted reader could fail to feel empathy for Sidney Carton as he approaches the guillotine. One who *empathizes* suffers along with the one who feels the sensations directly. *Empathy* is similar to *sympathy,* but empathy usually suggests stronger, more instinctive feeling. So a person who feels sympathy, or pity, for victims of a war in Asia may feel empathy for a close friend going through the much smaller disaster of a divorce.

telepathic \\,te-lə-'pa-thik\ Involving apparent communication from one mind to another without speech or signs.

* After ten years of marriage, their communication is virtually telepathic, and each always seems to know what the other is thinking.

Since *tele-* means "distant" (see TELE, p. 417), you can see how *telepathy* means basically "feeling communicated from a distance." The word was coined around 1880, when odd psychic phenomena were being widely discussed by people hoping that researchers might find a scientific basis for what they believed they themselves were experiencing. Today, when people talk about extrasensory perception, or ESP, telepathy is usually what they're talking about. In recent years, the notion of *memes*—ideas that might somehow physically fly from brain to brain so that people all over the world might have the same idea at about the same time without any obvious communication—has been widely discussed. Even though scientists haven't been able to establish the existence of telepathy, about 30% of Americans continue to believe in it.

PEN/PUN comes from the Latin words *poena,* "penalty," and *punire,* "to punish." A *penalty* is, of course, a *punishment.*

penal \\'pē-nəl\\ Having to do with punishment or penalties, or institutions where punishment is given.

* The classic novels *Les Misérables* and *The Count of Monte Cristo* portray the terrible conditions in French penal institutions in the 19th century.

A state or country's *penal code* defines its crimes and describes its punishments. During the 18th and 19th centuries, many countries established penal colonies, where criminals were sent as punishment. Often these were unbearably severe; but it was to such colonies that some of Australia's and the United States' early white inhabitants came, and the convicts provided labor for the European settlement of these lands.

impunity \\im-'pyü-nə-tē\\ Freedom from punishment, harm, or loss.

* Under the flag of truce, the soldiers crossed the field with impunity.

Impunity is protection from punishment, just as immunity is protection from disease. Tom Sawyer, in Mark Twain's novel, broke his Aunt Polly's rules with near impunity because he could usually sweet-talk her into forgiving him; if that failed, he had enjoyed himself so much he didn't care what *punishment* she gave him.

penance \\'pe-nəns\\ An act of self-punishment or religious devotion to show sorrow or regret for sin or wrongdoing.

* In the Middle Ages bands of pilgrims would trudge to distant holy sites as penance for their sins.

Penance as a form of apology for a mistake can be either voluntary or ordered by someone else. Many religions include penance among the ways in which believers can show *repentance* or regret for a misdeed. The Christian season of Lent, 40 days long, is traditionally a time for doing penance.

punitive \\'pyü-nə-tiv\\ Giving, involving, or aiming at punishment.

• The least popular teachers are usually the ones with punitive attitudes, those who seem to enjoy punishing more than teaching.

Punitive is an important word in the law. When you sue a person or company for having wronged you in some way, you normally ask for something of value equal to what you were deprived of by the other party. But when the defendant has done something particularly bad, you may also ask for *punitive damages,* money over and above the actual cost of the harm done, intended to teach the defendant a lesson. Punitive damages are fairly rare, but when they're actually granted they may be as much as four times the size of the basic damages.

Quizzes

A. Fill in each blank with the correct letter:

a. impunity   e. empathy
b. apathetic   f. penal
c. punitive   g. pathos
d. telepathic   h. penance

1. You can't go on breaking the speed limit with _____ forever.
2. He had covered disasters before, but the _____ of the situation in Haiti was beyond description.
3. In some households, grounding is a severe form of _____ action.
4. The mildest of the federal _____ institutions are the so-called "country club" prisons.
5. The public's response to studies predicting dangerous climate change was _____ for many years.
6. As _____ during the period of Lent, Christians may give up a favorite food.
7. Almost everyone feels some _____ for a child's misery.
8. Identical twins have claimed to experience _____ communication about important events.

B. Complete the analogy:

1. passionate : emotional :: apathetic : _____
   a. caring b. unjust c. indifferent d. dominant

---

2. fine : speeding :: penance : _____
   a. misdeed b. credit card c. fee d. behavior
3. humor : laughter :: pathos : _____
   a. comedy b. ridicule c. death d. pity
4. immunity : sickness :: impunity : _____
   a. death b. flood c. punishment d. sleep
5. kindness : cruelty :: empathy : _____
   a. pity b. heartlessness c. emotion d. tears
6. educational : school :: penal : _____
   a. judge b. police c. prison d. sentence
7. telephonic : electric :: telepathic : _____
   a. extrasensory b. superhuman c. airborne d. sci-fi
8. encouraging : reward :: punitive : _____
   a. damage b. penalty c. praise d. jury

MATR/MATER comes from the Greek and Latin words for "mother."
A *matron* is a mature woman with children. And *matrimony* is marriage itself, the traditional first step toward motherhood.

maternity \mə-ˈtər-nə-tē\ The state of being a mother; motherhood.

• It's quite possible that the *Mona Lisa* is a portrait of maternity, and
  that the painting marks the recent birth of her child Andrea.

Maternity is used as both a noun and an adjective. *Maternity benefits* are benefits specially provided by employers for women having babies, and usually include *maternity leave,* time off work. With maternity come *maternal* feelings, which are shown by all species of warm-blooded animals as well as a few reptiles such as crocodiles and alligators.

matriarch \ˈmā-trē-ˌärk\ A woman who controls a family, group, or government.

• Every August all the grown children and their families are summoned to the estate by the matriarch.

A *matriarchy* is a social unit governed by a woman or group of women. It isn't certain that a true *matriarchal* society has ever existed, so matriarchy is usually treated as an imaginative concept. But there are societies in which relatedness through women rather than men is stressed, and elements of matriarchy may be stronger in certain societies than they are in most of the Western world. And most of us can point to families in which a woman has become the dominant figure, or grande dame, or matriarch.

matrilineal \ˌma-trə-ˈli-nē-əl\ Based on or tracing the family through the mother.

• Many of the peoples of Ghana in Africa trace their family through matrilineal connections.

A person's *lineage* is his or her *line* of ancestors. So *matrilineal* means basically "through the mother's line," just as *patrilineal* means "through the father's line." *Matrilineality* is an important concept in anthropology; among other things, it usually determines who will inherit property on a person's death. Though families that follow the European model take the father's name and are therefore patrilineal, matrilineal societies have existed around the world, including among various American Indian tribes.

matrix \ˈmā-triks\ (1) Something (such as a situation or a set of conditions) in which something else develops or forms. (2) Something shaped like a pattern of lines and spaces.

• The country's political matrix is so complex that no one who hasn't lived there could possibly understand it.

In ancient Rome, a *matrix* was a female animal kept for breeding, or a plant (sometimes called a "parent plant" or "mother plant") whose seeds were used for producing other plants. In English the word has taken on many related meanings. Mathematicians use it for a rectangular organization of numbers or symbols that can be used to make various calculations; geologists use it for the soil or rock in which a fossil is discovered, like a baby in the womb. And *matrix* was a good choice as the name of the reality in which all humans find themselves living in a famous series of science-fiction films.

AQU comes from *aqua*, the Latin word for "water." We keep pet fish in an *aquarium* at home or visit larger sea animals in a building with that name. Water sports such as swimming, canoeing, and sailing are sometimes called *aquatics*. In Scandinavia there's a popular drink called *aquavit*, the name coming from the Latin *aqua vitae*, "water of life"—though instead of water it mostly consists of alcohol.

aquaculture \ˈä-kwə-ˌkəl-chər\ The farming of plants and animals (such as kelp, fish, and shellfish) that live in the water.

• The farming of oysters by the Romans was an early form of aquaculture that has continued to the present day.

For most of the modern history of aquaculture, only costly fish and shellfish like salmon and shrimp were harvested. But new technologies are allowing cheaper and more efficient cultivation of fish for food, and such common fish as cod are now being farmed. Seaweeds and other algae are also being grown—for food (mostly in Asia), cattle feed, fertilizer, and experimentally as a source of energy. Aquaculture is now the world's fastest-growing form of food production.

aquanaut \ˈä-kwə-ˌnȯt\ A scuba diver who lives and works both inside and outside an underwater shelter for an extended time.

• Each scientist at the laboratory spent two weeks a year as an aquanaut living in the deep-sea station.

Aquanaut combines *aqua* with the Greek *nautes*, meaning "sailor." Like *astronaut* and *aeronaut*, the word may remind you of those mythical Greek heroes known as the Argonauts, who sailed with Jason on his ship, the *Argo*, in quest of the Golden Fleece. Various underwater habitats for aquanauts, such as Conshelf, SEALAB, and MarineLab, have captured the public imagination since the 1960s.

aqueduct \ˈa-kwə-ˌdəkt\ (1) A pipe or channel for water. (2) A bridgelike structure for carrying water over a valley.

• Roman aqueducts were built throughout the empire, and their spectacular arches can still be seen in Greece, France, Spain, and North Africa.

Based party on the Latin *ducere*, meaning "lead" or "conduct" (see DUC, p. 35), the word *aqueduct* named an ancient civil-engineering marvel. You may have seen photos of the great arches of ancient aqueducts spanning valleys in countries throughout the old Roman Empire, practical pipelines that are also regarded as works of timeless beauty. From the 20th century, the 242-mile Colorado River Aqueduct, the 336-mile Central Arizona Project, and the 444-mile California Aqueduct are considered wonders of American engineering, but they are not renowned for their beauty. Most aqueducts today either are riverlike channels or run underground, perhaps appearing simply as a long mound.

aquifer \\'a-kwə-fər\\ A layer of rock, sand, or gravel that can absorb and hold water.

• Cities without access to a nearby lake or river must rely on underground aquifers to meet their water needs.

The vast but relatively shallow Ogallala Aquifer lies beneath the Great Plains, under portions of eight states. Its thickness ranges from a few feet to more than a thousand feet. The Ogallala yields about 30 percent of the nation's groundwater used for irrigation in agriculture, and provides drinking water for most of the people within the area. But for many years more water has been extracted from the Ogallala than has been returned, and the situation today is of great concern.

Quizzes

A. Choose the closest definition:

1. matriarch   a. goddess b. mermaid c. bride d. grande dame
2. aquaculture   a. aquarium design b. reef diving c. pearl fishing d. water farming
3. matrilineal   a. through the mother's family b. graduating c. adopted d. female
4. aqueduct   a. channel b. dam c. dike d. reservoir
5. matrix   a. formula b. alternate reality c. scheme d. source
6. aquanaut   a. swimmer b. diver c. surfer d. pilot
7. maternity   a. motherhood b. nightgown c. women's club d. marriage
8. aquifer   a. waterway b. fishpond c. spring d. underground reservoir

B. Fill in each blank with the correct letter:

a. aquifer	e. matrilineal
b. aquaculture	f. matriarch
c. maternity	g. aqueduct
d. matrix	h. aquanaut

1. Marriage didn't seem to affect her much, but _____ has changed her completely.

2. After five years living in the suburb, they felt they had become part of a complex social _____.
3. As an _____ she often lives underwater for several days at a time.
4. The _____ they depend on for irrigation is slowly being depleted, and the farmers are being forced to cut back on water use.
5. Wild salmon has become an expensive rarity, and _____ is the source of most of the salmon we now eat.
6. The tribe seemed to be _____, with all inheritances passing through the females rather than the males.
7. The _____ that runs through the city is an open concrete-lined river.
8. He'd been married to Cynthia for three years, but she hadn't yet dared to introduce him to her great-aunt, the family _____.

Words from Mythology

cereal \\'sir-ē-əl\\ (1) A plant that produces grain that can be eaten as food, or the grain it produces. (2) The food made from grain.

*   Rice is the main food cereal of Asia, whereas wheat and corn are the main food cereals of the West.

The Roman goddess Ceres, the equivalent of the Greek Demeter, was a calm goddess who didn't take part in the quarrels of the other gods. Her particular responsibility was the food-giving plants, and for that reason the food grains came to carry her name. Cereals of the ancient Romans included wheat, barley, spelt, oats, and millet—but not corn (maize), which was a cereal of the Americas.

Junoesque \\,jü-nō-'esk\\ Having mature, poised, and dignified beauty.

*   In 1876, as a centennial gift, the French sent to America a massive statue of a robed Junoesque figure representing Liberty, to be erected in New York Harbor.

Juno was the wife of Jupiter, the chief of the Roman gods. As the first among goddesses, her power gave her particular dignity; and as goddess of women and marriage, she was a mature matron. But such younger goddesses as Diana, goddess of the hunt, perhaps came closer to today's ideals of slim and athletic female beauty.

martial \\'mär-shəl\\ Having to do with war and military life.

* The stirring, martial strains of "The British Grenadiers" echoed down the snowy street just as dawn was breaking.

Mars was the Roman god of war and one of the patron gods of Rome itself. He was responsible for everything military, from warriors to weapons to marching music. Thus, *martial arts* are skills of combat and self-defense also practiced as sport. When *martial law* is declared, a country's armed forces take over the functions of the police. And a *court-martial* is a military court or trial.

Promethean \\prə-'mē-thē-ən\\ New or creative in a daring way.

* The Promethean energy of Beethoven's symphonies was a revelation to European audiences in the early years of the 19th century.

Prometheus was a Titan, a generation older than Zeus. When Zeus overthrew his own father Cronus and seized power, Prometheus fought on the side of the gods and against his fellow Titans. But when Zeus later wanted to destroy the race of humans, Prometheus saved them by stealing fire for them from the gods. He also taught them how to write, farm, build houses, read the stars and weather, cure themselves when sick, and tame animals—in short, all the arts and skills that make humans unique. So inventive was he that anything of great creativity and originality can still be called Promethean. But Prometheus had taken a terrible risk; enraged by his disobedience, Zeus had him chained to a rocky cliff, where for many long centuries an eagle daily tore at his liver.

Sisyphean \\ˌsi-sə-'fē-ən\\ Endless and difficult, involving many disappointments.

* After twenty years, many researchers had begun to think that defeating the virus was a Sisyphean task that would never succeed.

Reputedly the cleverest man on earth, King Sisyphus of Corinth tricked the gods into bringing him back to life after he had died. For this they punished him by sending him back to the underworld, where he must eternally roll a huge rock up a long, steep hill, only to watch it roll back to where he started. Something Sisyphean demands the same kind of unending, thankless, and ultimately unsuccessful efforts.

titanic \tī-'ta-nik\ Having great size, strength, or power; colossal.

• The titanic floods of 1993 destroyed whole towns on the Mississippi River.

In Greek mythology, the Titans were the generation of giant creators that produced the younger, stronger, cleverer gods, who soon overpowered and replaced them (see *Promethean* above). In 1911 the largest ship that had ever been built was christened the *Titanic* for its unmatched size and strength. But the name may have proved unlucky; on its maiden voyage in 1912 a massive iceberg ripped a fatal hole in the great ship, and it sank in the icy waters off Newfoundland.

Triton \'trī-tən\ (1) A being with a human upper body and the lower body of a fish; a merman. (2) Any of various large mollusks with a heavy, conical shell.

• In one corner of the painting, a robust Triton emerges from the sea with his conch to announce the coming of the radiant queen.

Triton was originally the son of the sea god Poseidon (or Neptune). A guardian of the fish and other creatures of the sea, he is usually shown as hearty, muscular, and cheerful. Like his father, he often carries a trident (three-pronged fork) and may ride in a chariot drawn by seahorses. Blowing on his conch shell, he creates the roar of the ocean. As a decorative image, Tritons are simply the male version of mermaids. The handsome seashells that bear their name are the very conchs on which they blow. Triton has also given his name to the planet Neptune's largest moon.

vulcanize \'vəl-kə-ˌnīz\ To treat crude or synthetic rubber or plastic so that it becomes elastic and strong and resists decay.

• The native islanders had even discovered how to vulcanize the rubber from the local trees in a primitive way.

The Roman god Vulcan (the Greek Hephaestus) was in charge of fire and the skills that use fire, especially blacksmithing. When

Charles Goodyear almost accidentally discovered how to vulcanize rubber in 1839, he revolutionized the rubber industry. He called his process *vulcanization* because it used fire to heat a mix of rubber and sulfur. Vulcanized rubber was soon being used for shoes and other products, and in the Civil War balloons made of this new, stronger rubber carried Union spies over the Confederate armies. The material's importance increased greatly over the years, and today vulcanized rubber remains in use for automobile tires and numerous other products.

Quiz

Fill in each blank with the correct letter:

a.	Promethean	e.	Sisyphean
b.	titanic	f.	vulcanize
c.	Triton	g.	cereal
d.	Junoesque	h.	martial

1. For a mother of nine, laundry and ironing can seem _____ in their endlessness and drudgery.
2. One clear and beautiful morning, a series of _____ waves swept the entire village into the sea.
3. The aging jazz singer acquired a certain _____ quality in her mature years.
4. On each arm of the great candelabra was carved a _____ blowing on his conch.
5. Corn, unknown in ancient Europe, has become a staple _____ of the modern world.
6. When Goodyear discovered how to _____ rubber, he made Henry Ford's Model T possible.
7. In some ways, Edison's mind may have been the most _____ since Leonardo da Vinci's.
8. The _____ arts of the Far East have become popular in the West as means of self-defense.

Review Quizzes

A. Indicate whether the following pairs of words have the same or different meanings:

1. aquamarine / navy blue   same ___ / different ___
2. subterranean / underground   same ___ / different ___
3. physiology / sports medicine   same ___ / different ___
4. disrepute / disgrace   same ___ / different ___
5. empathy / sentimentality   same ___ / different ___
6. Junoesque / slender   same ___ / different ___
7. Promethean / creative   same ___ / different ___
8. penance / regret   same ___ / different ___
9. mariner / sailor   same ___ / different ___
10. pathos / anger   same ___ / different ___
11. titanic / powerful   same ___ / different ___
12. vulcanize / organize   same ___ / different ___
13. terrestrial / earthly   same ___ / different ___
14. impunity / freedom from harm   same ___ / different ___
15. penal / legal   same ___ / different ___
16. matrix / puzzle   same ___ / different ___
17. marina / dock   same ___ / different ___
18. putative / natural   same ___ / different ___
19. terrarium / garden   same ___ / different ___
20. apathetic / indifferent   same ___ / different ___

B. Choose the word that does not belong:

1. Sisyphean   a. difficult b. unending c. demanding
   d. rolling
2. maternity   a. femininity b. parenthood
   c. motherliness d. motherhood
3. mariner   a. sailor b. seaman c. crew member
   d. archer
4. cereal   a. corn b. eggplant c. rice d. barley
5. reputed   a. known b. reported c. believed d. thought
6. ideology   a. essay b. philosophy c. principles
   d. beliefs
7. punitive   a. disciplinary b. punishing
   c. correctional d. encouraging
8. empathy   a. fascination b. pity c. concern
   d. compassion

9. maritime   a. coastal   b. nautical   c. oceangoing
     d. lakeside

10. apathetic   a. unfortunate   b. unconcerned
     c. uncaring   d. uninterested

C. Match the definition on the right to the correct word on the left:

1.	impute	a.	fancy garden
2.	martial	b.	through the mother's line
3.	parterre	c.	assign
4.	maritime	d.	nautical
5.	penal	e.	related to war
6.	matrilineal	f.	disciplinary
7.	terrestrial	g.	procedure
8.	methodology	h.	earthly

UNIT

11

CANT, from the Latin verb *cantare*, meaning "sing," produces several words that come directly from Latin. But some others came to English by way of French, which added an *h* to the root, giving us such words as *chant* and *chantey*.

cantata \kən-ˈtä-tə\ A musical composition, particularly a religious work from the 17th or 18th century, for one or more voices accompanied by instruments.

- Composers of the 18th century composed sacred cantatas by the dozen, and Bach's friend G. P. Telemann actually wrote over a thousand.

A cantata is sung, unlike a sonata, which is played on instruments only. The most famous cantatas are by Johann Sebastian Bach, who wrote the music for about 200 religious cantatas, using hymns and new religious poems as his texts. His cantatas consisted of several different sections for different voices—solos, duets, and choruses. Some of his nonreligious cantatas have been performed like mini-operas.

incantation \ˌin-ˌkan-ˈtā-shən\ (1) A use of spells or verbal charms spoken or sung as part of a ritual of magic. (2) A formula of words used in, or as if in, such a ritual.

- He repeated the words slowly over and over like an incantation.

Incantation comes directly from the Latin word *incantare*, "enchant." *Incantare* itself has *cantare* as a root, which reminds us that magic and ritual have always been associated with chanting and music. Incantations have often been in strange languages; "Abracadabra" is a not-so-serious version of an incantation.

cantor \\'kan-tər\\ An official of a Jewish synagogue who sings or chants the music of the services and leads the congregation in prayer.

- The congregation waited for the cantor to begin the prayers before joining in.

The cantor is, after the rabbi, the most important figure in a Jewish worship service. A cantor not only must possess an excellent singing voice but also must know by heart long passages of Hebrew. Cantors such as Jan Peerce and Richard Tucker became international opera stars. The comedian and singer Edward Israel Iskowitz renamed himself Eddie Cantor for his original profession and became enormously popular on stage, screen, radio, and television for over 40 years.

descant \\'des-ˌkant\\ An additional melody sung above the principal melody.

- The soprano added a soaring descant to the final chorus that held the listeners spellbound.

The prefix *des-*, meaning "two" or "apart," indicates that the descant is a "second song" apart from the main melody. In popular songs a descant will often be sung at the very end to produce a thrilling climax.

LINGU comes from the Latin word that means both "tongue" and "language," and in English today *tongue* can still mean "language" (as in "her native tongue"). Our expression "slip of the tongue" is just a translation of the Latin phrase *lapsus linguae*. The root even shows up in a slangy-sounding word like *lingo*. And since *lingu-* changed to *langu-* in French, our word *language* is related as well.

---

linguistics \\liŋ-'gwi-ˌstiks\\ The study of human speech.

- The new speechwriter, who had majored in linguistics, was soon putting his knowledge of the deceptive tricks of language to good use.

Any analysis of language, including 8th-grade grammar, can be called linguistics. As recently as 200 years ago, ordinary grammar was about the only kind of linguistics there was. Today a *linguist* may be a person who learns foreign languages, but the term usually refers to people who devote themselves to analyzing the structure of language. Many linguists concentrate on the history of a language; others study the way children learn to speak; others analyze the sounds of a language—and still others just study English grammar, a subject so big that you could easily spend your entire life on it.

multilingual \məl-tē-'liŋ-gwəl\ Using or able to use several languages.

• She soon discovered that he was truly multilingual, fluent in not only the German and Polish he had grown up speaking but in English and Arabic as well.

The roots of *multilingual* come from Latin (see MULTI, p. 582). If you happen to prefer Greek, use the synonym *polyglot*, in which *poly-* has the same meaning as *multi-*, and *-glot* means the same thing as *-lingual*. The best way to become multilingual is probably to be born in a *bilingual* (two-language) household; learning those first two seems to give the mind the kind of exercise that makes later language-learning easy.

lingua franca \'liŋ-gwə-'fraŋ-kə\ A language used as a common or commercial language among peoples who speak different languages.

• That first evening in Tokyo, she heard English being spoken at the next table, and realized it was serving as a lingua franca for a party of Korean and Japanese businessmen.

In the Middle Ages, the Arabs of the eastern Mediterranean referred to all Europeans as Franks (the name of the tribe that once occupied the land we call France). Since there was plenty of Arab-European trade, the traders in the Mediterranean ports eventually developed a trading language combining Italian, Arabic, and other languages, which almost everyone could more or less understand, and it became known as the "Frankish language," or lingua franca. Some languages actually succeed in becoming lingua francas without changing much. So, when the Roman empire became vast and mighty, Latin became the important lingua franca; and at a meeting between Japanese and Vietnamese businesspeople today, English may well be the only language spoken.

linguine \lin-¹gwē-¹nē\ A narrow, flat pasta.

- As a test of her clients' table manners, she would serve them challenging dishes and watch to see how gracefully they could handle chopsticks or deal with long, slithery linguine.

The modern language closest to Latin is Italian, and the Italian word *linguine* means literally "little tongues." Linguine is only one of the types of pasta whose names describes their shapes. Others include *spaghetti* ("little strings"), *fettuccine* ("little ribbons"), *penne* ("little quills"), *orzo* ("barley"), *farfalle* ("butterflies"), *vermicelli* ("little worms"), *capellini* ("little hairs"), *fusilli* ("little spindles"), and *radiatori* ("little radiators"). If you're thinking about learning Italian, you could make a good start by just visiting an Italian restaurant.

Quizzes

A. Choose the closest definition:

1. descant   a. climb downward   b. added melody
       c. supposed inability   d. writing table
2. linguistics   a. language study   b. reading
       c. mouth surgery   d. tongue exercise
3. incantation   a. ritual chant   b. ceremony
       c. solemn march   d. recorded song
4. linguine   a. slang   b. pasta   c. Italian dessert
       d. common language
5. cantata   a. snack bar   b. pasta dish
       c. sung composition   d. farewell gesture
6. lingua franca   a. Old French   b. common language
       c. Italian casserole   d. French coin
7. cantor   a. singer   b. refusal   c. traitor   d. gallop
8. multilingual   a. highly varied   b. in separate parts
       c. born with multiple tongues   d. fluent in several
   languages

B. Indicate whether the following pairs of words have the same or different meanings:

1. lingua franca / pasta dish   same ___ / different ___
2. incantation / sacred dance   same ___ / different ___
3. linguine / Italian language   same ___ / different ___
4. descant / enchant   same ___ / different ___

5. linguistics / science of singing   same __ / different __
6. cantata / sonata   same __ / different __
7. cantor / conductor   same __ / different __
8. multilingual / using
   several fingers   same __ / different __

SPIR comes from the Latin words meaning "breath" and "breathe." When we *inspire* others—that is, give them *inspiration*—it's as though we're breathing new energy and imagination into them. When you *expire*, or die, you "breathe out" your soul in your last breath. A license, membership, credit card, or free offer may also expire, at a time indicated by its *expiration* date.

spirited \'spir-ə-təd\ Full of energy or courage; very lively or determined.

• The team put up a spirited defense, but they were doomed from the start.

You may see *spirited* used to describe a conversation, a debate, a horse, or a campaign. And it often shows up in such words as *high-spirited* ("bold and energetic"), *mean-spirited* ("spiteful"), and *public-spirited* ("generous to a community"), all of which reflect the original meaning of *spirit*, a notion much like "soul" or "personality."

dispiriting \di-'spir-ə-tiŋ\ Causing a loss of hope or enthusiasm.

• It was terribly dispiriting for them to lose yet another game, and he had to reassure his daughter that she'd actually done a great job as goalie.

Lots of things can be dispiriting: a bad job interview, an awful film, a relationship going sour. Maybe for that reason, *dispiriting* has lots of synonyms: *discouraging, disheartening, demoralizing, depressing*, etc.

respirator \'re-spə-ˌrā-tər\ (1) A device worn over the nose and mouth to filter out dangerous substances from the air. (2) A device for maintaining artificial respiration.

- His lungs had been terribly damaged by decades of heavy smoking, and he'd been living on a respirator for the last year.

Respiration means simply "breathing." We usually come across the word in *artificial respiration,* the lifesaving technique in which you force air into the lungs of someone who's stopped breathing. Respirators can take several different forms. Scuba-diving equipment always includes a respirator, though it doesn't actually do the breathing for the diver. Medical respirators, which are used especially for babies and for emergency care and actually take over the job of getting oxygen into the lungs, are today usually called ventilators, so as to distinguish them from simple oxygen systems (which merely provide a steady flow of oxygen into the nostrils) and face masks.

transpire \tran-'spīr\ (1) To happen. (2) To become known.

- We kept up our questioning, and it soon transpired that the boys had known about the murder all along.

Since the prefix *trans-* means "through" (see TRANS, p. 626), *transpire*'s most literal meaning is something like "breathe through." Thus, the original meaning of the English word—still used today—is to give off a watery vapor through a surface such as a leaf. From there, it came to mean also the gradual appearance of previously secret information, as if leaking out of the pores of a leaf (as in "It transpired that she was not only his employee but also his girlfriend"). And soon it was being used to mean simply "happen" (as in "I wondered what had transpired in the cafeteria at lunchtime").

VER comes from the Latin word for "truth." A *verdict* in a trial is "the truth spoken" (see DICT, p. 272). But a just verdict may depend on the *veracity,* or "truthfulness," of the witnesses.

---

verify \'ver-ə-ˌfī\ (1) To prove to be true or correct. (2) To check or test the accuracy of.

- It is the bank teller's job to verify the signature on a check.

During talks between the United States and the former Soviet Union on nuclear weapons reduction, one big problem was how to verify that weapons had been eliminated. Since neither side wanted the other to know its secrets, *verification* of the facts became a difficult issue. Because of the distrust on both sides, many doubted that the real numbers would ever be *verifiable*.

aver \ə-ˈvər\ To state positively as true; declare.

• The defendant averred that she was nowhere near the scene of the crime on the night in question.

Since *aver* contains the "truth" root, it basically means "confirm as true." You may aver anything that you're sure of. In legal situations, *aver* means to state positively as a fact; thus, Perry Mason's clients aver that they are innocent, while the district attorney avers the opposite. If you make such a statement while under oath, and it turns out that you lied, you may have committed the crime of perjury.

verisimilitude \ˌver-ə-sə-ˈmi-lə-ˌtüd\ (1) The appearance of being true or probable. (2) The depiction of realism in art or literature.

• By the beginning of the 20th century, the leading European painters were losing interest in verisimilitude and beginning to experiment with abstraction.

From its roots, *verisimilitude* means basically "similarity to the truth." Most fiction writers and filmmakers aim at some kind of verisimilitude to give their stories an air of reality. They need not show something actually true, or even very common, but simply something believable. A mass of good details in a play, novel, painting, or film may add verisimilitude. A spy novel without some verisimilitude won't interest many readers, but a fantastical novel may not even attempt to seem true to life.

veracity \və-ˈra-sə-tē\ (1) Truth or accuracy. (2) The quality of being truthful or honest.

• We haven't been able to check the veracity of most of his story, but we know he wasn't at the motel that night.

People often claim that a frog placed in cold water that then is gradually heated will let itself be boiled to death, but the story actually lacks veracity. We often hear that the Eskimo (Inuit) peoples have dozens of words for "snow," but the veracity of the statement is doubtful, since Eskimo languages seem to have no more snow words than English (with *flake, blizzard, powder, drift, freezing rain,* etc.). In 2009 millions accepted the veracity of the claim that, against all the evidence, the elected president wasn't a native-born American. Not all the "facts" we accept without thinking are harmless.

Quizzes

A. Fill in each blank with the correct letter:

a. transpire   e. spirited
b. aver   f. veracity
c. respirator   g. dispiriting
d. verify   h. verisimilitude

1. Maybe some new information will _____ when they question the family tomorrow.

2. The company was doing badly, and she'd been having problems with her boss, so all in all it had been a _____ week at work.

3. The prosecutor expected the witness to _____ that the suspect was guilty.

4. Critics complained about the lack of _____ in his crime writing, saying it sounded as if he'd never even been inside a police station.

5. There's always a _____ exchange of opinions around the Thanksgiving table, but nobody ever takes offense.

6. His father has been living on a _____ for the last two weeks, but now his lungs seem to be improving.

7. She was never able to _____ anything he had told her about his past.

8. The boys claim they never went near the river that afternoon, but we suspect their _____.

B. Complete the analogy:

1. believe : doubt :: aver : _____
   a. state b. mean c. deny d. subtract

2. transfer : hand over :: transpire : _____
   a. breathe out b. cross c. encourage d. come to light

3. illusion : fantasy :: verisimilitude : _____
   a. appearance b. realism c. style d. proof

4. gloomy : glum :: spirited : _____
   a. spiraling b. alcoholic c. lively d. complex

5. loyalty : treason :: veracity : _____
   a. dishonesty b. truthfulness c. ideals d. safekeeping

6. exciting : thrilling :: dispiriting : _____
   a. dreary b. calming c. relaxing d. soothing

7. praise : ridicule :: verify : _____
    a. testify b. contradict c. establish d. foretell
8. pacemaker : heart :: respirator : _____
    a. kidneys b. brain c. liver d. lungs

TURB comes from the Latin verb *turbare,* "to throw into confusion or upset," and the noun *turba,* "crowd" or "confusion." So a *disturbance,* for example, confuses and upsets normal order or routine.

---

turbid \'tər-bid\ (1) Thick or murky, especially with churned-up sediment. (2) Unclear, confused, muddled.

• The mood of the crowd was restless and turbid, and any spark could have turned them into a mob.

The Colorado River in spring, swollen by melting snow from the high mountains, races through the Grand Canyon, turbid and churning. A chemical solution may be described as turbid rather than clear. And your emotions may be turbid as well, especially where love is involved: What did he mean by that glance? Why did she say it like that?

perturb \pər-'tərb\ To upset, confuse, or disarrange.

• News of the new peace accord was enough to perturb some radical opponents of any settlements.

With its *per-* prefix, *perturb* meant originally "thoroughly upset," though today the word has lost most of its intense edge. *Perturb* and *perturbation* are often used by scientists, usually when speaking of a change in their data indicating that something has affected some normal process. When someone is referred to as *imperturbable*, it means he or she manages to remain calm through the most trying experiences.

turbine \'tər-₁bīn\ A rotary engine with blades made to turn and generate power by a current of water, steam, or air under pressure.

• The power plant used huge turbines powered by water going over the dam to generate electricity.

The oldest and simplest form of turbine is the waterwheel, which is made to rotate by water falling across its blades and into buckets suspended from them. Hero of Alexandria invented the first steam-driven turbine in the 1st century A.D., but a commercially practical steam turbine wasn't developed until 1884; steam turbines are now the main elements of electric power stations. Jet engines are gas turbines. A *turbojet* engine uses a turbine to compress the incoming air that feeds the engine before being ejected to push the plane forward; a *turboprop* engine uses its exhaust to drive a turbine that spins a propeller. A wind turbine generates electricity by being turned by the wind; the largest now have vanes with a turning diameter of over 400 feet.

turbulent \'tər-byü-lənt\ (1) Stirred up, agitated. (2) Stirring up unrest, violence, or disturbance.

• The huge ocean liner *Queen Elizabeth II* was never much troubled by turbulent seas that might have sunk smaller boats.

Some people lead turbulent lives, and some are constantly in the grip of turbulent emotions. The late 1960s are remembered as turbulent years of social revolution in America and Europe. Often the captain of an airplane will warn passengers to fasten their seatbelts because of upper-air *turbulence,* which can make for a bumpy ride. El Niño, a seasonal current of warm water in the Pacific Ocean, may create turbulence in the winds across the United States, affecting patterns of rainfall and temperature as well.

VOLU/VOLV comes from the Latin verb *volvere,* meaning "to roll, wind, turn around, or twist around." Thus, *revolve* simply means "turn in circles." And a *volume* was originally a scroll or roll of papyrus.

---

voluble \'väl-yù-bəl\ Speaking readily and rapidly; talkative.

• He proved to be a voluble informer who would tell stories of bookies, smugglers, and hit men to the detectives for hours.

A voluble person has words "rolling" off his or her tongue. In O. Henry's famous story "The Ransom of Red Chief," the kidnappers nab a boy who turns out to be so unbearably voluble that they can hardly wait to turn him loose again.

devolve \di-'välv\ (1) To pass (responsibility, power, etc.) from one person or group to another person or group at a lower level of authority. (2) To gradually go from an advanced state to a less advanced state.

- Since 1998, considerable power has been devolving from the British government in London to the new Scottish Parliament in Edinburgh.

With its *de-* prefix (see DE-, p. 601), *devolution* implies moving backward. Once powers have been centralized in a unified government, giving any powers back—that is, devolving the power—to a smaller governmental unit can seem to be reversing a natural development. In a somewhat similar way, a job that your boss doesn't want to do may devolve upon you. But *devolve* and *devolution* are also treated nowadays as the opposites of *evolve* and *evolution*. So we may also speak of moral devolution, such as occurred in Germany in the 1930s, when a country with an extraordinary culture became a brutal dictatorship. And parents may watch their slacker teenager and wonder if devolution is occurring right in front of their eyes.

evolution \ˌe-və-ˈlü-shən\ A process of change from a lower, simpler, or worse state to one that is higher, more complex, or better.

- Thomas Jefferson and the other Founding Fathers believed that political evolution reached its highest form in democracy.

Part of the humor of the old *Flintstones* cartoon show is that it contradicts what is known about biological evolution, since humans actually *evolved* long after dinosaurs were extinct. *Evolution* can also be used more broadly to refer to technology, society, and other human creations. For example, an idea may evolve, even in your own mind, as the months or years pass. And though many people don't believe that human beings truly become better with the passing centuries, many will argue that our societies tend to evolve, producing more goods and providing more protection for more people.

convoluted \ˈkän-və-ˌlü-təd\ (1) Having a pattern of curved windings. (2) Involved, intricate.

- After 10 minutes, Mr. Collins's strange story had become so convoluted that none of us could follow it.

Convolution originally meant a complex winding pattern such as those visible on the surface of the brain. So a convoluted argument or a convoluted explanation is one that winds this way and that. An official document may have to wind its way through a convoluted process and be stamped by eight people before being approved. Convoluted language makes many people suspicious; as a great philosopher once said, "Anything that can be said can be said clearly."

Quizzes

A. **Choose the closest definition:**

1. convoluted   a. spinning b. babbling c. grinding
   d. winding
2. turbine   a. whirlpool b. engine c. headdress
   d. carousel
3. evolution   a. process of development b. process of
   democracy c. process of election d. process of
   elimination
4. perturb   a. reset b. inset c. preset d. upset
5. voluble   a. whirling b. unpleasant c. talkative
   d. garbled
6. turbulent   a. churning b. turning c. yearning
   d. burning
7. turbid   a. flat b. calm c. confused d. slow
8. devolve   a. hand down b. hand in c. turn up
   d. turn around

B. **Match the word on the left to the correct definition on the right:**

1. voluble   a. murky
2. turbine   b. chatty
3. evolution   c. seething
4. turbid   d. complicated
5. devolve   e. turning engine
6. perturb   f. degenerate
7. convoluted   g. disturb
8. turbulent   h. progress

FAC comes from the Latin verb *facere,* meaning "to make or do." Thus, a *fact* was originally simply "something done." A *benefactor* is someone who does good. And to *manufacture* is to make, usually in a *factory.*

factor \\'fak-tər\ Something that contributes to producing a result: ingredient.

- The most important factor in the success of the treaty talks was the physical presence of the two presidents.

In Latin *factor* means simply "doer." So in English a factor is an "actor" or element or ingredient in some situation or quantity. Charm can be a factor in someone's success, and lack of exercise can be a factor in producing a poor physique. In math we use *factor* to mean a number that can be multiplied or divided to produce a given number (for example, 5 and 8 are factors of 40). And in biology a gene may be called a factor, since genes are ingredients in the total organism.

factotum \fak-'tō-təm\ A person whose job involves doing many different kinds of work.

- Over the years she had become the office factotum, who might be doing legal research one day and organizing the company picnic the next.

This odd word doesn't come from ancient Latin, but it was coined to look as if it did. The term *Johannes factotum*, meaning "Jack-of-all-trades," first shows up in writing in 1592 to describe none other than Shakespeare himself. The word *gofer* is similar to *factotum* but a bit less dignified. In other words, a factotum is an assistant, but one who may have taken over some fairly important functions.

facile \\'fa-səl\ (1) Easily accomplished. (2) Shallow, superficial.

- The principal made a facile argument for the school's policy, but no one was convinced.

A facile suggestion doesn't deal with the issue in any depth, and a facile solution may be only temporarily effective. A facile writer is one who seems to write too quickly and easily, and a careful reader may discover that the writer hasn't really said very much.

facilitate \fə-'si-lə-ˌtāt\ To make (something) easier; to make (something) run more smoothly.

- Her uncle hadn't exactly gotten her the job, but he had certainly facilitated the process.

Facilitating is about getting things done. Clever employees are quietly facilitating all kinds of useful activity within their organizations all the time. People who lead therapy groups or workshops are often called *facilitators*, since their job isn't to teach or to order but rather to make the meetings as productive as possible. Even businesses now use facilitators in meetings where they don't want any person's particular desires to outweigh anyone else's. The *facilitation* of a rewarding discussion should be a facilitator's only goal. Today, in recognition of the many different situations that may call for a facilitator, there is even an International Association of Facilitators.

LUM comes from the Latin noun *lumen*, meaning "light." Thus, our word *illuminate* means "to supply with light" or "make clear," and *illumination* is light that shines on something.

---

lumen \\'lü-mən\\ In physics, the standard unit for measuring the rate of the flow of light.

• The lumen is a measure of the perceived power of light.

There are two common units for measuring light, the candela and the lumen. Both are recognized as standard international units, which also include the second (for time), the kilogram (for weight), and the meter (for length). The *candela* is a measure of intensity; an ordinary candle gives off light with the intensity of about one candela. The lumen is a measure of "luminous flux"; a standard 100-watt lightbulb gives off 1500–1700 lumens. Luminous flux indicates how much light is actually perceived by the human eye. Technologies vary in how efficiently they turn electricity into light; halogen lights produce about 12 lumens per watt, ordinary incandescent lightbulbs produce about 15 lumens per watt, and compact fluorescent bulbs produce about 50 lumens per watt.

luminous \\'lü-mə-nəs\\ (1) Producing or seeming to produce light. (2) Filled with light.

• She ended her recital with a luminous performance of Ravel's song cycle, and the crowd called her back for repeated encores.

Luminous, like its synonyms *radiant, shining, glowing,* and *lustrous*, is generally a positive adjective, especially when it describes something that doesn't literally glow, such as a face, a performance, or a poem. Luminous signs depend on a gas such as neon, krypton, argon, xenon, or radon—and you can use luminous (DayGlo) paint to make your own signs. New technologies have now given us luminous fabrics, which are being used to produce striking or creepy effects in clothing, upholstery, and interior surfaces.

bioluminescent \ˌbī-ō-ˌlü-mə-ˈne-sᵊnt\ Relating to light given off by living organisms.

- Most of the light emitted by bioluminescent marine organisms is blue or blue-green.

Bio- comes from the Greek word for "life" (see BIO, p. 407). On land, fireflies, glowworms, and the fox-fire fungus are all known for their *bioluminescence*. In the sea, bioluminescent life-forms include plankton, squid, and comb jellies, as well as some unusual fish. Most deep-sea animals are bioluminescent, but single-celled algae living at or near the surface can also create a remarkable show, as they often do in Bioluminescent Bay on the Puerto Rican island of Vieques. But bioluminescence is unknown in true plants, and mammals, birds, reptiles, and amphibians never got the knack of it either.

luminary \ˈlü-mə-ˌner-ē\ A very famous or distinguished person.

- Entering the glittering reception room, she immediately spotted several luminaries of the art world.

The Latin word *luminaria* could mean either "lamps" or "heavenly bodies." For medieval astrologers, the luminaries were the sun and the moon, the brightest objects in the heavens. Today a luminary is usually a person of "brilliant" achievement: a celebrity, a "leading light," or a "star."

Quizzes

A. Fill in each blank with the correct letter:

a. lumen
b. bioluminescent
c. luminary
d. luminous

e. facile
f. factor
g. factotum
h. facilitate

1. The light output of an ordinary candle provided the basis for the light unit called the _____ .
2. Her _____ voice was all the critics could talk about in their reviews of the musical's opening night.

3. She was quick-witted, but her reasoning was often _____ and not deeply thoughtful.
4. The _____ insects that he studies use their light for mating.
5. The support of the financial industry would greatly _____ the passage of the bill.
6. He had just been introduced to another _____ of the literary world and was feeling rather dazzled.
7. The main _____ in their decision to build was their desire for a completely "green" home.
8. As the company's _____, she often felt overworked and underappreciated.

B. Indicate whether the following pairs of words have the same or different meanings:

1. facilitate / ease   same ___ / different ___
2. lumen / lighting   same ___ / different ___
3. factor / element   same ___ / different ___
4. luminary / star   same ___ / different ___
5. factotum / expert   same ___ / different ___
6. luminous / glowing   same ___ / different ___
7. facile / practical   same ___ / different ___
8. bioluminescent / brilliant same ___ / different ___

Words from Mythology and History

muse \\'myüz\\ A source of inspiration; a guiding spirit.

• At 8:00 each morning he sat down at his desk and summoned his muse, and she almost always responded.

The Muses were the nine Greek goddesses who presided over the arts (including *music*) and literature. A shrine to the Muses was called in Latin a *museum*. An artist or poet about to begin work would call on his particular Muse to inspire him, and a poem itself might begin with such a call; thus, Homer's *Odyssey* begins, "Sing to me of the man, Muse" (that is, of Odysseus). Today a muse may be one's special creative spirit, but some artists and writers have also chosen living human beings to serve as their muses.

iridescent \\ˌir-ə-'de-sənt\\ Having a glowing, rainbowlike play of color that seems to change as the light shifts.

- The children shrieked with glee as the iridescent soap bubbles floated away in the gentle breeze.

Iris, the Greek goddess of the rainbow, took messages from Mount Olympus to earth, and from gods to mortals or other gods, using the rainbow as her stairway. *Iridescence* is thus the glowing, shifting, colorful quality of a rainbow, also seen in an opal, a light oil slick, a butterfly wing, or the mother-of-pearl that lines an oyster shell.

mausoleum \ˌmȯ-zə-ˈlē-əm\ (1) A large tomb, especially one built aboveground with shelves for the dead. (2) A large, gloomy building or room.

- The family's grand mausoleum occupied a prominent spot in the cemetery, for all the good it did the silent dead within.

Mausolus was ruler of a kingdom in Asia Minor in the 4th century B.C. He beautified the capital, Halicarnassus, with all sorts of fine public buildings, but he is best known for the magnificent monument, the Mausoleum, that was built by his wife Artemisia after his death. With its great height (perhaps 140 feet) and many beautiful sculptures, the Mausoleum was declared one of the Seven Wonders of the Ancient World. Though Halicarnassus was repeatedly attacked, the Mausoleum would survive for well over 1,000 years.

mentor \ˈmen-ˌtȯr\ A trusted counselor, guide, tutor, or coach.

- This pleasant old gentleman had served as friend and mentor to a series of young lawyers in the firm.

Odysseus was away from home fighting and journeying for 20 years, according to Homer. During that time, the son he left as a babe in arms grew up under the supervision of Mentor, an old and trusted friend. When the goddess Athena decided it was time to complete young Telemachus's education by sending him off to learn about his father, she visited him disguised as Mentor and they set out together. Today, anyone such as a coach or tutor who gives another (usually younger) person help and advice on how to achieve success in the larger world is called a mentor. And in recent years we've even been using the word as a verb, and now in business we often speak of an experienced employee *mentoring* someone who has just arrived.

narcissism \ˈnär-si-ˌsi-zəm\ (1) Extreme self-centeredness or fascination with oneself. (2) Love or desire for one's own body.

- His girlfriend would complain about his narcissism, saying he spent more time looking at himself in the mirror than at her.

Narcissus was a handsome youth in Greek mythology who inspired love in many who saw him. One was the nymph Echo, who could only repeat the last thing that anyone said. When Narcissus cruelly rejected her, she wasted away to nothing but her voice. Though he played with the affections of others, Narcissus became a victim of his own attractiveness. When he caught sight of his own reflection in a pool, he sat gazing at it in fascination, wasting away without food or drink, unable to touch or kiss the image he saw. When he finally died, the gods turned him into the flower we call the *narcissus*, which stands with its head bent as though gazing at its reflection. People with "*narcissistic* personality disorder" have a somewhat serious mental condition, according to psychologists, but the rest of us are free to call anyone who seems vain and self-centered a *narcissist*.

tantalize \\'tan-tə-ˌlīz\\ To tease or torment by offering something desirable but keeping it out of reach.

- The sight of a warm fire through the window tantalized the little match girl almost unbearably.

King Tantalus, according to Greek mythology, killed his son Pelops and served him to the gods in a stew for dinner. Almost all the gods realized what was happening and refused the meal, though only after Demeter had taken a nibble out of Pelops's shoulder. After they had reconstructed him, replacing the missing shoulder with a piece of ivory, they turned to punishing Tantalus. In Hades he stands in water up to his neck under a tree laden with fruit. Each time he stoops to drink, the water moves out of reach; each time he reaches up to pick something, the branches move beyond his grasp. He is thus eternally tantalized by the water and fruit. Today anything or anyone that tempts but is unobtainable is tantalizing.

thespian \\'thes-pē-ən\\ An actor.

- In summer the towns of New England welcome troupes of thespians dedicated to presenting plays of all kinds.

Greek drama was originally entirely performed by choruses. According to tradition, the Greek dramatist Thespis, of the 6th century B.C., was the inventor of tragedy and the first to write roles for the individual actor as distinct from the chorus, and the actor's exchanges with the chorus were the first dramatic dialogue. Since

Thespis himself performed the individual parts in his own plays, he was also the first true actor. Ever since choruses disappeared from drama, thespians have filled all the roles in plays. *Thespian* is also an adjective; thus, we can speak of "thespian ambitions" and "thespian traditions," for example.

zephyr \\ˈze-fər\\ (1) A breeze from the west. (2) A gentle breeze.

• Columbus left Genoa sailing against the zephyrs that continually blow across the Mediterranean.

The ancient Greeks called the west wind Zephyrus and regarded him and his fellows—Boreas (god of the north wind), Eurus (god of the east wind), and Notus (god of the south wind)—as gods. A zephyr is a kind wind, bringer of clear skies and beautiful weather.

Quiz

Fill in each blank with the correct letter:

a. mausoleum	e. muse
b. thespian	f. mentor
c. iridescent	g. zephyr
d. tantalize	h. narcissism

1. At the middle of the cemetery stood the grand _____ of the city's wealthiest family.
2. On fair days a gentle _____ would blow from morning until night.
3. The company president took the new recruit under her wing and acted as her _____ for the next several years.
4. He would often _____ her with talk of traveling to Brazil or India, but nothing ever came of it.
5. The oil slick on the puddle's surface became beautifully _____ in the slanting light.
6. After his last book of poetry was published, his _____ seemed to have abandoned him.
7. In everyone there is a bit of the _____ yearning for a stage.
8. By working as a model, she could satisfy her _____ while getting paid for it.

Review Quizzes

A. Choose the correct definition:

1. voluble   a. argumentative b. mumbly c. speechless
   d. talkative
2. facilitate   a. guide b. build c. order d. obstruct
3. verify   a. reverse b. mislead c. prove d. test
4. zephyr   a. stormy blast b. icy rain c. light shower
   d. gentle breeze
5. aver   a. reject b. detract c. deny d. assert
6. turbulent   a. unending b. swirling c. muddy d. angry
7. facile   a. tough b. quiet c. familiar d. easy
8. perturb   a. soothe b. restore c. park d. upset
9. devolve   a. decay b. turn into c. suggest d. improve
10. convoluted   a. disorderly b. complex c. discouraged
    d. superior
11. muse   a. singer b. poetry c. inspiration d. philosopher
12. tantalize   a. visit b. satisfy c. tease d. watch
13. iridescent   a. shimmering b. drab c. striped d. watery
14. mentor   a. translator b. interpreter c. guide d. student
15. factotum   a. manufacturer b. untruth c. dilemma
    d. assistant

**B. Indicate whether the following pairs of terms have
the same or different meanings:**

1. thespian / teacher   same __ / different __
2. facile / handy   same __ / different __
3. evolution / extinction   same __ / different __
4. verify / prove   same __ / different __
5. turbine / plow   same __ / different __
6. spirited / energetic   same __ / different __
7. incantation / chant   same __ / different __
8. turbid / muddy   same __ / different __
9. transpire / ooze   same __ / different __
10. aver / claim   same __ / different __

C. Fill in each blank with the correct letter:

a. lingua franca   g. facilitate
b. narcissism   h. linguistics
c. descant   i. cantor
d. verisimilitude   j. devolve
e. cantata   k. turbine
f. veracity   l. mausoleum

1. The defense lawyers knew the jury might be doubtful about the next witness's _____.

2. They were a very attractive couple, but their _____ often annoyed other people.

3. The university chorus was going to perform a Bach _____ along with the Mozart *Requiem*.

4. They finally realized they would need a real-estate agent to _____ the sale of the property.

5. He began his singing career as a _____ in Brooklyn and ended it as an international opera star.

6. She had hired a highly experienced deputy, hoping to _____ many of her responsibilities onto him.

7. One day in the cemetery the _____ door was open, and he peered in with horrified fascination.

8. Never having studied _____, he didn't feel able to discuss word histories in much depth.

9. The Spaniards and Germans at the next table were using English as a _____.

10. Her films showed her own reality, and she had no interest in _____.

11. The roar of the _____ was so loud they couldn't hear each other.

12. As part of their musical training, she always encouraged them to sing their own _____ over the main melody.

UNIT

12

UMBR comes from the Latin *umbra,* meaning "shadow." Thus, the familiar *umbrella,* with its ending meaning "little," casts a "little shadow" to keep off the sun or the rain.

---

umber \\'əm-bər\ (1) A darkish brown mineral containing manganese and iron oxides used for coloring paint. (2) A color that is greenish brown to dark reddish brown.

• Van Dyke prized umber as a pigment and used it constantly in his oil paintings.

The mineral deposits of Italy provided sources of a number of natural pigments, among them umber. Since the late Renaissance, umber has been in great demand as a coloring agent. When crushed and mixed with paint, it produces an olive color known as *raw umber;* when crushed and burnt, it produces a darker tone known as *burnt umber.*

adumbrate \\'a-dəm-brāt\ (1) To give a sketchy outline or disclose in part. (2) To hint at or foretell.

• The Secretary of State would only adumbrate his ideas for bringing peace to Bosnia.

A synonym for *adumbrate* is *foreshadow,* which means to present a shadowy version of something before it becomes reality or is provided in full. Tough questioning by a Supreme Court justice may adumbrate the way he or she is planning to rule on a case. A bad review by a critic may adumbrate the failure of a new film. And rats scurrying off a ship were believed to adumbrate a coming disaster at sea.

penumbra \pə-'nəm-brə\ (1) The partial shadow surrounding a complete shadow, as in an eclipse. (2) The fringe or surrounding area where something exists less fully.

• This area of the investigation was the penumbra where both the FBI and the CIA wanted to pursue their leads.

Every solar eclipse casts an *umbra,* the darker central area in which almost no light reaches the earth, and a penumbra, the area of partial shadow where part of the sun is still visible. *Penumbra* can thus be used to describe any "gray area" where things aren't all black and white. For example, the right to privacy falls under the penumbra of the U.S. Constitution; though it isn't specifically guaranteed there, the Supreme Court has held that it is implied, and thus that the government may not intrude into certain areas of a citizen's private life. Because its existence is still shadowy, however, the Court is still determining how much of an individual's life is protected by the right to privacy.

umbrage \'əm-brij\ A feeling of resentment at some slight or insult, often one that is imagined rather than real.

• She often took umbrage at his treatment of her, without being able to pinpoint what was offensive about it.

An umbrage was originally a shadow, and soon the word also began to mean "a shadowy suspicion." Then it came to mean "displeasure" as well—that is, a kind of shadow blocking the sunlight. *Umbrage* is now generally used in the phrase "take umbrage at." An overly sensitive person may take umbrage at something as small as having his or her name pronounced wrong.

VEST comes from the Latin verb *vestire,* "to clothe" or "to dress," and the noun *vestis,* "clothing" or "garment." *Vest* is the shortest English word we have from this root, and is the name of a rather small piece of clothing.

---

divest \dī-'vest\ (1) To get rid of or free oneself of property, authority, or title. (2) To strip of clothing, ornaments, or equipment.

- In protest against apartheid, many universities in the 1980s divested themselves of all stock in South African companies.

If you decide to enter a monastery, you may divest yourself of most of your possessions. When a church is officially abandoned, it's usually divested of its ornaments and furnishings. A company that's going through hard times may divest itself of several stores, and investors are constantly divesting themselves of stocks that aren't performing well enough. And when it turns out that athletes have been using steroids, they're usually divested of any awards they may have won.

investiture \in-'ves-tə-ˌchùr\ The formal placing of someone in office.

- At an English monarch's investiture, he or she is presented with the crown, scepter, and sword, the symbols of power.

In its original meaning, an *investiture* was the clothing of a new officeholder in garments that symbolized power. The Middle Ages saw much debate over the investiture of bishops by kings and emperors. These rulers felt that high religious offices were theirs to give as rewards for someone's loyal service or as bribes for someone's future support; the popes, on the other hand, regarded these investitures as the improper buying and selling of church offices. The investiture struggle caused tension between popes and monarchs and even led to wars.

transvestite \tranz-'ves-ˌtīt\ A person, especially a male, who wears clothes designed for the opposite sex.

- In Handel's operas, the heroic male leading roles are today often sung by female transvestites, since he originally wrote them for the soprano range.

Transvestite includes the prefix *trans-*, "across," and thus means literally "cross-dresser" (and the word *cross-dresser* is in fact now commonly used in place of *transvestite*). In the theater, from ancient Greece to Elizabethan England, *transvestism* was common because all parts—even Juliet—were played by men. Traditional Japanese Kabuki and Noh drama still employ transvestism of this sort. In everyday life, women's clothing includes fashions so similar to men's fashions that both *transvestite* and *cross-dresser* are generally applied only to men. The much newer word *transgender* describes people whose gender identity differs from the sex they had or were identified as having at birth.

travesty \\'tra-vəs-tē\ (1) An inferior or distorted imitation. (2) A broadly comic imitation in drama, literature, or art that is usually grotesque and ridiculous.

• The senator was shouting that the new tax bill represented a travesty of tax reform.

The word *travesty* comes from the same prefix and root as *transvestite*. Since cross-dressing often isn't very convincing, the word has usually referred to something absurd. So a verdict that angers people may be denounced as a "travesty of justice." *Saturday Night Live* specializes in dramatic travesties mocking everything from political figures and issues to popular culture—"disguised" versions intended for entertainment. *Travesty* may also be a verb; thus, Mel Brooks has travestied movie genres of all kinds—westerns, thrillers, and silent films, among others.

Quizzes

A. Fill in the blank with the correct letter:

a. penumbra e. divest
b. transvestite f. umber
c. investiture g. umbrage
d. travesty h. adumbrate

1. All the pigments—crimson, russet, _____, cobalt blue, and the rest—were mixed by his assistants.
2. The _____ of the prime minister was an occasion of pomp and ceremony.
3. Some people are quick to take _____ the moment they think someone might have been disrespectful.
4. Since all the judges were cronies of the dictator, the court proceedings were a _____ of justice.
5. The new director planned to _____ the museum of two of its Picassos.
6. The farther away a source of light is from the object casting a shadow, the wider will be that shadow's _____.

7. The young model became a notorious success when she was discovered to be a _____.

8. The increasing cloudiness and the damp wind seemed to _____ a stormy night.

B. Match the definition on the left to the correct word on the right:

1. resentment   a. penumbra
2. brownish color   b. travesty
3. installing in office   c. transvestite
4. cross-dresser   d. adumbrate
5. bad imitation   e. divest
6. get rid of   f. umbrage
7. near shadow   g. investiture
8. partially disclose   h. umber

THE/THEO comes from the Greek word meaning "god." *Theology,* the study of religion, is practiced by *theologians. Monotheism* is the worship of a single god; Christianity, Islam, and Judaism are *monotheistic* religions, and all three worship the same god. *Polytheistic* religions such as those of ancient Greece and Rome, on the other hand, worship many gods.

---

apotheosis \ə-ˌpä-thē-ˈō-səs\ (1) Transformation into a god. (2) The perfect example.

• Abraham Lincoln's apotheosis after his assassination transformed the controversial politician into the saintly savior of his country.

In ancient Greece, historical figures were sometimes worshipped as gods. In Rome, apotheosis was rare until the emperor Augustus declared the dead Julius Caesar to be a god, and soon other dead emperors were being *apotheosized* as well. In older paintings you may see a heroic figure—Napoleon, George Washington, or Shakespeare, for example—being raised into the clouds, symbolizing his or her apotheosis. But today any great classic example of something can be called its apotheosis. You might hear it said, for example, that Baroque music reached its apotheosis in the works of J. S. Bach, or that the Duesenberg Phaeton was the apotheosis of the touring car.

atheistic \ˌā-thē-ˈis-tik\ Denying the existence of God or divine power.

- The atheistic Madalyn Murray O'Hair successfully sought the removal of prayer from American public schools in the 1960s.

In the Roman Empire, early Christians were called atheistic because they denied the existence of the Roman gods. And once the Christian church was firmly established, it condemned the Romans as *atheists* because they didn't believe in the Christian God. In later centuries, English-speaking Christians would often use the words *pagan* and *heathen* to describe such non-Christians, while *atheist* would be reserved for those who actually denied the existence of any god. *Atheism* is different from *agnosticism,* which claims that the existence of any higher power is unknowable; and lots of people who simply don't think much about religion often call themselves *agnostics* as well.

pantheon \ˈpan-thē-än\ (1) A building serving as the burial place of or containing memorials to the famous dead of a nation. (2) A group of notable persons or things.

- A Hall of Fame serves as a kind of pantheon for its field, and those admitted in the early years are often the greatest of all.

Each of the important Roman gods and goddesses had many temples erected in their name. But in 27 B.C. a temple to all the gods together was completed in Rome; twice destroyed, it was ultimately replaced by a third temple around A.D. 126. This extraordinary domed structure is still one of the important sights of Rome, and the burial place for the painters Raphael and Carracci and two kings. In Paris, a great church was completed in 1789–90; named the Panthéon, it was announced as the future resting place of France's great figures, and the bodies of Victor Hugo, Louis Pasteur, Marie Curie, and many others now rest within its walls.

theocracy \thē-ˈä-krə-sē\ (1) Government by officials who are regarded as divinely inspired. (2) A state governed by a theocracy.

- The ancient Aztecs lived in a theocracy in which guidance came directly from the gods through the priests.

In the Middle Ages, the Muslim empires stretching around much of the Mediterranean were theocracies, and the pope ruled most of modern-day Italy. But theocracies are rare today. Modern Iran and Saudi Arabia (and perhaps half a dozen others) are usually regarded as *theocratic* governments, since, even though Iran's president is elected by popular vote and Saudi Arabia is ruled by a royal family, the countries' laws are religious laws. But when a government tries to follow all the teachings of a single religion, things usually don't work out terribly well, so U.S. Constitution and Bill of Rights forbid using religion as the principal basis for democracy.

ICON comes from the Greek *eikon*, which led to the Latin *icon*, both meaning "image." Though the *icon-* root hasn't produced many English words, the words that is does appear in tend to be interesting.

---

icon \ˈī-ˌkän\ (1) A religious image usually painted on a small wooden panel: idol. (2) Emblem, symbol.

• Henry Ford's assembly line captured the imagination of the world, and he and his company became icons of industrial capitalism.

In the Eastern Orthodox church, much importance is given to icons, usually small portraits on wood—sometimes with gold-leaf paint—of Jesus, Mary, or a saint, which hang in churches and in the houses of the faithful. The Orthodox church favors icons partly because they communicate directly and forcefully even to uneducated people. They are regarded as sacred; some believers actually pray to them, and many believe that icons have carried out miracles. The common modern uses of *icon* grew out of this original sense. The fact that Orthodox icons have a symbolic role led to *icon* being used to mean simply "symbol." Because of the icon's sacredness, the term also came to mean "idol." And once we began to use *idol* to refer to pop-culture stars, it wasn't long before we began using *icon* the same way. But for the little computer-desktop images that you click on, the older meaning of "symbol" is the one we're thinking of.

iconic \ī-ˈkä-nik\ (1) Symbolic. (2) Relating to a greatly admired and successful person or thing.

• The 1963 March on Washington was the iconic event in the history of the civil-rights movement, now familiar to all American schoolchildren.

The original meaning of *iconic* was essentially "resembling an icon," but today it more often seems to mean "so admired that it could be the subject of an icon." And with that meaning, *iconic* has become part of the language of advertising and publicity; today companies and magazines and TV hosts are constantly encouraging us to think of some consumer item or pop star or show as first-rate or immortal or flawless—absolutely "iconic"—when he or she or it is actually nothing of the kind.

iconoclast \ī-'kä-nə-ˌklast\ (1) A person who destroys religious images or opposes their use. (2) A person who attacks settled beliefs or institutions.

• She's always rattling her friends by saying outrageous things, and she enjoys her reputation as an iconoclast.

When the early books of the Bible were being written, most of the other Middle Eastern religions had more than one god; these religions generally encouraged the worship of idols of the various gods, which were often regarded as magical objects. But in the Ten Commandments given to Moses in the Old Testament, God prohibits the making of "graven images" or "idols" for worship, proclaiming that the Jews are to worship only one God, who is too great to be represented in an idol. However, by the 6th century A.D., Christians had begun to create religious images in order to focus the prayers of the faithful. Opposition to icons led to the *Iconoclastic* Controversy in A.D. 726, when, supported by the pope, iconoclasts began smashing and burning the images in churches and monasteries (*clast-* comes from the Greek word meaning "to break"). In time, peace was restored, and almost all Christians have since accepted depictions of Jesus, Mary, and the saints. Today an iconoclast is someone who constantly argues with conventional thinking, refusing to "worship" the objects of everyone else's "faith."

iconography \ˌī-kə-'nä-grə-fē\ (1) The imagery and symbolism of a work of art or an artist. (2) The study of artistic symbolism.

• Today scholars pore over the advertisements in glossy magazines, studying the iconography for clues to the ads' hidden meanings.

If you saw a 17th-century painting of a man writing at a desk with a lion at his feet, would you know you were looking at St. Jerome, translator of the Bible, who, according to legend, once pulled a thorn from the paw of a lion, which thereafter became his devoted friend? And if a painting showed a young woman reclining on a bed with a shower of gold descending on her, would you recognize her as Danaë, locked up in a tower to keep her away from the lustful Zeus, who then managed to gain access to her by transforming himself into golden light (or golden coins)? An *iconographic* approach to art can make museum-going a lot of fun—and amateur *iconographers* know there are also plenty of symbols lurking in the images that advertisers bombard us with daily.

Quizzes

A. Fill in each blank with the correct letter:

a. pantheon	e. icon
b. iconic	f. apotheosis
c. atheistic	g. iconoclast
d. iconography	h. theocracy

1. Her personal ____ of actresses included Vanessa Redgrave, Helen Mirren, Emma Thompson, and Maggie Smith.
2. He enjoyed being an ____, since he had a lot of odd ideas and arguing suited his personality well.
3. His well-known ____ beliefs meant that he couldn't hope for great success in politics.
4. Thirty years later, his great speech was viewed as an ____ moment in modern American history.
5. Being inducted into the Hall of Fame is as close as a modern ballplayer can come to ____.
6. The strange ____ of the painting had caught her attention years ago, and she continued to puzzle over the obviously symbolic appearance of various odd objects.
7. They had come back from Russia with a beautiful ____ of Mary and another of St. Basil.
8. The high priest in this medieval ____ was equivalent to a dictator.

B. Match the word on the left to its definition on the right:

1. icon   a. state ruled by religion
2. pantheon   b. symbolic
3. apotheosis   c. symbol
4. iconography   d. nonbelieving
5. atheistic   e. artistic symbolism
6. iconoclast   f. hall of fame
7. theocracy   g. dissenter
8. iconic   h. perfect example

URB comes from the Latin noun for "city." Our word *urban* describes cities and the people who live in them. With its *sub-* prefix (see SUB, p. 455), a *suburb* is a town "near" or "under" a larger city, and *suburban* houses are home to *suburbanites.*

urbane \ˌər-ˈbān\ Sophisticated and with polished manners.

• He was remembered as a gentlemanly and urbane host of elegant dinner parties.

Urbane's synonyms include *suave, debonair,* and especially *cosmopolitan. Urbanity* was a trait of such classic movie stars as Fred Astaire, Cary Grant, William Powell, Leslie Howard, Charles Boyer, and George Sanders. (Notice that, for some reason, *urbane* is almost always used to describe men rather than women.) Teenagers in the 1960s read James Bond novels and watched his character onscreen to get tips about acquiring an urbane identity. But it's hard to acquire urbanity without actually having had wide social experience in sophisticated cities. And, since times have changed, the whole notion doesn't seem to attract young people quite the way it used to.

exurban \ek-ˈsər-bən\ Relating to a region or settlement that lies outside a city and usually beyond its suburbs and often is inhabited chiefly by well-to-do families.

• Exurban areas typically show much higher education and income levels than closer-in suburbs or nearby rural counties.

With its prefix *ex-*, ("outside of," the noun *exurb* was coined around 1955 to describe the ring of well-off communities beyond the suburbs that were becoming commuter towns for an urban area. Most exurbs were probably quiet little towns before being discovered by young city dwellers with good incomes looking for a pleasant place to raise their children. Planners, advertisers, and political strategists today often talk about such topics as exurban development, exurban trends, exurban migration, and exurban voters.

interurban \ˌin-tər-ˈər-bən\ Going between or connecting cities or towns.

• Businesspeople in the two cities have been waiting for decades for a true high-speed interurban railway on the Japanese model.

Interurban is generally used to describe transportation. As a noun (as in "In those days you could take the interurban from Seattle to Tacoma"), *interurban* has meant a fairly heavy but fast electric train, something between an urban trolley and a full-fledged long-distance train, that offers more frequent service than an ordinary railway. Interurban transit today may include bus, ferry, and limousine— and, in a few lucky areas, a regional railway. With oil supplies dwindling, there's hope that interurban railways will be coming back into wider use.

urbanization \ˌər-bə-nə-ˈzā-shən\ The process by which towns and cities are formed and become larger as more and more people begin living and working in central areas.

• The area has been undergoing rapid urbanization, and six or seven of the old small towns are now genuine suburbs.

The word *urbanization* started appearing in print way back in the 1880s, which says something about the growth of American cities. The expansion of Los Angeles was an early example of uncontrolled urbanization. Urbanization is often seen as a negative trend, with bad effects on quality of life and the environment. But apartments require much less heat than houses, and commuting by mass transit rather than cars can reduce pollution and energy use, and cities offer improved opportunities for jobs (and often for education and housing as well), so city growth doesn't make everyone unhappy.

CULT comes from the Latin *cultus*, meaning "care." So *cultivation* is care of something, such as a garden, in a way that encourages its growth. And *culture* is what is produced by cultivating human knowledge, skills, beliefs, manners, science, and art over many years.

acculturation \ə-ˌkəl-chə-ˈrā-shən\ (1) Modification of the culture of an individual, group, or people by adapting to or borrowing traits from another culture. (2) The process by which a human being acquires the culture of a particular society from infancy.

• The old Eastern European bagel has gone through an acculturation in America, where it has acquired a soft texture, a white interior, and fillers like eggs and peanut butter.

Whenever people come in close contact with a population that's more powerful, they're generally forced to *acculturate* in order to survive. Learning a new language is usually part of the acculturation process, which may also include adopting new clothing, a new diet, new occupations, and even a new religion. An older generation often fails to acculturate thoroughly, but their children often pick up the new ways quickly.

cross-cultural \ˈkròs-ˈkəlch-rəl\ Dealing with or offering comparison between two or more different cultures or cultural areas.

• A cross-cultural study of 49 tribes revealed a tight relationship between the closeness of mother-infant bonding in a given tribe and that tribe's peacefulness toward its neighbors.

If you've ever traveled in a foreign country, you've found yourself making some cross-cultural comparisons: Why are huge family dinners so much more common in Italy than back home? Why do Mexican teenagers seem to play with their little relatives so much more than teenagers in the U.S.? Cross-cultural analysis has produced extremely interesting data about such things as the effects of various nations' diets on their populations' health. Though *cross-cultural* was originally used by anthropologists to refer to research comparing aspects of different cultures, it's also often used to describe the reality that lots of us face daily while simply walking the streets of a big American city.

horticulture \ˈhòr-tə-ˌkəl-chər\ The science and art of growing fruits, vegetables, flowers, or ornamental plants.

- He considered majoring in botany, but has decided instead on horticulture, hoping he can spend more time in a greenhouse than in the library or the lab.

Hortus is Latin for "garden," and the first gardens were planted about 10,000 years ago in what is often called the Fertile Crescent—the crescent-shaped area stretching from Israel north through Syria and down Iraq's two great rivers to the Persian Gulf. Probably more fertile in previous centuries than it is today, it was the original home of such food plants as wheat, barley, peas, and lentils or their ancient ancestors (not to mention the ancestors of cows, pigs, sheep, and goats as well). Many *horticulturists* today work as researchers or plant breeders or tend orchards and greenhouses—but most American households contain at least one amateur horticulturist.

subculture \\'səb-ˌkəl-chər\ A group whose beliefs and behaviors are different from the main groups within a culture or society.

- Members of the emo subculture at her high school recognized each other by their skinny jeans, dyed hair, and canvas sneakers.

This common meaning of *subculture* (it has an older biological meaning) only appeared in the 1930s, and for about 20 years it was used mostly by sociologists, psychologists, and anthropologists. But in the 1950s, as America's wealth led to more and more teenagers getting their own cars and thus their independence, not to mention the arrival of rock 'n' roll, people noticed something unusual happening among young people, and began to speak of the "youth subculture." As the country's wealth and freedom of movement continued to increase, we realized that the U.S. had become home to a large number of subcultures. Today the Web makes possible more than anyone could have dreamed of back in the 1950s. When we happen to stumble on a subculture—bodybuilders, Trekkies, hackers, Airstreamers, anime lovers, motocross enthusiasts—we may realize with astonishment that we had never even imagined that it might exist.

Quizzes

A. Choose the closest definition:

1. cross-cultural   a. combining art and music b. between two or more cultures c. combining fruits and vegetables d. intensively cultivated
2. interurban   a. densely populated b. between cities c. from the inner city d. within the city
3. urbanization   a. moving to cities b. street construction c. becoming citylike d. mass transit
4. horticulture   a. intellectual knowledge b. science of growing plants c. animal science d. horse breeding
5. acculturation   a. developing cultural institutions b. turning woods into farmland c. acquiring aspects of another culture d. appreciation of music and dance
6. urbane   a. foolish b. old-fashioned c. dependable d. sophisticated
7. subculture   a. group within a culture b. cultivation below ground c. goth kids d. small garden
8. exurban   a. high-rise b. crowded c. above the city d. beyond the suburbs

B. Fill in each blank with the correct letter:

a. exurban   e. interurban
b. urbane   f. urbanization
c. acculturation   g. horticulture
d. cross-cultural   h. subculture

1. In their ____ home, 25 miles from the city, they looked out on a small field and woods.
2. ____ had proceeded swiftly over the previous ten years, and shopping malls had replaced the cozy streets of the old suburb.
3. A ____ study had revealed far greater levels of anxiety in middle-class Americans than in middle-class Scandinavians.
4. Their next-door neighbors were an ____ couple who threw lively parties where you could meet writers, artists, designers, and media people.
5. His wife's background in ____ led them to plant a large fruit orchard and build a huge greenhouse for flower cultivation.

6. After the island was acquired by Japan around 1910, the population began undergoing rapid ____, eventually giving up its native language.

7. In his teens he became part of a Web-based ____ whose members were devoted to raising poisonous reptiles.

8. ____ railways have begun making a comeback as city dwellers have become increasingly concerned about climate change.

DEM/DEMO comes from the Greek word meaning "people." "Government by the people" was invented by the ancient Greeks, so it's appropriate that they were the first to come up with a word for it: *demokratia*, or *democracy*.

---

demographic \ˌde-mə-ˈgra-fik\ Having to do with the study of human populations, especially their size, growth, density, and patterns of living.

• Each year the state government uses the most current demographic figures to determine how to distribute its funding for education.

Demographic analysis, the statistical description of human populations, is a tool used by government agencies, political parties, and manufacturers of consumer goods. Polls conducted on every topic imaginable, from age to toothpaste preference, give the government and corporations an idea of who the public is and what it needs and wants. The government's census, which is conducted every ten years, is the largest demographic survey of all. Today *demographic* is also being used as a noun; so, for example, TV advertisers are constantly worrying about how to appeal to "the 18-to-24-year-old demographic."

endemic \en-ˈde-mik\ (1) Found only in a given place or region. (2) Often found in a given occupation, area, or environment.

• Malaria remains endemic in tropical regions around the world.

With its *en-* prefix, *endemic* means literally "in the population." Since the Tasmanian devil is found in the wild exclusively in Tasmania, scientists say it is "endemic to" that island. But the word can also mean simply "common" or "typical"; so we can say that corruption is endemic in the government of a country, that colds are "endemic in" nursery school, or that love of Barbie dolls is "endemic among" young American girls. Don't confuse *endemic* with *epidemic*; something can be endemic in a region for centuries without ever "exploding."

demagogue \ˈde-mə-ˌgäg\ A political leader who appeals to the emotions and prejudices of people in order to arouse discontent and to advance his or her own political purposes.

• His supporters called him a "man of the people"; his enemies called him a lying demagogue.

Demagogue was once defined by the writer H. L. Mencken as "one who will preach doctrines he knows to be untrue to men he knows to be idiots," and Mencken's definition still works quite well. The "doctrines" (ideas) preached by demagogues will naturally always be the kind that appeal directly to the ordinary voter, the "common man" or "little guy." Appealing to the common people is not itself a bad thing, but it has often been used by those who calculate that *demagoguery* (or *demagogy*) is the easiest way to power. In most countries, fear of *demagogic* leaders is so strong that voters aren't even permitted to vote directly for the nation's leader, but instead vote only for a local representative.

demotic \di-ˈmä-tik\ Popular or common.

• Partly because of television, the demotic language and accents of America's various regions have become more and more similar.

For many years *demotic* was used only to describe the writing of ancient Egypt, as the name of the script used by ordinary Egyptians rather than by their priests. *Demotic* is still an intellectual word, but it can now be used to describe any popular style in contrast to a style associated with a higher class, especially a style of speech or writing. So, for example, demotic Californian is different from demotic Texan. The most demotic dress today is probably blue jeans and sneakers, and those who wear them have demotic taste in fashion. The problem is, in American society it can sometimes be hard to find a style that *can't* be described as demotic.

POPUL comes from the Latin word meaning "people," and in fact forms the basis of the word *people* itself. So the *population* is the people of an area, and *popular* means not only "liked by many people" but also (as in *popular culture*) "relating to the general public."

---

populist \\'pä-pyə-list\\ A believer in the rights, wisdom, or virtues of the common people.

- He knew he would have to campaign as a populist in order to appeal to the working-class voters.

The word *populist* first appeared in the 1890s with the founding of the Populist Party, which stood for the interests of the farmers against the big-money interests. In later years *populism* came to be associated with the blue-collar class in the cities as well. Populism can be hard to predict. It sometimes has a religious tendency; it usually isn't very interested in international affairs; it has sometimes been unfriendly to immigrants and blacks; and it's often anti-intellectual. So populism often switches between liberal and conservative. But the *populist* style always shows its concern with Americans with average incomes as opposed to the rich and powerful.

populace \\'pä-pyü-ləs\\ (1) The common people or masses. (2) Population.

- Perhaps Henry Ford's major achievement was to manufacture a car that practically the entire populace could afford—the Model T.

Populace is usually used to refer to all the people of a country. Thus, we're often told that an educated and informed populace is essential for a healthy American democracy. Franklin D. Roosevelt's famous radio "Fireside Chats" informed and reassured the American populace in the 1930s as we struggled through the Great Depression. We often hear about what "the general populace" is thinking or doing, but generalizing about something so huge can be tricky.

populous \\'pä-pyü-ləs\\ Numerous, densely settled, or having a large population.

- Most Americans can't locate Indonesia, the fourth most populous country in the world, on a map.

With a metropolitan area of more than 20 million people, Mexico City could be called the world's second or third most populous city. And the nearby Aztec city of Tenochtitlán was one of the largest cities in the world even when Hernán Cortés arrived there in 1519. But by the time Cortés conquered the city in 1521 it wasn't nearly so populous, since European diseases had greatly reduced the population. Avoid confusing *populous* and *populace*, which are pronounced exactly the same.

vox populi \\'väks-'pä-pyü-,lī\ Popular sentiment or opinion.

- Successful politicians are always listening to the vox populi and adjusting their opinions or language accordingly.

Dating from at least the time of Charlemagne, the Latin saying "Vox populi, vox Dei" means literally "The voice of the people is the voice of God"—in other words, the people's voice is sacred, or the people are always right. Today, by means of modern opinion polls, we seem to hear the vox populi (or *vox pop* for short) year-round on every possible issue. But maybe we should occasionally keep in mind that full Charlemagne-era quotation: "Those people should not be listened to who keep saying the voice of the people is the voice of God, since the riotousness of the crowd is always very close to madness."

Quizzes

A. Choose the closest definition:

1. demagogue   a. medium-sized city b. fiery politician
   c. democratic socialist d. new democracy
2. populace   a. politics b. numerous c. masses
   d. popularity
3. endemic   a. common b. absent c. infectious
   d. occasional
4. demotic   a. devilish b. common c. cultural d. useful
5. populous   a. well-liked b. foreign c. numerous
   d. obscure
6. demographic   a. describing politics b. describing
   populations c. describing policies d. describing
   epidemics
7. populist   a. communist b. campaigner c. socialist
   d. believer in the people
8. vox populi   a. public policy b. public survey c. public
   opinion d. public outrage

B. **Indicate whether the following pairs of words have the same or different meanings:**

1. demotic / common   same __ / different __
2. populist / politician   same __ / different __
3. endemic / locally common   same __ / different __
4. populace / popularity   same __ / different __
5. demographic / phonetic   same __ / different __
6. vox populi / mass sentiment same __ / different __
7. demagogue / prophet   same __ / different __
8. populous / well-loved   same __ / different __

Animal Words

aquiline \\'a-kwə-ˌlīn\\ (1) Relating to eagles. (2) Curving like an eagle's beak.

• The surviving busts of noble Romans show that many of the men had strong aquiline noses.

Aquiline, from the Latin word meaning "eagle," is most often used to describe a nose that has a broad curve and is slightly hooked, like a beak. The aquiline figure on the U.S. seal brandishes the arrows of war and the olive branch of peace. The word for eagle itself, *Aquila,* has been given to a constellation in the northern hemisphere.

asinine \\'a-sə-ˌnīn\\ Foolish, brainless.

• He's not so great when he's sober, but when he's drunk he gets truly asinine.

The donkey, or *ass,* has often been accused of stubborn, willful, and stupid behavior lacking in logic and common sense. Asinine behavior exhibits similar qualities. Idiotic or rude remarks, aggressive stupidity, and general immaturity can all earn someone (usually a man) this description. If you call him this to his face, however, he might behave even worse.

bovine \\'bō-ˌvīn\\ (1) Relating to cows and oxen. (2) Placid, dull, unemotional.

• In that part of Texas, many of the veterinarians specialize in bovine conditions and won't even deal with dogs or cats.

Bovine comes from the Latin word for "cow," though the biological family called the Bovidae actually includes not only cows and oxen but also goats, sheep, bison, and buffalo. So *bovine* is often used technically, when discussing "bovine diseases," "bovine anatomy," and so on. It can also describe a human personality, though it can be a rather unkind way to describe someone. When Hera, the wife of Zeus, is called "cow-eyed," though, it's definitely a compliment, and Zeus fairly melts when she turns those big bovine eyes on him.

canine \\'kā-ˌnīn\\ Relating to dogs or the dog family; doglike.

- Pleasure in getting their tummies rubbed must be a basic canine trait, since all our dogs have loved it.

Dogs are prized for their talents and intelligence but aren't always given credit for their independence. Instead, tales of canine devotion and attachment are legendary; the old *Lassie* and *Rin-Tin-Tin* television series featured at least one heroic act of devotion per show. So we often hear people described as having "doglike devotion" or "doglike loyalty." But *canine* itself, unlike *doglike*, usually refers to four-legged creatures. *Canine* is not only an adjective but also a noun. Dogs and their relatives in the Canidae family—the wolves, jackals, foxes, and coyotes—are often called canines. And so are those two slightly pointed teeth a bit to the right and left of your front teeth.

feline \\'fē-ˌlīn\\ (1) Relating to cats or the cat family. (2) Like a cat in being sleek, graceful, sly, treacherous, or stealthy.

- The performers moved across the high wire with feline grace and agility.

Cats have always provoked a strong reaction from humans. The Egyptians worshiped them, leaving thousands of feline mummies and idols as evidence. In the Middle Ages, *felines* were feared as agents of the devil, and were thought to creep around silently at night doing evil. (Notice that *feline* is also a noun.) The fascinating family called the Felidae includes about 40 species of superb hunters, including the lions, tigers, jaguars, cheetahs, cougars, bobcats, and lynxes, and almost all of them are smooth, silent, and independent.

leonine \\'lē-ə-ˌnīn\\ Relating to lions; lionlike.

- As he conducted, Leonard Bernstein would fling his leonine mane wildly about.

The Latin word for "lion" is *leon,* so the names Leon, Leo, and Leona all mean "lion" as well. A leonine head usually has magnificent hair, like a male lion's mane. The leonine strength of Heracles (Hercules) is symbolized by the lion's pelt that he wears, the pelt of the fabled Nemean Lion which he had slain as one of his Twelve Labors. But leonine courage is what is so notably lacking in *The Wizard of Oz*'s Cowardly Lion.

porcine \\'pȯr-ˌsīn\\ Relating to pigs or swine; piglike.

- She describes her landlord's shape as porcine, and claims he has manners to match.

Pigs are rarely given credit for their high intelligence or their friendliness as pets, but instead are mocked for their habit of cooling themselves in mud puddles and the aggressive way they often go after food. While *porcine* isn't as negative a term as *swinish*, it may describe things that are fat, greedy, pushy, or generally piggish—but primarily fat. Porky Pig and Miss Piggy aren't particularly porcine in their behavior, only in their appearance—that is, pink and pudgy.

vulpine \\'vəl-ˌpīn\\ (1) Relating to foxes; foxlike. (2) Sneaky, clever, or crafty; foxy.

- She'd already decided she didn't like anything about him, especially the twitchiness, that vulpine face, and those darting eyes.

Foxes may be sleek and graceful runners with beautiful coats and tails, but they're almost impossible to keep out of the henhouse. Over the centuries they have "outfoxed" countless farmers. Because of the quick intelligence in their faces and their cunning nighttime raids, *vulpine* today almost always describes a face or manner that suggests a person capable of the same kind of sly scheming.

Quiz

Fill in each blank with the correct letter:

a. leonine   e. canine
b. aquiline   f. feline
c. porcine   g. vulpine
d. asinine   h. bovine

1. Collies and chow chows often have splendid _____ neck ruffs.
2. The dancers, in their black leotards, performed the piece with slinky, _____ grace.
3. Proud of the _____ curve of his nose, the star presents his profile to the camera in old silent films at every opportunity.
4. The slick fellow offering his services as guide had a disturbingly _____ air about him.
5. Some of the most beloved _____ traits, such as loyalty and playfulness, are often lacking in humans.
6. The last applicant she had interviewed struck her as passive and _____ and completely lacking in ambition.
7. Jeff and his crowd were in the balcony, catcalling, throwing down cans, and being generally _____.
8. She peeked out to see her _____ landlord climbing the stairs slowly, gasping for breath, with the eviction notice in his hand.

Review Quizzes

A. Choose the closest definition:

1. vulpine   a. reddish b. sly c. trustworthy d. furry
2. atheistic   a. boring b. godless c. roundabout d. contagious
3. adumbrate   a. revise b. punish c. advertise d. outline
4. populous   a. numerous b. populated c. popular d. common
5. iconoclast   a. icon painter b. dictator c. dissident d. tycoon

6. endemic   a. local b. neighborly c. sensational
    d. foreign
7. iconic   a. wealthy b. famous c. indirect d. symbolic
8. feline   a. sleek b. clumsy c. crazy d. fancy
9. pantheon   a. mall b. road race c. trouser store
    d. hall of fame
10. icon   a. psychic b. leader c. symbol d. prophet
11. urbane   a. calm b. elegant c. excited d. secure
12. horticulture   a. interior decoration b. food science
    c. horse breeding d. plant growing
13. demotic   a. reduced b. common c. upper-class
    d. demented
14. luminary   a. ruler b. lantern c. lighting designer
    d. celebrity
15. travesty   a. farce b. outfit c. transportation d. success
16. divest   a. add on b. take off c. take in d. add up

B. Fill in each blank with the correct letter:

a. populist   f. apotheosis
b. demographic   g. bovine
c. theocracy   h. populace
d. investiture   i. vulpine
e. aquiline   j. cross-cultural

1. The ____ of the great Albert Einstein seemed to occur
    while he was still living.
2. ____ surveys often divide the U.S. population by
    income and education.
3. Nothing ever seemed to disturb her pleasant but ____
    manner.
4. He was interested in ____ studies that showed that
    these kinds of cancers don't appear in African tribal
    populations.
5. The ____ of the society's new leader was a secret and
    solemn event.
6. With his ____ nose, he looked like a member of the
    ancient Roman senate.
7. He had a nervous, ____ manner, with a tense alertness
    and shifty eyes.
8. She ran her campaigns as a ____, a champion of the
    common man, though she herself had a great deal of
    money.

9. The general ____ has never cared much about foreign policy except when the country goes to war.

10. In a true ____, the legal punishments are often those called for in the holy books.

C. Match the word on the left to the correct definition on the right:

1. porcine   a. half-shadow
2. divest   b. doglike
3. asinine   c. brown
4. penumbra   d. public opinion
5. leonine   e. cross-dresser
6. umber   f. symbolic
7. vox populi   g. foolish
8. iconic   h. plump
9. transvestite   i. lionlike
10. canine   j. get rid of

UNIT

13

CORD, from the Latin word for "heart," turns up in several common English words. So does its Greek relative *card-*, which is familiar to us in words such as *cardiac*, "relating to the heart."

---

accord \ə-ˈkȯrd\ (1) To grant. (2) To be in harmony; agree.

• What she told police under questioning didn't accord with the accounts of the other witnesses.

A new federal law may accord with—or be in *accordance* with—the guidelines that a company has already established. The rowdy behavior of the hero Beowulf accords with Norse ideals of the early Middle Ages; but such behavior wouldn't have been in accordance with the ideals of a later young lord from the same general region, Shakespeare's Prince Hamlet. *Accord* is also a noun, meaning "agreement." Thus, we often hear of two countries signing a peace accord; and we also frequently hear of two things or people being "in accord with" each other.

concord \ˈkän-ˌkȯrd\ (1) A state of agreement: harmony. (2) A formal agreement.

• In 1801 Napoleon signed a concord with the pope reestablishing the Catholic Church in France.

The roots of *concord* suggest the meaning "hearts together." At the very outset of the American Revolution, the town of Concord, Massachusetts, was the site of a famous battle—obviously not exactly in keeping with its name. It shares that name with the capital of New Hampshire and a few other towns and cities, and *Concordia*, the original Latin word for "concord," is the name of several Lutheran universities. Today *concord* is a rather formal term, probably most often used to mean a specific agreement; thus, two countries may sign a concord on matters that have led to trouble in the past.

cordial \\'kȯr-jəl\\ Warm, friendly, gracious.

• After the meeting, the president extended a cordial invitation to everyone for coffee at her own house.

Anything that is cordial comes from the heart. Cordial greetings to friends on the street, or cordial relations between two countries, are warm without being passionate. *Cordial* is also a noun, which originally meant any stimulating medicine or drink that was thought to be good for the heart. Today a cordial is a liqueur, a sweetened alcoholic drink with interesting flavoring. Cordials such as crème de menthe, Drambuie, or Benedictine are alcoholic enough to warm the spirits and the heart.

discordant \\dis-'kȯr-dənt\\ Being at odds, conflicting, not in harmony.

• The first discordant note at dinner was struck by my cousin, when he claimed the president was only interested in taking away our guns.

Discord, a word more common in earlier centuries than today, means basically "conflict," so *discordant* often means "conflicting." The opinions of Supreme Court justices are frequently discordant; justices who disagree with the Court's decision usually write a dissenting opinion. *Discordant* is often used with a somewhat musical meaning, suggesting that a single wrong note or harmony has been heard in the middle of a performance—even though musical words such as *chord* actually come from a different Latin word, meaning "cord" or "string" (a reference to the strings of ancient instruments such as the lyre).

CULP comes from the Latin word for "guilt." Its best-known appearance in English is probably in *culprit,* meaning someone who is guilty of a crime.

---

culpable \\'kəl-pə-bəl\\ Deserving to be condemned or blamed.

- The company was found guilty of culpable negligence in allowing the chemical waste to leak into the groundwater.

Culpable normally means simply "guilty." To a lawyer, "culpable negligence" is carelessness so serious that it becomes a crime—for instance, building a swimming pool in your suburban yard with no fence around it, so that a neighbor's child could fall in and drown. But degrees of *culpability* are important in the law; someone who intended to do harm always faces a more serious challenge in court than someone who was merely careless.

exculpate \'ek-skəl-ˌpāt\ To clear from accusations of fault or guilt.

- The girls aren't proud of what they did that night, but they've been exculpated by witnesses and won't be facing criminal charges.

Exculpate gets its meaning from the prefix *ex-*, which here means "out of" or "away from." A suspected murderer may be exculpated by the confession of another person. And *exculpatory* evidence is the kind that defense lawyers are always looking for.

inculpate \in-'kəl-ˌpāt\ To accuse or incriminate; to show evidence of someone's involvement in a fault or crime.

- It was his own father who finally inculpated him, though without intending to.

Inculpate is the opposite of *exculpate,* just as *inculpatory* evidence is the opposite of *exculpatory* evidence. By inculpating someone else, an accused person may manage to exculpate himself. Through plea bargaining, the prosecution can often encourage a defendant to inculpate his friends in return for a lighter sentence.

mea culpa \ˌmā-ə-'kul-pə\ An admission of personal fault or error.

- The principal said his mea culpa at the school board meeting, but not all the parents were satisfied.

Mea culpa, Latin for "through my fault," comes from the prayer in the Catholic mass in which, back when Latin was still the language of the mass, one would confess to having sinned "mea culpa, mea culpa, mea maxima culpa" ("through my fault, through my fault, through my most grievous fault"). When we say "Mea culpa" today, it means "I apologize" or "It was my fault." But *mea culpa* is also common as a noun. So, for instance, a book may be a long mea culpa for the author's past treatment of women, or an oil-company may issue a mea culpa after a tanker runs aground.

Quizzes

A. Choose the closest definition:

1. exculpate   a. convict b. prove innocent c. suspect
     d. prove absent
2. discordant   a. insulting b. relieved c. unlimited
     d. conflicting
3. culpable   a. disposable b. refundable c. guilty
     d. harmless
4. cordial   a. hateful b. friendly c. fiendish d. cool
5. inculpate   a. incorporate b. resist c. accuse
     d. offend
6. concord   a. generosity b. straightness c. agreement
     d. pleasure
7. mea culpa   a. rejection b. apology c. excuse
     d. forgiveness
8. accord   a. harmonize b. accept c. distress d. convince

B. Match the definition on the left to the correct word on the right:

1. accuse   a. accord
2. excuse   b. concord
3. goodwill   c. mea culpa
4. heartfelt   d. discordant
5. grant   e. culpable
6. blamable   f. cordial
7. disagreeing   g. inculpate
8. confession   h. exculpate

DICT comes from *dicere*, the Latin word meaning "to speak." So a *dictionary* is a treasury of words for speaking. And a *contradiction* (with its prefix *contra-*, "against") speaks against or denies something.

diction \\'dik-shən\\ (1) Choice of words, especially with regard to correctness, clearness, or effectiveness. (2) Clarity of speech.

• Our CEO is determined to appear in some TV ads, but he first needs to work on his diction with a vocal coach.

When your English teacher complains about some of the words you chose to use in an essay, she's talking about your diction. She may also use the term when commenting on the word choices made by a poet, and why a particular word was the best one possible in a particular line. (Compare *syntax*, p. 660.) But the second meaning of *diction* is just as common, and your English teacher might use that one on you as well, especially when she's asked you to read something aloud and you mumble your way through it.

edict \\'ē-ˌdikt\\ (1) An official announcement that has the force of a law. (2) An order or command.

• In 1989 an edict by the leader of Iran pronouncing a death sentence on a British novelist stunned the world.

Edicts are few and far between in a democracy, since very few important laws can be made by a president or prime minister acting alone. But when a crisis arose in the Roman Republic, the senate would appoint a *dictator,* who would have the power to rule by edict. The idea was that the dictator could make decisions quickly, issuing his edicts faster than the senate could act. When the crisis was over, the edicts were canceled and the dictator usually retired from public life. Things are different today: dictators almost always install themselves in power, and they never give it up.

jurisdiction \\ˌjür-is-'dik-shən\\ (1) The power or right to control or exercise authority. (2) The territory where power may be exercised.

• Unluckily for the defendants, the case fell within the jurisdiction of the federal court rather than the more tolerant state court.

Questions of jurisdiction are generally technical legal matters. The most important ones include which court will hear a given case and which law-enforcement agency can get involved. But although they may seem like mere technicalities, *jurisdictional* matters sometimes turn out to be all-important in the final outcome. Jurisdiction may depend on where you are (for example, in which state), on who you are (if you're a juvenile, for example, you may only be tried in juvenile court), and on what the subject is (for example, cases involving the estate left by someone who has died are dealt with in probate court).

dictum \ˈdik-təm\ A formal and authoritative statement.

• It has long been a dictum of American foreign policy that the government doesn't negotiate with kidnappers and terrorists.

The word *dictum* is frequently used in philosophy, but also in economics, political science, and other fields. Almost any condensed piece of wisdom—"The perfect is the enemy of the good," "Buy low, sell high," "All politics is local," etc.—can be called a dictum. In the law, judges may often add to a written opinion an *obiter dictum*, or "statement made in passing"—a strong statement that isn't directly relevant to the case being decided. If they're well thought out and eloquent, *obiter dicta* (notice the plural form) may be referred to by later judges and lawyers for years afterward.

GNI/GNO comes from a Greek and Latin verb meaning "to know," and can be found at the root of *know* itself. Among other words built from this root, you may *recognize* ("know again") some and be *ignorant* of ("not know") others. But only an *ignoramus* would know absolutely none of them.

cognitive \ˈkäg-nə-tiv\ (1) Having to do with the process of knowing, including awareness, judgment, and understanding. (2) Based on factual knowledge that has been or can be gained by experience.

• A child isn't a computer; a third-grader's cognitive abilities are highly dependent on his or her upbringing and happiness.

Cognitive skills and knowledge involve the ability to acquire factual information, often the kind of knowledge that can easily be tested. So *cognition* should be distinguished from social, emotional, and creative development and ability. *Cognitive science* is a growing field of study that deals with human perception, thinking, and learning.

agnostic \ag-ˈnä-stik\ A person who believes that whether God exists is not known and probably cannot be known.

• Both of them were always agnostics, but after they had children they started attending church again.

The words *agnostic* and *agnosticism* were coined around 1870 by the great English biologist T. H. Huxley, who had just spent a decade defending the works of Charles Darwin against the attacks of the church. Scientists often put a high value on evidence when arguing about religion, and many *agnostic* thinkers believe that human minds simply aren't equipped to grasp the nature of God. But agnostics differ from *atheists*, who actually claim that no God exists and may even think they can prove it. You may have seen the similar word *gnostic*, the name for followers of certain religious sects from around the time of Christ that sought spiritual knowledge and rejected the material world. An increasing interest in *gnosticism* today can be seen in the popular novels of Philip Pullman, Dan Brown, and Neil Gaiman.

incognito \ˌin-ˌkäg-ˈnē-tō\ In disguise, or with one's identity concealed.

• Years after her reign as a top Hollywood star, she was discovered working incognito as a bartender in Manhattan while living in cheap hotels.

In a famous myth, Zeus and Hermes visit a village incognito to test the villagers. The seemingly poor travelers are turned away from every household except that of Baucis and Philemon. This elderly couple, though very poor themselves, provide the disguised gods with a feast. When the gods finally reveal themselves, they reward the couple generously for their hospitality, but destroy the rest of the village.

prognosis \präg-ˈnō-səs\ (1) The chance of recovery from a given disease or condition. (2) A forecast or prophecy.

• The prognosis for a patient with chicken pox is usually excellent; the prognosis for someone with liver cancer is terrible.

With its prefix *pro-*, meaning "before," *prognosis* means basically "knowledge beforehand" of how a situation is likely to turn out. *Prognosis* was originally a strictly medical term, but it soon broadened to include predictions made by experts of all kinds. Thus, for example, economists are constantly offering prognoses (notice the irregular plural form) about where the economy is going, and climate scientists regularly *prognosticate* about how quickly the earth's atmosphere is warming.

Quizzes

A. Fill in each blank with the correct letter:

a. agnostic   e. diction
b. dictum   f. incognito
c. cognitive   g. edict
d. jurisdiction   h. prognosis

1. Psychology is not entirely a ____ science, since it deals with behavior as well as the mind.
2. He often repeated Balzac's famous ____: "Behind every great fortune is a great crime."
3. Movie stars often go out in public ____, in faded sweatshirts, worn-out pants, and sunglasses.
4. When their dictatorial grandfather issued an ____, everyone obeyed it.
5. She has strong opinions about lots of public issues, but she's an ____ about foreign policy.
6. The ____ for the world's climate in the next century is uncertain.
7. He complains about his students' ____, saying they mumble so much that he often can't understand them.
8. The judge refused to consider two elements in the case, saying that they lay outside his ____.

B. Indicate whether the following pairs of words have the same or different meanings:

1. agnostic / complex   same ___ / different ___
2. cognitive / digestive   same ___ / different ___
3. diction / wordiness   same ___ / different ___
4. dictum / declaration   same ___ / different ___
5. incognito / hospitable   same ___ / different ___
6. jurisdiction / authority   same ___ / different ___
7. prognosis / outlook   same ___ / different ___
8. edict / order   same ___ / different ___

GRAPH comes from the Greek verb *graphein*, "to write." Thus, a *biography* is a written account of someone's life (see BIO, p. 407), a *discography* is a written list of recordings on disc (records or CDs), and a *filmography* is a list of motion pictures. But lots of uses of -*graph* and -*graphy* don't mean literally "writing" (as in *autograph* or *paragraph*), but instead something more like "recording," as in *photography*, *seismograph*, or *graph* itself.

calligraphy \kə-ˈli-grə-fē\ The art of producing beautiful handwriting.

• Calligraphy can be seen today in event invitations, logo designs, and stone inscriptions.

Kalli- is a Greek root meaning "beautiful," and "beautiful" in the case of *calligraphy* means artistic, stylized, and elegant. Calligraphy has existed in many cultures, including Indian, Persian, and Islamic cultures; Arabic puts a particularly high value on beautiful script, and in East Asia calligraphy has long been considered a major art. Calligraphers in the West use pens with wide nibs, with which they produce strokes of widely differing width within a single letter.

hagiography \ˌha-gē-ˈä-grə-fē\ (1) Biography of saints. (2) Biography that idealizes or idolizes.

• According to the new biography, which should really be called a hagiography, the former prime minister doesn't seem to have done anything small-minded or improper in his entire life.

For those able to read, reading stories of the lives of the saints was a popular pastime for centuries, and books collecting short saints' biographies were best sellers. These often included terrifically colorful stories (about slaying dragons, magically traveling through space, etc.) that were perhaps a bit too good to be strictly true, and after finding God not one of them ever did a single thing that wasn't saintly—and some of them may not have actually existed. Still today, *hagiographic* accounts of the lives of politicians and pop-culture stars are being written, though there now seems to be a bigger audience for biographies that seek out the not-so-wholesome secrets of the person's life, sometimes even making up a few of them.

choreography \ˌkȯr-ē-ˈä-grə-fē\ (1) The art of composing and arranging dances and of representing them in symbolic notation. (2) The movements by dancers in a performance.

- The reviews praised the show for its eye-catching choreography, calling it the best element of the whole musical.

In ancient Greece, a *choreia* was a circular dance accompanied by a singing *chorus*. But the actual notating of dances by means of symbols didn't begin until the 17th or 18th century, when ballet developed into a complex art form in France. The *choreographer* of a major ballet, which might run to an hour or more, will always record his or her work in notation, though *choreographing* a five-minute segment for a TV talent show usually doesn't require any record at all.

lithograph \ˈli-thə-ˌgraf\ A picture made by printing from a flat surface (such as a smooth stone) prepared so that the ink will only stick to the design that will be printed.

- To make a lithograph, the artist first draws an image, in reverse, on a fine-grained limestone or aluminum plate.

Lithos is Greek for "stone," and a stone surface has traditionally been involved in lithography, though a metal plate may take its place today. The *lithographic* process was invented around 1796 and soon became the main method of printing books and newspapers. Artists use *lithography* to produce prints (works intended to be sold in many copies), and art lithographs sometimes resemble older types of prints, including etchings, engravings, and woodcuts. Pablo Picasso, Marc Chagall, Joan Miró, and M. C. Escher are among the many artists who have used lithography to produce important original works. Today lithographic printing accounts for over 40% of all printing, packaging, and publishing.

ART comes from the Latin word for "skill." This reminds us that, until a few centuries ago, almost no one made a strong distinction between skilled craftsmanship and what we would now call "art." And the word *art* itself could also mean simply "cleverness." The result is that this root appears in some words where we might not expect it.

---

artful \ˈärt-fəl\ (1) Skillful. (2) Wily, crafty, sly.

- It was an artful solution: each side was pleased with the agreement, but it was the lawyer himself who stood to make the most money off of it.

A writer may produce an artful piece of prose, one that's clearly and elegantly written. The same writer might also make an artful argument, one that cleverly leaves out certain details and plays up others so as to make a stronger case. In the first instance, the prose is well crafted; in the second, the argument might instead be called crafty. But even though both uses are correct, most of us still use *artful* somewhat differently from *artistic*.

artifact \'är-ti-ˌfakt\ A usually simple object made by human workmanship, such as a tool or ornament, that represents a culture or a stage in a culture's development.

• Through the artifacts found by archaeologists, we now know a considerable amount about how the early Anasazi people of the Southwest lived.

One of the things that make humans unique is their ability to make and use tools, and ever since the first rough stone axes began to appear about 700,000 years ago, human cultures have left behind artifacts from which we've tried to draw a picture of their everyday life. The roots of artifact mean basically "something made with skill"; thus, a mere stone that was used for pounding isn't an artifact, since it wasn't shaped by humans for its purpose—unlike a ram's horn that was polished and given a brass mouthpiece and was blown as part of a religious ritual.

artifice \'är-tə-fəs\ (1) Clever skill. (2) A clever trick.

• By his cunning and artifice, Iago convinces Othello that Desdemona has been unfaithful.

Artifice can be a tricky word to use. It combines the same roots as *artifact,* so it's sometimes seen in descriptions of craftsmanship ("The artifice that went into this jewelry can still astound us," "The chef had used all his artifice to disguise the nature of the meat"). But it can also be used for many situations that don't involve physical materials ("They had gotten around the rules by a clever artifice," "The artifice of the plot is ingenious"). Like its adjective, *artificial*, *artifice* isn't necessarily either positive nor negative. But both words can make us slightly uncomfortable if we like to think of simplicity and naturalness as important values.

artisan \'är-tə-zən\ A skilled worker or craftsperson.

- At the fair, they saw examples of the best carving, pottery, and jewelry by local artisans.

Artisans aren't the same as *artists*, but it can sometimes be hard to tell the difference. In the Middle Ages, artisans organized themselves into guilds. In every city each group of artisans—weavers, carpenters, shoemakers, and so on—had its own guild, which set wages and prices, kept standards high, and protected its members from outside competitors. In America, however, most artisans have always been fiercely independent. Today, when factories produce almost all of our goods, artisans usually make only fine objects for those who can afford them. And we now even include food among the artisan's crafts, so you can buy *artisanal* cheeses, breads, and chocolates—but probably not if you're watching your budget.

Quizzes

A. Fill in each blank with the correct letter:

a.	choreography	e.	calligraphy
b.	lithograph	f.	hagiography
c.	artful	g.	artifact
d.	artisan	h.	artifice

1. The strangest _____ they had dug up was a bowl on which an extremely odd animal was painted.

2. A signed _____ by Picasso wouldn't be valued nearly as highly as one of his paintings.

3. She admired the _____, but the dancers didn't seem to have practiced enough.

4. He'd done an _____ job of writing the proposal so as to appeal to each board member who would have to approve it.

5. In his spare time he practiced _____, using special pens to write short quotations suitable for framing.

6. Each room in the palace was a masterpiece of _____, from its wall paintings to its chandeliers to its delicate furniture.

7. Each worker at the tiny textile workshop thought of himself or herself as an _____.

8. The book was pure _____, painting its statesman hero as not only brilliant but saintly.

B. Match the definition on the left to the correct word on the right:

1.	craftsperson	a.	artful
2.	saint's biography	b.	artifice
3.	ingenious	c.	lithograph
4.	print	d.	choreography
5.	clever skill	e.	artisan
6.	beautiful handwriting	f.	hagiography
7.	man-made object	g.	calligraphy
8.	dance design	h.	artifact

FORT comes from *fortis*, Latin for "strong." The familiar noun *fort*, meaning a building strengthened against possible attacks, comes directly from it. And our verb *comfort* actually means "to give strength and hope to."

fortify \\'för-tə-ˌfī\\ To strengthen.

• Fortified by a good night's sleep and a big breakfast, they set off for the final 20 miles of their journey.

Medieval cities were fortified against attack by high walls, and volunteers may fortify a levee against an overflowing river by means of sandbags. Foods can be fortified by adding vitamins, but "fortified wines," such as sherry and port, have brandy (a "stronger" drink) rather than vitamins added to them. By adopting good exercise habits, you can fortify your body against illness. And fortifying needn't always be physical. An author's reputation may be fortified by the success of his new book, or a prosecutor can fortify a case against a suspect by finding more evidence.

fortification \\ˌför-tə-fə-'kā-shən\\ (1) The building of military defenses to protect a place against attack. (2) A structure built to protect a place.

• The city's fortifications had withstood powerful assaults by catapults, battering rams, and tall siege towers that rolled up to release soldiers onto the top of the walls.

In the Middle Ages, many European cities were entirely enclosed by sturdy walls, with walkways along the top and towers at intervals, designed to make an invasion impossible. A water-filled ditch, or moat, might run alongside the wall for added defense. Such defenses turned the entire city into a *fort*, or *fortress*. Over the centuries, fortifications changed steadily with the development of new weaponry. In World War II, the German fortification of the French coast included antitank barriers, bunkers, minefields, and underwater obstacles, but it wasn't enough to turn back the immense force of the Allied invasion on D-day.

forte \\'fôrt, 'fôr-ˌtā, fôr-'tā\\ Something that a person does particularly well; one's strong point.

• Her forte was statistics, and she was always at a disadvantage when the discussion turned to public policy.

In the Middle Ages, swords were often known to break in battle, so the strongest part of a sword's blade—the part between the handle (or hilt) and the middle of the blade—was given a name, the *forte*. Today a forte is usually a special strength. But no one can agree on how to pronounce it: all three pronunciations shown above are heard frequently. Part of the problem is confusion with the Italian musical term *forte* (always pronounced /'fôr-ˌtā/), meaning "loud."

fortitude \\'fôr-tə-ˌtüd\\ Mental strength that allows one to face danger, pain, or hardship with courage.

• He's just too nice, and we worry that he won't have the fortitude to deal with the monsters in that office.

How many people know that the famous marble lions that guard the steps of the New York Public Library in Manhattan are named Patience and Fortitude? In Latin, the quality of *fortitudo* combines physical strength, vigor, courage, and boldness, but the English *fortitude* usually means simply firmness and steadiness of will, or "backbone." The philosopher Plato long ago listed four essential human virtues—prudence (i.e., good judgment), justice (i.e., ability to be fair in balancing between one's own interests and others'), temperance (i.e., moderation or restraint), and fortitude, and in Christian tradition these became known as the four "cardinal virtues."

CIS comes from the Latin verb meaning "to cut, cut down, or slay." An *incisor* is one of the big front biting teeth; beavers and wood-chucks have especially large ones. A *decision* "cuts off" previous discussion and uncertainty.

---

concise \kən-'sīs\ Brief and condensed, especially in expression or statement.

• Professor Childs's exam asked for a concise, one-page summary of the causes of the American Revolution.

Many students think that adding unnecessary sentences with long words will make their writing more impressive. But in fact almost every reader values *concision*, since concise writing is usually easier to read, better thought out, and better organized—that is, simply better writing. Words such as *short* don't have the full meaning of *concise*, which usually means not just "brief" but "packed with information."

excise \'ek-ˌsīz\ To cut out, especially surgically.

• The ancient Minoans from the island of Crete apparently excised the hearts of their human sacrifices.

Excise takes part of its meaning from the prefix *ex-*, "out." A writer may excise long passages of a novel to reduce it to a reasonable length, or a film director may excise a scene that might give offense. A surgeon may excise a large cancerous tumor, or make a tiny *excision* to examine an organ's tissue. *Excise* is also a noun, meaning a tax paid on something manufactured and sold in the U.S. Much of what consumers pay for tobacco or alcohol products go to cover the excise taxes that the state and federal government charge the manufacturers. But it's only accidental that this noun is spelled like the verb, since it comes from a completely different source.

incisive \in-'sī-siv\ Impressively direct and decisive.

• A few incisive questions were all that was needed to expose the weakness in the prosecutor's case.

From its roots, *incise* means basically "to cut into." So just as a doctor uses a scalpel to make an *incision* in the skin, an incisive remark cuts into the matter at hand. A good analyst makes incisive comments about a news story, cutting through the unimportant details, and a good critic *incisively* identifies a book's strengths and weaknesses.

precision \pri-ˈsi-zhən\ Exactness and accuracy.

• By junior year she was speaking with greater precision, searching for exact words in place of the crude, awkward language of her friends.

Many of us often use *precision* and *accuracy* as synonyms, but not scientists and engineers. For them, accuracy describes a particular measurement—that is, how close it is to the truth. But precision describes a measurement system—that is, how good it is at giving the same result every time it measures the same thing. This may be why even nonscientists now often speak of "precision instruments" for measuring, "precision landings" made by airplanes, "precision drilling" for natural gas, and so on.

Quizzes

A. Fill in each blank with the correct letter:

a. forte   e. concise
b. fortify   f. excise
c. fortification   g. incisive
d. precision   h. fortitude

1. Ms. Raymond's report was _____ but managed to discuss all the issues.

2. Carpentry isn't his _____, but he could probably build something simple like a bed.

3. They could _____ their theory by positive results from some more experiments.

4. The judge was deeply knowledgeable about the case, and his questions to both lawyers were _____.

5. The last Spanish _____ along the river proved to be the most difficult one for the French forces to take.

6. Whenever she was on the verge of despair, she remembered her grandfather's words about _____ being the character trait most important for success.

7. Before eating an apple, some people carefully _____ the brown spots.

8. What the tipsy darts players lacked in _____ they made up for in enthusiasm.

B. Choose the closest definition:

1. precision   a. accuracy b. beauty c. brilliance
   d. dependence
2. fortitude   a. armor b. endurance c. skill d. weapon
3. excise   a. add b. examine c. refuse d. cut out
4. forte   a. discipline b. force c. castle d. special
   strength
5. incisive   a. damaging b. sharp c. lengthy d. definite
6. fortification   a. diet b. exercise c. stronghold d. belief
7. concise   a. concentrated b. sure c. shifting d. blunt
8. fortify   a. attack b. strengthen c. struggle d. excite

Animal Words

apiary \\'ā-pē-ˌer-ē\\ A place where bees are kept for their honey.

• Apple orchards are excellent sites for apiaries, since the bees keep the apple trees productive by pollinating them.

Beekeeping, or *apiculture*, is the care of honeybees that ensures that they produce more honey than they can use. An apiary usually consists of many separate beehives. The social life of a hive is strange and marvelous. The queen bee, who will become the mother of an entire colony, is actually created by being fed "royal jelly" while she is still only a larva. The tens of thousands of worker bees are underdeveloped females; only a handful of the bees are male, and they do no work at all. The workers defend the hive by kamikaze means, stinging any intruder and dying as they do so. There's more drama in a quiet-looking apiary than the casual observer might notice.

caper \\'kā-pər\\ (1) A playful leap. (2) A prank or mischievous adventure.

• For their caper in the girls' bathroom, all three seniors were suspended for a week.

Caper in Latin means "a male goat." Anyone who has watched a young goat frolic in a field or clamber onto the roof of a car knows the kind of crazy fun the English word *caper*—which is also a verb—

is referring to. A *capriole* is a backward kick done in midair by a trained horse. *Capricorn,* meaning "horned goat," is a constellation and one of the signs of the zodiac. And a *capricious* act is one that's done with as little thought as a frisky goat might give it.

equestrian \i-ˈkwes-trē-ən\ Of or relating to horseback riding.

• The circus's equestrian acts, in which bareback riders performed daring acrobatic feats atop prancing horses, were her favorites.

Equestrian comes from *equus,* Latin for "horse." Old statues of military heroes, like the famous one of General Sherman on New York's Fifth Avenue, are frequently equestrian. In these sculptures the man always sits nobly upright on a horse, but the horse's stance varies; depending on whether the rider was killed in battle or survived, was victorious or defeated, the horse traditionally stands with four, three, or two hooves on the ground. Equestrian statues have been popular through the centuries, because until the 20th century almost every officer in Europe and America was trained in equestrian skills and combat.

lupine \ˈlü-ˌpīn\ Like a wolf; wolfish.

• Doctors reported that the boy showed lupine behavior such as snarling and biting, and walked with his knees bent in a kind of crouch.

Lupine comes from *lupus,* Latin for "wolf," and its related adjective *lupinus,* "wolfish." Lupine groups have a highly organized social structure, with leaders and followers clearly distinguished; dogs, since they're descended from wolves, often show these lupine patterns when living in groups. Stories of children raised by wolves (the most famous being Romulus, the legendary founder of Rome) have generally been hard to prove, partly because "wild" children lack human language abilities and can't describe their experiences. *Lupine* is also a noun, the name of a well-known garden flower, which was once thought to drain, or "wolf," the soil of its nutrients.

ovine \ˈō-ˌvīn\ Of, relating to, or resembling sheep.

• In her veterinary practice she specialized in ovine medicine, but often treated cows and pigs as well.

Sheep belong to the same family of mammals as goats, antelope, bison, buffalo, and cows. The genus *Ovis* includes at least five species, including the domestic sheep. Some 12,000 years ago, in the area now known as Iraq, sheep became one of the first animals to be domesticated; only the dog is known to have been tamed earlier. At first, they were valued for their milk, skin, and meat (mutton and lamb); not until about 1500 B.C. did the weaving of wool begin. Today a billion sheep are being farmed worldwide. The term *ovine* (which is a noun as well as an adjective) is mostly used in scientific and medical writing—which means you could impress your friends by dropping it into a casual conversation.

ornithologist \ˌȯr-nə-ˈthä-lə-jist\ A person who studies birds.

• John James Audubon, the great painter of the birds of early America, was also a writing ornithologist of great importance.

The Greek root *ornith-* means "bird," so *ornithology* is the study of birds. Amateur ornithology, usually called *birding* or *birdwatching,* is an extraordinarily popular pastime in America, where over 40 million people pursue it. Roger Tory Peterson's many field guides have long been some of the amateur ornithologist's most useful tools. Amateurs often make essential contributions to serious ornithology, as in the annual Christmas Bird Count, when tens of thousands of birders fan out across North and South America to produce a kind of census of all the species in the New World.

serpentine \ˈsər-pən-ˌtīn\ Like a snake or serpent in shape or movement; winding.

• The Great Wall of China, the greatest construction of all time, wends its serpentine way for some 4,000 miles across the Chinese landscape.

A snake moves by curving and winding along the ground. Roads through the Pyrenees, the mountains that separate Spain from France, tend to be serpentine, curving back and forth on themselves up and down the steep slopes. *Serpentine* has other meanings as well. As a noun, it's the name for a soft green mineral, and also for the party streamers you might throw at midnight on New Year's Eve. The *serpentine belt* under the hood in your car is the long, looping belt that most of the car's accessories—the AC, the power steering, the alternator, and so on—depend on to get their power.

simian \ˈsi-mē-ən\ Having to do with monkeys or apes; monkey-like.

• Every afternoon the pale youth could be found watching the simian antics in the Monkey House with strange intensity.

The Latin word for "ape" is *simia*, which itself comes from *simus,*
"snub-nosed." *Simian* is usually a scientific word; thus, for instance,
biologists study simian viruses in the search for cures to AIDS and
other diseases. But *simian* can be used by the rest of us to describe
human behavior. Human babies often cling to their mothers in a
simian way, and kids playing on a jungle gym may look like *sim-
ians*. But if you notice that a friend has a simian style of walking or
eating bananas, it might be best not to tell him.

Quiz

**Indicate whether the following pairs have the same
or different meanings:**

1. equestrian / horselike   same ___ / different ___
2. ornithologist / studier of birds   same ___ / different ___
3. lupine / apelike   same ___ / different ___
4. apiary / monkey colony   same ___ / different ___
5. ovine / goatlike   same ___ / different ___
6. caper / leap   same ___ / different ___
7. simian / catlike   same ___ / different ___
8. serpentine / winding   same ___ / different ___

Review Quizzes

A. Fill in each blank with the correct letter:

a. artisan   i. inculpate
b. edict   j. serpentine
c. equestrian   k. precision
d. artifact   l. artifice
e. discordant   m. prognosis
f. cognitive   n. simian
g. apiary   o. jurisdiction
h. exculpate

1. The farmer tended his _____ lovingly and gathered delicious wildflower honey every year.

2. In trying to _____ herself, she only made herself look guiltier.

3. They arrived in time to see the top riders compete in the championship _____ event.

4. The doctor's _____ is guarded, but she is cautiously optimistic that recovery will be complete.

5. It was a tall vase, with elaborate _____ shapes winding around it from top to bottom.

6. Each side's anger at the other has set a sadly _____ tone for the negotiations.

7. We set the clock with great _____ on the first day of every new year.

8. He's trying hard to _____ as many of his friends in the crime as he can.

9. These beautiful handblown goblets were obviously made by a talented _____.

10. The final _____ from the presidential palace commanded every citizen to wear a baseball cap at all times.

11. The child scrambled over the wall with _____ agility.

12. They're worried about their son's mental health, though the doctors say his _____ skills are fine.

13. She found a small clay _____ in the shape of a bear at the site of the ancient temple.

14. He used every _____ imaginable to hide his real age from the television cameras.

15. Firing local teachers falls outside the superintendant's actual _____.

B. Choose the correct *antonym*:

1. accord   a. harmonize b. strengthen c. differ d. agree
2. incisive   a. dull b. noble c. faulty d. exceptional
3. artful   a. lovely b. sly c. talented d. awkward
4. forte   a. weak point b. sword c. quarrel d. pinnacle
5. cordial   a. lazy b. cool c. terrific d. heartfelt
6. incognito   a. indoors b. in disguise c. as oneself d. as you were
7. fortify   a. construct b. reinforce c. supply d. weaken
8. concise   a. lengthy b. wide c. dated d. brief

9. culpable   a. prisonlike b. misleading c. guilty
   d. innocent
10. concord   a. belief b. conflict c. deception d. peace

C. Choose the closest definition:

1. ornithologist   a. student of fish b. student of words
   c. student of birds d. student of wolves
2. mea culpa   a. through my eyes b. through my fault
   c. through my door d. through my work
3. lupine   a. foxy b. horselike c. sheepish d. wolfish
4. discordant   a. energetic b. temporary c. phony
   d. clashing
5. jurisdiction   a. area of power b. area of coverage
   c. area of damage d. area of target
6. excise   a. call out b. hold out c. cut out d. fold out
7. choreography   a. book design b. dance script c. choir
   practice d. bird study
8. ovine   a. oval b. egglike c. sheep-related d. birdlike
9. dictum   a. word b. statement c. update d. answer
10. caper   a. wolf b. goat c. character d. prank

UNIT

14

CRYPT comes from the Greek word for "hidden." To *encrypt* a message is to encode it—that is, to hide its meaning in code language. When a scientific term begins with *crypto-,* it always means that there's something hidden about it.

---

crypt \'kript\ (1) A room completely or partly underground, especially under the main floor of a church. (2) A room or area in a large aboveground tomb.

• His old nightmare was of being locked in a crypt with corpses as his only companions.

Hidden under the main floor of a great church is often a large room, often with a tomb as its centerpiece. Many major European churches were built over the remains of a saint—the Vatican's great St. Peter's Basilica is an example—and instead of having the coffin buried, it was often given its spacious room below ground level. In a large aboveground tomb, or *mausoleum*, there may be several small chambers for individual coffins, also called crypts; when the comic book *Tales from the Crypt* made its first appearance in 1950, it was this meaning that the authors were referring to.

encrypt \in-'kript\ (1) To convert into cipher. (2) To convert a message into code.

• Messages on the group's Web site are encrypted in code words to keep law-enforcement agents from understanding them.

Codes aren't always in another language; people have always been able to communicate in ways that conceal their real meaning. In countries ruled by dictators, novelists and playwrights have sometimes managed to encrypt their messages, conveying political ideas to their audiences so that the authorities never notice. But *encryption* today usually refers to a complex procedure performed on electronic text to make sure the wrong people—whether a nation's enemies or a business competitor (most businesses use encryption today)—can't read it. And sensitive data that merely resides on a company's own computers is often encrypted as well.

cryptic \'krip-tik\ (1) Mysterious; puzzlingly short. (2) Acting to hide or conceal.

• From across the room, Louisa threw Philip a cryptic look, and he puzzled over what she was trying to tell him.

Until the writing on the famous Rosetta Stone was finally translated in the early 19th century, Egyptian hieroglyphic writing was entirely cryptic, its meaning hidden from the modern world. In the same way, a cryptic comment is one whose meaning is unclear, and a cryptic note may leave you wondering. Cryptic coloring among plants and animals acts like camouflage; so, for example, some moths that are tasty to blue jays are *cryptically* colored to look like bugs that jays won't touch.

cryptography \krip-'tä-grə-fē\ (1) Secret writing. (2) The encoding and decoding of messages.

• As a graduate student in mathematics, she never dreamed she would end up working in cryptography for the Defense Department.

During World War II, cryptography became an extremely complex science for both the Allied and Axis powers. The Allies managed to secretly crack the code produced by the Nazis' Enigma machine, and thereby may have shortened the war by two years. The Axis *cryptographers,* on the other hand, never managed to crack the Americans' ultimate code—the spoken languages of the Navajo and other American Indians. In the age of computers, cryptography has become almost unbelievably complex; it's widely used in peacetime in such areas as banking telecommunications.

AB/ABS comes to us from Latin, and means "from," "away," or "off." *Abuse* is the use of something in the wrong way. To *abduct* is to "lead away from" or kidnap. *Aberrant* behavior is behavior that "wanders away from" what is acceptable. But there are so many words that include these roots that it would be *absurd* to try to list them all here.

abscond \ab-'skänd\ To depart in secret and hide.

- They discovered the next morning that their guest had absconded with most of the silverware during the night.

Wagner's massive four-part opera *The Ring of the Nibelung* begins with a dwarf absconding with gold which he turns into a magic ring. And in J. R. R. Tolkien's *The Hobbit,* Bilbo Baggins absconds from Gollum's caves with the ring he has found, the ring Gollum calls "my precious"; what follows is detailed in the three-volume *Lord of the Rings.* (Tolkien knew Wagner's opera well.) A young couple might abscond from their parents to get married, but sooner or later they must face those parents again.

abstemious \ab-'stē-mē-əs\ Restrained, especially in the consumption of food or alcohol.

- Her parents had left her two million dollars when they died, having been so abstemious for years that their neighbors all assumed they were poor.

Many 14th-century monks lived by the Rule of St. Benedict, which demands an abstemious life of obedience and poverty. But not all monks could maintain such abstemious habits. Chaucer's *Canterbury Tales* contains a portrait of a fat monk who is supposed to follow a vegetarian diet but instead is an enthusiastic hunter who loves a juicy swan best. He justifies breaking the Rule by saying that it's old-fashioned and that he's just keeping up with modern times. *Abstemious* itself has a slightly old-fashioned sound today, especially in a country where everyone is constantly encouraged to consume.

abstraction \ab-'strak-shən\ The consideration of a thing or idea without associating it with a particular example.

- All the ideas she came up with in class were abstractions, since she had no experience of actual nursing at all.

From its roots, *abstraction* should mean basically "something pulled or drawn away." So *abstract* art is art that has moved away from painting objects of the ordinary physical world in order to show something beyond it. Theories are often abstractions; so a theory about economics, for instance, may "pull back" to take a broad view that somehow explains all of economics (but maybe doesn't end up explaining any of it very successfully). An *abstract* of a medical or scientific article is a one-paragraph summary of its contents—that is, the basic findings "pulled out" of the article.

abstruse \ab-ˈstrüs\ Hard to understand; deep or complex.

• In every class he fills the blackboard with abstruse calculations, and we usually leave more confused than ever.

The original meaning of *abstruse,* coming almost straight from the Latin, was "concealed, hidden." It's easy to see how the word soon came to describe the kind of language used by those who possess certain kinds of expert knowledge (and don't necessarily want to share it with other people). Scientific writing is often filled with the kind of abstruse special vocabulary that's necessary for exact and precise descriptions. Unfortunately, the language of a science like quantum physics can make an already difficult subject even more abstruse to the average person.

Quizzes

A. Match the definition on the left to the correct word on the right:

1.	mysterious	a.	encrypt
2.	code writing	b.	abstraction
3.	translate to code	c.	abscond
4.	difficult	d.	cryptic
5.	tomb	e.	abstruse
6.	generalization	f.	crypt
7.	self-controlled	g.	cryptography
8.	flee	h.	abstemious

B. Fill in each blank with the correct letter:

a. cryptic   e. cryptography
b. abscond   f. abstemious
c. abstraction   g. encrypt
d. crypt   h. abstruse

1. She had failed to ____ the file when she put it on her hard drive, and her secretary had secretly copied it.
2. His answer was so short and ____ that I have no idea what he meant.
3. The great, echoing ____ of St. Stephen's Cathedral could have held hundreds of people.
4. That's a clever ____, but in the real world things work very differently.
5. The ____ vocabulary of the literature professor led many students to drop her class.
6. He's given up drinking and leads an ____ life these days, rarely thinking about his former high living.
7. Their ____ hasn't been revised in two years, and we've been worried about the security of the data.
8. The bride is so shy that her mother fears she'll ____ from the reception.

PED comes from the Greek word for "child." The same root also has the meaning "foot" (see p. 78), but in English words it usually isn't hard to tell the two apart.

pedagogy \\'pe-də-ˌgō-jē\\ The art, science, or profession of teaching.

• His own pedagogy is extremely original; it sometimes alarms school officials but his students love it.

Since in Greek *agogos* means "leader," a *paidagogos* was a slave who led boys to school and back, but also taught them manners and tutored them after school. In time, *pedagogue* came to mean simply "teacher"; today the word has an old-fashioned ring to it, so it often means a stuffy, boring teacher. The word *pedagogy*, though, is still widely used, and often means simply "teaching." And *pedagogic* training is what everyone majoring in education receives.

pedant \\\'pe-dənt\\ (1) A formal, unimaginative teacher. (2) A person who shows off his or her learning.

* At one time or another, every student encounters a pedant who can make even the most interesting subject tedious.

It isn't always easy to tell a *pedantic* teacher from one who is simply thorough. Some professors get an undeserved reputation for *pedantry* from students who just don't like the subject much. Regardless of that, a pedant need not be a teacher; anyone who goes around displaying his or her knowledge in a boring way can qualify.

pediatrician \\ˌpē-dē-ə-ˈtri-shən\\ A doctor who specializes in the diseases, development, and care of children.

* Children in the U.S. usually see a pediatrician until they turn at least 15 or 16.

Since *iatros* means "physician" in Greek (see IATR, p. 615), words such as *pediatric* naturally refer to "children's medicine." *Pediatrics* is a fairly new medical specialty; until about 1900, children were considered small adults and given the same medical treatment, only milder. Benjamin Spock was the most famous pediatrician of the 20th century, and his book *Baby and Child Care* changed the way millions of Americans raised their children.

encyclopedic \\in-ˌsī-klə-ˈpē-dik\\ (1) Of or relating to an encyclopedia. (2) Covering a wide range of subjects.

* Someone with the kind of encyclopedic knowledge she has should be competing on *Jeopardy*.

In Greek, *paidaea* meant not simply "child-rearing" but also "education," and *kyklios* meant "general"; thus, an encyclopedia is a work broad enough to provide a kind of general education. The world's most eminent general encyclopedia, the *Encyclopaedia Britannica,* is a huge work that covers every field of human knowledge. But *encyclopedic* doesn't have to refer to books; it's often used to describe the wide-ranging knowledge that certain types of minds just can't stop acquiring.

TROP comes from the Greek *tropos*, meaning "turn" or "change." The *troposphere* is the level of the atmosphere where most weather changes—or "turns in the weather"—occur. And the *Tropics* of Cancer and Capricorn are the lines of latitude where the sun is directly overhead when it reaches its northernmost and southernmost points, on about June 22 and December 22 every year—that is, the point where it seems to turn and go back the other way.

---

tropism \\'trō-ˌpi-zəm\\ Automatic movement by an organism unable to move about from place to place, especially a plant, that involves turning or growing toward or away from a stimulus.

- The new president was soon showing a tropism for bold action, a tendency that seemed more the result of instinct than of careful thought.

In *hydrotropism*, a plant's roots grow in the direction of increasing moisture, hoping to obtain water. In *phototropism*, a plant (or fungus) moves toward light, usually the sun—perhaps because, in the colder climates where such plants are usually found, concentrating the sun's warmth within the sun-seeking flower can create a warm and inviting environment for the insects that fertilize it. In *thigmotropism*, the organism moves in response to being touched; most climbing plants, for example, put out tiny tendrils that feel around for something solid and then attach themselves or curl around it. When microbiologists talk about tropism, however, they're often referring instead to the way a virus will seek out a particular type of cell to infect. And when intellectuals use the word, they usually mean a tendency shown by a person or group which they themselves might not even be aware of.

entropy \\'en-trə-pē\\ (1) The decomposition of the matter and energy in the universe to an ultimate state of inactive uniformity. (2) Chaos, randomness.

- The apartment had been reduced to an advanced state of entropy, as if a tiny tornado had torn through it, shattering its contents and mixing the pieces together in a crazy soup.

With its Greek prefix *en-*, meaning "within," and the *trop-* root here meaning "change," *entropy* basically means "change within (a closed system)." The closed system we usually think of when speaking of entropy (especially if we're not physicists) is the entire universe. But entropy applies to closed systems of any size. Entropy is seen when the ice in a glass of water in a warm room melts—that is, as the temperature of everything in the room evens out. In a slightly different type of entropy, a drop of food coloring in that glass of water soon spreads out evenly. However, when a nonphysicist uses the word, he or she is usually trying to describe a large-scale collapse.

heliotrope \\'hē-lē-ə-ˌtrōp\\ Any of a genus of herbs or shrubs having small white or purple flowers.

• A long bank of purple heliotrope lined the walkway, and her guests were always remarking on the flowers' glorious fragrance.

Helios was the god of the sun in Greek mythology, and *helio-* came to appear in a number of sun-related English words. The genus known as the heliotropes consists of about 250 species; many are thought of as weeds, but the best-known species, garden heliotrope, is a popular and fragrant perennial that resembles the forget-me-not. The heliotrope tends to follow the sun—that is, turn its blossoms toward the sun as it travels from East to West every day. But the fact is, *heliotropism*—turning toward the sun—is common among flowers (and even leaves), and some, like the sunflower, are more dramatically *heliotropic* than the heliotrope. Those in the far North actually use their petals to reflect the sun's heat onto the flower's central ovary during the short growing season.

psychotropic \\ˌsī-kə-'trō-pik\\ Acting on the mind.

• My mother is taking two drugs that may produce psychotropic side effects, and I'm worried that they might be interacting.

Psychotropic is used almost always to describe substances that we consume. Such substances are more numerous than you might think, and some have been known for thousands of years. Native American religions, for example, have used psychotropic substances derived from certain cactuses and mushrooms for centuries. Caffeine and nicotine can be called psychotropic. Psychotropic prescription drugs include antidepressants (such as Prozac) and tranquilizers (such as Valium). Any medication that blocks pain, from aspirin to the anesthetics used during surgery, can be considered a psychotropic drug. Even children are now prescribed psychotropic drugs, often to treat attention deficit disorder. And all recreational drugs are psychotropic. *Psychoactive* is a common synonym of *psychotropic*.

Quizzes

A. Indicate whether the following pairs of words have the same or different meanings:

1. psychotropic / mind-altering   same ___ / different ___
2. encyclopedic / important   same ___ / different ___
3. entropy / disorder   same ___ / different ___
4. heliotrope / sunflower   same ___ / different ___
5. pediatrician / foot doctor   same ___ / different ___
6. tropism / growth   same ___ / different ___
7. pedagogy / teaching   same ___ / different ___
8. pedant / know-it-all   same ___ / different ___

B. Match the definition on the left to the correct word on the right:

1. thorough   a. entropy
2. decay   b. pediatrician
3. boring teacher   c. heliotrope
4. fragrant flower   d. encyclopedic
5. automatic motion   e. tropism
6. education   f. pedant
7. affecting the mind   g. psychotropic
8. children's doctor   h. pedagogy

NEO comes from the Greek *neos*, meaning "new." *Neo-* has become a part of many English words. Some are easy to understand; for example, *neo-Nazi*. Some are less so; you might not immediately guess that *neotropical* means "from the tropics of the New World," or that a *neophyte* is a "newcomer." When William Ramsay discovered four new gases, he named them all using Greek roots that at first glance might sound slightly mysterious: *argon* ("idle"), *krypton* ("hidden"), *xenon* ("strange")—and *neon* ("new").

---

neoclassic \ˌnē-ō-ˈkla-sik\ Relating to a revival or adaptation of the styles of ancient Greece and Roman, especially in music, art, or architecture.

• He had always admired the paintings of the French neoclassical masters, especially Poussin and Ingres.

In the arts and architecture, a style that has existed for a long time usually produces a reaction against it. So after the showy style of Europe's so-called baroque era (from about 1600 to the early 1700s), the reaction came in the form of the neoclassical movement, bringing order, restraint, and simpler and more conservative structures, whether in plays, sonatas, sculptures, or public buildings. Its inspiration was the art of ancient Greece and Rome—that is, of *classical* antiquity. Why *classical*? In Latin *classicus* meant "of the highest *class*," so in English *classic* and *classical* originally described the best ancient Greek and Latin literature, but soon came to mean simply "of ancient Greek and Rome," since these were already seen as the highest and best cultures. *Neoclassic* generally describes artworks from the 1700s or early 1800s (by the painter David, the composer Mozart, the sculptor Canova, etc.), but also works from the 20th century that seem to have been inspired by the ideals of Greece and Rome.

Neolithic \ˌnē-ə-ˈlith-ik\ Of or relating to the latest period of the Stone Age, when polished stone tools were used.

• Around the Mediterranean, the Neolithic period was a time of trade, of stock breeding, and of the first use of pottery.

Since *lithos* in Greek means "stone," the Neolithic period is the "new" or "late" period of the Stone Age, in contrast to the Paleolithic period ("old" or "early" period—see PALEO, p. 646) and the Mesolithic period ("middle" period) of the Stone Age. The use of polished stone tools came to different parts of the world at different times, but the Neolithic Age is usually said to begin around 9000 B.C. and to end around 3000 B.C., when the Bronze Age begins. The Neolithic is the era when the farming of plants and animals begins, and when, as a result, humans first begin to create permanent settlements.

neoconservative \ˌnē-ō-kən-ˈsər-və-tiv\ A conservative who favors strongly encouraging democracy and the U.S. national interest in world affairs, including through military means.

• Many believed that foreign policy in those years had fallen into the hands of the neoconservatives, and that the war in Iraq was one result.

In the 1960s several well-known socialist intellectuals, including Norman Podhoretz and Irving Kristol, alarmed by growing political extremism on the left, began to move in the other direction. Soon the term *neoconservative* (or *neocon* for short) was being attached to them. Rather than simply drifting toward the political center, Podhoretz and Kristol actually moved far to the right, especially on the issue of maintaining a strong military stance toward the rest of the world. The main magazine of *neoconservatism* became Podhoretz's *Commentary*; it was later joined by the *Weekly Standard*, edited by Kristol's son William. Not everyone agrees on how to define these terms; still, it's clear that today you don't have to be a former liberal in order to be a neoconservative.

neonatal \ˌnē-ō-ˈnā-t²l\ Of or relating to babies in the first month after their birth.

- The hospital's newest addition is a neonatal intensive-care unit, and newborns in critical condition are already being sent there from considerable distances.

Partly based on the Latin *natus*, "born," *neonatal* means "newly born." Neonatal babies themselves are called *neonates*. Most hospitals now offer neonatal screening, which is used to detect diseases that are treatable only if identified during the first days of life, and specialized neonatal nursing as well. But despite spending much money on neonatal care, the U.S. still ranks lower than some much less wealthy countries (such as the Czech Republic, Portugal, and Cuba) in infant mortality (infant deaths).

NOV comes from the Latin word *novus*, meaning "new." To *renovate* an old house is to "make it new again"—that is, put it back in tip-top shape. The long-running PBS show *Nova* keeps its large audience up to date on what's new in the world of science. And when the British king sent Scottish settlers to a large island off Canada's Atlantic coast in the 17th century, he named it *Nova Scotia*, or "New Scotland."

---

novice \ˈnä-vəs\ (1) One who has no previous training or experience in a specific field or activity; beginner. (2) A new member of a religious order who is preparing to become a nun or monk.

- It's hard to believe that a year ago she was a complete novice as a gardener, who couldn't identify a cornstalk.

Among the ancient Romans, a novice (*novicius*) was usually a newly imported slave, who had to be trained in his or her duties. Among

Catholics and Buddhists, if you desire to become a priest, monk, or nun, you must serve as a novice for a period of time, often a year (called your *novitiate*), before being ordained or fully professing your vows. No matter what kind of novice you are—at computers, at writing, at politics, etc.—you've got a lot to learn.

novel \\\'nä-vəl\\ (1) New and not resembling something formerly known or used. (2) Original and striking, especially in conception or style.

• His techniques for dealing with these disturbed young people were novel, and they caught the attention of the institute's director.

If someone tells you that you've come up with a novel idea or a novel interpretation of something, it's probably a compliment: not everyone is capable of original thinking. But not everything new is terribly worthwhile; a *novelty,* for example, is often a cute (or maybe just silly) little object that you might put on a display shelf in your house. It may seem surprising that the familiar noun *novel* is related as well. In the 14th century, Italian writers began writing collections of short tales, each of which they called a *novella* because it represented a new literary form; from this word, three centuries later, the English coined the noun *novel*.

innovation \\ˌi-nə-'vā-shən\\ (1) A new idea, device, or method. (2) The introduction of new ideas, devices, or methods.

• "Smooshing" bits of candy into ice cream while the customer watched was just one of his innovations that later got copied by chains of ice-cream outlets.

Innovation is a word that's almost always connected with business. In business today, it's almost a rule that a company that doesn't *innovate* is destined for failure. The most important and successful businesses were usually started by *innovators*. And company managers should always at least listen to the *innovative* ideas of their employees.

supernova \\ˌsü-pər-'nō-və\\ (1) The explosion of a star that causes it to become extremely bright. (2) Something that explodes into prominence or popularity.

• After exploding, a nova leaves a "white dwarf" which may explode again in the future, but a supernova destroys the entire star.

A *nova*, despite its name, isn't actually a "new" star, but rather one that wasn't noticed until it exploded, when it may increase in brightness by a million times before returning to its previous state a few days later. A supernova is far larger; a star in its supernova state may emit a billion times as much light as previously. After a few weeks it begins to dim, until it eventually ceases to exist; it's often replaced by a black hole. (Though remains that were shot out into space may survive; those of a great supernova seen in A.D. 1054 are now known as the Crab Nebula.) All this may serve as a warning to those human stars whose fame explodes too rapidly; supernovas of this kind have sometimes vanished by the following year.

Quizzes

A. Fill in each blank with the correct letter:

a. Neolithic   e. supernova
b. novice   f. neoconservative
c. novel   g. neoclassic
d. neonatal   h. innovation

1. My father subscribes to the ____ magazines and still thinks we had no choice but to invade Iraq.
2. The building's style is ____, with Roman columns and with white statues on either side of the entrance.
3. In his youth he had intended to join the priesthood, and he even served as a ____ for six months before giving it up.
4. They're now working at a ____ site in Syria, where they've found evidence of goat, pig, and sheep farming.
5. The baby might not have survived if the hospital hadn't had an excellent ____ ward.
6. The ____ seen by Asian astronomers in 1054 was four times as bright as the brightest planet.
7. The company had a history of ____ that had earned it immense respect and attracted many of the brightest young engineers.
8. She often comes up with ____ interpretations of the evidence in cases like this, and she's sometimes proven correct.

B. Match the word on the left to the correct definition on the right:

1. novice	a. star explosion
2. innovation	b. new invention or method
3. neoclassic	c. beginner
4. neoconservative	d. newborn
5. neonatal	e. ancient
6. novel	f. cleverly new
7. supernova	g. favoring aggressive foreign policy
8. Neolithic	h. resembling Greek and Roman style

POS comes from the Latin verb *ponere,* meaning "to put" or "to place." You *expose* film by "placing it out" in the light. You *compose* a song by "putting together" a series of notes. And you *oppose* locating a new prison in your town by "putting yourself against" it.

impose \im-ˈpōz\ (1) To establish or apply as a charge or penalty or in a forceful or harmful way. (2) To take unfair advantage.

* After seeing her latest grades, her parents imposed new rules about how much time she had to spend on homework every night.

The Latin *imposui* meant "put upon," and that meaning carried over into English in *impose.* A CEO may impose a new manager on one of the company's plants. A state may impose new taxes on luxury items or cigarettes, and the federal government sometimes imposes trade restrictions on another country to punish it. A polite apology might begin with "I hope I'm not imposing on you" (that is, "forcing my presence on you"). And a *self-imposed* deadline is one that you decide to hold yourself to.

juxtapose \ˈjək-stə-ˌpōz\ To place side by side.

* You won't notice the difference between the original and the copy unless you juxtapose them.

Since *juxta* means "near" in Latin, it's easy to see how *juxtapose* was formed. Juxtaposing is generally done for examination or effect. Interior designers constantly make decisions about juxtaposing objects and colors for the best effect. Juxtaposing two video clips showing the different things that a politician said about the same subject at two different times can be an effective means of criticizing. The *juxtaposition* of two similar X-rays can help medical students distinguish between two conditions that may be hard to tell apart. And advertisements frequently juxtapose "before" and "after" images to show a thrilling transformation.

transpose \trans-ˈpōz\ (1) To change the position or order of (two things). (2) To move from one place or period to another.

• She rechecked the phone number and discovered that two digits had been transposed.

Though transposing two digits can be disastrous, transposing two letters in a word often doesn't matter too much. (You can prboalby raed tihs setnence witohut too mcuh toruble.) Transposing two words or sounds—as in "Can I sew you to another sheet?"—has been a good source of humor over the years. Doctors sometimes discover that something in the body—a nerve, an organ, etc.—has been transposed, or moved away from its proper place. For musicians, transposing means changing the key of a piece; if you can do this at a moment's notice, you've been well trained.

superimpose \ˌsü-pər-im-ˈpōz\ To put or place one thing over something else.

• Using transparent sheets, she superimposes territory boundaries on an outline of Africa, showing us how these changed in the late 19th and early 20th century.

Superimposition was one of the magical effects employed by early filmmakers. Using "mirror shots," with semitransparent mirrors set at 45° angles to the scene, they would superimpose shadowy images of ghosts or scenes from a character's past onto scenes from the present. Superimposing your own ideas on something, such as a historical event, has to be done carefully, since your ideas may change whenever you learn something new about the event.

TEN, from the Latin verb *tenere*, basically means "hold" or "hold on to." A *tenant* is the "holder" of an apartment, house, or land, but not necessarily the owner. A *lieutenant* governor may "hold the position" ("serve in lieu") of the governor when necessary.

tenure \\'ten-yər\\ (1) The amount of time that a person holds a job, office, or title. (2) The right to keep a job, especially the job of teacher or professor.

- I know two assistant professors who are so worried about being denied tenure this year that they can't sleep.

Tenure is about holding on to something, almost always a job or position. So you can speak of someone's 30-year tenure as chairman, or someone's brief tenure in the sales manager's office. But *tenure* means something slightly different in the academic world. In American colleges and universities, the best (or luckiest) teachers have traditionally been granted a lifetime appointment known as tenure after about six years of teaching. Almost nobody has as secure a job as a *tenured* professor, but getting tenure can be difficult, and most of them have earned it.

tenacious \\tə-'nā-shəs\\ Stubborn or determined in clinging to something.

- He was known as a tenacious reporter who would stay with a story for months, risking his health and sometimes even his life.

Success in most fields requires a tenacious spirit and a drive to achieve. Nowhere is this more apparent than in the entertainment business. Thousands of actors and actresses work *tenaciously* to build a TV or film career. But without talent or beauty, *tenacity* is rarely rewarded, and only a few become stars.

tenable \\'te-nə-bəl\\ Capable of being held or defended; reasonable.

- She was depressed for weeks after her professor said that her theory wasn't tenable.

Tenable means "holdable." In the past it was often used in a physical sense—for example, to refer to a city that an army was trying to "hold" militarily against an enemy force. But nowadays it's almost always used when speaking of "held" ideas and theories. If you hold an opinion but evidence appears that completely contradicts it, your opinion is no longer tenable. So, for example, the old ideas that cancer is infectious or that being bled by leeches can cure your whooping cough now seem *untenable*.

tenet \'te-nət\ A widely held principle or belief, especially one held in common by members of a group or profession.

• It was soon obvious that the new owners didn't share the tenets that the company's founders had held to all those years.

A *tenet* is something we hold, but not with our hands. Tenets are often ideals, but also often statements of faith. Thus, we may speak of the tenets of Islam or Hinduism, the tenets of Western democracy, or the tenets of the scientific method, and in each case these tenets may combine elements of both faith and ideals.

Quizzes

A. Choose the closest definition:

1. impose   a. force b. request c. seek d. hint
2. tenacious   a. stubborn b. intelligent c. loving
      d. helping
3. superimpose   a. surpass b. put into c. place over
      d. amaze
4. juxtapose   a. place on top of b. put away c. place side
      by side d. put into storage
5. transpose   a. emerge b. change into c. cross d. switch
6. tenable   a. decent b. tough c. reasonable
      d. controllable
7. tenet   a. claw b. belief c. renter d. shelter
8. tenure   a. strong hold b. permanent appointment
      c. lengthy period d. male voice

B. Indicate whether the following pairs have the same or different meanings:

1. impose / remove   same ___ / different ___
2. tenet / principle   same ___ / different ___
3. transpose / exchange   same ___ / different ___
4. tenure / absence   same ___ / different ___
5. superimpose / offend deeply   same ___ / different ___
6. tenacious / sensible   same ___ / different ___
7. juxtapose / switch   same ___ / different ___
8. tenable / reasonable   same ___ / different ___

Number Words

MONO comes from the Greek *monos*, meaning "alone" or "single." So a *monorail* is a railroad that has only one rail; a *monocle* is an old-fashioned eyeglass that a gentleman used to squeeze into his eye socket; a *monotonous* voice seems to have only one tone; and a *monopoly* puts all ownership of a type of product or service in the hands of a single company.

monogamous \mə-ˈnä-gə-məs\ Being married to one person or having one mate at a time.

• Geese, swans, and most other birds are monogamous and mate for life.

American marriage is by law monogamous; people are permitted to have only one spouse at a time. There are cultures with laws that permit marriage to more than one person at a time, or *polygamy*. Although the term *polygamy* may refer to *polyandry* (marriage to more than one man), it is more often used as a synonym for *polygyny* (marriage to more than one woman), which appears to have once been common in most of the world and is still found widely in some cultures.

monoculture \ˈmä-nə-ˌkəl-chər\ (1) The cultivation of a single crop to the exclusion of other uses of land. (2) A culture dominated by a single element.

• Monoculture is practiced on a vast scale in the American Midwest, where nothing but corn can be seen in the fields for hundreds of square miles.

The Irish Potato Famine of 1845–49, which led to the deaths of over a million people, resulted from the monoculture of potatoes, which were destroyed by a terrible blight, leaving farmers nothing else to eat. Almost every traditional farming society has practiced crop rotation, the planting of different crops on a given piece of land from year to year, so as to keep the soil from losing its quality. But in the modern world, monoculture has become the rule on the largest commercial farms, where the same crop can be planted year after year by means of the intensive use of fertilizers. Modern monoculture has produced huge crops; on a large scale, it permits great efficiency in planting, pest control, and harvesting. But many experts believe this all comes at a huge cost to the environment.

monolithic \ˌmä-nə-ˈli-thik\ (1) Appearing to be a huge, feature-less, often rigid whole. (2) Made up of material with no joints or seams.

• The sheer monolithic rock face of Yosemite's El Capitan looks impossible to climb, but its cracks and seams are enough for experienced rock climbers.

The *-lith* in *monolith* comes from the Greek *lithos*, "stone," so *monolith* in its original sense means a huge stone like those at Stonehenge. What's so impressive about monoliths is that they have no separate parts or pieces. To the lone individual, any huge institution or government bureaucracy can seem monolithic. But the truth may be different: The former U.S.S.R. once seemed monolithic and indestructible to the West, but in the 1990s it crumbled into a number of independent republics.

monotheism \ˈmä-nō-thē-ˌi-zəm\ The doctrine or belief that there is a single god.

• The earliest known instance of monotheism dates to the reign of Akhenaton of Egypt in the 14th century B.C.

Monotheism, which is characteristic of Judaism, Islam, and Chris-tianity, is distinguished from *polytheism*, belief in or worship of more than one god. The monotheism that characterizes Judaism began in ancient Israel with the adoption of Yahweh as the single object of worship and the rejection of the gods of other tribes and nations without, initially, denying their existence. Islam is clear in acknowledging one, eternal, unbegotten, unequaled God, while Christianity holds that a single God is reflected in the three persons of the Holy Trinity.

UNI comes from the Latin word for "one." A *uniform* is a single design worn by everyone. A *united* group has one single opinion, or forms a single *unit*. A *unitard* is a one-piece combination leotard and tights, very good for skating, skiing, dancing—or riding a one-wheeled *unicycle*.

---

unicameral \ˌyü-ni-ˈka-mə-rəl\ Having only one lawmaking chamber.

• In China, with its unicameral system of government, a single group of legislators meets to make the laws.

Unicameral means "one-chambered," and the term almost always describes a governing body. Our federal legislature, like those of most democracies, is *bicameral,* with two legislative (lawmaking) bodies—the Senate and the House of Representatives. And except for Nebraska, all the state legislatures are also bicameral. So why did the nation decide on a bicameral system? Partly in order to keep some power out of the hands of ordinary voters, who the Founding Fathers didn't completely trust. For that reason, the original Constitution states that senators are to be elected by the state legislatures; not until 1914, after passage of a Constitutional amendment, did we first cast direct votes for our senators.

unilateral \ˌyü-ni-ˈla-tə-rəl\ (1) Done by one person or party; one-sided. (2) Affecting one side of the body.

• The Japanese Constitution of 1947 includes a unilateral rejection of warfare as an option for their country.

The world is a smaller place than it used to be, and we get uncomfortable when a single nation adopts a policy of *unilateralism*—that is, acting independently with little regard for what the rest of the world thinks. A unilateral invasion of another country, for instance, usually looks like a grab for power and resources. But occasionally the world welcomes a unilateral action, as when the U.S. announced unilateral nuclear-arms reductions in the early 1990s. Previously, such reductions had only happened as part of *bilateral* ("two-sided") agreements with the old Soviet Union. *Multilateral* agreements, on issues such as climate change, often involve most of the world's nations.

unison \ˈyü-nə-sən\ (1) Perfect agreement. (2) Sameness of musical pitch.

• Unable to read music well enough to harmonize, the village choir sang only in unison.

This word usually appears in the phrase "in unison," which means "together, at the same time" or "at the same musical pitch." So an excited crowd responding to a speaker may shout in unison, and a group of demonstrators may chant in unison. The old church music called Gregorian chant was written to be sung in unison, with no harmonizing voices, and kindergarten kids always sing in unison (at least when they can all find the same pitch). In a similar way, an aerobics class moves in unison following the instructor, and a group or even a whole town may work in unison when everyone agrees on a common goal.

unitarian \ˌyü-nə-ˈter-ē-ən\ Relating or belonging to a religious group that believes that God exists only in one person and stresses individual freedom of belief.

• With his unitarian tendencies, he wasn't likely to get into fights over religious beliefs.

Unitarianism, originally a sect of Christianity believing in a single or *unitary* God, grew up in 18th-century England and developed in America in the early 19th century. Though they believe in Christ's teaching, they reject the idea of the three-part Trinity—God as father, son, and holy spirit—and thus deny that Christ was divine, so some people don't consider them truly Christian. In this century the Unitarians joined with the *Universalist* Church, a movement founded on a belief in *universal* salvation—that is, the saving of every soul from damnation after death. Both have always been liberal and fairly small; today they count about half a million members. Without a capital letter, *unitarian* refers simply to belief in a *unitary* God, or in *unity* within some nonreligious system.

Quiz

Fill in each blank with the correct letter:

a. monotheism   e. unitarian
b. unilateral   f. monoculture
c. monolithic   g. unicameral
d. unison   h. monogamous

1. The president is allowed to make some _____ decisions without asking Congress's permission.
2. The relationship was unbalanced: she was perfectly _____, while he had two other women in his life.
3. In rejecting a _____ legislature, America seemed to follow Britain's lead.
4. The sheer mountain face, _____ and forbidding, loomed over the town.

5. As a strict Catholic, she found ____ beliefs unacceptable.
6. Most religious groups in this country practice one or another form of ____.
7. Corn was a ____ in the village, and the farmers would simply move to a new field each year to keep the soil from wearing out.
8. At Halloween and Thanksgiving assemblies, the children would recite holiday poems in ____.

Review Quizzes

A. Choose the correct synonym:

1. unilateral   a. one-sided b. sideways c. complete d. multiple
2. cryptography   a. gravestone writing b. physics writing c. code writing d. mathematical writing
3. monotheism   a. nature worship b. worship of one god c. worship of pleasure d. sun worship
4. abscond   a. steal b. discover c. retire d. flee
5. transpose   a. send out b. take place c. overcome d. switch
6. tenet   a. shelter b. principle c. choice d. landlord
7. pedagogy   a. study b. teaching c. research d. child abuse
8. unison   a. solitude b. melody c. collection d. agreement
9. crypt   a. code b. granite c. tomb d. church
10. superimpose   a. increase b. lay over c. improve d. excel
11. monogamous   a. with one spouse b. without a spouse c. with several spouses d. with someone else's spouse
12. tenable   a. available b. unbearable c. agreeable d. reasonable

B. Fill in each blank with the correct letter:

a. tenure   f. abstraction
b. pediatrician   g. tenacious
c. pedant   h. cryptic
d. unitarian   i. encyclopedic
e. impose   j. abstruse

1. Their son had just called to tell them that the university had decided to grant him _____.
2. Tuesday the baby sees the _____ for her immunizations and checkups.
3. The only clues for the treasure hunt were in a _____ poem that his father had written.
4. By the time she was 25 she had an _____ knowledge of her state's history.
5. The notion of a savior was foreign to his _____ beliefs.
6. The legislature is threatening to _____ strict limits on this kind of borrowing.
7. The speech contained one _____ after another, but never a specific example.
8. At the age of 72 he was regarded by most of the students as a boring _____.
9. The sick child's _____ grip on life was their only hope now.
10. The researcher's writing was _____ but it was worth the effort to read it.

C. Indicate whether the following pairs of words have the same or different meanings:

1. monotheism / growing of
   one crop   same ___ / different ___
2. unison / unitedness   same ___ / different ___
3. cryptic / gravelike   same ___ / different ___
4. monolithic / boring   same ___ / different ___
5. abstemious / self-controlled   same ___ / different ___
6. tenet / ideal   same ___ / different ___
7. crypt / tomb   same ___ / different ___
8. tenable / reasonable   same ___ / different ___
9. unicameral / one-chambered   same ___ / different ___
10. abstruse / difficult   same ___ / different ___

UNIT

15

TERM/TERMIN comes from the Latin verb *terminare*, "to limit, bound, or set limits to," and the noun *terminus*, "limit or boundary." In English, those boundaries or limits tend to be final. A *term* goes on for a given amount of time and then ends, and to *terminate* a sentence or a meeting or a ballgame means to end it.

---

terminal \\ˈtər-mə-nəl\\ (1) Forming or relating to an end or limit. (2) Fatal.

• She knows she's in the late stages of a terminal illness, and has already drawn up a will.

A terminal disease ends in death. If you're *terminally* bored, you're "bored to death." For many students, a high-school diploma is their terminal degree (others finish college before *terminating* their education). A bus or train *terminal* is the endpoint of the line. A computer terminal was originally the endpoint of a line connecting to a central computer. A terminal ornament may mark the end of a building, and terminal punctuation ends this sentence.

---

indeterminate \\ˌin-di-ˈtər-mə-nət\\ Not precisely determined; vague.

• The police are looking for a tall white bearded man of indeterminate age who should be considered armed and dangerous.

When you *determine* something, you decide on what it is, which means you put limits or boundaries on its identity. So something indeterminate lacks identifying limits. A mutt is usually the product of indeterminate breeding, since at least the father's identity is generally a mystery. A painting of indeterminate origins is normally less valued than one with the painter's name on it. And if negotiations are left in an indeterminate state, nothing has been decided.

interminable \in-'tər-mə-nə-bəl\ Having or seeming to have no end; tiresomely drawn out.

• The preacher was making another of his interminable pleas for money, so she snapped off the TV.

Nothing is literally endless, except maybe the universe and time itself, so *interminable* as we use it is always an exaggeration. On an unlucky day you might sit through an interminable meeting, have an interminable drive home in heavy traffic, and watch an interminable film—all in less than 24 hours.

terminus \'tər-mə-nəs\ (1) The end of a travel route (such as a rail or bus line), or the station at the end of a route. (2) An extreme point; tip.

• They've been tracking the terminus of the glacier for 20 years, in which time it has retreated 500 yards.

This word comes straight from Latin. In the Roman empire, a terminus was a boundary stone, and all boundary stones had a minor god associated with them, whose name was Terminus. Terminus was a kind of keeper of the peace, since wherever there was a terminus there could be no arguments about where your property ended and your neighbor's property began. So Terminus even had his own festival, the Terminalia, when images of the god were draped with flower garlands. Today the word shows up in all kinds of places, including in the name of numerous hotels worldwide built near a city's railway terminus.

GEO comes from the Greek word for "Earth." *Geography* is the science that deals with features of the Earth's surface. *Geologists* study rocks and soil to learn about the Earth's history and resources. *Geometry* was originally about measuring portions of the Earth's surface, probably originally in order to determine where the boundaries of Egyptians' farms lay after the annual flooding by the Nile River.

---

geocentric \ˌjē-ō-ˈsen-trik\ Having or relating to the Earth as the center.

• He claims that, if you aren't a scientist, your consciousness is mostly geocentric for your entire life.

The idea that the Earth is the center of the universe and that the sun revolves around it is an ancient one, probably dating back to the earliest humans. Not until 1543 did the Polish astronomer Copernicus publish his calculations proving that the Earth actually revolves around the sun, thus replacing the geocentric model with a *heliocentric* model (from *Helios*, the Greek god of the sun). But *geocentrism* remains central to various religious sects around the world, and still today one in five adult Americans believes the sun revolves around the Earth.

geophysics \ˌjē-ə-ˈfi-ziks\ The science that deals with the physical processes and phenomena occurring especially in the Earth and in its vicinity.

• Located in the heart of oil and gas country, the university offers a degree in geophysics and many of its graduates go straight to work for the oil and gas industry.

Geophysics applies the principles of physics to the study of the Earth. It deals with such things as the movement of the Earth's crust and the temperatures of its interior. Another subject is the behavior of the still-mysterious *geomagnetic* field. Some *geophysicists* seek out deposits of ores or petroleum; others specialize in earthquakes; still others study the water beneath the Earth's surface, where it collects and how it flows.

geostationary \ˌjē-ō-ˈstā-shə-ˌner-ē\ Being or having an orbit such that a satellite remains in a fixed position above the Earth, especially having such an orbit above the equator.

• It was the science-fiction writer Arthur C. Clarke who first conceived of a set of geostationary satellites as a means of worldwide communication.

We don't give much thought to geostationary satellites, but many of us rely on them daily. Anyone who watches satellite TV or listens to satellite radio is dependent on them; the weather photos you see on TV are taken from geostationary satellites; and military information gathering via satellite goes on quietly day after day. (Though the satellites that provide GPS service for your car or cell phone actually aren't geostationary, since they orbit the Earth twice a day.) By 2009 there were about 300 geostationary satellites in operation, all of them moving at an altitude of about 22,000 miles. Since they hover above the same spot on Earth, your receiving dish or antenna doesn't have to turn in order to track them.

geothermal \ˌjē-ō-ˈthər-məl\ Of, relating to, or using the natural heat produced inside the Earth.

- Geothermal power plants convert underground water or steam to electricity.

Geothermal comes partly from the Greek *thermos*, "hot" (see THERM/THERMO, p. 51). Most geothermal electricity is provided by power plants situated in areas where there is significant activity of the Earth's great tectonic plates—often the same areas where volcanoes are found. But hot water from deep underground may be used by cities far from volcanoes to heat buildings or sidewalks. And a newer source of geothermal energy relies on a less dramatic kind of heat: Individual homeowners can now install heat pumps that take advantage of the 50°–60° temperature of the soil near the surface to provide heating in cold weather (and air-conditioning in the warm months). These very small-scale geothermal systems may eventually supply more useful energy than the large power plants.

Quizzes

A. Choose the closest definition:

1. terminus   a. heat source b. endpoint c. final exam
        d. period
2. interminable   a. remarkable b. unthinkable
        c. reliable d. eternal
3. geocentric   a. moonlike b. near earth's core
        c. mathematical d. earth-centered
4. geophysics   a. physical geometry b. earth science
        c. material science d. science of shapes
5. geostationary   a. polar b. hovering over one
        location c. space-station-related d. equatorial

6. terminal   a. fatal b. technical c. verbal d. similar
7. indeterminate   a. lengthy b. uncertain c. unending
      d. likely
8. geothermal   a. globally warmed b. using earth's
      heat c. solar-powered d. tropical

B. Fill in each blank with the correct letter:

a. geophysics   e. indeterminate
b. terminus   f. geocentric
c. geothermal   g. terminal
d. interminable   h. geostationary

1. Tens of millions of people couldn't watch TV if it
    weren't for a fleet of _____ satellites.
2. Their house is mostly heated by a _____ heat pump, so
    they pay almost nothing for fuel.
3. Most of us are _____ in our thinking until a grade-school
    teacher tells us about how the earth revolves around the
    sun.
4. Their land extends all the way out to the _____ of the
    little peninsula.
5. He was a man of _____ age, and mysterious in other ways
    as well.
6. It was the mystery of the earth's magnetic field that
    eventually led him into the field of _____.
7. He gave _____ lectures, and I usually dozed off in the
    middle.
8. Last week we assumed his condition was _____; today no
    one is making predictions.

SPHER comes from the Greek word for "ball." A ball is itself a
sphere, as is the ball that we call Earth. So is the *atmosphere,* and
so are several other invisible "spheres" that encircle the Earth.

---

spherical \\'sfir-ə-kəl\\ Relating to a sphere; shaped like a sphere
or one of its segments.

• The girls agreed that the spacecraft had been deep blue and
  perfectly spherical, and that its alien passengers had resembled
  large praying mantises.

Something spherical is like a *sphere* in being round, or more or less round, in three dimensions. Apples and oranges are both spherical, for example, even though they're never perfectly round. A *spheroid* has a roughly spherical shape; so an asteroid, for instance, is often *spheroidal*—fairly round, but lumpy.

stratosphere \\'stra-tə-ˌsfir\\ (1) The part of the earth's atmosphere that extends from about seven to about 30 miles above the surface. (2) A very high or the highest region.

• In the celebrity stratosphere she now occupied, a fee of 12 million dollars per film was a reasonable rate.

The stratosphere (*strato-* simply means "layer" or "level") lies above the earth's weather and mostly changes very little. It contains the ozone layer, which shields us from the sun's ultraviolet radiation except where it's been harmed by manmade chemicals. The levels of the *atmosphere* are marked particularly by their temperatures; *stratospheric* temperatures rise only to around 32°—very moderate considering that temperatures in the *troposphere* below may descend to about −70° and those in the *ionosphere* above may rise to 1000°.

biosphere \\'bī-ə-ˌsfir\\ (1) The part of the world in which life can exist. (2) Living things and their environment.

• The moon has no biosphere, so an artificial one would have to be constructed for any long-term stay.

The *lithosphere* is the solid surface of the earth (*lith-* meaning "rock"); the *hydrosphere* is the earth's water (*hydro-* means "water"), including the clouds and water vapor in the air; and the *atmosphere* is the earth's air (*atmos-* meaning "vapor"). The term *biosphere* can include all of these, along with the 10 million species of living things they contain. The biosphere recycles its air, water, organisms, and minerals constantly to maintain an amazingly balanced state; human beings should probably do their best to imitate it. Though the word has a new sound to it, it was first used over a hundred years ago.

hemisphere \\'he-mə-ˌsfir\\ Half a sphere, especially half the global sphere as divided by the equator or a meridian.

- A sailor who crosses the equator from the northern to the southern hemisphere for the first time is traditionally given a special initiation.

Hemisphere includes the prefix *hemi-*, meaning "half." The northern and southern hemispheres are divided by the equator, the circle halfway between Earth's two poles. The eastern and western hemispheres aren't divided so exactly, since there are no poles in the Earth's east-west dimension. Often the dividing line is said to be the "prime meridian"—the imaginary north-south line that runs through Greenwich, England, from which all longitude is calculated (itself being the 0° meridian). But for simplicity's sake, the eastern hemisphere is often said to include all of Europe, Africa, Australia, and Asia, while the western hemisphere contains North and South America and a great deal of ocean.

VERT comes from the Latin verb *vertere,* meaning "to turn" or "to turn around." *Vertigo* is the dizziness that makes it seem as if everything is turning around you. And an *advertisement* turns your attention to a product or service.

---

divert \dī-'vərt\ (1) To turn from one purpose or course to another. (2) To give pleasure to by distracting from burdens or distress.

- The farmers had successfully diverted some of the river's water to irrigate their crops during the drought.

The Roman circus was used to provide *diversion* for its citizens—and sometimes to divert their attention from the government's failings as well. The diversion was often in the form of a fight—men pitted against lions, bears, or each other—and the audience was sure to see blood and death. A *diverting* evening these days might instead include watching the same kind of mayhem on a movie screen.

converter \kən-'vər-tər\ A device that changes something (such as radio signals, radio frequencies, or data) from one form to another.

- She was so indifferent to television that she hadn't even bought a converter, and her old TV sat there useless until she finally lugged it down to the recycling center.

Converters come in many forms. Travelers to foreign countries who bring along their electric razors or hair dryers always pack a small electric converter, which can change direct current to alternating current or vice versa. In 2009 millions of Americans bought digital-analog converters, small box-shaped devices that change the new broadcast digital signal to the analog signal that older TV sets were made to receive. A *catalytic converter* is the pollution-control device attached to your car's exhaust system that converts pollutants such as carbon monoxide into harmless form.

avert \ə-'vərt\ (1) To turn (your eyes or gaze) away or aside. (2) To avoid or prevent.

• General Camacho's announcement of lower food prices averted an immediate worker's revolt.

Sensitive people avert their eyes from gory accidents and scenes of disaster. But the accident or disaster might itself have been averted if someone had been alert enough. Negotiators may avert a strike by all-night talks. In the Cuban missile crisis of 1962, it seemed that nuclear catastrophe was barely averted. *Aversion* means "dislike or disgust"—that is, your feeling about something you can't stand to look at.

revert \ri-'vərt\ (1) To go back or return (to an earlier state, condition, situation, etc.). (2) To be given back to (a former owner).

• Control of the Panama Canal Zone, first acquired by the U.S. in 1903, reverted to the local government in 1999.

Since the prefix *re-* often means "back" (see RE-, p. 635), the basic meaning of *revert* is "turn back." *Revert* and *reversion* often show up in legal documents, since property is often given to another person on the condition that it will revert to the original owner at some future date or when something happens (usually the death of the second person). In nonlegal uses, the word tends to show up in negative contexts. Many reformed drinkers, for example, eventually revert to their old ways, and most people revert to smoking at least once or twice before succeeding in quitting for good.

Quizzes

A. Fill in each blank with the correct letter:

a. revert   e. divert
b. avert   f. converter
c. hemisphere   g. spherical
d. biosphere   h. stratosphere

1. Every living thing that we know of inhabits the earth's ____.
2. The generals had discussed what would be involved if they tried to ____ 10,000 troops from Afghanistan to Iraq.
3. The ____ contains the ozone layer, which guards the earth against excessive ultraviolet radiation.
4. She's praying that her daughter doesn't ____ to her old habit of partying several nights a week.
5. As soon as his normal baseball season is over, my nephew joins a team in the southern ____, where spring training is just starting.
6. Only by seizing a cord dangling beside the window did he manage to ____ disaster.
7. By federal law, every gasoline-powered vehicle must have a catalytic ____ to reduce pollution.
8. Football and rugby balls are ovoid, unlike the ____ balls used in other sports.

B. Match the word on the left to the correct definition on the right:

1. avert   a. go back
2. spherical   b. upper atmosphere
3. divert   c. device for adapting
4. hemisphere   d. avoid
5. revert   e. half-sphere
6. biosphere   f. entertain
7. stratosphere   g. globelike
8. converter   h. life zone

MORPH comes from the Greek word for "shape." *Morph* is itself an English word with a brand-new meaning, which was needed when we began to digitally alter photographic images or shapes to make them move or transform themselves in often astonishing ways.

---

amorphous \ə-ˈmȯr-fəs\ Without a definite shape or form; shapeless.

• Picking up an amorphous lump of clay, she molded it swiftly into a rough human shape.

According to the Greek myths of the creation, the world began in an amorphous state; and the Bible states that, at the beginning, "the earth was without form, and void." Most of us have had nightmares that consist mostly of just a looming amorphous but terrifying thing. A plan may have so little detail that critics call it amorphous. And a new word may appear to name a previously amorphous group of people, such as *yuppie* in 1983 and *Generation X* six years later.

anthropomorphic \ˌan-thrə-pə-ˈmȯr-fik\ (1) Having or described as having human form or traits. (2) Seeing human traits in nonhuman things.

• The old, diseased tree had always been like a companion to her, though she didn't really approve of such anthropomorphic feelings.

Anthropomorphic means a couple of different things. In its first sense, an anthropomorphic cup is a cup in the shape of a human, and anthropomorphic gods are human in appearance—like the Greek and Roman gods, for example, even though Socrates and others believed that their fellow Greeks had created the gods in their own image rather than the other way around. In its second sense, the animal characters in Aesop's fables are anthropomorphic since they all have human feelings and thoughts even though they don't look like humans. Thus, when the fox calls the grapes sour simply because they're out of reach, it's a very human response. Thousands of years after Aesop, *anthropomorphism* is still alive and well, in the animal stories of Beatrix Potter, George Orwell's *Animal Farm,* and hundreds of cartoons and comic strips.

metamorphosis \ˌme-tə-ˈmȯr-fə-səs\ (1) A physical change, especially one supernaturally caused. (2) A developmental change in an animal that occurs after birth or hatching.

- Day by day the class watched the gradual metamorphosis of the tadpoles into frogs.

Many ancient myths end in a metamorphosis. As Apollo is chasing the nymph Daphne, she calls on her river-god father for help and he turns her into a laurel tree to save her. Out of anger and jealousy, the goddess Athena turns the marvelous weaver Arachne into a spider that will spin only beautiful webs. But natural substances may also *metamorphose,* or undergo metamorphosis. Heat and pressure over thousands of years may eventually turn tiny organisms into petroleum, and coal into diamonds. And the most beloved of natural metamorphoses (notice how this plural is formed) is probably the transformation of caterpillars into butterflies.

morphology \mȯr-ˈfä-lə-jē\ (1) The study of the structure and form of plants and animals. (2) The study of word formation.

- The morphology of the mouthparts of the different mayfly species turns out to be closely related to what they feed on and their methods of eating.

Within the field of biology, morphology is the study of the shapes and arrangement of parts of organisms, in order to determine their function, their development, and how they may have been shaped by evolution. Morphology is particularly important in classifying species, since it can often reveal how closely one species is related to another. Morphology is studied within other sciences as well, including astronomy and geology. And in language, morphology considers where words come from and why they look the way they do.

FORM is the Latin root meaning "shape" or "form." When you march in *formation,* you're moving in ordered patterns. And a *formula* is a standard form for expressing information, such as a rule written in mathematical symbols, or the "Sincerely yours" that often ends a letter.

---

format \ˈfȯr-ˌmat\ (1) The shape, size, and general makeup of something. (2) A general plan, arrangement, or choice of material.

- The new thesaurus would be published in three formats: as a hardcover book, a large paperback, and a CD-ROM.

Format is a word that seems to gain more uses with every decade. Traditionally, people used the word simply to refer to the design of a book or newspaper page, but today that's only one of its many meanings. TV news shows seem to change their format, or general form, as often as their anchorpeople, and show types such as situation comedy and crime drama are often called formats. When a radio station gives up playing pop music to become a talk station, it's said to be switching formats. In the electronic age, *format* has also become widely used as a verb; thus, organizing electronic data for storage or other special uses is called formatting (or *reformatting*).

conform \kən-ˈfȯrm\ (1) To be similar or identical; to be in agreement or harmony. (2) To follow ordinary standards or customs.

• My family was too odd to really conform to the little town's ideas about proper behavior, but it didn't seem to bother our neighbors too much.

Conform, with its prefix *con-,* "with" or "together," means basically "to adopt the form of those around you." Thus, employee behavior must usually conform with basic company policies. A certain philosophy may be said to conform with American values (even if we sometimes have a hard time agreeing on exactly what those are). And a Maine Coon cat or a Dandie Dinmont terrier must conform to its breed requirements in order to be registered for breeding purposes. Being a *conformist* is usually a safe bet; being a *nonconformist,* who ignores society's standards and the whole idea of *conformity,* can be a bit dangerous but also sometimes more fun.

formality \fȯr-ˈma-lə-tē\ (1) An established custom or way of behaving that is required or standard. (2) The following of conventional rules.

• The bride and groom wanted a small, intimate wedding without all the usual formalities.

Formal behavior follows the proper *forms* or customs, and *informal* behavior feels free to ignore them. The formality of a dinner party is indicated by such formalities as invitations, required dress, and full table settings. Legal formalities, or technicalities, may turn out to be all-important even if they often seem minor. America requires fewer formalities than many other countries (in Germany, for example, you may know someone for years before using his or her first name), but even in relaxed situations Americans may be observing invisible formalities.

formative \ˈfȯr-mə-tiv\ (1) Giving or able to give form or shape; constructive. (2) Having to do with important growth or development.

• She lived in Venezuela during her formative years and grew up speaking both Spanish and English.

Whatever gives shape to something else may be called formative: for example, the Grand Canyon is a product of the formative power of water, and the automobile was a huge formative influence on the design of America's cities. But it usually applies to some kind of shaping that isn't physical. An ambitious plan, for example, goes through a formative stage of development. The formative years of the U.S. included experimentation with various forms of government. And the most important formative experiences in our own lives tend to take place in the first 20 years or so.

Quizzes

A. Indicate whether the following pairs of words have the same or different meanings:

1. formative / form-giving   same ___ / different ___
2. morphology / shapeliness   same ___ / different ___
3. conform / agree   same ___ / different ___
4. anthropomorphic / man-shaped   same ___ / different ___
5. format / arrangement   same ___ / different ___
6. amorphous / shapeless   same ___ / different ___
7. formality / convention   same ___ / different ___
8. metamorphosis / hibernation   same ___ / different ___

B. Fill in each blank with the correct letter:

a. morphology   e. conform
b. formative   f. amorphous
c. metamorphosis   g. formality
d. format   h. anthropomorphic

1. No one was surprised when WTFX's new _____ turned out to be exactly the same as that of the company's 70 other stations.
2. The job description seemed a bit _____, and she wondered what she would really be doing.

3. While on the base, visitors are expected to _____ with all official rules and regulations.
4. Her poodle really does have some _____ traits, but I'm not sure he really appreciates Beethoven.
5. He seemed to undergo a complete _____ from child to young adult in just a few months.
6. The new couple found the _____ of the elegant dinner a little overwhelming.
7. He had written his senior thesis on the _____ of a species of dragonfly.
8. Among her _____ influences she included her favorite uncle, her ballet classes, and the Nancy Drew series.

DOC/DOCT comes from the Latin *docere*, which means "to teach." So, for instance, a *doctor* was originally a highly educated person capable of instructing others in a field—which usually wasn't medicine.

doctrine \ˈdäk-trən\ (1) Something that is taught. (2) An official principle, opinion, or belief.

• According to the 19th-century doctrine of "papal infallibility," a pope's official statements on matters of faith and morals must be regarded as the absolute truth.

The original doctrines were those of the Catholic Church, especially as taught by the so-called *doctors* (religious scholars) of the Church. But today a doctrine can come from many other sources. Old and established legal principles are called legal doctrine. Traditional psychiatrists still follow the doctrines of Sigmund Freud. Communist doctrine in the 1920s and '30s was often the teachings of Lenin, which were then regarded in the Soviet Union as almost sacred. U.S. presidents have given their names to doctrines as well: In 1823 the Monroe Doctrine stated that the United States would oppose European influence in the Americas, and in 1947 the Truman Doctrine held that America would support free countries against enemies outside and inside.

docent \ˈdō-sᵊnt\ (1) Teacher, lecturer. (2) A person who leads guided tours, especially through a museum.

- Visitors to Istanbul's great Topkapi Museum often decide they need to hire an English-speaking docent.

The title of docent is used in many countries for what Americans would call an associate professor—that is, a college or university teacher who has been given tenure (see *tenure*, p. 306) but hasn't yet achieved the rank of full professor. But in the U.S. a docent is a guide who works at a museum, a historical site, or even a zoo or a park. Docents are usually volunteers, and their services are often free of charge.

doctrinaire \,däk-trə-'ner\ Tending to apply principles or theories without regard for practical difficulties or individual circumstance.

- She had never taken a doctrinaire approach to teaching, since education theories didn't always match the reality of instructing 25 lively students.

Someone doctrinaire sticks closely to official doctrines or principles. A doctrinaire judge will give identical sentences to everyone found guilty of a particular crime. A doctrinaire feminist may treat all men as if they were identical. A doctrinaire economist might call for a single solution for the economic problems in all countries, regardless of their social and cultural history. As you might guess, the word isn't often used in positive contexts.

indoctrinate \in-'däk-trə-,nāt\ (1) To teach, especially basics or fundamentals. (2) To fill someone with a particular opinion or point of view.

- In the Army's basic training, sergeants have 11 weeks to indoctrinate their new recruits with army attitudes and discipline.

Indoctrinate simply means "brainwash" to many people today. We frequently hear, for example, of religious cults that indoctrinate their members to give up their freedom and individuality and to work hard only for a leader's goals. But its meaning wasn't originally negative at all. And the fact is that every society indoctrinates its young people with the values of its culture; in the U.S. we tend to be indoctrinated to love freedom, to be individuals, and to work hard for success, among many other things. But we now rarely use *indoctrinate* (or its noun, *indoctrination*) in a positive way; instead we usually stick to the simpler and safer *teach* or *instruct*.

TUT/TUI comes from a Latin verb meaning "to look after," and in English the root generally shows up in words that include the meaning "guide," "guard," or "teach"—such as *tutor*, the name for a private teacher who guides a student (or *tutee*) through a subject.

tutorial \tü-ˈtȯr-ē-əl\ (1) A class for one student or a small group of students. (2) An instructional program that gives information about a specific subject.

• He'd been taking tutorials with the same graduate student for two years, and learning far more than he'd ever learned in his large classes.

Tutorials with live tutors are useful for both advanced students and struggling ones. Many computer programs include electronic tutorials to help the new user get used to the program, leading him or her through all its functions, often by means of pictures and short videos. But a really difficult program may still require a real-life tutor to be fully understood.

tuition \tü-ˈwi-shən\ (1) The act of teaching; instruction. (2) The cost of or payment for instruction.

• As she happily flipped through her college catalogs, her parents sat quietly but uneasily calculating the total tuition costs.

The sense of *tuition* meaning "teaching" or "instruction" is mostly used in Britain today. In the U.S., *tuition* almost always means the costs charged by a school, college, or university for that teaching. Those costs have tended to rise at an alarming rate in recent years. Around 2010 a student could receive a four-year college education (tuition, room, and board) at an inexpensive public university for less than $50,000, but might have to pay more than $200,000 at an expensive private college or university.

intuition \ˌin-tü-ˈwi-shən\ (1) The power of knowing something immediately without mental effort; quick insight. (2) Something known in this way.

• She scoffed at the notion of "women's intuition," special powers of insight and understanding in personal relations that women are supposed to have.

Intuition is very close in meaning to *instinct*. The moment a man enters a room you may feel you know *intuitively* or instinctively everything about him—that is, you may *intuit* his basic personality. Highly rational people may try to ignore their intuition and insist on being able to explain everything they think, but artists and creative thinkers often tend to rely on their *intuitive* sense of things. Intuition can be closely related to their imagination, which seems to come from somewhere just as mysterious. Some psychologists claim that the left brain is mainly involved in logical thinking and the right brain in intuitive thinking; but the brain is terribly complex, and even if there's some truth to this idea, it's not terribly obvious how to make use of it.

tutelage \'tü-tə-lij\ Instruction or guidance of an individual; guardianship.

• Under the old man's expert tutelage, they had learned to carve and paint beautiful and realistic duck decoys.

Tutelage usually means specialized and individual guidance. Alexander the Great was under the tutelage of the philosopher Aristotle between the ages of 13 and 16, and his *tutor* inspired him with a love of philosophy, medicine, and science. At 16 he commanded his first army, and by his death 16 years later he had founded the greatest empire ever seen. But it's not so easy to trace the effects of the brilliant tutelage he had received in his youth.

Quizzes

A. Choose the closest definition:

1. docent   a. leader b. scholar c. guide d. minister
2. tuition   a. requirement b. instruction c. resolution d. housing
3. indoctrinate   a. medicate thoroughly b. research thoroughly c. instruct thoroughly d. consider thoroughly
4. tutelage   a. responsibility b. protection c. instruction d. safeguard
5. doctrine   a. solution b. principle c. religion d. report
6. tutorial   a. small class b. large class c. night class d. canceled class

7. doctrinaire a. by the way b. by the by c. by the
   rule d. by the glass
8. intuition a. ignorance b. quick understanding
   c. payment d. consideration

**B. Match the word on the left to the correct definition
on the right:**

1.	indoctrinate	a. instruction costs
2.	tutelage	b. guide
3.	doctrine	c. fill with a point of view
4.	tutorial	d. insight
5.	doctrinaire	e. guardianship
6.	intuition	f. official teaching
7.	docent	g. individual instruction
8.	tuition	h. rigidly principled

Number Words

DI/DUP, Greek and Latin prefixes meaning "two," show up in both
technical and nontechnical terms, with *dup-* sometimes shortened to
du-. So a *duel* is a battle between two people. A *duet* is music for a
duo, or pair of musicians. A *duplicate* is an exact copy, or twin. And
if you have *dual* citizenship, you belong to two countries at once.

dichotomy \dī-'kä-tə-mē\ (1) A division into two often contradic-
tory groups. (2) Something with qualities that seem to contradict
each other.

• Already in her first job, she noticed a dichotomy between the
  theories she'd been taught in college and the realities of professional life.

In the modern world there's a dichotomy between fast and intense
big-city life and the slower and more relaxed life in the country.
But the dichotomy is nothing new: the Roman poet Horace was
complaining about it in the 1st century B.C. Among other eternal
dichotomies, there's the dichotomy between wealth and poverty,
between the policies of the leading political parties, between a
government's words and its actions—and between what would be

most fun to do right this minute and what would be the mature and sensible alternative.

dimorphic \dī-'mȯr-fik\ Occurring in two distinguishable forms (as of color or size).

• One of a birder's challenges is identifying birds of the less colorful sex in dimorphic species.

Dimorphism varies greatly in the animal kingdom. Among mammals, the male is generally larger than the female, but other differences in appearance tend to be modest. But birds are usually noticeably dimorphic, with the male being the more colorful sex; when we imagine a pheasant, a mallard, a cardinal, or a peacock, we're almost always picturing the male rather than the female. Among spiders the situation is often reversed. The golden orb-weaver spider, for example, is spectacularly dimorphic: the female may be 20 times the size of the male, and she usually ends up eating him, sometimes even while he's mating with her. Many sea creatures, including many fish, take care of gender problems by simply changing from one sex into the other.

duplex \'dü-ˌpleks\ (1) Having two principal elements; double. (2) Allowing electronic communication in two directions at the same time.

• The upper floor of their splendid duplex apartment had a panoramic view of Paradise Park.

Duplex can describe a confusing variety of things, depending on the technical field. Most of us use it as a noun: a *duplex* can be either a two-family house or a two-story apartment. In computer science and telecommunications, duplex (or *full-duplex*) communication can go in both directions at once, while *half-duplex* communication can go only one way at a time. In other areas, just translate *duplex* as "double" and see if the sentence makes sense.

duplicity \dů-'pli-sə-tē\ Deception by pretending to feel and act one way while acting in another.

• By the time Jackie's duplicity in the whole matter had come to light, she had left town, leaving no forwarding address.

The Greek god Zeus often resorted to duplicity to get what he wanted, and most of the time what he wanted was some woman.

His duplicity usually involved a disguise: he appeared to Leda as a swan, and to Europa as a bull. Sometimes he had to be *duplicitous* to get around his wife, Hera. After he had had his way with Io and was about to get caught, he turned her into a cow to avoid Hera's anger.

BI/BIN also means "two" or "double." A *bicycle* has two wheels, and *binoculars* consist of two little telescopes. *Bigamy* is marriage to two people at once. And a road built through the middle of a neighborhood *bisects* it into two pieces.

---

bipartisan \ˌbī-ˈpär-tə-zən\ Involving members of two political parties.

• The president named a bipartisan commission of three Republicans and three Democrats to look into the issue.

Partisan means basically "belonging to a party," so something bipartisan combines two parties. Since the United States today operates with a two-party system of government (even though the Constitution says nothing about parties at all), legislation often must have some bipartisan support in order to pass into law. Bipartisan committees review legislation, compromising on some points and removing or adding others in order to make the bill more agreeable to both parties and make bipartisan support from the entire legislature or Congress more likely.

binary \ˈbī-nə-rē\ (1) Consisting of two things or parts; double. (2) Involving a choice between two alternatives.

• The Milky Way contains numerous binary stars, each consisting of two stars orbiting each other.

Binary has many uses, most of them in technical terms. Almost all computer software, for example, is written in *binary code*, which uses only two digits, 0 and 1, 0 standing for a low-voltage impulse ("off") and 1 standing for a high-voltage impulse ("on"). All information is kept in this form. The word "HELLO," for example, looks like this: 1001000 1000101 1001100 1001100 1001111.

biennial \ˌbī-ˈe-nē-əl\ (1) Occurring every two years. (2) Continuing or lasting over two years.

- The great biennial show of new art in Venice usually either puzzles or angers the critics.

Biennial conventions, celebrations, competitions, and sports events come every two years. *Biennials* are plants that live two years, bearing flowers and fruit only in the second year. (Carrots and sugar beets are two examples; since we're only interested in their roots, we don't wait another year to see their flower and fruit.) In contrast, *semiannual* means "twice a year." But no one can agree whether *biweekly* means "twice a week" or "every two weeks," and whether *bimonthly* means "twice a month" or "every two months." Maybe we should stop using both of them until we can decide.

bipolar \ˌbī-ˈpō-lər\ Having two opposed forces or views; having two poles or opposed points of attraction.

- Our bipolar Earth spins on an axis that extends between the North and South Poles.

Magnets are always bipolar: one pole attracts and the other repels or drives away. And the Cold War arms race was bipolar, since it mainly involved the opposing powers of the U.S. and the Soviet Union. But the word is encountered most often today in *bipolar disorder,* the newer name of what used to be called *manic-depressive illness,* in which the person tends to swing between the two extremes, or poles, of high intensity and deep depression, with depression being the main condition. Though an extremely serious illness, bipolar disorder can often be controlled by the drug lithium.

Quiz

Fill in each blank with the correct letter:

a. bipolar
b. duplex
c. biennial
d. duplicity
e. dimorphic
f. binary
g. dichotomy
h. bipartisan

1. The new bill, with its thoroughly ____ backing, passed through Congress easily.
2. Parrots are strikingly ____, unlike canaries, in which you can't tell the sexes apart until the male starts singing.

3. Powerful drugs like lithium are often prescribed for _____ depression.

4. A liar's _____ usually catches up with him sooner or later.

5. At the very heart of the computer revolution was the _____ number system.

6. Democracies must always deal with the difficult _____ between individual liberties and social order.

7. They shared the modest _____ with another family of four, who they often met when going in and out.

8. Every two years we get to hear Mildred McDermot sing "Moonlight in Vermont" at the _____ town picnic.

Review Quizzes

A. Fill in each blank with the correct letter:

a.	anthropomorphic	k.	avert
b.	doctrine	l.	revert
c.	tuition	m.	conform
d.	interminable	n.	intuition
e.	duplex	o.	indeterminate
f.	binary	p.	bipartisan
g.	formative	q.	metamorphosis
h.	biennial	r.	dichotomy
i.	doctrinaire	s.	tutelage
j.	spherical	t.	hemisphere

1. This marble was limestone before it underwent _____.

2. The computer works by making choices between _____ opposites.

3. The main piano competition is _____, but there are smaller ones on the off-years.

4. The lab results were _____, and he was told to wait a week before having another blood test.

5. We failed to get the contract because our equipment didn't _____ to the company's specifications.

6. She managed to _____ a very awkward meeting by slipping out a side door just as he was coming in.

7. I had an ____ wait in the doctor's office and didn't get home until 6:00.

8. What he later learned about her past had confirmed his original ____ that she was not to be trusted.

9. The ____ between good and evil has been dealt with by different religions in many different ways.

10. Let's not ____ to the kind of name-calling we had to put up with at the last meeting.

11. To keep the issue as nonpolitical as possible, the governor named a ____ committee to study it.

12. At boarding schools, ____ isn't separated from fees for room and board.

13. The ____ was roomy, but a great deal of noise came through the wall separating them from the other family.

14. Under the great man's ____, he slowly learned how to develop his musical ideas into full-fledged sonatas.

15. As a practicing Catholic, she thought frequently about the church ____ that life begins at conception.

16. Michelangelo's great painting shows an ____ God touching Adam's finger.

17. A ____ interpretation of these rules will leave no room for fun at all.

18. My trip to Australia was the first time I had left this ____.

19. The assignment was to write an essay about the most ____ experience of her later teenage years.

20. The stone was roughly ____, but it didn't roll easily.

B. Choose the correct synonym and the correct antonym:

1. intuition   a. instruction   b. payment   c. logic   d. sixth sense

2. divert   a. please   b. entertain   c. bore   d. send

3. amorphous   a. beginning   b. shapeless   c. shaping   d. formed

4. terminal   a. first   b. final   c. highest   d. deathlike

5. duplicity   a. desire   b. two-facedness   c. honesty   d. complexity

6. formality   a. convention   b. black tie   c. rationality   d. casualness

7. conform   a. rebel   b. shape   c. greet   d. fit in

8. dichotomy   a. operation b. negotiation c. contradiction d. agreement
9. avert   a. face b. wonder c. avoid d. claim
10. doctrinaire   a. relaxed b. strict c. written d. religious

C. Choose the closest definition:

1. format   a. design b. formality c. formation d. concept
2. biosphere   a. life cycle b. environment c. natural bubble d. evolution
3. morphology   a. study of structure b. study of woods c. study of butterflies d. study of geometry
4. avert   a. embrace b. prevent c. claim d. escape
5. bipolar   a. double-jointed b. snowy c. opposing d. two-handed
6. indoctrinate   a. teach b. demonstrate c. infiltrate d. consider
7. metamorphosis   a. condition b. independence c. technique d. transformation
8. duplicity   a. doubleness b. dishonesty c. photocopy d. second opinion
9. tutorial   a. penalty b. teacher c. classroom d. small class
10. stratosphere   a. cloud level b. sea level c. atmospheric layer d. outer space

UNIT

16

TOP comes from *topos,* the Greek word for "place." A *topic* is a subject rather than a place; to the Greeks, the original word meant more or less "about one place or subject (rather than another)"—which just goes to show that it's not always easy to trace a word's meaning from its roots.

topical \ˈtä-pə-kəl\ (1) Designed for local application to or treatment of a bodily part. (2) Referring to the topics of the day.

• If the topical ointment doesn't work on the rash, the doctor will prescribe an antibiotic pill.

Like a topical medicine, a topical reference or story applies to something specific, focusing on a *topic* that's currently in the news. TV comedians often use topical humor, making jokes about a currently popular movie or the latest political scandal—if possible, one that just broke that same day. Topical humor has a short lifespan, though, because the news keeps changing and the new hot topics just keep coming. The medical meaning of *topical* stays closer to the meaning of the root, since it describes something that's put right on the place that seems to need it.

ectopic \ek-ˈtä-pik\ Occurring or originating in an abnormal place.

• A pacemaker was installed to correct her ectopic heartbeat.

Ectopic is a medical word that means basically "out of place." An ectopic kidney is located in an abnormal position. In patients with an ectopic heartbeat, the electrical signals that trigger the heart muscles originate in an abnormal area of the heart. But *ectopic* most commonly describes a pregnancy in which the fertilized egg begins to develop in an area outside the uterus, such as in a fallopian tube; such pregnancies may lead to serious problems if not treated.

utopian \yu̇-ˈtō-pē-ən\ Relating to an imaginary place in which the government, laws, and social conditions are perfect.

• Some of the new mayor's supporters had gotten increasingly unrealistic, and seemed to expect that she could turn the city into a utopian community.

In 1516 Thomas More published *Utopia*, a description of a fictional island in the Atlantic with an ideal society, in order to draw a sharp contrast with the disorderly political situation of his own time. He created the name from *topos* ("place") and *ou*, Greek for "no," since he was well aware that nowhere so perfect was likely to exist on earth. People have long dreamed of creating utopian communities; some of them have joined communes, societies where other idealists like themselves have chosen to live in a cooperative way according to certain principles. Not just communes but plans of all kinds have been labeled utopian by critics. But we can dream, can't we?

topography \tə-ˈpä-grə-fē\ (1) The art of showing the natural and man-made features of a region on a map or chart. (2) The features of a surface, including both natural and man-made features.

• Planning the expedition involved careful study of the region's topography.

Topography combines *top-* with *graph-*, a root meaning "write" or "describe." The topography of the Sahara Desert features shifting sand dunes and dry, rocky mountains. A *topographic* (or *topo*) map not only shows the surface features of a region but also indicates the contours and approximate altitude of every location, by means of numerous curving lines, each indicating a single elevation. In other words, it shows a "three-dimensional" picture on a two-dimensional surface. Topo maps are commonly used by hikers, surveyors, government workers, and engineers, among other people.

CENTR/CENTER comes from the Greek *kentron* and the Latin *centrum,* meaning "sharp point" or "center point of a circle." A *centrifuge* is a spinning machine that throws things outward from the *center*; the apparent force that pushes them outward is called *centrifugal* force.

---

eccentric \ik-'sen-trik\ (1) Not following an established or usual style or conduct. (2) Straying from a circular path; off-center.

• She keeps a dozen stray cats in her house and is rather eccentric, but her neighbors say she's very pleasant and completely harmless.

An eccentric wheel spins unevenly, and an eccentric person is similarly a little off-center. Most *eccentricities* are inoffensive to others, and some may even do some good. For instance, riding a bicycle to work might be considered eccentric by some people, but it's good exercise and it cuts down on pollution. Some *eccentrics* are just ahead of their time.

epicenter \'e-pi-ˌsen-tər\ (1) The location on the earth's surface directly above the focus of an earthquake. (2) The center or focus of activity.

• The destruction caused by Mexico City's earthquake was extensive because the city was at the quake's epicenter.

The meaning of *epi-* in *epicenter* is "over," so the epicenter of an earthquake lies over the center or "focus" of the quake. *Epicenter* can also refer to the centers of things that may seem in their own way as powerful—though not as destructive—as earthquakes. Wall Street, for example, might be said to lie at the epicenter of the financial world.

egocentric \ˌē-gō-'sen-trik\ Overly concerned with oneself; self-centered.

• He's brilliant but completely egocentric, and the only things he'll talk about are his own life and work.

Ego means "I" in Latin. To an egocentric person, *I* is the most important word in the language. Great artists and writers are often *egocentrics;* such people can be hard to live with, though their *egocentricity,* an unfortunate side effect of their talent, is often forgiven. But ordinary egocentricity, which shows up as selfishness, lack of sympathy, and lack of interest in other people, usually has little to do with any personal talent or success.

ethnocentric \\ˌeth-nō-ˈsen-trik\\ Marked by or based on the attitude that one's own group is superior to others.

- Some reviewers criticized the ethnocentric bias that came through in the way the film portrayed immigrants.

The Greek word *ethnos* means "nation" or "people." So *ethnocentricity* shows itself in a lack of respect for other ways of life, and an ethnocentric person feels that his or her own nation or group is the cultural center of the world. *Ethnocentric* describes the kind of person who behaves badly when traveling in foreign countries, often called an "Ugly American" (from a book and movie of the same name). Whenever you hear someone making fun of the way a foreigner speaks English, just remember that it's the foreigner, not the person laughing at him, who actually can speak a foreign language.

Quizzes

A. Fill in each blank with the correct letter:

a. epicenter	e. topography
b. ectopic	f. egocentric
c. ethnocentric	g. topical
d. utopian	h. eccentric

1. She claims that his remarks show an _____ bias against foreign cultures.
2. The _____ of a river valley often includes a wide, fertile floodplain.
3. The earth's orbit around the sun is _____ rather than perfectly circular.
4. An _____ pregnancy is an unusual event that poses serious medical problems.
5. Since he hates needles, he asks his dentist to use only a _____ anesthetic inside his mouth.
6. There's nothing wrong with liking yourself so long as you don't become _____.
7. In 1970 they founded a _____ community on a 400-acre farm, where all property was to be owned in common.
8. Luckily, the quake's _____ was far away from any human settlement.

> **B. Match the word on the left to the correct definition on the right:**
>
> 1. topical   a. central point
> 2. egocentric   b. centered on one's own group
> 3. utopian   c. away from its usual place
> 4. ethnocentric   d. self-centered
> 5. topography   e. of current interest
> 6. eccentric   f. ideal
> 7. ectopic   g. placed off-center
> 8. epicenter   h. landscape features

DOM comes from the Latin *domus,* "house," and *dominus,* "master," and the two are indeed related. In the Bible, King Ahasuerus, angered by his queen's disobedience, proclaims that "every man is to be master of his own house," and in the Roman empire no one doubted that this was how it was meant to be. A *domain* is the area where a person has authority or is *dominant*—but we no longer think of a house as the domain of a single dominant member of a family.

---

dominion \də-ˈmin-yən\ (1) An area over which one rules; domain. (2) Supreme authority.

* The Roman empire had dominion over the entire Mediterranean, which the Romans called *mare nostrum,* "our sea."

The ruler of a region has dominion over it, and the area itself may be called the ruler's dominion. In the days of the British Empire, England had dominion over many countries throughout the world. Though Canada has been quite independent of Great Britain since the 19th century, it was generally referred to as the Dominion of Canada in official documents until at least the 1950s. The word has an old-fashioned sound today, and probably shows up in history books, historical novels, and fantasy video games more often than in discussions of modern nations.

predominant \prē-ˈdä-mə-nənt\ Greater in importance, strength, influence, or authority.

- The predominant color of the desert landscape was a rusty brown.

Something predominant stands out above all the rest. The predominant theme in an essay is the one that *predominates*—the main idea that the writer wants to express. (Notice the difference between the adjective and the verb; be sure not to spell the adjective with an *-ate* ending.) The word is widely used in many fields. For example, the predominant language of Switzerland is German; the predominant cause of obesity in children is a bad diet; and your predominant reason for wanting a larger vocabulary may be to simply be a better-educated person—though the positive effects of a large vocabulary on one's romantic life are well known.

domineering \ˌdä-mə-ˈnir-iŋ\ Tending to control the behavior of others in a bossy manner.

- His mother was a domineering type, and not even his stepfather dared do anything without her permission.

To be domineering is to behave like a lord. (The word *lordly* doesn't express quite the same thing.) Someone who tells you what you can wear or what friends you can spend time with could be called domineering; so could someone who always decides what you're going to do with your free time. Those of us who grow up with a domineering parent usually flee as soon as we're old enough.

domination \ˌdä-mə-ˈnā-shən\ (1) Supremacy or power over another. (2) The exercise of governing or controlling influence.

- The region was under the domination of a single nation, even though it hadn't yet invaded its neighbors.

Domination may sound like something that's achieved by military force. The total domination of Europe, for example, has never been achieved: The Roman empire could never fully *dominate* the northern Germanic tribes; Napoleon couldn't conquer Spain; and although Adolf Hitler was briefly *dominant* over most of the continent, he never managed to overpower England. But the word's earliest appearances don't necessarily involve physical force; Chaucer, for instance, speaks of a mind's domination by strong drink. So we may observe that a great tennis player has continued his domination of the world's courts this season, or that the domination of popular music by rock and roll was obvious by the end of the 1950s.

OMNI comes from the Latin word *omnis*, meaning "all." So in English words, *omni-* can mean "in all ways," "in all places," or "without limits." An *omnidirectional* antenna, for example, is one that receives or sends radio waves equally well in all directions. And *Omni* by itself has been used repeatedly as a brand name for things as different as a hotel chain and a science magazine.

omnivore \ˈäm-ni-ˌvȯr\ An animal that eats both plants and other animals.

• If we're all natural omnivores, she kept asking herself, then why wouldn't her toddler eat anything but cashews and peanut butter until the age of four?

Human beings seem to be classic omnivores. Originally living as "hunter-gatherers," we hunted and fished when possible but also gathered nuts, berries, fruits, seeds, and roots for much of our diet. We're physically well suited for both tasks; our hands are perfect for picking things, and our build is ideal for running down even the fastest game animals because of our great stamina. Some 10,000 years ago humans began practicing agriculture involving both animals and plants. The other *omnivorous* mammals include chimpanzees, pigs, opossums, porcupines, bears, raccoons, skunks, chipmunks, mice and rats, and skunks. But even many mammals classed as *carnivorous* (see VOR, p. 69) turn out to be capable of shifting to plant foods when necessary.

omnipotent \äm-ˈni-pə-tənt\ Having complete or unlimited power; all-powerful.

• What really scares these men is the nightmare of an omnipotent state, and they think that with their guns they'll be able to keep the government's forces at bay when the time comes.

If you know that *potens* means "power" in Latin (see POT, p. 516), it's not hard to guess the meaning of *omnipotent*. In Christian services and prayers, the Latin *omnipotens* is translated as "almighty" and always applied to God. But *omnipotence* in a government or ruler is naturally a bit scary; as a British lord observed a century ago, "Power tends to corrupt, and absolute power corrupts absolutely." So democracies do their best to make omnipotence impossible.

omnibus \ˈäm-ni-bəs\ Of or including many things.

Eager to go home for vacation, Senate leaders assembled an omnibus bill to tie up the loose ends on dozens of unrelated projects.

In Latin, *omnibus* means "for all." So an omnibus bill in Congress packages several measures together, an omnibus survey may poll the public on a wide range of issues, and an omnibus edition of a writer's stories may bring together just about all of them. As a noun, *omnibus* used to mean a large vehicle for public transportation— that is, "for all" who could pay the fare—but around 1900 the word began to be shortened to simply *bus*.

omniscient \äm-ˈni-shənt\ Knowing everything; having unlimited understanding or knowledge.

• Brought up in a strict Christian family, he knew that an omniscient God was watching him every second of his life.

Omniscience is something that a totalitarian state may try to achieve by means of informers, cameras, and monitoring of electronic communication. If your English teacher tells you that a novel has an "omniscient narrator," she means that the voice telling the story isn't one of the characters but instead knows what each of them is doing and thinking, with the point of view constantly shifting from one to another.

Quizzes

A. Choose the closest definition:

1. domination   a. name   b. control   c. attraction
      d. movement
2. omnipotent   a. almighty   b. all-knowing
      c. all-seeing   d. all-round
3. domineering   a. owning   b. homelike   c. royal   d. bossy
4. omniscient   a. immense   b. all-knowing   c. universal
      d. unlimited
5. dominion   a. weakness   b. kingdom   c. game   d. habit
6. omnibus   a. immense   b. transporting
      c. all-inclusive   d. worldwide
7. predominant   a. longest   b. lightest   c. strongest
      d. earliest

8. omnivore   a. world traveler b. meat- and plant-eater
   c. universe d. bottom-feeder

B. Complete the analogy:

1. educated : unschooled :: omniscient : _____
   a. commanding b. lazy c. ignorant d. know-it-all
2. selective : limited :: omnibus : _____
   a. everyday b. all-time c. oversized d. comprehensive
3. persuasion : influence :: domination : _____
   a. household b. country c. command d. outlaw
4. weak : feeble :: omnipotent : _____
   a. timid b. all-powerful c. global d. huge
5. obedient : tame :: domineering : _____
   a. sweet b. easygoing c. obnoxious d. controlling
6. human : deer :: omnivore : _____
   a. plant-eater b. elk c. ape d. dieter
7. property : estate :: dominion : _____
   a. attitude b. difference c. realm d. country
8. larger : smaller :: predominant : _____
   a. secondary b. necessary c. primary d. demanding

HOL/HOLO, meaning "whole," comes from the Greek word *holos*, with the same meaning. The root can be found in *catholic*. When capitalized, *Catholic* refers to the worldwide Christian church based in Rome, which was once the "whole"—that is, the only—Christian church. Without the capital letter, *catholic* means simply "universal" or, when describing a person, "broad in one's interests or tastes."

holistic \hō-ˈlis-tik\ Relating to or concerned with wholes or with complete systems rather than with the analysis of, treatment of, or dissection into parts.

• Environmental scientists tend to be holistic in their views, even when they're only studying a tiny patch of ground.

"The whole is greater than the sum of its parts" expresses the essence of *holism*, a term coined by the great South African general and statesman Jan Smuts in 1926. Holism generally opposes the Western tendency toward analysis, the breaking down of wholes into parts sometimes to the point that "you can't see the forest for the trees." Holism is an important concept in the sciences and social sciences, and especially in medicine. Holistic medicine tries to treat the "whole person" rather than focusing too narrowly on single symptoms. It emphasizes the connections between the mind and the body, avoids the overuse of drugs, and has borrowed such practices from Eastern traditions as acupuncture and yoga.

hologram \\'hō-lə-ˌgram\ A three-dimensional image reproduced from a pattern of interference produced by a beam of radiation such as a laser.

• When holograms are used for data storage, the entire bulk of the storage material can be used rather than just its surface.

A hologram is a picture of a "whole" object, showing it in three dimensions. We've all seen cheap *holographic* images on credit cards and ID cards (where they help prevent copying). Far more impressive are large holograms that take the form of a ghostly 3-D moving figure that you can walk around to see from all angles. Holograms were invented in 1947 but only perfected after the invention of the laser in 1960. Today they're used in such technologies as compact-disc players and checkout scanners, and holograms can be created of the inside of live internal organs to permit doctors to examine the organs in great detail. And soon televisions with hologram technology may enable us to watch in "3-D."

Holocene \\'hō-lə-ˌsēn\ Of, relating to, or being the present geologic epoch.

• As the Holocene epoch began, the glaciers were swiftly retreating, forests were taking over the bare land, and human beings were moving northward again in large numbers.

To geologists, we live today in the Holocene epoch, the period that began about 10,000 years ago, at the end of the last ice age, when humans first began practicing agriculture. But what does Holocene have to do with "whole"? Well, in geological language, the Holocene epoch follows the *Paleocene* ("remotely recent"), the *Eocene* ("early recent"), the *Oligocene* ("scarcely recent"), the *Miocene* ("less recent"), the *Pliocene* ("more recent"), and the *Pleistocene* ("most recent") epochs—so the Holocene is the "wholly recent" period of geological time.

holocaust \\'hō-lə-ˌkȯst\ (1) (usually capitalized) The mass slaughter of European civilians and especially Jews by the Nazis during

World War II. (2) A thorough destruction involving extensive loss of life, especially through fire.

• Her parents had escaped the Holocaust in Poland by fleeing into the forest and surviving there with hundreds of others for two years.

The Greek word *holokaustos* means "burnt whole." For the early Jews who followed the laws given in the first books of the Bible, a holocaust was a sacrifice to God, the burning on an altar of a lamb, goat, or young bull. The word is used about 200 times in the traditional Greek version of the Old Testament, though it rarely appears in English translations. In the 1700s *holocaust* began to be used to refer to the mass destruction of life. But no mass murder in Western history ever approached the scale achieved by the Nazis. As many as 6 million Jews may have died at their hands; when the slaughter of non-Jews is included, the number of murdered victims may have amounted to over 15 million.

RETRO means "back," "backward," or "behind" in Latin. *Retro* in English is generally a prefix, but has also become a word in its own right, usually used to describe old styles or fashions.

---

retroactive \\,re-trō-ˈak-tiv\\ Intended to apply or take effect at a date in the past.

• The fact that the tax hike was retroactive annoyed the public the most.

We normally think of time as constantly moving forward. Since *retroactive* seems to defy time's forward movement, retroactive taxes, laws, and regulations are often seen as particularly obnoxious and unfair. (See also *ex post facto*, p. 64.) But nobody ever objects to receiving a retroactive raise at work. When we judge historical people and events in terms of present-day morality and attitudes, our retroactive judgments may indicate that we're too impressed with ourselves and ignorant of history.

retrofit \\ˈre-trō-,fit\\ To furnish something with new or modified parts or equipment that was optional or unavailable at the time of manufacture.

• The office building has been retrofitted with air-conditioning, but the result has been a mixed success.

The concept of retrofitting became an urgent necessity during World War II, when weapons technology was advancing at an intense pace and planes and ships were becoming outdated even before their construction was complete, and the only solution was to retrofit the completed craft with the brand-new technology. Retrofitting was revived on a massive scale during the energy crisis of the 1970s, when new features were added to millions of old houses to make them more energy-efficient. Retrofitting is thus different from merely *renovating*, which may not involve any new technology at all.

retrogress \ˌre-trō-ˈgres\ To return to an earlier and usually worse or more primitive state.

• According to the tests, the sophomores had actually retrogressed in the course of spring term.

As you might guess, *retrogress* is the opposite of *progress*. *Retrogression* is usually an undesirable decline from a higher or advanced level. So, for instance, in difficult social situations an adolescent can retrogress to a childish level of maturity. And under the extreme conditions of total war, a whole society may retrogress to a primitive state. The increasing number of poor or homeless people has been seen as evidence of modern social retrogression, and the rise of loud, name-calling TV and radio personalities strikes many people as a sign of political retrogression.

retrospective \ˌre-trə-ˈspek-tiv\ A generally comprehensive exhibition or performance usually covering an artist's output to date.

• A retrospective covering the photographer's entire career is forcing critics to revise their earlier estimates of her status as an artist.

Retrospective is partly rooted in the Latin verb *specere,* "to look," so a retrospective is a look back at an artist's career. The subject of a retrospective is usually an older living artist, or one who has recently died. Galleries and museums honor painters and sculptors, film festivals honor directors and actors, and concert organizations honor composers. Retrospectives can be difficult and expensive to assemble, so they're rarely put together except for deserving artists; the result is that they frequently win many new fans for the person's achievement.

Quizzes

A. Fill in each blank with the correct letter:

a.	retrospective	e.	hologram
b.	holistic	f.	retrogress
c.	retrofit	g.	Holocene
d.	holocaust	h.	retroactive

1. She turns 70 this year, and the museum is honoring her with a huge _____.

2. He likes wearing a T-shirt with a large _____ on the chest and watching people's reactions to the way it changes as they walk by.

3. The navy plans to _____ a fleet of 25-year-old ships to increase their speed and monitoring capacity.

4. His doctor favors a _____ approach to achieving wellness, but she'll prescribe standard drugs for serious illnesses.

5. In *Lord of the Flies*, a group of English schoolboys manages to _____ to a barely civilized state within a few months.

6. There are still a few hunting-and-gathering tribes on earth who live the way all of humankind lived at the beginning of the _____.

7. Although the tax increase wasn't passed until June, its effect was _____ to the first of the year.

8. The creation of the United Nations was intended to, among other things, prevent another _____ from ever occurring.

B. Match the word on the left to the correct definition on the right:

1.	retrogress	a.	3-D image
2.	holocaust	b.	effective as of earlier
3.	retrospective	c.	mass destruction
4.	retrofit	d.	concerned with the whole
5.	holistic	e.	review of a body of work
6.	Holocene	f.	revert to an earlier state
7.	retroactive	g.	current human era
8.	hologram	h.	modernize

TEMPOR comes from the Latin *tempus,* meaning "time." A *temporary* repair is meant to last only a short time. The *tempo,* or speed, of a country-and-western ballad is usually different from that of a hip-hop number. The Latin phrase *Tempus fugit* means "Time flies," an observation that seems more true during summer vacation than in the dead of winter.

temporal \ˈtem-pə-rəl\ (1) Having to do with time as opposed to eternity; having to do with earthly life as opposed to heavenly existence. (2) Having to do with time as distinguished from space.

• The quick passing of the seasons as we grow older makes us feel the fleeting nature of temporal existence.

Temporal existence is often contrasted with spiritual existence, which many religions teach is eternal. The American system of government features a separation of church and state—that is, a separation of spiritual and temporal authority. But such separation is relatively recent. In past centuries, the Roman Catholic Church exerted temporal authority—that is, political power—throughout much of Europe, and the Church of England has always been officially headed by the temporal ruler of Great Britain. *Temporal* isn't always used in religious contexts; for example, child psychologists often measure "temporal processing"—that is, speed of thinking—in children with mental difficulties. Note that *temporal* may also mean "near the temples (of the head)"; thus, your brain's *temporal lobes* are situated at your temples. But this *temporal* is based on a different Latin root.

contemporary \kən-ˈtem-pə-ˌrer-ē\ (1) Occurring or existing during the same period of time. (2) Having to do with the present period; modern or current.

• The two scientists were contemporary with each other, but neither seemed to have heard of the other's existence.

Contemporary can be confusing because of its slightly different meanings. In everyday use, it generally means simply "modern" or "new." But before the 20th century it instead referred only to things from the same era as certain other things; so, for instance, Jesus was contemporary with the Roman emperors Augustus and Tiberius, and Muhammad was contemporary with Pope Gregory the Great. And *contemporary* is also a noun: thus, Jane Austen's *contemporaries* included Coleridge and Wordsworth, and your own contemporaries were born around the same year that you were.

extemporaneous \ek-ˌstem-pə-ˈrā-nē-əs\ (1) Composed, performed, spoken, or done on the spur of the moment; impromptu or improvised. (2) Carefully prepared but delivered without notes.

- It was once common in middle-class homes to make extemporaneous speeches, recite poetry, and give little solo song recitals after a dinner with guests.

The ability to speak well *extemporaneously* is an important talent for politicians, especially when participating in debates. (Though it's also a good idea to have a "spin doctor" who can go out afterward and tell everyone what the candidate *really* meant to say.) Some people claim there's a difference between *extemporaneous* and *impromptu,* saying that an extemporaneous speech is planned beforehand but not written down, while an impromptu speech is genuinely unprepared or off-the-cuff, but today the two words are mostly used as synonyms.

temporize \ˈtem-pə-ˌrīz\ (1) To act in a way that fits the time or occasion; to give way to current opinion. (2) To draw out discussions to gain time.

- The legislature was accused of temporizing while the budget deficit continued to worsen.

The Latin word that *temporize* comes from meant simply "to pass the time"; the meaning of the English word is different but obviously related. People aren't usually admired for temporizing. A political leader faced with a difficult issue may temporize by talking vaguely about possible solutions without actually doing anything. The point is to avoid taking an action that lots of people aren't going to like, in hopes that the problem will somehow go away, but the effect is often just to make matters worse.

CHRON comes from the Greek word for "time." A *chronicle* records the events of a particular time, which is why so many newspapers have the name *Chronicle*. A *chronometer* is a device for measuring time, usually one that's more accurate (and more expensive) than an ordinary watch or clock.

---

chronic \ˈkrä-nik\ (1) Lasting a long time or recurring frequently. (2) Always present; constantly annoying or troubling; habitual.

- He had stopped to pick up ice-cream cones for the kids, hoping it would give him a temporary rest from their chronic bickering.

Chronic coughing goes on and on; chronic lateness occurs day after day; chronic lameness never seems to get any better. Unfortunately, situations that we call chronic almost always seem to be unpleasant. We never hear about chronic peace, but we do hear about chronic warfare. And we never speak of chronic health, only of chronic illness.

chronology \krə-ˈnä-lə-jē\ (1) A sequence of events in the order they occurred. (2) A table, list, or account that presents events in order.

• The scandal had gotten so complex that the newspaper had to print a chronology showing the order of the numerous events involved.

History is much more than a simple chronology of events, but keeping events in *chronological* order is the first essential step in thinking about it. When, for example, historians try to show how World War I prepared the way for World War II, tracking the chronology of the events in the years between the two wars can help in explaining a complicated historical era.

anachronism \ə-ˈna-krə-ˌni-zəm\ (1) The error of placing a person or thing in the wrong time period. (2) A person or thing that is out of its own time.

• A Model T Ford putt-putting down the highway at 25 miles per hour was an anachronism by 1940.

In Shakespeare's time, playwrights didn't worry much about anachronisms. When Shakespeare saw his plays performed, all the characters, even Romans and Greeks, would have been dressed in the clothes of his own period. *Macbeth*, which is set in the 11th century, contains *anachronistic* references to clocks and cannons, which the real Macbeth would have known nothing about. Today, a writer may spend months doing research in order to avoid anachronisms in the historical novel she's working on. Using the second meaning of the word, we could say that manual typewriters and slide rules are anachronisms in these days of computers and calculators, and a person who likes doing things the old-fashioned way might himself be described as an anachronism.

synchronous \ˈsiŋ-krə-nəs\ (1) Happening or existing at exactly the same time; simultaneous. (2) Recurring or acting at exactly the same intervals.

- The theory depends on whether the chemical appeared in synchronous deposits worldwide seven million years ago.

Communications satellites are usually put into a synchronous (or *geosynchronous*) orbit, circling the earth once every 24 hours and so appearing to hover over a single spot on the surface. This type of *synchronized* movement is important, since you have to know where to aim your satellite dish. In the computer field, *synchronous* usually refers to the use of a simple timing signal that permits very rapid exchange of data between computers. The kind of mysterious coincidence sometimes called *synchronicity*—such as the appearance of two different comic-book characters named Dennis the Menace in the U.S. and Britain within three days of each other in 1951—has fascinated people for centuries.

Quizzes

A. Complete the analogy:

1. antique : ancient :: contemporary : _____
   a. simultaneous b. modern c. fragile d. warped
2. foreigner : country :: anachronism : _____
   a. antique b. novelty c. watch d. time period
3. argue : agree :: temporize : _____
   a. discuss b. negotiate c. conclude d. grow cold
4. drama : scenes :: chronology : _____
   a. events b. clock c. length d. sequence
5. sudden : expected :: extemporaneous : _____
   a. sudden b. rehearsed c. off-the-cuff d. off-the-wall
6. infrequent : occasional :: chronic : _____
   a. short b. surprising c. continuous d. noisy
7. temporary : enduring :: temporal : _____
   a. modern b. existing c. arising d. eternal
8. amorphous : shapeless :: synchronous : _____
   a. simultaneous b. in sequence c. out of order
   d. always late

B. Match the word on the left to the correct definition on the right:

1. chronic   a. current
2. temporal   b. order of events

3. anachronism	c. ongoing
4. extemporaneous	d. happening at the same time
5. synchronous	e. talk to fill time
6. temporize	f. improvised
7. chronology	g. measurable by time
8. contemporary	h. misplacement in time

Number Words

TRI means "three," whether derived from Greek or Latin. A *tricycle* has three wheels. A *triangle* has three sides and three angles. And a *triumvirate* is a board or government of three people.

triad \\'trī-ˌad\ (1) A group of three usually related people or things. (2) A secret Chinese criminal organization.

* The kids in the garage band next door seemed to know six or seven triads and a couple of seventh chords.

The best-known type of triad is a type of musical chord consisting of three notes. A D-major triad is made up of the notes D, F-sharp, and A; an F-minor triad is made up of F, A-flat, and C; and so on. Major and minor triads form the basis of tonal music, and songs and other pieces usually end with a *triadic* harmony. In medicine, a triad is a set of three symptoms that appear together. The Chinese criminal organizations called triads got their name from the triangular symbol that they used back when they began, centuries ago, as patriotic organizations. Today, with over 100,000 members, the triads operate in the U.S., Canada, and many other countries.

trilogy \\'tri-lə-jē\ A series of three creative works that are closely related and develop a single theme.

* William Faulkner's famous "Snopes trilogy" consists of the novels *The Hamlet*, *The Town*, and *The Mansion*.

Dozens of tragic trilogies were written for the Greek stage, though only one, Aeschylus's great *Oresteia* (consisting of *Agamemnon*, *The Libation Bearers*, and *The Eumenides*), has survived complete. Authors in later years have occasionally chosen to create trilogies to allow themselves to develop a highly complex story or cover a long span of time. Tolkien's *Lord of the Rings* wasn't actually intended as a trilogy, but since it was published in three volumes it's usually called one. George Lucas's three original *Star Wars* movies are an example of a film trilogy (which he followed many years later by another).

triceratops \ˌtrī-ˈser-ə-ˌtäps\ One of a group of large dinosaurs that lived during the Cretaceous period and had three horns, a bony crest or hood, and hoofed toes.

• The triceratops probably used its three horns for defense against the attacks of meat-eating dinosaurs.

The name *triceratops,* meaning literally "three-horned face," refers to the two horns above its eyes and the smaller third horn on its snout. Just as striking was the frilled hood or ruff that rose behind its head, though no one is quite sure what it was for. The triceratops was one of the last dinosaurs to evolve and also one of the last to become extinct. It could reach lengths of 30 feet and could stand nearly eight feet high. Despite its ferocious looks and three-foot-long horns, the triceratops was actually a vegetarian.

trident \ˈtrī-dənt\ A three-pronged spear, especially one carried by various sea gods in classical mythology.

• The bronze statue at the middle of the great fountain depicted a sea god emerging from the water, wreathed in seaweed and carrying a large trident.

A trident has three prongs or teeth, as the root *dent,* "tooth," tells us. The trident has long been used to spear fish in different parts of the world, so there's no mystery about why the Greek sea god Poseidon and his Roman counterpart Neptune both carry a trident as their symbol. In some gladiator exhibitions in ancient Rome, one gladiator, called a *retiarius* ("net man"), would be equipped as though he were a fisherman, with a weighted net and a trident; with his net he would snare his sword-wielding opponent, and with his trident he would spear his helpless foe.

trimester \trī-ˈmes-tər\ (1) A period of about three months, especially one of three such periods in a human pregnancy. (2) One of three terms into which an academic year is sometimes divided.

• Most women experience morning sickness in the first trimester of pregnancy.

Semester, which comes from the Latin words for "six" and "month," has come to mean half an academic year when the year is divided into two segments. When an academic year is divided into three segments, each is called a trimester (which is usually a bit more accurate, since each segment often is close to three months in length). Some colleges operate on the "quarter" system, with the summer being the fourth quarter, but this just means that each quarter is basically a trimester. In a human pregnancy, a trimester is three months long, representing one-third of the nine months that a typical pregnancy lasts.

trinity \ˈtri-nə-tē\ (1) (capitalized) The unity of Father, Son, and Holy Spirit as three persons in one God in Christian belief. (2) A group of three people.

• In Christian art depicting the Trinity, the Holy Spirit is almost always shown as a radiant dove.

The nature of the Trinity (or Holy Trinity) has caused centuries of argument and division within the Christian faith. The word doesn't actually appear in the Bible itself, but the New Testament does speak of the Father, Son, and Holy Spirit together; the Father is understood as the protector of the Jews, the Son as the savior of mankind, and the Holy Spirit as the preserver of the church. Almost all the major Christian sects may be called *trinitarian.* The island of Trinidad is one of many places named with the Spanish translation of *Trinity.*

triptych \ˈtrip-tik\ (1) A picture or carving made in the form of three panels side by side. (2) Something composed or presented in three sections.

• The Renaissance produced many beautiful triptychs portraying religious scenes that are still used as altarpieces.

Triptych contains the root *-ptyche,* the Greek word for "fold." So a traditional painted or carved triptych has three hinged panels, and the two outer panels fold in toward the central one. Most triptychs were intended to be mounted over a church altar. Many great triptychs were produced in the Renaissance, perhaps the most famous being Hieronymus Bosch's *Garden of Earthly Delights.* But major triptychs continued to be produced throughout the 20th century by such painters as Francis Bacon.

trivial \ˈtri-vē-əl\ Of little value or importance.

- She was so caught up in the trivial details of the trip that she hardly noticed the beautiful scenery.

Trivial comes from a Latin word meaning "crossroads"—that is, where three roads come together. Since a crossroads is a very public place where all kinds of people might show up, *trivialis* came to mean "commonplace" or "vulgar." Today the English word has changed slightly in meaning and instead usually describes something barely worth mentioning. Mathematicians use the word to refer to some part of a proof or definition that's extremely simple and needn't be explained, but the rest of us tend to use it just to mean "unimportant." "Small talk" at a party, for example, is usually trivial conversation, though a trivial excuse for not going on a date ("I have to wash my hair") might hide an emotion that isn't so trivial ("I can't stand the sight of you"). To *trivialize* something is to treat it as if it didn't matter, as if it were just another *triviality*.

Quiz

Choose the closest definition:

1. trimester   a. a three-masted sailing ship b. a period of about three months c. a three-cornered hat d. a three-minute egg
2. trivial   a. crossed b. indented c. unimportant d. found
3. triad   a. three-striped flag b. three-headed monster c. three-note chord d. three-month delay
4. trinity   a. romantic triangle b. three-part recipe c. group of three d. triplets
5. trident   a. three-toothed hag b. three-pronged spear c. triple portion d. threesome
6. trilogy   a. three-person conversation b. three-hour nap c. three-volume story d. three-ton truck
7. triceratops   a. three-foot alligator b. three-set tennis match c. three-topped tree d. three-horned dinosaur
8. triptych   a. three-week travel voucher b. three-part painting c. three-phase rocket d. three-handed clock

Review Quizzes

A. Fill in each blank with the correct letter:

a. topical
b. contemporary
c. temporize
d. synchronous
e. topiary
f. epicenter
g. dominion
h. chronic
i. retrofit
j. trivial
k. eccentric
l. retroactive
m. extemporaneous
n. predominant
o. trilogy

1. She constantly assured her employees that their opinions were never _____ or unimportant.

2. England, though a small nation, once had _____ over a great empire.

3. It cost millions to _____ each fighter jet with new navigational instruments.

4. For high-school dancers, their movements were remarkably _____.

5. When the last volume of her _____ was published, her fans snapped it up eagerly.

6. Before beginning to drill, the dentist applies a _____ anesthetic.

7. The doctor told him his condition was _____ and untreatable but not life-threatening.

8. Having left his notes at home, he had to give an entirely _____ lecture.

9. The book was criticized for having too many subjects and no _____ theme.

10. The city maintains a small _____ garden full of trees and bushes in all sorts of shapes.

11. No matter how long you _____ and stall for time, the problem won't go away.

12. Since his salary review was delayed by a few weeks, his boss made the raise _____ to the beginning of the month.

13. His habit of wearing purple socks and white sneakers to the office was considered harmlessly _____.

14. Several other great Dutch artists were _____ with Rembrandt.

15. She works hard at being outrageous, and it's not the first time she's been at the _____ of a controversy.

B. Choose the closest definition:

1. egocentric   a. group-centered   b. centered on the mind   c. self-centered   d. mentally ill.
2. retrofit   a. insert   b. dress up   c. update   d. move back
3. retrospective   a. backward glance   b. exhibit of an artist's work   c. illusion of depth   d. difference of opinion
4. anachronism   a. electronic clock   b. literary theory   c. misplacement in time   d. current topic
5. triceratops   a. winged dragon   b. dinosaur   c. three-part work   d. climbing gear
6. triad   a. triplet   b. chord   c. third rail   d. three-pointed star
7. temporal   a. religious   b. ideal   c. time-related   d. durable
8. holistic   a. wholesome   b. herbal   c. complete   d. whole-oriented
9. ectopic   a. amazing   b. current   c. reserved   d. out of place
10. triptych   a. three-part painting   b. triple window   c. computer switch   d. multivolume work

C. Match each word on the left to the correct definition on the right:

1.	Holocene	a.	land's features
2.	predominant	b.	group-centered
3.	retrogress	c.	three-pronged spear
4.	domination	d.	principal
5.	chronology	e.	group of three
6.	ethnocentric	f.	go backward
7.	trimester	g.	order of events
8.	topography	h.	school-year term
9.	trinity	i.	recent era
10.	trident	j.	control

UNIT

17

ANIM comes from the Latin *anima*, meaning "breath" or "soul." So, for example, an *animal* is a living, breathing thing—though human animals have often argued about whether other species actually have souls.

animated \ˈa-nə-ˌmā-təd\ (1) Full of life; lively, vigorous, active. (2) Seeming or appearing to be alive.

• Her gestures as she talked were so animated that even people across the room were watching her.

Animated cartoon characters have been "given life" by film techniques, though the *animation* of drawings actually goes back to handheld toys in the 1830s. A child watching the cartoon may also be animated—squealing, laughing, and jumping around—as can a crowd of hockey fans or a rock-concert audience. And the best discussions and arguments are often highly animated.

magnanimous \mag-ˈna-nə-məs\ (1) Showing a lofty and courageous spirit. (2) Generous and forgiving.

• She was magnanimous in victory, saying she'd been lucky to win and praising her opponent's effort.

The basic meaning of *magnanimity* is "greatness of spirit." Thus, magnanimity is the opposite of pettiness or "smallness." A truly magnanimous person can lose without complaining and win without gloating. Angry disputes can sometimes be resolved when one side makes a magnanimous gesture toward the other. And it's the mark of magnanimity to give credit to everyone who worked on a project even if you'd rather it all went to you.

animosity \ˌa-nə-ˈmä-sə-tē\ Ill will or resentment.

• Legend has it that the animosity between the Greeks and the Trojans began with the stealing of the beautiful Helen from her husband, Menelaus.

The important Latin word *animus* (very closely related to *anima*) could mean a great many things having to do with the soul and the emotions, one of them being "anger." As an English word, *animus* has generally meant "ill will," so it isn't mysterious that *animosity* means basically the same thing. Animosity can exist between two people, two groups or organizations, or two countries, and can sometimes lie hidden for years before reappearing. The deep animosities that exist between certain ethnic and religious groups sometimes seem as if they will last forever.

inanimate \i-ˈna-nə-mət\ (1) Not alive; lifeless. (2) Not lively; dull.

• The sculptures of Rodin are so expressive that, although inanimate, they seem full of life and emotion.

The couch you sit on while you watch TV is an inanimate object, as is your footrest, your bag of snacks, and your remote control. Spend too much time on that couch and you risk becoming a couch potato. (A potato is an inanimate object.)

FIG comes from a Latin verb meaning "to shape or mold" and a noun meaning "a form or shape." So a *figure* is usually a shape. A *transfiguration* transforms the shape or appearance of something. And a *disfiguring* injury changes the appearance of part of the body for the worse.

figurative \ˈfi-gyu̇-rə-tiv\ (1) Representing form or figure in art. (2) Saying one thing in terms normally meaning or describing another thing.

• When the poet says he's been living in the desert, it's a figurative reference to his emotional life.

Words and phrases can have both literal and figurative meanings, and we all use words with both kinds of meanings every day of our lives. We can literally close the door to a room, or we can *figuratively* close the door to further negotiations—that is, refuse to take part in them. Figurative language includes *figures* of speech, such as similes ("she's been like a sister to me") and metaphors ("a storm of protest"). And sometimes it's hard to tell whether a phrase is literal or figurative: If I say I "picked up" a little Spanish in Mexico, is that literal or figurative? You've probably noticed that lots of the definitions in this book show both a literal meaning (often something physical) and a figurative meaning (often nonphysical).

configuration \kən-ˌfi-gyu̇-ˈrā-shən\ An arrangement of parts or elements; shape, design.

• We've changed the configuration of the office so that employees will have more privacy at their desks.

The term is very common in computer science and mathematics, and in scientific and technological fields in general. Thus, for example, two scientists won a 1962 Nobel Prize for their description of the configuration of the DNA molecule. Since then, researchers have studied what different configurations within the DNA strands mean and what they control, and genetic engineers have tried to *configure* or *reconfigure* DNA in new ways to prevent or treat diseases.

effigy \ˈe-fə-jē\ An image of a person, especially a crude representation of a hated person.

• The night before the big game, an effigy of the rival coach was burned on a huge bonfire.

It was the practice of the ancient Egyptians to bury an effigy of a dead person along with that person's body. The idea was that if anything happened to the body in the afterlife, the effigy could be used as a spare. *Effigy* now usually refers to crude stuffed figures of the kind that get abused by angry protestors and unruly college students. But the small dolls that witches have used to bring pain and death on their victims can be called effigies as well. Actually, those witches and college kids seem to use their effigies for pretty much the same thing.

figment \ˈfig-mənt\ Something made up or imagined.

- His preference for Cindy is a figment of your imagination; believe me, he barely knows she exists.

A figment is something formed from imaginary elements. Daydreams are figments; nightmares are figments that can seem very real. Most figments are everyday fears and hopes about small things that turn out to be imaginary. But when the radio play "The War of the Worlds" aired in 1938, it caused a panic among thousands of people who didn't realize the Martian invasion was just a figment of the author's imagination.

Quizzes

A. Fill in each blank with the correct letter:

a. inanimate   e. figment
b. figurative   f. magnanimous
c. animated   g. configuration
d. effigy   h. animosity

1. The _____ form of the dog lay stretched in front of the fire for hours.

2. The _____ of the new aircraft's wings was one of the Defense Department's most closely held secrets.

3. Inviting her former rival to take part in the conference was a _____ gesture.

4. Don't tell him, but his popularity is just a _____ of his imagination.

5. He only meant the remark in a _____ sense, but lots of people thought he meant it literally.

6. Another _____ discussion about politics was going on when they arrived at the bar that evening.

7. The best negotiators always make a serious study of the basic causes of the _____ between feuding partners.

8. Every Halloween they would set a crude _____ of a farmer on their porch, though they never really knew why.

B. Indicate whether the following pairs of terms have the same or different meanings:

1. figment / fruitcake   same ___ / different ___
2. animosity / hatred   same ___ / different ___

3. figurative / mathematical	same ___ / different ___
4. magnanimous / petty	same ___ / different ___
5. effigy / bonfire	same ___ / different ___
6. animated / lively	same ___ / different ___
7. configuration / list of parts	same ___ / different ___
8. inanimate / not alive	same ___ / different ___

ANN/ENN comes from Latin *annus*, meaning "year." An *annual* event occurs yearly. An *anniversary* is an example of an annual event, although the older you get the more frequent they seem to be.

---

annuity \ə-'nü-ə-tē\ Money that is payable yearly or on some regular basis, or a contract providing for such payment.

* Throughout her working career she invested regularly in annuities that would support her after retirement.

Annuities are handy things to have when you retire, since they provide an income on an *annual* basis or more frequently. Annuities are normally contracts with life-insurance companies that specify that payments begin at retirement. Company pensions are traditionally doled out in the form of annuities, and sweepstakes jackpots may also come as annuities. An annuity can be a wise idea if you think you're going to live a long time; however, annuities can be tricky and should only be purchased after carefully comparing the products offered by various companies.

superannuated \ˌsü-pər-'an-yu̇-ˌwā-təd\ (1) Outworn, old-fashioned, or out-of-date. (2) Forced to retire because of old age or infirmity.

* He called himself a car collector, but his backyard looked like a cemetery for superannuated clunkers.

A superannuated style is out-of-date—its time has come and gone. And a person who has passed an age limit and been forced to retire may technically be called superannuated. But more often *superannuated* describes people who seem somehow to belong to the past. So a 55-year-old surfer might be regarded as superannuated by the young crowd riding the waves in Santa Cruz, and a superannuated hippie might still be dressing the way he did in 1972.

millennium \mə-'le-nē-əm\ (1) A period of time lasting 1,000 years, or the celebration of a 1,000-year anniversary. (2) A period of great happiness and perfection on earth.

• The first millennium B.C. saw the rise of important civilizations in Greece, Rome, India, Central America, and China.

Since in Latin *mille* means "thousand" (see MILL, p. 448), a millennium lasts 1,000 years. Thus, we're living today at the beginning of the third millennium since the birth of Christ. But some religious sects, relying on a prophecy in the biblical Book of Revelation, speak of a coming millennium when Jesus will return to reign on earth for 1,000 years, evil will be banished, and all will live in peace and happiness. Members of these sects who keep themselves in a constant state of preparedness are called *millenarians* or *millennialists*.

perennial \pə-'re-nē-əl\ (1) Continuing to grow for several years. (2) Enduring or continuing without interruption.

• "See You in September" is a perennial summertime hit among lovesick teenagers.

A perennial garden is full of *perennials* like delphiniums and asters, flowers that continue to bloom year after year. (*Annuals*, by contrast, grow for only a single season and must be replanted *annually*, and *biennials* die after two years.) Evergreens are *perennially* green; for that reason, they're perennial favorites for Christmas wreaths and decorations. In a similar way, taxes are a perennial political issue; and a perennial political candidate may come back over and over claiming he's the only one who can save us from them.

EV comes from the Latin *aevum,* "age" or "lifetime." Though the root occurs in only a few English words, it's related to the Greek *aion,* "age," from which we get the word *eon,* meaning "a very long period of time."

coeval \kō-'ē-vəl\ Having the same age or lasting the same amount of time; contemporary.

• Homer's *Iliad* and *Odyssey,* probably written around 700 B.C., are coeval with portions of the Hebrew Bible, or Old Testament.

Coeval usually describes things that existed together for a very long time or that originated at the same time in the distant past. Thus, astronomers might speak of one galaxy as being coeval with another, and a period in the history of one civilization might be coeval with a similar period in another. As a noun, however, *coeval* may describe people as well; so, for example, two artists who lived and worked at the same time might be described as *coevals*.

longevity \län-ˈje-və-tē\ (1) A long duration of life. (2) Length of life; long continuance.

- Picasso had a career of remarkable longevity, and was producing plentifully until his death at 91.

As living conditions improve and the science of medicine advances, the longevity of the average American has increased greatly, from about 45 years in 1900 to over 75 years today. But the most impressive human longevity is nothing compared to the 400-year lifespan of an ocean clam found near Iceland, or the 5,000-year lifespan of the bristlecone pine, a tree found in the western U.S. We may use *longevity* to talk not only about actual lives but also of the useful "life" of things: the life of your car's tires or the shingles on your roof, for example.

medieval \ˌmē-dē-ˈē-vəl\ (1) Relating to the Middle Ages of European history, from about A.D. 500 to 1500. (2) Extremely out-of-date.

- The great cathedral at Chartres in France, finished in 1220, is a masterpiece of medieval architecture.

With its roots *medi-*, meaning "middle," and *ev-*, meaning "age," *medieval* literally means "of the Middle Ages." In this case, *middle* means "between the Roman empire and the Renaissance"—that is, after the fall of the great Roman state and before the "rebirth" of culture that we call the Renaissance. This same period used to be called the "Dark Ages," since it was believed that in these years civilization all but vanished. And indeed, for most Europeans in these centuries, it was a time of poverty, famine, plague, and superstition, rather than the age of magic, dazzling swordplay, towering castles, and knights in splendid armor displayed in today's graphic novels and video games.

primeval \prī-ˈmē-vəl\ (1) Having to do with the earliest ages; primitive or ancient. (2) Existing from the beginning.

• When European settlers first arrived in North America, they found vast tracts of primeval forest, seemingly untouched by human influence.

With its *prim-* prefix, meaning "first," *primeval* obviously refers to an original age. So the word often suggests the earliest periods in the earth's history. Myths are often stories of the creation of the world and of its primeval beings. The trees in a primeval forest (few of which remain today in most countries) may be 400 years old—not as old as the world, but maybe as old as they ever live to. According to scientists, life on earth began in the protein-rich waters of the primeval seas and swamps, and the decay of their tiny organisms and plant matter over millions of years produced our petroleum and coal.

Quizzes

A. Choose the closest definition:

1. perennial   a. flowerlike   b. excellent   c. everlasting
    d. thorough
2. longevity   a. extent   b. life length   c. longitude
    d. longing
3. superannuated   a. amazing   b. huge   c. aged
    d. perennial
4. coeval   a. ancient   b. simultaneous   c. same-sized
    d. continuing
5. millennium   a. thousand   b. century   c. era
    d. a thousand years
6. annuity   a. annual event   b. annual payment   c. annual
    income   d. annual garden
7. medieval   a. antiquated   b. middle-aged   c. romantic
    d. knightly
8. primeval   a. wicked   b. elderly   c. primitive   d. muddy

B. Match the definition on the left to the correct word on the right:

1. ancient   a. perennial
2. of the same age   b. longevity
3. yearly payment   c. primeval
4. era of earthly paradise   d. coeval

5.	of the Middle Ages	e.	millennium
6.	worn out	f.	annuity
7.	length of life	g.	medieval
8.	continuing	h.	superannuated

CORP comes from *corpus,* the Latin word for "body." A *corpse* is a dead body. A *corporation* is also a kind of body, since it may act almost like an individual. And a *corps* is a "body" of soldiers.

corporeal \kȯr-ˈpȯr-ē-əl\ Having or relating to a physical body; substantial.

• In paintings, angels usually look very much like corporeal beings, often with actual feathered wings.

In various religions, including Christianity, *corporeal* existence is often called the opposite of *spiritual* existence, and corporeal existence, unlike spiritual existence, is often said to be contaminated with evil. The word is also often used by philosophers, especially when considering the nature of reality. For lawyers, *corporeal* describes physical property such as houses or cars, as opposed to something valuable but nonphysical like a good reputation.

corpulent \ˈkȯr-pyü-lənt\ Having a large, bulky body; obese.

• Squire Jenkins had often been described as "stout" or "portly," but more recently the word his acquaintances were using was usually "corpulent," or even "fat."

The Duchess of Windsor may have said that you can never be too rich or too thin, but that's a rather modern point of view. In earlier times in Europe, being overweight was considered a sign of wealth and well-being, as demonstrated by the *corpulence* of many European kings. Still today, corpulence is thought to be superior to thinness in some of the world's cultures. But *corpulent* and *corpulence* are less often used than they once were, and we're now probably more likely to say "obese" and "obesity."

corporal \ˈkȯr-pə-rəl\ Relating to or affecting the body.

• She was reminded that, in the public-school system, shaking a child was now regarded as unacceptable corporal punishment.

The adjective *corporal* today usually appears in the phrase *corporal punishment,* which means "bodily punishment." This used to include such acts as mutilation, branding, imprisonment, and even death. But today execution comes under the separate heading of "capital punishment," which originally involved losing your head (*capit-* meaning "head"). Milder forms of corporal punishment are used by American parents, and were once common in schools as well. *Corporal* is occasionally used in other ways; in the traditional church, the "corporal works of mercy" include seven helpful acts such as sheltering the homeless and burying the dead. *Corporal* as a military rank actually comes from *caporal*—which has the same root as *capital*.

incorporate \in-ˈkòr-pə-ˌrāt\ (1) To blend or combine into something already existing to form one whole. (2) To form or form into a corporation.

- The new edition incorporates many suggestions and corrections received by the author from his readers.

From its roots, *incorporate* means basically "add into a body" or "form into a body." So, for example, a chef might decide to incorporate a couple of new ingredients into an old recipe, and then might incorporate that new item into the restaurant's dinner menu. The restaurant itself was probably *incorporated* at the beginning, and so is now a *corporation*—that is, a "body" that's legally allowed to act like a single person in certain ways, even if it may have many individual employees. As you can see, the two meanings turn out to be fairly different.

TANG/TACT comes from the Latin words *tangere,* "to touch," and *tactus,* "sense of touch." So, for instance, to make *contact* is to touch or "get in touch with."

---

tact \ˈtakt\ The ability to deal with others without offending them.

- Already at 16 his daughter showed remarkable tact in dealing with adults, which she certainly hadn't gotten from him.

This word came to English directly from French (a Latin-based language), where it can also mean simply "sense of touch." Dealing with difficult situations involving other people can require the kind of extreme sensitivity that our fingertips possess. As Lincoln once said, "Tact is the ability to describe others as they see themselves," which doesn't usually come naturally. Someone *tactful* can soothe the feelings of the most difficult people; a *tactless* person will generally make a bad situation worse.

tactile \'tak-təl\ (1) Able to be perceived by touching. (2) Relating to the sense of touch.

• He always enjoyed the tactile sensation of running his hand over the lush turf.

If you set your cell phone to vibrate rather than ring, you're taking the tactile option. Educators believe that some students are naturally "tactile learners," much better at "hands-on" learning than at tasks that involve patient listening and reading. Many longtime readers resist using e-books, saying they miss the tactile sensations of leafing through an actual book. And the blind, using the raised dots of the braille alphabet, rely entirely on their tactile sense to read; some can actually read as fast as the average person can read out loud.

tangential \tan-'jen-shəl\ Touching lightly; incidental.

• The government is trying to determine if the extremists were deeply involved or if their relationship to the suspect was merely tangential.

In geometry, a *tangent* is a straight line that touches a curve at a single point. So we say that someone who starts talking about one thing and gets sidetracked has gone off on a tangent. The new subject is tangential to the first subject—it touches it and moves off in a different direction.

tangible \'tan-jə-bəl\ Able to be perceived, especially by touch; physical, substantial.

• The snow was tangible evidence that winter had really come.

Something that's literally tangible can be touched. A rock is tangible, and so is a broken window; if the rock is lying next to the window, it could be tangible evidence of vandalism. When we say that the tension in a room is tangible, we mean we feel it so strongly that it seems almost physical. But if we're being literal, tension, like hope, happiness, and hunger, is literally *intangible*—it may be real, but it can't be touched. When lawyers talk about an intangible asset, they might mean something like a company's good reputation—very valuable, but not quite touchable.

Quizzes

A. Fill in each blank with the correct letter:

a.	incorporate	e.	corporeal
b.	tangible	f.	tangential
c.	corporal	g.	tact
d.	tactile	h.	corpulent

1. The question was only _____ to the main subject, but he answered it anyway.

2. The flogging of sailors was once a common form of _____ punishment in the British navy.

3. The district attorney realizes that they don't have much _____ evidence, and he's desperate to dig up more.

4. At 300 pounds, President Taft was often referred to as _____, especially by his enemies.

5. Brain surgeons have highly developed _____ sensitivities.

6. We hope to _____ suggestions from everyone on the board into our final proposal.

7. The footprints on the rug suggested that their mysterious nighttime visitor had been something more _____ than a ghost.

8. She's never had much _____, and her big mouth is always getting her into trouble.

B. Indicate whether the following pairs of terms have the same or different meanings:

1. corpulent / boring   same ___ / different ___
2. tangential / touching lightly same ___ / different ___
3. incorporate / leave out   same ___ / different ___
4. tact / cleverness   same ___ / different ___
5. corporeal / substantial   same ___ / different ___
6. corporal / military   same ___ / different ___
7. tactile / sticky   same ___ / different ___
8. tangible / touchable   same ___ / different ___

CODI/CODE comes from the Latin *codex,* meaning "trunk of a tree" or "document written on wooden tablets." A *code* can be either a set of laws or a system of symbols used to write messages. To *encode* a message is to write it in code. A genetic code, transmitted by genes, is a set of instructions for everything from blood type to eye color.

codex \\'kō-ˌdeks\\ A book in handwritten form, especially a book of Scripture, classics, or ancient texts.

• There on the shelves of the monastery library they saw codex after codex, all carefully copied and illustrated by hand.

In the 3rd and 4th centuries A.D., the codex began to replace the older scroll as the preferred form for longer writings. Unlike the scroll, this wonderful invention permitted writing on both sides of a sheet, made it easy to locate a particular passage, and could contain a very long piece of writing. Codices (note this unusual plural form) were usually written on parchment, the specially prepared skin of a sheep or goat, or papyrus, the ancestor of paper. Because codices were handwritten, there were few copies of any single codex, and sometimes only a single copy. Today we no longer write our books in longhand, but the modern book has kept basically the same form as the original codices.

codicil \\'kä-də-səl\\ (1) An amendment or addition made to a will. (2) An appendix or supplement.

• With the birth of each new grandchild, the old man added a new codicil to his will.

A codicil is literally a "little *codex,*" a little bit of writing on a small piece of writing material, used to add to or change something about a larger piece of writing. A codicil to a will can change the terms of the original will completely, so it generally requires witnesses just like the will itself, though in some states a handwritten codicil may not. In mystery novels, such changes have been known to cause murders; in real life, codicils aren't usually quite that exciting.

codify \\'kä-də-ˌfī\\ To arrange according to a system; classify.

• In the 6th century B.C., the great statesman Solon newly codified the laws of Athens, replacing the harsh legal code of Draco.

A *code* is a collection of laws arranged in an orderly way; famous examples include the Code of Hammurabi, from about 1760 B.C. in ancient Babylon, and the Napoleonic Code, produced at Napoleon's orders in 1804. Laws that have been included in a code have been codified. The rules of baseball differed greatly from one place to another until they were codified by Alexander Cartwright in 1845; they haven't changed much since, though we don't know what Cartwright would say about the designated hitter.

decode \di-ˈkōd\ (1) To put a coded message into an understandable form. (2) To find the underlying meaning of; decipher.

• The Allies were able to decode many important secret messages sent by the Germans and Japanese in World War II.

To *decode* is to take out of *code* and put into understandable language. (Its opposite is *encode*, "to put into coded form.") But dreams may sometimes also be decoded; psychologists often try to decode the images of their patients' dreams so as to understand the emotions behind them. And readers must often decode what a novel or story or poem is telling them, which may require two or three readings. *Decipher* is often a synonym, though we now use it when talking about reading difficult handwriting.

SIGN comes from the Latin noun *signum,* "mark or sign." A *signal* is a kind of sign. Your *signature* is your own personal sign. And an architect's *design* marks out the pattern for a building.

---

signify \ˈsig-nə-ˌfī\ (1) To be a sign of something; to mean something. (2) To show or make known, especially by a sign.

• The improved performance of the students signifies that the new approach may be working.

Signify basically means "to make a sign or signal." One of its synonyms is *indicate*; the *index finger* is the finger you point with, so to indicate is essentially to point to something. *Significant* means "important" and *significance* means "importance"; similarly, *insignificant* means "unimportant" and *insignificance* means "lack of importance."

insignia \in-ˈsig-nē-ə\ A badge of authority or honor; a distinguishing sign or mark.

- Peering closely at the photograph, he could now see clearly the insignia of the Nazi SS on his grandfather's chest.

Insignia are the official signs of rank, titles, or awards. Medals are an example, as are the crowns of monarchs. The Catholic church employs such insignia as the red robes of cardinals. U.S. presidents have the presidential seal, which appears on the stand when they're giving a speech. But most of us think first of the bars, stripes, badges, and patches of military rank.

signatory \\\|sig-nə-,tȯr-ē\\ A person or government that signs an agreement with others; especially a government that agrees with others to abide by a signed agreement.

- More than a dozen countries were signatories to the agreement setting limits on fishing in international waters.

A signatory puts his or her *signature* on a document that is also *signed* by others. In 1215 the English barons revolted against King John and forced him to join them as a signatory to the Magna Carta. This agreement stated the barons' own duties to the King but also *assigned* the barons clear rights and limited the King's power over them. Though the Magna Carta did nothing for the common people, it's often been called the first step toward democracy in the English-speaking countries.

signet \\\|sig-nət\\ (1) A seal used instead of a signature to give personal or official authority to a document. (2) A small engraved seal, often in the form of a ring.

- The charters of lands and rights of the early American colonies were confirmed with the king's signet.

Signets have been used for thousands of years. The design of a signet is personalized for its owner, and no two are alike. The ancients used signets to mark their possessions and to sign contracts. In later years signets were used to stamp a blob of hot wax sealing a folded secret document so that it couldn't be opened and read without the design being broken. The Pope still wears a signet, called the Fisherman's Ring, which is carved with a figure of St. Peter encircled with the Pope's name; after a Pope's death, the ring is destroyed and a new one is made.

Quizzes

A. Choose the closest definition:

1. codify   a. conceal b. list c. disobey d. interpret
2. signet   a. stamp b. gold ring c. Pope's sign d. baby
   swan
3. codicil   a. small fish b. one-tenth c. amendment to a
   will d. legal objection
4. signify   a. sense b. remind c. sign d. mean
5. insignia   a. indication b. signal c. badge d. rank
6. codex   a. private seal b. handwritten book c. secret
   letter d. coded message
7. signatory   a. document b. agreement c. banner
   d. cosigner
8. decode   a. explain b. conceal c. symbolize d. disguise

**B. Match the word on the left to the correct definition
on the right:**

1. insignia   a. interpret
2. codex   b. addition
3. signatory   c. emblem of honor
4. decode   d. engraved seal
5. signet   e. old type of book
6. codify   f. signer
7. signify   g. organize laws
8. codicil   h. indicate

Number Words

QUADR/QUART comes from Latin words meaning "four" or
"fourth." In English, a *quart* is one-fourth of a gallon, just as a
quarter is one-fourth of a dollar. A *quadrangle* has four sides and
angles but isn't necessarily square. And *quadruplets* are four babies
born at the same time.

quadrant \ˈkwä-drənt\ (1) A quarter of a circle. (2) Any of the four
quarters into which something is divided by two lines intersecting
at right angles.

- Washington, D.C., like a number of other cities, is divided into quadrants called Northwest, Northeast, Southwest, and Southeast.

This word is used for a traditional instrument, used to make calculations of altitude and traditionally employed by sailors to navigate, which has a piece shaped like a quarter of a circle. A quadrant shower is a shower that fits snugly into a bathroom corner and displays a curved front, making a quadrant shape on the floor. But perhaps *quadrant* is used most often today to name a particular quarter of a city.

quadrille \kwä-ˈdril\ A square dance popular in the 18th and 19th century, made up of five or six patterns for four couples.

- Quadrilles were very popular at balls in the American South before the Civil War.

The quadrille, named for its four couples that form the sides of a square, seems to have begun as a French country dance. In the 18th century it became fashionable among the French nobility; as performed by elegantly dressed aristocrats, it became slow and formal. It crossed over to England and from there to New England, where it turned back into a dance for the common people. It soon evolved into the American square dance, a lively type of dance that employs a "caller" to make sure everyone remembers the steps.

quadriplegic \ˌkwä-drə-ˈplē-jik\ Paralyzed in both arms and both legs.

- A motorcycle accident in her teens had killed her boyfriend and left her a quadriplegic.

Quadriplegia is the result of injury or illness, almost always affecting the spine. Though a *paraplegic* has lost the use only of his or her legs, *quadriplegics* are paralyzed in all four limbs. Today voice-activated wheelchairs help the quadriplegic get around, and houses can be equipped with similar systems to operate lights and appliances; monkeys have even been trained to assist quadriplegics with everyday tasks. The work of the quadriplegic actor Christopher Reeve has led to remarkable advances in developing new nerve connections, enabling some determined paraplegics and quadriplegics to walk again.

quartile \ˈkwȯr-ˌtīl\ One of four equal groups each containing a quarter of a statistical population.

- The schools in our town always average in the lowest quartile in both reading and math achievement.

A quartile is a *quarter* of a specific group that has been tested or evaluated in specific ways. The first quartile is the one that scores highest and the fourth quartile scores lowest. For achievement and proficiency tests, the first quartile is the place to be; for blood pressure or cholesterol, the third quartile is healthier.

TETR comes from the Greek word for "four." In the immensely popular video game *Tetris*, for example, each of the pieces the game is played with has four segments. But the root usually shows up in long chemical names.

---

tetracycline \ˌte-trə-ˈsī-ˌklēn\ A yellow broad-spectrum antibiotic.

- He was sent home with a prescription for tetracycline and some advice about how to avoid Lyme disease in the future.

Most chemical names are made up of two or more Greek and Latin roots strung together. Thus, *tetracycline*, with its *cycl-* root from the Greek word for "circle," means "four-ringed"—that is, "consisting of four fused hydrocarbon rings." Antibiotics work against bacteria and other tiny organisms (but not viruses); tetracycline, which comes from a kind of soil bacteria, is one of the most used of the antibiotics. "Broad-spectrum" antibiotics work well on numerous organisms; thus, tetracycline has proved effective against acne, chlamydia, cholera, rickets, and various lung and eye infections, among many other conditions.

tetrahedron \ˌte-trə-ˈhē-drən\ A solid shape formed by four flat faces.

- Her son's box kite was a tetrahedron, and its pyramid shape was easy to pick out among the traditional designs flown by the other children.

The simplest tetrahedron is made of four equal-sided triangles: one is used as the base, and the other three are fitted to it and each other to make a pyramid. But the great pyramids of Egypt aren't tetrahedrons: they instead have a square base and four triangular faces, and thus are five-sided rather than four-sided.

tetralogy \te-ˈtra-lə-jē\ A set of four connected literary, artistic, or musical works.

• *The Raj Quartet,* Paul Scott's long and complex tetralogy of India, was made into a highly praised television series.

Vivaldi's *Four Seasons* could be called a tetralogy, since it's a set of four violin concertos, one for each season of the year. Eight of Shakespeare's history plays are often grouped into two tetralogies. Wagner's great *Ring of the Nibelung,* an opera tetralogy based on Norse mythology, contains about 18 hours of music. The original tetralogies, however, were sets of four plays by the same author performed together in ancient Greece; the first three were always tragedies, and the last was a wild comedy. Tetralogies were written by such great dramatists as Aeschylus, Sophocles, and Euripedes; unfortunately, none of them have survived in their entirety.

tetrapod \ˈte-trə-ˌpäd\ A vertebrate with two pairs of limbs.

• His special study was the great seismosaurus, probably the largest tetrapod—and the largest land animal—that ever lived.

The earliest tetrapods, or "four-footed" animals, were mammal-like reptiles that evolved before the rise of the dinosaurs and ranged from mouse-sized to cow-sized. Today the tetrapods include the reptiles, the amphibians, the birds, and the mammals—including humans. Though the fish aren't classified as tetrapods, it's quite possible that our own limbs began as paired fins hundreds of millions of years ago.

Quiz

Match the definition on the left to the correct word on the right:

1. four-sided solid   a. quadriplegic
2. square dance   b. tetralogy
3. one-fourth of a group   c. quadrant
4. four connected works   d. tetrapod
5. paralyzed in four limbs   e. quartile
6. quarter   f. tetrahedron
7. antibiotic   g. quadrille
8. four-limbed animal   h. tetracycline

Review Quizzes

A. Choose the correct synonym and the correct antonym:

1. decode   a. translate b. recover c. encode d. transmit
2. animated   a. colorful b. lifeless c. smiling d. vigorous
3. tangible   a. readable b. touchable c. eternal
      d. nonphysical
4. animosity   a. affection b. mammal c. dedication
      d. hatred
5. corpulent   a. slim b. spiritual c. overweight d. bodily
6. figurative   a. modeled b. literal c. painted d. symbolic
7. corporal   a. military b. bodily c. nonphysical
      d. reasonable
8. perennial   a. two-year b. lasting c. temporary
      d. flowering
9. longevity   a. anniversary b. shortness
      c. uncertainty d. permanence
10. primeval   a. recent b. antique c. ancient d. swamplike

B. Fill in each blank with the correct letter:

a. magnanimous   k. medieval
b. codicil   l. codex
c. corporeal   m. figment
d. intact   n. quartile
e. quadriplegic   o. tetrapod
f. effigy   p. coeval
g. inanimate   q. tetracycline
h. tactile   r. superannuated
i. millennium   s. incorporate
j. tetrahedron   t. signify

1. When she woke from her coma, she reported the experience of floating in the air and looking down on her _____ body.
2. The year 2000 marked the start of the third _____ A.D.
3. In _____ Europe, great walls were erected around entire cities for the protection of the people.

4. Every large land animal is a _____, as is every bird.

5. In his victory speech he was _____ to his opponents, promising them an important role in his government.

6. In these auctions, bidders _____ that they're raising their bids by holding up a paddle with a number on it.

7. In this report she hoped to _____ all the research she'd been doing for the last year.

8. In the rare-book room of the library, he found another _____ containing three long poems in Old English.

9. A grade-point average that falls in the top _____ earns a student special privileges.

10. A _____ can be a strong and stable structure, since it's made of four triangles.

11. For the homecoming celebration, we made an _____ of our opponents' mascot and draped it in black.

12. We all know it's ridiculous to curse at _____ objects when it's just our own clumsiness that's at fault.

13. A _____ to the environmental treaty provided for a special exception for three African countries.

14. Because of technological advances and access laws, the life of a _____ is far less restricted than it once was.

15. Being blind, his _____ sense was extremely well developed.

16. It was a terrible experience, but they came through it with their sense of humor _____.

17. The idea that my parents don't like you is a _____ of your imagination.

18. She knows that creaky old chair is _____, but she loves it and wouldn't give it up for anything.

19. That tree was planted when I was born, so it and I are _____.

20. Penicillin and _____ are among the most useful of the antibiotics.

C. **Match the definition on the left to the correct word on the right:**

1. incidental   a. configuration
2. will addition   b. tetralogy
3. politeness   c. annuity
4. arrangement   d. tact
5. regular payment   e. codify
6. formal dance   f. quadrille
7. four-part work   g. tangential
8. seal   h. signet
9. signer   i. codicil
10. classify   j. signatory

UNIT

18

CAPIT, from the Latin word for "head," *caput,* turns up in some important places. The head of a ship is its *captain*, and the *capital* of a state or country is where the "head of state" works. A *capital* letter stands head and shoulders above a lowercase letter, as well as at the head (beginning) of a sentence.

---

capitalism \\'ka-pə-tə-ˌli-zəm\\ An economic system based on private ownership, private decisions, and open competition in a free market.

• In the 1980s, the leaders of the free world had faith that capitalism and a free-market economy would solve all our problems.

Capital is wealth—that is, money and goods—that's used to produce more wealth. Capitalism is practiced enthusiastically by *capitalists*, people who use capital to increase production and make more goods and money. Capitalism works by encouraging competition in a fair and open market. Its opposite is often said to be socialism. Where a *capitalist* economy encourages private actions and ownership, socialism prefers public or government ownership and control of parts of the economy. In a pure capitalist system, there would be no public schools or public parks, no government programs such as Social Security and Medicare, and maybe not even any public highways or police. In a pure socialist system, there wouldn't be any private corporations. In other words, there's just about no such thing as pure capitalism or pure socialism in the modern world.

capitulate \kə-'pi-chə-ˌlāt\ To surrender or stop resisting; give up.

• At 2:00 a.m. the last three senators finally capitulated, allowing the bill to move forward.

Capitulation often refers to surrender on the battlefield. Originally it only referred to surrender according to an agreement, though that part of the meaning is often absent. Today a teacher can capitulate to her students' cries of protest against a homework assignment, or a father can capitulate to his kids' pleas to stop for ice cream, when the only terms of the agreement are that they'll stop complaining.

decapitate \di-'ka-pə-ˌtāt\ (1) To cut off the head; behead. (2) To destroy or make useless.

• The leaders of the uprising were decapitated, and their heads were mounted on long poles on London Bridge as a warning to the people.

Decapitation is a quick and fairly painless way to go, so it was once considered suitable only for nobles like Sir Walter Raleigh, Mary Queen of Scots, and two of Henry VIII's unfortunate wives. The invention of the guillotine in the 18th century was meant to make execution swifter and more painless than hanging or a badly aimed blow by the executioner's sword.

recapitulate \ˌrē-kə-'pi-chə-ˌlāt\ To repeat or summarize the most important points or stages.

• At the end of his talk, the president carefully recapitulated the main points in order.

Capitulation originally meant the organizing of material under headings. So *recapitulation* usually involves the gathering of the main ideas in a brief summary. But a recapitulation may be a complete restatement as well. In many pieces of classical music, the recapitulation, or *recap,* is the long final section of a movement, where the earlier music is restated in the main key.

ANTHROP comes from the Greek word for "human being." So an *anthropomorphic* god, such as Zeus or Athena, basically looks and acts like a human. And in Aesop's fables and many animated cartoons, animals are usually *anthropomorphized* and behave exactly like furry, four-legged human beings.

anthropoid \\'an-thrə-ˌpȯid\ Any of several large, tailless apes.

- The chimpanzees, gorillas, orangutans, gibbons, and bonobos are all classified as anthropoids.

With its suffix *-oid*, meaning "resembling," the word *anthropoid* means literally "resembling a human being." Anthropoid apes are so called because they resemble humans more closely than do other primates such as monkeys and lemurs. Some even spend a good deal of time walking on their hind legs. Anthropoids are, of course, highly intelligent (though maybe no more so than many monkeys), and some of them use sticks and stones as tools. (But if you call someone an anthropoid, you're probably not complimenting his intelligence.)

anthropology \\ˌan-thrə-'pä-lə-jē\ The science and study of human beings.

- By studying the cultures of primitive peoples, anthropology may give us a better understanding of our own culture.

Anthropologists, those who study the whys and wherefores of human existence, today look not only at the tribes of the Amazon but also at the neighborhoods of Brooklyn or Santa Monica. Every group and every culture now seems to be possible material for anthropology. Some anthropologists specialize in the study of human evolution, some study human language, some study archaeology, and some study human culture through the ages. Unlike historians, they tend to focus less on what has been recorded in writings than on what can be discovered in other ways.

misanthropic \\ˌmi-sən-'thrä-pik\ Hating or distrusting humans.

- Few characters in literature are more misanthropic than Ebenezer Scrooge, who cares for nothing but money.

Jonathan Swift was famous for the *misanthropy* of works such as *Gulliver's Travels* which make fun of all kinds of human foolishness. But in spite of his apparent misanthropic attitude, he spent a third of his income on founding a hospital and another third on other charities—certainly not the acts of a true *misanthrope*. Today we often use synonyms such as *cynic* and *grinch* for misanthropic types—while hoping we don't meet too many of them.

lycanthropy \lī-ˈkan-thrə-pē\ (1) A delusion that one has become a wolf. (2) Transformation into a wolf through witchcraft or magic.

• The local farmers avoided the residents of the village in the next valley, who had long been suspected of grave robbing and lycanthropy.

The Greek word for "wolf," *lykos*, combines with the *anthro-* root to produce the meaning "wolfman." In European folklore, dating back to the ancient Greeks and Romans, there are men who change into wolves at night and devour animals, people, or graveyard corpses before returning to human form at dawn. Werewolves, or *lycan-thropes*, may be evil and possessed by the devil, or may instead be the victims of a werewolf bite and thereby cursed to change into wolf form at the full moon. The werewolf's evil intention is shown by its eating only part of the animal or corpse, rather than all of it like a truly hungry wolf.

Quizzes

A. Fill in each blank with the correct letter:

a. misanthropic
b. capitalism
c. lycanthropy
d. capitulate
e. recapitulate
f. anthropology
g. decapitate
h. anthropoid

1. She's too proud to _____ to her rivals on this point without getting something major in return.
2. In the years when new primitive cultures were being discovered regularly, _____ must have been a very exciting field.
3. _____ is the economic system in most of the world's countries today, but in many of these the government also plays a large role.
4. The gorilla is classified as an _____ because of its relatively close resemblance to humans.
5. The guillotine was used in France to _____ criminals before capital punishment was outlawed there.
6. By the time he turned 80 he was genuinely bitter and _____ and disliked by all his neighbors.

7. All the sports channels constantly _____ the highlights
    of recent games.
8. In these mountains, where wolves can be heard baying
    at the moon every night, many of the villagers believe
    in _____.

**B. Match the word on the left to the correct definition
    on the right:**

1. recapitulate   a.   free-market system
2. misanthropic   b.   human-wolf transformation
3. capitalism   c.   surrender
4. anthropoid   d.   summarize
5. decapitate   e.   antisocial
6. anthropology   f.   study of cultures
7. capitulate   g.   ape
8. lycanthropy   h.   behead

KINE comes from the Greek word *kinesis*, meaning "movement."
Kinetic energy is the energy of motion (as opposed to potential
energy, the kind of energy held by a stretched elastic band). Kinetic
art is art that has moving parts, such as Alexander Calder's famous
mobiles. And *cinema*, the art of moving pictures, actually comes
from the same *kine-* root as well.

---

kinesiology \kə-ˌnē-sē-ˈä-lə-jē\ The scientific study of human
movement.

• With a kinesiology degree in hand, she landed a job as a rehab
  therapist for patients following heart surgery.

Kinesiologists study the acquisition of motor skills, the mechanical
aspects of movement, and the body's responses to physical activity.
A kinesiologist may work in a public-school fitness program, design
exercise programs for people with and without disabilities, or work
with patients recovering from disease, accidents, and surgery. As a
field of research, kinesiology focuses particularly on the mechanics
of muscular activity.

hyperkinetic \ˌhī-pər-kə-ˈne-tik\ (1) Relating to or affected with
hyperactivity. (2) Characterized by fast-paced or frantic activity.

- *Noises Off* is a hyperkinetic stage farce that moves at a breathless pace for a full hour and a half.

Since the prefix *hyper-* means "above, beyond" (see HYPER, p. 457), *hyperkinetic* describes motion beyond the usual. The word is usually applied to children, and often describes the condition of almost uncontrollable activity or muscular movements called *attention-deficit/hyperactivity disorder* (ADHD). Kids with ADHD are usually not just hyperkinetic but also inattentive, forgetful, and flighty. Though they're often treated with drugs, many experts believe there are better ways of dealing with the problem. Lots of people now shorten both *hyperactive* and *hyperkinetic* to simply *hyper* ("He's been hyper all morning"), but usually don't mean it too seriously.

kinescope \\'ki-nə-ˌskōp\\ A motion picture made from an image on a picture tube.

- In the archives she turned up several kinescopes of Ernie Kovacs's 1950s show, which she thought had been dumped into New York Harbor decades ago.

Kinescope, originally a trademark for the cathode-ray tube in a TV, later became the name for a film of a TV screen showing a live broadcast. In order for a program to be seen beyond New York in the early days of TV, a kinescope had to be shipped from station to station. Though grainy and fuzzy, these were for a time the only way of capturing live shows. But in 1951 Desi Arnaz and Lucille Ball decided to film their comedy show rather than to broadcast it live, and in a few years live broadcast comedy and drama had vanished from the airwaves.

telekinesis \\ˌte-li-kə-'nē-səs\\ The movement of objects without contact or other physical means, as by the exercise of an occult power.

- Fascinated by telekinesis as a boy, he'd spent hours in his room trying to push a pencil off the table using only his mind.

Tele- in Greek means "far off" (see TELE, p. 417). The eternally appealing idea of moving an object remotely, using only psychic powers, has had a long life in films, TV shows, stories and novels, video games, and comics. But although some researchers believe in the existence of telekinesis (also known as *psychokinesis*), most scientists believe that any reported experiences have been the result of fraud, wishful thinking, or naturally explainable events.

DYNAM comes from the Greek *dynamis*, meaning "power." A *dyne* is a unit used in measuring force; an instrument that measures force is called a *dynamometer*. And when Alfred Nobel invented a powerful explosive in 1867, he named it *dynamite*.

---

dynamic \dī-'na-mik\ (1) Relating to physical force or energy. (2) Continuously and productively active and changing; energetic or forceful.

- The situation has entered a dynamic phase, and what we knew about it last week has changed considerably by now.

Dynamic is the opposite of *static,* which means "not moving or active." So all living languages, for example, are dynamic rather than static, changing from year to year even when they don't appear to be. A bustling commercial city like Hong Kong is intensely dynamic, constantly changing and adapting. A dynamic relationship—for example, the relationship between housing values and interest rates charged by banks—is one that changes all the time. Unfortunately, the word has been used so much by advertisers that we tend to forget its basic meaning.

dynamo \'dī-nə-ˌmō\ (1) A power generator, especially one that produces direct electric current. (2) A forceful, energetic person.

- Even as they entered the power plant, the roar of the water covered the sound of the immense dynamos.

The dynamo was introduced in 1832 to produce electricity for commercial use. Like all later generators, the original dynamos changed mechanical energy (produced by steam, which was itself produced by burning coal) into electricity. The word is less used today than it once was, since it's often applied only to generators that produced direct electric current (DC) rather than alternating current (AC), which is now the standard. A human dynamo is a person who seems to have unlimited energy, such as New York's legendary mayor Fiorello La Guardia, whose forcefulness and vigor matched that of his intensely *dynamic* city.

aerodynamics \͵er-ō-dī-ˈna-miks\ (1) A science that studies the movement of gases such as air and the way that objects move through such gases. (2) The qualities of an object that affect how easily it is able to move through the air.

• Early automobile designs were based on the boxlike carriages drawn by horses, back when no one was even thinking about aerodynamics.

Aerodynamics began as a science around the time of the Wright brothers' first manned flights. Since then, it's become important to the building not only of aircraft and automobiles but also of rockets and missiles, trains, ships, and even such structures as bridges and tall buildings, which often have to withstand strong winds. An *aerodynamic* vehicle is one whose design helps it achieve the greatest speed and most efficient use of fuel. But although we might casually call any sleek car design aerodynamic, true aerodynamics is practiced not by artistic product designers but instead by highly trained scientists, and many people's lives depend on their work.

hydrodynamic \͵hī-drō-dī-ˈna-mik\ Having to do with the science that studies fluids in motion and the forces that act on bodies surrounded by fluids.

• Building levees to contain a flood presents complicated hydrodynamic problems.

Bernoulli's principle, which is basic to the science of *hydrodynamics,* says that the faster a fluid substance flows, the less outward pressure it exerts. It shows the close relationship between *hydrodynamics* and *aerodynamics* (which deals with the movement of air and other gases), since it can partly explain how air will "lift" an airplane by the way it flows over the wings, and how a spoiler helps keep a race car's wheels pressed to the ground as it accelerates. Hydrodynamics is sometimes applied today in studying the surface of the planets and even the stars. As used informally by boaters, *hydrodynamic* often means "hydrodynamically efficient."

Quizzes

A. Choose the closest definition:

1. dynamo   a. powerhouse b. force unit c. time interval d. power outage

2. kinesiology   a. science of planetary motion b. atomic motion c. study of human movement d. history of film

3. aerodynamic   a. glamorously smooth b. relating to movement through air c. using oxygen for power d. atmospherically charged

4. telekinesis   a. moving of objects by mental power b. broadcasting of films c. distant motion d. electronic control from afar

5. hyperkinetic   a. overgrown b. large-bodied c. intensely active d. projected on a large screen

6. hydrodynamic   a. relating to moving fluids b. water-resistant c. relating to boats d. relating to water

7. kinescope   a. light meter b. peep show c. early movie camera d. camera for live TV

8. dynamic   a. explosive b. energetic c. excited d. dangerous

B. Indicate whether the following pairs have the same or different meanings:

1. hydrodynamic / tidal   same ___ / different ___
2. hyperkinetic / overactive   same ___ / different ___
3. kinescope / motion-
   triggered camera   same ___ / different ___
4. aerodynamic / air-powered   same ___ / different ___
5. kinesiology / sports history   same ___ / different ___
6. dynamo / generator   same ___ / different ___
7. telekinesis / electronic
   broadcasting   same ___ / different ___
8. dynamic / electric   same ___ / different ___

GRAD comes from the Latin noun *gradus,* "step" or "degree," and the verb *gradi,* "to step, walk." A *grade* is a step up or down on a scale of some kind, and a *gradual* change takes place in small steps.

gradation \grā-'dā-shən\ (1) A series made up of successive stages. (2) A step in an ordered scale.

• In the fall, the leaves show gradations of color from deepest red to brightest yellow.

In the Boy Scouts, gradations of rank move upward from Tenderfoot to Eagle Scout. A violin or a voice can produce gradations of musical pitch too small to appear in written music. In the 18th century Jonathan Swift could even write of "the several kinds and gradations of laughter, which ladies must daily practice by the looking-glass."

degrade \di-'grād\ (1) To treat someone or something poorly and without respect. (2) To make the quality of something worse.

• They had feared for years that television was degrading the mental capacities of their children.

In Shakespeare's *King Lear,* the old king is degraded by the daughters he has given his kingdom to. He finds it *degrading,* for instance, when the number of his guards is reduced from 100 to 25. His *degradation* seems complete when, after going mad, he's reduced to living in the wilderness. As you can see, *degrade* is often a synonym for *humiliate.*

gradient \'grā-dē-ənt\ (1) Slope, grade. (2) A continuous change in measure, activity, or substance.

• Steep temperature gradients in the atmosphere are usually associated with unstable conditions.

Any slope can be called a gradient. In the interstate highway system, the maximum gradient is 6 percent; in other words, the highway may never ascend more than 6 vertical feet over a distance of 100 feet. Any rate of change that's shown on a graph may have a sloped gradient. Suppose the graph's horizontal axis shows the passage of time and its vertical axis shows some activity; if the activity is happening very fast, then the gradient of the line on the graph will be steep, but if it's slow the gradient will be gentle, or *gradual.*

retrograde \\'re-trō-ˌgrād\ (1) Moving or performed in a direction that is backward or opposite to the usual direction. (2) Moving toward a worse or earlier state.

- For the government to cover up the findings of its scientific research institutes was clearly a retrograde step.

Retrograde describes backwardness of one kind or another. If a country decided to go back to amputating the limbs of criminals, we might call that policy retrograde. A retrograde view of women might be one that sees them basically as housekeepers. Mars and Jupiter show retrograde (backward) motion at some stages of their orbits, though this is only because of the way we see them from the earth, not because of any real backward movement.

REG, from the Latin *regula*, meaning "rule," has given us many English words. Something *regular* follows a rule of some kind, even if it's just a law of nature. A *regime* can be a form of rule or government. To *regulate* an industry means to make and enforce rules, or *regulations*, for it; removing such rules is called *deregulation*.

---

regimen \\'re-jə-mən\ A regular course of treatment, usually involving food, exercise, or medicine.

- As part of his training regimen, he was now swimming two miles, running seven miles, and bicycling 15 miles every day.

Americans love self-improvement, so they're constantly adopting regimens: skin-care regimens, low-cholesterol regimens, weight-loss regimens, and the like. A course of medication may be complicated enough to deserve the name *regimen*, and a rehab regimen may require having your activities monitored at a treatment center. Mental regimens can also be valuable; researchers are finding that minds that get the most exercise seem to last the longest.

interregnum \ˌin-tə-ˈreg-nəm\ (1) The time during which a throne is vacant between two successive reigns or regimes. (2) A period during which the normal functions of government or control are suspended.

- During the weeklong interregnum between the CEO's death and the appointment of a new CEO, she felt that she was really running the whole show.

Eyery time a pope dies, there's an interregnum period before a
new one is elected by the cardinals. In most democratic systems,
however, the law specifies who should take office when a president
or prime minister dies unexpectedly, and since the power usually
passes automatically, there's no true interregnum. The question of
succession—that is, of who should take over when a country's leader
dies—has often presented huge problems for countries that lacked
a constitution, and in monarchies it hasn't always been clear who
should become king or queen when a monarch dies. The interregnum
following the death of Edward VI in 1553, for instance, was briefly
suspended when Lady Jane Grey was installed as Queen; nine days
later she was replaced by Mary Tudor, who sent her straight to the
Tower of London.

regalia \ri-ˈgāl-yə\ (1) The emblems and symbols of royalty.
(2) Special or official dress.

- The governor seems to enjoy life in the governor's mansion and
  all the regalia of office more than actually doing his job.

Just as *regal* describes a king or queen—that is, a ruler—*regalia*
originally meant the things, and especially the dress and decoration, that belong exclusively to a monarch. The British monarchy's
regalia include the crown jewels (crown, scepter, orb, sword, etc.)
that lend luster to royal coronations. Academic regalia—the caps,
gowns, and hoods worn by students receiving their degrees—link
institutions to their past by preserving the dress worn at universities
since their beginnings in the Middle Ages, when long hooded robes
were needed for warmth.

regency \ˈrē-jən-sē\ A government or period of time in which a
regent rules in place of a king or queen.

- Since the future king was only four when Louis XIV died, France
  spent eight years under a regency before he took the throne at 13
  as Louis XV.

In Britain, the years from the time when George III was declared
insane until his death (1811–1820) are known as the Regency period,
since in these years his son, the future George IV, served as Prince
Regent, or acting monarch. (Sometimes the term covers the period
up to the end of George IV's own reign in 1830.) The Regency is
remembered for its elegant architecture and fashions, its literature
(especially the works of Jane Austen), and its politics. Today hotels,

furniture, and businesses on both sides of the Atlantic carry the name "Regency" to identify with the period's style, and hundreds of modern romance novels—called simply "Regencies"—have been set in the period. Though there have been dozens of European regencies over the centuries, for Americans today there seems to be only one Regency.

Quizzes

A. Choose the closest definition:

1. regency   a. monarch   b. acting government
   c. crowning   d. royal style
2. degrade   a. reduce in size   b. raise in esteem   c. lower in rank   d. increase in importance
3. regimen   a. army unit   b. dynasty   c. rule book
   d. routine
4. gradient   a. graph   b. slope   c. road   d. steps
5. interregnum   a. vacation   b. recess   c. period without a leader   d. period of peace
6. gradation   a. program in a series   b. stage in a series
   c. eventual decline   d. definite improvement
7. regalia   a. royalty   b. set of rules   c. training schedule
   d. trappings of office
8. retrograde   a. moving in reverse   b. grading again
   c. primitive   d. switching grades

B. Fill in each blank with the correct letter:

a. regimen   e. retrograde
b. gradation   f. interregnum
c. regency   g. gradient
d. degrade   h. regalia

1. At a ceremonial occasion such as this, every officer would be present, in full _____.
2. Each subtle _____ of color seemed more beautiful as the sun slowly set.
3. Every pope's death is followed by a short _____ while the cardinals prepare to choose a new pope.
4. The trail's _____ for the first part of the race was gentle, but after three miles it became quite steep.

5. His 20-year-old daughter took over the company when he died, but her first couple of years were really a _____ under the senior vice president.
6. Once a thriving democracy, the country lapsed into dictatorship in the 1970s, a _____ step that it's still recovering from.
7. Her new _____ included a yoga session and a one-hour bike ride every day.
8. By all means apologize for your mistake, but don't _____ yourself.

CRIT comes from a Greek verb that means "to judge" or "to decide." So a film *critic* judges a movie and tells us what's good or bad about it. Her *critical* opinion may convince us not to go, or we may overlook any negative *criticism* and see it anyway.

criterion \krī-'tir-ē-ən\ A standard by which a judgment or decision is made.

• He's one of those readers whose main criterion for liking a book is whether it confirms his prejudices.

One person's principal criterion for a new car may be its gas mileage, while someone else's may be whether it has room for four children. When filling a job opening, employers usually look for several criteria (notice the plural form) in the applicants; and when college admissions officers are reading student applications, they likewise always keep a few basic criteria in mind. And when interviewing an applicant, one criterion for both the employer and the admissions officer might include the size of the applicant's vocabulary!

critique \kri-'tēk\ A judgment or evaluation, especially a rating or discussion of merits and faults.

• Whenever he reads his latest story in the fiction-writing seminar, one of the other students always delivers a nasty critique.

Even though *criticize* means to judge something negatively, a critique can be completely positive—or completely negative. Usually it's somewhere in between. When a paper of yours receives a critique from a teacher, you should read it carefully, and then reread it; getting mad or offended is the worst way to react. *Critique* is often a verb as well. Thus, writers and artists often form groups solely to critique each other's work, and scientific articles frequently get critiqued in letters to the editor in the following issue of the journal.

hypercritical \ˌhī-pər-ˈkri-tə-kəl\ Overly critical.

• Most teachers do their best to correct their students' mistakes without seeming hypercritical.

The important prefix *hyper-* means "excessive" or "beyond" (see HYPER, p. 457), so *hypercritical* means basically "too fussy." In TV and film comedies, the mother-in-law is just about always hypercritical, since the person her child married is never good enough for her. But other parents, spouses, and even children can be just as bad, so we should all be careful. If your father asks what you think of his new experimental meatloaf and you say it needs a pinch of oregano, you're being constructive; if you say he should cut down on the sawdust next time, you're probably being hypercritical.

hematocrit \hi-ˈma-tə-ˌkrit\ The ratio of the volume of red blood cells to whole blood.

• The latest blood test had revealed that her hematocrit had risen considerably and was almost back to normal.

Our blood is mostly made up of four components: plasma, red blood cells, white blood cells, and colorless blood cells called platelets. An instrument called a hematocrit (because it "judges" the blood) is used to separate a sample of blood into its components. The normal hematocrit for men is about 48%, for women about 38%. An abnormal proportion of red blood cells, either too many or too few, is a good early indicator of many diseases. So when you give blood as part of a physical exam, your hematocrit is one of the findings your doctor will often check.

JUR comes from the Latin verb *jurare,* "to swear, take an oath," and the noun *jus,* "right or law." A *jury,* made up of *jurors,* makes judgments based on the law. And a personal *injury* was originally something done to you that a court would find unjust.

---

jurisprudence \ˌjr-is-ˈprü-dəns\ (1) A system of law. (2) The study and philosophy of law.

- As a young lawyer his heroes were the crusaders of 20th-century jurisprudence, especially Louis Brandeis and Thurgood Marshall.

Jurisprudence as a study may have begun in the Roman empire, where schools of law were first established. And Roman jurisprudence, like so many other things the Romans created, served as the model in later centuries throughout the Western world. And like many other legal words, *jurisprudence* is used only in formal writing.

abjure \ab-ˈjür\ To reject formally.

- The Spanish Inquisition forced many Jews to abjure their religion and adopt Christianity or be burned at the stake.

From its Latin roots, *abjure* would mean literally "to swear away." Thus, after the holidays many people abjure all sweets and fattening foods, often making their vow in front of friends or relatives. *Abjure* is often confused with *adjure,* which means "to command solemnly, as if under oath." Thus, a judge might adjure a criminal to change his ways; but it's up to the criminal to abjure a life of crime.

perjury \ˈpər-jə-rē\ The crime of telling a lie under oath.

- Found guilty of perjury for lying under oath in front of a Congressional committee, he was sentenced to two years in prison.

The prefix *per-* in Latin often meant "harmfully." So witnesses who *perjure* themselves do harm to the truth by knowingly telling a lie. Not all lying is perjury, only lying under oath; so perjury generally takes place either in court or before a legislative body such as Congress. To avoid committing perjury, a witness or defendant may "take the Fifth": that is, refuse to answer a question because the answer might be an admission of guilt, and the Fifth Amendment to the Constitution forbids forcing a citizen to admit to being guilty of a crime.

de jure \dē-ˈjür-ē\ Based on or according to the law.

- The country is a de jure democracy, but since one party controls all the media outlets it really isn't one.

Coming straight from Latin, *de jure* is a term used mostly, but not always, in legal writing. Sometimes it's not enough to have something written into law; if a law isn't enforced, it might as well not exist. And if ordinary citizens are too scared of what would happen to them if they exercised their rights, then they don't really have those rights at all. Unfortunately, many countries have constitutions and laws that sound good but turn out not to have much effect. So *de jure* is almost always used in contrast to something else; its opposite is *de facto* (see p. 63).

Quizzes

A. Indicate whether the following pairs have the same or different meanings:

1. de jure / based on law   same ___ / different ___
2. hematocrit / test tube   same ___ / different ___
3. jurisprudence / legal beliefs   same ___ / different ___
4. hypercritical / untruthful   same ___ / different ___
5. perjury / testimony   same ___ / different ___
6. criterion / standard   same ___ / different ___
7. abjure / reject   same ___ / different ___
8. critique / evaluation   same ___ / different ___

B. Fill in each blank with the correct letter:

a. hematocrit   e. abjure
b. jurisprudence   f. hypercritical
c. criterion   g. perjury
d. de jure   h. critique

1. He had never learned how to make his criticism seem constructive rather than _____.
2. As soon as the party agrees to _____ violence, we're ready to allow them to participate in elections.
3. The judges gave a thorough and helpful _____ of each contestant's work.
4. Although her own philosophy of _____ is liberal, most observers think her interpretations of the law as a judge have been balanced.
5. What shall we use as the basic _____ for this award?
6. The _____ power of the prime minister was considerable, but all real power was held by the army.

7. The _____ showed an abnormal ratio of red blood cells.

8. She was probably committing _____ when she swore that she had spent the night alone at home.

Number Words

PENT comes from the Greek word for "five." The *Pentagon* in Washington, D.C., the world's largest office building, has five sides just like any other pentagon. And a *pentatonic* scale in music has only five notes, rather than the seven notes of the major or minor scale.

pentathlon \pen-ˈtath-ˌlän\ An athletic contest in which each athlete competes in five different events.

• The modern Olympic pentathlon includes swimming, cross-country running, horseback riding, fencing, and target shooting.

The Greek word *athlos* means "contest or trial," so to be an *athlete* you had to compete in physical contests. The ancient Greek pentathlon tested warriors' skills in sprinting, long jumping, javelin throwing, discus throwing, and wrestling, none of which are part of today's Olympic pentathlon. But a *pentathlete* must still have muscles and reflexes suited to almost any kind of physical feat. See also *decathlon*, p. 425.

Pentateuch \ˈpen-tə-ˌtük\ The first five books of the Old Testament, traditionally said to have been written by Moses.

• The Pentateuch takes us from the creation of the world up to the Israelites' arrival in the Promised Land.

Pentateuch means simply "five books." In Greek, the Pentateuch (which Jews call the Torah) includes the books of Genesis, Exodus, Leviticus, Numbers, and Deuteronomy. These contain some of the oldest and most famous stories in the Bible, including those of Adam and Eve, Jacob and his brothers, and Moses, as well as some of the oldest codes of law known, including the Ten Commandments.

pentameter \pen-'ta-mə-tər\ A line of poetry consisting of five metrical feet.

• Shakespeare's tragedies are written mainly in blank verse, which is unrhymed iambic pentameter.

In a line of poetry written in perfect *iambic pentameter*, there are five unstressed syllables, each of which is followed by a stressed syllable. Each pair of syllables is a metrical foot called an *iamb*. Much of the greatest poetry in English has been written in iambic pentameter; Chaucer, Shakespeare, and Milton used it more than any other meter. Robert Frost's line "I'm going out to clean the pasture spring" is an example of it; his "And miles to go before I sleep" is instead an example of iambic *tetrameter,* with only four accented syllables.

Pentecostal \ˌpen-ti-'käs-tᵊl\ Of or relating to any of various fundamentalist sects that stress personal experience of God and vocal expression in worship.

• Their neighbors belonged to a Pentecostal sect and homeschooled their daughters, who never wore clothes more revealing than floor-length skirts and long pants.

In ancient Greek, *pentekoste* meant "fiftieth day"—that is, the fiftieth day after Easter (counting Easter itself). On that day, Christians celebrate an event described in the Bible that took place fifty days after Christ's resurrection, when the apostles heard the rush of a mighty wind, saw tongues of fire descending on them, and heard the Holy Spirit speaking from their own mouths but in other tongues (languages). "Speaking in tongues," when everyone in a congregation may begin talking in languages that no one can understand, is the best-known practice of *Pentecostals*. Pentecostals belong to many different denominations; with growing numbers especially in Latin America and Africa, there may be over 500 million Pentecostals worldwide.

QUINT comes from the Latin word meaning "five." *Quintuplets* are babies that come in sets of five; about 60 U.S. families increase in size by that number every year.

---

quincentennial \ˌkwin-sen-'te-nē-əl\ A 500th anniversary, or the celebration of such an event.

402   **Unit 18**

- In 1992 Americans celebrated the quincentennial of Christopher Columbus's first voyage to the New World.

The United States is such a young country that it will be quite some time before we reach our quincentennial as a nation: 2276 A.D., to be exact. Some American cities will celebrate their quincentennials long before that, but even St. Augustine, Florida, the nation's oldest city, will have to wait until 2065. Meanwhile, many young people can look forward happily to our national *tricentennial* in 2076; and their grandchildren may be around for our *quadricentennial* in 2176.

quintessential \ˌkwin-tə-ˈsen-chəl\ Representing the purest or most perfect example of something.

- As a boy, he had thought of steak, eggs, and home fries as the quintessential Saturday breakfast.

The philosophers and scientists of the ancient world and the Middle Ages believed that the world we inhabit was entirely made up of four elements: earth, air, fire, and water. Aristotle added a fifth element, the *aether* or *ether*, by which he meant the material that fills the rest of space, mostly invisibly but sometimes taking the form of stars and planets. Many writers described the element as a kind of invisible light or fire. In the Middle Ages, it was referred to as the *quinta essentia* ("fifth element"). It isn't surprising that the *quinta essentia* came to stand for anything so perfect that it seemed to surpass the limitations of earth. Today we generally use *quintessential* rather freely to describe just about anything that represents the best of its kind.

quintet \kwin-ˈtet\ (1) A musical piece for five instruments or voices. (2) A group of five, such as the performers of a quintet or a basketball team.

- The team's five starters are considered one of the most talented quintets in professional basketball.

A classical quintet is usually written for strings (usually two violins, two violas, and a cello) or woodwinds (flute, oboe, clarinet, bassoon, and horn), but brass quintets (two trumpets, horn, trombone, and tuba) have also become popular in North America recently. In jazz, Miles Davis led two famous quintets. In pop music, the Miracles, the Temptations, and the Jackson 5 were immensely popular vocal quintets. In rock, one of the most common instrumental lineups has been a quintet consisting of two guitars, a bass, a keyboard, and drums; famous rock quintets have included the Grateful Dead and the Beach Boys.

quintile \\'kwin-ˌtīl\\ One or another of the values that divide a tested population into five evenly distributed classes, or one of these classes.

* According to the tests, their one-year-old boy ranks high in the second quintile for motor skills.

Americans love statistics about themselves, whether they inform us about our income, ice-cream consumption, or trash production. And any such rating can be divided into fifths, or quintiles. The fifth or lowest quintile would include the 20 percent of the population who make the least money or eat the least ice cream or generate the least trash, and the first quintile would include the 20 percent who make, eat, or generate the most.

Quiz

Match the definition on the left to the correct word on the right:

1. evangelically Christian   a. quintet
2. most typical   b. quintile
3. event with five contests   c. Pentateuch
4. 500th birthday   d. pentathlon
5. composition for five   e. quincentennial
6. poetic rhythm   f. Pentecostal
7. first books of the Bible   g. quintessential
8. one fifth of a group   h. pentameter

Review Quizzes

A. Choose the correct synonym:

1. degrade   a. praise   b. outclass   c. lose   d. lower
2. capitulate   a. nod   b. yield   c. resist   d. fall in
3. hypercritical   a. pretended   b. complimentary
    c. underdeveloped   d. overly harsh
4. criterion   a. argument   b. scolding   c. standard
    d. critical review
5. retrograde   a. failing   b. forward   c. sideways
    d. backward
6. abjure   a. take up   b. damn   c. reject   d. include
7. perjury   a. cleansing   b. lying under oath   c. theft
    d. court decision
8. misanthropic   a. humanitarian   b. wretched
    c. antisocial   d. monumental
9. de jure   a. by a judge   b. by a lawyer   c. by law
    d. by a jury
10. pentathlon   a. five competitions   b. five-note scale
    c. five-month period   d. five-sided figure

B. Fill in each blank with the correct letter:

a. decapitate		i. recapitulate
b. anthropology		j. hyperkinetic
c. dynamic		k. criterion
d. gradient		l. quintessential
e. regency		m. hematocrit
f. critique		n. pentathlon
g. Pentecostal		o. quintet
h. quintile		

1. Her main _____ for a boyfriend was a great sense of humor.
2. In Japan, the track for a mountain cable car climbs at a _____ of an astonishing 31 degrees.
3. Our professor is always careful to _____ her main points at the end of each class.
4. He would write a lengthy _____ on every term paper, though he suspected few of the students ever read them.
5. For her, *The Night of the Living Dead* remained the _____ horror film, against which she judged all the others.

6. The _____ lasted several years, as the boy king passed through an awkward preadolescent stage to emerge as a serious and dignified 20-year-old.

7. The concert ended with a string _____ by Beethoven.

8. For his graduate work in _____, he's been doing research on societies in India's tribal areas.

9. She's having her bloodwork done and is waiting anxiously to hear her _____.

10. In their harsh justice system, the standard practice was to lop off the hands of minor offenders and _____ serious criminals.

11. The test results placed her in the highest _____ of the population.

12. By all accounts, he was a _____ and forceful individual.

13. At 25 he was still as _____ as a 14-year-old, constantly fidgeting at his desk, with his leg bouncing up and down.

14. They grew up attending a _____ church, watching their father speak in tongues on most Sundays.

15. Track stars with superb all-round training usually try out for the _____ competition.

C. Choose the closest definition:

1. anthropoid   a. tapirs and antelopes b. cats and dogs c. chimpanzees and gorillas d. salamanders and chameleons

2. gradation   a. step in a series b. show in a series c. novel in a series d. speech in a series

3. quintile   a. fifteenth b. five-spot c. group of five d. one fifth

4. quintessential   a. fifth b. being c. ideal d. important

5. Pentateuch   a. New Testament books b. five-sided figure c. Old Testament books d. five-pointed star

6. capitalism   a. free-enterprise system b. common-property state c. socialist democracy d. controlled economy

7. dynamo   a. explosive b. missile c. generator d. electric weapon

8. quincentennial   a. 5th anniversary b. 15th anniversary c. 50th anniversary d. 500th anniversary

9. pentameter   a. five-line stanza   b. five-word sentence   c. five-beat poetic line   d. five-sided shape

10. regalia   a. monarchy   b. official costume   c. regularity   d. solemn dignity

11. criterion   a. dinosaur   b. mourning   c. criticism   d. gauge

12. jurisprudence   a. legal philosophy   b. legal agreement   c. senior judge   d. cautious ruling

13. regimen   a. daily plan   b. strict order   c. ruling family   d. officers' club

14. perjury   a. suing   b. cursing   c. misleading   d. lying

15. critique   a. mystique   b. commentary   c. argument   d. defense

UNIT

19

BIO comes from the Greek word for "life," and forms the base for many English words. *Biology*, for instance, is the study of living forms and life processes; the *biosphere* is the entire area of and above the earth where life can exist; and *biotechnology* is the use of living organisms to create useful products.

---

bionic \bī-'ä-nik\ Made stronger or more capable by electronic or mechanical devices.

- Bionic feet and hands for amputees have ceased to be mere sci-fi fantasies and are becoming realities.

The science of *bionics* uses knowledge about how biological systems work to help solve engineering problems. The material Velcro, for example, was inspired by the way burrs behave when they stick to your clothes, and some computer chips are now wired in ways that imitate the "wiring" of the brain and nervous system. But in popular use, the adjective *bionic* almost always describes artificial limbs or other bodily parts that work as much like real ones as possible. A perfect bionic arm would move and function as easily as a real arm—a goal we're rapidly getting closer to.

biopsy \'bī-ˌäp-sē\ The removal and examination of tissue, cells, or fluids from a living body.

- Everyone felt relieved when the results of the biopsy showed the tumor wasn't cancerous.

Matter examined in a biopsy is always taken from a living organism. Most biopsies are done by using a needle to extract tissue or fluid, but some may instead require cutting, and others may amount to nothing more than swabbing the inside of the patient's cheek. Biopsies are best known as a means of detecting cancer, but a doctor may also take a biopsy of heart muscle to investigate suspected heart disease, for example, or perform a biopsy on a pregnant woman to test for disorders in the fetus.

biodegradable \ˌbī-ō-di-ˈgrā-də-bəl\ Able to be broken down into harmless substances by microorganisms or other living things.

• Though the advertisements promised that the entire package was biodegradable, environmentalists expressed their doubts.

In *biodegradable,* with its root *grad,* "to step or move," and its prefix *de-* "downward," we get an adjective describing things that can be broken down into basic substances through normal environmental processes. Animal and plant products are normally biodegradable, but mineral substances such as metals, glass, and plastics usually are not. Newly developed biodegradable plastics are now appearing in numerous products. However, "biodegradable" products can vary greatly in how long they take to break down. A loaf of bread may require only a couple of weeks, and a piece of paper may vanish in a couple of months, but some "biodegradable" plastic milk cartons may take four or five years.

symbiosis \ˌsim-bē-ˈō-səs\ (1) The close living together of two different forms of life in a way that benefits both. (2) A cooperative relationship between two people or groups.

• The lichen that grows on rocks is produced by the symbiosis of a fungus and an alga, two very different organisms.

With its prefix *sym-,* "with," *symbiosis* expresses the notion of cooperation between living things. *Symbiotic* associations are found throughout the plant and animal world. You may have read, for instance, of the little blackbird plover, which picks the teeth of the fierce African crocodile. Or the bird called the African honeyguide, which leads a little mammal called the ratel to a bees' nest, which the ratel, protected from the bees by its thick fur, then breaks open, and both it and the honeyguide feast on the honey. Or even our own bodies, which are home to millions of bacteria—especially the bacterium *E. coli* in our intestines—and neither we nor *E. coli* could live without the other. You can probably think of plenty of human relationships that could be called symbiotic as well.

GEN, which comes from the Greek *genos*, meaning "birth," has *generated* dozens of English words. A set of *genes,* for instance, gives birth to a living being. And a *genealogy* is a historical map of your family, showing how each *generation* gave birth to the next.

---

genesis \\'je-nə-səs\\ Origin, beginning.

• The genesis of the project dates back to 1976, when the two young men were roommates at Cornell University.

The traditional Greek name for the first and best-known book of the Bible is Genesis, meaning "origin." Genesis tells the stories of the creation, Adam and Eve, Cain and Abel, Noah's ark, the Tower of Babel, Abraham and his sons, and more—the stories that explain how the world and humanity were created, as well as much about how humanity, and especially the descendants of Abraham, relate to the rest of the world. Today we use *genesis* to refer to the creative beginnings of much smaller things, but never unimportant ones.

generator \\'je-nə-ˌrā-tər\\ A machine by which mechanical energy is changed into electrical energy

• The jungle settlement depended on a large generator, which provided electricity for a couple of hours each morning and evening.

Generators work by rotating a coil of wire in a magnetic field, causing a current to flow in the wire. A generator may be a huge spinning turbine powered by water, wind, steam, gas, or nuclear reactions, which sends electricity out through power lines to thousands of customers. But normally when we use the word, we're thinking of a small machine powered by gasoline or diesel, such as you might keep in your basement for those times when a storm knocks out your power, to create electricity right in front of your eyes. A special kind of generator called an alternator powers a car's electrical system (including its lights, power steering, etc.) while the car is running.

genre \\'zhän-rə\\ Kind, sort; especially a distinctive type or category of literature, art, or music.

- Opera was a new genre for her, since all her compositions up until then had been songs and chamber music.

Genre, as you might guess from the way it sounds, comes straight from French, a language based on Latin. It's closely related to *genus*, a word you may have encountered in biology class. Both words contain the *gen-* root because they indicate that everything in a particular category (a genre or a genus) belongs to the same "family" and thus has the same origins. So the main genres of classical music would include symphonies, sonatas, and opera, and the major genres of literature would include novels, short stories, poetry, and drama. But within the category of novels, we could also say that detective novels, sci-fi novels, romance novels, and young-adult novels are separate genres.

carcinogenic \ˌkär-sə-nō-ˈje-nik\ Producing or causing cancer.

- Although she knows all too well that the tobacco in cigarettes is carcinogenic, she's too addicted to quit.

It sometimes seems as if the list of carcinogenic substances gets longer every day. A substance such as a food additive that's been in common use for years may unexpectedly show signs of being carcinogenic in laboratory experiments. When that happens, the suspected *carcinogen* will often have to be withdrawn from the market. When a building material like asbestos turns out to be a carcinogen, it may also have to be physically removed from buildings. English has hundreds of other scientific words ending in *-genic* (such as *allergenic*), and in almost all of them the ending means "causing."

Quizzes

A. Fill in each blank with the correct letter:

a.	genre	e.	biopsy
b.	symbiosis	f.	genesis
c.	carcinogenic	g.	bionic
d.	biodegradable	h.	generator

1. The _____ of the idea for his first novel lay in a casual remark by a stranger one afternoon in the park.

2. Scientists are working on new _____ devices to enable amputees to do detailed manual work.

3. Any insecticides that are known to be _____ have supposedly been banned by the federal government.

4. Just about everything in our bodies is _____ except the fillings in our teeth.

5. She had a physical last week, and the doctor ordered a _____ of a suspicious-looking patch of skin.

6. After 50 years of marriage, the _____ between them is just about total.

7. About once a year, an ice storm knocks out the electricity, and we haul out the _____ to get everything going again.

8. She loved various kinds of classical music, but the string quartet was one _____ that she could never warm up to.

B. Indicate whether the following pairs have the same or different meanings:

1. genesis / birth   same ___ / different ___
2. biopsy / life story   same ___ / different ___
3. generator / electricity-
    producing machine   same ___ / different ___
4. biodegradable / readily
    broken down   same ___ / different ___
5. carcinogenic / cancer-causing   same ___ / different ___
6. symbiosis / shared existence   same ___ / different ___
7. genre / animal group   same ___ / different ___
8. bionic / fantastic   same ___ / different ___

FUNCT comes from the Latin verb *fungi,* "to perform, carry out." If your car is *functional,* it's able to perform its *function* of providing transportation. But a *functional illiterate* is a person who, for all practical or functional purposes, might as well not be able to read or write at all.

---

functionary \'fəŋk-shə-ˌner-ē\ (1) Someone who performs a certain function. (2) Someone who holds a position in a political party or government.

- He was one of a group of party functionaries assigned to do the dirty work of the campaign.

For most of us, being described as a *functionary* wouldn't be a compliment. The word refers especially to a person of lower rank, with little or no authority, who must carry out someone else's orders. *Bureaucrat* is often a synonym. However, *functionary* can also refer to the world beyond government and offices; a character in a play, for example, could be called a functionary if it was obvious that her sole function was to keep the plot moving.

malfunction \ˌmal-ˈfəŋk-shən\ To fail to operate in the normal or usual manner.

- An examination of the wreck revealed that the brakes may have malfunctioned as the truck started down the hill.

A malfunctioning switch might keep us from turning on a light. A malfunctioning heart valve might require replacement with an artificial valve, and if your immune system malfunctions it may start to attack healthy cells. And a *malfunction* in a voting machine could result in hundreds of votes being miscounted.

defunct \di-ˈfəŋkt\ No longer, living, existing, or functioning.

- The company, which had once had annual sales of $150 million, was now defunct.

If you know that *de-* often means "the opposite of" (see DE-, p. 601), it's easy to guess the meaning of *defunct*. Shakespeare seems to have been the first writer to use this adjective, in *Henry V.* Defunct American political parties include the Greenback Party, the Readjuster Party, and the Nullifier Party. Defunct Academy Awards categories include Best Dance Direction and Best Assistant Director. Defunct U.S. auto models include the Dudly Bug, the LuLu, the Hupmobile, the Gas-au-lec, and the Nu-Klea Starlite. But to speak of a person as defunct would sound disrespectful—which is how it sounds in e. e. cummings's famous poem "Buffalo Bill's defunct."

dysfunctional \dis-ˈfəŋ(k)-shnəl\ (1) Showing abnormal or unhealthy behaviors and attitudes within a group of people. (2) Being unable to function in a normal way.

- A psychologist would call their family dysfunctional, but even though there's a lot of yelling and slamming of doors, they seem pretty happy to me.

Dysfunctional and *dysfunction* have been used for almost a hundred years, often in medical writing ("brain dysfunction," "a dysfunctional liver") but also by social scientists ("a dysfunctional city council," "diplomatic dysfunction"). But they only really entered the general vocabulary in the 1980s, when therapists and talk-show hosts began talking about dysfunctional families. The signs of family dysfunction turned out to be numerous, and it soon began to seem as if pretty much all our families could be called dysfunctional.

MUT comes from the Latin *mutare*, "to change." Plenty of science-fiction movies—*Godzilla, The Fly, The Incredible Shrinking Man*—used to be made on the subject of weird *mutations,* changes in normal people or animals that usually end up causing death and destruction. What causes the unfortunate victim to *mutate* may be a mysterious or alien force, or perhaps invisible radiation. Though the science in these films isn't always right on target, the scare factor of an army of *mutants* can be hard to beat.

---

commute \kə-ˈmyüt\ (1) To exchange or substitute; especially to change a penalty to another one that is less severe. (2) To travel back and forth regularly.

- There was a public outcry at the harshness of the prison sentence, and two days later the governor commuted it to five years.

When you commute between a suburb and a city, you're "exchanging" one location for another. When a chief executive substitutes a life sentence for the death sentence handed down by a court, he or she is commuting the original sentence. Most such *commutations* are the result of the prisoner's good behavior. A *commutator* is a device in many electric motors that regularly changes alternating current to direct current.

immutable \i-ˈmyü-tə-bəl\ Not able or liable to change.

- Early philosophers believed there was an immutable substance at the root of all existence.

Mutable means simply "changeable," so when the negative prefix *im-* is added we get its opposite. In computer programming, an immutable object is one that can't be changed after it's been created. In a constantly changing world, people who hunger for things as immutable as the laws of nature may try to observe an immutable moral code and set of values. Unfortunately, *immutability* isn't a basic quality of many things in this world.

permutation \ˌpər-myu̇-ˈtā-shən\ A change in the order of a set of objects; rearrangement, variation.

* They had rearranged the rooms in the house plans four or five times already, but the architect had come up with yet another permutation.

There are six permutations of the letters A, B, and C, selected two at a time: AB, AC, BC, BA, CA, and CB. As you see, order is important in permutations. (By contrast, there are only three *combinations*: AB, AC, and BC.) Permutation is an important concept in mathematics, especially in the field of probability. But we can use the word more generally to mean any change produced by rearranging existing parts without introducing new ones. Some soap operas, for example, love permutations; the cast of regulars is constantly being rearranged into new pairs, and even triangles.

transmute \trans-ˈmyüt\ (1) To change in shape, appearance, or nature, especially for the better; to transform. (2) To experience such a change.

* Working alone in his cluttered laboratory in 15th-century Milan, he spent twenty years searching for a method of transmuting lead into gold.

Transmutation changes something over into something else. Thus, a writer may transmute his life into stories or novels, and an arranger might transmute a lively march tune into a quiet lullaby. In the "Myth of Er" at the end of Plato's *Republic,* for example, human souls are transmuted into the body and existence of their choice. Having learned from their last life what they do *not* want to be, many choose transmutation into something that seems better. A meek man chooses to be transmuted into a tyrant, a farmer into a dashing (but short-lived) warrior, and so on. But very few seem to have learned anything from their former life that would make their choice a real improvement.

Quizzes

A. Choose the closest definition:

1. defunct   a. dead b. depressed c. defective d. deserted
2. permutation   a. evolution b. rearrangement
    c. approval d. inflation
3. functionary   a. bureaucrat b. hard worker
    c. activist d. executive
4. transmute   a. reconsider b. send away c. silence
    d. convert
5. dysfunctional   a. untrained b. divorced c. performing
    poorly d. unfamiliar
6. immutable   a. unchangeable b. immature c. noisy
    d. defiant
7. malfunction   a. work slowly b. work improperly
    c. work efficiently d. work mechanically
8. commute   a. deposit b. invest c. discuss d. change

B. Complete the analogies:

1. hostile : friendly :: immutable : _____
    a. changeable b. decaying c. breathable d. out of date
2. wounded : healed :: dysfunctional : _____
    a. lame b. healthy c. crippled d. unsteady
3. permit : allow :: commute : _____
    a. review b. claim c. substitute d. send
4. healthy : vigorous :: defunct : _____
    a. brainless b. failed c. strong d. unhappy
5. order : sequence :: permutation : _____
    a. addition b. notion c. rearrangement d. removal
6. soldier : army :: functionary : _____
    a. anthill b. stadium c. vacation d. organization
7. transmit : send :: transmute : _____
    a. transit b. transform c. transfer d. transport
8. misbehave : scold :: malfunction : _____
    a. function b. fix c. exchange d. rearrange

FRACT comes from the Latin verb *frangere,* "to break or shatter." A *fraction* is one of the pieces into which a whole can be broken, and a *fracture* is a break in a wall, a rock, or a bone.

---

fractious \'frak-shəs\ (1) Apt to cause trouble or be unruly. (2) Stirring up quarrels; irritable.

• Shopping with a fractious child is next to impossible.

One of the earliest meanings of *fraction* was "a break in good feeling"—that is, an argument or conflict. So a person who starts fights could be called fractious. A fractious horse is one that hasn't been properly broken or trained. A fractious political party is one whose members keep fighting among themselves. And a fractious baby is one that's always breaking the home's peace and quiet with angry squalling.

fractal \'frak-tᵊl\ An irregular shape that looks much the same at any scale on which it is examined.

• He was showing her the fractals in the local ferns, in which each leaf reproduced the shape of the entire fern.

This term was coined in 1975 to describe shapes that seem to exist at both the small-scale and large-scale levels in the same natural object. Fractals can be seen in snowflakes, in which the microscopic crystals that make up a flake look much like the flake itself. They can also be seen in tree bark and in broccoli buds. Coastlines often represent fractals as well, being highly uneven at both a large scale and a very small scale. Fractal geometry has been important in many fields, including astronomy, physical chemistry, and fluid mechanics. And even some artists are benefiting, creating beautiful and interesting abstract designs by means of fractals.

infraction \in-'frak-shən\ The breaking of a law or a violation of another's rights.

• The assistant principal dealt with any students who had committed minor infractions of the rules.

An infraction is usually the breaking of a law, rule, or agreement. So a nation charged with an infraction of an international treaty will usually have to pay a penalty. In Federal law, an infraction is even smaller than a misdemeanor, and the only penalty is a fine. Most of us occasionally commit infractions of parking laws and get ticketed; speeding tickets are usually for infractions as well, though they go on a permanent record and can end up costing you money for years to come. The closely related word *infringement* generally refers to a violation of a right or privilege; use of another's writings without permission, for example, may be an infringement of the copyright.

refraction \ri-ˈfrak-shən\ The change of direction of a ray of light or wave of energy as it passes at an angle from one substance into another in which its speed is different.

• From where I was standing, the refraction made it look as if her legs underwater were half their actual length.

The root of *refraction* is seen in the notion that the path of a ray of light or wave of energy is "broken" when it is deflected or turned. The effects of refraction can be seen in a rainbow, which is formed when light rays passing into (and reflecting out of) water droplets are bent at different angles depending on their color, so that the light separates into bands of color. The amount of refraction depends on the angle and the type of matter; refraction can occur even when passing through different kinds of air. A mirage, such as you might see in the desert or over a patch of asphalt in the summer, occurs when light passing through warm air meets the very hot air near the surface; reflecting the sky, it often resembles a lake.

TELE has as its basic meanings "distant" or "at a distance." A *telescope* is for looking at far-off objects; a camera's *telephoto* lens magnifies a distant scene for a photograph; and a *television* lets us watch things taking place far away.

---

telegenic \ˌte-lə-ˈje-nik\ Well-suited to appear on television, especially by having an appearance and manner attractive to viewers.

• The local anchorpeople all have telegenic faces and great hair, though they don't always seem to know a lot about the economy or political science.

The word *telegenic,* a blend of "*tele*vision" and "photo*genic,*" first appeared back in the 1930s, before hardly anyone owned a TV. With the supreme importance of TV cameras in politics, people running for political office today worry about being telegenic enough to have a successful career. Even events have been described as telegenic;

unfortunately, such events are often human tragedies, such as fires, earthquakes, or floods, which happen to broadcast well and capture the interest of the viewers.

teleological \ˌtē-lē-ə-ˈlä-ji-kəl\ Showing or relating to design or purpose, especially in nature.

• Many naturalists object to the teleological view that sees everything in nature as part of a grand design or plan.

Teleology has the basic meaning "the study of ends or purposes." So Aristotle's famous "teleological argument" claims that anything complex must have a creator, and thus that God exists. And a teleological explanation of evolutionary changes claims that all such changes occur for a definite purpose. But the type of morality called "teleological ethics" doesn't involve God at all: instead, it claims that we should judge whether an act is good or bad by seeing if it produces a good or bad result, even if the act involves harming or killing another person.

telemetry \tə-ˈle-mə-trē\ The science or process of measuring such things as pressure, speed, or temperature, sending the result usually by radio to a distant station, and recording the measurements there.

• The telemetry of the satellite had gone dead in 1999, and its fate remains a mystery.

Telemetry is used to obtain data on the internal functioning of missiles, rockets, unmanned planes, satellites, and probes, providing data on such factors as position, altitude, and speed as well as conditions like temperature, air pressure, wind speed, and radiation. Weather forecasters rely on telemetry to map weather patterns. Astronauts on the space shuttle are monitored with telemetry that measures and transmits readings on their blood pressure, respiration, and heart rates. Similar kinds of telemetry are used by biologists to study animals in the wild and keep track of their populations and movements. Telemetry is also widely used in modern agriculture, often to regulate irrigation.

telecommute \ˈte-li-kə-ˌmyüt\ To work at home using an electronic link with a central office.

- A dozen of our employees are now telecommuting, and we calculate that altogether they're saving 25 gallons of gasoline and its pollution every day.

This word has been around since the early 1970s, when computer terminals in the home first began to be connected to so-called mainframe computers by telephone lines. Since the creation of the World Wide Web in 1991, and with the widening access to broadband connections, telecommuting has grown to the point that the U.S. is now home to many millions of occasional *telecommuters*. Telecommuting can make work much easier for people with young children and people with disabilities, and because of its obvious environmental benefits and the lessening of traffic congestion, telecommuting is now officially encouraged by federal legislation. Still, only a fraction of those who could be telecommuting are actually doing so.

Quizzes

A. Fill in each blank with the correct letter:

a. telecommute	e. infraction
b. fractious	f. teleological
c. telegenic	g. refraction
d. fractal	h. telemetry

1. Under the microscope, the bark revealed its _____ nature, reproducing its visible surface at the microscopic level.
2. The philosopher's argument was _____ in that it looked for a design or purpose in natural phenomena.
3. It's a _____ team, and there often seems to be no cooperation between them at all.
4. Her boss has given her permission to _____ two days a week, using a computer hookup from home.
5. _____ of sunlight through water droplets is what produces rainbows.
6. Wildlife zoologists use _____ to track the migration habits of the caribou.
7. That last _____ of the rules cost their team 15 yards.
8. Some newscasters seem to have been hired for nothing more than their _____ smiles.

B. **Match each word on the left to the correct definition on the right:**

1.	telecommute	a.	self-reproducing shape
2.	refraction	b.	quarrelsome
3.	telemetry	c.	work electronically from home
4.	fractal	d.	bending of light rays
5.	telegenic	e.	violation
6.	fractious	f.	well-suited to television
7.	teleological	g.	long-distance measurement
8.	infraction	h.	relating to design or purpose

PHIL comes from the Greek word meaning "love." In *philosophy,* it's joined with *sophia,* "wisdom," so philosophy means literally "love of wisdom." When joined with *biblio-,* "book," the result is *bibliophile,* or "lover of books." And *Philadelphia,* containing the Greek word *adelphos,* "brother," was named by its Quaker founder, William Penn, as the city of "brotherly love."

---

oenophile \ˈē-nə-ˌfīl\ A person with an appreciation and usually knowledge of fine wine.

• As an amateur oenophile, he was constantly talking to his friends in the vocabulary of wine tasting.

The root *oeno-* comes from the Greek word meaning "wine." The oenophile should be distinguished from the *oenologist,* or "student of wine," who has a technical knowledge of the cultivation of wine grapes and of the whole winemaking process. Oenophiles may not know how to make a great wine, but they know one when they taste it. Not only that, but they can describe it using nouns like *nose, finish,* and *bouquet,* as well as adjectives such as *woody, full-bodied, robust,* and *noble.*

philatelist \fə-ˈla-tə-list\ A person who collects or studies stamps.

• The U.S. Postal Service issues first-day covers of each new stamp design especially for philatelists.

The first postage stamps were made available on May 1, 1840, in England, and it didn't take long for the hobby of stamp collecting to arise. Within a year, a young London lady was letting it be known in a newspaper advertisement that she was "desirous of covering her dressing room with cancelled postage stamps." *Philately* has been alive and well ever since, though modern philatelists—including rock stars, English kings, and American presidents—are more likely to put the stamps they collect in special albums.

Anglophile \\'aŋ-glə-ˌfīl\\ A person who greatly admires or favors England and English things.

• His grandparents were Anglophiles, and whenever they had guests in the afternoon the beautiful silver tea service would come out.

Even after fighting two wars against Britain, Americans continued to regard England with more fondness than perhaps any other country. For much of our history, Americans have sought to imitate the British in any number of ways—American movie stars even used to adopt British accents—and the two countries have long been close allies. But Britain isn't the only country Americans fall in love with; *Francophiles* (France-lovers), *Germanophiles* (Germany-lovers), and *Italophiles* (Italy-lovers) are also common. In the 19th century, Russian *Slavophiles* called for rejecting European culture in favor of homegrown Russian culture (Slavs being those who speak a Slavic language such as Russian or Polish). Occasionally *phil-* words are turned around; thus, someone who is *philosemitic* is a lover of Jewish culture.

philanthropy \\fə-'lan(t)-thrə-pē\\ (1) A charitable act or gift. (2) An organization that distributes or is supported by charitable contributions.

• Her last philanthropy was dedicated to protecting a vast area in central Africa where many of the great apes lived.

With its *anthro-* root (see ANTHROP, p. 384), *philanthropy* means literally "love of mankind." Thus, philanthropy is giving money for a purpose or cause benefiting people who you don't personally know. (Animals are usually included as well.) Individuals have often set up their own permanent *philanthropic* organizations in the form of foundations. The greatest American *philanthropists* have included Warren Buffett, Bill Gates, Andrew Carnegie, and

John D. Rockefeller, but tens of millions of us could be considered philanthropists on a much smaller scale.

NEG and its variants *nec-* and *ne-* are prefixes of denial or refusal in Latin, and the Latin verb *negare* means "to say no." To *negate* something is to make it ineffective, and something *negative* denies, contradicts, refuses, or reverses.

---

negligent \'ne-gli-jənt\ (1) Failing to take proper or normal care. (2) Marked by or likely to show neglect.

• The Army Corps of Engineers was found negligent for having failed to keep the New Orleans levees in good repair.

To be negligent is to be *neglectful*. *Negligence* is an important legal concept; it's usually defined as the failure to use the care that a normally careful person would in a given situation. Negligence is a common claim in lawsuits regarding medical malpractice, auto accidents, and workplace injuries. But you can also be negligent about answering your e-mail, or negligent in the way you dress. (The original garment called a *negligee* was worn by women who had neglected to get fully dressed.) The legal meanings of *negligent* and *negligence*, however, tend to be the ones we most often encounter nowadays.

abnegation \ˌab-ni-'gā-shən\ Self-denial.

• She's been denying herself pleasures since she was a child, so she's actually attracted by the life of abnegation that a nun leads.

Abnegation plays an important part in the teachings of all the major religions. The founder of Buddhism was a prince who gave up all his worldly goods when he discovered the world of poverty that lay outside the palace gates, and abnegation has been a Buddhism practice ever since. Hinduism has an even older tradition of abnegation. Special periods of abnegation and fasting may even be included in a religion's yearly calendar; serious Christians give up some pleasure for the 40-day period of Lent, for instance, and Muslims are forbidden to eat during daylight hours during the month of Ramadan.

negligible \'ne-gli-jə-bəl\ So small as to be neglected or disregarded.

- Local weather forecasters had made it sound like the blizzard of the century, but the amount of snow turned out to be negligible.

Negligible comes from the same Latin verb as *neglect,* so something negligible is literally "neglectable." If an accident results in negligible damage to your car, you should be thankful. If two years of intense focus on testing in the classroom results in a negligible improvement in student test scores, it's probably time to try something new.

renege \ri-ˈneg\ To go back on a promise or commitment.

- If his partners renege at this point, the whole project will probably fall through.

To renege on a bet is to refuse to pay up when you lose. To renege on a promise of marriage, or on a deal of any kind, is to pull out. History is full of promises and commitments and treaties that were reneged on, such as the many treaties with Native Americans that American settlers and the U.S. government went back on over a period of almost 300 years. A synonym is *welsh* ("He always welshes on his deals"); however, since that word may have come from *Welsh,* meaning a native of Wales in Britain, some people think it might be offensive.

Quizzes

A. Choose the closest definition:

1. Anglophile   a. amateur fisherman b. geometry fan
    c. England-lover d. non-Hispanic
2. negligible   a. small b. correctable c. noteworthy
    d. considerate
3. oenophile   a. pig lover b. book lover c. word lover
    d. wine lover
4. negligent   a. penniless b. careless c. criminal
    d. decent
5. philatelist   a. stamp collector b. gem collector c. wine
    collector d. coin collector

6. abnegation   a. abundance   b. abruptness   c. self-
   denial   d. self-satisfaction
7. philanthropy   a. stamp collecting   b. pleasure
   c. dignity   d. generosity
8. renege   a. repeat   b. go back on   c. renegotiate
   d. overturn

**B. Indicate whether the following pairs have the same
   or different meanings:**

1. negligent / neglectful   same ___ / different ___
2. philatelist / postman   same ___ / different ___
3. philanthropy / wealth   same ___ / different ___
4. renege / return   same ___ / different ___
5. oenophile / wine expert   same ___ / different ___
6. abnegation / absence   same ___ / different ___
7. Anglophile / fish-lover   same ___ / different ___
8. negligible / unimportant   same ___ / different ___

Number Words

DEC comes from both Greek and Latin and means "ten." So a
decade lasts for ten years; the *decimal* system is based on ten; and
a *decahedron* is a geometrical shape with ten sides.

decalogue \'de-kə-ˌlòg\ (1) (capitalized) The Ten Commandments. (2) Any basic set of rules that must be obeyed.

• At 15 she posted a decalogue of life rules on her bedroom door,
  starting with "1. Be respectful to teachers."

In *decalogue* the root *deca-* is combined with *logos,* Greek for
"word." In the Biblical book of Exodus, the original Decalogue,
or Ten Commandments, was handed to Moses by God atop Mount
Sinai. In Jewish and Christian tradition, the Ten Commandments
are regarded as laws handed down from the highest authority and as
the foundation of morality. They include commands to honor God,
the Sabbath day, and one's parents, and bans on worshiping images,
swearing, murder, adultery, theft, lying about others, and envying
what others have. Individuals have often had their own personal

decalogues; Thomas Jefferson's "ten commandments" started off with "Never put off till tomorrow what you can do today."

decathlon \di-'kath-ˌlän\ An athletic contest made up of ten parts.

* Though the U.S. has dominated the Olympic decathlon for its whole modern history, the 1948 victory by the 17-year-old Bob Mathias still astonished the world.

Decathlon from *deca-* and *athlon,* "contest," means "ten contests." The ancient Greek Olympics held five-contest competitions, or *pentathlons*, that were based on the skills needed in battle. The modern Olympic decathlon, which was born in 1912, consists of the 100-meter run, 400-meter run, 1500-meter run, 110-meter high hurdles, javelin throw, discus throw, shot put, pole vault, high jump, and long jump. The original winner was the legendary Jim Thorpe, who would later be judged the greatest American athlete of the 20th century. And ever since, the Olympic decathlon winner has been called the finest all-around athlete in the world.

decibel \'de-sə-bəl\ A unit based on a scale ranging from 0 to about 130 used to measure the loudness of sound, with 0 indicating the least sound that can be heard and 130 the average level that causes pain.

* She worries about the damage that high decibel levels can cause, and always wears ear protection when mowing the lawn.

The *bel* in *decibel* honors the inventor of the telephone, Alexander Graham Bell. Decibels work on a logarithmic scale (you may need to look up *logarithm*), so 20 decibels is 10 times as strong as 10 decibels, and 50 decibels is 1,000 times as strong as 20 decibels. The decibel readings of some everyday sounds make for interesting comparisons. Whispers and rustling leaves usually register under 20 decibels, the average level of conversation is about 50 decibels, and noisy factories or office machinery may have decibel levels of 90 to 100. In the category of sounds between 100 and 120 decibels, which can eventually cause deafness, we find elevated trains, artillery— and rock concerts.

decimate \'de-sə-ˌmāt\ To reduce drastically or destroy most of.

- Before the developments of modern medicine, diphtheria and typhoid could decimate the populations of entire towns and cities.

Commanders in the Roman army took discipline seriously. Mutiny in the ranks was dealt with by selecting, through drawing lots, one soldier in every ten and making the other nine club or stone the unfortunate winner of this gruesome lottery to death. The *dec-* in *decimate* thus reflects this Roman practice, which was ordered by such well-known leaders as Crassus, Mark Antony, and Augustus. But over time, the word's meaning has shifted, and today it almost always describes great destruction or loss of life. So, for example, we can say that a wave of layoffs has decimated a company's workforce, the populations of some of Africa's greatest wild animals have been decimated by poaching, or aerial bombardment has decimated whole sections of a city.

CENT, from the Latin *centum,* means "one hundred." A dollar is made up of a hundred *cents,* though other monetary systems use *centavos* or *centimes* as the smallest coin. A *centipede* has what appears to be a hundred feet, though the actual number varies greatly. But there really are a hundred years in a *century.*

---

centenary \sen-ˈte-nə-rē\ A 100th anniversary or the celebration of it; a centennial.

- The company is celebrating the centenary of its founding with a lavish banquet.

A *centenary,* like its cousin *centennial,* is an anniversary. Thus, the year 2013 may mark the centenary of a town's founding, and the year-long calendar of public events that the town sponsors for the occasion—that is, the celebration of the anniversary—can also be called a centenary. Individuals have their own centenaries, which usually celebrate their births; thus, Gerald Ford's centenary will occur in 2013, and John Kennedy's in 2017. And if you live long enough to be a *centenarian,* you'll be around to join the celebrations.

centigrade \ˈsen-tə-ˌgrād\ Relating to a temperature scale in which 0° is the freezing point of water and 100° is its boiling point.

- The normal temperature of a human body is 37° centigrade.

The centigrade scale is essentially identical to the *Celsius* scale, the standard scale by which temperature is measured in most of the world. Anders Celsius of Sweden first devised the centigrade scale in the early 18th *century*. But in his version, 100° marked the freezing point of water, and 0° its boiling point. Later users found it less confusing to reverse these two. To convert Fahrenheit degrees to centigrade, subtract 32 and multiply by 5/9. To convert centigrade to Fahrenheit, multiply by 9/5 and add 32.

centimeter \\'sen-tə-ˌmē-tər\\ A length measuring 1/100th of a meter, or about 0.39 inch.

- There are 2.54 centimeters in an inch, 30.48 centimeters in a foot.

In the metric system, which is used in most countries of the world, each basic unit of measure of length, area, or volume can be divided into centimeters. A meter consists of 100 centimeters, a square meter consists of 10,000 square centimeters, and a cubic meter consists of 1,000,000 cubic centimeters.

centurion \\sen-'chûr-ē-ən\\ The officer in command of a Roman century, originally a troop of 100 soldiers.

- Centurions and their centuries were the backbone of the great Roman armies.

In ancient Rome, a *century* was approximately equal to a company in the U.S. Army, and a centurion was roughly equivalent to a captain. Centurions play a role in the New Testament; Jesus performs a miracle for a centurion in Capernaum, centurions are present at the crucifixion, and in later years St. Paul is arrested by centurions. According to a writer of the time, centurions were chosen for their size and strength, their abilities at swordplay and at throwing missiles, and the quality of their discipline, which was partly shown by how well their soldiers kept their own armor polished.

Quiz

Fill in each blank with the correct letter:

a. centurion   e. decathlon
b. decimate   f. centimeter
c. centigrade   g. Decalogue
d. decibel   h. centenary

1. The ear can usually hear the difference between noises that differ in intensity by a single _____.
2. No one bothers to compete in the _____ who isn't an extraordinary natural athlete.
3. The company celebrated its _____ this month, and one of the founder's elderly children was able to come.
4. The _____ in the Old Testament is matched by the Beatitudes in the New Testament.
5. Rain is likely to become snow at about 0° _____.
6. An earthquake can easily _____ the buildings of an entire city.
7. The legion commanders decided that each _____ should divide up the food within his own century.
8. Last week's rainfall in Paris measured less than a _____.

Review Quizzes

A. Choose the correct synonym:

1. immutable   a. unalterable b. transformable
   c. inaudible d. audible
2. dysfunctional   a. working badly b. unresponsive
   c. healthy d. uncaring
3. permutation   a. continuation b. splendor c. disorder
   d. rearrangement
4. defunct   a. working b. rotten c. useless d. dreary
5. fractious   a. smiling b. peaceable c. angry
   d. troublesome
6. infraction   a. lawful act b. arrest c. piece d. violation

7. abnegation   a. position b. self-indulgence c. self-denial d. refusal

8. symbiosis   a. musical instrument b. independence c. community d. interdependence

9. decimate   a. destroy b. pair up c. multiply d. remove

10. renege   a. afford b. honor c. flee d. deny

B. Fill in each blank with the correct letter:

a.	commute	i.	refraction
b.	functionary	j.	telepathic
c.	telegenic	k.	malfunction
d.	carcinogenic	l.	oenophile
e.	Anglophile	m.	biopsy
f.	biodegradable	n.	decathlon
g.	decibel	o.	centurion
h.	centenary		

1. Their bags are made of _____ plastic that they claim will break down within two months.

2. Somethng that was downloaded is causing parts of the operating system to _____.

3. Since tobacco is well known to be a _____ substance, it's surprising that smoking is still legal.

4. He's so serious about wines that it's hard to be his friend if you're not an _____.

5. That music might sound better if the sound were turned down a _____ or two.

6. Which of the ten events in the _____ is your favorite?

7. The _____ of light in a glass of water appears to bend a pencil or spoon where it enters the water.

8. Doctors recommended a _____ in case the X-ray had missed something.

9. A low-level _____ in the company handles such complaints.

10. The experiment showed that her claim to have _____ powers was false.

11. My grandfather celebrates his _____ in May.

12. He was successful in radio but not _____ enough to succeed on television.

13. The _____ and his soldiers had proved themselves skilled fighters in the battles on the eastern frontier.

14. Filled with books about Queen Victoria, Churchill, and Henry VIII, the house was clearly home to an _____.
15. After having reviewed the new evidence that had come to light, the governor decided to _____ the sentence.

C. **Indicate whether the following pairs of terms have the same or different meanings:**

1. transmute / endanger   same ___ / different ___
2. bionic / artificial   same ___ / different ___
3. telemetry / space travel   same ___ / different ___
4. centimeter / $1/1000$ of a meter   same ___ / different ___
5. philatelist / dancer   same ___ / different ___
6. teleological / systematic   same ___ / different ___
7. decalogue / set of rules   same ___ / different ___
8. negligible / ignorable   same ___ / different ___
9. infraction / split   same ___ / different ___
10. functionary / bureaucrat   same ___ / different ___

UNIT

20

NOM comes from the Latin word for "name." A *nominee* is a person "named"—or *nominated*—to run for or serve in office. A *binomial* ("two names") is the scientific name for a species: *Felis catus* for the house cat, for example. A *polynomial,* with "many names," is an algebra expression involving several terms: $2x^2 + 9y - z^3$, for instance.

---

nominal \\ˈnä-mə-nəl\\ (1) Existing in name or form only and not in reality. (2) So small as to be unimportant; insignificant.

• The actor himself was the nominal author, but 90 percent of the prose was the work of his ghostwriter.

Something nominal exists only in name. So the nominal ruler in a constitutional monarchy is the king or queen, but the real power is in the hands of the elected prime minister. In the United Kingdom, the British monarch is also the nominal head of the Church of England; and those baptized in the Church who aren't really churchgoers might be called nominal Christians. A fee can be called nominal when it's small in comparison to the value of what it buys. So, for example, you might sell a friend a good piece of furniture for a nominal amount. And the charge for a doctor's visit might be a nominal $20, since most of the cost is covered by an insurance plan.

nomenclature \\ˈnō-mən-ˌklā-ˌchùr\\ (1) A name or designation, or the act of naming. (2) A system of terms or symbols used in biology, where New Latin names are given to kinds and groups of animals and plants.

- Naming newly discovered plants or animals requires close study of the system of nomenclature.

Various specialized fields have their own particular nomenclatures, or sets of terms. In particle physics, for instance, the elementary particles known as quarks, which are believed to come in pairs, have acquired such names as "up" and "down," "strange" and "charm," and "truth" and "beauty"—which is all most of us know about quarks and all we need to know. But *nomenclature* is used most often for the system of biological classification created by Linnaeus. In Linnaeus's system, each species has its own two-word name, the first word being the name of its genus. Thus, the genus *Equus* includes the horse *(Equus caballus)* and the mountain zebra *(Equus zebra)*. But since broccoli, cauliflower, and cabbage actually all belong to the same species *(Brassica oleracea),* they each need a third name to distinguish themselves.

ignominious \ˌig-nə-ˈmi-nē-əs\ (1) Marked with shame or disgrace; dishonorable. (2) Humiliating or degrading.

- If Attila the Hun was truly murdered by his bride on their wedding night, it was a most ignominious death for a warrior.

The Latin *nomen* could mean both "name" and "good reputation," and even today we can say that someone who has been disgraced has "lost his good name." With its negative prefix *ig-, ignominious* indicates the "namelessness" that goes with shame or dishonor. A person who suffers an ignominious fate may die nameless and forgotten. In the former Soviet Union, party leaders who fell out of favor, even if they avoided being imprisoned or executed, became nonpersons. Their names were removed from official records and history books and they were treated as if they had never existed.

misnomer \ˌmis-ˈnō-mər\ A wrong name, or the use of a wrong name.

- Calling the native peoples of the western hemisphere "Indians" was one of the great misnomers in recorded history.

Historians have long noted that the Holy Roman Empire in its later years was neither holy, Roman, nor an empire. The Battle of Bunker Hill was actually fought on nearby Breed's Hill. And the famous

Woodstock Festival was actually held in the town of Bethel. But misnomers aren't limited to history. The Pennsylvania Dutch are actually of German ancestry. Koala bears aren't bears—they're marsupials. And in the world of food, the Rocky Mountain oyster, as diners have sometimes discovered too late, aren't really oysters.

PATER/PATR comes from both the Greek and the Latin word for "father." So a *patron,* for example, is someone who assumes a fatherly role toward an institution or project or individual, giving moral and financial support.

---

patrician \pə-ˈtri-shən\ A person of high birth or of good breeding and cultivation; an aristocrat.

• They passed themselves off as patricians, and no one looked too closely at where their money came from.

A patrician was originally a descendant of one of the original citizen families of ancient Rome. Until about 350 B.C., only patricians could hold the office of senator, consul, or pontifex (priest). Later, the word was applied to members of the nobility created by the Roman emperor Constantine. As time went by, other nobles, such as those in medieval Italian republics and in German city-states, also came to be known as patricians. Today someone's appearance, manners, or tastes can be described as *patrician*, whether the person is actually of high birth or not. The actress Grace Kelly, an immigrant's daughter, was admired for her *patrician* beauty even before she became Princess Grace of Monaco, with classic features worthy of ancient Rome's finest sculptors.

patriarchy \ˈpā-trē-ˌär-kē\ (1) A family, group, or government controlled by a man or a group of men. (2) A social system in which family members are related to each other through their fathers.

• She spent the 1980s raging against the patriarchy, which she claimed had destroyed the lives of millions of women.

With its root -*arch*, meaning "ruler, leader," a *patriarch* is a man who dominates something, even if it's just a family. In Christianity, the term is used for a few leading figures who appear early in the Old Testament, including Methuselah, Abraham, Isaac, and Jacob; in the Eastern Orthodox church, a patriarch is usually the equivalent of a bishop. Outside of the field of anthropology, *patriarchy* didn't start to be used much until the 1970s, when the women's movement gained a huge following. Many feminists have claimed that all Western societies are *patriarchal*—that is, that they systematically enable men to dominate women. But there's plenty of disagreement about how this is done, and the word isn't discussed as often as it used to be.

expatriate \ek-ˈspā-trē-ət\ A person who has moved to a foreign land.

• As he got to know his fellow expatriates in Morocco, he found himself wondering what had led each of them to leave America.

Expatriate combines the prefix *ex-*, "out of" or "away from," with the Latin *patria,* "fatherland." A famous colony of expatriates was the group of writers and artists who gathered in Paris between the two world wars, including Ernest Hemingway, F. Scott Fitzgerald, and Gertrude Stein. Unlike an exile or an emigrant, an expatriate's residence abroad is usually voluntary and extended but not permanent, and expatriates—often called *expats*—generally keep their original national identity and eventually end their self-imposed exiles by *repatriating* themselves.

paternalistic \pə-ˌtər-nə-ˈlis-tik\ Tending to supply the needs of or regulate the activities of those under one's control.

• Some still accuse the university of being too paternalistic in regulating student living arrangements.

A good father shows *paternal* concern about his children, just as a good mother often acts out of *maternal* feeling. But *paternalistic* has a negative sound nowadays, since paternalistic people or institutions seek—often with decent intentions—to control many aspects of the lives of those under their control. In the 19th century, mill owners actually often provided cheap housing for the mill's employees. Today companies frequently have strict rules regarding personal appearance, or against marriages within the company. Colleges and universities used to practice a kind of *paternalism,* especially in trying to keep men and women out of each other's dorms, but a changing society has mostly put an end to that.

Quizzes

A. Fill in each blank with the correct letter:

a. patriarchy
b. misnomer
c. expatriate
d. nominal

e. ignominious
f. paternalistic
g. nomenclature
h. patrician

1. It's a community pool, and the fee we pay each time we use it is only _____.
2. At Christian colleges, policies tend to be rather strict and _____.
3. "Friend" is a _____ for Charlotte; "rival" is more like it.
4. The country could still be called a _____, with men being completely dominant both at home and in the government.
5. The first public attempts to test the antiballistic missiles ended in _____ failure.
6. He soon discovered that he wasn't the only American _____ living in the Guatemalan village.
7. The person who discovers a previously unknown plant usually gets to name it, but the _____ must follow a strict set of rules.
8. His family and upbringing were _____, but he still considered himself a man of the people.

B. Match the word on the left to the correct definition on the right:

1. paternalistic
2. nomenclature
3. patriarchy
4. misnomer
5. expatriate
6. nominal
7. ignominious
8. patrician

a. wrong name
b. aristocrat
c. exercising fatherly authority
d. rule by men
e. naming system
f. humiliating
g. in name only
h. person living abroad

LEGA comes from the Latin *legare,* meaning "to appoint" or "to send as a deputy." The same root actually shows up in such words as *legal*—but how the law connects with sending deputies can get awfully complicated and probably isn't worth going into.

---

legate \ˈle-gət\ An official representative, such as an ambassador.

• All the important European powers sent legates of some kind to the peace conference.

Legate is a somewhat old-fashioned word, less used today than it was a century ago. More common is the synonym *envoy*. In the days before electronic communications, a legate often had particularly large responsibilities, since he couldn't check with his government to be sure he was doing the right thing. The Vatican still sends papal legates to represent the pope's point of view in negotiations.

legacy \ˈle-gə-sē\ (1) Something left to a person in a will. (2) Something handed down by an ancestor or predecessor or received from the past.

• The Stradivarius family of violin makers left a priceless legacy of remarkable instruments.

In its basic meaning, a legacy is a gift of money or other personal property that's granted by the terms of a will—often a substantial gift that needs to be properly managed. But the word is used much more broadly as well. So, for instance, much of Western civilization—law, philosophy, aesthetics—could be called the undying legacy of ancient Greece. And the rights and opportunities that women enjoy today are partly the legacy of the early suffragists and feminists.

delegation \ˌde-li-ˈgā-shən\ A group of people chosen to represent the interests or opinions of others.

• Each American colony sent a delegation to the Second Continental Congress, and in its second year all 56 delegates approved Jefferson's Declaration of Independence.

The task of a delegation—each member of which can be called a *delegate*—is to represent a larger group, often at a conference. Thus, a delegation of nondoctors to a medical convention may want to make sure the rights and needs of patients aren't ignored, just as a delegation of laypeople may attend a religious conference to express the concerns of other laypeople.

relegate \\'re-lə-ˌgāt\\ (1) To remove or assign to a less important place. (2) To refer or hand over for decision or for carrying out.

• First-year students were relegated to the back of the line so that all the upper classes could eat first.

Originally *relegate* meant "to send into exile, banish." So when you relegate an old sofa to the basement, you're sending it to home-decorating Siberia. When confronted with a matter that no one really wants to face, a chief executive may relegate it to a committee "for further study," which may manage to ignore it for years. It may be annoying to read a newspaper article about a pet project and find that your own contributions have been relegated to a short sentence near the end.

GREG comes from the Latin *grex,* "herd" or "flock." Bees, starlings, cows—any creatures that like to live together in flocks or herds—are called *gregarious*, and the same word is used for people who enjoy companionship and are happiest when they're in the middle of a rowdy herd.

---

aggregate \\'a-grə-gət\\ A collection or sum of units or parts.

• His lawyers realize that the aggregate of incriminating details is now pointing toward a conviction.

An aggregate is often an example of something being greater than the sum of its parts. For instance, even if no individual element in a person's background would assure a criminal career, the aggregate of factors could make a life of crime seem unavoidable. *Aggregate* is often used in the phrase "in the aggregate," as in "Her achievements were, in the aggregate, impressive enough to earn her a scholarship." *Aggregate* is also an adjective, meaning "total"; so, for instance, economists often discuss aggregate demand for goods and services in the country's economy, just as you yourself might speak about your father's aggregate income from his three jobs.

congregation \\ˌkän-gri-'gā-shən\\ (1) A gathering of people, especially for worship or religious instruction. (2) The membership of a church or temple.

- That Sunday the congregation was especially large, and the minister delivered one of his best sermons.

The verb *congregate* may be used for spontaneous gatherings. A crowd quickly congregates at the scene of an accident, for example, just as cows, sheep, or horses tend to congregate during a storm. And under military rule, citizens are often forbidden to congregate on street corners or anywhere else. But a congregation is generally a group that has gathered for a formal purpose, usually in church. The Congregational Church was originally the church of the Puritan settlers, in which each congregation governed its own church independent of any higher authority.

egregious \i-'grē-jəs\ Standing out, especially in a bad way; flagrant.

- Many of the term papers contained egregious grammatical errors.

Since *egregious* begins with a short version of *ex-*, meaning "out of," the word should mean literally "out of the herd." So something egregious possesses some quality that sets it apart from others. Originally, that distinguishing quality was something good, but by the 16th century the word's meaning had taken a U-turn and the word was being applied to things that were outrageously bad. This has remained the most common sense. Thus, an egregious fool is one who manages to outdo run-of-the-mill fools, and egregious rudeness sets a new standard for unpleasant salesclerks.

segregate \'se-grə-ˌgāt\ (1) To separate from others or from the general mass; isolate. (2) To separate along racial lines.

- Some schools are experimenting with gender segregation, claiming that both sexes learn better in classrooms from which the other sex is absent.

The prefix *se-* means "apart," so when you segregate something you set it apart from the herd. The word typically means separating something undesirable from the healthy majority. During the apple harvest, damaged fruit is segregated from the main crop and used for cider. In prisons, hardened criminals are segregated from youthful offenders. Lepers used to be segregated from the general population because they were thought to be highly infectious. The opposite of *segregate* is often *integrate*, and the two words were in the news almost daily for decades as African-Americans struggled to be admitted into all-white schools and neighborhoods.

Quizzes

A. Complete the analogy:

1. habit : custom :: legacy : _____
   a. descendant b. tradition c. transit d. deputy
2. obedient : tame :: egregious : _____
   a. crowded b. uncrowded c. blatant d. fair
3. governor : executive :: legate : _____
   a. letter b. priest c. deputy d. bandit
4. series : sequence :: aggregate : _____
   a. individual b. collection c. attack d. annoyance
5. flock : group of sheep :: delegation : _____
   a. group of candidates b. group of worshippers
   c. group of runners d. group of representatives
6. tear : mend :: segregate : _____
   a. mix b. sort c. send away d. refine
7. revise : amend :: relegate : _____
   a. vanish b. banish c. tarnish d. varnish
8. location : place :: congregation : _____
   a. birds b. whales c. group d. temple

B. Fill in each blank with the correct letter:

a. congregation   e. legacy
b. relegate   f. aggregate
c. segregate   g. legate
d. delegation   h. egregious

1. The child had tried to hide his mistake with an _____ lie.
2. The king's _____ arrived two weeks early in order to negotiate the agreement that the king would later sign in person.
3. Battlefield medics were forced to _____ the hopeless cases from the other casualties.
4. The government is struggling to overcome a _____ of corruption that goes back a hundred years or more.

5. Taken in the _____, these statistics are very disturbing.
6. At the conference a carefully chosen _____ presented its views to the president.
7. The _____ grew silent as the first strains of the wedding march sounded.
8. There in the corner, where the shopkeeper had decided to _____ him, sat a stuffed bear with a mournful face.

FLU comes from the Latin verb *fluere,* "to flow." So a *flume* is a narrow gorge with a stream flowing through it. A *fluent* speaker is one from whom words *flow* easily. *Influence* originally referred to an invisible *fluid* that was believed to flow from the stars and to affect the actions of humans. A mysterious outbreak of disease in 15th-century Italy led Italians to blame it on the stars' *influenza*—and the name stuck.

affluence \ˈa-ˌflü-əns\ An abundance of wealth.

• The affluence of the city's northern suburbs is indicated by the huge houses there.

Affluence comes from the Latin verb *affluere,* "to flow abundantly." Thus, someone or something blessed with affluence has received an incoming *flood* of riches. Since the *affluent* residents of suburbs often work in the central city but pay taxes back home, the wealth of some metropolitan areas tends to *flow* in one direction—out.

effluent \ˈe-ˌflü-ənt\ Polluting waste material discharged into the environment.

• The effluent from the mill had long ago turned this once-beautiful stream into a foul-smelling open-air sewer.

Effluent comes from the Latin verb *effluere,* "to flow out." In an older meaning, an effluent was a stream flowing out of a river or lake. But nowadays *effluent* almost always means wastes that pour into our water and air. Liquid factory waste, smoke, and raw sewage can all be called effluents. An effluent filter keeps treated waste flowing out of a septic tank from clogging up its drainage pipes.

confluence \ˈkän-ˌflü-əns\ (1) A coming or flowing together at one point. (2) A place of meeting, especially of two streams.

- The confluence of several large economic forces led to the "perfect storm" that shook the world economy in 2008.

The joining of rivers—as at Harpers Ferry, West Virginia, where the Shenandoah and Potomac Rivers flow together spectacularly—was the original meaning of *confluence*, and in its later meanings we still hear a strong echo of the physical merging of waters. So today we can speak of a confluence of events, a confluence of interests, a confluence of cultures, and so on, from which something important often emerges.

mellifluous \me-ˈli-flü-wəs\ Flowing like honey; sweetened as if with honey.

- His rich, mellifluous voice is familiar to us from countless voice-overs for commercials, station breaks, and documentaries.

With its root *mel-,* meaning "honey," *mellifluous* means literally "flowing like honey." The word usually applies to sound; it has often been used to describe voices such as Renee Fleming's or Barbra Streisand's, or pieces by composers such as Ravel and Debussy. The DJ on a radio station that plays soft music may have a voice so mellifluous that it almost puts the listener to sleep.

PREHEND/PREHENS comes from the Latin verb *prehendere,* "to seize." Most of the English words where it appears are closely related to the ones discussed below.

---

prehensile \prē-ˈhen-səl\ Adapted for grasping, especially by wrapping around.

- The squid has eight short "arms" but also two long prehensile tentacles that it uses for catching its prey.

Howler monkeys are among the American monkeys with prehensile tails. Famous for their booming howls, howlers can wrap their tails around a nearby branch while using their prehensile feet and hands for picking lice from their fur or lobbing a coconut at an unwelcome tourist. Our own hands are prehensile, of course. Our feet are not; on the other hand, they're much better for running than the prehensile feet of a monkey or ape.

apprehend \ˌa-pri-ˈhend\ (1) Arrest, seize. (2) Understand.

- It was a few minutes before she managed to apprehend the meaning of what she had just seen.

To *apprehend* is to seize, either physically or mentally. So to apprehend a thief is to nab him. But to apprehend a confusing news story, or to apprehend a difficult concept in physics, is to understand it—that is, to "grasp" it mentally. If you're *apprehensive* about something that's about to happen, it means you've grasped all the unpleasant possibilities and are waiting with anxiety or dread.

comprehend \ˌkäm-pri-ˈhend\ (1) To grasp the meaning of; understand. (2) To take in or include.

- In the days following the dropping of the atomic bomb on Hiroshima, the public slowly began to comprehend the fact that the nuclear age had arrived.

To comprehend is to mentally grasp something's complete nature or meaning. *Comprehend* is thus often a bit stronger than *understand*: for example, you may understand the instructions in a handbook without completely comprehending their purpose. *Comprehend*'s second meaning is much less common. Using that sense of the word, we could say that good manners comprehends (that is, includes) more than simple table etiquette, for example, or that true courage comprehends more than just physical showing off. And something *comprehensive* includes a great deal: so a comprehensive exam, for instance, includes all the material that was studied in the course.

reprehensible \ˌre-pri-ˈhen-sə-bəl\ Deserving stern criticism or blame.

- Whether or not he ever broke the law, his treatment of his first wife was thoroughly reprehensible.

From its prefix *re-*, meaning "back," *reprehend* would mean literally "to hold back, restrain"; but even the Latin version of the verb had come to mean "to scold, blame"—in other words, to restrain bad behavior by expressing disapproval. *Reprehensible* is applied to both things and people—that is, both the sin and the sinner. So a senator might be scolded for reprehensible conduct, but might also be called a thoroughly reprehensible person. And most of us would call dogfighting morally reprehensible, and would use the same word to describe those who put the dogs up to it.

Quizzes

A. Choose the closest definition:

1. apprehend   a. seize   b. insist   c. understand   d. deny
2. confluence   a. support   b. joining   c. certainty
    d. outflow
3. reprehensible   a. understandable   b. worthy of blame
    c. worthy of return   d. inclusive
4. comprehend   a. take   b. understand   c. compress
    d. remove
5. mellifluous   a. flowing slowly   b. flowing outward
    c. flowing smoothly   d. flowing downward
6. effluent   a. wastewater   b. wealth   c. trash   d. sewer
7. prehensile   a. able to peel   b. able to swing   c. able to
    howl   d. able to grasp
8. affluence   a. suburb   b. excess   c. wealth   d. mall

B. Indicate whether the following pairs of words have the same or different meanings:

1. prehensile / dropping   same ___ / different ___
2. mellifluous / smooth   same ___ / different ___
3. reprehensible / unusual   same ___ / different ___
4. effluent / pollutant   same ___ / different ___
5. comprehend / include   same ___ / different ___
6. confluence / understanding   same ___ / different ___
7. apprehend / arrest   same ___ / different ___
8. affluence / wealth   same ___ / different ___

TEMPER comes from the Latin verb *temperare,* "to moderate or keep within limits" or "to mix." Most of the world's people live in the *temperate* zone—that is, the zone where the *temperature* is moderate, between the hot tropics and the icy Arctic and Antarctic Circles. It's less easy to see how we get *temperature* from this root; the word actually used to refer to the mixing of different basic elements in the body, and only slowly came to mean how hot or cold that body was.

temper \\'tem-pər\\ To dilute, qualify, or soften by adding something more agreeable; to moderate.

• A wise parent tempers discipline with love.

The *temper* root keeps its basic meaning—"to mix" or "to keep within limits"—in the English word *temper*. When you temper something, you mix it with some balancing quality or substance so as to avoid anything extreme. Thus, it's often said that a judge must temper justice with mercy. Young people only gradually learn to temper their natural enthusiasms with caution. And in dealing with others, we all try to temper our honesty with sensitivity.

temperance \\'tem-prəns\\ (1) Moderation in satisfying appetites or passions. (2) The drinking of little or no alcohol.

• Buddhism teaches humankind to follow "the middle way"—that is, temperance in all things.

Since *temperance* means basically "moderation," you might assume that, with respect to alcohol, *temperance* would mean moderate consumption, or "social drinking." Instead, the word has usually meant the prohibition of all alcohol. To temperance leaders such as Carry Nation, the safest form of drinking was no alcohol at all. Believing she was upholding the law, Nation began her hatchet-swinging attacks on saloons, known as "hatchetations," in the 1890s. National prohibition did eventually come—and go—but largely through the efforts of more *temperate* (that is, moderate) reformers.

intemperate \\in-'tem-pə-rət\\ Not moderate or mild; excessive, extreme.

• Lovers of fine wines and scotches are almost never intemperate drinkers.

Since the prefix *in-* generally means "not," *intemperate* is the opposite of *temperate*. Someone intemperate rejects moderation in favor of excess. A religious fanatic is likely to preach with intemperate zeal, and a mean theater critic may become intemperate in her criticism of a new play, filling her review with intemperate language. And both *temperate* and *intemperate* also often refer to weather; a region with an intemperate climate isn't where all of us would choose to build a house.

distemper \dis-ˈtem-pər\ (1) A highly contagious viral disease, especially of dogs. (2) A highly contagious and usually fatal viral disease, especially of cats, marked by the destruction of white blood cells.

• An epidemic of feline distemper had swept the country, and its cat population had plummeted.

Back when doctors believed that our moods were affected by an imbalance of mysterious fluids in the body, or "humors," distemper often meant moodiness, as when Shakespeare's Hamlet is asked "What is the source of your distemper?" Today the word is used only for true physical conditions. The distemper that affects dogs, often called canine distemper, also affects foxes, wolves, mink, raccoons, and ferrets. It can be treated with medication, but is generally fatal if not treated. Distemper in cats, known as feline distemper or *panleukopenia*, actually isn't related to canine distemper. If caught quickly, it too can be treated. And both types can be prevented by vaccination, so all responsible pet owners get their animals vaccinated.

PURG comes from the Latin verb *purgare,* "to clean or cleanse." Almost all the English words where it shows up are closely related to those discussed below.

---

purge \ˈpərj\ (1) To clear of guilt or sin. (2) To free of something unwanted or considered impure.

• During the 1930s, Stalin purged the Soviet communist party of thousands of members who he suspected of disloyalty.

In some cultures, a ritual bath or prayer is performed to purge guilt or evil spirits. The Minoans of ancient Crete may have used human sacrifice as a way of purging the entire community, which is fine for the community but rough on the victims. In many cultures, people periodically purge themselves physically—that is, clean out their digestive tracts—by taking strong laxatives; this used to be a popular springtime ritual, and herbal *purgatives* were readily available.

expurgate \ˈek-spər-ˌgāt\ To cleanse of something morally harmful or offensive; to remove objectionable parts from.

• In those years, high-school English classes only used expurgated editions of Chaucer's *Canterbury Tales*.

Expurgation has a long and questionable history. Perhaps history's most famous *expurgator*, or censor, was the English editor Thomas Bowdler, who in 1818 published the *Family Shakespeare,* an expurgated edition of Shakespeare's plays that omitted or changed any passages that, in Bowdler's opinion, couldn't decently be read aloud in a family. As a result, the term *bowdlerize* is now a synonym of *expurgate.*

purgative \\'pər-gə-tiv\\ (1) Cleansing or purifying, especially from sin. (2) Causing a significant looseness of the bowels.

• I'm afraid my ten-year-old discovered the purgative effect of too many apples after a lazy afternoon in the orchard.

Purgative can be used as a noun as well as an adjective. For centuries, doctors prescribed purgatives—that is, laxatives—for all kinds of ailments, not knowing anything better to do. Physical cleansing has always reminded people of emotional and spiritual cleansing, as expressed in the saying "Cleanliness is next to godliness." So we may say, for example, that confession has a purgative effect on the soul. Some psychologists used to claim that expressing your anger is purgative; but in fact it may generally be no better for your emotional life than taking a laxative, and can sometimes really foul things up.

purgatory \\'pər-gə-ˌtòr-ē\\ (1) According to Roman Catholic doctrine, the place where the souls of those who have died in God's grace must pay for their sins through suffering before ascending to heaven. (2) A place or state of temporary suffering or misery.

• For both of them, filled with anxiety, the long, sleepless night felt like purgatory.

Purgatory is the place where the soul is cleansed of all impurities, as Dante described in his great poem *The Divine Comedy.* Today *purgatory* can refer to any place or situation in which suffering and misery are felt to be sharp but temporary. Waiting to hear the results of a test, or whether you got a good job, can be a purgatory. And an endless after-dinner speech can make an entire roomful of people feel as if they're in purgatory.

Quizzes

A. Fill in each blank with the correct letter:

a. intemperate   e. purgatory
b. expurgate   f. temper
c. temperance   g. purgative
d. purge   h. distemper

1. For a sick person, waiting for medical test results can feel like _____.
2. Don thinks we had better _____ our enthusiasm for this scheme with a large dose of skepticism.
3. When taken in moderate quantities, the _____ effects of bran can be healthful.
4. The widow leaped to her feet and launched into a shockingly _____ tirade at the jury.
5. Filmmakers must sometimes _____ entire scenes from their films to receive an acceptable rating.
6. Her eternal watchword was _____, and no one ever saw her upset, worn out, angry, or tipsy.
7. Concerned that the workers might be forming a union, the president considered trying to _____ the entire department.
8. That year, the local raccoon population had been severely reduced by an epidemic of _____.

B. Match the definition on the left to the correct word on the right:

1. place of misery   a. distemper
2. unrestrained   b. purge
3. remove offensive material   c. temperance
4. mix or moderate   d. purgative
5. purifying   e. temper
6. moderation   f. expurgate
7. remove impure elements   g. intemperate
8. animal disease   h. purgatory

Number Words

MILL means either "a thousand" or "a thousandth." A *millennium* is a thousand years, and a *million* is a thousand thousands. But a *milligram* is a thousandth of a gram, a *milliliter* a thousandth of a liter, and a *millimeter* a thousandth of a meter.

millefleur \mēl-ˈflər\ Having a pattern of small flowers and plants all over.

• She was painstakingly embroidering a millefleur pattern on a pillow casing.

Millefleur came into French from the Latin *mille flores* ("a thousand flowers"), and from French directly into English. You may have seen the famed Unicorn Tapestries, in which the unicorn is seen frolicking, relaxing, being hunted, and being caught, all against a beautiful millefleur background. Italian has given us the similar word *millefiori*; though *fiori*, like *fleurs*, means "flowers," *millefiori* actually refers to a type of multicolored ornamental glass. And the borrowed French word *mille-feuille* (*feuille* meaning "leaf") is the name of a dish made with puff pastry, the kind of pastry whose flakes resemble thin dry leaves.

millenarianism \ˌmi-lə-ˈner-ē-ə-ˌni-zəm\ (1) Belief in the 1,000-year era of holiness foretold in the Book of Revelation. (2) Belief in an ideal society to come, especially one brought about by revolution.

• Millenarianism is one of the future-oriented beliefs common in the New Age movement.

Originally the *millennium* was not simply any thousand-year period, but instead the thousand years prophesied in the biblical Book of Revelation, when holiness will prevail on earth and Jesus Christ will preside over all. Later, *millennium* was extended to mean any period—always in the future—marked by universal happiness and human perfection. On several occasions over the centuries, members of Christian sects have become convinced that the biblical millennium was arriving and gathered together to await it. But nonreligious millenarians have also believed in a future society marked by human perfection. Even if they regard this future as certain, they've generally been willing to help it along by working for a political, social, or economic revolution. The millennium always seems to be approaching; to date, it hasn't arrived.

millipede \\'mi-lə-ˌpēd\\ Any of a class of many-footed arthropods that have a cylindrical, segmented body with two pairs of legs on each segment, and, unlike centipedes, no poison fangs.

• As they turned over rocks and bricks in their search for the lost bracelet, millipedes of various sizes went scurrying off.

The earth is home to about 10,000 species of millipedes. Though they have no poison fangs, many of them can, when threatened, emit a liquid or gas poisonous to their enemies. If their structure were true to their name, millipedes would have a thousand legs, but in fact they have far fewer. Even so, a millipede in motion is a sight to ponder: How can it possibly coordinate all those legs so that it doesn't trip over itself? Like some tiny conga line or bunny hop, it scuttles away to a rhythm only it can hear.

millisecond \\'mi-lə-ˌse-kənd\\ One thousandth of a second.

• A lightning bolt lasts only about 20 milliseconds, though the image may stay in one's eye for much longer.

A millisecond isn't long enough for the blink of an eye, but a few milliseconds may determine the winner of a swim race or a hundred-yard dash. With the ever-increasing speed of modern technology, even a millisecond has started to seem a little sluggish; computer operations are now measured in nanoseconds—that is, billionths of a second.

HEMI/SEMI means "half." *Hemi-* comes from Greek, *semi-* from Latin. A *hemisphere* is half a sphere, and a *semicircle* is half a circle. (The French prefix *demi-*, which probably developed from Latin as well, also means "half"—as in *demitasse*, a little after-dinner coffee cup half the size of a regular cup.)

semitone \\'se-mē-ˌtōn\\ The tone at a half step.

• The ancient piano in the great music room had been allowed to fall terribly out of tune, with every note at least a semitone flat.

A semitone (sometimes called a *half tone* or a *half step*) is the distance from a white key to a neighboring black key on the piano keyboard—for example, from G to G-sharp or from E to E-flat.

In an octave (from G to the next G above, for instance), there are twelve semitones. Semitones are the smallest intervals that are used intentionally in almost any of the music you'll normally hear. Two semitones equal a *whole tone*—the distance from G up to A or from E down to D, for example.

semicolon \\'se-mē-,kō-lən\\ The punctuation mark ; , used chiefly to separate major sentence elements such as independent clauses.

• Some young vandal had done a search-and-replace on Mr. Marsh's computer file, and in place of every semicolon was the mysterious message "Hendrix RULES!"

The semicolon was introduced into modern type by an Italian printer around 1566. But since it's actually the same symbol as the ancient Greek question mark, it's older than the colon (:), which first appears around 1450. Don't mix the two up. A colon introduces something: usually a list, sometimes a statement. A semicolon separates two independent but related clauses; it may also replace the comma to separate items in a complicated list.

hemiplegia \\,he-mi-'plē-jə\\ Total or partial paralysis of one side of the body that results from disease of or injury to the motor centers of the brain.

• She's starting to regain the use of her right hand, and some of the therapists think her hemiplegia might eventually be reversed.

Hemi-, unlike *semi*, almost always appears in scientific or technical words, including medical terms such as this one. A *hemiplegic*, like a paraplegic (who has lost the use of both legs), has usually suffered brain damage, often from a wound or blood clot. Other conditions that affect one side of the body are *hemihypertrophy* (excessive growth on one side), *hemiatrophy* (wasting on one side), and *hemiparesis* (weakness or partial paralysis).

semiconductor \\,se-,mē-kən-'dək-tər\\ A solid that conducts electricity like a metal at high temperatures and insulates like a nonmetal at low temperatures.

• Silicon, which makes up 25% of the earth's crust, is the most widely used semiconductor, and as such has formed the basis for a revolution in human culture.

A semiconductor is a crystal material whose ability to conduct electricity rises as its temperature goes up. That is, it sometimes acts as a conductor and sometimes as an insulator. Its conducting ability can be much increased by chemical treatment. A manufactured chip of silicon, less than half an inch square, may contain millions of microscopic transistors, which can serve control and memory functions when installed in a computer, automobile, cell phone, DVD player, or microwave oven.

Quiz

Fill in each blank with the correct letter:

a. millefleur
b. semiconductor
c. millisecond
d. semitone

e. semicolon
f. millenarianism
g. hemiplegia
h. millipede

1. _____ increased dramatically as the year 2000 approached.
2. In most integrated circuits, silicon is used as the _____.
3. The poison from the largest tropical centipedes can be lethal to small children, but a _____ could never kill a human.
4. Seeing that the highest note was out of her comfortable range, she asked her pianist to play the whole song a _____ lower.
5. For the baby's room they chose wallpaper with a dainty _____ design.
6. A childhood disease had resulted in the crippling _____ that had confined him to a wheelchair for ten years.
7. Some Olympic races have been extremely close, but no one has ever won by a single _____.
8. The meaning of a clause rarely depends on whether it ends with a colon or a _____.

Review Quizzes

A. Complete the analogy:

1. repulsive : attractive :: ignominious : _____
   a. favorite b. honorable c. horrible d. disgraceful

2. obnoxious : pleasant :: egregious : _____
   a. boring b. bothersome c. unpleasant
   d. unnoticeable

3. milliliter : volume :: millisecond : _____
   a. distance b. weight c. time d. mass

4. enthusiastic : eager :: intemperate : _____
   a. calm b. amused c. restrained d. uncontrolled

5. paraplegia : legs :: hemiplegia : _____
   a. paralysis b. stroke c. lungs d. left or right side

6. erase : delete :: expurgate : _____
   a. confess b. read c. censor d. scrub

7. allow : permit :: apprehend : _____
   a. accept b. ignore c. figure out d. examine

8. split : separation :: confluence : _____
   a. breakup b. division c. flow d. merging

9. repair : fix :: purge : _____
   a. purify b. smooth c. weaken d. support

10. present : gift :: legacy : _____
    a. ownership b. legal settlement c. will d. inheritance

B. Choose the closest definition:

1. patrician a. patriot b. aristocrat c. father
   d. grandfather

2. congregation a. anthill b. gathering c. hearing
   d. church

3. temperance a. wrath b. modesty c. moderation
   d. character

4. nominal a. trifling b. important c. by name d. serious

5. legate a. heritage b. gift c. ambassador d. letter

6. comprehend a. misjudge b. confirm c. grasp
   d. gather

7. effluent a. discharge b. effort c. excess d. wealth

8. purgative a. secret agent b. bleaching agent c. road
   agent d. cleansing agent

9. semicolon a. small intestine b. punctuation mark
   c. low hill d. small bush

10. reprehensible   a. understandable   b. reptilian
    c. disgraceful   d. approachable
11. distemper   a. anger   b. hysteria   c. disease   d. weakness
12. millipede   a. thousand-year blight   b. many-legged
    arthropod   c. hundred million   d. obstacle
13. purgatory   a. near heaven   b. place of punishment
    c. evacuation   d. place of earthly delights
14. semitone   a. soft sound   b. half note   c. shade of
    color   d. half step
15. aggregate   a. nuisance   b. assembly   c. pile   d. sum total

C. Fill in each blank with the correct letter:

a.	mellifluous	i.	temper
b.	expatriate	j.	misnomer
c.	millefleur	k.	semiconductor
d.	paternalistic	l.	legacy
e.	affluence	m.	prehensile
f.	purge	n.	millenarianism
g.	nomenclature	o.	delegation
h.	segregate		

1. Thousands of microscopic transistors partly made of the
   same _____ are embedded in each chip.
2. Each generation hopes to leave the next a _____ of
   peace and prosperity.
3. Each time a new insect is discovered, strict rules
   of _____ help determine what its name will be.
4. We sent a two-person _____ off to the restaurant to
   choose supper for everyone.
5. The hands of even a newborn infant are _____ and
   surprisingly strong.
6. Let's _____ the bad fruit from the rest to prevent the
   rot from spreading.
7. The company's _____ attitudes toward its employees
   were at times helpful and at times just irritating.
8. The _____ tones of a Mozart flute concerto poured
   from the window.
9. "Panama hat" is a _____, since the hats have actually
   always been made in Ecuador.
10. Imperial Rome was a city of great _____ as well as
    terrible poverty.

11. Many of us take milk or cream with our coffee to _____ its acidity.
12. The outburst seemed to _____ the crowd of its anger.
13. Since everyone interprets the Bible's prophecies differently, _____ has broken out at many different times through the centuries.
14. She soon realized that she wasn't the only American _____ in her Kenyan village.
15. A design with a detailed _____ background is a challenge for even a needlepoint expert.

UNIT

21

SUB means "under." So a *subway* runs under the streets, and a *submarine* moves under the ocean's surface. A *subject* is a person under the authority of another. A movie's *subplot* is lower in importance than the main plot. *Subscribe* once meant "to write one's name underneath," so *subscription* was the act of signing a document or agreement.

---

subconscious \ˌsəb-ˈkän-shəs\ Existing in the mind just below the level of awareness.

• After dropping three dishes in a week, she began thinking there might be some kind of subconscious agitation behind her case of butterfingers.

We're rarely aware, or at least fully aware, of our subconscious mental activity. But subconscious thought does affect our feelings and behavior, and it's often revealed in dreams, artistic expression, and slips of the tongue. The subconscious mind can be a hiding place for anxiety, a source of creativity, and often the reason behind our own mysterious behavior.

subjugate \ˈsəb-jə-ˌgāt\ To bring under control and rule as a subject; conquer, subdue.

• The country's government claimed it was just trying to protect national security, but some saw its actions as an attempt to subjugate the news media.

Since *jugus* means "yoke" in Latin, *subjugate* means literally "bring under the yoke." Farmers control oxen by means of a heavy wooden yoke over their shoulders. In ancient Rome, conquered soldiers, stripped of their uniforms, might actually be forced to pass under an ox yoke as a sign of submission to the Roman victors. Even without an actual yoke, what happens to a population that has come under the control of another can be every bit as humiliating. In dozens of countries throughout the world, ethnic minorities are denied basic rights and view themselves as subjugated by their country's government, army, and police.

subliminal \sə-ˈbli-mə-nəl\ Not quite strong enough to be sensed or perceived consciously.

* A few worried parents claimed that some heavy-metal songs contain subliminal messages—in the form of words recorded backwards—that urge young fans to take up devil worship.

Since the Latin word *limen* means "threshold," something subliminal exists just below the threshold of conscious awareness. The classic example of a subliminal message is "Eat popcorn" flashed on a movie screen so quickly that the audience doesn't even notice it consciously. Actually, no such advertising has ever been shown to work. But ordinary ads, both in print and on TV, do contain all kinds of images that shape our response to the product being advertised even when we don't realize it. Try looking carefully at some ads that you like, in order to discover how many ways they may be *subliminally* affecting you.

subversion \səb-ˈvər-zhən\ (1) An attempt to overthrow a government by working secretly from within. (2) The corrupting of someone or something by weakening their morals, loyalty, or faith.

* It's sometimes easier for a government to combat attack from outside than subversion from within.

Subversion is literally the "turning over" of something. In the 1950s and '60s, many people worried about communist subversion of the U.S. government, though they often saw *subversive* activities where none existed. Nondemocratic governments often claim that anyone who disagrees with them or joins a demonstration is a *subversive*. But subversion isn't always quite so serious a matter; when words like *weekend, sandwich, job,* and *camping* started being used by the French, for example, some of them began claiming that America was *subverting* their language.

HYPER is a Greek prefix that means "above or beyond," so *hyper-* often means about the same thing as *super-*. *Hyperinflation* is inflation that's growing at a very high rate. To be *hypercritical* or *hypersensitive* is to be critical or sensitive beyond the normal. And if you *hyperextend* a knee or elbow, it means you're actually bending it backward.

---

hyperactive \ˌhī-pər-ˈak-tiv\ Excessively active.

• Stephen King's hyperactive imagination has produced dozens of fantastical stories, not to mention countless nightmares in his readers.

For doctors and psychologists, *hyperactive* describes a condition with unpleasant consequences. Hyperactive children usually have a very short attention span and can't sit still, and *hyperactivity* can lead to difficulty in learning or just get them in trouble for disturbing their classes. But not every high-spirited child is hyperactive. Having a high energy level is pretty normal for children, and some parents think that prescribing drugs for hyperactivity is mostly just good for the drug companies.

hyperbole \hī-ˈpər-bə-lē\ Extreme exaggeration.

• The food at Chez Pierre was good, but it couldn't live up to the hyperbole of the restaurant critics.

Advertisers and sports commentators make their living by their skillful use of hyperbole. Presenting each year's Superbowl as "the greatest contest in the history of sports" certainly qualifies as hyperbole, especially since the final scores are usually so lopsided. Equally *hyperbolic* are advertisers' claims that this year's new car model is "the revolutionary vehicle you've been waiting for" when it's barely different from last year's—which of course was once described in the same glowing terms. Politicians love hyperbole too; some of them seem convinced that calling a new bill "the worst bill ever passed by Congress" or comparing the president to Hitler is a great way to win votes.

hypertension \ˌhī-pər-ˈten-shən\ High blood pressure.

- Pregnancy is often accompanied by mild hypertension that doesn't threaten the mother's life.

You might have thought that hypertension was what a movie audience feels near the climax of a thriller, but you would have been wrong. High blood pressure—that is high pressure against the walls of your veins and arteries caused by blood flow—often occurs when the arteries or veins become blocked or narrowed, making the heart work harder to pump blood. But many cases seem to be the result of smoking or taking in too much salt, and many are genetically caused. Hypertension is serious, since it can lead to heart attacks and strokes. Though it often produces no warning symptoms, your blood pressure can be checked quickly and easily by a nurse. If it's high, it can usually be controlled by stopping smoking, losing weight, lowering your salt intake, and exercising—and if all else fails, by medication.

hyperventilate \ˌhī-pər-ˈven-tə-ˌlāt\ To breathe rapidly and deeply.

- They laughed so hard they began to hyperventilate and feel giddy.

Hyperventilating can be a response to fear and anxiety. A test pilot who panics and hyperventilates faces a dangerous situation. When the level of carbon dioxide in your blood goes down and the oxygen level goes up, blood vessels constrict because of the chemical changes and the body can't get enough oxygen (even though it's there in the blood), and the pilot can become lightheaded and may even faint. To guard against this, pilots are taught to control their breathing. On the ground, the usual remedy for *hyperventilation* is breathing into a paper bag, which raises the level of carbon dioxide and restores normal breathing.

Quizzes

A. **Fill in each blank with the correct letter:**

a. hyperactive   e. subjugate
b. subliminal   f. hyperventilate
c. hypertension   g. subconscious
d. subversion   h. hyperbole

1. Stealing elections through fraud represents a _____ of democracy.
2. She's warned me that there's plenty of _____ in her brother's big talk and that I shouldn't take it too seriously.
3. Accident-prone people may have a _____ desire to do themselves harm.
4. In yoga class we're often warned not to _____ during our breathing exercises.
5. Napoleon hoped to _____ all of Europe and make it his empire.
6. Both my parents are on medication for _____, and the doctor monitors their blood pressure regularly.
7. He claims the ice cubes in whiskey ads contain images that send _____ messages to readers.
8. A _____ imagination can transform every creak and rustle in a dark house into a threat.

B. **Match the word on the left to the correct definition on the right:**

1. hyperactive   a. breathe deeply and rapidly
2. subjugate   b. secret effort to overthrow
3. hyperventilate   c. extreme overstatement
4. subconscious   d. not strong enough to be sensed
5. hypertension   e. beneath the level of consciousness
6. subversion   f. overly active
7. hyperbole   g. conquer
8. subliminal   h. high blood pressure

PRE, one of the most common of all English *prefixes,* comes from *prae,* the Latin word meaning "before" or "in front of." So a *prediction* forecasts what will happen before it occurs. The 5:00 TV news *precedes* the 6:00 news. And someone with a *prejudice* against a class of people has judged them before having even met them.

preclude \pri-'klüd\ To make impossible beforehand; prevent.

• If we accept this cash offer from the company, that will preclude our joining in the big suit against it with the other investors.

Preclude is often used in legal writing, where it usually refers to making something legally impossible. A new law may be passed by Congress to preclude any suits of a certain kind against a federal agency, for example. Some judges have found that the warnings on cigarette packs preclude any suits against the tobacco companies by lung-cancer sufferers. But there are plenty of nonlegal uses as well. Bad weather often precludes trips to the beach, and a lack of cash might preclude any beach vacation at all.

precocious \prē-'kō-shəs\ Showing the qualities or abilities of an adult at an unusually early age.

• Everyone agrees that their seven-year-old daughter is smart and precocious, but she's also getting rather full of herself.

Growing from a child to an adult is like the slow ripening of fruit, and that's the image that gave us *precocious*. The word is based on the Latin verb *coquere,* meaning "to ripen" or "to cook," but it comes most directly from the adjective *praecox,* which means "ripening early or before its time." *Precocity* can occasionally be annoying; but precocious children don't come precooked, only "preripened."

predispose \ˌprē-di-'spōz\ (1) To influence in advance in order to create a particular attitude. (2) To make one more likely to develop a particular disease or physical condition.

• Growing up in a house full of sisters had predisposed her to find her friendships with other women.

Predispose usually means putting someone in a frame of mind to be willing to do something. So a longtime belief in the essential goodness of people, for example, will predispose us to trust a stranger. Teachers know that coming from a stable family generally predisposes children to learn. And viewing television violence for years may leave young people with a *predisposition* to accept real violence as normal. The medical sense of the word is similar. Thus, a person's genes may predispose her to diabetes or arthritis, and malnutrition over a long period can predispose you to all kinds of infections.

prerequisite \prē-ˈre-kwə-zət\ Something that is required in advance to achieve a goal or to carry out a function.

• In most states, minimal insurance coverage is a prerequisite for registering an automobile.

Prerequisite is partly based on *requirere,* the Latin verb meaning "to need or require." So a prerequisite can be anything that must be accomplished or acquired before something else can be done. Possessing a valid credit card is a prerequisite for renting a car. A physical exam may be a prerequisite for receiving a life-insurance policy. And successful completion of an introductory course is often a prerequisite for enrolling in a higher-level course.

PARA is a Greek prefix usually meaning "beside" or "closely related to." So *parallel* lines run beside each other. And a Greek *paragraphos* was originally a line written beside the main text of a play to show where a new person begins speaking; today we just start a new *paragraph* on a new line.

---

paraphrase \ˈper-ə-ˌfrāz\ To restate the meaning (of something written or spoken) in different words.

• She started off the class by asking one of the students to paraphrase the Tennyson poem, to make sure everyone understood its basic meaning.

When we paraphrase, we provide a version that can exist beside the original (rather than replace it). We paraphrase all the time. When you tell a friend what someone else has said, you're almost always paraphrasing, since you're not repeating the exact words. If you go to hear a talk, you might paraphrase the speaker's main points afterward for your friends. And when writing a paper on a short story, you might start off your essay with a *paraphrase* of the plot. Paraphrasing is especially useful when dealing with poetry, since poetic language is often difficult and poems may have meanings that are hard to pin down.

paralegal \ˌpa-rə-ˈlē-gəl\ Of, relating to, or being a trained assistant to a lawyer.

• Part of the firm's business involved researching real-estate properties, which the senior lawyers regarded as paralegal work.

Much of the work in a law office can be done by paralegal assistants, also called legal aides or simply *paralegals*, who work alongside licensed lawyers. Often a paralegal is trained in a narrow field and then entrusted with it. In this respect, paralegals are similar to *paraprofessionals* in other fields, such as engineering. Paraprofessionals used to be trained in the office itself, but today it's common to study for a paraprofessional certificate or degree at a community college or university.

paramedic \ˌpa-rə-ˈme-dik\ A specially trained medical technician licensed to provide a wide range of emergency services before or during transportation to a hospital.

• Five ambulances had already arrived, and a dozen paramedics were crouched over the victims with bandages and IVs.

In ground warfare, wounded troops must usually be transported from the front lines back to field hospitals, and trained *paramedical* personnel—that is, nondoctors, usually known as *medics* or *corpsmen*—were first widely used in such situations. It took many decades for the wartime model to be applied effectively to ordinary peacetime medicine. With advances in medical technology (such as defibrillators, for restarting a heart after a heart attack), paramedics became an essential part of emergency medicine, and today hundreds of thousands of people owe their lives to paramedics. *Paraprofessionals* who work only in hospitals and clinics usually go by other titles.

paramilitary \ˌpa-rə-ˈmi-lə-ˌter-ē\ Relating to a force formed on a military pattern, especially as a possible backup military force.

• In the country's most remote regions, the real power was held by large landowners, who actually kept paramilitary forces, their own private armies, on their estates.

This term *paramilitary* can take in a wide range of organizations, but is usually applied to forces formed by a government. Groups opposing a government, even when organized along military lines, are more often referred to as guerrillas or insurgents. In countries with weak central governments (such as, in recent times, Afghanistan, Somalia, Iraq, or Congo), warlords may form their own paramilitary forces and take over all local police and military functions. *Paramilitary* often has a sinister sound today, since it's also applied to groups of off-duty military or police personnel who carry out illegal violence, often at night, with the quiet support of a government.

Quizzes

A. Choose the closest definition:

1. prerequisite   a. pattern   b. requirement   c. preference
     d. direction
2. paramedic   a. medical technician   b. hypodermic
     c. surgeon   d. nurse's aide
3. predispose   a. recycle   b. eliminate   c. demonstrate
     d. influence
4. paraphrase   a. spell out   b. shorten   c. lengthen
     d. reword
5. preclude   a. come before   b. come after   c. prevent
     d. predict
6. paralegal   a. lawful   b. lawyer-assisting
     c. above the law   d. barely legal
7. precocious   a. nearly cooked   b. maturing early
     c. self-contradictory   d. necessary
8. paramilitary   a. basic-training   b. skydiving
     c. semimilitary   d. police

B. Fill in each blank with the correct letter:

a. paraphrase   e. predispose
b. preclude   f. paramedic
c. precocious   g. prerequisite
d. paralegal   h. paramilitary

1. No one in her class of high-school seniors was able
   to _____ the proverb "Blood is thicker than water."
2. At 13 she was _____ enough to mingle with the guests
   at her parents' cocktail parties.
3. Everything I had heard about the guy from my friends
   didn't exactly _____ me to like him.

4. After a year as a _____ she knew she had the stomach for anything a doctor might have to face.
5. Any felony conviction in your past would _____ your getting a job with the state government.
6. At his law firm they treated almost everything involving real estate as _____ work.
7. The only _____ for taking the Galaxies course is a strong background in high-school math and physics.
8. Many of the crimes are apparently being carried out by members of secret _____ organizations made up of off-duty police and former soldiers.

META is a prefix in English that generally means "behind" or "beyond." In medicine, for example, the *metacarpal* bones are the hand bones that come right after, or beyond, the *carpal* or wrist bones. And *metalanguage* is language used to talk about language, which requires going beyond normal language.

---

metadata \ˌme-tə-ˈdā-tə\ Data that provides information about other data.

• Before putting videos up on the Web site, she always tags them with a decent set of metadata.

Metadata is electronic data that somehow describes an electronic file or its contents, and is usually included in the file itself. An important use for metadata is for searching. A piece of metadata might identify the file, its size, the date it was compiled, its nature, and so on. Metadata is particularly important for making pictures searchable; since a picture of a landscape in the Southwest, for example, can't be "read" by a search engine, data tags such as "Southwest," "mesa," and "arroyo" might be included in the digitized image file. The same can be done for audio files; the tags for a speech might read "Gore," "climate," and "Copenhagen." Metadata tags for a Web page, including tags identifying its most important content, ensure that the page won't be overlooked by a search engine.

metaphorical \ˌme-tə-ˈfȯr-i-kəl\ Relating to a figure of speech in which a word or phrase meaning one kind of object or idea is used in place of another to suggest a similarity between them.

- He always points out to his classes that metaphors can be found in poetry of all kinds, from "The eyes are the windows of the soul" to "You ain't nothin' but a hound dog."

Metaphor comes from a Greek word meaning "transfer" (or, to stay close to its roots, "carry beyond"). Thus, a metaphor transfers the meaning of one word or phrase to another. Metaphors often include a form of the verb *be* (as in the examples above), and they're often contrasted with similes, which are usually introduced by *like* or *as* ("O, my luve's like a red, red rose"). But, they don't have to include *be*; when you say that the teacher gave us a mountain of homework or that we're drowning in paperwork, these too are *metaphorical* statements.

metaphysics \,me-tə-'fi-ziks\ The part of philosophy having to do with the ultimate causes and basic nature of things.

- Most of the congregation prefers to hear their minister preach about virtue, and they get restless when his sermons head in the direction of metaphysics.

Just as *physics* deals with the laws that govern the physical world (such as those of gravity or the properties of waves), metaphysics describes what is beyond physics—the nature and origin of reality itself, the immortal soul, and the existence of a supreme being. Opinions about these *metaphysical* topics vary widely, since what's being discussed can't be observed or measured or even truly known to exist. So most metaphysical questions are still as far from a final answer as they were when Plato and Aristotle were asking them.

metonymy \mə-'tä-nə-mē\ A figure of speech in which the name of one thing is used for the name of something else that is associated with it or related to it.

- When Wall Street has the jitters, the White House issues a statement, and the people wait for answers from City Hall, metonymy is having a busy day.

At first glance, *metaphor* and *metonymy* seem close in meaning, but there are differences. In a metaphor we substitute one thing for something else that's usually quite different; for example, *Web* for a worldwide network of linked computers and their technology. In metonymy, we replace one word or phrase (such as "stock market" or "local government officials" in the examples above) with another word or phrase associated with it. Most familiar *metonyms* are place-names, such as *Hollywood* for "the film industry," or *K Street* for "Washington lobbyists." But saying "the press" to refer to the news media, or "sweat" to refer to hard work, could also be called metonymy.

PER is a Latin preposition that generally means "through," "throughout," or "thoroughly." Thus, *perforate* means "to bore through," *perennial* means "throughout the years," and *permanent* means "remaining throughout." And the "thoroughly" sense shows up in *persuade,* for "thoroughly advise," and *perverted,* "thoroughly turned around."

---

percolate \\'pər-kə-ˌlāt\\ (1) To trickle or filter through something porous. (2) To become spread through.

* She tells herself that the money she spends on luxuries eventually percolates down to the needy.

Percolate comes from a Latin verb meaning "to put through a sieve." Something that percolates filters through something else, just as small particles pass through a sieve. Water is drawn downward through the soil, and this *percolation* usually cleans the water. A slow rain is ideal for percolating into the soil, since in a violent rainstorm most of it quickly runs off. For this reason, drip irrigation is the most effective and water-conserving form of irrigation. Percolation isn't always a physical process; awareness of an issue may percolate slowly into the minds of the public, just as Spanish words may gradually percolate into English, often starting in the Southwest.

pervade \\pər-'vād\\ To spread through all parts of something.

* We all knew that more job cuts were coming, and the entire office was pervaded with anxiety.

Pervade can be used to describe something physical: a chemical odor may pervade a building, for example, and most scientists believe that outer space is pervaded by mysterious "dark matter." But the word usually doesn't refer to anything that could be detected by scientific instruments. Thus, humor may pervade a novel, gloom may pervade a gathering, and corruption may pervade a government. And something *pervasive* exists in every part of something: fatherlessness may be a pervasive problem in poor neighborhoods, for instance, and pervasive optimism sometimes causes the stock market to soar.

permeate \\'pər-mē-ˌāt\ (1) To spread throughout. (2) To pass through the pores or small openings of.

- On Saturday mornings back in those days, the aroma of fresh pies and breads would permeate almost every house on the block.

Permeate is often a synonym for *pervade.* We could say, for example, that at exam time the campus is either "permeated" or "pervaded" by a sense of dread. But the two words aren't identical. For one thing, *permeate* can mean simply "pass through," and is often used when talking about liquids; thus, a boot can be permeated by water, though certain oils make leather less *permeable,* and you might just want to buy boots made of *impermeable* material. And things may "pass through" in a nonphysical way as well; so you might say that anxiety about climate change has started to permeate into the public's consciousness—but once anxiety has become *pervasive* it's pretty much taken over.

persevere \ˌpər-sə-'vir\ To keep at something in spite of difficulties, opposition, or discouragement.

- For ten years she persevered in her effort to find out what the government knew about her husband's disappearance.

The early settlers of the New World persevered in the face of constant hardship and danger. The Pilgrims of Plymouth Plantation lost half their number in the first winter to disease and hunger, but their *perseverance* paid off, and within five years their community was healthy and self-sufficient. Perhaps more remarkable are all the solitary inventors who have persevered in pursuing their visions for years, lacking any financial support and laughed at by the public.

Quizzes

A. Fill in each blank with the correct letter:

a.	metaphorical	e.	permeate
b.	persevere	f.	metonymy
c.	metaphysics	g.	pervade
d.	percolate	h.	metadata

1. None of his audio or photo files have any _____ associated with them, so it's impossible to find them via an ordinary Web search.
2. She's extremely stubborn, so I'm sure she's going to _____ until the whole thing is completed.
3. When the Gypsy Carmen sings "Love is a wild bird," she's being _____.
4. We know that drugs now _____ the blue-collar workplace in many small Midwestern towns.
5. "Green Berets," the nickname for the U.S. Army Special Forces, is a good example of _____.
6. Before the Internet, it took many years before these ideas began to _____ the barriers that the government had set up.
7. In philosophy he loved _____ most, because it dealt with the deepest mysteries.
8. The liquid began to _____ through the blend of herbs and spices, giving off a delicious scent.

B. Match the word on the left to the correct definition on the right:

1.	persevere	a.	seep
2.	metonymy	b.	equating one thing with another
3.	permeate	c.	spread into
4.	metaphysics	d.	keep going
5.	pervade	e.	use of an associated term
6.	percolate	f.	study of the nature of things
7.	metaphorical	g.	information about other information
8.	metadata	h.	fill with something

ANT/ANTI is a Latin prefix meaning "against." An *anticlimax* is the opposite of a climax. An *antiseptic* or *antibiotic* fights germs. An *antacid* attacks acid in the stomach. And an *antidote* works against the effects of a poison.

antagonist \an-ˈta-gə-nist\ A person who opposes or is unfriendly toward another; an opponent.

* With supplies ordered from the Acme Company, Road Runner's constant antagonist, Wile E. Coyote, attempts one dastardly deed after another.

On the stage or screen, in a story or a novel, the *protagonist* is the main character and the antagonist is the opposing one. *Pro-* and *ant-* usually mark the good and bad characters, but not always; there may occasionally be an evil protagonist and a good antagonist. In the drama of the real world, it's especially hard to sort out which is which, so we usually speak of both parties to a conflict as antagonists. During a strike, for example, representatives of labor and management become antagonists; they often manage to *antagonize* each other, and the *antagonism* often remains after the strike is over.

antigen \ˈan-ti-ˌjen\ A chemical substance (such as a protein) that, when introduced into the body, causes the body to form antibodies against it.

* When the immune system is weak, it may not be able to produce enough antibodies to combat the invading antigens.

An *antibody* is a protein produced by your immune system to fight outside invaders. Since the enemy substance actually triggers the production of antibodies, such substances are called antigens—*anti-* being short for *antibody*, and *-gen* meaning "producer." (In a similar way, an *allergen* produces an allergy, and a *pathogen* produces a pathology or disease.) Antigens are often rodlike structures that stick out from the surface of an invading organism—usually a bacterium or a virus—and allow it to attach itself to cells in the invaded body. But unfortunately for them, in doing so they let the immune system know they're present, and the body is flooded with an army of Pac-Man-like antibodies.

antipathy \an-'ti-pə-thē\ A strong dislike.

- It seemed odd that he could feel such intense antipathy for someone he'd only met once, and we suspected there was more to the story.

When the nation of Yugoslavia was created in 1945, it combined a number of ethnic groups with a history of violent antipathy toward each other. In 1991–92 four regions of the country announced that they would become independent nations; a bloody six-year war followed, fueled by these ancient and powerful antipathies. The American Civil War similarly resulted from antipathy between the North and the South. But in the U.S.'s relations with its next-door neighbors, it's been a long time since emotions have gotten much stronger than annoyance.

antithesis \an-'ti-thə-səs\ (1) The contrast or opposition of ideas. (2) The exact opposite.

- Life on the small college campus, with its personal freedom and responsibility, was the antithesis of what many students had known in high school.

Writers and speechmakers use the traditional pattern known as antithesis for its resounding effect; John Kennedy's famous "ask not what your country can do for you—ask what you can do for your country" is an example. But *antithesis* normally means simply "opposite." Thus, war is the antithesis of peace, wealth is the antithesis of poverty, and love is the antithesis of hate. Holding two *antithetical* ideas in one's head at the same time—for example, that you're the sole master of your fate but also the helpless victim of your terrible upbringing—is so common as to be almost normal.

CONTRA is the Latin equivalent of *anti-*, and it too means essentially "against" or "contrary to." A *contrast* "stands against" something else that it's compared to. And *contrapuntal* music, as in the music of Bach, sets one melody against another played at the same time and produces harmony (which no one is opposed to).

---

contraband \'kän-trə-ˌband\ Goods that are forbidden by law to be owned or brought into or out of a country; smuggled goods.

- Late at night he would go driving through the desert on the interstate, peddling his contraband to wary gas-station attendants.

In Latin a *bannus* was an order or decree, so a *contrabannum* was something that went against a decree. This led to the Italian word *contrabbando,* from which we get *contraband*. Contraband items aren't always illegal; they may simply be things (such as cigarettes) that are meant to be taxed. So a dealer in untaxed contraband can charge a little less and still make enormous profits. Of course, if the item is actually forbidden, like illegal drugs, then the profits could be much greater.

contraindication \ˌkän-trə-ˌin-də-ˈkā-shən\ Something (such as a symptom or condition) that makes a particular treatment, medication, or procedure likely to be unsafe.

• A history of stomach ulcers is a contraindication to regular use of aspirin.

For doctors, an *indication* is a symptom or circumstance that makes a particular medical treatment desirable. Serious anxiety, for example, is often an indication for prescribing a tranquilizer. A contraindication, then, is a symptom or condition that makes a treatment risky, such as taking certain other medications at the same time. Drugs and conditions that are *contraindicated* for a medication are listed on its label, and reeled off at high speed in TV ads. Patients can guard against the dangers of drug interaction by reading labels carefully and making sure their doctors know what else they're currently taking.

contravene \ˌkän-trə-ˈvēn\ (1) To go against or act contrary to; to violate. (2) To oppose in an argument, to contradict.

• The power company was found to be contravening state and federal environmental standards for wastewater discharged into bodies of water.

Contravene is most often used in reference to laws. So a government may take a company to court claiming that its policies are in *contravention* of national labor laws. The contravention of copyright laws is a big topic today especially where electronic information is involved. And a country might be punished if a trade organization finds that it's contravening international trade agreements.

contrarian \kən-ˈtrer-ē-ən\ A person who takes a contrary position or attitude, especially an investor who buys shares of stock when most others are selling or sells when others are buying.

- My father was basically a contrarian, who never accepted the common wisdom and loved nothing so much as a good argument.

Anyone who thinks that most of what the public believes is wrong would be called a contrarian. And *contrarian* is a basic term in the vocabulary of investing. In fact, most successful investors often behave like contrarians by "buying low and selling high"—that is, buying stocks that are cheap because most investors put a low value on them but that have the possibility of rising, and selling stocks that most investors are valuing highly but that seem likely to decline. The word may be most common as an adjective; so you may express a *contrarian* opinion, hold a contrarian view, or pursue a contrarian investment strategy.

Quizzes

A. Complete the analogy:

1. champion : hero :: antagonist : _____
   a. comrade b. supporter c. opponent d. thug
2. harm : benefit :: contraindication : _____
   a. denial b. refusal c. injection d. indication
3. truth : fact :: antithesis : _____
   a. same b. opposite c. enemy d. friend
4. opposite : equal :: contrarian : _____
   a. contrast b. conformist c. contradiction d. conflict
5. misery : joy :: antipathy : _____
   a. disgust b. confusion c. opposition d. liking
6. accept : oppose :: contravene : _____
   a. go around b. violate c. obey d. distrust
7. cause : effect :: antigen : _____
   a. germs b. blood c. antibody d. genes
8. idol : adored :: contraband : _____
   a. useful b. opposed c. smuggled d. expensive

B. Indicate whether the following pairs of words have the same or different meanings:

1. antithesis / opposite   same ___ / different ___
2. contrarian / opponent   same ___ / different ___
3. antipathy / affection   same ___ / different ___
4. contraindication / benefit   same ___ / different ___

5.	contravene / violate	same ___ / different ___
6.	antigen / antibody	same ___ / different ___
7.	antagonist / enemy	same ___ / different ___
8.	contraband / antidote	same ___ / different ___

Greek and Latin Borrowings

in memoriam \\ˌin-mə-ˈmȯr-ē-əm\ In memory of.

- The message on the pedestal begins "In memoriam" and then lists the names of the local young men who died in World War I.

Since the days of the Roman empire, the words *In memoriam*, followed by a name, have been found on monuments and gravestones. They may also appear in the dedication of a book or poem; Alfred Tennyson's greatest poem is his immense *In Memoriam*, written over a period of 17 years to mourn the death of his dear friend Arthur Hallam.

magnum opus \ˈmag-nəm-ˈō-pəs\ A great work, especially the greatest achievement of an artist, composer, or writer.

- No one was exactly sure what the massive novel was about, but everyone was certain that it was his magnum opus.

The greatest work of a great artist may be hard to agree on. Many would pick Rembrandt's *The Night Watch*, Mozart's *Don Giovanni,* Ovid's *Metamorphoses,* Dante's *Divine Comedy,* Wren's St. Paul's Cathedral, and Michelangelo's Sistine Chapel murals. But for Shakespeare, would it be *Hamlet* or *King Lear*? For Mahler, *The Song of the Earth* or the Ninth Symphony? For the Marx Brothers, *A Day at the Races* or *A Night at the Opera*?

memento mori \mə-ˈmen-tō-ˈmȯr-ē\ A reminder of mortality, especially a human skull symbolizing death.

- The first twinges of arthritis often serve as a vivid memento mori for middle-aged jocks trying to ignore their advancing years.

Memento mori literally means "Remember you must die." The early Puritan settlers were particularly aware of death and fearful of what it might mean, so a Puritan tombstone will often display a memento mori intended for the living. These death's-heads or skulls may strike us as ghoulish, but they helped keep the living on the straight and narrow for fear of eternal punishment. In earlier centuries, an educated European might place an actual skull on his desk to keep the idea of death always present in his mind.

habeas corpus \\ˈhā-bē-əs-ˈkȯr-pəs\\ An order to bring a jailed person before a judge or court to find out if that person should really be in jail.

• The country has a primitive legal system with no right of habeas corpus, and suspects often are shot before they ever see a judge.

The literal meaning of *habeas corpus* is "You shall have the body"— that is, the judge must have the person charged with a crime brought into the courtroom to hear what he's been charged with. Through much of human history, and in many countries still today, a person may be imprisoned on the orders of someone in the government and kept behind bars for years without ever getting a chance to defend himself, or even knowing what he's done wrong. In England, the right to be brought before a judge to hear the charges and answer them was written into law over 300 years ago, and the U.S. adopted the British practice in its Constitution.

rigor mortis \\ˈri-gər-ˈmȯr-təs\\ The temporary rigidity of muscles that sets in after death.

• The coroner could tell from the progress of rigor mortis that death had occurred no more than six hours earlier.

Rigor mortis, which translates from Latin as "stiffness of death," sets in quickly and usually ends three or four days after death. The condition results from a lack of certain chemicals in the muscles; it may be affected by muscular activity before death as well as the external temperature. Mystery writers frequently make use of rigor mortis as a means by which the detective or the examiner can determine the time of the victim's death, which often turns out to be all-important in solving the case.

sine qua non \\ˌsi-ni-ˌkwä-ˈnōn\\ An essential thing.

• Good planning is the sine qua non of a successful dinner party.

Sine qua non can be translated literally as "Without which, not." Though this may sound like gibberish, it means more or less "Without (something), (something else) won't be possible." *Sine qua non* sounds slightly literary, and it shouldn't be used just anywhere. But it actually shows up in many contexts, including business ("A solid customer base is the sine qua non to success"), show business ("A good agent is a sine qua non for an actor's career"), and politics ("His support was really the sine qua non for her candidacy").

tabula rasa \\'ta-byu̇-lə-'rä-sə\\ (1) The mind in its blank or unmarked state before receiving any impressions from outside. (2) Something existing in its original pure state.

• As for knowing what life outside of his little village was like, he was practically a tabula rasa.

In ancient Rome, a student in class would write on a wax-covered wooden tablet, or *tabula*, using a sticklike implement. At the end of the day, the marks could be scraped off, leaving a fresh, unmarked tablet—a *tabula rasa*—for the next day's lessons. But even before the Romans, the Greek philosopher Aristotle had called the mind at birth an "unmarked tablet." We still use the term today, but usually not very seriously; with what we know about biology and genetics, most of us don't really think there's nothing in a mind at birth.

terra incognita \\'ter-ə-ˌin-ˌkäg-'nē-tə\\ An unexplored country or field of knowledge.

• We've been to Phoenix once, but otherwise Arizona is terra incognita.

When Roman mapmakers drew a land area that no one had yet explored, they often labeled it "Terra Incognita"—that is, "Unknown Territory"—and the term continued to be used for centuries afterward. When Columbus and his successors first crossed the Atlantic, they entered upon terra incognita, a land that came to be called the "New World." But the term is just as useful for mental exploration. For most of us, subjects such as particle physics, French 17th-century drama, and soil mechanics are terra incognita, and we can only hope to live long enough to be able to explore some of them someday.

Quiz

Fill in each blank with the correct letter:

a. rigor mortis   e. in memoriam
b. magnum opus   f. terra incognita
c. sine qua non   g. memento mori
d. habeas corpus   h. tabula rasa

1. The entire field of quantum physics is _____ to me.
2. She claimed there was no such thing as the _____ of a successful novel, since great novels are so different.
3. *The Rite of Spring* is often regarded as Igor Stravinsky's _____.
4. To judge from the degree of _____, she appeared to have died no later than 4:00 a.m.
5. The monument listed the brave men and women who had died in the war, under the words "_____."
6. As for knowledge about home repair, his mind is a _____.
7. In legal systems without _____, individuals are often locked up for years without ever knowing the charges against them.
8. Just accept those first gray hairs as a little _____.

Review Quizzes

A. Complete the analogy:

1. brief : extended :: hyperactive : _____
   a. exaggerated b. young c. required d. calm
2. unconscious : aware :: subliminal : _____
   a. underneath b. noticeable c. deep d. regular
3. prefer : favor :: preclude : _____
   a. assume b. expect c. prevent d. avoid
4. awareness : ignorance :: hyperbole : _____
   a. exaggeration b. understatement c. calm
   d. excitement
5. permit : allow :: permeate : _____
   a. ignore b. move c. penetrate d. recover

6. night : dark :: sine qua non : _____
   a. necessary b. nonessential c. thorough
   d. objective
7. fondness : affection :: antipathy : _____
   a. love b. rejection c. solution d. distaste
8. edit : revise :: paraphrase : _____
   a. dedicate b. praise c. restate d. compose
9. tolerate : accept :: contravene : _____
   a. argue b. violate c. oppose d. throw out
10. dispute : argument :: antithesis : _____
    a. dislike b. agreement c. danger d. opposite

B. Fill in each blank with the correct letter:

a. pervade   i. rigor mortis
b. memento mori   j. contraindication
c. metaphysics   k. antigen
d. antagonist   l. subconscious
e. metadata   m. metaphorical
f. in memoriam   n. contrarian
g. precocious   o. subjugate
h. hyperventilate

1. She was a smart and _____ child who could read by
   the age of three.
2. He senses that a negative tone has begun to _____ the
   school in the last couple of years.
3. The preserved body sits on a chair behind glass in
   public view like a strange _____.
4. In Iraq, many years of government brutality failed to
   fully _____ the people called the Kurds.
5. There's so much difficult _____ language in the poem
   that critics have had a hard time interpreting it.
6. The death was so recent that _____ hadn't yet set in.
7. Late-night discussions in the dorm often became
   arguments about deep topics such as _____.
8. Pregnancy is a _____ to taking the measles vaccine.
9. The initial tests look for the _____ associated with
   tumors of this kind.
10. The _____ for the photos on his blog site includes
    identification of every single person in them.
11. At the end of each year, the magazine includes a section
    called "_____," which lists all the important figures
    who died that year.

12. The chief _____ of the Republican Party is the Democratic Party, and vice versa.

13. He keeps dinner parties lively with his _____ arguments, which nobody ever agrees with.

14. When my 12-year-old gets anxious, he often starts to _____, and it's caused him to pass out a couple of times.

15. Was it some _____ fear that made her forget the interview?

C. Choose the closest definition:

1. metaphorical   a. symbolic b. literary c. descriptive d. extensive

2. subversion   a. sabotage b. undertow c. turnover d. overture

3. predispose   a. recycle b. subdue c. spread d. influence

4. sine qua non   a. requirement b. exception c. allowance d. objection

5. antithesis   a. opponent b. opposite c. disadvantage d. argument

6. precocious   a. previous b. ripe c. early-maturing d. clever

7. tabula rasa   a. partial truth b. complete ignorance c. slight contamination d. pure trash

8. percolate   a. boil b. spread c. restore d. seep

9. contravene   a. go against b. retrieve c. dance d. object

10. terra incognita   a. new information b. unknown cause c. unexplored territory d. old suspicion

11. contraband   a. smuggled goods b. trade surplus c. customs d. imports

12. prerequisite   a. requirement b. reservation c. influence d. decision

13. metonymy   a. rate of growth b. exaggeration c. model of perfection d. use of a related word

14. persevere   a. carry off b. resume c. inquire d. carry on

15. hypertension   a. anxiety b. tightness c. high blood pressure d. duodenal ulcer

UNIT

22

ACER/ACR comes from the Latin adjective *acer*, meaning "sharp" or "sour." Grapefruit and limes have an *acid* taste; *acid* can also describe a person's sense of humor (other words for it might be *sharp* or *biting*). The *acidity* of the soil often indicates whether it's good for growing certain crops; blueberries, for instance, love acid soil, so they're more likely to be found east of the Mississippi River, where acid soil is the rule.

---

acerbic \ə-ˈsər-bik\ Sharp or biting in temper, mood, or tone.

- She had enjoyed his acerbic humor for years, but then a friend told her about the nasty jokes he was making about her behind her back.

Acerbic often describes wit. An acerbic critic won't make many friends among the writers or artists whose work is being criticized, but often keeps his or her readers amused and entertained. *Acerbity* may be slightly less sharp than sarcasm, but not much; both words have roots meaning basically "cut."

acrid \ˈa-krəd\ Unpleasantly sharp and harsh; bitter.

- The acrid odor of gunpowder hung in the air long after the shots' echoes had died away.

Acrid exactly fits the smoke from a fire—a burning building or forest, for example. Dense smog may cast an acrid pall over a city, making throats burn and eyes sting. But, like *acid* and *acerbic*, *acrid* sometimes also describes nonphysical things, such as the remarks of a bitter person.

acrimony \ˈa-krə-ˌmō-nē\ Harsh or bitter sharpness in words, manner, or temper.

• Town meetings here were usually civilized, and no one could recall an issue that had ever aroused such intense acrimony as the new pulp mill.

Acrimony is angry harshness that usually springs from intense personal dislike. An *acrimonious* exchange is full of cutting, unpleasant remarks designed to hurt. Civil wars are often more acrimonious and bloody than foreign wars. In the same way, a bad divorce may be more acrimonious than any other kind of legal battle.

exacerbate \ig-ˈza-sər-ˌbāt\ To make worse, more violent, or more severe.

• The increase in coal-burning power plants has greatly exacerbated the buildup of greenhouse gases.

To exacerbate is not to cause, but only to make something bad even worse. So the loss of a major industry in a city may exacerbate its already serious unemployment problem. A vicious remark can exacerbate a quarrel. Building a new mall may exacerbate an area's existing traffic problems. A new drug can exacerbate the side effects of the drug a patient is already taking. It used to be thought that too much blood in the body exacerbated a fever, so the patient's blood would be drained, often by means of leeches—and not all patients survived.

STRICT comes from the Latin verb meaning "to draw tight, bind, or tie." So the English word *strict* means "tightly controlled." And when someone begins a sentence "Strictly speaking, . . ." you know he or she is going to be talking about a word or idea in its most limited sense, "drawing tight" the meaning till it's as narrow as possible.

stricture \ˈstrik-chər\ (1) A law or rule that limits or controls something; restriction. (2) A strong criticism.

• There are severe legal strictures on the selling of marijuana in almost every state.

Stricture has meant many things through the centuries, and its "restriction" meaning—probably the most common one today—is actually the most recent. High-school teachers often put strictures on texting during class. Cities concerned about their murder rate have slapped strictures on the possession of handguns. And the United Nations may vote to put strictures on arms sales to a country that keeps violating international treaties. With the meaning "strong criticism," *stricture* is slightly old-fashioned today, but it's still used by intellectuals. So, for example, an article may amount to a harsh stricture on the whole medical profession, or an art review may just express the critic's strictures on sentimental paintings of cute little houses with glowing windows.

restrictive \ri-'strik-tiv\ (1) Serving or likely to keep within bounds. (2) Serving or tending to place under limits as to use.

• The deed to the property had a restrictive covenant forbidding any development of the land for 50 years.

Restrictive covenants (that is, agreements) in real-estate deeds were once used to forbid the buyer from ever selling the property to anyone of another race. These are now illegal, though other kinds of restrictive covenants are very common; in some neighborhoods, they may even tell you what colors you can't paint your house. In grammar, a restrictive clause is one that limits the meaning of something that comes before it. In the sentence "That's the professor who I'm trying to avoid," "who I'm trying to avoid" is a restrictive clause, since it's what identifies the professor. But in the sentence "That's my History professor, who I'm trying to avoid," the same clause is *nonrestrictive*, since the professor has already been identified as "my History professor." There should always be a comma before a nonrestrictive clause, but not before a restrictive clause.

constrict \kən-'strikt\ (1) To draw together or make narrow. (2) To limit.

• She felt that small towns, where everyone seems to know every move you make and is just waiting to gossip about it, can constrict your life terribly.

Arteries constricted by cholesterol slow the flow of blood, just as traffic arteries or highways constricted by accidents slow the flow of traffic. But *constriction* isn't always physical. Economic growth may be constricted by trade barriers. A narrow, constricted life may be the result of poverty or lack of opportunity. And an actress may feel constricted by a role she played as a child or by her TV character from years ago, which the public refuses to forget.

vasoconstrictor \ˌvā-zō-kən-ˈstrik-tər\ Something such as a nerve fiber or a drug that narrows a blood vessel.

• For operations like this, my dentist likes to use a vasoconstrictor to keep bleeding to a minimum.

Our blood vessels are constantly narrowing and widening in response to our activity or our environment, constricting in order to retain body heat and widening to get rid of excess heat. So when we're hot our skin flushes, and when we're very cold we become pale. Since the width of the blood vessels affects blood pressure, vasoconstrictors are prescribed to treat low blood pressure. Vasoconstrictors include antihistamines and amphetamines, as well as nicotine and caffeine; we commonly buy them for our runny noses and bloodshot eyes as well. The opposite of vasoconstrictors are *vasodilators*, which are commonly used to treat high blood pressure.

Quizzes

A. Indicate whether the following pairs of words have the same or different meanings:

1. exacerbate / worsen   same __ / different __
2. acrid / dry   same __ / different __
3. acrimony / divorce payment   same __ / different __
4. acerbic / harsh   same __ / different __
5. constrict / assemble   same __ / different __
6. restrictive / limiting   same __ / different __
7. vasoconstrictor /
   Amazon snake   same __ / different __
8. stricture / tightening   same __ / different __

B. Fill in each blank with the correct letter:

a. stricture   e. acerbic
b. vasoconstrictor   f. acrimony
c. constrict   g. acrid
d. stringent   h. exacerbate

1. The list of new demands only served to _____ the crisis.
2. The _____ that Olympic athletes be amateurs would sometimes get an athlete banned because of a few dollars he or she had earned as a professional.
3. The _____ fumes in the plant irritated his eyes and nose for several days.
4. With four or five _____ comments she managed to annoy or insult almost everyone in the room.
5. Soon after the banking scandal hit the newspapers, a new set of _____ regulations was announced.
6. She was given a _____ for the tooth extraction, but there was some bleeding anyway.
7. These deposits are beginning to _____ the coronary arteries to a dangerous degree.
8. Even for a child-custody case, the _____ between the parties was unusual.

STRU/STRUCT comes from the Latin verb *struere*, meaning "to put together, build, arrange." A *structure* is something that's been *constructed*,—that is, built or put together. *Instructions* tell how the pieces should be arranged. Something that *obstructs* is a barrier that's been "built" to stand in your way. And something *destructive* "unbuilds."

deconstruction \ˌdē-kən-ˈstrək-shən\ Analysis of texts, works of art, and cultural patterns that is intended to expose the assumptions on which they are based, especially by exposing the limitations of language.

• Deconstruction has been performed on *Huckleberry Finn* by English professors so many times that it's a wonder there's anything left of it.

Deconstruction doesn't actually mean "demolition"; instead it means "breaking down" or analyzing something (especially the words in a work of fiction or nonfiction) to discover its true significance, which is supposedly almost never exactly what the author intended. A feminist may *deconstruct* an old novel to show how even an innocent-seeming story somehow depends on the oppression of women. A new western may deconstruct the myths of the old West and show lawmen as vicious and criminals as flawed but decent. Table manners, *The Sound of Music,* and cosmetics ads have all been the subjects of *deconstructionist* analysis. Of course, not everyone agrees with deconstructionist interpretations, and some people reject the whole idea of deconstruction, but most of us have run into it by now even if we didn't realize it.

infrastructure \\'in-frə-ˌstrək-chər\ (1) The underlying foundation or basic framework. (2) A system of public works.

• The public loved her speeches about crime but dozed off when she brought up highway repair and infrastructure deterioration.

Infra- means "below"; so the infrastructure is the "underlying structure" of a country and its economy, the fixed installations that it needs in order to function. These include roads, bridges, dams, the water and sewer systems, railways and subways, airports, and harbors. These are generally government-built and publicly owned. Some people also speak about such things as the intellectual infrastructure or the infrastructure of science research, but the meaning of such notions can be extremely vague.

construe \kən-'strü\ (1) To explain the arrangement and meaning of words in a sentence. (2) To understand or explain; interpret.

• She asked how I had construed his last e-mail, and I told her that something about it had left me very worried.

Construe can usually be translated as "interpret." It's often used in law; thus, an Attorney General might construe the term "serious injury" in a child-abuse law to include bruises, or a judge might construe language about gifts to "heirs" to include spouses. The IRS's *construal* of some of your activities might be different from your own—and much more expensive at tax time. Construing is also close to translating; so when the British say "public school," for instance, it should be construed or translated as "prep school" in American terms.

instrumental \ˌin-strə-'men-təl\ (1) Acting as a means, agent, or tool. (2) Relating to an instrument, especially a musical instrument.

• His mother had been instrumental in starting the new arts program at the school, for which she was honored at the spring ceremony.

An *instrument* is a tool, something used to *construct*. It's often a tool for making music. A musical saw happens to be a carpenter's tool that can be played with a violin bow (though you probably wouldn't want to play a wrench or a pair of pliers). The musical meanings of *instrumental*, as in "It starts with an instrumental piece" or "a jazz *instrumental*," are common. But the meanings "helpful," "useful," and "essential," as in "He was instrumental in getting my book published," are just as common.

PROP/PROPRI comes from the Latin word *proprius*, meaning "own." A *proprietor* is an owner, and *property* is what he or she owns. And the original meaning of *proper* was "belonging to oneself'," so a writer around the year 1400 could say "With his own proper sword he was slain," even if we might not say it quite the same way today.

---

proprietary \prə-ˈprī-ə-ˌter-ē\ (1) Relating to an owner or proprietor; made or sold by one who has the sole right to do so. (2) Privately owned and run as a profit-making organization.

• The local hospital was a not-for-profit institution, whereas the nearby nursing homes were proprietary.

A proprietary process is a manufacturing process that others are forbidden to use, and a proprietary trademark is a name that only the owner can use. Legal rights of this kind are ensured by copyrights and patents. After a certain period of time, inventions and processes lose their legal protection, cease to be proprietary, and enter the "public domain," meaning that everyone can use them freely. Baseball fans often take a proprietary attitude toward their favorite team—that is, they behave more or less as if they own it, even though the only thing they may own is the right to yell from a bleacher seat till the end of a game.

propriety \prə-ˈprī-ə-tē\ (1) The state of being proper; appropriateness. (2) Acting according to what is socially acceptable, especially in conduct between the sexes.

• Propriety used to forbid a young unmarried man and woman to go almost anywhere without an adult.

In an earlier era, when social manners were far more elaborate than they are today, *propriety* and *impropriety* were words in constant use. Today we're more likely to use them in other contexts. We may talk about the propriety of government officials' dealings with private citizens, the propriety of the relationship between a lawyer and a judge, or the impropriety of speaking out of turn in a meeting that follows Robert's rules of order. Relations between men and women still present questions of propriety, but today it's often in the workplace rather than in social settings. Wherever rules, principles, and standard procedures have been clearly stated, propriety can become an issue. Something *improper* usually isn't actually illegal, but it makes people uncomfortable by giving the impression that something isn't quite right.

appropriate \ə-ˈprō-prē-ˌāt\ (1) To take exclusive possession of, often without right. (2) To set apart for a particular purpose or use.

- It was one of those insulting words that sometimes get appropriated by a group that it's meant to insult, which then starts using it proudly and defiantly.

From its roots, the verb *appropriate* would mean basically "make one's own"—that is, "take," or sometimes "grab." Each year the President and Congress create a budget and appropriate funds for each item in it, funds which mostly come in the form of taxes from the public. In the House of Representatives, the powerful *Appropriations* Committee often gets the last word on how much money goes to each program. "*Misappropriation* of funds," on the other hand, is a nice way of saying "theft." If someone appropriated pieces of your novel, you might take him or her to court; and if you appropriated trade secrets from your former employers, you might be the one sued.

expropriate \ek-ˈsprō-prē-ˌāt\ (1) To take away the right of possession or ownership. (2) To transfer to oneself.

- It was only when the country's new government threatened to expropriate the American oil refineries that Congress became alarmed.

In ancient Rome, an emperor could condemn a wealthy senator, have him killed, and expropriate his property. In 1536 Henry VIII declared himself head of the new Church of England and expropriated the lands and wealth of the Roman Catholic monasteries. And nearly all of North America was expropriated from the American

Indians, usually without any payment at all. Today, democratic governments only carry out legal *expropriations*, in which the owners are *properly* paid for their land—for example, when a highway or other public project needs to be built.

Quizzes

A. Complete the analogy:

1. grant : award :: expropriate : _____
   a. find b. want c. move d. claim

2. consumer goods : cars :: infrastructure : _____
   a. foundation b. surface c. bridges d. boats

3. accept : receive :: appropriate : _____
   a. send b. lose c. take d. offer

4. solve : figure out :: construe : _____
   a. build b. misspell c. tighten d. interpret

5. habit : practice :: propriety : _____
   a. appropriateness b. property c. behavior
   d. proportion

6. description : portrayal :: deconstruction : _____
   a. demolition b. interpretation c. transference
   d. translation

7. monetary : money :: proprietary : _____
   a. prosperity b. property c. profit d. protection

8. practical : effective :: instrumental : _____
   a. hardworking b. tool-shaped c. instructional
   d. useful

B. Indicate whether the following pairs of terms have the same or different meanings:

1. proprietary / public   same ___ / different ___
2. construe / explain   same ___ / different ___
3. appropriate / take   same ___ / different ___
4. infrastructure / dome   same ___ / different ___
5. propriety / ownership   same ___ / different ___
6. instrumental / melodic   same ___ / different ___
7. expropriate / seize   same ___ / different ___
8. deconstruction / demolition   same ___ / different ___

TORT comes from a form of the Latin verb *torquere*, meaning "to twist, wind, or wrench." In *torture*, parts of the body may be wrenched or twisted or stretched; so those "Indian sunburns" that schoolkids give by twisting in different directions on some unlucky guy's wrist stay pretty close to *torture*'s original meaning.

tort \\'tòrt\\ A wrongful act that does not involve breach of contract and for which the injured party can receive damages in a civil action.

• The manufacturer was almost bankrupted by the massive tort actions brought by employees harmed by asbestos.

Tort came into English straight from French many centuries ago, and it still looks a little odd. Its root meaning of "twisted" (as opposed to "straight") obviously came to mean "wrong" (as opposed to "right"). Every first-year law student takes a course in the important subject of torts. Torts include all the so-called "product-liability" cases, against manufacturers of cars, household products, children's toys, and so on. They also cover dog bites, slander and libel, and a huge variety of other very personal cases of injury, both mental and physical—Torts class is never dull. If you're sued for a tort and lose, you usually have to pay "damages"—that is, a sum of money—to the person who you wronged.

extort \\ik-'stòrt\\ To obtain from a person by force, threats, or illegal power.

• She had tried to extort money from a film star, claiming that he was the father of her baby.

To extort is literally to wrench something out of someone. *Extortion* is a mainstay of organized crime. Just as the school bully extorts lunch money from the smaller kids in exchange for not beating them up, thugs extort "protection" money from business owners with threats of violence. But that's only one kind of extortion; a mobster might extort favors from a politician with threats of revealing some dark secret, just as you might extort a favor from a brother or sister by promising not to tell on them.

contort \\kən-'tòrt\\ To twist in a violent manner.

• The governor's explanation of his affair was so contorted that it only made matters worse for him.

Circus *contortionists* are known for twisting their bodies into pretzels; such *contortions* tend to be easier for females than for males, and much easier for the young than for the old. When trying to say something uncomfortable or dishonest, people often go through verbal contortions. But when someone else "twists" something you said or did, we usually say instead that they've *distorted* it.

tortuous \'tȯr-chə-wəs\ (1) Having many twists, bends, or turns; winding. (2) Crooked or tricky; involved, complex.

* The road over the mountains was long and dangerously tortuous, and as you rounded the sharp corners you could never see whether a huge truck might be barreling down toward you.

A labyrinth is a tortuous maze. The first labyrinth was built as a prison for the monstrous Minotaur, half bull and half man; only by holding one end of a thread was the heroic Theseus able to enter and slay the Minotaur and then exit. A tortuous problem, a tortuous history, and the tortuous path of a bill through Congress all have many unexpected twists and turns; a tortuous explanation or argument may be too crooked for its own good. Don't confuse *tortuous* with *torturous*, which means "tortured" or "painfully unpleasant"; *tortuous* has nothing to do with torture.

VIV comes from *vivere*, the Latin verb meaning "to live or be alive." A *survivor* has lived through something terrible. A *revival* brings something back to life, whether it's an old film, interest in a long-dead novelist, or religious enthusiasm in a group, maybe in a huge tent in the countryside.

---

vivacious \vī-'vā-shəs\ Lively in an attractive way.

* For the cheerleading squad, only the most outgoing, energetic, and vivacious of the students get chosen.

Vivacious can be used to describe a piece of music or writing, but it's generally used today to describe people, and particularly women. The main female characters in Shakespeare's plays—Beatrice in *Much Ado About Nothing*, Rosalind in *As You Like It,* and Portia in *The Merchant of Venice*, for example—are often full of humor, spirit, and *vivacity*.

bon vivant \ˌbän-vē-'vänt\ A sociable person with a love of excellent food and drink.

- My uncle and aunt were bons vivants, and could usually be found in the evening at a swank midtown bar surrounded by a crowd of tipsy merrymakers.

Bon vivant comes straight from French, where it means literally "good liver," and is still pronounced in the French way, though we've actually been using it in English since the 17th century. A proper bon vivant has some money and lots of friends and plenty of style and knows a good wine and can tell a great story and loves to laugh. Because of all these requirements, true bons vivants are rather rare—but that doesn't mean there aren't plenty of people who hope to be one someday.

revivify \rē-ˈvi-və-ˌfī\ To give new life to; bring back to life.

- All their efforts to revivify the boys' club seemed to be getting them nowhere, till one of the board members had a great idea.

Worn-out soil may be revivified by careful organic tending. A terrific new recruit can revivify a discouraged football team, and an imaginative and energetic new principal can revivify a failing high school. After World War II, one European country after another was slowly revivified, their economies and cultural life gradually coming back to life. Notice that *revivify* looks like some other words with very similar meanings, such as *revive, revitalize,* and *reinvigorate.*

vivisection \ˈvi-və-ˌsek-shən\ Operation on living animals, often for experimental purposes.

- The lab attempts to avoid vivisection in its research, concentrating instead on alternative methods that have been developed.

Vivisection includes the Latin root *sect,* meaning "cut." The Greek physician Galen, who lived during the 2nd century A.D., practiced vivisection on live monkeys and dogs to learn such things as the role of the spinal cord in muscle activity and whether veins and arteries carry air or blood; his findings formed the basis of medical practice for more than a thousand years. Vivisection continues to be used in drug and medical research today, but often in secret, since it makes most people very uncomfortable and some groups are violently opposed to it.

Quizzes

A. Fill in each blank with the correct letter:

a. revivify   e. extort
b. tort   f. vivisection
c. vivacious   g. contort
d. tortuous   h. bon vivant

1. He was horrified by _____, and even protested the dissecting of frogs in biology class.
2. She was able to _____ her body so as to fit entirely into a box 20 inches square.
3. As the daughter of a _____, she was used to having her parents leave her with a babysitter most evenings while they enjoyed themselves in the downtown bars and restaurants.
4. A group of new young teachers had managed to _____ the school.
5. In a _____ case, unlike a criminal case, the government doesn't get involved.
6. We carefully made our way down the steep and _____ trail.
7. Marie is the _____ one and Jan is the serious one.
8. He tried to _____ a B from his math teacher by saying that, if he couldn't play because of bad grades, they'd lose and everyone would blame her.

B. Choose the closest definition:

1. vivacious   a. sweet-tempered   b. loud   c. lively d. gluttonous
2. extort   a. obtain by force   b. pay up   c. engage in crime   d. exterminate
3. vivisection   a. living area   b. animal experimentation   c. experimental treatment   d. removal of organs
4. contort   a. perform   b. twist   c. squeeze   d. expand
5. bon vivant   a. dieter   b. partyer   c. chocolate candy d. nightclub act
6. tortuous   a. painful   b. winding   c. harmful d. monstrous
7. revivify   a. revive   b. reclaim   c. retain   d. restrain
8. tort   a. deformity   b. law   c. product   d. wrongful act

SERV means "to be subject to." A *servant* is the person who *serves* you with meals and provides other necessary *services*. A tennis or volleyball *serve* puts the ball in play, much as a servant puts food on the table.

serviceable \\'sər-və-sə-bəl\\ (1) Helpful or useful. (2) Usable.

• In the attic they found some chairs and a table, which, with a new coat of paint, became quite serviceable for informal get-togethers.

Someone who speaks serviceable Spanish isn't fluent in it but gets by pretty well. A serviceable jacket is practical and maybe even rugged. But *serviceable* sometimes damns with faint praise. A serviceable performance is all right but not inspired. Serviceable curtains aren't the ideal color or pattern, but they *serve* their purpose. A serviceable pair of shoes is sturdy but won't win you any fashion points.

servile \\'sər-ˌvīl\\ (1) Suitable to a servant. (2) Humbly submissive.

• The dog's manner was servile, and it lacked a healthy independence.

During the Middle Ages, most of the farming was done by a servile class known as *serfs,* who enjoyed hardly any personal freedom. This began to change in the 14th century; but the Russian serfs weren't freed until the 1860s, when the servile class in the U.S. was also freed. But *servile* today usually refers to a personal manner; a person who shows *servility* usually isn't a *servant,* but simply seems too eager to please and seems to lack self-respect.

servitude \\'sər-və-ˌtüd\\ A state or condition of slavery or bondage to another.

• She spent an entire summer working at a resort under conditions that felt like utter servitude.

Servitude is slavery or anything resembling it. The entire black population of colonial America lived in permanent servitude. And millions of the whites who populated this country arrived in "indentured servitude," obliged to pay off the cost of their journey with several years of labor. Servitude comes in many forms, of course: in the bad old days of the British navy, it was said that the difference between going to sea and going to jail was that you were less likely to drown in jail.

subservient \səb-ˈsər-vē-ənt\ (1) Serving or useful in an inferior situation or capacity. (2) Slavishly obedient.

• Many have wondered why Congress always seems subservient to the financial industry, supporting it even when the voters are angrily calling for reforms.

Since *sub-* means "below," it emphasizes the lower position of the person in the subservient one. Soldiers of a given rank are always subservient to those of a higher rank; this *subservience* is symbolized by the requirement that they salute their superior at every opportunity. Women have often been forced into subservient relationships with men. A small nation may feel subservient to its more powerful neighbor, obliged to obey even when it doesn't want to. So subservience usually brings with it a good dose of resentment.

CLUS comes from the Latin *claudere*, "to close." Words based on the Latin verb often have forms in which the *d* becomes an *s*. So, for example, *include*, which once meant "to shut up or enclose" and now means "to contain," has the related word *inclusive*, which means "including everything."

---

occlusion \ə-ˈklü-zhən\ An obstruction or blockage; the act of obstructing or closing off.

• The doctors worry that a loosened piece of plaque from the artery wall could lead to an occlusion of a brain artery, resulting in a stroke.

Occlusion, formed with the prefix *ob-*, here meaning "in the way," occurs when something has been closed up or blocked off. Almost all heart attacks are the result of the occlusion of a coronary (heart) artery by a blood clot, and many strokes are caused by an occlusion in an artery serving the brain. When a person's upper and lower teeth form a *malocclusion*, they close incorrectly or badly. An occlusion, or *occluded* front, happens when a fast-moving cold front overtakes a slow-moving warm front and slides underneath it, lifting the warm air and blocking its movement.

exclusive \iks-ˈklü-siv\ (1) Not shared; available to only one person or group, especially those from a high social class. (2) Full and complete.

• That technology is exclusive to one cell-phone manufacturer, but some of the others are dying to use it.

In words such as *expel*, *export*, and *exclusive*, the prefix *ex-* means "out of, outside." Thus, to *exclude* means basically to close the door in order to keep someone or something out. When the word appears in an advertisement, it's often making an appeal to snobs. An "exclusive" offer is supposedly made to only a few people; not so many years ago, "exclusive" housing developments excluded those of a certain race or color. If a product is being sold *exclusively* by one store, you won't be able to find it anywhere else. When a newspaper or news show has an *exclusive*, it's a story that no one else has yet reported. *Exclusive*'s antonym is *inclusive*; an inclusive policy, an inclusive church, or an inclusive approach is one that aims to include as many people as possible.

recluse \ˈre-ˌklüs\ A person who lives withdrawn from society.

• The lonely farmhouse was home to a middle-aged recluse, a stooped, bearded man who would never answer the door when someone knocked.

Greta Garbo and Howard Hughes were two of the most famously *reclusive* celebrities of modern times. She had been a great international star, called the most beautiful woman in the world; he had been an aircraft manufacturer and film producer, with one of the greatest fortunes in the world. It seems that Garbo's *reclusiveness* resulted from her desire to leave her public with only the youthful image of her face. Hughes was terrified of germs, though that was the least of his problems.

seclusion \si-ˈklü-zhən\ (1) A screening or hiding from view. (2) A place that is isolated or hidden.

• The police immediately placed him in seclusion in a hospital room, with armed guards at the door.

With its prefix *se-*, "apart," *seclusion* has the basic meaning of a place or condition that's "closed away." A lone island may be *secluded*, and its seclusion might be what its owner prizes most about it. Presidents and their staffs may go into seclusion before making critical decisions. Monastery life is purposely secluded, and monks may have taken vows to live lives of seclusion. The deadly brown *recluse* spider prefers seclusion but is sometimes disturbed by very unlucky people.

Quizzes

A. Complete the analogy:

1. freedom : liberty :: servitude : _____
   a. determination b. arrangement c. slavery d. work
2. inclusive : many :: exclusive : _____
   a. everyone b. numerous c. few d. snobbish
3. considerate : thoughtless :: subservient : _____
   a. boastful b. bossy c. decisive d. unique
4. monk : pray :: recluse : _____
   a. deny b. receive c. reclaim d. hide
5. fashionable : stylish :: serviceable : _____
   a. useless b. devoted c. fundamental d. adequate
6. progress : advance :: occlusion : _____
   a. dismissal b. obstruction c. prevention d. denial
7. dominant : aggressive :: servile : _____
   a. saving b. sensitive c. obedient d. forgetful
8. conclusion : ending :: seclusion : _____
   a. refusal b. relaxation c. isolation d. denial

B. Indicate whether the following pairs of words have the same or different meanings:

1. occlusion / stroke   same ___ / different ___
2. subservient / military   same ___ / different ___
3. recluse / hermit   same ___ / different ___
4. serviceable / usable   same ___ / different ___
5. exclusive / sole   same ___ / different ___
6. servitude / enslavement   same ___ / different ___
7. seclusion / solitude   same ___ / different ___
8. servile / humble   same ___ / different ___

Greek and Latin Borrowings

acme \ˈak-mē\ Highest point; summit, peak.

- Last Saturday's upset victory over Michigan may prove to have been the acme of the entire season.

In Greek, *acme* meant a mountain peak, but in English we hardly ever use it in the physical sense. Instead we speak of someone's new job as the acme of her career, or of a certain leap as the acme of classical dance technique. In old Road Runner cartoons, the Acme Company is the provider of every ingenious device imaginable. But the word can't always be taken quite literally as a brand or company name; it's possible, for instance, that something called the Acme Bar & Grill may not be the absolutely highest and best example of a bar and grill. And don't confuse *acme* with *acne,* the skin disorder—even though both actually come from the same word.

catharsis \kə-ˈthär-səs\ A cleansing or purification of the body, emotions, or spirit.

- Having broken down sobbing at the funeral, he said afterwards that it had felt like a catharsis.

One of the earliest uses of *catharsis* is in Aristotle's *Poetics,* where the philosopher claims that watching a tragedy provides the spectators with a desirable catharsis because of the buildup and release of the emotions of pity and fear. Sigmund Freud borrowed the term as a name for the process of bringing a set of unconscious desires and ideas back into consciousness in order to eliminate their bad effects. Today some people claim it's *cathartic* to merely express your anger or grief, since it "gets it out of your system." Laxatives are also called cathartic, since they provide a physical catharsis that some people believe to be healthful. But there's no general agreement about any of this, and the notion of catharsis remains a very personal one.

colossus \kə-ˈlä-səs\ (1) A gigantic statue. (2) A person or thing that resembles such a statue in size or activity or influence.

- Even if *Citizen Kane* had been his only movie, Orson Welles would be regarded as a colossus in the history of film.

The original colossi (notice the plural form) were the larger-than-life statues made by the Greeks and Romans. The most famous of these was the Colossus of Rhodes, a statue of the sun god Helios built on the Greek island of Rhodes around 280 B.C. that was over 100 feet tall and took more than 12 years to build. The Statue of Liberty is a modern colossus, enormous and stately, at the entrance to New York Harbor. And someone who has played a *colossal* role in history, such as Winston Churchill, may be called a colossus as well.

detritus \di-ˈtrī-təs\ Loose material that results from disintegration; debris.

• The base of the cliff was littered with the detritus of centuries of erosion.

After the first hard freeze of fall, gardens are sadly littered with the detritus of the summer's plants and produce: stalks, leaves, vines, rotted vegetables, and maybe even a hand trowel left behind. As the flooding Mississippi River retreats back to its ordinary course, it leaves detritus behind in its wake, debris gathered from everywhere by the raging waters. The detritus of civilization may include junkyards and abandoned buildings; mental detritus may includes all kinds of useless trivia. Notice how this word is pronounced; for some reason, people often try to accent the first syllable rather than the second.

hoi polloi \ˌhȯi-pə-ˈlȯi\ The general population; the masses.

• He's a terrible snob, the kind of person who thinks it's funny to say things like "the riffraff" and "the hoi polloi" and "the great unwashed."

In Greek, *hoi polloi* means simply "the many." (Even though *hoi* itself means "the," in English we almost always say "the hoi polloi.") It comes originally from the famous Funeral Oration by Pericles, where it was actually used in a positive way. Today it's generally used by people who think of themselves as superior—though it's also sometimes used in Pericles' democratic spirit. By the way, it has no relation to *hoity-toity*, meaning "stuck-up," which starts with the same sound but has nothing to do with Greek.

kudos \ˈkü-ˌdōz\ (1) Fame and renown that result from an achievement; prestige. (2) Praise.

• His first film earned him kudos at the independent film festivals, and the big studios were soon calling him up.

Kudos is an odd word in English. In Greek, *kydos* meant "glory" or "prestige"; in other words, it wasn't something you could count. But in English *kudos* looks like a plural and is therefore often treated as one. So people now sometimes use the form *kudo,* with *kudos* as its plural.

onus \ˈō-nəs\ A disagreeable necessity or obligation; responsibility.

• Now that Congress has passed the bill, the onus is on the President to live up to his promise and sign it into law.

In Latin *onus* means literally a "burden," like a particularly heavy backpack. But in English an onus is more often a burden of responsibility or blame. In legal language, the *onus probandi* is the "burden of proof," meaning the big job of assembling enough evidence to prove a person's guilt, since the accused is innocent until proved guilty.

stigma \ˈstig-mə\ A mark of shame: stain.

• In these small villages, the stigma of pregnancy is a terrible thing for an unmarried girl.

In Greek and Latin, a stigma was a mark or brand, especially one that marked a slave, so a stigma marked a person as inferior. When the plural form *stigmata* is used, it usually refers to the nail wounds on Christ's hands and feet, wounds which have sometimes reappeared on the hands or feet of later worshippers such as St. Francis. When *stigma* began to be used in English, it usually meant the kind of mark or stain you can't actually see. So today we hear about the stigma of homelessness, the stigma of overweight, and the stigma of mental illness. People may be so afraid of being *stigmatized* for losing a job that they'll put on their office clothes and drive out their driveways every weekday morning so that the neighbors won't know.

Quiz

Fill in each blank with the correct letter:

a. kudos   e. hoi polloi
b. colossus   f. detritus
c. acme   g. stigma
d. catharsis   h. onus

1. Now that they have apologized, the _____ is on you to do the same.
2. The storm waves had left the beach littered with _____.
3. For many years Microsoft has remained the _____ of the software industry, feared by all its competitors.
4. In the 1950s the _____ of divorce was strong enough that a divorced man almost couldn't run for high office.
5. She says she and her fellow stars would never go near a restaurant where the _____ might be eating.
6. At the _____ of his racing career, Bold Ruler won the Kentucky Derby.
7. His painting is obviously a kind of _____ for him, and his works are filled with violent images.
8. A young Korean pianist has been winning _____ from critics worldwide.

Review Quizzes

A. Complete the analogy:

1. rule : regulation :: stricture : _____
   a. criticism   b. injury   c. dislike   d. bravery
2. demanding : effortless :: tortuous : _____
   a. twisting   b. winding   c. straight   d. descending
3. expensive : costly :: exclusive : _____
   a. indirect   b. fantastic   c. experienced   d. fashionable
4. criticism : error :: kudos : _____
   a. praise   b. prestige   c. blame   d. achievement
5. experiment : subject :: vivisection : _____
   a. botany   b. biology   c. bacteria   d. animals

6. inspect : examine :: construe : _____
   a. condemn b. continue c. contend d. interpret
7. appropriate : take :: expropriate : _____
   a. proclaim b. seize c. expel d. complete
8. funny : comical :: acerbic : _____
   a. distrustful b. sarcastic c. witty d. cheerful
9. praise : compliment :: onus : _____
   a. load b. habit c. obligation d. reputation
10. capable : helpless :: serviceable : _____
    a. useless b. useful c. practical d. formal

B. Fill in each blank with the correct letter:

a. extort
b. exacerbate
c. appropriate
d. constrict
e. detritus
f. convivial
g. servitude
h. infrastructure
i. tortuous
j. seclusion
k. vivacious
l. colossus
m. restrictive
n. propriety
o. occlusion

1. The collapsing bridge was only the latest evidence of the city's deteriorating _____.
2. She began a long and _____ explanation of why she had stayed out so late, but her parents weren't buying it.
3. The _____ of the mountain hut was just what she needed to begin serious work on her book.
4. The children at the orphanage lived in a condition of genuine _____, often working from dawn to dusk.
5. They often joined their neighbors for a _____ evening of Scrabble or charades.
6. The steep bank had become a dumping ground, and _____ of all kinds lay at the bottom.
7. His diet had been terrible for years, so he wasn't surprised when the doctor reported a near _____ of one coronary artery.
8. The company's new standards of _____ prohibited taking any large gifts from salespeople.
9. There were several _____ clauses in the house contract, including one that required weekly mowing of the lawn.
10. The statue for the plaza would be a 30-foot-high _____ representing Atlas holding the globe.

11. She had been a _____ teenager, but had become rather quiet and serious by her thirties.

12. She was forced to practically _____ the money from her husband with threats.

13. Dr. Moss warned him that any drinking would only _____ his condition.

14. The legislature had decided to _____ funds for new harbor facilities.

15. She feared that marriage and a family would _____ her life unbearably.

C. Choose the closest definition:

1. acerbic   a. spicy b. tangy c. mild d. stinging
2. deconstruction   a. analysis b. destruction
   c. breaking d. theory
3. acme   a. monument b. peak c. honor d. award
4. subservient   a. arrogant b. submissive
   c. demanding d. underneath
5. contort   a. torture b. twist c. turn d. twirl
6. instrumental   a. instructive b. intelligent
   c. helpful d. fortunate
7. catharsis   a. explosion b. cleansing c. pollution
   d. cough
8. acrid   a. pleasant b. crazed c. irritating d. soothing
9. stigma   a. sting b. statue c. stain d. stalk
10. recluse   a. spider b. hermit c. request d. hiding place
11. acrimony   a. breakup b. dispute c. bitterness
    d. custody
12. propriety   a. misbehavior b. suitability c. harassment
    d. drama
13. servile   a. efficient b. pleasant c. humble
    d. unnerving
14. tort   a. cake b. twist c. wrong d. law
15. revivify   a. retreat b. rewrite c. reappear d. refresh

UNIT

23

TEXT comes from a Latin verb that means "to weave." So a *textile* is a woven or knitted cloth. The material it's made from determines its *texture,* the smoothness or roughness of its surface. And individual words are "woven" into sentences and paragraphs to form a *text.*

---

textual \\'teks-chə-wəl\\ Having to do with or based on a text.

- A textual analysis of 1,700 lipstick names, including Hot Mama and Raisin Hell, suggested to the author that the women buying them lack a healthy sense of self-worth.

Before the invention of the printing press, books were produced by hand. When the *text* of a book is copied this way, textual errors can creep in, and a text that's been copied again and again can contain many such errors. By comparing different copies of a work, textual critics try to figure out where the copyists went wrong and restore the text to its original form so that modern readers can again enjoy the correct versions of ancient texts. When a class performs textual analysis of a poem, however, they are looking closely at its individual words and phrases in an effort to determine the poem's meanings.

context \\'kän-ˌtekst\\ (1) The surrounding spoken or written material in which a word or remark occurs. (2) The conditions or circumstances in which an event occurs; environment or setting.

- The governor claimed that his remarks were taken out of context and that anyone looking at the whole speech would get a different impression.

Context reveals meaning. The context of an unfamiliar word can give us *contextual* clues to help us determine what the word means. Taking a remark out of context can change its meaning entirely. Likewise, people's actions sometimes have to be understood as having occurred in a particular context. The behavior of historical figures should be seen in the context of their time, when standards may have been very different from our own.

hypertext \\'hī-pər-ˌtekst\\ A database format in which information related to that on a display screen can be accessed directly from the screen (as by a mouse click).

- Three days ago my mother was asking me why some of the words are underlined in blue, but by yesterday she was already an expert in hypertext.

Since *hyper-* generally means "above, beyond" (see HYPER, p. 457), hypertext is something that's gone beyond the limitations of ordinary text. Thus, unlike the text in a book, hypertext permits you, by clicking with a mouse, to immediately access text in one of millions of different electronic sources. Hypertext is now so familiar that most computer users may not even know the word, which was coined by Ted Nelson back in the early 1960s. It took a few more years for hypertext to actually be created, by Douglas Engelbart, and then quite a few more years before the introduction of the World Wide Web in 1991.

subtext \\'səb-ˌtekst\\ The underlying meaning of a spoken or written passage.

- The tough and cynical tone of the story is contradicted by its romantic subtext.

A literary text often has more than one meaning: the literal meaning of the words on the page, and their hidden meaning, what exists "between the lines"—the subtext. Arthur Miller's play *The Crucible,* for example, is about the Salem witchcraft trials of the 17th century, but its subtext is the comparison of those trials with the "witch hunts" of the 1950s, when many people were unfairly accused of being communists. Even a social conversation between a man and a woman may have a subtext, but you may have to listen very closely to figure out what it is. Don't confuse *subtext* with *subplot,* a less important plot that moves along in parallel with the main plot.

PLAC comes from the Latin *placere*, "to please or be agreeable to," or *placare*, "to soothe or calm." *Pleasant*, *pleasurable*, and *pleasing* all derive from this root, even though their spelling makes it hard to see.

placate \'plā-ˌkāt\ To calm the anger or bitterness of someone.

• The Romans had a number of ways of placating the gods, which occasionally included burying slaves alive.

Politicians are constantly having to placate angry voters. Diplomats frequently need to placate a country's allies or possible enemies. Parents are always placating kids who think they've been unfairly denied something. And lovers and spouses are some of the champion placaters. It's no secret that people with the best social skills are often the best at placating other people—and that they themselves may be the ones who benefit the most by it.

placebo \plə-'sē-bō\ A harmless substance given to a patient in place of genuine medication, either for experimental purposes or to soothe the patient.

• The placebo worked miraculously: his skin rash cleared up, his sleep improved, and he even ceased to hear voices.

Doctors doing research on new treatments for disease often give one group a placebo while a second group takes the new medication. Since those in the placebo group usually believe they're getting the real thing, their own hopeful attitude may bring about improvement in their condition. Thus, for the real drug to be considered effective, it must produce even better results than the placebo. Placebos have another use as well. A doctor who suspects that a patient's physical symptoms are psychologically produced may prescribe a placebo in the hope that mentally produced symptoms can also be mentally cured.

placidity \pla-'si-də-tē\ Serene freedom from interruption or disturbance; calmness.

• Her placidity seemed eerie in view of the destruction she had witnessed and the huge loss she had suffered.

A placid lake has a smooth surface untouched by wind. A placid scene is one in which everything seems calm; it may even include a meadow with a few placid cows grazing on it. Someone with a *placid* personality has an inner peacefulness that isn't easily disturbed. As a personality trait, *placidity* is surely a lot better than some of the alternatives; however, the word sometimes describes people who are also a bit passive, like those contented cows.

implacable \im-ˈpla-kə-bəl\ Not capable of being pleased, satisfied, or changed.

• Attempts to negotiate a peace settlement between such implacable enemies seem doomed to failure.

Implacable, with its negative prefix *im-*, describes something or someone that can't be calmed or soothed or altered. A person who carries a grudge feels an implacable resentment—a resentment that can't be soothed. An implacable foe is one you can't negotiate with, perhaps one who's fueled by implacable hatred. And *implacable* sometimes describes things that only seem to be alive: an implacable storm is one that seems as if it will never let up, and an implacable fate is one that you can't outrun or hide from.

Quizzes

A. Fill in each blank with the correct letter:

a. placebo   e. subtext
b. textual   f. implacable
c. placate   g. hypertext
d. context   h. placidity

1. When the sentence was taken out of _____, it sounded quite different.
2. An _____ mob had been demonstrating outside the presidential palace for two weeks now, with their numbers growing from day to day.
3. Many young people wonder how anyone ever did research without the benefit of _____ links.
4. It took a week of bringing flowers home every day to _____ his wife.
5. The deeper meaning of many literary works lies in their _____.
6. The group of patients who were given a _____ did as well as those who were given the real drug.

7. The study of poetry normally requires careful _____ analysis.

8. The _____ of the quiet countryside was soothing after a week in the city.

B. Match the word on the left to the correct definition on the right:

1. placate   a. relating to written matter
2. context   b. unyielding
3. placebo   c. underlying meaning
4. textual   d. soothe
5. placidity   e. setting of spoken or written words
6. subtext   f. harmless substitute
7. implacable   g. computer links
8. hypertext   h. peacefulness

AUT/AUTO comes from the Greek word for "same" or "self." Something *automatic* operates by itself, and an *automobile* moves by itself, without the help of a horse. An *autograph* is in the handwriting of the person him- or herself, and an *autopsy* is an inspection of a corpse by an examiner's own eyes.

---

automaton \ȯ-ˈtä-mə-tən\ (1) An automatic machine, especially a robot. (2) An individual who acts mechanically.

• The work he used to do as a welder in the assembly plant has been taken over by a sophisticated automaton designed overseas.

The idea of the automaton has fascinated people for many centuries. A traveler to the emperor's court in Byzantium in A.D. 949 reported that mechanical birds sat in a golden tree singing the songs of their species; that mechanical lions flanked the throne, roaring and switching their great tails; and that, as he stood watching, the emperor's throne suddenly shot upward toward the high ceiling, and when it slowly descended the emperor was wearing new robes. Early automata (notice the common plural form) often relied on water, steam, or falling weights to power them. Today automata, often called robots, are used in manufacturing plants to build not only vehicles but also much smaller electronic equipment.

autoimmune \,ȯ-tō-im-'yün\ Of, relating to, or caused by antibodies that attack molecules, cells, or tissues of the organism producing them.

- His doctors suspected that the strange combination of symptoms might be those of an autoimmune disease.

Any healthy body produces a variety of antibodies, proteins in the blood whose job is to protect the body from unwanted bacteria, viruses, and cancer cells. The cells and organs that deal with such infections make up the immune system. In some people and animals, for various reasons, the antibodies become overactive and turn on the body's healthy tissues as well; the result is an autoimmune disease—an immune response directed against one's own self. More than eighty autoimmune diseases have been identified, the best-known being type 1 diabetes, multiple sclerosis, lupus, and rheumatoid arthritis.

autonomy \ȯ-'tä-nə-mē\ (1) The power or right of self-government. (2) Self-directing freedom, especially moral independence.

- Though normally respectful of their son's autonomy, the Slocums drew the line at his request to take a cross-country motorcycle trip.

Since *nomos* is Greek for "law," something *autonomous* makes its own laws. The amount of autonomy enjoyed by French-speaking Quebec, or of Palestinians in certain towns in Israel, or of independent-minded regions of Russia, have become major issues. The autonomy of individual states in the United States has posed serious constitutional questions for two centuries. The autonomy of children is almost always limited by their parents. But when those parents are elderly and begin driving poorly and getting confused about their finances, their children may see the need to limit their autonomy in much the same way.

autism \'ȯ-,ti-zəm\ A condition that begins in childhood and causes problems in forming social relationships and in communicating with others and includes behavior in which certain activities are constantly repeated.

- She was beginning to think that her four-year-old's strange behavior and complete lack of interest in his playmates might be due to autism.

Autism, in its strict sense, becomes evident before the age of 3. The autistic child generally refuses to talk, becomes obsessive about toys, resists any change vehemently, and sometimes flies into unexplained rages. Autism is believed to be biological in origin, and seems to be related to several milder conditions such as Asperger's syndrome. As many as 1 in 100 children, mostly boys, may have autism, Asperger's, or a related condition. About one in ten autistic children turns out to have a remarkable mental gift, such as the ability to play a difficult piece on the piano after a single hearing or repair a complex machine without any training. Many *autistic* children seem to grow out of it as they become adults, and some autistic adults manage to live independently. *Autistic* is sometimes used loosely to describe a much more common kind of psychological withdrawal in adults.

GRAT comes from the Latin words *gratus,* meaning "pleasing, welcome, or agreeable," and *gratia,* meaning "grace, agreeableness, or pleasantness." A meal that's served *graciously* will be received with *gratitude* by *grateful* guests; those who show no appreciation could be called *ingrates.*

gratify \\'gra-tə-ˌfī\\ (1) To be a source of pleasure or satisfaction; give pleasure or satisfaction to. (2) To give in to; indulge or satisfy.

• It gratified him immensely to see his daughter bloom so beautifully in high school.

A *gratifying* experience is quietly pleasing or satisfying. But gratifying an impulse means giving in to it, which isn't always such a good idea, and "instant *gratification*" of every desire will result in a life based on junk food and worse. Truly gratifying experiences and accomplishments usually are the result of time and effort.

gratuity \\grə-'tü-ə-tē\\ Something, especially a tip, given freely.

• After sitting for three hours over a six-course meal at Le Passage, we always leave the waiter a very generous gratuity.

Gratuity is a fancier and more formal word than *tip.* It occurs most often in written notices along the lines of "Gratuities accepted." Its formality makes it best suited for describing tips of the dignified, expensive variety. For the taxi driver who takes you to the superb

Belgian restaurant, it's a tip; for the restaurant's maitre d', it's a gratuity.

gratuitous \grə-ˈtü-ə-təs\ Not called for by the circumstances.

- Members of the committee were objecting to what they considered gratuitous violence on television.

In its original sense, *gratuitous* can refer to anything given freely, like a tip. But the word now almost always applies to something that's seen as not only unnecessary (like a tip, which you don't really have to give) but also unwelcome. To insult or criticize someone *gratuitously* is to make a hurtful remark that's uncalled for and undeserved. But scenes in a film that you yourself might call gratuitous were, unfortunately, probably put there to attract an audience that wants to see them.

ingratiate \in-ˈgrā-shē-ˌāt\ To gain favor or acceptance by making a deliberate effort.

- None of her attempts to ingratiate herself with the professor seemed to improve her grades.

To ingratiate yourself is to put yourself in someone's good *graces*—that is, to gain someone's approval. People often try to ingratiate themselves by engaging in an activity known by such names as *bootlicking, apple-polishing,* and *brownnosing.* But some people are able to win favor just by relying on their *ingratiating* smiles.

Quizzes

A. Complete the analogy:

1. favor : prefer :: gratify : _____
   a. use b. please c. thank d. repay
2. liberty : freedom :: autonomy _____
   a. government b. car science c. independence
   d. robot
3. entertain : joke :: ingratiate : _____
   a. flatter b. devour c. vibrate d. criticize
4. worker : laborer :: automaton : _____
   a. robot b. computer c. gadget d. employee

5. necessary : needed :: gratuitous : _____
    a. thankless b. unthinking c. welcome d. uncalled-for
6. immune : infections :: autoimmune : _____
    a. bacteria b. viruses c. epidemic d. body tissues
7. bonus : salary :: gratuity : _____
    a. obligation b. thankfulness c. refusal d. bill
8. paranoia : suspicion :: autism : _____
    a. sleep b. withdrawal c. anger d. fear of cars

B. Indicate whether the following pairs of words have the same or different meanings:

1. automaton / robot   same ___ / different ___
2. gratuity / tip   same ___ / different ___
3. autoimmune / invulnerable   same ___ / different ___
4. gratuitous / deserved   same ___ / different ___
5. autonomy / freedom   same ___ / different ___
6. gratify / gladden   same ___ / different ___
7. autism / dictatorship   same ___ / different ___
8. ingratiate / contribute   same ___ / different ___

CLAM/CLAIM comes from the Latin verb *clamare*, meaning "to shout or cry out." To *claim* often means "to call for." And an *exclamation* is a cry of shock, joy, or surprise.

---

clamor \\'kla-mər\ (1) Noisy shouting; loud, continuous noise. (2) Strong and active protest or demand.

• The clamor in the hallways between classes was particularly loud that morning as news of the state championship swept through the student body.

The clamor on Broadway at midday can be astonishing to a tourist from a midwestern town; if they happen to be digging up the street with jackhammers, the clamor can be even worse. The clamor on the floor of a stock exchange goes on without stopping for seven hours every day. A clamor of protest may sometimes be quieter, but is often just as hard to ignore. A politican who receives a thousand e-mails a day *clamoring* for his resignation might as well be listening to an angry crowd.

acclamation \\,a-klə-'mā-shən\ (1) A loud, eager indication of approval, praise, or agreement. (2) An overwhelming yes vote by cheers, shouts, or applause.

• To the principal's suggestion that Friday be a holiday to honor the victors in the national math olympics, the students yelled their approval in a long and loud acclamation.

Approval can come from a single person, but acclamation requires a larger audience. An *acclaimed* movie is widely praised, and critical *acclaim* can lead to box-office success. When a popular proposal comes up in a legislature, the speaker may ask that it be passed "by acclamation," which means that everyone just gets to yell and cheer in approval and no one bothers counting the votes at all.

declaim \di-'klām\ To speak in the formal manner of someone delivering a speech.

• Almost any opinion can sound convincing if it's declaimed loudly and with conviction.

Declaiming suggests an unnatural style of speech best suited to a stage or podium. Listening to an actor declaim a passage in a Shakespeare play can be enjoyable. Listening to Aunt Ida at Sunday dinner declaiming on the virtues of roughage might not be. Most people don't appreciate being treated as an audience, and good advice is usually more welcome when it's not given in a *declamatory* style.

proclaim \prō-'klām\ To declare or announce publicly, officially, or definitely.

• He burst into the dorm room, jumped onto his bed, and proclaimed that he had just aced the sociology exam.

The *pro-* in *proclaim* means "forward, out," so a *proclamation* is an "outward" statement intended for the public. We often think of proclamations as something issued by monarchs or dictators, but Lincoln was able to issue his Emancipation Proclamation because as president he had the power to free the slaves in certain areas. At a slightly lower level, a governor may proclaim a day in honor of the state's firemen, a movie critic may proclaim a director to be the best of all, or you may proclaim your New Year's resolutions to a crowd of friends.

CRAC/CRAT comes from the Greek word meaning "power." Attached to another root, it indicates which group holds the power. With *demos*, the Greek word for "people," it forms *democracy*, a form of government in which the people rule. A *theocracy*, from the Greek *theos*, "god," is government based on divine guidance. In a *meritocracy*, people earn power by their own merit.

aristocrat \ə-'ris-tə-ˌkrat\ The highest social class in a country, usually because of birth and wealth.

* A wealthy aristocrat from a famous European family, she surprised everyone by becoming a supporter of little-known jazz musicians.

Since *aristos* means "best" in Greek, ancient Greeks such as Plato and Aristotle used the word *aristocracy* to mean a system of rule by the best people—that is, those who deserved to rule because of their intelligence and moral excellence. But this kind of "best" soon became something you could inherit from your parents. The United States has no formal aristocracy—no noble titles such as *baron* or *marquis* that stay in the family—but certain American families have achieved an almost *aristocratic* status because of the wealth they've held onto for generations.

autocratic \ˌȯ-tə-'kra-tik\ (1) Having to do with a form of government in which one person rules. (2) Resembling the ruler of such a government.

* It's hard to believe that a guy who seems so nice to his friends is an autocratic boss who sometimes fires people just because he's in a bad mood.

Autos in Greek means "same" or "self," so in an autocratic government all the power is held by the leader him- or herself. Autocratic governments are often called dictatorships, or sometimes *autocracies*. In everyday life, a teacher, a parent, or a football coach can all behave like autocrats as well.

bureaucrat \'byu̇r-ə-ˌkrat\ (1) An appointed government official. (2) An official of a government or system that is marked by fixed and complex rules that often result in long delays.

* To settle his insurance claim he had to make his way through four or five bureaucrats, every one of them with a new form to fill out.

In French, a *bureau* is a desk, so *bureaucracy* means basically "government by people at desks." Despite the bad-mouthing they often get, partly because they usually have to stick so close to the rules, bureaucrats do almost all the day-to-day work that keeps a government running. The idea of a bureaucracy is to split up the complicated task of governing a large country into smaller jobs that can be handled by specialists. *Bureaucratic* government is nothing new; the Roman empire had an enormous and complex bureaucracy, with the bureaucrats at lower levels reporting to bureaucrats above them, and so on up to the emperor himself.

plutocracy \plü-ˈtä-krə-sē\ (1) Government by the wealthy. (2) A controlling class of wealthy people.

- Theodore Roosevelt sought to limit the power held by the plutocracy of wealthy industrialists.

Ploutos was Greek for "wealth," and Plouton, or Pluto, was one of the names used for the Greek god of the underworld, where all the earth's mineral wealth was stored. So a plutocracy governs or wields power through its money. The economic growth in the U.S. in the late 19th century produced a group of enormously wealthy *plutocrats*. Huge companies like John D. Rockefeller's Standard Oil gained serious political power, and Rockefeller was able to influence lawmakers in states where his businesses operated. For this reason, it was said in 1905 that Ohio and New Jersey were plutocracies, not democracies.

Quizzes

A. Fill in each blank with the correct letter:

a.	plutocracy	e.	proclaim
b.	declaim	f.	bureaucrat
c.	aristocrat	g.	acclamation
d.	clamor	h.	autocratic

1. She hates being thought of as a _____, but in these huge government offices with long rows of desks it's hard for her to think of herself as anything else.
2. The assembly approved the proposal by enthusiastic _____.

3. Her father had been harsh and _____, and her mother and brothers had barely opened their mouths when he was around.

4. I got tired of hearing him _____ about how much better things were when he was young.

5. His parents had been London shopkeepers, but many who met him assumed from his fine manners and accent and dress that he was an _____.

6. The networks could _____ the winner of the election as early as 7:00 p.m.

7. The country is supposedly a democracy, but it's really run as a _____ by about twenty extremely wealthy families.

8. The proposed new tax was met with a _____ of protest.

B. Match the word on the left to the correct definition on the right:

1. autocratic   a. declare
2. declaim   b. noble
3. plutocracy   c. noisy din
4. acclamation   d. government official
5. proclaim   e. speak formally
6. bureaucrat   f. ruled by one person
7. clamor   g. rule by the rich
8. aristocrat   h. acceptance with cheers

PUNC comes from the Latin noun *punctum,* meaning "point." A period is a form of *punctuation* that's literally a point, and a *punctured* tire has been pricked by a sharp point.

punctilious \ˌpəŋk-ˈti-lē-əs\ Very careful about the details of codes or conventions.

• A proofreader has to be punctilious about spelling and punctuation.

A *punctilio* is a small point—a minor rule, or a little detail of conduct in a ceremony. A person who pays close attention to such minor details is punctilious. *Punctiliousness* can be valuable, especially for certain kinds of tasks, as long as you don't become so concerned about small points that you fail to pay attention to the large ones.

punctual \\'pəŋk-chə-wəl\\ Being on time; prompt.

- The company had become much more punctual under the new president, and every meeting started precisely on time.

The original meaning of *punctual* described a *puncture* made by a surgeon. The word has meant lots of other things through the centuries, usually involving being precise about small points. And today *punctuality* is all about time; a punctual train or a punctual payment or a punctual person shows up "on the dot."

compunction \\kəm-'pəŋk-shən\\ (1) Anxiety caused by guilt. (2) A slight misgiving.

- Speeding is something many people seem to do without compunction, their only concern being whether they'll get caught.

Compunction is most often used in describing people who don't feel it—that is, who aren't "stung" or "pricked" by conscience. Ruthless businessmen steal clients and contracts from other businessmen without compunction, and hardened criminals have no compunctions about armed robbery and worse. Notice how compunction can be used in a noncountable way, like *guilt* ("He killed without compunction"), or in the plural, like *qualm* ("She had no compunctions about lying"). But words like *guilt, qualm, regret, remorse, doubt,* and *unease,* unlike *compunction,* are often used when talking about people who actually suffer from them.

acupuncture \\'a-kyə-ˌpəŋ(k)-chər\\ A method of relieving pain or curing illness by inserting fine needles through the skin at specific points.

- As a last resort he agreed to try acupuncture treatment with Dr. Lu, and his pain vanished like magic.

In Latin, *acus* means "needle," and the English word *acupuncture* was coined way back in the 17th century to describe a technique the Chinese had already been using for 2,000 years. An *acupuncturist* may insert many extremely fine needles at a time; the treatment is usually uncomfortable but not truly painful. In China today, even major surgery is often carried out using only acupuncture to kill the pain; it's also used for many other conditions, including insomnia, depression, smoking, and overweight. Acupuncture is based on ancient theories of bodily energy that few Western doctors have ever accepted; but even though attempts to explain its effects by

Western science have been unsuccessful, it's now widely recognized by doctors as effective for pain reduction.

POT comes from the Latin adjective *potens*, meaning "able." Our English word *potent* means "powerful" or "effective," whether for good or bad. A potent new antibiotic might be able to deal with infections that have developed resistance to older drugs; an industrial gas might be identified as a potent contributor to climate change; and a potent drink might leave you staggering.

---

potential \pə-ˈten-shəl\ (1) The possibility that something will happen in the future. (2) A cause for hope.

- If the plan works we'll be millionaires, but the potential for disaster is high.

Potential can be either good or bad. Studying hard increases the potential for success, but wet roads increase the potential for accidents. But when a person or thing "has potential," we always expect something good from it in the future. As an adjective (as in "potential losses," "potential benefits," etc.), *potential* usually means simply "possible." In science, however, the adjective has a special meaning: *Potential energy* is the kind of stored energy that a boulder sitting at the top of a cliff has (the opposite of *kinetic energy,* which is what it has as it rolls down that cliff).

impotent \ˈim-pə-tənt\ Lacking power or strength.

- The government now knows it's utterly impotent to stop the violence raging in the countryside, and has basically retreated to the capital city.

A police department may be impotent to stop the flow of drugs into a neighborhood. A group of countries may be impotent to force another country to change its human-rights policies. The *impotence* of a prime minister may be shown by her inability to get an important piece of legislation passed. *Impotent* and *impotence* may also have a special meaning, when they refer to a man's inability to have sexual intercourse.

plenipotentiary \ˌple-nə-pə-ˈten-shə-rē\ A person, such as a diplomat, who has complete power to do business for a government.

- In the Great Hall, in the presence of the Empress, the plenipotentiaries of four European nations put their signatures on the treaty.

Back in the 12th century, when the Roman Catholic Church in some ways resembled the powerful Roman empire that had come before it, the Church revived the Roman concept of an official with *plena potens*—"full powers"—to negotiate agreements (see PLE/PLEN, p. 117). Whereas an ambassador could only make offers that a faraway ruler had specified, often weeks or months earlier, a plenipotentiary could negotiate an entire agreement without checking back constantly with his ruler. Today, with instant electronic communications, this distinction has generally lost its importance, but there are still ambassadors who wouldn't be allowed at a negotiating table.

potentate \\'pō-t³n-ˌtāt\\ A powerful ruler.

- After 18 years as president of the college, he wielded power like a medieval potentate, and no one on the faculty or staff dared to challenge him.

Like such titles as *grand vizier, caliph,* and *khan*, *potentate* summons up thoughts of absolute rulers of an earlier age in such lands as Turkey, Persia, and India. It often suggests a person who uses power or authority in a cruel and unjust way—that is, a tyrant. Today, though it's still used as a title by the organization called the Shriners, it's more often used humorously ("Supreme Intergalactic Potentate," "Potentate of Pasta," etc.).

Quizzes

A. Choose the closest definition:

1. impotent   a. antique b. weak c. broken d. skimpy
2. punctual   a. deflated b. cranky c. prompt d. careful
3. potentate   a. ruler b. bully c. warrior d. prime minister
4. acupuncture   a. massage technique b. arrow hole c. pinprick d. needle therapy
5. punctilious   a. pointed b. careful c. prompt d. unusual
6. plenipotentiary   a. monarch b. ambassador c. fullness d. likely possibility

7. compunction   a. desire b. bravery c. qualm
   d. conviction
8. potential   a. privilege b. prestige c. power
   d. possibility

**B. Indicate whether the following pairs of words have
    the same or different meanings:**

1. acupuncture / precision   same ___ / different ___
2. plenipotentiary / emperor   same ___ / different ___
3. punctual / on time   same ___ / different ___
4. potentate / monarch   same ___ / different ___
5. compunction / threat   same ___ / different ___
6. impotent / powerless   same ___ / different ___
7. punctilious / speedy   same ___ / different ___
8. potential / influence   same ___ / different ___

Greek and Latin Borrowings

ambrosia \am-ˈbrō-zhə\ (1) The food of the Greek and Roman
gods. (2) Something extremely pleasant to taste or smell.

• After two days lost in the woods, the simple stew tasted like
  ambrosia to them.

Ambrosia literally means "immortality" in Greek, and in Greek and
Roman mythology only the immortals—the gods and goddesses—
could eat ambrosia or drink *nectar.* Both may have been divine
forms of honey. The gods also used nectar and ambrosia like oils
for ceremonial anointing, and a mixture of water, oil, and fruits
called ambrosia came to be used in human ceremonies as well.
Since we can't know what the mythical ambrosia tasted or smelled
like, we mere mortals are free to give the name to our favorite
ambrosial dessert—perhaps one involving oranges, coconut, and
heavy cream.

dogma \ˈdȯg-mə\ (1) Something treated as established and
accepted opinion. (2) A principle or set of principles taught by a
religious organization.

• New findings about how animals communicate are challenging
  the current dogma in the field.

Religious dogma and scientific dogma are sometimes at odds, as in arguments between those who believe in the biblical story of creation and those who believe in evolution. Since all dogma resists change, arguments of any kind are harder to resolve when both sides are *dogmatic* in their beliefs. *Dogma* and *dogmatic* are generally used disapprovingly; it's always other people who believe unquestioningly in dogma and who take a dogmatic approach to important issues.

gratis \\ˈgra-təs\\ Without charge; free.

• The service is gratis, since it comes as part of a package deal.

Gratis comes from the Latin word for "favor"; so in English a party favor is a small item given gratis to everyone attending a party. *Gratis* is used as both an adjective ("The drinks were gratis") and an adverb ("Drinks were served gratis"). But however it's used, it means "free."

eureka \\yu̇-ˈrē-kə\\ An exclamation used to express triumph and delight on a discovery.

• The mountain town of Eureka, California, was named for the cries of delight by prospectors when they discovered gold in them thar hills.

Eureka means "I have found" in Greek. The story goes that the Greek inventor Archimedes, given the task of determining the purity of gold in a crown, shouted "Eureka!" one day after stepping into a bath and making water slop over the side, when he suddenly realized that the weight of water displaced indicated the bulk of his body, but that a larger body made of lighter matter might weigh the same but would displace more water. Thus, a crown in which lighter metal had secretly been mixed with the gold would reveal itself in the same way. The story may not be true, but we still shout "Eureka!" when we make a sudden, welcome discovery.

per se \\pər-ˈsā\\ By, of, or in itself; as such.

• He claims that the reason for the invasion wasn't oil per se, but rather the country's dangerous military power, which had been made possible by its oil.

We generally use *per se* to distinguish between something in its narrow sense and some larger thing that it represents. Thus, you may have no objection to educational testing per se, but rather to the way testing is done. An opposition party may attack a president's policy not because they dislike the policy per se but because they want to weaken the president. And when New York's police chief decided to crack down on small crimes, it wasn't the small crimes per se that were his target, but instead the larger crimes which he believed would be reduced because of this new approach.

opus \\ˈō-pəs\\ A creative work, especially a musical composition or set of compositions numbered in order of publication.

• Beethoven's Ninth Symphony is also known as Opus (Op.) 125.

A literary opus is often a single novel, though the word may sometimes refer to all of a writer's works. But *opus* normally is used for musical works. Mendelssohn's Opus 90 is his *Italian Symphony,* for example, and Brahms's Op. 77 is his Violin Concerto. Since many composers' works were never given opus numbers in an orderly way, they now often have catalog numbers assigned by later scholars. So Haydn's Symphony No. 104 is Hob.104 (Hob. is short for Anthony van Hoboken, the cataloger), and Mozart's *Marriage of Figaro* is K.492 (K. stands for Ludwig Köchel).

impetus \\ˈim-pə-təs\\ (1) A driving force or impulse; something that makes a person try or work hard; incentive. (2) Momentum.

• The promise of a nice bonus gave us all an added impetus for finishing the project on time.

An impetus can be something positive and pleasant, or something negative and unpleasant, but in either case it stimulates action. The need to earn a living provides many people with the impetus to drag themselves out of bed five mornings a week. On the other two days, the impetus might be the smell of bacon cooking, or the idea of an early-morning round of golf. *Impetus* can be used either with *an* or *the* in front of it ("The accident provided an impetus for changing the safety regulations") or without them ("His discoveries have given impetus to further research").

thesis \\ˈthē-səs\\ (1) An opinion or proposition that a person presents and tries to prove by argument. (2) An extended paper that contains the results of original research, especially one written by a candidate for an academic degree.

• She's done all the coursework needed for her master's degree but hasn't yet completed her thesis.

In high school, college, or graduate school, students often have to write a thesis on a topic in their major field of study. In many fields, a final thesis is the biggest challenge involved in getting a master's degree, and the same is true for students studying for a Ph.D. (a Ph.D. thesis is often called a *dissertation*). But a thesis may also be an idea; so in the course of the paper the student may put forth several theses (notice the plural form) and attempt to prove them.

Quiz

Fill in each blank with the correct letter:

a.	gratis	e.	thesis
b.	ambrosia	f.	opus
c.	per se	g.	eureka
d.	impetus	h.	dogma

1. His latest _____ is a set of songs on poetry by Pablo Neruda.
2. This sauce tastes like _____!
3. Treating epilepsy and depression by stimulating the muscles with electrical current was medical _____ for years, but today no one is doing it anymore.
4. The article isn't really about surgery _____, but it talks about several issues that are closely related to it.
5. She wrote her _____ on the portrayal of women in the works of Nathaniel Hawthorne.
6. _____! I knew I'd find that file sooner or later!
7. The souvenirs were distributed _____ to anyone who stopped to see the display.
8. The _____ for this latest big research effort is a prize that's being offered by a foundation.

Review Quizzes

A. Complete the analogy:

1. shout : whisper :: clamor : _____
   a. noise   b. din   c. murmur   d. confusion
2. barrier : stop :: impetus : _____
   a. force   b. drive   c. trip   d. work
3. approval : permission :: autonomy : _____
   a. satisfaction   b. independence   c. slavery   d. poverty
4. helpful : servant :: autocratic : _____
   a. friend   b. enemy   c. teacher   d. tyrant
5. turmoil : conflict :: placidity : _____
   a. peace   b. dullness   c. trouble   d. smoothness
6. alas : disappointment :: eureka : _____
   a. distress   b. woe   c. distance   d. discovery
7. gladden : delight :: gratify : _____
   a. please   b. depress   c. amaze   d. surprise
8. strong : vigorous :: impotent : _____
   a. healthy   b. fragile   c. powerful   d. weak

B. Fill in each blank with the correct letter:

a.	acclamation	i.	plutocracy
b.	ingratiate	j.	thesis
c.	potentate	k.	autonomy
d.	context	l.	placate
e.	declaim	m.	punctilious
f.	ambrosia	n.	subtext
g.	automaton	o.	autocratic
h.	dogma		

1. She can work like an _____ for eight hours a day, in constant motion, never pausing to speak to a fellow worker.
2. Her boss had flown into a rage that morning, and it had taken her two hours to _____ him.
3. By taking his remarks out of _____, the papers made him look like a crook.
4. The _____ that controls the government also controls all the country's news media.
5. Her attempts to _____ herself with the new management were resented by the other workers.

6. She was so _____ about the smallest office policies that everyone went to her when they had forgotten one of them.

7. He had to revise his _____ twice before being granted his master's degree.

8. He holds court in his vast 15th-floor office like an oriental _____, signing documents and issuing commands.

9. Huge cheering crowds in the streets greeted him on his return from exile, and he was swept into office almost by _____.

10. The dinner was nothing special, but the dessert was pure _____.

11. Replacing an _____ government with a democracy is never easy if the country is unfamiliar with democratic procedures.

12. She stood before the crowd and began to _____ in the tones of a practiced politician.

13. Several remote tribes have been granted limited _____, including self-policing rights and freedom from taxation.

14. Her theory was hotly debated, since it disagreed with the established _____.

15. She claims that the novel has a _____ that no one has ever noticed, and pointed out the clues that the author had provided.

C. Choose the closest definition:

1. aristocrat   a. noble   b. power   c. ruler   d. office worker

2. gratuitous   a. pleasant   b. unnecessary   c. happy   d. satisfying

3. gratuity   a. fee   b. service   c. obligation   d. tip

4. opus   a. achievement   b. composition   c. burden   d. talent

5. per se   a. if not   b. of course   c. free of charge   d. as such

6. compunction   a. confidence   b. misgiving   c. condition   d. surprise

7. autism   a. self-absorption   b. self-governance   c. authenticity   d. authority

8. gratis   a. irritating   b. grateful   c. inexpensive   d. free

9. gratify   a. unify b. donate c. satisfy d. modify
10. factotum   a. computer printout b. carved pole
        c. plumber d. assistant
11. implacable   a. impossible to place b. impossible to
        change c. impossible to say d. impossible to like
12. textual   a. of an idea b. of a manuscript c. on an
        assumption d. on a hunch
13. placebo   a. one-celled animal b. medical instrument
        c. harmless substance d. peaceful mood
14. potential   a. regulation b. influence c. impact
        d. possibility
15. bureaucrat   a. furniture maker b. politician
        c. official d. servant

UNIT

24

MAND comes from *mandare*, Latin for "entrust" or "order." A *command* is an order; a *commandment* is also an order, but usually one that comes from God. And a *commando* unit carries out orders for special military actions.

---

mandate \\'man-ˌdāt\\ (1) A formal command. (2) Permission to act, given by the people to their representatives.

• The new president claimed his landslide victory was a mandate from the voters to end the war.

A mandate from a leader is a command you can't refuse. But that kind of personal command is rarely the meaning of *mandate* today; much more common are connected with institutions. Thus, the Clean Air Act was a mandate from Congress to clean up air pollution—and since *mandate* is also a verb, we could say instead that the Clear Air Act *mandated* new restrictions on air pollution. Elections are often interpreted as mandates from the public for certain kinds of action. But since a politician is not just a symbol of certain policies but also an individual who might happen to have an awfully nice smile, it can be risky to interpret most elections as mandating anything at all.

mandatory \\'man-də-ˌtȯr-ē\\ Required.

• If attendance at the meeting hadn't been mandatory, she would have just gone home.

Something mandatory is the result of a *mandate* or order, which usually comes in the form of a law, rule, or regulation. Today there seem to be a lot of these mandates, so mandatory seat belts, mandatory inspections for industries, and mandatory prison sentences for violent crimes are regularly in the news. But mandatory retirement at age 65, which used to be common, is now illegal in most cases.

commandeer \ˌkä-mən-ˈdir\ To take possession of something by force, especially for military purposes.

- No sooner had they started their meeting than the boss showed up and commandeered the conference room.

Military forces have always had the power to commandeer houses. The Declaration of Independence complains about the way the British soldiers have done it, and the third Amendment to the Constitution states that the commandeering of people's houses shall be done only in a way prescribed by law. Almost anything—food, supplies, livestock, etc.—can be militarily commandeered when the need arises. But you don't have to be in the military for someone to "pull rank" on you: Your father may commandeer the car just when you were about to take it out for the evening, your teacher may commandeer your cell phone as you're texting in the middle of class, or your older sister may commandeer the TV remote to watch some lousy dancing competition.

remand \ri-ˈmand\ (1) To order a case sent back to another court or agency for further action. (2) To send a prisoner back into custody to await further trial or sentencing.

- The state supreme court had remanded the case to the superior court, instructing it to consider the new evidence.

Remand means "order back" or "send back." After losing a case in a lower court, lawyers will frequently appeal it to a higher court. If the higher court looks at the case and sees that the lower court made certain kinds of errors, it will simply remand it, while telling the lower court how it fell short the first time: by not instructing the jury thoroughly, for example, or by not taking into account a recent related court decision.

UND comes into English from the Latin words *unda*, "wave," and *undare*, "to rise in waves," "to surge or flood." *Undulations* are waves or wavelike things or motions, and to *undulate* is to rise and fall in a wavelike way.

---

undulant \ˈən-jə-lənt\ (1) Rising and falling in waves. (2) Wavy in form, outline, or surface.

• The man's undulant, sinister movements reminded her of a poisonous snake about to strike.

The surface of a freshly plowed field is undulant. A range of rolling hills could be called undulant, as could the shifting sands of the Sahara. A waterbed mattress is often literally undulant. And a field of wheat will *undulate* or sway in the wind, like the waves of the sea.

inundate \ˈi-nən-ˌdāt\ (1) To cover with a flood or overflow. (2) To overwhelm.

• As news of the singer's death spread, retailers were inundated with orders for all his old recordings.

In the summer of 1993, record rains in the Midwest caused the Mississippi River to overflow its banks, break through levees, and inundate the entire countryside; such an *inundation* hadn't been seen for at least a hundred years. By contrast, the Nile River inundated its entire valley every year, bringing the rich black silt that made the valley one of the most fertile places on earth. (The inundations ceased with the completion of the Aswan High Dam in 1970.) Whenever a critical issue is being debated, the White House and Congressional offices are inundated with phone calls and e-mails, just as a town may be inundated with complaints when it starts charging a fee for garbage pickup.

redound \ri-ˈdau̇nd\ (1) To have an effect for good or bad. (2) To rebound or reflect.

• Each new military victory redounded to the glory of the king, whose brilliance as a leader was now praised and feared throughout Europe.

Redound has had a confusing history. Its original meaning was simply "overflow." But since the prefix *re-* often means "back," the later meaning "result" may have arisen because flowing back—on a beach, for example—is a result of the original flowing. *Redound* has long been confused with other words such as *resound* and *rebound*, so today "rebound" is another of its standard meanings. As examples of its usual meaning, we could say that the prohibition of alcohol in 1919 redounded unintentionally to the benefit of gangsters such as Al Capone—and that Capone's jailing on tax-evasion charges redounded to the credit of the famous "Untouchables."

redundancy \ri-ˈdən-dən-sē\ (1) The state of being extra or unnecessary. (2) Needless repetition.

• A certain amount of redundancy can help make a speaker's points clear, but too much can be annoying.

Redundancy, closely related to *redound*, has stayed close to the original meaning of "overflow" or "more than necessary." Avoiding redundancy is one of the prime rules of good writing. "In the modern world of today" contains a redundancy; so does "He died of fatal wounds" and "For the mutual benefit of both parties." But redundancy doesn't just occur in language. "Data redundancy" means keeping the same computer data in more than one place as a safety measure, and a backup system in an airplane may provide redundancy, again for the sake of safety.

Quizzes

A. Fill in each blank with the correct letter:

a. redound   e. remand
b. commandeer   f. inundate
c. undulant   g. mandate
d. mandatory   h. redundancy

1. "Each and every" is an example of a _____ that almost everyone uses.
2. A group of four gunmen tried to _____ the jet soon after takeoff.
3. In the second movement, the composer depicts the waves of the ocean by means of lines that rise and fall in _____ patterns.
4. The court's decision represents a _____ to continue working toward absolute equality in the workplace.
5. Sportsmanship and generosity always _____ to the credit of both the team and the school.

6. The judge will probably _____ this case to the lower court for further study.
7. Piles of job applications _____ the office every day.
8. The session on business ethics is _____ for all employees.

B. Match the definition on the left to the correct word on the right:

1. needless repetition   a. mandate
2. required   b. undulant
3. flood   c. commandeer
4. take over   d. redundancy
5. reflect   e. inundate
6. command   f. remand
7. wavy   g. mandatory
8. send back   h. redound

SANCT, meaning "holy," comes from the Latin word *sanctus*. Thus, *sanctity* means "holiness." In ancient Greece, a spot could be *sanctified*, or "made holy," by a group of priests who carried out a solemn ritual; these might be spots where fumes arose from a crack in the earth or where a spring of clear water flowed out of the ground, and a temple might be built there for worship of a god.

---

sanction \\'saŋk-shən\\ To give approval to.

• The bill's opponents claimed that removing criminal penalties for drug possession would amount to sanctioning drug use.

Sanction originally meant "make holy" or "give official church approval to." The word still has a solemn sound to it, so sanctioning is something generally done by an institution or government, though not necessarily by a church. So a college may sanction—or "give its blessing to"—the use of office space by a gay organization, or a hot-rod association may sanction two new tracks for official races. But *sanction* is also a noun, which may have two near-opposite meanings, "approval" and "penalty." Thus, a company may be accused of giving its *sanction* to illegal activities. But when two or more countries impose sanctions on another country, it often involves cutting off trade. No wonder *sanction* is such a tricky word for so many of us.

sanctimonious \ˌsaŋk-tə-ˈmō-nē-əs\ Pretending to be more religiously observant or morally better than other people.

• The candidates' speeches were sanctimonious from beginning to end, filled with stories about how their deep faith was the basis for everything they did.

Making a show of your religious morality has always struck some people the wrong way, including Jesus. In his Sermon on the Mount, Jesus preaches that, when we give away money for charity, we shouldn't let our left hand know what our right hand is doing—that is, the giving should be done for its own sake and other people shouldn't be told about it. Those who make a display of how good and pious they are are called hypocrites. But *sanctimony*, or *sanctimoniousness*, has often been a good strategy for American politicians, many of whom have found it a great way to win votes.

sacrosanct \ˈsa-krō-ˌsaŋkt\ (1) Most sacred or holy. (2) Treated as if holy and therefore immune from criticism or disturbance of any kind.

• Lots of experts have criticized the governor's education program, but it's regarded as sacrosanct by members of her own party.

Sacrosanct means literally "made holy by a sacred rite," and in its original use the word was reserved for things of the utmost holiness. But *sacrosanct* is now used to describe a questionable sacredness which nevertheless makes something immune from attack or violation; that is, the person using the word usually doesn't regard the thing as sacred at all. So to call a government program sacrosanct is to imply that others regard it as untouchable. And a piece of writing is more likely to be thought of as sacrosanct by its author than by the editor who has to fix it up.

sanctuary \ˈsaŋk-chə-ˌwer-ē\ (1) A holy place, such as a church or temple, or the most holy part of one. (2) A place of safety, refuge, and protection.

• The midtown park is a tranquil sanctuary amidst the city's heat, noise, and bustle.

Historically, churches have been places where fugitives could seek at least temporary protection from the law. In Anglo-Saxon England, churches and churchyards generally provided 40 days of immunity, and neither the sheriffs nor the army would enter to seize the outlaw.

But gradually the right of sanctuary was eroded. In 1486 sanctuary for the crime of treason was disallowed, and sanctuary for most other crimes was severely restricted by Henry VIII and later abolished. In the 1980s many U.S. churches provided sanctuary to political refugees from Central America, and the U.S. government mostly chose not to interfere. Today, wildlife sanctuaries provide protection for the species within its boundaries, and farm-animal sanctuaries now rescue livestock from abuse and starvation.

LOQU comes from the Latin verb *loqui*, "to talk." An *eloquent* preacher speaks fluently, forcefully, and expressively. And a dummy's words come out of a *ventriloquist*'s mouth—or perhaps out of his belly (in Latin, *venter*).

---

colloquium \kə-'lō-kwē-əm\ A conference in which various speakers take turns lecturing on a subject and then answering questions about it.

• There's a colloquium at Yale on Noah Webster in September, where she's scheduled to deliver a paper.

A *colloquy* is a conversation, and especially an important, high-level discussion. *Colloquy* and *colloquium* once meant the same thing, though today *colloquium* always refers to a conference. Because of its old "conversation" meaning, however, a colloquium is a type of conference with important question-and-answer periods.

soliloquy \sə-'li-lə-kwē\ A dramatic speech that represents a series of unspoken thoughts.

• Film characters never have onscreen soliloquies, though they may tell us their thoughts in a voiceover.

Since *solus* means "alone" in Latin, soliloquies take place when a character is alone onstage, or maybe spotlighted off to one side of a dark stage. Novels have no trouble in expressing to the reader a character's personal thoughts, but such expression is less natural to stage drama. The soliloquies of Shakespeare—in *Hamlet* ("To be or not to be"), *Macbeth* ("Tomorrow and tomorrow and tomorrow"), *Romeo and Juliet* ("But soft! what light from yonder window breaks"), etc.—are the most famous, but modern playwrights such as Tennessee Williams, Arthur Miller, and Sam Shepard have also employed them.

colloquial \kə-ˈlō-kwē-əl\ Conversational in style.

• The author, though obviously a professional writer, uses a colloquial style in this new book.

Since *colloquy* means basically "conversation," colloquial language is the language almost all of us speak. It uses contractions ("can't," "it's," "they've"), possibly some slang, lots of short words and not many long ones. But our language usually changes when we write, becoming more formal and sometimes even "literary." Except in e-mails and text messages, many people never write a contraction or use the word "I", and avoid informal words completely. But colloquial language isn't necessarily bad in writing, and it's sometimes more appropriate than the alternative.

loquacious \lō-ˈkwā-shəs\ Apt to talk too much; talkative.

• She had hoped to read quietly on the plane, but the loquacious salesman in the next seat made it nearly impossible.

A loquacious speaker can leave a big audience stifling its yawns after the first 45 minutes, and the *loquaciousness* of a dinner guest can keep everyone else from getting a word in edgewise. Loquacious letters used to go on for pages, and a loquacious author might produce a 1,200-page novel. Lincoln's brief 269-word Gettysburg Address was delivered after a two-hour, 13,000-word speech by America's most famous orator, a windbag of *loquacity*.

Quizzes

A. Choose the closest definition:

1. sanction   a. pray b. warn c. trade d. approve
2. soliloquy   a. love poem b. monologue c. lullaby
   d. conversation
3. sanctimonious   a. hypocritical b. holy c. solemn
   d. divine
4. sacrosanct   a. sacred b. churchlike c. Christian
   d. priestly
5. loquacious   a. abundant b. silent c. talkative
   d. informative
6. sanctuary   a. belief b. holiness c. cemetery d. refuge

7. colloquial a. slangy b. disrespectful
   c. conversational d. uneducated
8. colloquium   a. field of study b. university c. college
   d. scholarly discussion

B. Indicate whether the following pairs of words have the same or different meanings:

1. soliloquy / praise   same ___ / different ___
2. sanction / dedicate   same ___ / different ___
3. loquacious / long-winded   same ___ / different ___
4. sacrosanct / heavenly   same ___ / different ___
5. colloquium / temple   same ___ / different ___
6. sanctuary / shelter   same ___ / different ___
7. colloquial / informal   same ___ / different ___
8. sanctimonious / passionate   same ___ / different ___

VIR is Latin for "man." A *virtue* is a good quality—originally, the kind of quality an ideal man possessed. And *virtuous* behavior is morally excellent. All in all, the Romans seem to have believed that being a man was a good thing.

---

virility \və-'ri-lə-tē\ Energetic, vigorous manhood; masculinity.

• For his entire life he believed that anyone who had been a Marine had established his virility beyond any doubt.

Luckily, there's no doubt about what virility is, since it's depicted on the covers of dozens of new romance novels every month! A masterful and dominating manner, a splendid bared chest, a full head of lustrous hair, and an array of stunning costumes seem to be what's required. (*Virile* traits often missing in these men are hair on the chest and any hint of future baldness.) High-school football provides a showplace for demonstrations of adolescent virility, and for years afterward virile high-school players can keep using football language in their business life: "get to the red zone," "Hail Mary pass," "move the ball," and on and on.

---

triumvirate \trī-'əm-və-rət\ (1) A commission or government of three. (2) A group or association of three.

• A triumvirate slowly emerged as the inner circle of the White House, and the vice president wasn't among them.

The first triumvirate of the Roman Republic, which consisted of Julius Caesar, Pompey, and Crassus, was simply an alliance or partnership, not a formal institution of the government. The alliance didn't last long, however, and Caesar eventually emerged with total power. This led to his assassination, after which a second triumvirate took over, with Octavian, Mark Antony, and Lepidus dividing the Roman world among themselves. But these *triumvirs* also soon turned on one another, with Octavian alone taking power; in time he would become Rome's first emperor.

virago \və-ˈrä-gō\ A loud, bad-tempered, overbearing woman.

• The staff called her a virago and other things behind her back, but everyone was respectful of her abilities.

The original Latin meaning of *virago* was "female warrior." But in later centuries the meaning shifted toward the negative. The most famous virago in English literature is the ferocious Kate in Shakespeare's *The Taming of the Shrew*. Some historical viragoes have also become famous. Agrippina poisoned her husband, the Emperor Claudius, so that her son Nero could take his place (but it was Nero himself who eventually had her assassinated). And Queen Eleanor of Aquitaine, a powerful virago of the 12th century, was imprisoned by her husband, King Henry II of England, after she encouraged their sons to rebel against him. Today some people are beginning to use *virago* admiringly again.

virtuosity \ˌvər-chü-ˈä-sə-tē\ Great technical skill, especially in the practice of a fine art.

• Playing with the band, his virtuosity doesn't show through; you really have to hear him solo to appreciate him.

Virtuosity is used particularly to describe musicians, but also often for writers, actors, dancers, and athletes. A *virtuoso* is a highly skilled performer, and a *virtuoso* performance is one that astonishes the audience by its feats. In ancient Greece the cities would hold male competitions in acrobatics, conjuring, public reciting, blowing the trumpet, and acting out scenes from Homer's epics, the winners of which would have been praised as *virtuous*, or "full of manly virtues."

VAL has as its basic meaning "strength," from the Latin verb *valere*, meaning "to be worthy, healthy, or strong" and "to have power or influence." So *evaluating* a house involves determining how healthy it is. A *valid* license or credit card is one that's still in effect, and a valid proof is one that provides strong evidence.

---

valor \\'va-lər\\ Personal bravery in the face of danger.

* The gun duels of the Old West were invented by a novelist inspired by the valor of the knights in medieval tournaments.

Valor in uniform is still rewarded by medals. Many American civic organizations award a Medal of Valor for physical courage, and the Air Force Medal of Honor displays the single word "Valor." The somewhat old-fashioned adjective *valorous* more often describes warriors of the past. But *valiant* is still in common use, though it less often describes military courage than other kinds of bravery or effort.

equivalent \\i-'kwi-və-lənt\\ (1) Equal in force, amount, value, area, or volume. (2) Similar or virtually identical in effect or function.

* A square can be equivalent to a triangle in area, but not in shape.

Modern democracies have institutions and offices that are roughly equivalent to those found in others: the president of the United States has his British equivalent in the prime minister, for instance, and the U.S. Congress finds its equivalent in the British Parliament. The heavily armored knight on his great armored horse has been called the Middle Ages' equivalent of the army tank. In none of these examples are the two things identical to each other; they're simply very similar in their effect or purpose or nature, which is what *equivalence* usually implies.

prevalent \\'pre-və-lənt\\ Widely accepted, favored, or practiced; widespread.

* On some campuses Frisbees seem to be more prevalent than schoolbooks, especially in the spring.

Many diseases that were prevalent a century ago have been controlled by advances in medicine. Smallpox was prevalent on several continents for many centuries, and when Europeans brought it with them to the Americas, it killed more American Indians than the armed settlers did. But *prevalent* doesn't just describe diseases. One ideal of male or female beauty may be prevalent in a particular society and quite a different ideal in another. In the 1950s and '60s, there was a prevalent notion that if you went swimming less than an hour after eating you might drown because of stomach cramps—which goes to show that not every prevalent idea is exactly true.

validate \\'va-lə-ˌdāt\\ (1) To make legally valid; give official approval to. (2) To support or confirm the validity of.

• It will take many more research studies to validate a theory as far-reaching as this one.

Validating a pass might require getting an official stamp on it. Validating experimental data might require checking it against data from further experiments. An A on a test might validate your study methods. And you might go to a trusted friend to validate your decision to get rid of your boyfriend, buy a pet iguana, or sell everything and move to Las Vegas.

Quizzes

A. Fill in each blank with the correct letter:

a. virago
b. virtuosity
c. triumvirate
d. virility

e. valor
f. validate
g. prevalent
h. equivalent

1. Some people think a man's _____ fades with age.
2. An election worker at the next table will _____ each voter's ID.
3. The orchestra will be performing with a solo violinist whose _____ has already made her a star.
4. Colds and flu threaten to be unusually _____ this winter.
5. The ranch is owned by Mamie Peabody, a brawny _____ who sometimes competes in the men's events at the rodeo.
6. We may not be able to find an identical chair, but we'll find an _____ one.
7. The company is really run by a _____: Bailey, Sanchez, and Dr. Ross.

8. At a memorial ceremony, the slain guard who had tried to stop the gunman was honored for _____.

B. Match the word on the left to the correct definition on the right:

1. prevalent		a.	courage
2. virago		b.	masculinity
3. virtuosity		c.	confirm
4. virility		d.	strong woman
5. valor		e.	skill
6. triumvirate		f.	widespread
7. equivalent		g.	three-person board
8. validate		h.	similar in value

CRE/CRET comes from the Latin verb *crescere*, which means both "to come into being" and "to grow." So a *crescendo* in music occurs when the music is growing louder, and a *decrescendo* when it's growing softer.

---

crescent \\'kre-sənt\\ (1) The moon between the new moon and first quarter, and between the last quarter and the next new moon. (2) Anything shaped like the crescent moon.

• The symbol of Islam is a crescent moon with a star between the points, an astronomical impossibility.

Crescent means basically "growing," since a crescent moon is in the process of "growing" to a full moon. A *crescent wrench*, with its open end (unlike the kind of wrench that has an almost circular end), can be found in almost any household. A *croissant,* or crescent pastry, is a breakfast staple. The curving region called the Fertile Crescent, which stretches from the Persian Gulf up through Iraq, across to Lebanon and Israel, and down into Egypt's Nile River valley, was the birthplace of civilization, where weaving, pottery, domesticated livestock, irrigation farming, and writing all first appeared.

accretion \\ə-'krē-shən\\ (1) Growth or enlargement by gradual buildup. (2) A product of such buildup.

• The house and barn were linked by an accretion of outbuildings, each joined to the next.

The slow accretion of scientific knowledge over many centuries has turned into an avalanche in our time. Any accretion of ice on a grounded jet will result in takeoff delays because of the danger it poses. The land area of the Mississippi Delta increases every year from the accretion of soil washed down the Mississippi River, though the accretions happen so slowly that it's difficult to detect any increase at all. *Accretion* is often used in scientific writing; its usual verb form, *accrue*, is more often used in financial contexts ("This figure doesn't count the accrued interest on the investments").

excrescence \ek-'skre-səns\ (1) A projection of growth, especially when abnormal. (2) A disfiguring, unnecessary, or unwanted mark or part.

• The new warehouse squatted like some hideous excrescence on the landscape.

Warts and pimples are common excrescences that can usually be wiped out with medication; other excrescences such as cysts and tumors need to be removed surgically. Mushrooms are the excrescences of underground fungus networks. Some people consider slang words to be vulgar excrescences on the English language, but others consider slang the most colorful vocabulary of all.

increment \'iŋ-krə-mənt\ (1) Something gained or added, especially as one of a series of regular additions or as a tiny increase in amount. (2) The amount or extent of change, especially the positive or negative change in value of one or more variables.

• Her bank account has grown weekly by increments of $50 for the past two years.

Increment is used in many technical fields, but also nontechnically. *Incremental* increases in drug dosages are used for experimental purposes. Incremental tax increases are easier to swallow than sudden large increases. Incremental changes of any kind may be hard to notice, but can be very significant in the long run. Rome wasn't built in a day, but was instead built up by increments from a couple of villages in the 10th century B.C. to the capital of the Mediterranean world in the 1st century A.D.

FUS comes from the Latin verb *fundere*, "to pour out" or "to melt." A *fuse* depends on melting metal to break an overloaded circuit. Nuclear *fusion* involves the "melting" together of light nuclei to form heavier nuclei, and fusion cuisine brings together the cooking of two or more cultures.

---

transfusion \trans-ˈfyü-zhən\ (1) The process of transferring a fluid and especially blood into a blood vessel. (2) Something transfused.

• The transfusion gave her an immediate burst of energy, and her friends were astonished when they arrived at the hospital that afternoon.

When blood transfusions were first attempted by Europeans in the early 1600s, they were met with skepticism, since the established practice was to bleed patients, not *transfuse* them with blood. Some patients were transfused with animal blood, and so many died as a result that by 1700 transfusions had been widely outlawed. Not until 1900 were the major blood groups (A, B, AB, and O) recognized, making transfusions safe and effective.

effusive \i-ˈfyü-siv\ (1) Given to excessive display of feeling. (2) Freely expressed.

• At the victory party she lavished effusive praise on all her supporters for almost half an hour.

Since to *effuse* is to "pour out," an effusive person makes a habit of pouring out emotions. Greeting someone *effusively* may include great hugs and wet kisses. Academy Award winners tend to become embarrassingly effusive once they've got the microphone. But at least *effusiveness* is generally an expression of positive rather than negative emotions.

profusion \prə-ˈfyü-zhən\ Great abundance.

• In May the trees and flowers bloom with almost delirious profusion.

A profusion is literally a "pouring forth," so a profusion of gifts is a wealth or abundance of gifts. A *profusely* illustrated book is filled to overflowing with pictures. A bad social error should be followed by *profuse* apologies, and profound gratitude should be expressed with profuse thanks.

suffuse \sə-ˈfyüz\ To spread over or fill something, as if by fluid or light.

- As the soft light of dawn suffused the landscape, they could hear the loons crying over the lake.

The odors of baking may suffuse a room, and so may the light of a sunset. A face may be suffused (that is, filled, but also probably flushed) with joy, or hope, or love. A novel may be suffused with Irish humor, and a room may be suffused with firelight. Scientists may even describe an insect's gray wings as being suffused with tinges of red.

Quizzes

A. Choose the closest definition:

1. excrescence   a. disgust b. outgrowth c. extremity
      d. garbage
2. suffuse   a. overwhelm b. flow c. spread through
      d. inject
3. accretion   a. agreement b. eruption c. decision
      d. buildup
4. effusive   a. emotional b. gradual c. continual
      d. general
5. increment   a. entrance b. slight increase
      c. construction d. income
6. transfusion   a. revision b. change c. transfer
      d. adjustment
7. crescent   a. semicircle b. pastry c. sickle shape
      d. buildup
8. profusion   a. distinction b. abundance c. addition
      d. completion

B. Indicate whether the following pairs of words have the same or different meanings:

1. effusive / gushy   same ___ / different ___
2. crescent / pinnacle   same ___ / different ___
3. transfusion / improvement   same ___ / different ___
4. excrescence / ugliness   same ___ / different ___
5. suffuse / fill   same ___ / different ___
6. increment / excess   same ___ / different ___
7. profusion / amount   same ___ / different ___
8. accretion / destruction   same ___ / different ___

Greek and Latin Borrowings

apologia \\ˌa-pə-ˈlō-jē-ə\\ A defense, especially of one's own ideas, opinions, or actions.

- His resignation speech was an eloquent apologia for his controversial actions as chairman.

An apologia and an *apology* usually aren't the same thing. An apology includes an admission of wrongdoing, but an apologia rarely *apologizes* in this sense, instead seeking to justify what was done. So, for example, in 1992 some of the books published for the 500th anniversary of Columbus's voyage were apologias explaining why European powers such as Spain acted as they did in the New World: because, for example, the Aztecs were a cruel people, practicing human sacrifice in grotesque ways (victims were skinned, and their skins were worn by the high priests), and Christianity hoped to reform them. Of course, the Spanish Inquisition was torturing and executing nonbelievers at the same time—but that would be the subject of other apologias.

atrium \\ˈā-trē-əm\\ (1) An open rectangular patio around which a house is built. (2) A court with a skylight in a many-storied building.

- Best of all, their new home had a large atrium, where they could eat breakfast in the fresh air in spring and summer.

In malls and grand office buildings today, the enclosed atrium, often with full-size trees growing in it and high indoor balconies with hanging vines, has become a common architectural feature. But the original atria (notice the unusual plural) were open to the sky and occupied the center of a house or villa in ancient Rome. The open Roman courtyard allowed air to circulate and light to enter, and even its plantings helped cool the house. Situating the cooking fireplace in the atrium was another way of keeping the house itself cool. Still today, houses around the Mediterranean Sea and in tropical Latin America often have internal courtyards.

oligarchy \\ˈä-lə-ˌgär-kē\\ A government in which power is in the hands of a small group.

- The population was shackled by an iron-willed oligarchy that dictated every aspect of their lives and ruthlessly crushed any hint of rebellion.

Oligarchy combines roots from the Greek words *oligos*, meaning "few," and *archos*, meaning "leader or ruler." In ancient Greece, an *aristocracy* was government by the "best" (in Greek, *aristos*) citizens. An oligarchy was a corrupted aristocracy, one in which a few evil men unjustly seized power and used it to further their own ends. Since at least 1542, *oligarchy* has been used in English to describe oppressive governments of the kind that serve the interests of a few very wealthy families.

encomium \en-ˈkō-mē-əm\ Glowing, enthusiastic praise, or an expression of such praise.

• The surprise guest at the farewell party was the school's most famous graduate, who delivered a heartfelt encomium to the woman he called his favorite teacher of all.

Encomium comes straight from Latin. Mark Antony's encomium to the dead Caesar in Shakespeare's *Julius Caesar* ("Friends, Romans, countrymen, lend me your ears") is one of the most famous encomiums of all time, while Ben Jonson's encomium to the dead Shakespeare ("He was not of an age, but for all time") has also been widely read and discussed. The British poet laureate is expected to compose poetic encomiums to mark special events or to praise a person honored by the state. And any awards banquet is thick with encomiums, with each speaker trying to outdo the last in praise of those being honored.

neurosis \nu̇-ˈrō-səs\ A mental and emotional disorder that is less severe than a psychosis and may involve various pains, anxieties, or phobias.

• He has a neurosis about dirt, and is constantly washing his hands.

A neurosis is a somewhat mild mental disorder; unexplained anxiety attacks, unreasonable fears, depression, and physical symptoms that are mentally caused are all examples of *neurotic* conditions. A superstitious person who compulsively knocks on wood or avoids anything with the number 13 might be suffering from a harmless neurosis. But a severe neurosis such as agoraphobia (see p. 587) can be very harmful, making a person a prisoner of his or her home. *Neurosis* is based on the Greek word for "nerve," since until quite recently neurotic behavior was often blamed on the nerves. Neurosis is usually contrasted with *psychosis*, which includes a considerably more serious group of conditions.

opprobrium \ə-ˈprō-brē-əm\ (1) Something that brings disgrace. (2) A public disgrace that results from conduct considered wrong or bad.

- The writers of the New Testament hold the Pharisees up to opprobrium for their hypocrisy and hollow spirituality.

Witches have long been the objects of opprobrium; in Europe in the 16th and 17th centuries, women thought to be witches were burned by the thousands. The *opprobrious* crime of treason could likewise result in the most hideous torture and execution. In *The Scarlet Letter,* the sin of adultery in Puritan times brought opprobrium on Hester Prynne. Today the country of Israel is the object of opprobrium in many countries, while the Palestinians suffer similar opprobrium in others. And mere smokers, or even overweight people, may sometimes feel themselves to be the objects of mild opprobrium.

referendum \ˌre-fə-ˈren-dəm\ (1) The referring of legislative measures to the voters for approval or rejection. (2) A vote on such a measure.

- The referendum on the tax needed for constructing the new hospital passed by seven votes.

Referendum is a Latin word, but its modern meaning only dates from the 19th century, when a new constitution adopted by Switzerland stated that the voters could vote directly on certain issues. Thus, a referendum is a measure that's *referred* (that is, sent on) to the people. Since the U.S. Constitution doesn't provide for referenda (notice the common plural form) at the national level, referenda tend to be on local and state issues. In most locales, a few questions usually appear on the ballot at election time, often involving such issues as new zoning ordinances, new taxes for schools, and new limits on spending.

ultimatum \ˌəl-tə-ˈmā-təm\ A final proposal, condition, or demand, especially one whose rejection will result in forceful action.

- The ultimatum to Iraq in 1991 demanding that it withdraw from Kuwait was ignored, and a U.S.-led invasion was the response.

An ultimatum is usually issued by a stronger power to a weaker one, since it wouldn't carry much weight if the one giving the ultimatum couldn't back up its threat. Near the end of World War II, the Allied powers issued an ultimatum to Japan: surrender completely or face the consequences. Japan rejected the ultimatum, and within days the U.S. had dropped atomic bombs on Hiroshima and Nagasaki, killing some 200,000 people.

Quiz

Fill in each blank with the correct letter:

a. encomium   e. apologia
b. ultimatum   f. oligarchy
c. neurosis   g. referendum
d. atrium   h. opprobrium

1. His particular _____ was a fear of heights.
2. The country has a president, of course, but everyone knows he's just the front man for a shadowy _____.
3. The committee voted to submit the new zoning plan to the voters in a special _____.
4. The new office building was designed around a wide, sunlit _____ with a fountain and small trees.
5. His book is an _____ for his entire life, which may cause his enemies to rethink their opinion of him.
6. _____ has been heaped on the school board from angry parents on both sides of the issue.
7. When peace negotiations fell apart, an angry _____ was issued by the government.
8. Most of her speech was devoted to a glowing _____ to her staff members.

Review Quizzes

A. Complete the analogy:

1. church : temple :: sanctuary : _____
   a. destination b. parish c. destiny d. refuge

2. relaxed : stiff :: colloquial : _____
   a. conversational b. talkative c. casual d. formal

3. portion : segment :: increment : _____
   a. inroad b. inflation c. increase d. instinct

4. reprimand : scolding :: encomium : _____
   a. warm drink b. warm thanks c. warm toast
   d. warm praise

5. truce : treaty :: ultimatum : _____
   a. decision b. negotiation c. threat d. attack

6. donate : contribute :: remand : _____
   a. pass over b. send back c. take on d. give up

7. monarchy : king :: oligarchy : _____
   a. dictator b. ruling group c. emperor d. totalitarian

8. cavity : hole :: excrescence : _____
   a. growth b. deposit c. residue d. toad

9. rare : scarce :: prevalent : _____
   a. unique b. commonplace c. thick d. preferred

10. evaporate : dry up :: inundate : _____
    a. flood b. drain c. wash d. irrigate

11. order : demand :: commandeer : _____
    a. allow b. seize c. rule d. lead

12. vamp : sexy :: virago : _____
    a. loud b. attractive c. powerful d. elderly

13. generous : stingy :: effusive : _____
    a. emotional b. thoughtful c. restrained d. passionate

14. release : restrain :: sanction : _____
    a. disapprove b. request c. train d. decide

15. femininity : man :: virility : _____
    a. female b. girl c. woman d. lady

B. Fill in each blank with the correct letter:

a. referendum
b. profusion
c. crescent
d. validate
e. virtuosity
f. colloquium
g. redundancy
h. mandate
i. apologia
j. opprobrium
k. transfusion
l. equivalent
m. loquacious
n. sacrosanct
o. redound

1. Although he was shy the first time he came to dinner, he's usually downright _____ these days.

2. Three new young staff members were hired this year, and they've given the whole place a real _____ of energy.

3. If our researchers receive the Nobel Prize this year, it will _____ to the university's credit for years to come.

4. The hammer and sickle on the Soviet Union's flag oddly resembled the Islamic star and _____.

5. The planning board submitted its proposal to the voters as a nonbinding _____.

6. My professor is participating in the _____, and we're all required to attend.

7. Some politicians claim they have a _____ from the voters even when their margin of victory was actually small.

8. Under the new boss, no department here is _____ and almost any of them could be broken up tomorrow.

9. She was renowned for her _____ in the kitchen, whipping up delicious meals from any ingredients that came to hand.

10. The bower was hung with roses blooming in great _____.

11. At a scientific conference in July she delivered a convincing _____ for the unusual methods that had drawn so much criticism.

12. An endorsement from one of the major medical associations would help _____ the therapies we offer.

13. When a neo-Nazi group marched down Pennsylvania Avenue, it was greeted with loud _____ from egg-throwing anti-Nazi demonstrators.

14. The computer files contain a great deal of data _____ that isn't actually serving any purpose.

15. A speed of 100 kilometers per hour is _____ to about 60 miles per hour.

C. Match the definition on the left to the correct word on the right:

1.	open courtyard	a.	soliloquy
2.	emotional disorder	b.	undulant
3.	spread over	c.	valor
4.	accumulation	d.	triumvirate
5.	bravery	e.	suffuse
6.	monologue	f.	accretion
7.	hypocritical	g.	atrium
8.	wavelike	h.	neurosis
9.	required	i.	sanctimonious
10.	three-person group	j.	mandatory

UNIT

25

VERB comes from the Latin *verbum*, meaning "word." A *verb*—or action word—appears in some form in every complete sentence. To express something *verbally*—or to *verbalize* something—is to say it or write it.

---

verbose \vər-ˈbōs\ Using more words than are needed; wordy.

• The writing style in government publications has often been both dry and verbose—a deadly combination.

Americans brought up on fast-paced TV shows and action films have lost any patience they once had for *verbosity*. So most American writing is brisk, and American speakers usually don't waste many words. But many of us love our own voices and opinions and don't realize we're being verbose until our listeners start stifling their yawns. And students still try to fill up the pages of their term papers with unneeded verbosity.

proverb \ˈprä-ˌvərb\ A brief, often-repeated statement that expresses a general truth or common observation.

• "Waste not, want not" used to be a favorite proverb in many households.

Proverbs probably appeared with the dawn of language. Sayings such as "A stitch in time saves nine," or "Pride goeth before a fall," or "Least said, soonest mended," or "To everything there is a season" are easily memorized nuggets of wisdom. But the convenient thing about proverbs is that there's often one for every point of view. For every "Look before you leap" there's a "He who hesitates is lost." "A fool and his money are soon parted" can be countered with "To make money you have to spend money." A cynic once observed, "Proverbs are invaluable treasures to dunces with good memories."

verbatim \vər-ˈbā-təm\ In the exact words; word for word.

* It turned out that the writer had lifted long passages verbatim from an earlier, forgotten biography of the statesman.

Verbatim comes directly from Latin into English with the same spelling and meaning. Memorizing famous speeches, poems, or literary passages is a good way to both train the memory and absorb the classic texts of our literature and culture. At one time the ability to recite verbatim the Gettysburg Address, the beginning of the Declaration of Independence, and great speeches from Shakespeare was the mark of a well-educated person. But when that language was quoted by a writer, he or she was always careful to put quotation marks around it and tell readers who the true author was.

verbiage \ˈvər-bē-ij\ An excess of words, often with little content; wordiness.

* The agency's report was full of unnecessary verbiage, which someone should have edited out before the report was published.

Government reports are notorious for their unfortunate tendency toward empty verbiage, through part of the reason is simply that officials are anxious to be following all the rules. Legal documents are also generally full of verbiage, partly because lawyers want to be sure that every last possibility has been covered and no loopholes have been left. But writing that contains unneeded verbiage is often trying to disguise its lack of real substance or clarity of thought. And every writer, including government workers and lawyers, should be constantly on the lookout for opportunities to hit the Delete key.

SIMIL/SIMUL come from the Latin adjective *similis*, meaning "like, resembling, similar," and the verb *simulare*, "to make like." Two *similar* things resemble each other. Two *simultaneous* activities proceed at the same time. And a *facsimile*, such as you might receive from your *fax* machine, looks exactly the same as the original.

---

simile \\'si-mə-lē\ A figure of speech, introduced by *as* or *like,* that makes a point of comparison between two things different in all other respects.

• He particularly liked the simile he'd thought of for the last line of the song's chorus, "It felt like a bullet in his heart."

Fiction, poetry, and philosophy have been full of similes for centuries. In fact, the oldest literature known to us uses similes, along with their close relatives known as metaphors (see p. 464). This suggests that similes are an essential part of imaginative writing in all times and all cultures. When Tennyson, describing an eagle, writes "And like a thunderbolt he falls," he's using a simile, since the line makes a specific comparison. "The road was a ribbon of moonlight" could be called a metaphor, though "The road was like a ribbon of moonlight" would be a simile.

assimilate \ə-'si-mə-ˌlāt\ (1) To take in and thoroughly understand. (2) To cause to become part of a different society or culture.

• One of the traditional strengths of American society has been its ability to assimilate one group of immigrants after another.

Assimilate comes from the Latin verb *assimulare,* "to make similar," and it originally applied to the process by which food is taken into the body and absorbed into the system. In a similar way, a fact can be taken into the mind, thoroughly digested, and absorbed into one's store of knowledge. A newcomer to a job or a subject must assimilate an often confusing mass of information; only after it's been thoroughly absorbed can the person make intelligent use of it. An immigrant family assimilates into its new culture by gradually adopting a new language and the habits of their new neighbors—a process that's always easier for the children than for the parents.

simulacrum \ˌsim-yə-'la-krəm\ A copy, especially a superficial likeness or imitation.

• As a boy he had filled his bedroom with model fighter jets, and these simulacra had kept his flying fantasies active for years.

In its original meaning, a simulacrum is simply a representation of something else; so an original oil painting, marble statue, or plastic figurine could all be simulacra (notice the plural form) in the old sense. But today the word usually means a copy that's meant to substitute for the real thing—and usually a cheap and inferior copy, a pale imitation of the original. So in old Persia a beautifully laid out garden was a simulacrum of paradise. Some countries' governments are mere simulacra of democracy, since the people in power always steal the elections by miscounting the votes. And a bad actor might do a simulacrum of grief on the stage that doesn't convince anyone.

simulate \\'sim-yə-ˌlāt\ (1) To take on the appearance or effect of something, often in order to deceive. (2) To make a realistic imitation of something, such as a physical environment.

- The armed services have made extensive use of video games to simulate the actual experience of warfare for their recruits.

The zircon, that favorite of home shopping channels, simulates a diamond—more or less. A skilled furrier can dye lower-grade furs to simulate real mink. A skilled actress can simulate a range of emotions from absolute joy to crushing despair. And an apparatus that simulates the hazards of driving while intoxicated is likely to provide some very real benefits.

Quizzes

A. Fill in each blank with the correct letter:

a. simulacrum   e. proverb
b. verbiage   f. simile
c. simulate   g. verbose
d. verbatim   h. assimilate

1. Please quote me _____ or don't "quote" me at all.
2. Most students can't _____ so much information all at once, so they approach it gradually.
3. He turned out to be a _____ old windbag, and I slept through the whole talk.
4. That restaurant doesn't offer real maple syrup, just an unconvincing _____.
5. She did her best to _____ pleasure at the news, but could barely manage a smile.

6. "Nothing ventured, nothing gained" was a favorite _____ of my grandmother's.

7. Unnecessary _____ usually gets in the way of clarity in writing.

8. "A day without sunshine is like a chicken without a bicycle" has to be the oddest _____ of all time.

B. Complete the analogy:

1. garbage : food :: verbiage : _____
   a. boxes b. verbs c. words d. trash

2. create : invent :: assimilate : _____
   a. wring b. absorb c. camouflage d. drench

3. frequently : often :: verbatim : _____
   a. later b. closely c. differently d. exactly

4. painting : portrays :: simulacrum : _____
   a. imitates b. shows c. demonstrates d. calculates

5. sound bite : quotation :: proverb : _____
   a. saying b. sentence c. introduction d. phrase

6. inflate : expand :: simulate : _____
   a. reveal b. entrap c. devote d. imitate

7. scarce : sparse :: verbose : _____
   a. poetic b. wordy c. fictional d. musical

8. contrast : different :: simile : _____
   a. near b. distant c. alike d. clear

SCEND comes from the Latin verb *scandere,* "to climb." The staircase we *ascend* to our bedroom at night we will *descend* the next morning, since what goes up must come down.

transcend \tran-ˈsend\ To rise above the limits of; overcome, surpass.

• His defeat in the election had been terribly hard on him, and it took two years before he finally felt he had transcended the bitterness it had produced.

Great leaders are expected to transcend the limitations of politics, especially during wartime and national crises. A great writer may transcend geographical boundaries to become internationally respected. And certain laws of human nature seem to transcend historical periods and hold true for all times and all places.

condescend \ˌkän-di-ˈsend\ (1) To stoop to a level of lesser importance or dignity. (2) To behave as if superior.

- Every so often my big brother would condescend to take me to a movie, but only when my parents made him.

Back when society was more rigidly structured, *condescend* didn't sound so negative. People of higher rank, power, or social position had to overlook certain established rules of behavior if they wished to have social dealings with people of lower status, but such *condescension* was usually gracious and courteous. In today's more classless society, the term implies a manner that may be slightly offensive. A poor relation is unlikely to be grateful to a wealthy and *condescending* relative who passes on her secondhand clothes, and employees at an office party may not be thrilled when the boss's wife condescends to mingle with them. Often the word is used rather unseriously, as when a friend comments that a snooty sales clerk condescended to wait on her after ignoring her for several minutes.

descendant \di-ˈsen-dənt\ (1) One that has come down from another or from a common stock. (2) One deriving directly from a forerunner or original.

- Though none of the great man's descendants ever came close to achieving what he had, most of them enjoyed very respectable careers.

Descendant is the opposite of *ancestor*. Your grandparents' descendants are those who are descended from them—your parents, your brothers and sisters, and any children that any of you may have. It's been claimed that every person on earth is a descendant of Muhammad, and of every historical person before him—Julius Caesar, the Buddha, etc.—who started a line of *descent*. (Some of us still find this hard to believe.) And not all descendants are human; every modern thesaurus, for example, could be called the descendant of the one devised by Peter Mark Roget in 1852.

ascendancy \ə-ˈsen-dən-sē\ Governing or controlling interest; domination.

- Under Augustus, Rome succeeded in establishing its ascendancy over the entire Mediterranean by 30 BC.

In the course of a year, the sun appears to pass through the twelve constellations of the zodiac in sequence, and all the planets also lie close to the solar path. The constellation and planet that are just rising, or *ascendant*, above the eastern horizon in the sun's path at the moment of a child's birth are said by astrologers to exercise a lifelong controlling influence over the child. This is the idea that lies at the heart of *ascendancy*, though the word today no longer hints at supernatural powers.

ONYM comes from the Greek *onyma*, meaning "name, word." An *anonymous* donor or writer is one who isn't named. A *synonym* is a word with the same meaning as another word (see SYN, p. 660). And *homonyms* (see HOM/HOMO, p. 58) are words that look and sound alike but aren't actually related, such as *well* ("healthy") and *well* ("a deep hole with water in it").

antonym \\'an-tə-ˌnim\\ A word that means the opposite of some other word.

• There's no point in telling a three-year-old that *cat* isn't an antonym of *dog*, and *sun* isn't an antonym of *moon*.

Antonym includes the Greek prefix *ant-*, meaning "opposite" (see ANT/ANTI, p. 469). Antonyms are often thought of in pairs: *hot/cold, up/down, wet/dry, buy/sell, failure/success*. But a word may have more than one antonym (*old/young, old/new*), especially when one of the words has synonyms (*small/large, small/big, little/big*), and a word may have many approximate antonyms (*adore/hate, adore/detest, adore/loathe*). But although lots of words have synonyms, not so many have antonyms. What would be the antonym of *pink*? *weather*? *semipro*? *thirty*? *firefighter*? *wax*? *about*? *consider*?

eponymous \\i-'pä-nə-məs\\ Of, relating to, or being the person for whom something is named.

• Adjectives such as *Elizabethan, Victorian,* and *Edwardian* show how the names of certain British monarchs have become eponymous for particular time periods and styles.

Things as different as a bird, a river, and a drug may be named to honor someone. The Canadian city of Vancouver was named after the explorer George Vancouver; the diesel engine was named for its inventor, Rudolph Diesel; Alzheimer's disease was named after the physician Alois Alzheimer; and so on. Common eponymous terms include *Ohm's law, Parkinson's Law,* and the *Peter Principle.* And if the Beatles' famous "white album" actually has a name, it's usually called "The Beatles," which means that it's eponymous as well. Don't be surprised if *eponymous* turns out to be a hard word to use; lots of other people have discovered the same thing.

patronymic \ˌpa-trə-ˈni-mik\ Part of a personal name based on the name of one's father or one of his ancestors.

• Reading Tolstoy's vast novel, it can be helpful to know that Helene Vasilievna's second name is a patronymic, and thus that her father is named Vasili.

A patronymic, or *patronym* (see also PATER/PATR, p. 433), is generally formed by adding a prefix or suffix to a name. Thus, a few centuries ago, the male patronymic of Patrick was Fitzpatrick ("Patrick's son"), that of Peter was Peterson or Petersen, that of Donald was MacDonald or McDonald, and that of Hernando was Hernández. Today, of course, each of these is an ordinary family name, or *surname.* In Russia, both a patronymic and a surname are still used; in the name Peter Ilyich Tchaikovsky, for example, Ilyich is a patronymic meaning "son of Ilya."

pseudonym \ˈsü-də-ˌnim\ A name that someone (such as a writer) uses instead of his or her real name.

• Hundreds of Hardy Boys, Nancy Drew, and Bobbsey Twins novels were churned out under such pseudonyms as Franklin W. Dixon, Carolyn Keene, and Laura Lee Hope.

The Greek *pseudo-* is used in English to mean "false," or sometimes "resembling." A pseudonym is thus a false name, or alias. A writer's pseudonym is called a *pen name*, as in the case of Howard O'Brien (who usually writes as "Anne Rice" but sometimes under other names), and an actor's pseudonym is called a *stage name*, as in the case of Marion Morrison ("John Wayne"). A *cadre name* may be used for the sake of secrecy by a revolutionary plotter such as Vladimir Ulyanov ("Lenin") or Iosif Dzhugashvili ("Stalin"). And in many religious orders, members adopt *devotional names*, as Agnes Bojaxhiu did in 1931 ("Teresa," later known as "Mother Teresa").

Quizzes

A. Choose the closest definition:

1. ascendancy   a. growth b. climb c. dominance d. rank
2. eponymous   a. having several rulers b. written by three people c. borrowed from literature d. taken from a name
3. descendant   a. offspring b. ancestor c. cousin d. forerunner
4. patronymic   a. client's name b. name based on your father's c. last name d. first name
5. transcend   a. exceed b. astound c. fulfill d. transform
6. antonym   a. technical name b. third name c. word with opposite meaning d. word with related meaning
7. condescend   a. stoop b. remove c. agree d. reject
8. pseudonym   a. alias b. phony c. made-up word d. honorary title

B. Fill in each blank with the correct letter:

a. condescend   e. transcend
b. antonym   f. eponymous
c. ascendancy   g. descendant
d. patronymic   h. pseudonym

1. He's one of the few people in the office who manages to _____ all the unpleasantness that goes on around here.
2. The best _____ for "popular" is "unpopular," not "shy."
3. The Democrats are in the _____ at the moment, but they may not be next year.
4. She'll remind you that she's a _____ of some fairly famous people, but she won't mention that the family also has some criminals in its past.
5. In a Russian family in which the father is named Fyodor, a boy's _____ would be Fyodorovich and a girl's would be Fyodorevna.
6. He was born Vlad Butsky, but he writes under the _____ Vance Bond.
7. She lives in a very glamorous world these days, and she would never _____ to show up at a family reunion.
8. The Restaurant Alain Savoy is the _____ establishment belonging to the great French chef.

SCRIB/SCRIP comes from the Latin verb *scribere,* "to write." *Scribble* is an old word meaning to write or draw carelessly. A written work that hasn't been published is a *manuscript*. And to *describe* is to picture something in words.

conscription \kən-'skrip-shən\ Enforced enlistment of persons, especially for military service; draft.

• The first comprehensive system for nationwide conscription was instituted by France for the Napoleonic wars that followed the French Revolution.

With its *scrip-* root, *conscription* means basically writing someone's name on a list—a list that, unfortunately, a lot of people usually don't want to be on. Conscription has existed at least since ancient Egypt's Old Kingdom (27th century B.C.), though universal conscription has been rare throughout history. Forms of conscription were used by Prussia, Switzerland, Russia, and other European powers in the 17th and 18th centuries. In the U.S., conscription was first applied during the Civil War, by both the North and the South. In the North there were pockets of resistance, and the draft led to riots in several cities. The U.S. abandoned conscription at the end of the war and didn't revive it until World War I.

circumscribe \'sər-kəm-ˌskrīb\ (1) To clearly limit the range or activity of something. (2) To draw a line around or to surround with a boundary.

• Some children do best when their freedom is clearly circumscribed and their activities are supervised.

The prefix *circum-,* "around," is the key to *circumscribe*'s basic meaning. Thus, we could say that a boxing ring is circumscribed by ropes, just as the area for an archaeological dig may be. A governor's power is always circumscribed by a state's constitution. And a physician's assistant has a *circumscribed* role that doesn't include writing prescriptions.

inscription \in-'skrip-shən\ (1) Something permanently written, engraved, or printed, particularly on a building, coin, medal, or piece of currency. (2) The dedication of a book or work of art.

• All U.S. coins bear the Latin inscription "E pluribus unum"— "From many, one."

With its prefix *in-*, meaning "in" or "on," it's not surprising that an inscription is either written on or engraved into a surface. Inscriptions in the ancient world were always chiseled into stone, as inscriptions still may be today. The principal monument of the Vietnam memorial in Washington, D.C., for instance, is a black wall on which are *inscribed* the names of all the Americans who died during the war—each name in full, row upon seemingly endless row. But an inscription may also be a dedication, such as the words "For my wife" all by themselves on a page near the beginning of a book.

proscribe \prō-'skrīb\ To forbid as harmful or unlawful; prohibit.

• Despite thousands of laws proscribing littering, many of America's streets and public spaces continue to be dumping grounds.

The Latin prefix *pro-* sometimes meant "before," in the sense of "in front of" the people. So in ancient Rome *proscribere* meant to make public in writing the name of a person who was about to be executed, and whose property would be seized by the state. But the meaning of the English word soon shifted to mean simply "prohibit" instead. *Proscribe* today is actually often the opposite of the very similar *prescribe,* which means basically "require."

FALL comes from the Latin verb *fallere*, "to deceive." It's actually at the root of the word *false,* which we rarely use today to mean "deceptive," though that meaning does show up in older phrases: "Thou shalt not bear false witness against thy neighbor," for instance, or "A false-hearted lover will send you to your grave." *Fallere* is even at the root of *fail* and *fault*, though you might not guess it to look at them.

---

fallacy \'fa-lə-sē\ A wrong belief; a false or mistaken idea.

• In her new article she exposes yet another fallacy at the heart of these economic arguments.

Philosophers are constantly using the word *fallacy.* For them, a fallacy is reasoning that comes to a conclusion without the evidence to support it. This may have to do with pure logic, with the assumptions that the argument is based on, or with the way words are used, especially if they don't keep exactly the same meaning throughout the argument. There are many classic fallacies that occur again and again through the centuries and everywhere in the world. You may have heard of such fallacies as the "ad hominem" fallacy, the "question-begging" fallacy, the "straw man" fallacy, the "slippery slope" fallacy, the "gambler's" fallacy, or the "red herring" fallacy. Look them up and see if you've ever been guilty of any of them.

fallacious \fə-'lā-shəs\ Containing a mistake; not true or accurate.

• Any policy that's based on a lot of fallacious assumptions is going to be a bad one.

Fallacious is a formal and intellectual word. We rarely use it in casual speech; when we do, we risk sounding a bit full of ourselves and all-knowing. But it's used widely in writing, especially when one writer is arguing with another. And it's used to describe both errors in fact and errors in reasoning, including fallacies of the kind described in the previous entry.

fallibility \ˌfa-lə-'bi-lə-tē\ Capability of making mistakes or being wrong.

• Doctors are concerned about the fallibility of these tests, which seem unable to detect the virus about 20% of the time.

You'll find this word showing up in discussions of eyewitness testimony at crime scenes, of lie detectors, and of critical airplane parts. Some of us are most familiar with the fallibility of memory, especially when we remember something clearly that turns out never to have happened. Being *fallible* is part of being human, and sometimes the biggest errors are made by those who are thought of as the most brilliant of all.

infallible \in-'fa-lə-bəl\ (1) Not capable of being wrong or making mistakes. (2) Certain to work properly or succeed.

• Two college friends of mine claimed to have an infallible system for beating the odds at roulette in Las Vegas.

Watch out when you hear about infallible predictions, an infallible plan, an infallible cure, or even infallible lip gloss. *Infallible* isn't a claim that scientists, engineers, and doctors like to make, so you're probably getting better information when the word *not* comes first. You may have heard the phrase "papal *infallibility*," which refers to the official position of the Roman Catholic church, adopted in the

19th century, that certain solemn statements made by a Pope about faith or morals were not to be questioned. Popes since then have been careful not to make many of these statements.

Quizzes

A. Fill in each blank with the correct letter:

a. proscribe   e. infallible
b. fallacious   f. circumscribe
c. inscription   g. fallacy
d. fallibility   h. conscription

1. The college feels a strong responsibility for ensuring students' safety, but at the same time it doesn't want to _____ student life too much.
2. At first glance the article's claims sounded interesting, but it wasn't hard to discover the basic _____ they were based on.
3. She already knew the _____ she wanted on her gravestone: "She done the best she could."
4. The _____ of these tests has been shown again and again, but some doctors keep using them.
5. The number of fistfights and accidents at the games had finally forced officials to _____ beer drinking completely.
6. Since 1973 there's been no military _____ in the U.S., but that doesn't mean the draft won't come back someday.
7. Saying that one cool summer disproves the whole idea of global warming is obviously _____ and no one really believes it.
8. In his teens he had read book after book about gambling strategies, all of which were claimed by their authors to be _____.

B. **Match each word on the left with its correct definition on the right:**

1. fallacy   a. prohibit
2. proscribe   b. error
3. fallibility   c. epitaph
4. conscription   d. unreliability
5. fallacious   e. wrong
6. circumscribe   f. limit
7. infallible   g. perfect
8. inscription   h. draft

SOLU comes from the Latin verb *solvere,* "to loosen, free, release," and the root therefore may take the form *solv-* as well. So to *solve* a problem means to find its *solution,* as if you were freeing up a logjam. And a *solvent* is a chemical that *dissolves* or "loosens up" oil or paint.

soluble \\'säl-yə-bəl\\ (1) Able to be dissolved in a liquid, especially water. (2) Able to be solved or explained.

• To an optimistic young principal, the problems of a school like this one might seem challenging but soluble.

Soluble looks like a word that should be confined to chemistry labs, though it's often used by nonchemists as well to describe substances that can be dissolved in liquids. On the other hand, the sense of *soluble* meaning "solvable" is also quite common. In this sense, *soluble,* like its opposite, *insoluble,* is usually paired with *problem*. If only all life's problems were soluble by stirring them in a container filled with water.

absolution \\ˌab-sə-'lü-shən\\ The act of forgiving someone for their sins.

• Every week she would kneel to confess her little sins and receive absolution from the priest.

Since the Latin *absolutus* meant "set free," it's easy to see how *absolution* came to mean "set free from sin." (And also easy to see why *absolute* means basically "pure"—that is, originally, "free of sin.") The verb for *absolution* is *absolve.* Just as a priest absolves believers of their sins, you may absolve your brother of blame for a household disaster, or you yourself may in time be absolved for that scrape on the car backing out of a parking space.

dissolution \ˌdi-sə-ˈlü-shən\ The act or process of breaking down or apart into basic components, as through disruption or decay.

• The dissolution of the U.S.S.R. was probably the most momentous event of the last quarter of the 20th century.

Dissolution is the noun form of *dissolve*, but it's a much less common word. Still, we refer to the fact that the dissolution of American marriages became far more common in the later 20th century. Or that when India won its independence in 1948, the dissolution of the once-global British empire was all but complete. Or that factors such as crime and drugs might be contributing to the dissolution of contemporary society's moral fabric. A *dissolute* person is someone in whom all restraint has dissolved, and who now indulges in behavior that shocks decent people.

resolute \ˈre-zə-ˌlüt\ Marked by firm determination.

• After ten years of indecision, the Senate finally seems resolute about reaching an agreement.

Resolute comes from the same Latin verb as *resolved*, and the two words are often synonyms. So how did it get this meaning from the Latin? Essentially, when you resolve a question or problem, you come to a conclusion, and once you've reached a conclusion you can proceed to act. So in your New Year's *resolutions*, you resolve—or make up your mind—to do something. Unfortunately, New Year's resolutions aren't a good illustration of the meaning of *resolute*, since only about one in ten actually seems to succeed.

HYDR flows from the Greek word for "water." The "water" root can be found in the lovely flower called the *hydrangea*: its seed capsules resemble ancient Greek water vessels.

---

hydraulic \hī-ˈdrȯ-lik\ (1) Relating to water; operated, moved, or brought about by means of water. (2) Operated by the resistance or pressure of liquid forced through a small opening or tube.

• Without any hydraulic engineers, the country is unlikely to build many dams or reservoirs on its own.

By means of a hydraulic lift, the driver can lift the bed of a dump truck with the touch of a button. He might also repair the hydraulic steering, the hydraulic brake, or the hydraulic clutch—all of which, like the lift that holds everything up, take advantage of the way liquids act under pressure. Somewhat like a pulley or a lever, a hydraulic system magnifies the effect of moderate pressure exerted over a longer distance into powerful energy for a shorter distance.

dehydrate \dē-ʰhī-ˌdrāt\ (1) To remove water from. (2) To deprive of energy and zest.

* The boy appeared at dusk staggering out of the desert, dangerously sunburned and dehydrated.

Dehydrating food is a good way to preserve it; raisins, which are dehydrated grapes, are a good example. *Dehydration* through industrial processes makes it possible to keep food even longer and store it in a smaller space. Freeze-drying produces food that only needs *rehydration*—that is, the addition of water—to restore its original consistency. Runners, cyclists, and hikers fearful of dehydration seem to be constantly *hydrating* themselves nowadays, sometimes even using a shoulder pack with a tube going straight into the mouth. *Dehydrate* can also be used for making something "dry" or "lifeless"; thus, a dull teacher can dehydrate American history, and an unimaginative staging can dehydrate a great Shakespeare play.

hydroelectric \ˌhī-drō-i-ʰlek-trik\ Having to do with the production of electricity by waterpower.

* A massive African hydroelectric project is creating the world's largest manmade lake, and is said to hold the key to the future for the country.

The prime component of most hydroelectric systems is a dam. A high dam funnels water downward at high pressure to spin turbines, which in turn drive generators to produce high-voltage electricity. Mountainous countries with rushing rivers can produce the most *hydroelectricity*. Though hydroelectricity comes from a clean and completely renewable energy source, dams disrupt natural systems in a way that disturbs environmentalists.

hydroponics \ˌhī-drō-ʰpä-niks\ The growing of plants in nutrient solutions, with or without supporting substances such as sand or gravel.

- He had never thought hydroponics produced vegetables as tasty as those grown in soil, and the tomatoes seemed particularly disappointing.

Hydroponics, also known as *aquaculture* or *tank farming*, began as a way of studying scientifically the mechanisms of plant nutrition. Hydroponically grown plants may have no solid material under them at all; instead, their roots often simply hang in water with a rich mix of nutrients dissolved in it. The principal advantage to hydroponics is the savings from reduced labor costs, since it's generally carried on in enclosed areas and the irrigation and fertilizing are done mechanically. Peppers, cucumbers, and various other vegetables are produced *hydroponically* in huge quantities.

Quizzes

A. Complete the analogy:

1. freezing : melting :: dissolution : _____
   a. unification b. separation c. death d. defiance
2. pneumatic : air :: hydraulic : _____
   a. solid b. gas c. liquid d. evaporation
3. request : plea :: absolution : _____
   a. accusation b. forgiveness c. requirement d. loss
4. sterility : bacteria :: hydroponics : _____
   a. water b. soil c. air d. fire
5. determined : hesitant :: soluble : _____
   a. moist b. dry c. unexplainable d. possible
6. nuclear : uranium :: hydroelectric : _____
   a. coal b. petroleum c. dynamics d. water
7. puzzle : mystery :: resolution : _____
   a. determination b. delay c. detection d. demand
8. drain : replenish :: dehydrate : _____
   a. find b. dry out c. rehydrate d. add

> **B. Indicate whether the following pairs of words have the same or different meanings:**
>
> 1. hydraulic / electric   same __ / different __
> 2. soluble / explainable   same __ / different __
> 3. dehydrate / dry   same __ / different __
> 4. dissolution / disintegration   same __ / different __
> 5. hydroelectric / solar-powered   same __ / different __
> 6. resolution / attitude   same __ / different __
> 7. hydroponics / waterworks   same __ / different __
> 8. absolution / forgiveness   same __ / different __

Greek and Latin Borrowings

aegis \ˈē-jəs\ (1) Something that protects or defends; shield. (2) Sponsorship or guidance by an individual or organization.

• The conference was held under the aegis of the World Affairs Council, which provided almost all of the funding.

The original aegis was a goatskin shield or breastplate, symbolizing majesty, that was worn by Zeus and his daughter Athena in Greek mythology. Athena's aegis bore the severed head of the monstrous Medusa. *Aegis* came to be used for any kind of invulnerable shield. But today we almost always use the word in the phrase "under the aegis of . . . ," which means "under the authority, sponsorship, or control of."

charisma \kə-ˈriz-mə\ (1) An extraordinary gift for leadership that attracts popular support and enthusiasm. (2) A special ability to attract or charm; magnetism.

• Many later leaders have envied the charisma of Napoleon Bonaparte, who many of his followers genuinely believed to be immortal.

Charisma is Greek for "gift," but its traditional meaning comes from Christian belief, where it originally referred to an extraordinary power—the gift of healing, the gift of tongues, or the gift of prophecy—bestowed on an individual by the Holy Spirit. The first nonreligious use of *charisma* didn't appear until the 20th century, when it was applied to that mysterious personal magnetism that a lucky few seem to possess, especially the magnetism with which a political leader can arouse great popular enthusiasm. When John F. Kennedy was elected president in 1960, its use by journalists popularized the term in the mass media. Since then, actors, rock stars, athletes, generals, and entrepreneurs have all been said to possess charisma.

ego \\ˈē-gō\ (1) A sense of confidence and satisfaction in oneself; self-esteem. (2) An exaggerated sense of self-importance.

• His raging ego was what his fellow lawyers remembered about him—his tantrums, his vanity, his snobbery, and all the rest of it.

Ego is the Latin word for "I." So if a person seems to begin every sentence with "I," it's sometimes a sign of a big ego. It was the psychologist Sigmund Freud (well, actually his original translator) who put *ego* into the popular vocabulary, but what he meant by the word is complex, so only other psychologists really use it in the Freudian sense. The rest of us generally use *ego* simply to mean one's sense of self-worth, whether exaggerated or not. When used in the "exaggerated" sense, *ego* is almost the same thing as *conceit*. Meeting a superstar athlete without a trace of this kind of ego would be a most refreshing experience. But having a reasonable sense of your own worth is no sin. Life's little everyday victories are good—in fact, necessary—for a healthy ego.

ethos \\ˈē-ˌthäs\ The features, attitudes, moral code, or basic beliefs that define a person, a group, or an institution.

• The company's ethos has always been an interesting blend of greed and generosity.

Ethos means "custom" or "character" in Greek. As originally used by Aristotle, it referred to a man's character or personality, especially in its balance between passion and caution. Today *ethos* is used to refer to the practices or values that distinguish one person, organization, or society from others. So we often hear of the ethos of rugged individualism and self-sufficiency on the American frontier in the 19th century; and a critic might complain about, for example, the ethos of violence in the inner cities or the ethos of permissiveness in the suburbs.

hubris \\'hyü-brəs\\ Unreasonable or unjustified pride or self-confidence.

• Two hours later, the team's boastful pregame hubris bumped into the embarrassing reality of defeat.

To the Greeks, *hubris* referred to extreme pride, especially pride and ambition so great that they offend the gods and lead to one's downfall. Hubris was a character flaw often seen in the heroes of classical Greek tragedy, including Oedipus and Achilles. The familiar old saying "Pride goeth before a fall" is basically talking about hubris.

id \\'id\\ The part of a person's unconscious mind that relates to basic needs and desires.

• His own id often scared him, especially when a sudden violent impulse would well up out of nowhere.

In Latin, *id* means simply "it." Sigmund Freud (and his translator) brought the word into the modern vocabulary as the name of what Freud believed to be one of the three basic elements of the human personality, the other two being the *ego* (see p. 566) and the *superego*. According to Freud, the id is the first of these to develop, and is the home of the body's basic instincts, particularly those involving sex and aggression. Since the id lacks logic, reason, or even organization, it can contain conflicting impulses. Primitive in nature, it wants to be satisfied immediately. Although its workings are completely unconscious, Freud believed that its contents could be revealed in works of art, in slips of the tongue ("Freudian slips"), and in one's dreams.

libido \\lə-'bē-dō\\ (1) Sexual drive. (2) In psychoanalytic theory, energy that is derived from primitive biological urges and is usually goal-oriented.

• She would sit at home trying not to think about where his unmanageable libido had led him this time.

The Latin word *libido,* meaning "desire, lust," was borrowed by Sigmund Freud as the name for a concept in his own theories. At first he defined *libido* to mean the instinctual energy associated with the sex drive. Later he broadened the word's meaning and began using it to mean the mental energy behind purposeful human activity of any kind; in other words, the libido (for which Freud also used the term *eros,* a Greek word meaning "sexual love") came to be regarded as the life instinct, which included sex along with all the other impulses we rely on to keep us alive. But those of us who aren't psychologists use the word simply as a synonym for "sex drive."

trauma \\'trȯ-mə\ (1) A serious injury to the body. (2) An abnormal psychological state caused by mental or emotional stress or physical injury.

* Fifteen years later, their adopted Cambodian daughter was still having nightmares in which she relived the trauma of those terrible years.

Trauma is the Greek word for "wound." Although the Greeks used the term only for physical injuries, nowadays *trauma* is just as likely to refer to emotional wounds. We now know that a *traumatic* event can leave psychological symptoms long after any physical injuries have healed. The psychological reaction to emotional trauma now has an established name: *post-traumatic stress disorder,* or PTSD. It usually occurs after an extremely stressful event, such as wartime combat, a natural disaster, or sexual or physical abuse; its symptoms include depression, anxiety, flashbacks, and recurring nightmares.

Quiz

Fill in each blank with the correct letter:

a. charisma   e. ethos
b. libido   f. trauma
c. aegis   g. ego
d. id   h. hubris

1. It seems like _____ to brag about a victory before it has been won.
2. It took her just a few weeks to recover from the physical _____, but the emotional scars were still with her years later.
3. He has such a massive _____ that no praise seems to satisfy him.
4. Those who enter the monastery don't lose their _____, just their opportunity to satisfy it.

5. She's going on a speaking tour through the Middle East under the _____ of the State Department.
6. Attracting and motivating such a terrific faculty required a principal of great personal _____.
7. The wildest of these underground comic books seem to be a pure expression of the teenage _____.
8. She joined the church because of its _____ of tolerance and social service.

Review Quizzes

A. Complete the analogy:

1. tag : label :: pseudonym : _____
   a. last name b. title c. maiden name d. alias
2. drama : play :: trauma : _____
   a. wound b. harm c. mind d. emotion
3. allow : prohibit :: proscribe : _____
   a. hesitate b. stick c. permit d. lead
4. tune : melody :: proverb : _____
   a. poem b. song c. story d. saying
5. extent : length :: simile : _____
   a. shape b. contrast c. kind d. comparison
6. mob : crowd :: ego : _____
   a. self b. other c. friend d. same
7. deceive : mislead :: simulate : _____
   a. increase b. excite c. grow d. imitate
8. disease : cure :: dissolution : _____
   a. disintegration b. unification c. departure d. solidity
9. baby : mother :: descendant : _____
   a. brother b. offspring c. child d. ancestor
10. soak : drench :: dehydrate : _____
    a. liquidate b. dry c. dissolve d. adjust

B. Fill in each blank with the correct letter:

a.	transcend	i.	id
b.	libido	j.	condescend
c.	verbose	k.	hydroponics
d.	patronymic	l.	ethos
e.	circumscribe	m.	proscribe
f.	absolution	n.	resolution
g.	simile	o.	conscription
h.	verbatim		

1. The doctor warned her that her _____ would be reduced while she was on the medication.

2. The use of _____ and greenhouses enables the floral industry to operate year-round.

3. He'd been very nervous about seeing her again, so when she smiled at him it felt like a kind of _____.

4. Stevenson was originally a _____ ("Steven's son"), which was later sometimes shortened to Stevens.

5. Military professionals often dislike _____ because most of the recruits don't want to be in the armed services.

6. He invites his wife's family to their place on holidays, but he would never _____ to go to their house instead.

7. Since the tape recorder wasn't turned on, there's no _____ record of the meeting.

8. The worst _____ in the song is the one that compares his beloved to a really solid six-cylinder engine.

9. Occasionally the Congress will try to _____ the president's power, but they usually end up deciding they'd rather not have the new responsibilities themselves.

10. All the states now _____ smoking inside public buildings.

11. She hates school, and she lacks the _____ to complete her high-school equivalency degree on her own.

12. These made-for-TV movies are made for very little money and almost never _____ the lowest level of acting and production.

13. In my afternoon class there's an extremely _____ guy whose "questions" sometimes go on for five minutes.

14. The _____ is completely primitive and reacts unthinkingly according to the pleasure-pain principle.

15. There's something very wrong with a company's _____ when the employees who get ahead are the ones who tell on their friends.

C. Match each word on the left to its correct definition on the right:

1.	inscription	a.	domination
2.	verbiage	b.	personal magnetism
3.	dehydrate	c.	prohibit
4.	simulacrum	d.	replica
5.	soluble	e.	protection
6.	hubris	f.	mistake
7.	fallacy	g.	dissolvable
8.	dissolution	h.	breakup
9.	aegis	i.	excessive pride
10.	hydraulic	j.	involving liquid
11.	ascendancy	k.	absorb
12.	proscribe	l.	wordiness
13.	assimilate	m.	saying
14.	charisma	n.	dry
15.	proverb	o.	dedication

UNIT

26

MUR, from the Latin noun *murus*, meaning "wall," has produced a modest number of English words.

---

muralist \\'myùr-ə-list\\ A painter of wall paintings.

- She's enjoying her new career as a muralist, but it's terribly hard on her when she sees her works wrecked by vandals.

Any wall painting may be called a *mural*. Murals have been around since long before the framed painting. Scenic murals date back to at least 2000 B.C. on the island of Crete. Indoor murals for private homes were popular in ancient Greece and Rome, and many of those at Pompeii were preserved by the lava of Mt. Vesuvius. In the Renaissance the muralists Raphael and Michelangelo created great wall and ceiling paintings for the Catholic Church, and Leonardo da Vinci's *The Last Supper* became one of the most famous of all murals. Mural painting saw a great revival in Mexico beginning in the 1920s, when a group of muralists inspired by the Mexican Revolution, including Diego Rivera, J. C. Orozco, and D. A. Siqueiros, began taking their intensely political art to the public by creating giant wall paintings, sometimes on outdoor surfaces.

intramural \\ˌin-trə-'myùr-əl\\ Existing or occurring within the bounds of an institution, especially a school.

- At college he lacked the time to go out for sports in a serious way, but he did play intramural hockey all four years.

With its Latin prefix *intra-*, "within" (not to be confused with *inter-*, "between"), *intramural* means literally "within the walls." The word is usually used for sports played between teams made up only from students at one campus. Intramural athletics is often the most popular extracurricular activity at a college or university.

extramural \\,eks-trə-'myúr-əl\\ Existing outside or beyond the walls or boundaries of an organized unit such as a school or hospital.

• "Hospital Without Walls" is an extramural program that offers home health-care services.

Extramural contains the Latin *extra-*, meaning "outside" or "beyond" (see EXTRA, p. 163). The walls in *extramural* are usually those of schools, colleges, and universities, and the word is often seen in phrases like "extramural activities" and "extramural competition," referring to things that involve the world beyond the campus. Some institutions use the term "extramural study" for what others call "distance learning"—that is, teaching and learning by means of Web connections to the classroom and to videos of lectures. Money that flows into universities to support research (from foundations, government institutes, etc.) is usually called "extramural income."

immure \\i-'myúr\\ To enclose within, or as if within, walls; imprison.

• In Dumas's famous novel, the Count of Monte Cristo is in fact a sailor who had been unjustly immured in an island prison for 15 years before breaking out and taking his revenge.

In Eastern European legend, whenever a large bridge or fort was completed, a young maiden would be immured in the stonework as a sacrifice. (It's not certain that such things were actually done.) In Poe's grim story "A Cask of Amontillado," a man achieves revenge on a fellow nobleman by chaining him to a cellar wall and bricking him up alive. At the end of Verdi's great opera *Aida*, Aida joins her lover so that they can die immured together. But real-life examples of *immurement* as a final punishment are somewhat harder to find.

POLIS/POLIT comes from the Greek word for "city." The ancient Greek city-states, such as Athens, Thebes, and Sparta, operated much like separate nations, so all their *politics* was local, like all their public *policy*—and even all their *police*!

politic \ˈpä-lə-ˌtik\ (1) Cleverly tactful. (2) Wise in promoting a plan or plan of action.

• Anger is rarely a politic way to seek agreement, since it usually comes across as rude and self-righteous.

Politic behavior in class always requires a respectful attitude toward your teacher. It's never politic to ask for a raise when your boss is in a terrible mood. And once teenagers learn to drive, they quickly learn the politic way to ask for the car—that is, whatever gets the keys without upsetting the parents. As you can see, *politic* can be used for many situations that have nothing to do with public *politics*.

politicize \pə-ˈli-tə-ˌsīz\ To give a political tone or character to.

• By 1968 the Vietnam War had deeply politicized most of America's college campuses.

Sexual harassment was once seen as a private matter, but in the 1980s and '90s it became thoroughly politicized, with women loudly pressuring lawmakers to make it illegal. So, at the same time, the issue of sexual harassment politicized many women, who began to take an interest in political action because of it. In other words, we may speak of an issue becoming politicized, but also of a person or group becoming politicized.

acropolis \ə-ˈkrä-pə-ləs\ The high, fortified part of a city, especially an ancient Greek city.

• On the Athenian Acropolis, high above the rest of the city, stands the Parthenon, a temple to Athena.

The Greek root *acro-* means "high"; thus, an acropolis is basically a "high city." Ancient cities often grew up around a high point, in order that they could easily be defended. The Greeks and Romans usually included in their acropolises temples to the city's most important gods; so, for example, Athens built a great temple on its Acropolis to its protector goddess, Athena, from which the city took its name. Many later European cities cluster around a walled castle on a height, into which the population of the city and the surrounding area could retreat in case of attack, and even South American cities often contain a similar walled area on high ground.

megalopolis \ˌme-gə-ˈlä-pə-ləs\ (1) A very large city. (2) A thickly populated area that includes one or more cities with the surrounding suburbs.

- With its rapid development, the southern coast of Florida around Miami quickly became a megalopolis.

A "large city" named Megalopolis was founded in Greece in 371 B.C. to help defend the region called Arcadia against the city-state of Sparta. Though a stadium seating 20,000 was built there, indicating the city's impressive size for its time, Megalopolis today has only about 5,000 people. Social scientists now identify 10 megalopolises in the U.S., each with more than 10 million people. The one on the eastern seaboard that stretches from Boston to Washington, D.C., where the densely populated cities seem to flow into each other all along the coast, is now home to over 50 million people. But it's easily surpassed by the Japanese megalopolis that includes Tokyo, with more than 80 million inhabitants.

Quizzes

A. Fill in each blank with the correct letter:

a. muralist
b. politic
c. megalopolis
d. immure
e. extramural
f. acropolis
g. politicize
h. intramural

1. Chicago itself has fewer than 3 million inhabitants, but the _____ that includes Milwaukee and Madison has over 14 million.
2. Her fear of theft was so great that she actually intended to _____ all the gold and silver behind a brick wall in the basement, leaving clues to the location in her will.
3. He knew it was never _____ to mention his own children's achievements around his brother, whose oldest son was in prison.
4. They had hired a professional _____ to paint the walls of the staircase with a flowery landscape.
5. The city government buildings occupied an _____, high above the factories that lined the riverbank.
6. Women's softball was the most popular of the college's _____ sports.

7. Most voters thought it was unfortunate that the candidates had actually managed to _____ a traffic accident.

8. The government mental-health center in Washington, D.C., conducts its own research but also funds _____ research at universities across the country.

B. Match the word on the left with the correct definition on the right.

1. megalopolis
2. immure
3. intramural
4. politic
5. acropolis
6. politicize
7. muralist
8. extramural

a. within an institution
b. seal up
c. high part of a city
d. turn into a political issue
e. wall painter
f. huge urban area
g. shrewdly sensitive
h. outside an institution

NUMER comes from the Latin words meaning "number" and "to count." A *numeral* is the symbol that represents a number. *Numerous* means "many," and *innumerable* means "countless." *Numerical* superiority is superiority in numbers, and your numerical standing in a class is a ranking expressed as a number.

---

numerology \ˌnü-mə-ˈrä-lə-jē\ The study of the occult significance of numbers.

• Though he didn't believe in numerology as a mystical bond between numbers and living things, he never went out on Friday the 13th.

As an element of astrology and fortune-telling, numerology has long been employed to predict future events. For many early Christians, 3 represented the Trinity, 6 represented earthly perfection, and 7 represented heavenly perfection; and still today, many of us like to group things into sets of 3 or 7, for no particular reason. Numerology has also been used to interpret personality; in particular, *numerologists* may assign numbers to each letter of a person's name and use the resulting figures, along with the person's date of birth, as a guide to his or her character.

alphanumeric \\,al-fə-nü-'mer-ik\ Having or using both letters and numbers.

- Back in the 1950s, we always spoke our phone numbers in alphanumeric form, using the letters printed on the dial: for example, "TErrace 5-6642," instead of "835-6642."

Alphanumeric passwords are much harder for a hacker to crack than plain alphabetic passwords, since the number of possible combinations is so much greater. License plates usually contain both letters and numbers, since, for a big state or country, the plate wouldn't be large enough to fit enough numbers for everyone. In computing, the standard alphanumeric codes, such as ASCII, may contain not only ordinary letters and numerals but also punctuation marks and math symbols.

enumerate \i-'nü-mə-,rāt\ To specify one after another; list.

- The thing he hated most was when she would start enumerating his faults out loud, while he would sit scowling into the newspaper trying to ignore her.

In a census year, the U.S. government attempts to enumerate every single citizen of the country—a task that, even in the modern era of technology, isn't truly possible. Medical tests often require the *enumeration* of bacteria, viruses, or other organisms to determine the progress of a disease or the effectiveness of a medication. Despite its *numer-* root, you don't have to use numbers when enumerating. For students of government and law, the "enumerated powers" are the specific responsibilities of the Congress, as listed in the U.S. Constitution; these are the only powers that Congress has, a fact that the Tenth Amendment makes even more clearly.

supernumerary \\,sü-pər-'nü-mə-,rer-ē\ Exceeding the usual number.

- Whenever the workload for the city's courts and judges gets too large, supernumerary judges are called in to help.

Supernumerary starts off with the Latin prefix *super-*, "above" (see SUPER, p. 598). You may have heard of someone being born with supernumerary teeth, supernumerary fingers, or supernumerary toes. A supernumerary rainbow may show up as a faint line—red, green, or purple—just touching the main colored arc. *Supernumerary* is also a noun: A supernumerary is usually someone in a crowd scene onstage, otherwise known as an "extra" or a "spear-carrier."

KILO is the French version of the Greek word *chilioi*, meaning "thousand." France is also where the metric system originated, in the years following the French Revolution. So in English, *kilo-* shows up chiefly in metric-system units. Before the computer age, the most familiar *kilo-* words for English-speakers were probably *kilowatt*, meaning "1,000 watts," and *kilowatt-hour*, meaning the amount of energy equal to one kilowatt over the course of an hour.

---

kilobyte \\'ki-lə-ˌbīt\\ A unit of computer information equal to 1,024 bytes.

• A 200-word paragraph in the simplest text format takes up about a kilobyte of storage space on your hard drive.

Knowing the root *kilo-*, you might think a kilobyte would be exactly 1,000 bytes. But actually a kilobyte represents the power of 2 that comes closest to 1,000: that is, 2^{10} (2 to the 10th power), or $2 \times 2 \times 2 \times 2 \times 2 \times 2 \times 2 \times 2 \times 2 \times 2$, or 1,024. Why 2? Because the capacity of memory chips is always based on powers of 2. Locations in electronic memory circuits are identified by binary numbers (numbers that use only the digits 0 and 1), so the number of addressable locations becomes a power of 2.

kilometer \\kə-'lä-mə-tər\\ A unit of length equal to 1,000 meters.

• U.S. highway signs near the Canadian border often show distances in kilometers in addition to miles.

A kilometer is equal to about 62/100 of a mile, and a mile is equal to about 1.61 kilometers. The U.S. has been slow to adopt metric measures, which are used almost everywhere else in the world. Though our car speedometers are often marked in both miles and kilometers, the U.S. and Great Britain are practically the only developed nations that still show miles rather than kilometers on their road signs. But even in the U.S., footraces are usually measured in meters or kilometers, like the Olympic races. Runners normally abbreviate *kilometer* to *K*: "a 5K race" (3.1 miles), "the 10K run" (6.2 miles), and so on.

kilohertz \\'ki-lə-ˌhərts\\ A unit of frequency equal to 1,000 cycles per second.

• A drone aircraft nosedived and crashed after an onboard tape recorder turned out to be using a 10-kilohertz signal, the same frequency used by the aircraft's control system.

If your favorite AM radio station has a frequency of 680 kilohertz (kHz), that means the station's transmitter is oscillating (vibrating) at a rate of 680,000 cycles per second (i.e., 680,000 times a second). A related term is *megahertz* (MHz), meaning "*millions* of cycles per second." Shortwave radio operates between 5.9 and 26.1 MHz, and the FM radio band operates between 88 and 108 MHz. Garage-door openers work at about 40 MHz, baby monitors work at 49 MHz, and so on. The terms *hertz*, *kilohertz* and *megahertz* honor the great German physicist Heinrich Hertz, the first person to broadcast and receive radio waves.

kilogram \\'ki-lə-ˌgram\\ A unit of weight equal to 1,000 grams.

• The kilogram is the only base unit of measurement still defined by a physical object rather than a physical constant (such as the speed of light).

The original concept of the kilogram, as the mass of a cubic decimeter of water (a bit more than a quart), was adopted as the base unit of mass by the new revolutionary government of France in 1793. In 1875, in the Treaty of the Meter, 17 countries, including the U.S., adopted the French kilogram as an international standard. In 1889 a new international standard for the kilogram, a metal bar made of platinum iridium, was agreed to; President Benjamin Harrison officially received the 1-kilogram cylinder for the U.S. in 1890. But no one uses that bar very often; for all practical purposes, a kilogram equals 2.2 pounds.

Quizzes

A. **Match each word on the left to its correct definition on the right:**

1. kilobyte a. 3/5 of a mile
2. enumerate b. extra
3. supernumerary c. measure of electronic capacity
4. kilogram d. list
5. kilohertz e. occult use of numbers
6. numerology f. 1,000 vibrations per second
7. alphanumeric g. 2.2 pounds
8. kilometer h. combining numbers and letters

B. **Fill in each blank with the correct letter:**

a. supernumerary e. kilobyte
b. kilogram f. kilometer
c. enumerate g. alphanumeric
d. kilohertz h. numerology

1. Every Tuesday there's a 5-_____ race along the river, which is short enough that 10-year-olds sometimes run it.
2. For his annual salary review, his boss always asks him to _____ the projects he completed during the previous year.
3. On a hard drive, a _____ is enough capacity for a few sentences of text, but for audio or video it's too small to even mention.
4. As a child, she had a couple of _____ teeth, which the dentist pulled when she was 8 years old.
5. The broadcast frequencies of FM stations are required to be 200 _____ apart so as not to interfere with each other.
6. When they first moved to Berlin, it took them a few days to get used to buying potatoes and oranges by the _____ rather than the pound.
7. She occasionally visited a local fortune-teller, who would use playing cards and _____ to predict her future.
8. The Web site uses six-character _____ passwords, of which there are enough for tens of millions of users.

MICRO, from the Greek *mikros*, meaning "small," is a popular English prefix. A *microscope* lets the eye see *microscopic* objects, and libraries store the pages of old newspapers on *microfilm* at 1/400th of their original size. And we continue to attach *micro-* to lots of familiar words; most of us could figure out the meaning of *microbus* and *microquake* without ever having heard them before. Scientists often use *micro-* to mean "millionth"; thus, a *microsecond* is a millionth of a second, and a *micrometer* is a millionth of a meter.

microbe \\'mī-ˌkrōb\\ An organism (such as a bacterium) of microscopic or less than microscopic size.

• Vaccines reduce the risk of diseases by using dead or greatly weakened microbes to stimulate the immune system.

A hint of the Greek word *bios*, meaning "life," can be seen in *microbe*. Microbes, or *microorganisms*, include bacteria, protozoa, fungi, algae, amoebas, and slime molds. Many people think of microbes as simply the causes of disease, but every human is actually the host to billions of microbes, and most of them are essential to our life. Much research is now going into possible *microbial* sources of future energy; algae looks particularly promising, as do certain newly discovered or created microbes that can produce cellulose, to be turned into ethanol and other biofuels.

microbiologist \\ˌmī-krō-bī-'ä-lə-jist\\ A scientist who studies extremely small forms of life, such as bacteria and viruses.

• Food microbiologists study the tiny organisms that cause spoiling and foodborne illness.

Since microorganisms are involved in almost every aspect of life on earth, microbiologists work across a broad range of subject areas. Some study only viruses, some only bacteria. A marine microbiologist studies the roles of microbial communities in the sea. A soil microbiologist might focus on the use and spread of nitrogen. Veterinary microbiologists might research bacteria that attack racehorses or diagnose anthrax in cows. And the government puts microbiologists to work studying whether microbes could adapt to life on the surface of Mars, and how to defend ourselves against the possibility of germ warfare.

microbrew \\'mī-krō-ˌbrü\\ A beer made by a brewery that makes beer in small amounts.

• As a city of 75,000 people with eight breweries, it offers a greater variety of microbrews per capita than any other place in America.

Microbrews are usually beers or ales made with special malts and hops, unfiltered and unpasteurized, and thus distinctive in their aroma and flavor. Many microbreweries double as bar/restaurants, called *brewpubs*, where the gleaming vats may be visible behind a glass partition. "Craft brewing" and the opening of local brewpubs began in earnest in the U.S. in the 1980s. But not everyone is willing to pay extra for a beer, and lots of people are simply used to the blander taste of the best-selling beers, so by 2008 microbrews still only accounted for about 4% of all beer sold in the U.S.

microclimate \\'mī-krō-ˌklī-mət\\ The essentially uniform local climate of a small site or habitat.

• Temperature, light, wind speed, and moisture are the essential components of a microclimate.

The microclimate of an industrial park may be quite different from that of a nearby wooded park, since the plants absorb light and heat while asphalt parking lots and rooftops radiate them back into the air. A microclimate can offer a small growing area for crops that wouldn't do well in the wider region, so skilled gardeners take advantage of microclimates by carefully choosing and positioning their plants. San Francisco's hills, oceanfront, and bay shore, along with its alternating areas of concrete and greenery, make it a city of microclimates.

MULTI comes from the Latin word *multus*, meaning "many." Thus, a *multicultural* society is one that includes people of several different countries, languages, and religions; a *multimedia* artwork uses two or more artistic media (dance, music, film, spoken text, etc.); and a *multitude* of complaints reaching your office would be a great many indeed.

---

multicellular \\ˌməl-tē-'sel-yə-lər\\ Consisting of many cells.

• Multicellular organisms—fungi, plants, and animals—have specialized cells that perform different functions.

Multicellular organisms are distinguished from the very primitive single-celled organisms—bacteria, algae, amoebas, etc. Even sponges, simple as they are, have specialized cell types such as digestive cells. In complex multicellular organisms, only the surface cells can exchange substances with the external environment, so the organisms have developed transport systems such as the circulatory system, in which the blood brings gases and nutrients to the cells and removes waste products from them.

multidisciplinary \ˌməl-tē-ˈdi-sə-plə-ˌner-ē\ Involving two or more subject areas.

• Her favorite class was Opera, a multidisciplinary class taught jointly by a music professor and a literature professor.

A *discipline* is a field of study. So a multidisciplinary (or *interdisciplinary*) course is a team-taught course in which students are asked to understand a single subject as it's seen by two or more traditional disciplines. Multidisciplinary teaching can open students' eyes to different views of a subject that they had never considered before. A multidisciplinary panel discussion, on the other hand, presents views from scholars in different fields but may leave any merging of the information to the audience.

multifarious \ˌməl-tə-ˈfer-ē-əs\ Having or occurring in great variety; diverse.

• Natives put the coconut palm to multifarious uses: using the nuts for eating, the juice for drinking, the wood for building huts, the leaves for thatch, the fiber for mats, and the shells for utensils.

Multifarious is a rather grand word, probably not for everyday use, but when you want to emphasize great variety—such as the huge number of uses to which a state-of-the-art cell phone can be put— it can be effective. Dictionary fans are constantly amazed by the multifarious meanings of the word *set* (47 of them in one unabridged dictionary), and thesaurus lovers may marvel at the multifarious synonyms for *drunk*.

multilateral \ˌməl-tē-ˈla-tə-rəl\ Involving more than two nations or parties.

• A couple of times a year, representatives of the large industrial democracies meet for a round of multilateral trade negotiations.

Since *lateral* means "side" (see LATER, p. 611), *multilateral* means basically "many-sided." The philosophy of *multilateralism* claims that the best solutions generally result when as many of the world's nations as possible are involved in discussions, and *multilateralists* often favor strengthening the United Nations. Today multilateralism can be seen at work in, for example, the World Health Organization, the World Trade Organization, and the International Criminal Court. But the U.S. doesn't always join the major multilateral organizations, instead often behaving as if a *unilateral* approach—that is, going it alone—was best for the interests of a powerful nation.

Quizzes

A. Fill in each blank with the correct letter:

a.	multicellular	e.	multidisciplinary
b.	microbrew	f.	microbiologist
c.	microbe	g.	microclimate
d.	multilateral	h.	multifarious

1. At the state fair their beer was judged Minnesota's best _____.
2. Researchers are interested in the role played in the disease by a _____ that no one had particularly noticed before.
3. The U.S. has been participating in _____ climate talks with the rest of the world's biggest polluters.
4. For a young _____ like herself, it seemed that the most interesting job possibilities lay in the study of viruses.
5. Arriving at college from his little high school, he was delighted but overwhelmed by the _____ course choices that were open to him.
6. Their 25-acre property, a bowl-shaped field surrounded by woods, had its own _____ which was perfect for certain fruit trees.
7. The subject of economics can often be approached in a _____ way, since it usually involves mathematics, sociology, political science, and other fields.
8. The smallest _____ organisms actually seem to have at least 1,000 cells, while the human body has trillions.

B. Choose the closest definition:

1. microbe   a. miniature ball   b. tiny organism
   c. infection   d. midget
2. multilateral   a. many-eyed   b. many-armed
   c. with many participants   d. many-angled
3. microclimate   a. short period of different weather
   b. weather in Micronesia   c. weather at the
   microscopic level   d. special climate of a small area
4. multifarious   a. odd   b. varied   c. evil   d. unusual
5. multicellular   a. bacterial   b. viral   c. consisting of
   many cells   d. huge
6. microbrew   a. small serving of beer   b. half-cup of
   coffee   c. beer from a small brewery   d. tea in a small
   container
7. multidisciplinary   a. punishment by several methods
   b. involving several subject areas   c. with many
   disciples   d. punishment by different people
8. microbiologist   a. one who studies small insects
   b. small scientist   c. one who grows small plants
   d. one who studies bacteria and viruses

PAR, from the Latin, means "equal." Our English word *par* means an amount taken as an average or a standard, and especially the standard score for each hole on a golf course—which is why the phrase "par for the course" means "about as well as expected." We *compare* things to see if they're equal; similar things can be called *comparable*—that is, "equal with." And "on a par with" means "comparable to."

parity \'per-ə-tē\ The state of being equal.

• That year the Canadian dollar reached parity with the U.S. dollar for the first time in three decades.

Parity has special meanings in such fields as physics, math, medicine, genetics, and marketing. Back when the Soviet Union and the U.S. were opposing superpowers, there was often talk of parity in nuclear weapons between the two sides. We sometimes hear about parity between mental and physical health in insurance coverage, or parity in colleges' funding of men's and women's athletics. But parity may be most common in discussions of currencies. The *exchange rate* between two national currencies often changes every day, as each drifts higher or lower, and occasionally two similar currencies, such as the euro and the U.S. dollar, will achieve parity, but it rarely lasts long.

disparity \di-'sper-ə-tē\ A noticeable and often unfair difference between people or things.

• He'd been noticing an increasing disparity between what the government was claiming and what he saw happening all around him.

Disparity contains the Latin *dis*, meaning "apart" or "non-" (see DIS, p. 60), so a disparity is a kind of "nonequality." The word is often used to describe a social or economic condition that's considered unfairly unequal: a racial disparity in hiring, a health disparity between the rich and the poor, an income disparity between men and women, and so on. Its adjective, *disparate* (accented on the first syllable), is often used to emphasize strong differences.

nonpareil \ˌnän-pə-'rel\ Someone or something of unequaled excellence.

• Critics seem to agree that this is the new nonpareil of video-game consoles, the one to beat.

American children learn this word (even if they can't pronounce it) as the name of the candies covered with white sugar pellets that they buy at the movie theater, and it's also the name of the pellets themselves. But the more general meaning is common too. *Nonpareil* is also an adjective. A famous boxing champion of the 1920s was known as Nonpareil Jack Dempsey, when he wasn't being called "the Manassa Mauler." Like its synonyms *paragon* and *peerless*, *nonpareil* is popular as a company and product name; it's also the name of a fruit, an almond, a bird, and a butterfly.

subpar \'səb-'pär\ Below a usual or normal level.

• Because of a severe cold, her performance that evening had been subpar, but the audience seemed to love it anyway.

Since *sub-* means "below" (see SUB, p. 455), almost anything that fails to measure up to a traditional standard may be called subpar. So you may hear of subpar ratings for a TV show, subpar care at a nursing home, subpar attendance at a concert, or subpar work by a contractor. If you played a subpar round of golf, though, you needed *more* strokes than you should have.

PHOB comes from the Greek noun *phobos*, "fear," and it shows up clearly in our noun *phobia*, meaning "unusual fear of a specific thing." Phobias vary greatly in seriousness and also in frequency. Most of us have experienced *claustrophobia* at some time, but few truly suffer from fear of the number 13, a condition known as *triskaidekaphobia*.

---

acrophobic \ˌa-krə-ˈfō-bik\ Fearful of heights.

- She's so acrophobic that, whenever she can't avoid taking the route that includes the high bridge, she asks the police to drive her across.

The Greek *akron* means "height" or "summit," and the *acro-* root can be seen in such words as *acrobat* and *Acropolis*. Almost everyone has some fear of heights, but an abnormal dread of high places, along with the vertigo (dizziness) that most *acrophobes* also experience, are common as well; in fact, *acrophobia* is one of the half-dozen most common recognized phobias. Acrophobia and claustrophobia both play a role in another well-known phobia: the fear of flying, itself often known as *aerophobia*.

agoraphobia \ˌa-gə-rə-ˈfō-bē-ə\ A fear of being in embarrassing or inescapable situations, especially in open or public places.

- After barely surviving a terrible attack of agoraphobia in the middle of the Sonoran Desert, he finally agreed to start seeing a psychologist.

The *agora* was the marketplace in ancient Greece; thus, agoraphobia often involves fear of public places and crowds. But it also may involve fear of being in shops, or even fear of being in open spaces, or fear of traveling alone. It may also be a fear of experiencing some uncontrollable or embarrassing event (like fainting) in the presence of others with no help available. Agoraphobia can be hard to understand for those who don't suffer from it, especially because it can take so many different forms, but it is often a serious and socially crippling condition.

xenophobe \\'ze-nə-ˌfōb\\ One who has a fear or hatred of strangers or foreigners.

- A Middle Easterner reading the U.S.'s visa restrictions might feel that the State Department was run by xenophobes.

Xenophobe is partly based on the Greek noun *xenos*, meaning "stranger, guest, foreigner." Unlike other phobias, *xenophobia* isn't really considered an abnormal condition; instead, it's generally thought of as just serious narrow-mindedness, the kind of thinking that goes along with racism and extreme patriotism. In times of war, a government will often actually try to turn all its citizens into xenophobes.

arachnophobia \\ə-ˌrak-nə-'fō-bē-ə\\ Having a fear or dislike of spiders.

- At 50, my sister still suffers from arachnophobia, and can't sleep in a room unless she knows it has no spiders.

In Greek mythology, Arachne was a weaver of such skill that she dared to challenge the goddess Athena at her craft. When she won their competition by weaving a tapestry disrespectful to the gods, the enraged Athena tore it to shreds, and in despair Arachne hanged herself. Out of pity, Athena loosened the rope, which became a cobweb, and changed Arachne into a spider. Today, the spiders, scorpions, mites, and ticks all belong to the class known as *arachnids*. Arachnophobia is the most common of the animal phobias; but many people suffer from similar phobias regarding snakes (*ophidiophobia*), dogs (*cynophobia*), and mice and rats (*musophobia*).

Quizzes

A. Fill in each blank with the correct letter:

a. acrophobic
b. parity
c. agoraphobia
d. disparity

e. xenophobe
f. nonpareil
g. arachnophobia
h. subpar

1. Customers kept complaining that the quality of the product was _____, so we eventually stopped selling it completely.

2. She still suffers from _____, even though she hasn't had spider nightmares for many years.

3. His _____ is so bad that he won't even accept an award at a ceremony.

4. She's concerned about the _____ between the performance on standardized tests and what she sees when she sits in on actual classes.

5. Immigration is almost the only thing he talks about these days, and he seems to have become a full-fledged _____.

6. For 25 years it has prided itself on being the _____ Japanese restaurant in the city.

7. He's so _____ that he had to stay in the car when we visited the Grand Canyon.

8. Since the 1970s women have been demanding _____ in pay with men, but they still lag well behind.

B. Match the definition on the left to the correct word on the right:

1.	fear of spiders	a.	agoraphobia
2.	gap	b.	xenophobe
3.	fear of open or public places	c.	nonpareil
4.	ideal	d.	acrophobic
5.	fearful of heights	e.	subpar
6.	equality	f.	parity
7.	one fearful of foreigners	g.	disparity
8.	inferior	h.	arachnophobia

Medical Words

HEM/HEMO comes from the Greek word for "blood" and is found at the beginning of many medical terms. By dropping the *h*-, the same word produced the suffix *-emia*, which likewise shows up in lots of "blood" words, including *anemia*, *leukemia* and *hyperglycemia*.

hemorrhage \\'hem-rij\\ (1) A large loss of blood from a blood vessel. (2) A rapid and uncontrollable loss or outflow.

- He arrived at the emergency room reporting headache, nausea, and drowsiness, and the doctor immediately suspected that he'd suffered a brain hemorrhage.

A hemorrhage usually results from either a severe blow to the body or from medication being taken for something else. Though many hemorrhages aren't particularly serious, those that occur in the brain (cerebral hemorrhages) can be life-threatening. In older people, hemorrhages are often caused by blood-thinning medication taken to prevent heart attacks. A bruise (or *hematoma*) is a hemorrhage close enough to the surface of the skin to be visible. *Hemorrhage* is also a verb, which isn't always used to talk about actual blood; thus, we may hear that a business is hemorrhaging money, or that the U.S. has been hemorrhaging industrial jobs for decades. Be careful when writing *hemorrhage*; it's not an easy word to spell.

hematology \ˌhē-mə-ˈtä-lə-jē\ The study of blood and blood-forming organs.

- Her specialty in hematology let her work with patients of all ages and types, since blood problems may affect almost anyone.

Blood is basic to almost all the body's functions, and a blood test can reveal more about your physical condition than almost any other kind of examination, so hematology is an important medical specialty, with many separate subjects. Since blood cells are formed in the bone marrow, the bones are one important focus for *hematologists*. The coagulation, or thickening, of the blood is another important subject, since coagulation is what keeps us from bleeding to death from even small wounds. And there are dozens of serious blood diseases, including anemia (a lack of red blood cells) and leukemia (cancer involving a buildup of white blood cells).

hemophilia \ˌhē-mə-ˈfi-lē-ə\ A bleeding disorder caused by the blood's inability to coagulate.

- When he was a child, his hemophilia had kept him from joining the other kids in rough play at recess.

The dreaded disease known as hemophilia is the result of an inherited gene, and almost always strikes boys rather than girls (though mothers may pass the gene to their sons). Since the blood lacks an ingredient that causes it to clot or coagulate when a blood vessel breaks, even a minor wound can cause a *hemophiliac* to bleed to death if not treated. Bleeding can be particularly dangerous when

it's entirely internal, with no visible wound, since the perso⸝
be aware it's happening. Queen Victoria transmitted the hemo⸝⸝
gene to royal families all across Europe; the hemophilia of a yo⸝⸝
Russian prince played a part in the downfall of the Russian czars.
Today, hemophiliacs take drugs that stop the bleeding by speeding
coagulation, and hemophiliac life expectancies in developed countries are almost as long as the average.

hemoglobin \\ˈhē-mə-ˌglō-bən\\ The element in blood that transports oxygen from the lungs to the body's tissues and transports
carbon dioxide from the tissues back to the lungs.

• Her doctor had noticed her low hemoglobin count and was insist-
  ing that she include more iron-rich vegetables in her diet.

When filled with oxygen, the hemoglobin in your blood is bright
red; returning to the lungs without its oxygen, it loses its brightness
and becomes somewhat bluish. Hemoglobin levels can change from
day to day, and may be affected by such factors as a lack of iron
in the diet, a recent loss of blood, and being pregnant. When you
give blood, a nurse first pricks your finger to test your hemoglobin
level; a low hemoglobin count indicates anemia and may mean that
you shouldn't give blood that day. Mild anemia is generally of little
importance, but some types can be very serious.

ITIS, a suffix found in both Greek and Latin, means "disease" or
"inflammation." In *appendicitis* your appendix is swollen and painful, and in *tonsillitis* the same is true of your tonsils. With *laryngitis*,
your throat and larynx may become so sore that it's difficult to
talk. Some of us enjoy making up our own *-itis* words; high-school
teachers, for example, long ago noticed that many of their seniors
tended to lose all interest in schoolwork and start skipping classes,
and labeled the condition *senioritis*.

bursitis \\bər-ˈsī-təs\\ Inflammation of a lubricating sac (bursa),
especially of the shoulder or elbow.

• My barber developed bursitis after many years of lifting his
  arms all day.

A bursa is a little pouch filled with fluid that sits between a tendon
and a bone. When the fluid becomes infected by bacteria or irritated
by too much movement, bursitis results. Throwing a baseball too

many times at one session, for example, may inflame and irritate one of the bursae (notice the plural form) in the shoulder. Bursitis in another part of the body may be known by a traditional name such as "housemaid's knee," "soldier's heel," or "tennis elbow." Bursitis generally goes away after a few weeks of resting the affected area, and the pain can be treated with ice packs and aspirin.

hepatitis \\,he-pə-'tī-təs\ Inflammation of the liver.

- His skin now had a yellowish tinge, as did the whites of his eyes, and his doctor immediately recognized the signs of advanced hepatitis.

The liver, the body's largest gland, performs many important tasks, but is also vulnerable to many illnesses. At least five types of hepatitis, labeled with the letters A–E, are caused by viruses. The most common are hepatitis A, acquired through contaminated food and water; hepatitis B, which usually travels via sexual activity or shared needles; and hepatitis C, generally passed through shared needles. Some other types, including alcoholic hepatitis (caused by drinking too much alcohol), aren't infectious. There are vaccines for types A and B, and drug treatments for A, B, and C, though the drugs aren't always effective.

bronchitis \brän-'kī-təs\ Inflammation of the bronchial tubes.

- Before the smoking ban went into effect, three flight attendants had sued the airline, claiming secondhand smoke was to blame for their bronchitis.

The *bronchial* tubes carry air into the tiny branches and smaller cells of the lungs. In bronchitis, the tubes become sore and you develop a deep cough. Bronchitis caused by bacteria can be treated with antibiotics, but there's no drug treatment for the more common kind caused by a virus. A bout of bronchitis may involve a couple of weeks of coughing (with no laughing allowed), weakness, and loss of energy and interest in doing things. Apart from that, bronchitis is rarely serious—at least if it doesn't progress to pneumonia.

tendinitis \\,ten-də-'nī-təs\ A painful condition in which a tendon in the arm or leg becomes inflamed.

- After years of tennis and bicycling, she now has tendinitis of both the elbow and the knee.

Tendinitis is often seen in active, healthy people who do something that requires repeated motion, including golfers and tennis players (especially those with improper form), carpenters, and violinists. It's usually treated by keeping the joint from moving, by means of a splint, cast, or bandage. If not dealt with in time, tendinitis can turn into the more serious *tendinosis*, or tendon degeneration.

Quiz

Fill in each blank with the correct letter:

a. hepatitis
b. hematology
c. bronchitis
d. hemophilia

e. bursitis
f. hemorrhage
g. hemoglobin
h. tendinitis

1. After a week of lifting boxes he got a case of ____, and they had to get movers in to finish the packing.
2. Blood samples get sent to the ____ department for analysis.
3. From the yellowness of her eyes, he suspected that it was a serious case of ____.
4. Soon after they start playing tennis and golf each spring, they both find they've developed ____ and have to give it up for a while.
5. He's a heavy smoker, and for several years he's been suffering from ____ several times a year.
6. Oxygen turns the ____ in the blood bright red; when the oxygen is removed, it becomes bluish.
7. The bleeding caused by the accident all seemed to be close to the surface, and there was no evidence of an internal ____.
8. The family had a history of ____, so she was naturally worried when her 3-year-old's wound kept bleeding for an hour.

Review Quizzes

A. Match the definition on the left to the correct word on the right:

1. one fearful of foreigners   a.   immure
2. list   b.   subpar
3. wall up   c.   xenophobe
4. 2.2 pounds   d.   enumerate
5. liver disease   e.   arachnophobia
6. varied   f.   parity
7. equality   g.   bronchitis
8. lung inflammation   h.   kilogram
9. fear of spiders   i.   hepatitis
10. inferior   j.   multifarious

B. Fill in each blank with the correct letter:

a. muralist   f. kilometer
b. agoraphobia   g. politicize
c. multidisciplinary   h. microclimate
d. nonpareil   i. intramural
e. supernumerary   j. disparity

1. By their careful planting on this south-facing hillside, they had created a _____ that was perfect for certain crops that no one else was able to grow.
2. Each year there seemed to be a larger _____ between their expected income and what they actually earned.
3. The college has had an _____ debating society for several years, but this year they've decided to challenge several nearby colleges in a debate competition.
4. Only six people could play on a side, so the _____ volleyball players had to wait five minutes before rotating into the game.
5. A _____ is more than half a mile but less than two-thirds of a mile.
6. The Congress has managed to _____ an issue that always used to be thought of as a private matter.
7. He has a good reputation as a _____ for the wall paintings he's done in public buildings.
8. Her _____ has gotten worse, and now she refuses to even leave the house.

9. She's a _____ classroom teacher—enthusiastic, knowledgeable, concerned, entertaining, funny, everything a teacher should be.

10. The journal is devoted to water, taking a _____ approach that involves chemistry, physics, biology, and environmental science.

C. Indicate whether the following pairs of terms have the same or different meanings:

1. immure / embrace   same ___ / different ___
2. subpar / below normal   same ___ / different ___
3. enumerate / solve   same ___ / different ___
4. acrophobic / fearful of heights   same ___ / different ___
5. supernumerary / extra   same ___ / different ___
6. hematology / liver medicine   same ___ / different ___
7. kilohertz / unit of frequency   same ___ / different ___
8. disparity / equality   same ___ / different ___
9. hemorrhage / blood circulation   same ___ / different ___
10. nonpareil / unlikely   same ___ / different ___

UNIT

27

NANO comes from the Greek *nanos*, meaning "dwarf." For a prefix meaning "small," English got by for centuries with the Greek *micro-*, and later *mini-* came to be used widely as well. But only recently, as a result of advances in scientific knowledge and technology, has there been a need for a prefix meaning "extremely small"—a need that's been filled by *nano-*, which today is being attached to all kinds of words, sometimes not very seriously (*nanoskirt*, *nanobrained*, etc.).

---

nanotechnology \ˌna-nō-tek-ˈnä-lə-jē\ The science of manipulating materials on an atomic or molecular scale, especially to build microscopic devices such as robots.

- Nanotechnology is now seen as contributing to numerous environmental solutions, from cleaning up hazardous waste sites to producing strong but lightweight materials for auto bodies.

Nanotechnology, or *nanotech* for short, deals with matter at a level that most of us find hard to imagine, since it involves objects with dimensions of 100 billionths of a meter (1/800th of the thickness of a human hair) or less. The chemical and physical properties of materials often change greatly at this scale. Nanotechnology is already being used in automobile tires, land-mine detectors, and computer disk drives. *Nanomedicine* is a particularly exciting field: Imagine particles the size of a blood cell that could be released into the bloodstream to form into tiny robots and attack cancer cells, or "machines" the size of a molecule that could actually repair the damaged interiors of individual cells.

nanosecond \\'na-nə-ˌse-kənd\\ One billionth of a second.

- When he finally asked if she would marry him, it took her about a nanosecond to say yes.

The nonserious use of *nanosecond* is probably much more common than the proper technical use. In measurement terms such as *nanosecond*, *nanogram*, and *nanometer*, *nano-* means "billionth"; in other kinds of words, its meaning isn't quite so precise. In computers, the speed of reading and writing to random access memory (RAM) is measured in nanoseconds. By comparison, the speed of reading or writing to a hard drive or a CD-ROM player, or for information to travel over the Internet, is measured in *milliseconds* (thousandths of a second), which are a million times longer than nanoseconds.

nanostructure \\'na-nə-ˌstrək-chər\\ An arrangement, structure, or part of something of molecular dimensions.

- In the 1990s the physics department, which had been doing extensive research on microstructures, began to get deeply involved in nanostructures, including nanofoam, nanoflakes, and nanofibers.

Two important types of nanostructure are *nanocrystals* (tiny crystals, often of semiconducting material) and *nanotubes* (tiny tubes, usually of pure carbon). Nanocrystals made from semiconductors change color depending on their size, and are being used for such tasks as detecting viruses in living cells. Nanotubes can conduct enormous amounts of electrical current, far more than metal wires. They are the basic material of tiny "paper" batteries, which can be rolled, folded, or cut while still producing power. Nanotubes are also now being used in materials for lightweight tennis rackets and golf clubs, and may soon enable the manufacture of TV screens no thicker than a film.

nanoparticle \\'na-nə-ˌpär-ti-kəl\\ A tiny particle whose size is measured in billionths of a meter.

- Nanoparticles of iron are being used to clean up soil pollution, helping break down molecules of dangerous substances into simple compounds.

Nanoparticles of a material usually have very different qualities from those that the material has at its ordinary scale, which is one reason why there's such excitement about the possibilities for how they might be used in future technologies. Many uses have already been developed. Aluminum nanoparticles added to rocket fuel can make the fuel burn twice as fast and release much more energy. Silicon nanoparticles are increasing the energy efficiency of solar cells by allowing the energy from ultraviolet light to be captured for the first time. Other nanoparticles are now helping prevent rust in metals, produce stronger batteries, enhance the diagnosis of cancer, and improve the filtering of water, and the number of other applications is growing fast.

SUPER, a Latin prefix meaning "over, higher, more than," has become one of the most familiar prefixes in English, one of those prefixes that we use to create new words all the time: *supermodel*, *superpowerful*, *superjock*, *supersize*, *supersweet*—the list goes on and on. This all seems to have started in 1903 when the playwright G. B. Shaw translated the German word *übermensch*, Nietzsche's famous term for the person who rises to heroic heights through discipline and creative power, in the title of his play *Man and Superman*. The comic-book character with the same name wouldn't make his appearance for another 30 years.

superfluous \sù-'pər-flü-əs\ Beyond what is needed; extra.

• My Freshman Comp professor removes all superfluous words from our essays, and usually ends up shortening mine by about 40 percent.

Since the Latin *fluere* means "to flow" (see FLU, p. 440), you can think of *superfluous* as describing a river with so much water that it's overflowing its banks. The word is used in all kinds of contexts. Superfluous characters in computer code may keep it from working. Most of the buttons on a remote control may strike us as superfluous, since we never use them. When a situation "speaks for itself," any comment may be superfluous. And whenever you yourself are feeling superfluous, as in a "Two's company, three's a crowd" situation, it's probably time to leave.

insuperable \in-'sü-pə-rə-bəl\ Incapable of being solved or overcome.

- In learning to speak again after suffering a massive stroke, he had overcome what seemed like insuperable odds.

From its roots, the literal meaning of *insuperable* would be something like "un-get-overable"; *insurmountable* is a fairly exact synonym. *Insuperable* is used to describe obstacles, difficulties, barriers, obstructions, problems, and objections. Americans love stories of people who succeed in spite of terrible handicaps, whether as a result of physical limitations, prejudice, poverty, or lack of opportunity; such rugged spirits may be called *indomitable*, "incapable of being subdued."

supersede \ˌsü-pər-ˈsēd\ To take the place of; to replace with something newer or more useful.

- The notorious decision in the Dred Scott case was superseded by the 14th Amendment to the Constitution, which stated that anyone born in the U.S. had all the rights of a citizen.

The Latin word *supersedere* means "sit on top of"—which is one way of taking someone else's place. Your boss may send around a memo that supersedes the memo she sent the day before (the one with all the errors in it). Every time the first-class postage rate goes up, the new stamps supersede the old ones. In science, a new theory often supersedes an older one; for example, the theory that a characteristic you acquire during your lifetime can be passed on biologically to your children (called *Lamarckism*) was superseded by Darwin's theory of evolution. Watch out when spelling this word; *supersede* is practically the only English word that ends in *-sede*.

superlative \sü-ˈpər-lə-tiv\ Supreme, excellent.

- The new restaurant turned out to be an elegant place, and we all agreed that the food and wine were superlative.

Superlative may sound high-flown when compared with a synonym like *outstanding*, but if your next paper comes back from your teacher with the comment "Superlative work!" at the top you probably won't complain. Since *superlative* means "best, greatest," it makes sense that *superlative* is also a term used in grammar for the highest degree of comparison. So for the adjective *simple*, for example, the comparative form is *simpler* and the superlative form is *simplest*; and for the adverb *boldly*, the comparative form is *more boldly* and the superlative is *most boldly*.

Quizzes

A. **Indicate whether the following pairs of terms have the same or different meanings:**

1. superfluous / enormous   same ___ / different ___
2. nanotechnology /
   computer science   same ___ / different ___
3. insuperable / impossible   same ___ / different ___
4. nanosecond / million seconds   same ___ / different ___
5. supersede / replace   same ___ / different ___
6. nanoparticle /
   thousand particles   same ___ / different ___
7. superlative / outstanding   same ___ / different ___
8. nanostructure / enclosed mall   same ___ / different ___

B. **Fill in each blank with the correct letter:**

a. nanoparticle   e. supersede
b. superlative   f. nanostructure
c. superfluous   g. insuperable
d. nanotechnology   h. nanosecond

1. Again and again she had overcome what seemed to be ___ odds.
2. Many scientists believe that ___ is the most exciting field in the physical sciences today, with possible uses in almost every aspect of life.
3. A ___ is something whose size is measured in billionths of a meter.
4. A lot of the language in these student essays is ___, since it just repeats things that have already been said in different words.
5. Each picture illustrates a different ___ (a nanotube, a nanorod, a nanowire, etc.), each of which has its own set of important uses.
6. He raced down the hall and was back in about a ___ with the good news.
7. This new set of regulations will ___ the ones we've been working under for the last five years.
8. The movie had received ___ reviews, and we were looking forward to seeing it.

DE in Latin means "down, away." So a *descent* is a downward slope or climb, and a *decline* is a downward slide (of health, income, etc.). To *devalue* something is to take value away from it. And you might describe a *depressed* friend as "down."

debase \di-ˈbās\ To lower the value or reputation of someone or something.

- Every year she complains about how Christmas has been debased by commercialism.

Debase is often used to talk about someone's lowered status or character. People are constantly blustering about the debased tastes of the ordinary American, and especially the debased music of America's youth. A commentator might observe that both candidates had managed to debase themselves by the end of a political campaign. *Debase* has a special meaning in economics: From time to time, governments find that they need to quietly debase their countries' currency by reducing the percentage of valuable metal in its coins; if they don't, the metal may become more valuable than the coin and people will begin melting the coins down and reselling the metal.

defamation \ˌde-fə-ˈmā-shən\ The harming of someone's reputation by libel or slander.

- In a famous case in 1735, the newspaper publisher J. P. Zenger was found not guilty of defamation because everything he had printed about the plaintiff was true.

Harming someone's reputation in speech with falsehoods is known as slander, and doing the same thing in writing is known as libel (which sometimes includes speech as well). Any ordinary citizen who can claim to have suffered harm as a result of such defamation may sue. So why aren't politicians suing all the time? Because an exception is made for "public persons" (a category that includes most other celebrities as well), who must also prove that any such statement was made with "reckless disregard for the truth." And although, even by that standard, public persons are *defamed* all the time, most of them have decided that it's better to just grin and bear it.

degenerative \di-ˈje-nə-rə-tiv\ Causing the body or part of the body to become weaker or less able to function as time passes.

- Alzheimer's is a degenerative disease of the brain, marked by the decline of mental and physical abilities.

Degenerative diseases—including cancer, glaucoma, Parkinson's, diabetes, arthritis, and leprosy—are usually contrasted with infectious diseases (diseases caused by bacteria, viruses, fungi, and protozoa). However, many infectious diseases (Lyme disease, AIDS, etc.) can cause a body or body part to *degenerate*, and infective organisms play a part in some degenerative diseases. Some degenerative diseases can be controlled; some can even be cured. But no one has yet discovered a way to reverse such degenerative conditions as multiple sclerosis, emphysema, or Alzheimer's.

dejection \di-ˈjek-shən\ Sadness, depression, or lowness of spirits.

- Her friends were puzzled by her frequent periods of dejection, which seemed to occur with no obvious cause.

Based partly on the Latin *iacere*, "to throw" (see JECT, p. 31), *dejection* means literally "cast down"—that is, "downcast." Like *melancholy*, *gloom*, and even *sadness*, *dejection* seems to have been declining in use for many years; instead, we now seem to prefer *depression* (whose roots mean basically "a pressing down"). Since *depression* is also the word used by doctors, lots of people now assume that anyone depressed should be taking an antidepressant; if we went back to *dejected* and *dejection*, we might not be so quick to make that assumption.

NUL/NULL comes from the Latin word *nullus*, "none," which is itself a combination of *ne-* ("not") and *ullus* ("any"). Have you ever noticed how many of our negative words start with *n-*? Think of *no*, *not*, *never*, *nothing*, *none*, *no one*, *nowhere*, and the hundreds of *non-* words—just about all of which go back to the same Greek root.

null \ˈnəl\ (1) Having no legal power; invalid. (2) Having no elements.

- If we can prove that you signed the contract because you were being physically threatened, it will automatically be declared null.

Null is used mostly by lawyers, mathematicians, and computer programmers. In law, it usually occurs in the phrase "null and void" (which means about the same thing as *null* itself). When one of the parties that has signed a contract doesn't hold up his or her part of the deal—for example, if a contract states that a supplier must supply a million screws of a certain quality of steel, and it turns out the screws supplied were of inferior steel—the other company can refuse to pay anything, claiming the contract is null and void. In mathematics, *null* means "lacking any elements"; a *null set* is a set of figures that's actually empty. In computer programming, a *null* is a character that doesn't actually show up as a character, but instead may just be required to show that a series of digits or characters is finished.

nullity \\'nə-lə-tē\\ (1) Nothingness. (2) A mere nothing.

• He couldn't believe she'd actually left him for that nullity—a guy with no style, no drive, no personality at all.

Intellectuals may speak of a book or a film as a nullity, claiming it possesses nothing original enough to justify its existence. Legal scholars also use the word; a law passed by a legislature may be called a nullity if, for example, it's so obviously unconstitutional that it's going to be shot down by the courts in no time. And if you're in an unkind mood, you're also free to call a person a nullity, if you're not instead calling him a nobody, a nonentity, or a zero.

nullify \\'nə-lə-ˌfī\\ (1) To cancel legally. (2) To cause something to lose its value or to have no effect.

• In soccer or water polo, a penalty can nullify a goal that has just been made.

A legislature may nullify a ban, a law, or a tax by simply passing a new law. Election results can be nullified if a court finds the voting process was improper, and a court ruling can be nullified by a higher court. Even the Supreme Court itself may have its decisions nullified by new laws passed by the Congress—though not if a decision is based on the Constitution. In the years leading up to the American Civil War, Southern states claimed the right to nullify any federal law (such as antislavery laws) that they believed to be unconstitutional, leading to the *Nullification* Crisis of 1832. *Annul* is a close synonym of *nullify* (with the same root), as are *abrogate* and *invalidate*.

annulment \ə-ˈnəl-mənt\ An official statement that something is no longer valid.

- He requested an annulment of the marriage from the Church, but his wife claimed that, after 15 years and two children, the idea of annulment was ridiculous.

Annulment usually applies to marriage. In some states an annulment may be carried out by a court ("judicial annulment"), but annulment is generally practiced by a church ("ecclesiastic annulment"), and principally the Roman Catholic Church, which traditionally hasn't permitted divorce. The usual acceptable reason for annulment is a "failure to consummate" the marriage by having children. Unlike a marriage that ends in divorce, an annulled marriage is considered never to have existed. Other things can be annulled as well, including a contract (if one party fails to comply with its terms) or an election (if it wasn't carried out properly).

Quizzes

A. Fill in each blank with the correct letter:

a. null	e. annulment
b. nullify	f. nullity
c. dejection	g. defamation
d. degenerative	h. debase

1. She's bringing suit against her former husband for _____, claiming that statements he had made to a reporter had caused her to lose her job.
2. If the judge's decision goes against the government, it will _____ a 10-year-old state law.
3. Her lawyer is going to argue that the first trial was a _____ because some of the jurors missed whole days of testimony.
4. Dogs often suffer from _____ joint diseases that get worse year by year.
5. His _____ after getting turned down by his top two colleges was so deep that he didn't smile for weeks.
6. We're claiming the contract is _____ and void because the other company failed to do what it had agreed to.

7. Her friends all told her that a star like her would just _____ herself by appearing in TV ads.

8. After five years and no children, she asked the church for an _____ of the marriage.

B. Match the definition on the left to the correct word on the right:

1. undo   a. annulment
2. weakening   b. defamation
3. nothingness   c. nullity
4. depression   d. debase
5. invalid   e. degenerative
6. cancellation   f. nullify
7. slander   g. dejection
8. disgrace   h. null

ARM comes from the Latin *arma*, meaning "weapons, tools." The root is seen in such English words as *arms* (i.e., weapons), *armed*, and *army*. It has nothing to do with the limb that starts at your shoulder; the name for that kind of arm comes from the Latin word meaning "shoulder."

armada \är-'mä-də\ A large group of warships or boats.

• The U.S. Navy hopes to build an electric armada, a new generation of ships driven by electric power.

A Spanish word that originally meant simply "armed," *armada* is now used in Spanish-speaking nations as the name of their national navies. In English, the word usually has historical overtones. The Great Armada of 1588 was a 120-ship fleet sent by Philip II of Spain in an attempt to invade Elizabethan England; it was defeated when British forces lit eight ships afire and sent them sailing into the Armada's midst, then blocked the passage to the south so that the remaining ships were forced to sail northward around Britain in order to return home, causing dozens more ships to be wrecked in the stormy northern seas. Today we sometimes use the word humorously for fleets of fishing boats, rowboats, or canoes.

armistice \'är-mə-stəs\ An agreement to stop fighting a war; a truce.

- Ambassadors from three neighboring countries were trying to arrange an armistice between the warring forces.

Just as the *solstice* is the time of year when the sun (Latin, *sol*) "stands still," an armistice is an agreement for armies to stop where they are and lay down their arms. The word is associated with the truce that marked the end of World War I on the Western Front, where the Allies had confronted Germany, in 1918. The day of the ceasefire, November 11th ("the eleventh day of the eleventh month"), was for many years called Armistice Day; today it's known as Veterans Day in the U.S. and as Remembrance Day in Canada and Australia.

armory \\ˈärm-rē\\ A place where weapons are made or stored.

- The great military rifles known as the Springfield 30.06 and the M1 were developed at the Springfield Armory in Massachusetts.

An armory has traditionally been a military storage compound where machine guns, rifles, pistols, ammunition, parts, and accessories are kept. In the U.S., National Guard and Reserve units often use armories as training headquarters in peacetime. Ever since George Washington established the country's first armory in Springfield in 1777, arsenals and armories of the Army Ordnance Corps have had a remarkable history of arms manufacture.

disarming \\dis-ˈärm-iŋ\\ Tending to remove any feelings of unfriendliness or distrust.

- All of us at the meeting were charmed by the new manager's disarming openness and modesty.

A defeated country is sometimes forced to *disarm* (give up its weapons), and research may be aimed at disarming a deadly virus (making it incapable of doing damage). But the meaning of the adjective *disarming* isn't quite so physical. If you say your nephew has a disarming smile, you mean that his smile's warmth and genuineness disarm the people he meets of any possible suspicion or criticism and of any verbal weapons they might have used against him.

SURG comes from the Latin verb *surgere*, meaning "to rise, spring up." Our noun *surge* means "a sudden, large increase," and the verb *surge* means "to move with a surge." A *storm surge* occurs when violent storm winds at sea cause the water to pile up higher than normal sea level. A *surge protector* keeps a spike in electrical current from "frying" your computer when a lightning strike sends a sudden surge down the wires.

upsurge \\'əp-ˌsərj\ A rapid or sudden increase or rise.

- Almost forgotten for years, at 76 he was offered a colorful role in an odd little film, which brought an upsurge in interest in his career.

An upsurge in drug use sometimes leads to an upsurge in crime. An upsurge of flu cases can be cause for alarm. And an upsurge of fury at overpaid CEOs might lead to new legislation to restrain high salaries. We seem to use *upsurge* more in negative contexts than in positive ones, but not always; we usually welcome an upsurge of consumer confidence, an upsurge in new-car sales, or an upsurge in the stock market.

insurgency \in-'sər-jən-sē\ A usually violent attempt to take control of a government; a rebellion or uprising.

- The Mexican press was fascinated by the armed insurgency's mysterious leader, who wore a mask and went by the name of Subcomandante Marcos.

Insurgencies fall into the category of "irregular warfare," since an insurgency normally lacks the organization of a revolution, even though it has the same aims. Revolutions often begin within a country's armed forces, whereas insurgencies often arise in remote areas, where they gain strength slowly by winning the confidence of rural populations. An insurgency may be based on ethnic or religious identity, or its roots may be basically political or economic. Since insurgencies are rarely strong enough to face a national army head-on, *insurgents* (often called *guerrillas*) tend to use such tactics as bombing, kidnapping, hostage taking, and hijacking.

counterinsurgent \ˌkaùn-tər-in-'sər-jənt\ A person taking military or political action against guerrillas or revolutionaries.

- Counterinsurgents who build trust with the local population will gradually begin to receive useful information.

A counterinsurgent is, as you might guess, someone who combats an insurgency. *Counterinsurgency* efforts often attempt to win the "hearts and minds" of a population by hiring and paying local villagers, opening health clinics and schools, organizing sports programs, and providing agricultural assistance. These terms were first used to describe the American effort to strengthen the South Vietnamese government against communist forces in the 1960s—an effort that eventually ended in defeat.

resurgent \ri-ˈsər-jənt\ Rising again into life, activity, or prominence.

- The country had let down its guard over the summer, and in the fall a resurgent flu virus overwhelmed the public-health system, killing tens of thousands.

Resurgent means literally a "rising again" (see RE, p. 634). We may speak of a resurgent baseball team, a resurgent steel industry, the *resurgence* of jogging, or a resurgence of violence in a war zone. *Resurgence* is particularly prominent in its Italian translation, *risorgimento*. In the 19th century, when the Italian peninsula consisted of a number of small independent states, a popular movement known as the Risorgimento managed to unify the peninsula and create the modern state of Italy in 1870.

Quizzes

A. Fill in each blank with the correct letter:

a. armistice   e. armada
b. insurgency   f. upsurge
c. armory   g. resurgent
d. counterinsurgent   h. disarming

1. The army was facing a large guerrilla _____ that had already taken over the fourth-largest city.
2. A cargo ship would suddenly be surrounded by an _____ of small pirate boats, against which it was impossible to defend itself.

3. The recent ____ in oil prices has alarmed investors, who worry that expensive oil will slow down the larger economy.

4. He's always had a ____ manner, and lots of people like him immediately because of his smile.

5. There seems to be a ____ interest in film musicals, after many years when none were being released at all.

6. The rebels were becoming stronger, and the country's army and police lacked the proper training to provide an effective ____ force.

7. The ____ that was signed that year had only prevented fighting for a few months.

8. Any ____ would have to be situated well away from the battlefront, since it would be a disaster if the enemy managed to seize it.

B. Indicate whether the following pairs of words have the same or different meanings:

1. armada / fleet   same ___ / different ___
2. disarming / trucelike   same ___ / different ___
3. upsurge / triumph   same ___ / different ___
4. counterinsurgent / guerrilla   same ___ / different ___
5. armory / battleship   same ___ / different ___
6. resurgent / revived   same ___ / different ___
7. armistice / treaty   same ___ / different ___
8. insurgency / inflation   same ___ / different ___

STRAT comes from the Latin word *stratum*, meaning "spread" or "bed." *Strata*, a form of the same word, came to be used by the Romans to mean "paved road"—that is, *street*.

stratum \\'strā-təm\\ (1) A layer of a substance, especially one of a series of layers. (2) A level of society made up of people of the same rank or position.

• Alcohol and drug abuse are found in every stratum of society.

In geology, a stratum is a layer of rock or soil that is distinct from those above and below it. Rock and soil *strata* (notice the plural form) can be seen in road cuts, cliffs, quarries, riverbanks, and sand dunes, and in pieces of limestone, slate, and shale. Archaeologists digging in historical sites are careful to note the stratum where each artifact is found. Earth scientists divide the earth's atmosphere into strata, just as oceanographers divide the ocean's depths into strata. And for social scientists, a stratum is a group of people who are similar in some way, such as education, culture, or income.

stratification \,stra-tə-fə-'kā-shən\ The process or state of being formed, deposited, or arranged in layers.

* The stratification of the lake in summer keeps oxygen-rich cold water at the bottom, where coldwater fish such as trout take refuge.

If you look for it, you'll find stratification almost everywhere. On a tall rain-forest tree, there may be different air plants clinging to it, different insects crawling on it, and different mammals making their homes at different levels. The earth beneath you may be *stratified* into several distinctive layers within the first 20 feet. If the wind you're feeling is moving at 10 miles per hour, at 30 feet above your head it may be 20 mph, and in the jet stream above that it may be 150 mph. If you climb a high mountain in Himalayas, you may begin in a lush, wet forest and end up in a windswept environment where not even lichen will grow.

substrate \'səb-,strāt\ (1) An underlying layer. (2) The base on which an organism lives.

* The soil is the substrate of most seed plants.

With its Latin prefix *sub-*, "below" (see SUB, p. 455), *substrate* obviously refers to a layer under something else. Rock may serve as the substrate for the coral in a coral reef. Tiny wafers of silicon (or another semiconductor) serve as the substrate for computer chips. *Substrate* may also mean *subsoil*—that is, the layer under the topsoil, lacking in organic matter or humus. *Substrate* is part of the vocabulary of various other sciences, including chemistry and biology. But although it's mostly a scientific term, writers may also use it to mean simply "foundation"—for instance, when observing that reading is the substrate on which most other learning is based.

stratocumulus \,strā-tō-'kyü-myə-ləs\ A low-lying cloud formation appearing as extensive and often dark horizontal layers, with tops rounded into large balls or rolls.

- A dark bank of stratocumulus clouds was moving in quickly, and in March that usually meant bad weather.

When a cloud type forms a broad "layer" over the earth, the *strat-* root shows up in its scientific name. The type called simply *stratus* forms a low layer of gray extending over a large area. *Cirrostratus* ("curl layer") clouds form a high, thin layer often covering the entire sky (but without the wispy curls of ice crystals that give pure *cirrus* clouds their name). *Altostratus* ("high layer") clouds form a darkish gray mid-altitude layer. *Nimbostratus* ("rainstorm layer") clouds form a low, dark layer of gray cloud that usually produces light but continuous rain, snow, or sleet (but not violent storms of the kind that give pure *nimbus* clouds their name). *Cumulus* ("heap") is the familiar puffy fair-weather type of cloud; stratocumulus is its more wintry version, which spreads out in a fairly flat layer, much less "heaped up," and sometimes dense enough to cover almost the whole sky.

LATER comes from the Latin adjective *lateralis*, meaning "side." The noun for "side" in Latin was *latus*, and the same word served as an adjective meaning "wide." The relationship between the two isn't hard to spot, since something wide extends far out to its sides. So lines of *latitude* extend east-west around the earth, in the dimension we tend to think of as its width (unlike lines of *longitude*, which extend north-south, in the dimension that, for some reason, we decided to think of as its "length").

---

lateral \ˈla-tə-rəl\ Of or relating to the side.

- Only in the lateral views did the X-rays reveal an suspicious-looking shadow on the lung.

Lateral shows up in all kinds of contexts. A lateral job change is one that keeps you at about the same job level and salary. A coach might have special drills to improve his players' lateral speed and agility. The British speak of "lateral thinking," thinking that grabs ideas that may not seem to be relevant but turn out to work well— what we might call "thinking outside the box." But we know *lateral* best from football. A lateral pass is a pass of the ball between teammates that usually goes to the side and slightly backward from the direction in which they're advancing; unlike a forward pass, a lateral may be made from any position, and any number may be made in a single play.

bilateral \bī-ˈla-tə-rəl\ Involving two groups or countries.

• Instead of working on a set of separate bilateral trade agreements, they propose bringing the countries of the region together to sign a single joint agreement.

Since the prefix *bi-* means "two" in Latin (see BI/BIN, p. 333), *bilateral* means essentially "two-sided." In the days when there were two superpowers, the U.S. and the Soviet Union regularly engaged in bilateral arms negotiations; such negotiations are much less common today. Sometimes *bilateral* refers to two sides of the same thing. A bilateral hip replacement, for instance, replaces both hip bones in the same operation. And *bilateral symmetry* (a term often used by biologists) refers to the fact that, in many organisms (such as humans), the left side is basically the mirror image of the right side.

collateral \kə-ˈla-tə-rəl\ (1) Associated but of secondary importance. (2) Related but not in a direct or close way.

• Though the army referred to the civilian deaths as "collateral damage," since civilians weren't the intended targets, the incident aroused intense anger among the survivors.

If an official talking about some policy refers to a collateral issue, he or she means something that may be affected but isn't central to the discussion. To an anthropologist, your cousin would be called a collateral relative, since he or she (unlike your grandmother, brother, or daughter) is "off to the side" of your direct line of descent. As a noun, *collateral* means something provided to a lender as a guarantee of repayment. So if you take out a loan or mortgage to buy a car or house, the loan agreement usually states that the car or house is collateral that goes to the lender if the sum isn't paid.

equilateral \ˌē-kwə-ˈla-tə-rəl\ Having all sides or faces equal.

• On her desk she kept an equilateral prism, through which every morning the sun would project the colors of the spectrum onto the far wall.

Since *equi-* means "equal" (see EQU, p. 113), the meaning of *equilateral* is easy to guess from its roots. The word is mostly used in geometry. The standard polygons (many-sided geometrical shapes)— the pentagon, hexagon, octagon, etc.—are assumed to be equilateral if we don't say otherwise; an equilateral rectangle has the special name *square*. But triangles are particularly important, and many triangles are not equal-sided. The standard polyhedrons (many-sided solids) are also equilateral. Most common is the cube, all of whose sides are square. The tetrahedron has four triangular sides and thus is a pyramid with a triangular base, unlike the pyramids of Egypt with their square bases.

Quizzes

A. Fill in each blank with the correct letter:

a. stratocumulus
b. equilateral
c. stratum
d. lateral
e. substrate
f. collateral
g. stratification
h. bilateral

1. His trainer is teaching him ____ weight lifts, in which you hold your arms out to the sides.

2. The Defense Department is headquartered in a huge building that forms an ____ pentagon.

3. It was a typical winter sky, covered in a gray layer of ____ clouds.

4. The coral may use any hard surface as its ____, so artificial reefs have been created by sinking old ships.

5. The departure of the factory cost the community 150 jobs, and the ____ effects on the town's economy were severe.

6. In old mill towns you could actually see the social ____, since the wealthy people lived on the high ground and the working class lived down below.

7. The two countries have been holding ____ talks, but the other countries in the region will be joining the process soon.

8. The ____ under the topsoil consisted of yellow lime mixed with gravel, and the one below that was of slatelike rock.

B. Indicate whether the following pairs of terms have the same or different meanings:

1. equilateral / equal-sided   same __ / different __
2. stratum / layer   same __ / different __
3. lateral / backward   same __ / different __
4. stratocumulus /
       puffy summer clouds   same __ / different __
5. bilateral / two-sided   same __ / different __
6. stratification / strategy   same __ / different __
7. collateral / many-sided   same __ / different __
8. substrate / topic   same __ / different __

TOM comes from the Greek root meaning "cut." Thus, the Latin word *anatomia*, from which we get *anatomy*, means "dissection"—that is cutting or separating the parts of an organism for detailed examination. In a *lobotomy*, the nerves linking a brain lobe to the rest of the brain are removed; even though lobotomies have hardly been performed in the last 50 years, the idea can still fill us with horror.

---

appendectomy \ˌa-pən-ˈdek-tə-mē\ Surgical removal of the human appendix.

* Appendectomy is an emergency procedure, since appendicitis can be fatal if its symptoms are ignored.

The *appendix* is a tiny tube attached to the large intestine that no longer has any real function. *Appendicitis*—inflammation and swelling of the appendix, usually as a result of bacterial infection—generally occurs between the ages of 10 and 19, and is the most common reason for emergency surgery in the U.S. today. Since the appendix has so little to do, appendectomies normally have no negative aftereffects at all. If appendicitis is ignored, bacteria may enter the blood and infect other parts of the body.

gastrectomy \ga-ˈstrek-tə-mē\ Surgical removal of all or part of the stomach.

* Gastrectomy is used to treat holes in the stomach wall, noncancerous tumors, and cancer, but is performed only when other treatments have been rejected.

Gastr- comes from the Greek word for "belly," and shows up in English in such words as *gastric* ("relating to the stomach") and *gastronomy* ("the cooking and eating of fine food"). Believe it or not, there are many people today who have had a gastrectomy and live without a stomach; some of them need to eat fairly steadily and carefully through the day, but many lead almost completely normal and even vigorous lives.

tonsillectomy \\,tän-sə-'lek-tə-mē\ Surgical removal of the tonsils.

• His daughter's usual doctor thought antibiotics could cure her swollen tonsils, but a specialist recommended tonsillectomy.

The tonsils are the areas of tissue that you can see in the mirror on both sides of your throat (not to be confused with the uvula, which hangs down in the middle). Tonsillectomy, the most common surgery performed on children in the U.S., is intended to relieve *tonsillitis*, or inflammation of the tonsils (usually by strep or staph bacteria). But the fact is, tonsillitis can often be successfully treated with antibiotics, which means that surgery, including the week or two of pain and discomfort that follows it, is generally unnecessary.

mastectomy \\ma-'stek-tə-mē\ Surgical removal of all or part of the breast.

• She has always dreaded being disfigured by mastectomy, but her talks with the surgeon have calmed her considerably.

Breast cancer is the most common cancer among American women. Early cases can often be treated with drugs or with a small operation called a *lumpectomy* (because it removes a lump). Though a "simple mastectomy" is larger than a lumpectomy, it allows the breast to be reconstructed, using artificial implants or tissue from elsewhere on the body. But "radical mastectomy," which is required when the cancer is at an advanced stage, takes much of the chest muscle and makes reconstruction impossible.

IATR, from the Greek *iatros*, "healer, physician," usually hides in the middle of words, where it isn't immediately noticed. A *pediatrician* treats children (see PED, p. 295). A *psychiatrist* is a physician who treats mental problems. (A psychologist, by contrast, doesn't have a medical degree and thus can't prescribe drugs.) And a *physiatrist* is a doctor who practices "physical medicine and rehabilitation," which may involve such things as testing various physical abilities, relieving pain through electric heat or massage, or training patients to exercise or to use an artificial limb.

---

iatrogenic \ī-ˌa-trə-ˈje-nik\ Caused accidentally by medical treatment.

• Most medical malpractice suits seek compensation for iatrogenic injury.

In the 21st century, patients with throat infections are no longer being bled to death by misguided doctors, like the unfortunate George Washington. But iatrogenic injury and death still remain serious risks. Because of a doctor's bad handwriting, a patient may be given the wrong powerful drug. The sheer number of drugs on the market has led to dangerous drug interactions, which often occur when one doctor doesn't know what another is doing. Too many patients go to the hospital for some common treatment and pick up an antibiotic-resistant staph infection. And let's not even think about those unlucky patients who wake up to find that the surgeon has removed the wrong foot.

bariatric \ˌber-ē-ˈa-trik\ Relating to or specializing in the treatment of obesity.

• In the type of bariatric surgery called gastric bypass, part of the stomach is actually stapled off.

Baros means "weight" in Greek; so, for example, a *barometer* is an instrument that measures air pressure or weight. *Bariatric* describes the medical treatment of serious overweight—that is, obesity. Bariatric surgery is only employed when other methods of weight loss have been tried and failed. Though stapling the stomach may seem extreme, we now know that obesity greatly increases the risk of heart disease, diabetes, cancer, and stroke, so stomach surgery doesn't just help people look and feel better—it's a potential lifesaver.

geriatric \ˌjer-ē-ˈa-trik\ Of or relating to old people.

• We guessed we were now in the hospital's geriatric wing, since all the patients seemed to be elderly.

Since most medical care is devoted to those over 65, *geriatrics*, the medical treatment of the elderly, is a highly important specialty. The specific problems of the elderly include physical inactivity and instability, which result from weakness and loss of energy. Weakness of the eyes and ears plays a role, and weakening of the immune system often leads to more disease. All these conditions can be made worse by mental problems, such as declining intellectual activity, declining memory, and depression, which may prevent the patient from taking action to improve his or her condition. But the effects of aging can be greatly relieved by proper care. And the greatest improvement often results when the patient is persuaded to become more physically, mentally, and socially active.

podiatrist \pə-'dī-ə-trist\ A doctor who treats injuries and diseases of the foot.

- Like most podiatrists, she spends a lot of time dealing with minor complaints like bunions, ankle sprains, arch pain, and hammertoes.

Most foot problems result from the fact that human feet were never designed to walk on asphalt and concrete or even to wear shoes (all that cushioning we demand in our shoes may be doing us more harm than good). So today we have an entire medical specialty devoted to feet. In the U.S., a podiatrist is a doctor of *podiatric* medicine (D.P.M.), who is licensed to perform surgery. The root *pod-* comes from the Greek word for "foot" (compare PED, p. 78). But in England a foot doctor is often called a *chiropodist*, a term that dates from the time when the same specialist treated hands as well, since *chiro-* means "hand."

Quiz

Fill in each blank with the correct letter:

a. iatrogenic	e. mastectomy
b. gastrectomy	f. podiatrist
c. appendectomy	g. tonsillectomy
d. bariatric	h. geriatric

1. Following his _____ surgery his weight dropped from 310 pounds to 220.
2. Because of the doctor's bad handwriting, the pharmacist had given her the wrong medicine, and she had sued, claiming her new condition was _____ in origin.
3. After her _____ the breast had been completely reconstructed.

4. He had undergone a ____ after tests had revealed tumors on the stomach wall.
5. After her last Kung Fu class she had a badly swollen foot, and her ____ was having some X-rays taken.
6. I myself had a ____ when I was 11, but my son's tonsils got better after a week of antibiotics.
7. With the growing elderly population, there's a crying need for more ____ specialists.
8. X-rays showed that the appendix was badly swollen, and they managed to schedule an ____ for that same afternoon.

Review Quizzes

A. Match the definition on the left to the correct word on the right:

1. layer
2. revived
3. not in effect
4. equal-sided
5. outstanding
6. doctor-caused
7. incidental
8. weapons depot
9. devalue
10. sidewise

    a. superlative
    b. equilateral
    c. lateral
    d. stratum
    e. armory
    f. iatrogenic
    g. null
    h. resurgent
    i. collateral
    j. debase

B. Fill in each blank with the correct letter:

a. insurgency
b. bariatric
c. substrate
d. armistice
e. superfluous

f. supersede
g. nanotechnology
h. disarming
i. defamation
j. geriatric

1. After seven long years of war, the news of the ____ was greeted with tears of joy.
2. Amateurs can often grow mushrooms successfully on a ____ of sawdust, hay, or even coffee grounds.

3. ____ patients receive most of the country's medical care every year.

4. The government had beaten back a major ____ in the 1990s, but the rebels had regrouped and new fighting had begun.

5. The new version of the software will naturally ____ any previous versions, even if some users think it's not an improvement.

6. She had been making outrageous statements about him to the newspapers, and he finally sued for ____ of character.

7. The possible future medical uses of the tiny particles and structures employed in ____ seem to be limited only by scientists' imaginations.

8. The advice my doctors have been giving me about my condition has been ____, since I've known all these facts for years.

9. She had been prepared to find him terrifying, but his manner was so ____ that she relaxed almost immediately.

10. After years of failure at reducing, she was finally told by her doctor that ____ surgery was probably her best hope.

C. Indicate whether the following pairs of words have the same or different meanings:

1. insurgency / uprising   same ___ / different ___
2. degenerative / corrupt   same ___ / different ___
3. podiatrist / children's doctor   same ___ / different ___
4. annulment / undoing   same ___ / different ___
5. bilateral / two-sided   same ___ / different ___
6. geriatric / bacterial   same ___ / different ___
7. upsurge / increase   same ___ / different ___
8. dejection / sadness   same ___ / different ___
9. armada / fleet   same ___ / different ___
10. insuperable / excellent   same ___ / different ___

UNIT

28

MEDI comes from the Latin *medius*, meaning "middle." Our word *medium* refers to something in a middle position. The *medieval* period of European history, also known as the Middle Ages, is the period between Greek and Roman antiquity and the "modern age." But why people around 1620 began to use the term "Middle Ages," because they regarded themselves as modern, is an interesting question.

median \\'mē-dē-ən\\ In the middle; especially, having a value that is in the middle of a series of values arranged from smallest to largest.

• The city's west side is well-off but its east side isn't, so the city's median house prices are typical for the region.

People often use the word *average* without realizing that there are two common forms of average. Suppose you want to find the average net worth of a group of people—that is, the average value of everything they possess. To find one type of average, called the *mean*, you'd simply add up the total value of money and property of everyone in the group and divide it by the number of people. To find the other type, called the *median*, you'd identify the net worth of the person who is richer than half the people and poorer than the other half. So if Warren Buffett drove through a tiny village in India, the mean net worth of those in the village would suddenly rise to perhaps a billion dollars, but their median net worth would remain close to zero. Which figure would be more meaningful?

mediate \ˈmē-dē-ˌāt\ (1) To work with opposing sides in an argument or dispute in order to get an agreement. (2) To achieve a settlement or agreement by working with the opposing sides.

- He was the third person who had attempted to mediate the dispute between the firm and its striking workers, the first two having given up in despair.

Mediation is often used in disputes between companies and labor unions, and the government actually provides *mediators* for such disagreements. The mediator tries to bring the two sides to an agreement, but doesn't have the power to actually order such an agreement. Mediators also sometimes have a role in international disputes; when two neighboring countries claim exclusive fishing rights in the same ocean waters, for example, they may invite a trained mediator to help settle the argument. *Arbitration* is similar to mediation, but in arbitration both parties in a dispute agree to accept the arbitrator's decision.

intermediary \ˌin-tər-ˈmē-dē-ˌer-ē\ A person who works with opposing sides in a dispute in order to bring about an agreement.

- The divorce had been bitter, and the two now communicated only through an old friend who they both trusted as an intermediary.

Since *inter-* means "between, among" (see INTER, p. 653), an intermediary is someone who moves back and forth in the middle area between two sides—a "go-between." *Mediator* (which shares the *medi-* root) is often a synonym, and so is *facilitator*; *broker* and *agent* are often others. Thus, a real-estate broker or agent shuttles between a house's buyer and seller, who may never even meet each other. Financial *intermediation* is what happens when you put money in a bank or investment firm, which then invests it in various companies; if you want, you can instead cut out the intermediary and invest the money directly in companies of your own choosing.

mediocrity \ˌmē-dē-ˈä-krə-tē\ The quality of being not very good.

- He's the kind of person who can get depressed by the mediocrity of a dinner, or even a wine.

People interested in words always point out that *mediocrity* doesn't mean quite what its main root would indicate: Why doesn't it describe something that's right in the middle of the pack, exactly what you would expect? Instead the words *mediocrity* and *mediocre* always suggest disappointment. A mediocre play is one you wish you hadn't wasted an evening on, and the mediocre actor in it should probably find another profession. A person can even be called a mediocrity, though it isn't very nice and you'd never do it to his face.

OID comes from the Greek word for "appearance" or "form." Since *aster* in ancient Greek meant "star," the small bodies orbiting between Mars and Jupiter that looked like stars through primitive telescopes were called *asteroids*. A *factoid* is a little bit of information that looks like a fact, whether it is or not. And some people these days will attach *-oid* to just about anything; you can probably figure out the meaning of *nutsoid*, *nerdoid*, and *freakazoid* without much help.

---

rhomboid \\'räm-ˌbȯid\\ In geometry, a shape with four sides where only the opposite sides and angles are equal.

• The flimsy picture frame had been damaged en route, and its rectangular shape was now a rhomboid.

Rhomboids, like triangles, may take various different shapes, but they always look like a lopsided diamond or rectangle. As both a noun and an adjective, *rhomboid* can be applied to anything with those shapes, such as certain muscles of the upper back when viewed from behind. Whenever you hear about rhomboid exercises, rhomboid strain, or rhomboid pain, it involves those muscles, which attach your shoulder blades to your spine and can be strained by carrying a heavy backpack, serving a tennis ball, or just slumping in your chair in front of a computer all day.

deltoid \\'del-ˌtȯid\\ A large muscle of the shoulder.

• In Anatomy class she had learned about the deltoids, which her trainer at the gym just called "delts."

The fourth letter of the Greek alphabet is *delta*, and a capital delta is triangle-shaped. In English, *delta* commonly means the sand deposits that form a huge triangle at the mouth of certain large rivers. *Deltoid* as an adjective means "having a triangular shape," and botanists often use the word to describe the shape of certain leaves. The triangular, swept-back wings seen on jet fighter aircraft are called *delta wings*. Your deltoid muscles—not far from your rhomboids—form a cap on your shoulders, and some gym trainers even treat *shoulder* and *deltoid* as synonyms. Can you guess the general shape of deltoids when seen from the side?

dendroid \\'den-ˌdrȯid\\ Resembling a tree in form.

- The reef was a fantastic jungle, its dendroid corals resembling luminous, poisonous trees in a landscape of bizarre beauty.

Dendrology is the study of trees, and those who do the studying are called *dendrologists*. So *dendroid* describes something that "branches" in all directions from a central "trunk" in an irregular way. The word is almost always used by biologists, who often speak of dendroid seaweeds, dendroid moss, and dendroid algae.

humanoid \\'hyü-mə-ˌnȯid\\ Looking or acting like a human.

- We slowly learn that most of Dr. Bennell's friends have been replaced by humanoid substitutes that have emerged from pods.

A humanoid robot, sometimes called an *android*, is a robot that resembles a human. Accounts of the yeti, Sasquatch, and Bigfoot continue to fascinate us mainly because of their humanoid characteristics. The idea of creating a monstrous *humanoid*, such as the Jewish golem or Victor Frankenstein's creation, has intrigued us for centuries. "Humanoid Animation" is a standard for creating humanlike figures for video that lets the same figure be used in a variety of 3-D games—some of which have nothing but humanoids for characters.

Quizzes

A. Fill in each blank with the correct letter:

a. mediocrity	e. intermediary
b. humanoid	f. dendroid
c. median	g. mediate
d. rhomboid	h. deltoid

1. Seen from up close, the mosses turn out to be _____, resembling a colony of tiny trees.
2. What he dislikes most about his body is his narrow shoulders, so the first thing he asked his trainer for was some good _____ exercises.

3. The school's wrestling team includes a couple of big guys, but the _____ weight is only about 160 pounds.

4. She'd been expecting a lot from the kids in the advanced-placement class, so she was dismayed by the _____ of the first papers they passed in.

5. If life is ever discovered on a distant planet, few scientists expect the life-forms to be _____, even if that's what sci-fi films always show.

6. The two kids are always fighting, and their father's main job is to _____ their disputes.

7. The antenna takes the shape of a _____, almost a diamond.

8. These illegal arms deals usually require an _____ who knows both languages and is trusted by both parties.

B. **Indicate whether the following pairs of words have the same or different meanings:**

1. mediate / exchange   same __ / different __
2. deltoid / shoulder muscle   same __ / different __
3. intermediary / agent   same __ / different __
4. dendroid / treelike   same __ / different __
5. mediocrity / ordinariness   same __ / different __
6. humanoid / manmade   same __ / different __
7. median / so-so   same __ / different __
8. rhomboid / shifting shape   same __ / different __

SCOP, which usually appears in a suffix, comes from the Greek *skopein*, meaning "to look at." In English we have the simple noun *scope*, along with some other words it sometimes stands for: *telescope*, *microscope*, *periscope*, and so on. And have you ever used a *stereoscope*, a device your great-grandparents probably enjoyed, which lets you look through a viewer at two slightly different photographs of the same thing, one with each eye, to enjoy the illusion that you're seeing it in three dimensions?

---

endoscope \\'en-də-ˌskōp\\ A lighted tubular medical instrument for viewing the interior or a hollow organ or body part that typically has one or more channels to permit passage of surgical instruments.

- Possible uses of the endoscope outside of medicine soon became apparent, and soon mechanics were using specially designed endoscopes to view the insides of jet engines.

The Greek prefix *endo-* means "within, inside," so around 1860 an early crude instrument for looking deep inside the body was named the endoscope. But modern *endoscopy* required the invention of the electric lightbulb and then fiber-optic cable, so the first modern endoscopes date only to 1967. An endoscope may be inserted through a natural passageway (for example, through the nose or down the esophagus) or through a tiny cut in the skin. A tiny camera with a light at the end of the cable sends back images onto a screen, and the surgeon uses special instruments that work through a tube alongside the cable. There are now specialized types of endoscopes for every part of the body, where they can take tissue samples, cut out small growths, or remove foreign objects.

arthroscopic \,är-thrə-'skä-pik\ Relating to a fiber-optic instrument that is inserted through an incision near a joint to examine the joint's interior.

- The day he scheduled the fourth arthroscopic operation on his knee was the day he decided to hang up his football cleats.

In Greek, *arthron* means "joint." *Arthritis* is a condition of swollen and painful joints, and *arthropods* are animals (including insects, arachnids, and crustaceans) that have a segmented body and jointed limbs. Arthroscopic surgery, or *arthroscopy*, has revolutionized the treatment of joint injuries. It's performed with an arthroscope, a specialized type of endoscope (see above). A tiny camera and a light are inserted through a small cut in the skin, and through another cut nearby a tiny surgical instrument, controlled through its own cable, is inserted. The surgeon then performs the operation, guided by the images sent back via the fiber-optic cable. Most patients walk out of the hospital on crutches the same day, though full recovery may take a couple of months.

laparoscopy \,la-pə-'räs-kə-pē\ Examination of the interior of the abdomen using a fiber-optic instrument inserted through a cut in the abdomen's wall.

- The initial laparoscopy involves inserting the cable through a tiny cut and inflating the internal area with carbon dioxide so that a good-sized area will become visible.

Since *laparo-* means "wall of the abdomen," a *laparoscope* is an endoscope designed especially to examine the abdomen. Common *laparoscopic* surgeries include removal of the gallbladder, appendix, or kidney, and removal of tumors from abdominal organs. Like the other endoscopic surgeries, laparoscopy, as compared to traditional surgery, reduces risk of bleeding, pain following the operation, patient recovery time, and length of hospital stays.

oscilloscope \ä-ˈsi-lə-ˌskōp\ An instrument that shows visual images of changing electrical current on a screen.

• An oscilloscope next to the bed was monitoring her vital signs, but otherwise it was hard for a visitor to be sure she was even alive.

In Latin *oscillare* means "to swing," and our word *oscillation* usually means "vibration" or "variation," especially in a changing flow of electricity. The oscilloscope basically draws a graph of an electrical signal. Since all kinds of physical phenomena can be converted into an electric voltage, oscilloscopes can be used to measure such things as sound, light, and heat. So an oscilloscope can analyze how one clarinet's sound is different from another's, or how one bulb's light differs from another's. Auto mechanics use oscilloscopes to measure engine vibrations; doctors use them to measure brain waves. Audio technicians use oscilloscopes to diagnose problems in audio equipment; TV and radio technicians use them to diagnose TV and radio problems. But oscilloscopes are most essential today to high-tech electronics experimentation.

TRANS comes from Latin to indicate movement "through, across, or beyond" something. *Translation* carries a writer's meaning from one language to another. A television signal is sent or *transmitted* through the air (or a cable) to your set. When making your way through a city on public *transportation*, you may have to *transfer* from one bus or subway to another.

---

transient \ˈtran-shē-ənt\ (1) Not lasting long; short-lived. (2) Passing through a place and staying only briefly.

• It's a college town, so much of its population is transient.

A transient mood is one that passes quickly. A brief stopover in a town on your way to somewhere else is a transient visit. A summer job on a farm is transient work, lasting only as long as the growing season. You may occasionally experience a transient episode of dizziness or weakness, which vanishes without a trace. As a noun, *transient* means a person who passes through a place, staying only briefly. The hoboes and tramps of earlier years were some of our most colorful transients, known for hopping freight trains, panhandling on the street, and stealing homemade pies cooling on the windowsill.

transfiguration \trans-ˌfi-gyə-ˈrā-shən\ A change in form or appearance; a glorifying spiritual change.

• Being in love caused a complete transfiguration of her personality.

The Gospels relate that one day Jesus took three disciples up a mountain, where they witnessed his transfiguration into divine form: his face shone like the sun, his garments became brilliantly white, and a voice from heaven proclaimed that this was the son of God. *Transfiguration* was first used in English as the name of this biblical event, and the Feast of the Transfiguration remains the name of a holy day. So the word has always kept a somewhat religious—and almost always positive—tone. A face may be transfigured by joy, and an "ugly duckling" may be slowly transfigured into a radiant beauty. And as Harry Potter fans know, transfiguration is a subject long taught at the Hogwarts School by Minerva McGonagall.

transponder \tran-ˈspän-dər\ A radio or radar set that emits a radio signal after receiving such a signal.

• When a patient is admitted to an emergency room, an implanted transponder can relay important data about his or her medical history.

This word was coined during World War II by simply joining pieces of the words *transmitter* and *responder*. Transponders are basic to modern aviation and communications satellites, and they're finding new uses in fields such as medicine as well. But they're now also part of everyday life. The "E-ZPass" that lets you drive right through turnpike tollbooths is a transponder, and the car you're driving may not even start unless it recognizes the signal from your personal key's transponder. In a big crowded foot race, you may carry a tiny transponder on your shoe that records when you cross both the starting line and the finish line.

transcendent \tran-ˈsen-dənt\ (1) Exceeding or rising above usual limits; supreme. (2) Beyond comprehension; beyond ordinary experience or material existence.

* Despite the chaos around her she remained calm, with a transcendent smile on her face.

The Latin verb *scandere* means "to climb," so *transcend* has the basic meaning of climbing so high that you cross some boundary. A transcendent experience is one that takes you out of yourself and convinces you of a larger life or existence; in this sense, it means something close to "spiritual." The American writers and thinkers known as the *Transcendentalists*, including Ralph Waldo Emerson and Henry David Thoreau, believed in the unity of all creation, the basic goodness of humankind, and the superiority of spiritual vision over mere logic. When we speak of the transcendent importance of an issue such as climate change, we may mean that everything else on earth actually depends on it.

Quizzes

A. Indicate whether the following pairs of words have the same or different meanings:

1. transient / temporary   same __ / different __
2. transcendent / sublime   same __ / different __
3. arthroscopic / insect-viewing   same __ / different __
4. oscilloscope /
       underwater viewer   same __ / different __
5. transfiguration / transformation same __ / different __
6. endoscope /
       electron microscope   same __ / different __
7. transponder / radio signaler   same __ / different __
8. laparoscopy /
       abdomen examination   same __ / different __

B. Fill in each blank with the correct letter:

a. transcendent   e. transponder
b. oscilloscope   f. laparoscopy
c. transient   g. transfiguration
d. arthroscopic   h. endoscope

1. The mechanic always lets her watch the screen of the _____ as he tries to diagnose the sources of her engine's problems.

2. Painters are well aware of how _____ the color effects of the sunset are, and how the sky often looks completely different after five minutes.

3. With _____ surgery, knee operations now take only an hour or so, and the patient leaves the office on crutches soon afterward.

4. The community is surrounded by a high wall, and the gate opens only when signaled by a resident's _____.

5. Today there's a specialized type of _____ for looking inside practically every part of the body.

6. On the rare occasions when he conducts nowadays, the critics rave about his _____ performances of the great Mahler symphonies.

7. The _____ revealed a small stomach tumor, which appeared not to be cancerous.

8. Painters have tried to depict Jesus' _____ on the mountaintop, while realizing that it's probably impossible to do with mere paint.

PRO is an important prefix, with a couple of quite different broad meanings. In this section, we'll look at words in which *pro-* has the basic meaning "for" or "favoring." Everyone knows words like *pro-democracy* and *pro-American*, but other *pro-* words may not be quite so self-explanatory.

---

proactive \prō-ˈak-tiv\ Acting in anticipation of future problems, needs, or changes.

• Our president prides himself on being proactive, and is always imagining situations the company might be facing in three or four years.

People who tend to *react* to a problem only when it's gotten serious could be called *reactive* people. Until recently, *reactive* (in this sense) didn't really have an antonym. So *proactive* was coined to describe the kind of person who's always looking into the future in order to be prepared for anything. A good parent attempts to be proactive on behalf of his or her children, trying to imagine the problems they might be facing in a few months or years. A company's financial officers study the patterns of the company's earnings to make sure it won't risk running short of cash at any point in the next year or two. *Proactive* has only been around a few decades, and it can still sometimes sound like a fashionable buzzword.

pro bono \ˌprō-ˈbō-nō\ Being, involved in, or doing professional work, and especially legal work, donated for the public good.

• The law firm allows her to do several hours of pro bono work every week, and she devotes it to helping poor immigrant families.

In Latin, *pro bono publico* means "for the public good"; in English we generally shorten the phrase to *pro bono*. Donating free legal help to those who need it has long been a practice of American law firms; the American Bar Association actually recommends that all lawyers donate 50 hours a year. Pro bono work is sometimes donated by nonlegal firms as well. For example, an advertising firm might produce a 60-second video for an environmental or educational organization, or a strategic-planning firm might prepare a start-up plan for a charity that funds shelters for battered women.

proponent \prə-ˈpō-nənt\ One who argues in favor of something: advocate.

• The new governor is a proponent of a longer school year, and he's gotten a lot of support from parents.

Proponent comes from the same Latin word as *propose*, so a proponent is someone who proposes something, or at least supports it by speaking and writing in favor of it. Thus, for example, proponents of casinos argue that they create jobs, whereas proponents of a casino ban—that is, casino *opponents*—argue that they're corrupting and they take money away from people who can't afford it. As a rule, just about anything important that gets proposed also gets *opposed*.

pro forma \prō-ˈfȯr-mə\ Done or existing as something that is required but that has little true meaning or importance.

• The letter she received from him after her husband's death struck her as pro forma, and she knew the old friendship between the two men had never really been repaired.

A lot of things are done for the sake of appearances. A teacher might get officially observed and evaluated every three years, even though everyone knows she's terrific and the whole thing is strictly pro forma. A critic might say that a orchestral conductor gave a pro forma performance, since his heart wasn't in it. A business owner might make a pro forma appearance at the funeral of a politician's mother, never having met her but maybe hoping for a favor from her son sometime in the future. In business, *pro forma* has some special meanings; a pro forma invoice, for example, will list all the items being sent but, unlike a true invoice, won't be an actual bill.

PRO, in its other broad meaning, means "before, in front of." So, for example, to *proceed* means "to move out in front"; to *progress* means to "to move forward"; and somebody *prominent* stands out, as if he or she were actually standing out in front of the crowd.

---

protrude \prō-'trüd\ To jut out from the surrounding surface or context.

* As he leaned over, she noticed something protruding from under his jacket, and realized with a sickening feeling that he was armed.

Since *trudere* means "to thrust" in Latin, *protrude* means basically "to thrust forward." If your neighbors' patio protrudes over your property boundary, you may want to discuss it with them. A *protruding* disc in your spine may have to be operated on sooner or later; superficial *protrusions*, such as corns or bunions, tend to be less serious than more deeply rooted ones.

prophylaxis \ˌprō-fə-'lak-səs\ Measures designed to preserve health and prevent the spread of disease.

* For rabies, prophylaxis in the form of vaccines for cats and dogs is much better than treating them after being bitten.

In Greek, *phylax* means "guard," so *prophylactic* measures guard against disease by taking action ahead of time. Thus, for example, before the polio vaccine became available, prophylaxis against polio included avoiding crowds and public swimming pools. These days a well-known kind of *prophylactic* is used to prevent sexually transmitted diseases; but prophylactic measures only work when people use them.

promulgate \\'prä-məl-ˌgāt\ (1) To proclaim or make public. (2) To put (a law) into effect.

• The country's new constitution was officially promulgated in a grand ceremony at the presidential palace.

All laws need to be made public in some way so that citizens may know if they're in danger of breaking them. Since they can't be expected to go into effect until the population knows they exist, *promulgate* has the two meanings "proclaim" and "put into effect." In ancient Greece and Rome, when most people couldn't read, a new written law would actually be proclaimed in a public place; we've all seen such scenes in historical movies. But today *promulgation* of a law generally occurs simply by its being published in an official government publication and on a government Web site. New laws are also often reported in newspapers and on TV, though rarely in complete form.

prologue \\'prō-ˌlȯg\ (1) An introduction to a literary work. (2) An introductory event or development.

• The Boston Tea Party of 1773 turned out to be a prologue to the American Revolution.

In ancient Greek drama, the *prologos* (a word that means basically "speaking before") was the opening portion of the play, before the entry of the all-important chorus. It might be spoken by a single actor, maybe playing a god, who would "set the scene" for the audience. Playwrights today instead often provide the same kind of "scene-setting" information through dialogue near the play's beginning; in movies, it may appear (as in the "Star Wars" series) in the form of actual written text. In a nonfiction book, the lead-in is now usually called a *preface* or *introduction*; novels rarely provide any introduction at all. Still, *prologue* remains a useful word for nonliterary purposes. The saying "The past is prologue" tells us that, in real life, almost everything can be a prologue to what follows it.

Quizzes

A. Fill in each blank with the correct letter:

a. pro bono
b. proponent
c. prophylaxis
d. promulgate

e. pro forma
f. prologue
g. proactive
h. protrude

1. For the doctor, _____ requires the use of gloves and sometimes masks, and constant hand washing throughout the day.
2. The only part of being a lawyer that she really liked was her _____ work helping poor families with their housing problems.
3. Talk-show hosts were helping to _____ a made-up story about a scandal involving the First Lady.
4. He claims we're falling behind in education, which is why he's a _____ of a longer school year.
5. Economists worry that these scattered bank failures may turn out to be a _____ to a serious financial crisis.
6. He's gotten terribly thin, and the bones of his arms now _____ from under his skin.
7. Her apology was strictly _____, and didn't sound sincere at all.
8. The company has never spent much time thinking about its future, and it really needs to become more _____.

B. Match the definition on the left to the correct word on the right:

1. disease prevention
2. formal
3. introduction
4. broadcast
5. backer
6. bulge
7. forward-looking
8. unpaid

a. prophylaxis
b. promulgate
c. prologue
d. pro bono
e. protrude
f. proponent
g. pro forma
h. proactive

RE is a prefix which, like *pro-* (see PRO, p. 629), has more than one meaning. In this section, we'll focus on the meaning "again." We use *re-* words with this meaning every day—*redo, reheat, recheck, reread, resell, repaint*, etc.—and we feel free to make up new ones as needed. But in plenty of other *re-* words, the meaning isn't so obvious.

---

remorse \ri-ˈmȯrs\ A deep regret arising from a sense of guilt for past wrongs.

• Remorse for the accident that occurred that night seems to have altered the course of the senator's life.

In Latin, *mordere* means "to bite"; thus, remorse is something that "gnaws" at you over and over. In criminal court, judges are always looking for signs that a convicted felon is suffering remorse for his crime; if not, the judge may well lengthen his sentence or deny him parole after serving part of it. Remorse is stronger than mere regret; real remorse is the kind of thing that may last a lifetime.

reiterate \rē-ˈi-tə-ˌrāt\ To state or do over again or repeatedly.

• At the end of every class, Professor Lewis reiterates that we should get an early start on our term papers.

In Latin, *iterum* means "again," so *reiterate* has the basic meaning of "repeat over and over." Our word *iteration* is used a lot by computer programmers today, often meaning a repeated response to program instructions that gets something closer to its final form, but also often meaning a new version of something, such as a program. But a *reiteration* is simply a repeat or several repeats.

rejuvenate \ri-ˈjü-və-ˌnāt\ To make young or youthful again; to give new vigor to.

• He was in bad shape after his wife's death, but everyone says he's been rejuvenated by his remarriage.

Juvenis, Latin for "young," can be seen in a word such as *juvenile*. *Rejuvenation* is something that can be carried out on a creaky old house, a clunker of a car, a sluggish career, a weak economy, or a company that's lost its edge, but *rejuvenate* and *rejuvenation* are probably used most often for talking about our physical selves. Ads for lotions promise skin rejuvenation; diet-book covers show rejuvenated (or maybe just young) models bursting with health. We still seem to be searching for that "Fuente de la Juventud" that Juan Ponce de León failed to discover five hundred years ago.

reconcile \\'re-kən-ˌsīl\\ (1) To make agree. (2) To make friendly again.

• Now she has to reconcile her liking for her brother-in-law with the news that he was picked up for armed robbery last week.

In Latin, *conciliare* means "to calm, soothe"; thus, *reconcile* means essentially "to calm again." Warring friends can often be reconciled by a nice note or apology. When you're faced with two things that don't square very well, you may have to reconcile them, the way a scientist might try to reconcile the differing results from two research projects. The U.S. House and Senate, in a process called *reconciliation*, try to produce one final bill from two different versions that they've passed separately. To reconcile yourself to something means to get used to it; thus, you may need to reconcile yourself to not getting to the beach next summer, or you may have reconciled yourself to the idea of your daughter in the Peace Corps marrying a Mongolian goat herder.

RE, in its other main sense, means "back" or backward." Since doing something again means going back to it, the two senses are actually related; still, the meaning of *re-* in most words is pretty clearly one or the other. So a *rebound* comes back at you; to *recall* means to "call back" a memory; and to *react* is to "act back" at someone else's action.

---

reciprocal \\ri-'si-prə-kəl\\ (1) Done, given, or felt equally by both sides. (2) Related to each other in such a way that one completes the other or is the equal of the other.

• They had done us a great favor, so as a reciprocal gesture we invited them for a weekend on the island.

In Latin, *reciprocus* means "returning the same way" or "alternating." So in a *reciprocating engine*, like the one in your car, the pistons move back and forth, and that motion is transformed into the rotary motion of the crankshaft. A *reciprocal* is a pair of numbers (such as 5/6 and 6/5) that can be multiplied to produce 1. *Reciprocity* (with the accent on the third syllable) between two nations means they agree to recognize certain things granted in one country as being valid in the other—for example, your driver's license.

rebut \ri-ˈbət\ (1) To oppose by argument. (2) To prove to be wrong.

• The claims about receiving payoffs from builders were eventually rebutted by the mayor's office, but the damage had been done.

The -*but* in *rebut* once meant basically "butt," so *rebut*'s original meanings were "to drive or beat back" and "to attack with violent language." *Rebuttals* can still be rather violent, as anyone who has watched some heated moments in a presidential debate can testify. The word is often used by lawyers, since the lawyer for the accused or for the party being sued almost always tries to rebut the charges against his or her client; but it's also used in plenty of contexts outside the courtroom.

revoke \ri-ˈvōk\ To officially cancel the power or effect of something (such as a law, order, or privilege).

• His real-estate license had been revoked after his conviction for fraud three years earlier.

Since *vocare* means "to call" in Latin (see VOC, p. 138), to revoke is to "call back." Your driver's license could be revoked after about three convictions for driving under the influence of alcohol; some people's licenses are even revoked for life. You could get your passport revoked if a judge thought you had violated the terms of your bail and suspected you might skip the country. And if you're out of prison on probation and violate the terms of probation, it will probably be revoked and you'll end up back in the slammer.

regress \ri-ˈgres\ To return to an earlier and usually worse or less developed condition or state.

• In the years since she had left, the country seemed to have regressed badly, and its corruption and dire poverty had gotten much harder to ignore.

As you might guess, *regress* is the opposite of *progress*. So if a disease regresses, that's generally a good thing, but in most other ways we prefer not to regress. If someone's mental state has been improving, we hope he or she won't start to regress; and when a nation's promising educational system begins to regress, that's a bad sign for the country's future. Economists often distinguish between a *progressive* tax and a *regressive* tax; in a progressive tax, the percentage that goes to taxes gets larger as the amount of money being taxed gets larger, while in a regressive tax the percentage gets smaller. (Rich people prefer regressive taxes.)

Quizzes

A. Fill in each blank with the correct letter:

a. remorse   e. reciprocal
b. rebut   f. regress
c. revoke   g. reconcile
d. reiterate   h. rejuvenate

1. State officials may ____ the factory's permit to release larger amounts of heated water into the river.
2. Her outburst at her daughter left her filled with ____ for days afterward.
3. These spas always promise to ____ your skin, and often your spirit as well.
4. She's trying to ____ the image she had of her friend with what she's recently learned about him.
5. The governor has been trying to ____ these new charges against him for days without success.
6. An American university may have a ____ arrangement with a European university, whereby each agrees to take the other's students for a year.
7. Sometimes our 15-year-old just seems to ____ and start acting the way he did when he was two years younger.
8. In almost every speech she tries to ____ the same few points, since she doesn't trust the voters to remember them otherwise.

B. Indicate whether the following pairs of words have the same or different meanings:

1. revoke / cancel   same ___ / different ___
2. regress / backslide   same ___ / different ___
3. remorse / regret   same ___ / different ___
4. rejuvenate / return   same ___ / different ___
5. reconcile / fight back   same ___ / different ___

6.	rebut / send back	same ___ / different ___
7.	reciprocal / mutual	same ___ / different ___
8.	reiterate / modernize	same ___ / different ___

DERM comes from the Greek *derma*, meaning "skin." For medical advice on a skin problem such as acne, we may go to a *dermatologist*, or skin specialist. When we get a shot, it's usually with a *hypodermic*, a needle that goes "under the skin" (see HYP/HYPO, p. 49). A *pachyderm* is a "thick-skinned" animal, which most of us just call an elephant.

dermal \ˈdər-məl\ Relating to the skin and especially to the dermis.

• The agency is always studying what can be done to prevent dermal exposure to chemicals in the workplace.

The word *dermal* often comes up nowadays in connection with cosmetic treatments. Dermal therapy usually means restoring moisture to dry, cracked skin. Dermal fillers such as collagen can be injected to fill in acne scars or reduce wrinkles. These have now been joined by treatments like Botox, which paralyzes facial dermal muscles, again in order to reduce wrinkles (since those dermal muscles are used to form expressions). A synonym for *dermal* is *cutaneous*.

epidermis \ˌe-pə-ˈdər-məs\ The outer layer of the skin.

• The epidermis is the body's first line of defense against infection, external injury, and environmental stresses.

Epidermis includes the Greek prefix *epi-*, meaning "outer" (see EPI, p. 46); thus, the epidermis overlies the *dermis*, or inner layer of skin. The epidermis itself consists of four or five layers; the outermost layer is made of dead cells, which are being shed continuously. The epidermis acts as a physical barrier—a protective wrap over the body's surface, which, by preventing water loss, allows vertebrates to live on land.

taxidermist \ˈtak-sə-ˌdər-mist\ One who prepares, stuffs, and mounts the skins of dead animals.

- The taxidermist suggested that the bobcat be displayed in the act of leaping fiercely toward the viewer.

Taxidermists are called on not only by sportsmen and collectors but by museums, movie studios, and advertisers. Taxidermists first remove the skin (with its fur, hair, or feathers), then create a plaster cast of the carcass with which to produce a "mannequin," on which they replace the skin. Producing trophies of lifelike quality that often recreate an exciting moment requires physical skill, attention to detail, and sometimes artistic talent.

dermatitis \ˌdər-mə-ˈtī-təs\ Inflammation of the skin.

- The only dermatitis she had ever suffered had been the result of playing in poison ivy when she was little.

Dermatitis usually appears as a rash, and may cause itching, blisters, swelling, and often scabbing and scaling. It often marks an allergic reaction of some kind. *Contact dermatitis* is caused by something (often a chemical) touching the skin. *Atopic dermatitis* usually affects the insides of the elbows, the backs of the knees, and the face; generally resulting from an inherited sensitivity, it's often triggered by inhaling something. Eczema, psoriasis, and dandruff are all forms of dermatitis. Even in the worst cases, dermatitis isn't infectious and doesn't produce serious health consequences.

ENDO comes from the Greek *endon*, meaning "within." In English it appears almost always in scientific terms, especially in biology. A nonscientific *endo-* word is *endogamy*, meaning marriage within a specific group as required by custom or law—one of the many customs that can be seen everywhere from the most remote tribes to the highest society in wealthy countries.

---

endocrine \ˈen-də-krən\ (1) A hormone. (2) Any of several glands (such as the thyroid) that pour their secretions directly into the blood or lymph.

- Since the endocrines are so vital to human life, affecting such things as cell growth and blood sugar, the chemicals known as endocrine disrupters can be destructive and even deadly.

The body's glands remove specific substances from the blood and alter them for rerelease into the blood or removal. Glands such as those that produce saliva and sweat secrete their products through tiny ducts or tubes on or near the body's surface. The glands without ducts, called the *endocrine* glands, instead secrete their products into the bloodstream; the *endo-* root indicates that the secretions are internal rather than on the surface. The endocrine system includes such glands as the pituitary (which controls growth, regulates the other endocrines, and performs many other tasks), the thyroid (another growth gland that also influences metabolism), the adrenals (which secrete adrenaline and steroids), the hypothalamus (which influences sleep and weight regulation), and the ovaries (which produce eggs). Endocrine problems are treated by *endocrinologists*.

endodontic \ˌen-də-ˈdän-tik\ Relating to a branch of dentistry that deals with the pulp of the teeth.

• Her dentist told her the problem was endodontic and that she should see a specialist soon to prevent loss of the tooth.

Endodontists, as you might expect from the *endo-* root, deal with the interior of the tooth. The tooth's enamel, on the outside, covers a thick layer called the *dentin*; this in turn surrounds the innermost part, called the *pulp*, a mass of soft tissue through which nerves and blood vessels run. When a tooth has been badly damaged by decay or cracking, producing a risk of dangerous infection of the pulp, a "root canal" procedure is performed by an endodontist. Try to avoid ever getting to know an endodontist; brush your teeth twice daily, floss before bedtime, and never let a cavity go unfilled for long.

endogenous \en-ˈdä-jə-nəs\ Developing or originating within a cell, organ, body, or system.

• Vitamin D can be obtained from food and supplements, but it's also an endogenous vitamin, produced by the body when the skin is exposed to sunlight.

When biologists need to make a distinction between things that are produced within a cell or organ and things that affect it from the outside, they use the terms *endogenous* and *exogenous*. It used to be thought, for instance, that mutations in cells always resulted from exogenous causes, until it was discovered that substances in the body, including those called oxidants, could cause them *endogenously* as well. "Circadian rhythms"—the regular cycles, roughly 24 hours in length, that plants, animals, and humans rely on to regulate their days—are endogenously generated and don't actually depend on the sun for their timing.

endorphin \en-'dòr-fən\ Any of a group of proteins in the brain that are able to relieve pain.

• On the final stretch of her daily five-mile run, she could usually count on the endorphins kicking in, giving her that beautiful "runner's high."

The word *endorphin* was coined, back when the substances were discovered in the 1970s, by joining pieces of *endogenous* and *morphine*, morphine being a narcotic that closely resembles the endorphins and relieves pain in a similar way. Studies suggest that the pain-relieving practice called acupuncture (see p. 515) works by releasing endorphins. Endorphins also seem to play an important role in pregnancy. Though much remains to be learned about the endorphins, the general public seems ready to give them credit for any all-natural high.

Quiz

Fill in each blank with the correct letter:

a. taxidermist   e. endocrine
b. endodontic   f. dermal
c. endogenous   g. endorphin
d. dermatitis   h. epidermis

1. He had a mild form of ____ that occasionally produced a rash on his upper arms.
2. To get rid of wrinkles, you can have a ____ filler injected into parts of your body.
3. This ____ is released in large quantities during serious physical activity and seems to have important painkilling effects.
4. She has always had bad teeth, and now she's finally having ____ work done on the really rotten ones.
5. Low growth rate in teenagers is often an ____ problem that can be fixed with hormones.
6. The ____ keeps the body waterproof and provides a barrier against infection.
7. They had come across a dead eagle in perfect condition, and a ____ had done a beautiful job of mounting it for display.

8. Vitamin D is an _____ vitamin, but bodies seem to require sunlight to produce it.

Review Quizzes

A. Match the definition on the left to the correct word on the right:

1.	go backward	a.	transient
2.	skin rash	b.	dendroid
3.	brief	c.	protrude
4.	tree-shaped	d.	regress
5.	internally produced	e.	reconcile
6.	repeat	f.	endogenous
7.	refresh	g.	reiterate
8.	declare publicly	h.	promulgate
9.	jut out	i.	dermatitis
10.	bring into agreement	j.	rejuvenate

B. Fill in each blank with the correct letter:

a.	pro forma	f.	pro bono
b.	reciprocal	g.	dermal
c.	proponent	h.	remorse
d.	endodontic	i.	reconcile
e.	revoke	j.	rebut

1. When she tried to _____ the claims her opponent had made, the crowd broke out in jeers.
2. He has always been a _____ of women's issues, particularly government-funded day care.
3. In the past she's gotten _____ silicone injections to erase her facial wrinkles.
4. Most of the _____ work he's done has been for environmental groups that can't afford legal fees.
5. The application process was just _____, since they had already promised her the job.
6. _____ over the accident seems to be the main cause of his depression.
7. They haven't been able to _____ the results of the two studies, which came to very different conclusions.

8. The tooth had been aching for several weeks, but he was still surprised when his dentist told him it would require ____ work.

9. Expensive golf courses sometimes have ____ agreements that enable members to use courses in other cities for the same price.

10. Because of numerous violations, the city is threatening to ____ the nightclub's license to operate.

C. Indicate whether the following pairs of terms have the same or different meanings:

1. prophylaxis / support   same ___ / different ___
2. prologue / extension   same ___ / different ___
3. epidermis / outer skin   same ___ / different ___
4. endogenous / produced inside   same ___ / different ___
5. reiterate / restate   same ___ / different ___
6. endodontic /
        relating to tooth enamel   same ___ / different ___
7. proactive / anticipating   same ___ / different ___
8. rejuvenate / renew   same ___ / different ___
9. rebut / disprove   same ___ / different ___
10. dermal / skin-related   same ___ / different ___

UNIT

29

NECRO comes from the Greek *nekros*, meaning "dead body," so it's not surprising that it shows up in some unappetizing places. A *necrophagous* insect, for instance, is one that feeds on dead bodies; when homicide investigators discover a corpse, they may use the insect evidence to figure out when the person died.

necrosis \nə-ˈkrō-səs\ Death of living tissue, usually within a limited area.

• He had ignored the spider bite for several days, and his doctor was alarmed to see that serious necrosis had set in.

Cells die naturally after a period of time, but may also die as a result of injuries, infections, or cancer. Burns produce necrosis, and the bedsores suffered by nursing-home patients are a form of necrosis. The dreaded condition known as gangrene, in which the dying tissue turns black or green, is another form. When untreated, the dying cells release substances that lead to the death of surrounding cells, so untreated necrosis can lead to death. Treatment usually requires the removal of the *necrotic* tissue, and in severe cases can even involve amputating a limb.

necromancer \ˈne-krə-ˌman-sər\ One who conjures the spirits of the dead in order to magically reveal the future or influence the course of events.

- Her specialty is communication with the dead, and she might once have been known as a necromancer, but her sign says simply "Psychic."

The practice of *necromancy* goes back as far as the ancient Assyrians and Babylonians and has continued through all the centuries since. In the Middle Ages it became associated with black magic; condemned by the church, it had to be practiced secretly. In Europe a necromancer might work in a remote graveyard at night, standing within a magical circle he had drawn to shield himself from the anger of the spirits. The grave of a person who had died suddenly or violently might be plundered for its body parts; the unused energy these were believed to contain made them valuable in the *necromantic* ceremony. But body parts aren't essential to necromancy, which is now practiced by channelers, mediums, and shamans, and even by groups of amateurs sitting around a Ouija board.

necropolis \nə-ˈkrä-pə-ləs\ A cemetery, especially a large, elaborate cemetery of an ancient city.

- On Sundays the downtown is like a necropolis, and he was always slightly disturbed by the complete absence of life among all those buildings.

With its *-polis* ending, meaning "city" (see POLIS/POLIT, p. 573), a *necropolis* is a "city of the dead." Most of the famous necropolises of Egypt line the Nile River across from their cities. In ancient Greece and Rome, a necropolis would often line the road leading out of a city; in the 1940s a great Roman necropolis was discovered under the Vatican's St. Peter's Basilica. Some more recent cemeteries especially deserve the name necropolis because they resemble cities of aboveground tombs, a necessity in low-lying areas such as New Orleans where a high water table prevents underground burial.

necropsy \ˈne-ˌkräp-sē\ An autopsy, especially one performed on an animal.

- Daisy's sudden death was so mysterious that we paid for a necropsy, and it turned out she'd been a victim of lethal chemicals in our imported dog food.

Human autopsies are generally performed either to determine the cause of death or to observe the deadly effects of a disease for research or education purposes. Autopsies may be necessary when tracking an epidemic; they're also performed to discover whether a death might actually have resulted from murder, and if so, what evidence it might reveal that could help catch the murderer. Animal necropsies are actually more common than human autopsies, since a farmer with livestock is always concerned that whatever killed one animal not pose a threat to the others.

PALEO comes from the Greek *palaios*, meaning "ancient"—that is, "older than old." The prefix sometimes gets attached to very recognizable words; *paleobiology*, for instance, deals with the biology of fossil organisms, *paleogeography* is the study of geography in earlier geological eras, and *paleoecology* is the study of the relationship of plants and animals to their environment in those eras.

Paleolithic \ˌpā-lē-ə-ˈli-thik\ Of or relating to the earliest period of the Stone Age, characterized by rough or chipped stone implements.

• He raves about the health benefits of his Paleolithic diet, the kind that our pre-agricultural, hunting-and-gathering Stone Age ancestors would have eaten.

Since *lithos* means "stone" in Greek, the name Paleolithic was given to the older part of the Stone Age. The first known period of human culture, the Paleolithic actually covers almost all of human history, from the first use of stone tools around 2.5 million years ago until the invention of agriculture around 10,000 years ago. For almost all that time, humans used the very crudest of stone tools, produced by chipping away flakes of stone in order to make an edge for an ax or knife. Near the end of the period, animal bones and antlers were being used for tools, especially pointed tools, and sculpted figures and cave art were being produced. The Paleolithic gave way to the Mesolithic ("Middle Stone Age") period, with its tools made of polished stone, wood, and bone.

paleography \ˌpā-lē-ˈä-grə-fē\ (1) The study of ancient writings and inscriptions. (2) Ancient writings.

• For her thesis on Central American paleography, she spent a winter in Honduras studying rock inscriptions 30 miles upriver from the nearest town.

The world's oldest literature dates from about 4,000 years ago, from the land known as Sumer (now southern Iraq). Early writing took the form of pictographs, very simple pictures that first represented things or ideas and later came to represent actual words. The first actual alphabet, in which each character represents a sound, appeared in the same general region about 500 years later. But writing developed in very different ways in different parts of the world, and 1,000 years later, when Europeans first arrived in the New World, alphabetic writing still wasn't being used anywhere in the Americas. Decoding some ancient languages has proven to be a huge task for *paleographers*, and determining the age and the source of a piece of writing can pose major challenges.

paleontology \ˌpā-lē-ˌän-ˈtä-lə-jē\ A science dealing with the life of past geological periods as known from fossil remains.

- Her obsession with dinosaurs as a child continued through her teens, and no one was surprised when she started graduate school in paleontology.

Until the 1820s, hardly anyone even suspected that dinosaurs had ever existed. In the years since, paleontology has sought to discover the entire history of life on earth, from the era of single-celled organisms up into the human era. *Paleontologists* continue to make remarkable discoveries, such as that a huge meteorite that fell in the Gulf of Mexico wiped out the dinosaurs—all except the birds, the only surviving dinosaurs. "Radiometric dating" can reveal the age (often tens of millions of years) of a rock or fossil or a tiny grain of pollen by measuring how much its radioactive elements have disintegrated. The study of molecules of DNA, RNA, and proteins has also become important for dating. Paleontologists often consult with geologists searching for oil, gas, and coal deposits, since all these "fossil fuels" were formed from plant and animal remains.

Paleozoic \ˌpā-lē-ə-ˈzō-ik\ The era of geological history, ending about 248 million years ago, in which vertebrates and land plants first appeared.

- His geological specialty was the beginning of the Paleozoic, from which the earliest fish fossils date.

The Greek root *zo-* means "animal," so names such as Paleozoic were invented to refer to a period in the development of animal life. For geologists, the Paleozoic era is followed by the Mesozoic (*meso-* meaning "middle"), which is followed by the Cenozoic (*cen-* meaning "recent"). Eras are huge stretches of time; geologists break eras down into smaller "periods" and "epochs." Thus, the Paleozoic ends with the Permian period, the Mesozoic ends with the Upper Cretaceous epoch, and the Cenozoic ends with the Holocene epoch—the epoch in which we are living. The Paleozoic era produced the first fish, the first land plants, the first insects, and the first amphibians and reptiles; the dinosaurs, birds, and mammals had to wait for the Mesozoic.

Quizzes

A. Fill in each blank with the correct letter:

a. Paleolithic
b. necrosis
c. Paleozoic
d. necropsy
e. paleography
f. necromancer
g. paleontology
h. necropolis

1. The frostbite was bad and there was a chance of _____ setting in, so we had to work fast.
2. With his specialty in _____, he spent much of his time on the rivers of Peru looking for rocks with ancient carvings.
3. Grief-stricken parents would go to the village _____, who would try to contact their dead children.
4. They were certain the cat hadn't died of natural causes, and the _____ revealed that they were right.
5. The men's graves in this Iron Age _____ held numerous weapons.
6. The wall paintings date from the end of the _____, just before the beginning of settled farming villages.
7. Millions of kids are fascinated by dinosaurs, but not many will go on to study _____ in college.
8. Insects, reptiles, amphibians, and primitive fish inhabited the earth during the _____ era, but not mammals.

B. Indicate whether the following pairs of terms have the same or different meanings:

1. Paleozoic / of the period
   about 10,000 years ago   same ___ / different ___
2. necropsy / autopsy   same ___ / different ___
3. necromancer / gravedigger   same ___ / different ___

4.   paleography / study of
     ancient writings   same ___ / different ___
5.   Paleolithic / Old Stone Age   same ___ / different ___
6.   necrosis / tissue death   same ___ / different ___
7.   necropolis / cemetery   same ___ / different ___
8.   paleontology / study of
     past geological periods   same ___ / different ___

CIRCU/CIRCUM comes from the Latin *circus*, meaning "circle." So a *circus* is traditionally held under a round tent. A *circuit* can be a tour around an area or territory, or the complete path of an electric current. To *circumnavigate* means "to navigate around"— often around the world.

circuitous \sər-ˈkyü-ə-təs\ (1) Having a circular or winding course. (2) Not forthright or direct in action.

• She sometimes arrives at her conclusions by circuitous reasoning that her students can't even follow.

Circuitous is usually the opposite of *direct*, and it's generally used to describe either roads or explanations. Detours are usually circuitous, and a circuitous path, twisting and turning and cutting back on itself, is the kind of route you'd expect to find in the mountains. Lawyers often find themselves making circuitous arguments, which may get most circuitous when they're defending particularly undesirable clients.

circumference \sər-ˈkəm-frəns\ (1) The perimeter or boundary of a circle. (2) The outer boundary or surface of a shape or object.

• To calculate the circumference of a circle, multiply its diameter by 3.1416.

Attempts have been made to measure the circumference of the earth since the time of Aristotle. The calculation that Columbus was relying on led him to think he could reach China by sailing west more quickly than by sailing east. But that measurement had calculated the earth's circumference as about a quarter too small, and the rest is history. Columbus wasn't the only one who got it wrong; many later attempts continued to produce different measurements for the earth's circumference—even though the Greeks had calculated it correctly way back in the 3rd century B.C.

circumspect \'sər-kəm-ˌspekt\ Careful to consider all circumstances and possible consequences; cautious.

• Her answer was careful and circumspect, and I couldn't help thinking she knew a lot more than she was telling.

Since *spect-* comes from the Latin word for "look," *circumspect* basically means "looking around" yourself before you act. Being a doctor has traditionally called for a circumspect personality, which gives their patients confidence in them. Scholars are known for their *circumspection*, since there's nothing worse for scholars' reputations than mistakes in the books or articles they've written. Bankers once had a reputation for great circumspection, but the financial disaster of 2008 earned some bankers a very different kind of reputation.

circumvent \'sər-kəm-ˌvent\ (1) To make a circuit around. (2) To manage to get around, especially by clever means.

• We knew there was a traffic jam on the highway and circumvented it by using back roads.

In mythology, a person's attempts to circumvent fate are almost always doomed. In the *Iliad* we're told of how Achilles' mother, Thetis, hoping to circumvent the prophecy that her child would die in a war against Troy, disguised the boy as a woman. But clever Odysseus, recruiting for the Greek army, arrived disguised as a peddler, and among the jewels he displayed to the women of the household he laid a sword. The young Achilles, ignoring the jewelry, immediately seized the sword, thereby identifying himself for what he was. Today we more often hear of attempts to circumvent the law, or at least some requirements that we'd rather not have to deal with.

MINI/MINU come from Latin words meaning "small" and "least." So the *minimum* is the least, and a *minute* amount is almost nothing. And *mini-* is all too familiar as a prefix that we've been applying to all kinds of things since the 1950s: *minivan*, *miniskirt*, *mini-mart*, *minipark*, and the rest.

minimalism \\'mi-nə-mə-ˌli-zəm\ A style or technique (as in music, literature, or design) that is characterized by extreme spareness and simplicity.

• He'd never understood what anyone liked about minimalism, since minimalist stories always seemed to leave out any description of people's characters and motivation and rarely even described their surroundings.

In the 1960s, a few composers, including Philip Glass, Steve Reich, and John Adams, began writing music inspired by the music of India and Southeast Asia, often with a quick pulsing beat and chords that are repeated quickly over and over while small changes are slowly introduced. *Minimalist* art, which began appearing around the same time, tries to strip away all personal elements, often leaving only pure geometric forms; you may have seen the plain silver boxes of Donald Judd, or the straight neon tubes of Bruce Nauman. In literature, the stripped-down fiction of Samuel Beckett and Raymond Carver is often considered minimalist. But there's a real question whether these various types of minimalism should even be considered the same concept.

minuscule \\'mi-nəs-ˌkyül\ Very small.

• For someone who had been living on a minuscule budget since graduating from college, even the paycheck for a minimum-wage job felt like wealth to her.

As a noun, *minuscule* means a style of ancient or medieval handwriting script with smaller letters than earlier scripts. There were actually several minuscules, but the most important was promoted from around A.D. 800 on by Charlemagne, who believed that any educated person in the Holy Roman Empire should be able to read the Latin written by anyone else. If you've ever looked at a medieval manuscript, you've probably seen minuscule script, along with so-called *majuscule* (for modern type, we would use the words *lower-case* and *capital* instead); even today most of us can read medieval minuscule and majuscule without too much trouble. Be careful about spelling *minuscule*; we tend to expect a word meaning "small" to begin with *mini-* rather than *minu-*.

minutiae \mə-'nü-shē-ˌē\ Very small or minor details.

• She likes "thinking big," and gets annoyed when her job requires her to deal with what she considers minutiae.

As you might guess, this word comes straight from Latin. The Romans used it in its singular form, *minutia*, to mean "smallness," and in the plural to mean "trifles"; today we almost always use it in the plural with that same "trifles" meaning. Hardly anyone ever talks about minutiae except to dismiss their importance. So you may talk about the minutiae of daily life or the minutiae of a contract, or about getting bogged down or buried in minutiae at the office. Just don't forget that the devil is often in the details.

diminutive \də-ˈmi-nyə-tiv\ (1) Indicating small size. (2) Very small.

• In German, Hänsel is a diminutive form of Hans (which is a diminutive form of Johannes), and Gretel is a diminutive form of Margaret.

Just as *diminish* means "to grow smaller," *diminutive* means "very small." When writing about language, *diminutive* as both an adjective and a noun refers to particular endings and the words made with them to indicate smallness. In English, such endings include *-et* and *-ette* (*piglet, dinette, cigarette, diskette*) as well as *-ie* and *-y* (*doggy, bootie, Bobby, Debbie*). However, *diminutives* are more common in many other languages. Outside of language, *diminutive* is used for many things, including people ("She noticed a diminutive figure standing shyly by the door"), but often not very seriously ("We were served some rather diminutive rolls").

Quizzes

A. Fill in each blank with the correct letter:

a. circumference	e. diminutive
b. minimalism	f. circumspect
c. circumvent	g. circuitous
d. minuscule	h. minutiae

1. He enjoys working on actual cases, but he gets worn down by the flood of _____ involved in billing his clients.

2. She's a big fan of _____ in Web design, and Google's white home page has always been her ideal.

3. The banking industry generally works hard to _____ any laws that tend to restrict their ability to make profits.

4. Whenever we asked where his income came from, he would say something vague and ____ and treat it as a joke.

5. We finally found the house, but only after getting completely lost and taking an extremely ____ route.

6. She can't stand it when they start arguing over ____ differences while ignoring the really important issues.

7. People often comment on the contrast between his ____ physique and the enormous power he wields on Capitol Hill.

8. The race course runs the entire ____ of the lake twice, a total of ten miles.

B. Match the definition on the left to the correct word on the right:

1.	cautious	a.	circumference
2.	roundabout	b.	circumvent
3.	rim	c.	minuscule
4.	details	d.	minutiae
5.	miniature	e.	circumspect
6.	style of extreme simplicity	f.	diminutive
7.	small	g.	circuitous
8.	get around	h.	minimalism

INTER comes straight from Latin. In English it has various meanings; all of them can be expressed broadly as "between," but they're still quite distinct: "moving between" (*intercity*), "communicating between" (*intercom*), "coming between" (*intercept*), and so on. No wonder so many English words begin with *inter-*.

intercede \ˌin-tər-ˈsēd\ (1) To act as a go-between between unfriendly parties. (2) To beg or plead in behalf of another.

• He had interceded for her with their boss on one important occasion, for which she was still grateful.

The Latin *cedere* means "to go," so "go between" is the most literal meaning of *intercede*. (The same *-cede* root can also be seen in such words as *precede* and *secede*.) If you've been blamed unfairly for something, a friend may intercede on your behalf with your coach or teacher. More often, it will be the coach or teacher who has to intercede in a student dispute. The *intercession* of foreign governments has sometimes prevented conflicts from becoming worse than they otherwise would have.

interstice \in-'tər-stəs\ A little space between two things; chink, crevice.

* All the interstices between the rocks have been filled with new cement, and the wall should be fine for another hundred years.

People often speak of interstices in the physical sense (referring to the interstices in surfaces, for example, or microscopic interstices between particles in chemical compounds), but also often in a less literal way (the interstices in a movie's plot, in the economy, in what's covered by a complicated tax law, etc.). The pronunciation of *interstice* is slightly unusual; you might not guess that it's accented on the second syllable. This is also true in the plural *interstices*, which is used more often than the singular form; note also that in *interstices* the final *e* is usually pronounced long, so that it rhymes with *bees*.

interdict \ˌin-tər-'dikt\ (1) To prohibit or forbid. (2) To destroy, damage, or cut off (as an enemy line of supply) by firepower to stop or hamper an enemy.

* All weapons trade with the country had been interdicted by the NATO alliance, and ships were actually being stopped and searched before being allowed to dock.

Interdict and *interdiction* are used for very serious prohibitions—more serious than, say, a professor telling the class that texting is forbidden during lectures. During the Middle Ages and Renaissance, an *interdict* was a sentence imposed by the powerful Catholic Church forbidding a person or place, and sometimes even an entire country, from receiving church privileges or participating in church functions. *Interdict* now often means "cut off" in a physically forceful way as well; interdictions are usually targeted at either arms supplies or illegal drug shipments.

interpolate \in-'tər-pə-ˌlāt\ To put something between other things or parts, especially to put words into a piece of writing or a conversation.

- On page 6, she noticed that someone had interpolated a couple of sentences that completely altered the meaning of her original text.

The meaning of *interpolate* is often entirely innocent. An *interpolation* in a text may have been approved by everyone concerned, and an interpolation in conversation is usually just an interruption. But in its older meaning, interpolating usually meant tampering with a text secretly to change its apparent meaning. Legislators are sometimes enraged to discover what someone has quietly interpolated into their favorite bill at the last minute. And any contract always has to be read carefully to make sure the other lawyer didn't slip in an undesirable interpolation.

SUR is actually a shortening of the Latin prefix *super-*, meaning "over, above" (see SUPER, p. 598), and has the same meaning. A *surface* is the face above or on the outside of something. A *surplus* is something above and beyond what is needed. And to *survey* a landscape is to look out over it.

---

surmount \sər-ˈmau̇nt\ To rise above; overcome.

- The story of how he surmounted poverty and crippling physical ailments to achieve what he achieved is almost unbelievable.

Our verb *mount*, meaning "ascend, get up onto," comes from the same Latin root as *mountain*, and we keep those images in mind when using *surmount*, since climbing up or over a mountain is a symbol of achievement. The word almost always refers to human effort, and almost always in a positive way; thus, we speak of surmounting difficulties, surmounting problems, surmounting hurdles, surmounting handicaps—you get the idea.

surcharge \ˈsər-ˌchärj\ An additional tax or charge.

- Checking the bill, she discovered two surcharges that no one had warned her about.

The Arab oil embargo of 1973 led airlines to add fuel surcharges to their passenger fares that were large enough to discourage air travel. Surcharges are usually added for special service. When you request a "rush job" from a service supplier, it will probably bring a surcharge along with it. A particularly difficult phone installation may carry a surcharge. An extra-large fine for a speeding offense after you've already had too many tickets could be called a surcharge. An added tax may be called a surcharge (or *surtax*) when it only affects people with incomes above a certain level. And if those low, low prices that show up in really big letters in ads for all kinds of services turn out to be misleading, it's probably because they don't include a bunch of surcharges that you won't find out about till later.

surfeit \\'sər-fət\\ A supply that is more than enough; excess.

• Whenever he glanced into his daughter's room, he was always astonished at the utter surfeit of things—dolls, dollhouses, stuffed animals, cushions, games, posters, and clothing strewn everywhere.

Book and film critics often use *surfeit* when complaining about how an author or director has given us too much of something. In our consumer society, we're always noticing a surfeit of one thing or another, such as breakfast cereals in the supermarket. Statistics are always indicating a surfeit of lawyers or doctors or accountants in some parts of the country and a lack of them in others. The death of a young star always results in a surfeit of articles and books about him or her. And a potluck supper usually results in a surfeit of food, which might leave you *surfeited*, or stuffed.

surreal \\sə-'rēl\\ Very strange or unusual; having the quality of a dream.

• In a surreal sequence, the main character gets a job on floor 7 1/2, which turns out to be only half as high as the other floors, so everyone must walk around stooped over.

In 1924 a group of European poets, painters, and filmmakers founded a movement that they called *Surrealism*. Their central idea was that the unconscious mind (a concept Sigmund Freud had recently made famous) was the source of all imagination, and that art should try to express its contents. The unconscious, they believed, revealed itself most clearly in dreams. The *Surrealist* painters included René Magritte, Joan Miró, and Salvador Dalí, whose "limp watches" painting became the best-known Surrealist image of all. Since those years, we've used *surreal* to describe all kinds of situations that strike us as dreamlike. And even though the Surrealist movement ended long ago, surrealism now seems to be everywhere—not just in painting, literature, and movies but also in blogs, video games, and graphic novels.

Quizzes

A. Fill in each blank with the correct letter:

a. surfeit
b. interdict
c. surcharge
d. interstice

e. interpolate
f. surreal
g. intercede
h. surmount

1. The door to the ruined barn was locked, but through an ____ in the wall I glimpsed an old tractor and several odd pieces of machinery.
2. Even though we know hardly any facts about the divorce, there's already been a ____ of talk on the radio about it.
3. The governor is calling for a ____ on all packaged snack foods with low nutritional value.
4. She would go on talking about her country by the hour, while I would occasionally ____ a comment to show that I was paying attention.
5. There was something ____ about gazing out from the deck of a luxurious cruise ship at the primitive huts lining the islands' shores.
6. The country's small coast guard hopes to ____ most of the arms at sea before they can reach the guerrilla fighters.
7. Only after I got the coach to ____ did the principal agree to change my suspension to probation.
8. When he was wheeled out to accept the award, most of the audience realized for the first time what terrible difficulties he had had to ____.

B. Match the word on the left to the correct definition on the right:

1. interdict
2. surcharge
3. surfeit
4. intercede
5. interpolate
6. surmount
7. surreal
8. interstice

a. rise above
b. block
c. excess
d. chink
e. dreamlike
f. extra fee
g. ask for mercy
h. stick in

CO is a Latin prefix that generally means "with, together," and we see it daily in such words as *costar*, *cofounder*, *co-owner*, and *coworker*. But many other *co-* words aren't quite so easy to understand when you first encounter them.

coalesce \ˌkō-ə-ˈles\ To come together to form one group or mass.

• Three local civic groups have recently coalesced to form a single organization, believing it will result in more effective campaigns.

Social movements are often said to coalesce when groups with somewhat different interests realize how much they have in common. Some physicists believe that planets coalesced not from space rocks but from icy clouds of cosmic dust. Some people even study how languages coalesce—for example, the fairly new language Afrikaans, a mixture of Dutch and native languages spoken in South Africa, which only really solidified about 150 years ago.

cogeneration \ˌkō-ˌje-nə-ˈrā-shən\ The production of electricity using waste heat (as in steam) from an industrial process, or the use of steam from electric power generation as a source of heat.

• With its new cogeneration system, the company reports converting over 65% of the energy in natural gas to electricity, making this the most efficient power plant ever built.

Cogeneration is basically the production of energy and usable heat (generally in the form of steam and hot water) in the same plant, usually by capturing heat that in older plants used to be simply wasted. It's one of the principal ways in which countries intend to reduce their greenhouse-gas emissions so as to slow climate change. Cogeneration plants are often small, and the fuels used in them are varied. Lumber mills, for instance, can operate their own cogeneration plants, feeding them with wood scraps and sawdust, and wastewater treatment plants generate gas that can likewise be used as a source of energy. Since it's hard to move heat long distances, cogeneration is most efficient when the heat can be used nearby. Though the general public today knows little about cogeneration, more and more of us will be benefiting from it in the coming years.

codependency \ˌkō-di-ˈpen-dən-sē\ A psychological condition or a relationship in which a person is controlled or manipulated by someone affected with a condition such as alcohol or drug addiction.

• She never knew what codependency was until her daughter took up with a mean, abusive alcoholic and refused to leave him.

Dependency on addictive substances has been known for centuries, but the concept of codependency got its name only as recently as 1979. For many of us, codependency isn't easy to understand; we may keep asking "Why doesn't she just leave him?" and find it hard to accept the answers we get. *Codependents* usually don't share their partners' addiction, but their lives tend to be taken over with the burden of caring for and protecting the spouse or partner. In recent years, people have started claiming that all kinds of conditions— anorexia, overeating, gambling, fear of intimacy, etc.—can result in codependency. Many experts think all of this has gone too far; still, almost everyone agrees that spouses of alcoholics and drug addicts face unique difficulties and should look for support and advice anywhere they can find it.

cohesion \kō-ˈhē-zhən\ (1) The action or state of sticking together. (2) Molecular attraction by which the particles of a body are united throughout the mass.

• The party's greatest strength was its cohesion and discipline, and on bill after bill that year not a single member voted with the other party.

Cohesion is one of the noun forms of *cohere*; the others are *cohesiveness* and *coherence*, each of which has a slightly different meaning. *Coherence* is often used to describe a person's speech or writing. An *incoherent* talk or blog post is one that doesn't "hang together"; and if the police pick up someone who they describe as *incoherent*, it means he or she isn't making sense. But to describe a group or team that always sticks together, you would use *cohesive*, not *coherent*. And the words you'd use in Chemistry class to describe the way molecules hang together—for example, the way water forms into beads and drops—are *cohesion*, *cohesive*, and *cohesiveness*.

SYN is a Greek and Latin prefix meaning "together" or "at the same time." So "in *sync*" (short for "in *synchronization*") means "together in time." And a *synonym* is a word that can be considered together with another word since it has the same meaning.

syntax \\'sin-ˌtaks\\ The way in which words are put together to form phrases, clauses, or sentences.

* The president's critics complain about his odd and confusing syntax when he speaks in public.

Syntax is basically about what word comes before and after another word; in other words, it's part of the larger subject of grammar. Syntax is often an issue in poetry, and it's usually discussed in connection with *diction*—that is, the poet's choice of words. So, for example, your English professor might point out the *syntactic* difference between "Whose woods these are I think I know" and "I think I know whose woods these are"; whereas if the discussion was about diction instead, the question might be about the choice of "woods" rather than "land," or "think" rather than "bet."

synthesize \\'sin-thə-ˌsīz\\ To make something by combining different things.

* From all the proposals put in front of us, we were asked to synthesize a plan that could get the support of the whole group.

Synthesize is a very common word in chemistry, since chemists are constantly synthesizing new compounds—that is, *synthetic* compounds—including drugs and industrial chemicals. It's also often used when talking about writing; nonfiction writers must often synthesize large amounts of material from many sources to produce a book—which represents a *synthesis* of the important materials. An electronic *synthesizer* creates new sounds (which may imitate the sounds of acoustic instruments) by generating different basic tones and then manipulating and merging them together with others.

synergy \\'si-nər-jē\\ The increased effectiveness that results when two or more people or businesses work together.

- With the first company's importance in print media and the second's success on the Web, everyone was convinced that the merger would result in an awesome synergy.

An old saying, "The whole is greater than the sum of its parts," expresses the basic meaning of *synergy*. The word is sometimes used in a purely physical sense, especially when talking about drugs; sometimes a "cocktail" of drugs may be more effective than the sum of the effectiveness of each of the separate drugs. But the word is best known in the world of business. The notion that, when the right two companies merge, they'll produce a profitable synergy seemed exciting in the 1990s, when *synergy* became a trendy buzzword (even though it's actually been around since the 17th century). The idea of synergy was one factor in what became a "merger mania"; unfortunately, business synergy often turned out to be harder to achieve than to imagine.

syndrome \\'sin-ˌdrōm\\ A group of signs and symptoms that occur together and characterize a particular abnormality or condition.

- When there is no trembling—the most obvious symptom of Parkinson's disease—most doctors fail to recognize the Parkinson's syndrome.

Combining its two Greek roots, *syndrome* means basically "running together." So when diagnosing a condition or disease, doctors tend to look for a group of symptoms existing together. As long as a set of symptoms remains mysterious, it may be referred to as a specific syndrome. But if that name is used for a while, it may become the condition's permanent name, even after an underlying cause has been found. So today we have *Down syndrome*, *acquired immune deficiency syndrome*, *Asperger's syndrome*, *carpal tunnel syndrome*, *chronic fatigue syndrome*, *Tourette's syndrome*, *sick building syndrome*, and many more. And since mental conditions often turn out to have physical causes, *syndrome* is used in psychology as well as in medicine.

Quizzes

A. Fill in each blank with the correct letter:

a. cohesion   e. cogeneration
b. syntax   f. synthesize
c. syndrome   g. synergy
d. coalesce   h. codependency

1. The book manages to ____ a great deal of material that has rarely been discussed together.
2. When foreign students speak, they often employ ____ that seems odd in English but would be completely natural in their own language.
3. Paper mills are increasingly starting up ____ projects to turn their waste wood products into electricity and steam.
4. Team ____ is always a problem early in the football season, since the kids may not know each other or understand each other's strengths and weaknesses.
5. Spouses of alcoholics and drug addicts meet every week in the church basement to discuss the problems of ____.
6. Officials worry that these individual terrorist groups may be starting to ____ into one large network.
7. It wasn't obvious what kind of ____ could be achieved by merging an office-supplies company with a tractor manufacturer.
8. Doctors had become concerned about a ____ involving fever, mental confusion, and extreme weakness that had been appearing in dozens of local residents.

B. Indicate whether the following pairs have the same or different meanings:

1. syndrome / depression   same ___ / different ___
2. coalesce / combine   same ___ / different ___
3. cohesion / sticking together   same ___ / different ___
4. codependency / reliance
    on two parents   same ___ / different ___
5. synergy / combined action   same ___ / different ___
6. cogeneration / two-source
    power production   same ___ / different ___
7. syntax / sentence structure   same ___ / different ___

8. synthesize / create from
   several ingredients   same ___ / different ___

Words from Mythology and History

Adonis \ə-ˈdä-nəs\ A very handsome young man.

• Conversation in the little clusters of girls suddenly stops whenever this Adonis—blond, muscular, with an athlete's gait—swaggers down the school corridor.

Adonis, like Narcissus (see p. 240), was a beautiful youth in Greek mythology. He was loved by both Aphrodite, goddess of love and beauty, and Persephone, goddess of the underworld. One day while hunting, he was killed by a wild boar. In answer to Aphrodite's pleas, Zeus allowed him to spend half the year with her and half in the underworld. Today a man called an Adonis probably has strikingly fine features, low body fat, rippling muscles—and a certain vain attitude of overconfidence. Adonises should beware; the boar that killed Adonis was sent by either the jealous Artemis (goddess of hunting) or the envious Ares (god of war).

amazon \ˈa-mə-ˌzän\ A tall, strong, often masculine woman.

• I was greeted by the team's captain, a robust, broad-shouldered amazon who gripped my hand with crushing force.

In Greek mythology, an Amazon was a member of a race of women warriors. One of the famous labors of Heracles (Hercules) was to obtain the sash of the Amazon queen Hippolyta, and the hero Theseus married Hippolyta's sister. The Amazon River got its name when, in 1542, the first Europeans to descend the river were attacked by Indian warriors who, even at close range, they believed to be women. The mystery of these warriors continues to this day. However impressive a figure they cut, though, not every tall and strong woman today would take it as a compliment to be called an amazon.

chimera \kī-ˈmir-ə\ An often grotesque creature of the imagination.

• This latest piece of legislation is a weird chimera, with sections devoted to agriculture, defense, welfare, law enforcement, and scientific research.

In Greek mythology, the Chimera was a fire-breathing she-monster with a lion's head, a goat's body, and a dragon's tail, which laid waste the countryside in southwestern Turkey. It was finally killed by the hero Bellerophon, whose flying horse, Pegasus, enabled him to attack from the air. Over time, *chimera* came to be used for any imaginary monster made up of strange and mismatched parts; today it's the name of several species of truly bizarre-looking fish. But more commonly a chimera is a fantasy, an illusion, a figment of the imagination, or a dream that will never come true.

cornucopia \ˌkȯr-nə-ˈkō-pē-ə\ (1) A container shaped like a hollow horn full of fruits, vegetables, and ears of grain. (2) An abundance of something desirable.

* These books were a cornucopia of wonderful stories and poems, and as a child I spent countless hours with them.

The Latin term *cornu copiae* meant "horn of plenty," and *cornucopia* and *horn of plenty* have both been used in English since the 16th century. Both terms refer to a hollow goat's horn, or a wicker basket shaped like one, overflowing with produce from the harvest. The cornucopia has been used as a decorative image to represent abundance since at least the 5th century B.C., when it represented a gift given by the infant god Zeus to his beloved nurse: a broken goat's horn that would always magically be filled with whatever she wanted. In the U.S., cornucopias are often seen on altars, in store-window displays, and as table centerpieces, especially at harvesttime or Thanksgiving.

Elysium \i-ˈli-zhē-əm\ A place or condition of ideal happiness; paradise.

* They had named their estate Elysium, and as we gazed out over its fountains, ponds, and sweeping lawns we could see why.

This word came into Latin from the Greek *Elysion*. In classical mythology, Elysium, or the *Elysian fields*, was the home of the blessed after death, the final resting place of the souls of the heroic and the pure. So it's easy to see how the word came to mean any place or state of bliss or delight. When we try to picture heaven, many of us probably see a lovely park; the great boulevard of Paris was named for the beautiful park that originally bordered it: the Champs-Elysées, or Elysian Fields.

epicure \\'e-pi-ˌkyür\ A person with cultivated taste, especially for food and drink; a gourmet.

- He reads trashy novels and watches junk on TV, but he has an epicure's love of fine cheeses and wines.

The Greek philosopher Epicurus was known for his original thinking about the nature of matter, but he's best remembered for his ideas about pleasure as the chief aim of life. By pleasure Epicurus chiefly meant the absence of pain and anxiety. However, over the years *Epicureanism* has come to mean a delight in fine sensual pleasures, and today an epicure is someone with refined taste, especially in food and wine. To display your own refined taste in language, you might try using *epicure* and *epicurean* in place of the overused *gourmet*.

exodus \\'ek-sə-dəs\ A situation in which many people leave a place at the same time.

- The war led to a mass exodus of Iraq's Christians.

The second book of the Old Testament tells of the departure of Moses and the Israelites from Egypt and their difficult journey across the Sinai Desert to Mount Sinai, from which they would eventually complete their journey to their home in Palestine. The book's original Hebrew name was Shemot, but it's known to English-speakers as Exodus, from the Greek *exodos*, "departure." Leon Uris chose the name *Exodus* for his powerful novel about the founding of Israel in the years after World War II, since the new state's postwar settlers had departed from many parts of the world for their new home in Palestine.

gorgon \\'gȯr-gən\ An ugly, repulsive, or terrifying woman.

- The beautiful star disappeared into the makeup room and emerged two hours later transformed into a gorgon.

The Gorgons were three monstrous sisters in Greek mythology, the most famous of whom was Medusa. They had snakes for hair, and anyone who looked directly at them was immediately turned to stone. Medusa herself was finally beheaded by the hero Perseus, who avoided looking straight at her by instead watching her reflection in his mirrorlike shield. Today the familiar types of jellyfish, with long snakelike tentacles descending from their headlike bodies, are known as medusas.

Quiz

Fill in each blank with the correct letter:

a. epicure   e. gorgon
b. Elysium   f. exodus
c. Adonis   g. chimera
d. amazon   h. cornucopia

1. Her boss was a _____ who terrorized the office.
2. As he aged he began to think the CIA was watching him, and even though it was just a _____ it caused him a lot of anxiety.
3. She spoke about her country place as an _____ where they could spend their lives surrounded by beauty.
4. He's a serious _____, and you have to be brave to invite him over for dinner.
5. When the economy is good, a job fair can be a _____ of employment opportunities.
6. Her departure from the company led to an _____ of other employees.
7. To everyone's surprise, he ended up marrying a robust, outdoorsy _____ an inch taller than he was.
8. Everyone thought her new boyfriend was an _____, and she liked watching girls' heads turn as they walked around campus together.

Review Quizzes

A. Choose the closest definition:

1. circumspect   a. lazy b. all-seeing c. careful
       d. winding
2. surmount   a. increase b. overcome c. look through
       d. reject
3. interdict   a. scold b. allow c. cut off d. intrude
4. diminutive   a. little b. cozy c. detailed d. comfortable
5. surreal   a. excessive b. artistic c. secret d. dreamlike

6. circuitous a. circular b. electrical c. roundabout
   d. circulating
7. surfeit a. surplus b. waves c. conclusion d. topic
8. coalesce a. begin b. merge c. cooperate d. end
9. interstice a. filling b. gap c. layer d. village
10. minutiae a. particles b. leftovers c. moments d. trivia

B. Fill in each blank with the correct letter:

a. cogeneration   f. surcharge
b. paleontology   g. circumvent
c. codependency   h. minimalism
d. syntax   i. interdict
e. Paleolithic   j. cohesion

1. He knew his daughter wasn't alcoholic, but he worried about the ___ he'd been noticing between her and her husband.
2. From the odd ___ of the sentences, she guessed that the writer didn't know English that well.
3. After going on a fossil dig in Africa in junior year, he decided to pursue graduate work in ___.
4. The college's new ___ system will use natural gas to produce both electricity and heat.
5. To help balance its budget, the city is now considering adding a ___ to all speeding tickets.
6. We found some chipped-stone arrowheads and took them to a local professor, who identified them as products of the ___ period.
7. More agents will be needed to ___ the drugs being carried north to Panama from Colombia.
8. Some people worry about the ___ of the European Union, especially as the number of member nations grows and national interests begin to shift.
9. Some outside hackers have managed to ___ the country's Internet censorship by clever electronic means.
10. The critics call her novels good examples of ___, since she barely describes people or scenes at all and the action is never really explained.

C. **Indicate whether the following pairs of words have
   the same or different meanings:**

1. minuscule / empty   same ___ / different ___
2. interpolate / fill up   same ___ / different ___
3. circumference / spiral   same ___ / different ___
4. intercede / invade   same ___ / different ___
5. synthesize / perform   same ___ / different ___
6. necropolis / graveyard   same ___ / different ___
7. syndrome / group of symptoms   same ___ / different ___
8. circumspect / visible from afar   same ___ / different ___
9. necrosis / black magic   same ___ / different ___
10. coalesce / come together   same ___ / different ___

UNIT

30

TOXI comes from the Greek and Latin words for "poison," something the Greeks and Romans knew a good deal about. Socrates died by taking a solution of poison hemlock, a flowering plant much like wild carrot that now also grows in the U.S. Rome's enemy Mithridates, king of Pontus, was obsessed with poisons, experimented with them on prisoners, and tried to make himself immune to them by eating tiny amounts of them daily. Nero's mother Agrippina poisoned several of her son's rivals to power—and probably did the same to her own husband, the emperor Claudius.

toxin \ˈtäk-sən\ A substance produced by a living organism (such as bacteria) that is highly poisonous to other organisms.

• Humans eat rhubarb stems without ill effects, while cattle may die from eating the leaves, which seem to contain two different toxins.

Long before chemists started creating poisons from scratch, humans were employing natural toxins for killing weeds and insects. For centuries South American tribes have used the toxin curare, extracted from a native vine, to tip their arrows. The garden flower called wolfsbane or monkshood is the source of aconite, an extremely potent toxin. The common flower known as jimsonweed contains the deadly poison scopolamine. And the castor-oil plant yields the almost unbelievably poisonous toxin called ricin. Today we hear health advisers of all kinds talk about ridding the body of toxins;

but they're usually pretty vague about which ones they mean, and most of these "toxins" wouldn't be called that by biologists.

toxicity \täk-'si-sə-tē\ The state of being poisonous; the degree to which something is poisonous.

* Though they had tested the drug on animals, they suspected the only way to measure its toxicity for humans was by studying accidental human exposures.

Toxicity is often a relative thing; in the words of a famous old saying, "The dose makes the poison." Thus, it's possible to die from drinking too much water, and lives have been saved by tiny doses of arsenic. Even though botulinum toxin is the most *toxic* substance known, it's the basic ingredient in Botox, which is injected into the face to get rid of wrinkles. With some poisons, mere skin contact can be lethal; others are lethal when breathed into the lungs in microscopic amounts. To determine if a chemical will be officially called a poison, researchers often use the "LD50" test: If 50 milligrams of the substance for every kilogram of an animal's body weight results in the death of 50% of test animals, the chemical is a poison. But there are problems with such tests, and toxicity remains a very individual concept.

toxicology \ˌtäk-si-'kä-lə-jē\ A science that deals with poisons and their effect.

* At medical school he had specialized in toxicology, hoping eventually to find work in a crime laboratory.

Even though most of us are aware of toxicology primarily from crime shows on TV, *toxicologists* actually do most of their work in other fields. Many are employed by drug companies, others by chemical companies. Many work for the government, making sure the public is being kept safe from environmental poisons in the water, soil, and air, as well as unhealthy substances in our food and drugs. These issues often have to do with quantity; questions about how much of some substance should be considered dangerous, whether in the air or in a soft drink, may be left to toxicologists. But occasionally a toxicology task may be more exciting: for instance, discovering that what looked like an ordinary heart attack was actually brought on by a hypodermic injection of a paralyzing muscle relaxant.

neurotoxin \ˌnu̇r-ō-ˈtäk-sən\ A poisonous protein that acts on the nervous system.

• From her blurred vision, slurred speech, and muscle weakness, doctors realized she had encountered a neurotoxin, and they suspected botulism.

The nervous system is almost all-powerful in the body: all five senses depend on it, as do breathing, digestion, and the heart. So it's an obvious target for poisons, and neurotoxins have developed as weapons in many animals, including snakes, bees, and spiders. Some wasps use a neurotoxin to paralyze their prey so that it can be stored alive to be eaten later. Snake venom is often *neurotoxic* (as in cobras and coral snakes, for example), though it may instead be *hemotoxic* (as in rattlesnakes and coppermouths), operating on the circulatory system. Artificial neurotoxins, called *nerve agents*, have been developed by scientists as means of chemical warfare; luckily, few have ever been used.

TEN/TENU comes from the Latin *tenuis*, meaning "thin." So to *extend* something is to stretch it, and lots of things get thin when they're stretched. The *ten-* root is even seen in *pretend*, which once meant to stretch something out above or in front; that something came to be a claim that you were something that you actually weren't.

---

tenuous \ˈten-yə-wəs\ Having little substance or strength; flimsy, weak.

• It's a rather tenuous theory, and the evidence supporting it has been questioned by several researchers.

Something tenuous has been stretched thin and might break at any time. A person with a tenuous hold on his sanity should be watched carefully. If a business is only *tenuously* surviving, it will probably go bankrupt in the next recession. If there seems to be only a tenuous connection between two crimes, it means the investigators have more work to do.

attenuated \ə-ˈten-yə-ˌwā-təd\ Thinned or weakened.

• The smallpox shot is an injection of the virus in an attenuated form too weak to produce an actual case of smallpox.

A friendship can become attenuated if neither person bothers to keep in touch. Radio waves can become attenuated by the shape of the landscape, by foliage, by atmospheric conditions, and simply by distance. Factory workers and rock musicians often use noise-attenuating ear plugs to save their hearing. To *attenuate* something isn't to stop it, just to tone it down.

extenuating \ik-ˈsten-yə-ˌwā-tiŋ\ Partially excusing or justifying.

• A good college rarely accepts someone who has dropped out of high school twice, but in his case there were extenuating circumstances, including the death of both parents.

Extenuating is almost always used today before "circumstances." Extenuating circumstances are an important concept in the law. If you steal to feed your children, you're naturally less guilty than someone who steals just to get richer; if you kill someone in self-defense, that's obviously an extenuating circumstance that makes your act different from murder. Juries will usually consider extenuating circumstances (even when they're instructed not to), and most judges will listen carefully to an argument about extenuating circumstances as well. And they work outside of the courtroom as well; if you miss your daughter's performance in the middle-school pageant, she may forgive you if it was because you had to race Tigger to the vet's emergency room.

distended \di-ˈsten-dəd\ Stretched or bulging out in all directions; swelled.

• All the children's bellies were distended, undoubtedly because of inadequate nutrition or parasites.

Before giving you a shot, the nurse may wrap a rubber tube around your upper arm to *distend* the veins. When the heart isn't pumping properly, the skin of the feet and ankles may become distended. A doctor who notices that an internal organ has become distended will always want to find out the cause. As you can see, *distended* tends to be a medical term.

Quizzes

A. Fill in each blank with the correct letter:

a. attenuated
b. toxicity
c. extenuating
d. toxicology

e. distended
f. neurotoxin
g. tenuous
h. toxin

1. Guidebooks warn against the _____ of the water hemlock, the deadliest plant in North America.
2. The dog we used to have bit everyone, and only my mother ever tried to come up with _____ circumstances for his behavior.
3. We used to play with our cousins a lot in our childhood, but all those old friendships have become _____ over the years.
4. He was now yelling, his face red and his veins _____, and I feared he might have a heart attack.
5. Sarin, a manmade _____ 500 times more powerful than cyanide, was outlawed by treaty in 1993.
6. The university offers a graduate degree in environmental _____, which deals with chemical and biological threats to public health.
7. Everyone knows that the ceasefire is _____ and would collapse if one armed soldier decided to go on a rampage.
8. Ricin, a _____ that comes from the castor bean, can be lethal if an amount the size of a grain of sand is inhaled.

B. Match the definition on the left with the correct word on the right:

1. flimsy
2. nerve poison
3. study of poisons
4. bulging
5. plant-based poison
6. poisonousness
7. weakened
8. justifying

a. toxicity
b. distended
c. attenuated
d. extenuating
e. toxin
f. tenuous
g. neurotoxin
h. toxicology

TECHNI/TECHNO comes from the Greek *techne*, meaning "art, craft, skill," and shows up in dozens of English words. Some, such as *technical*, *technology*, and *technique*, have long been familiar. Others, such as *techno-thriller*, were only coined in the current computer age, which has also seen the new cut-down terms *techno* (for *techno-pop*, the electronic dance music) and *tech* (for *technician* or *technology*).

---

technocrat \\'tek-nə-ˌkrat\\ A scientist or technical expert with power in politics or industry.

• The new president, a great fan of science, had surrounded himself with an impressive team of technocrats.

In 1919 W. H. Smyth coined the term *technocracy* to mean basically "management of society by technical experts." Technocracy grew into a movement during the Great Depression of the 1930s, when politicians and financial institutions were being blamed for the economic disaster, and fans of technocracy claimed that letting technical experts manage the country would be a great improvement. (They also suggested that dollars could be replaced by "energy certificates" representing energy units called *ergs*.) Today *technocrat* and *technocratic* are still popular words for experts with a highly rational and scientific approach to public policy issues. But these experts aren't always the best politicians, and when a terrific technological solution to a problem is opposed by a powerful group or industry, lawmakers find it easier to just ignore it.

technophobe \\'tek-nə-ˌfōb\\ One who fears or dislikes advanced technology or complex devices and especially computers.

• The new employee was a middle-aged technophobe, who seemed startled every time a new page popped up on her computer screen.

The condition known as *technophobia* got its name around 1965 (though its synonym *Luddite* had been around for a long time), and since then we've been flooded with electronic gadgetry. But even today few people actually understand any electrical technology more complicated than a lightbulb, so there's still plenty of technophobia around. And it isn't limited to computer users. The explosion of the atomic bomb made technophobes out of millions of people; and since human-caused climate change has been a result of technology, it's not surprising that it too has produced a *technophobic* response.

But if technology turns out to be part of a solution, maybe that will change.

technophile \'tek-nə-ˌfīl\ One who loves technology.

* Back in my day, the high-school technophiles subscribed to *Popular Mechanics*, built ham radios, and were always taking apart the engines of their clunkers.

The word *technophile* came along soon after *technophobe*, which seemed to need an antonym. Its own synonyms include *geek*, *gearhead*, and *propeller-head* (for the characters in 1950s comic books who wore propeller beanies to indicate that they were sci-fi fans). Even before American inventors began amazing the world with their "Yankee ingenuity" in the 19th century, most Americans could be described as technology lovers. Today, American *technophilia* may be seen most vividly when a new version of a popular video game sells millions of copies to young buyers on the day of its release.

pyrotechnic \ˌpī-rə-'tek-nik\ Of or relating to fireworks.

* Her astonishing, pyrotechnic performance in the concerto left the audience dazed.

You've read about funeral *pyres*, and you may even have survived a *pyromaniac* ("insane fire-starting") stage in your youth, so you might have guessed that *pyr* means "fire" in Greek. *Pyrotechnic* refers literally to fireworks, but always seems to be used for something else—something just as exciting, explosive, dazzling, sparkling, or brilliant. The performances of sports stars and dancers are often described as pyrotechnic, and a critic may describe the *pyrotechnics* of a rock guitarist's licks or a film's camerawork. A pyrotechnic performance is always impressive, but the word occasionally suggests something more like "flashy" or "flamboyant."

LONG comes from Latin *longus*, which, as you might guess, means "long." The English word *long* shows up in many compound terms such as *long-suffering* ("patiently enduring lasting offense or hardship") and *long-winded* ("boringly long in speaking or writing"), but the *long-* root also sometimes shows up less obviously. To *prolong* something is to lengthen it, for example, and a *chaise longue* (not *lounge!*) is "a long reclining chair."

longitude \\\ˈlän-jə-ˌtüd\\ Distance measured by degrees or time east or west from the prime meridian.

- Checking the longitude, she was surprised to see that the tip of South America is actually east of New York City.

The imaginary (but very important) lines of longitude run from the North Pole to the South Pole. Each is identified by the number of degrees it lies east or west of the so-called prime meridian in Greenwich, England (part of London). A circle is divided into 360°; so, for example, the longitude of the Egyptian city of Cairo is about 31°E—that is, about 31° east of London. The "long" sense of the root may be easier to see in some uses of the adjective *longitudinal*: A longitudinal study is a research study that follows its subjects over many long years, and a longitudinal engine is one that drives a crankshaft that runs lengthwise under a vehicle (as in rear-wheel-drive cars) rather than crosswise.

elongate \\i-ˈlȯŋ-ˌgāt\\ (1) To extend the length of; stretch. (2) To grow in length.

- When mammals gained the ability to fly, it wasn't by means of feathered wings; instead, over thousands of years the digits of their "hands" elongated and a web formed between them.

Elongate is often found in scientific writing, but the adjective *elongated* is more common, and frequently used to describe body parts in discussions of anatomy. This was even the case when the superhero Elongated Man made his appearance back in 1960. But some other characters with the same powers—Plastic Man, Elastic Lad, and Mr. Fantastic—ended up having longer careers.

longueur \\lōn-ˈgər\\ A dull and boring portion, as of a book.

- She tells me the book is extremely rewarding, in spite of some longueurs during which she occasionally drops off to sleep.

Longueur comes straight from French, a language based on Latin. When we borrow a foreign word, it's usually because English doesn't have a really good synonym, which is the case here. *Longueur* is used mostly when talking about books, but also when describing lectures and speeches. Like certain other French words, *longueur* tends to be used mainly by critics and professors—but lots of us who aren't either could find plenty of use for it too.

oblong \ä-ˌblȯŋ\ Longer in one direction than in the other.

* Their apartment was awkwardly oblong, with a long skinny hall running past the cramped rooms.

Oblong is a general but useful term for describing the shape of things such as leaves. There's no such thing as an oblong circle, since a stretched circle has to be called an oval, and any rectangle that isn't square is oblong, at least if it's lying on its side (such rectangles can actually be called *oblongs*). Pills are generally oblong rather than round, to slide down the throat more easily. An oblong table will often fit a living space better than a square or round one with the same area. And people are always buried in oblong boxes.

Quizzes

A. Indicate whether the following pairs of words have the same or different meaning:

1. technophobe / computer genius   same ___ / different ___
2. longueur / boring passage   same ___ / different ___
3. pyrotechnic / spectacular   same ___ / different ___
4. oblong / unnatural   same ___ / different ___
5. technocrat / mechanic   same ___ / different ___
6. elongate / stretch   same ___ / different ___
7. longitude / lines parallel
   to the equator   same ___ / different ___
8. technophile / technology hater   same ___ / different ___

B. Fill in each blank with the correct letter:

a. technocrat   e. oblong
b. longitude   f. technophobe
c. technophile   g. longueur
d. elongate   h. pyrotechnic

1. By following a few basic tips, you can _____ your laptop battery's life by a month or more.
2. Even the Greeks knew how to calculate latitude from the sun and stars, but no one managed to measure _____ accurately until the 18th century.
3. All through high school and college, computer jocks like him were called nerds or geeks, but he always preferred to be described as a _____.

4. The talk was just one _____ after another, and she finally got up and tiptoed out of the lecture hall.
5. The shields used by Celtic warriors were _____ rather than round, and thus able to protect much of the body.
6. As governor, he had the reputation of being a _____, convinced that much of the state's problems could be solved by using proper technology and data.
7. The debate between these two remarkable minds was a _____ display of brilliant argument and slashing wit.
8. My father is making a real effort to master e-mail, but my mother is a genuine _____ who just wishes the computer would go away.

IDIO comes from the Greek *idios*, meaning "one's own" or "private." In Latin this root led to the word *idiota*, meaning "ignorant person"— that is, a person who doesn't take in knowledge from outside himself. And that led to a familiar English word that gets used too often, usually to describe people who aren't ignorant at all.

idiom \\'i-dē-əm\\ An expression that cannot be understood from the meanings of its separate words but must be learned as a whole.

• As a teacher of foreign students, you can't use idioms like "Beats me!" and "Don't jump the gun" in class unless you want to confuse everyone.

If you had never heard someone say "We're on the same page," would you have understood that they weren't talking about a book? And the first time someone said he'd "ride shotgun," did you wonder where the gun was? A modern English-speaker knows thousands of idioms, and uses many every day. Idioms can be completely ordinary ("first off," "the other day," "make a point of," "What's up?") or more colorful ("asleep at the wheel," "bite the bullet," "knuckle sandwich"). A particular type of idiom, called a *phrasal verb*, consists of a verb followed by an adverb or preposition (or sometimes both); in *make over*, *make out*, and *make up*, for instance, notice how the meanings have nothing to do with the usual meanings of *over*, *out*, and *up*.

idiomatic \\,i-dē-ə-'ma-tik\\ In a manner conforming to the particular forms of a language.

- The instructions for assembling the TV probably sounded fine in the original Chinese but weren't exactly written in idiomatic English.

The speech and writing of a native-born English-speaker may seem crude, uneducated, and illiterate, but will almost always be idiomatic—that is, a native speaker always sounds like a native speaker. For a language learner, speaking and writing *idiomatically* in another language is the greatest challenge. Even highly educated foreign learners—professors, scientists, doctors, etc.—rarely succeed in mastering the kind of idiomatic English spoken by an American 7th-grader.

idiosyncrasy \ˌi-dē-ə-ˈsiŋ-krə-sē\ An individual peculiarity of a person's behavior or thinking.

- Mr. Kempthorne, whose idiosyncrasies are well known to most of us, has recently begun walking around town talking to two ferrets he carries on his shoulders.

Idiosyncrasies are almost always regarded as harmless. So, for example, filling your house with guns and Nazi posters might be called something stronger than *idiosyncratic*. But if you always arrange your Gummi candies in table form by color and type, then eat them in a special order starting with the pterodactyls (purple ones must die first!), you might qualify. Harmless though your strange habits might be, they may not be the kind of thing you'd tell people about; most Americans are careful to hide their idiosyncrasies, since our culture doesn't seem to value odd behavior. The British, however, are generally fond of their eccentrics, and English villages seem to be filled with them. By the way, few words are harder to spell than *idiosyncrasy*—be careful.

idiopathic \ˌi-dē-ə-ˈpa-thik\ Arising spontaneously or from an obscure or unknown cause.

- After her doctor hemmed and hawed and finally described her condition as "idiopathic," she realized she needed a second opinion.

Words with the *-pathy* suffix generally name a disease or condition (see PATH, p. 210), so you might think *idiopathic* should describe a disease or condition that's unique to an individual. But the word is actually generally used to describe any medical condition that no one has yet figured out. Most facial tics are called idiopathic by doctors, since no cause can be found. Other well-known conditions, including chronic fatigue syndrome, irritable bowel syndrome, and fibromyalgia, still perplex the medical community. And even though doctors expect that the causes of all of them will eventually be found, and that those causes will turn out to be the same for hundreds of thousands of people, the conditions are still called idiopathic.

AER/AERO comes from the Greek word for "air." The *aerospace* industry manufactures vehicles that travel through the atmosphere and beyond into space. *Aerodynamic* designs move through the air with maximum speed. And *aerophobia* is the technical name for what we usually just call fear of flying.

---

aerial \\'er-ē-əl\\ (1) Performed in the air. (2) Performed using an airplane.

- They're doing an aerial survey of the whale population, which involves scanning the ocean's surface from an airplane.

Shakespeare himself may have coined this word, in *Othello*, and later he gave the name Ariel to the famous air-spirit character in *The Tempest*. An *aerialist* is an acrobat who performs high above the audience. In painting, *aerial perspective* is the way an artist creates the illusion that a mountain or city is far away (something that early painters only slowly learned how to do), usually by making it slightly misty and bluish gray—as if seen through miles of air. An *aerial work platform*, or "cherry picker," supports a worker at a high elevation on the end of a crane. And *aerial* itself can be used as a noun, meaning a TV antenna, a forward pass in football, or a high-flying stunt performed by a skateboarder or snowboarder.

aerate \\'er-ˌāt\\ To supply with air or oxygen.

- The garden soil was well aerated, since they had recently plowed in all the compost and manure and even added a box of earthworms.

Faucet *aerators* and aerating showerheads can be easily installed by homeowners to cut water (and especially hot water) use by as much as 50%. A lawn aerator removes little plugs of soil in order to let air deep into the soil, greatly improving the quality of soil that may have gotten too compacted. And a pond aerator, such as a fountain, is a necessity for an ornamental pond with no stream feeding it, since oxygen in the water is necessary to prevent the growth of algae and allow fish to live.

aerobic \,er-'ō-bik\ (1) Living or occurring only in the presence of oxygen. (2) Involving or increasing oxygen consumption.

• Trainers measure a person's aerobic capacity by means of the VO_2 max ("maximum volume of oxygen") test.

Aerobic exercise is exercise that takes an extended amount of time—usually ten minutes or more—but is usually performed at only moderate intensity. Running, swimming, bicycling, and cross-country skiing are classic aerobic exercises. In 1968 a best-selling book called *Aerobics* introduced a system of exercise for increasing the body's ability to take in and use oxygen, and today aerobics classes, often mimicking such outdoor exercise as running and bicycling, take place every afternoon in thousands of gyms and YMCAs across the country. Aerobic exercise particularly strengthens the heart and lungs, but usually has many other good effects as well. Aerobic bacteria, which need oxygen to live, are essential for breaking down living matter so that it returns to the soil. They include the famous intestinal *E. coli*, as well as the staph and strep bacteria that can make a visit to the hospital risky.

anaerobic \,a-nə-'rō-bik\ (1) Living or occurring in the absence of oxygen. (2) Relating to activity in which the body works temporarily with inadequate oxygen.

• He's never run a mile in his life, and everything he does at the gym is anaerobic.

In Greek, the prefix *a-* or *an-* means "not" or "without," and *bios* means "life." Anaerobic sports and exercise, such as gymnastics, weight lifting, and sprinting, are of high intensity but short duration, so they don't involve much oxygen intake. Anaerobic exercise triggers a different type of cell activity from aerobic exercise. As a result, it doesn't do much for your heart and lungs and it doesn't burn off fat; what it does do is build muscle. Anaerobic bacteria are bacteria that live without oxygen. They're responsible for several nasty conditions, including tetanus, gangrene, botulism, and food poisoning. They often live in deep wounds, so a bad dog bite—or, even worse, a human bite—can be dangerous, since the mouth is full of anaerobic bacteria. But most anaerobic bacteria are harmless, and many are essential to our lives.

Quizzes

A. Fill in each blank with the correct letter:

a. idiomatic   e. aerial
b. aerate   f. idiom
c. anaerobic   g. idiosyncrasy
d. idiopathic   h. aerobic

1. My Italian friend sometimes says "According to me" when the _____ way of saying it would be "In my opinion."
2. One famous _____ of the great pianist was playing his instrument while wearing fingerless gloves.
3. When she suspected that a patient was just imagining his symptoms, she'd tell him the illness was unusual and _____ and give him some harmless drug.
4. Since oxygen improves the taste of most red wines, wine lovers will usually _____ a newly opened bottle for a few minutes before drinking.
5. _____ photos of the earthquake's destruction showed dramatically how it had cut straight through the city.
6. Most of us say things like "tongue in cheek" or "pound the pavement" without even knowing what an _____ is.
7. She goes running four times a week, and on the other days she does _____ workouts at the gym.
8. The only _____ exercise he gets is biking, but he goes so slowly that it hardly even counts.

B. Indicate whether the following pairs of words have the same or different meanings:

1. idiosyncrasy / quirk   same ___ / different ___
2. aerobic / involving oxygen   same ___ / different ___
3. idiomatic / foreign   same ___ / different ___
4. aerate / supply with air   same ___ / different ___
5. idiom / stupidity   same ___ / different ___
6. aerial / performed in the air   same ___ / different ___
7. anaerobic / inflated   same ___ / different ___
8. idiopathic / of unknown cause   same ___ / different ___

CAD comes from the Latin verb *cadere*, "to fall." Thus, a *cascade* is usually a waterfall, but sometimes a flood of something else that seems to pour on top of you: a cascade of new problems, a cascade of honors, and so on.

cadaver \kə-ˈda-vər\ A dead body, especially one that is to be dissected; a corpse.

• The cadaver she was given to work on, from the Manhattan morgue, was that of an unclaimed homeless woman.

Since a corpse is a body that has "fallen down dead," the root *cad-* seems at home here. For most of us, *cadaver* has an impersonal sound, and indeed the word is often used for a body whose identity isn't important: most medical students probably don't spend much time wondering who they're dissecting. Someone with *cadaverous* features looks like a corpse before he or she is dead.

decadent \ˈde-kə-dənt\ Marked by decay or decline, especially in morals.

• The French empire may have been at its most decadent just before the French Revolution.

To be decadent is to be in the process of *decay*, so a powerful nation may be said to be in a decadent stage if its power is fading. But the word is more often used to speak of moral decay. Ever since the Roman empire, we've tended to link Rome's fall to the moral decay of its ruling class, who indulged in extreme luxuries and unwholesome pleasures while providing the public with cruel spectacles such as the slaughter of the gladiators. But not everyone agrees on what moral *decadence* looks like (or even how it might have hastened the fall of Rome), though most people think it involves too many sensual pleasures—as, for instance, among the French and English poets and artists of the 1880s and '90s called the Decadents. These days, for some reason, people have decided *decadent* is the way to describe rich chocolate cakes.

cadence \ˈkā-dᵊns\ (1) The close of a musical phrase, especially one that moves to a harmonic point of rest. (2) The rhythmic flow of sound in language.

- As the piano came to a cadence, the singer ascended to a beautiful high note, which she held for several seconds until the piano came in again in a new key.

Most of us hear the ending of a piece of music as a fall to a resting place, even if the melody ends on a high note. And that's the way endings were being heard way back in the 16th century, when *cadence* first began to be used in English for musical endings. Most cadences are harmonic "formulas" (standard harmonic patterns that we've all heard thousands of times) and we don't expect them to be original; so whether you're consciously aware of it or not, a *cadential* passage is usually quite recognizable. When *cadence* means "speech rhythm," its *cad-* root refers to the way the accents "fall."

cadenza \kə-ˈden-zə\ A virtuosic flourish or extended passage by a soloist, often improvised, that occurs shortly before the end of a piece or movement.

- Each of her arias was greeted with greater applause, but it was the brilliant improvised cadenza of her final number that brought down the house.

A concerto is a large piece for an instrumental soloist (usually playing piano or violin) and orchestra. Concertos are often extremely demanding for the soloist, but the most difficult part of all may be the cadenza, when the orchestra drops out completely, leaving the soloist to dazzle the audience with a set of flourishes, often completely original, right before a movement ends. Cadenzas are also heard in many vocal arias, especially those of the 18th century. The word, borrowed from Italian, originally meant "cadence"; thus, the cadenza, even if it lasts for a couple of minutes, is essentially a decoration of the final important harmonic cadence of the piece.

TRIB comes from the Latin *tribuere*, meaning "to give" or "to pay." So a group that *distributes* food passes it out to those in need, and when you *contribute* to the group you give your money or energy to it.

---

tribute \ˈtri-ˌbyüt\ (1) Something (such as a gift or speech) that is given or performed to show appreciation, respect, or affection. (2) Something that proves the good quality or effectiveness of something.

- Near the end of his speech, he paid tribute to the two pioneers in the field who were in the audience.

Tribute originally took the form of things given from a weaker group to the dominant power of a region—a bit like the "protection money" the Mafia gets from small businesses after making them offers they can't refuse, though the older form of tribute actually did buy the weaker group some protection from enemy forces. Tribute could come in the form of valuables, cattle, or even produce, and might include the loan of warriors to strengthen the ruler's army. But when we "pay tribute" today, it's generally in the form of praise. And when we say, for instance, that a successful school "is a tribute to" the vision of its founder, we mean that its success is itself a form of praise for the person who founded it. And a "tribute band" is a rock group intended to honor a great band of the past.

tributary \\'tri-byə-₁ter-ē\ A stream flowing into a larger stream or a lake.

- The entire expedition had perished of fever attempting to reach the source of one of the Amazon's great tributaries.

A tributary was originally a person or state that owed tribute to a more powerful person or state. Ancient China, for instance, had dozens of *tributary* states, and the emperor would receive elephants from Siam or young girls from Korea as tribute. Just as a smaller power gave some of its wealth to a larger power, a small river contributes its waters to a larger one. A tributary can be a tiny stream, but some are immense rivers. The Missouri River, for example, could be called a tributary to the Mississippi, even though it's about 2,500 miles long and receives hundreds of tributaries itself.

attribute \ə-'tri-₁byüt\ (1) To explain by indicating a cause. (2) To regard as likely to be a quality of a person or thing.

- He attributed his long life to a good sense of humor and a glass of wine with lunch and dinner every day.

Attribute means something rather similar to "pay tribute." So, for example, an award winner who pays tribute to an inspiring professor is, in a sense, attributing her success to the professor. Though if you attribute your fear of dogs to an incident in your childhood, you're not exactly praising the nasty dog that bit you way back when. The second sense of *attribute* is slightly different: If you attribute bad motives to a politician, it means you think he or she is doing things for the wrong reasons (even if you don't have any proof). When *attribute* is accented on its first syllable, it's being used as a noun, usually as a synonym for *quality*. So, for instance, you may believe that an even temper is an attribute of the best presidents, or that cheerfulness is your spouse's best attribute.

retribution \ˌre-trə-ˈbyü-shən\ Something given in payment for a wrong; punishment.

- The victims' families have been clamoring for retribution, sometimes even interrupting the trial proceedings.

With its prefix *re-*, meaning "back," *retribution* means literally "payback." And indeed we usually use it when talking about personal revenge, whether it's retribution for an insult in a high-school corridor or retribution for a guerrilla attack on a government building. But retribution isn't always so personal: God takes "divine retribution" on humans several times in the Old Testament, especially in the great Flood that wipes out almost the entire human race. And retribution for criminal acts, usually in the form of a prison sentence, is taken by the state, not the victims.

Quizzes

A. Indicate whether the following pairs have the same or different meanings:

1. cadence / musical ending — same ___ / different ___
2. attribute / donate — same ___ / different ___
3. decadent / morally declining — same ___ / different ___
4. tributary / small lake — same ___ / different ___
5. cadaver / bodily organ — same ___ / different ___
6. tribute / praise — same ___ / different ___
7. cadenza / side table — same ___ / different ___
8. retribution / revenge — same ___ / different ___

B. Fill in each blank with the correct letter:

a. tributary   e. attribute
b. retribution   f. cadaver
c. cadenza   g. decadent
d. cadence   h. tribute

1. The soloist's ____ was breathtaking, and the audience burst into applause as he played his final notes.
2. The insult had left her seething, and within minutes she had begun planning her terrible ____.
3. As ____ to his huge achievements, the university announced that it would be naming the new science building for him.
4. It was a major ____ to the Amazon, but until 1960 no one but the native Indians had ever attempted to reach its source.
5. Every time it seemed as if the piece was reaching its final ____, the harmony would shift and the music would continue.
6. Her roommate's family struck her as ____, with the younger generation spending its huge allowances on expensive and unhealthy pleasures.
7. In those days grave robbers would dig up a ____ at night after the burial and deliver it to the medical school.
8. He wants to ____ his success entirely to his own brains and energy, forgetting that not everyone is born with $30 million to play with.

Words from Mythology and History

halcyon \\'hal-sē-ən\\ (1) Calm and peaceful. (2) Happy and successful.

- She looks back fondly on those halcyon childhood days when she and her sisters seemed to inhabit a magical world where it was always summer.

For the Greeks, the halcyon was a bird (probably the kingfisher) that was believed to nest on the Mediterranean Sea around the beginning of winter, and had the power to quiet the rough December waters around Sicily for about two weeks—the "halcyon days." Thus the adjective *halcyon* came to mean calm and serene. Today people especially use it to describe a golden time in their past.

meander \\mē-'an-dər\\ (1) To follow a winding course. (2) To wander slowly without a specific purpose or direction.

- A little-used trail meanders through the mountains, crossed by cowpaths onto which hikers often stray and get lost.

Now and then, geography contributes an ordinary word to the language. The Greek word *maiandros* came from the Maiandros River (now the Menderes River) in western Turkey, which rises in the mountains and flows 240 miles into the Aegean Sea. Meandering is a natural tendency especially in slow-moving rivers on flat ground with fine-grained sand, and the Maiandros was well known for its many windings and wanderings. Roads and trails, like rivers, can be said to meander, but so can relaxed music, lazy writing, and idle thoughts.

oedipal \\'e-də-pəl\\ Relating to an intense emotional relationship with one's mother and conflict with one's father.

- Already on her first visit she sensed a tense oedipal situation, with her boyfriend and his father barely getting through dinner without coming to blows.

In Greek mythology, the king of Thebes, in response to a dreadful prophecy, abandoned his infant son Oedipus, who was then brought up by shepherds. Grown to manhood, Oedipus slew his father almost accidentally, not recognizing him, and then married his mother. When the shameful truth was discovered, the mother committed suicide and Oedipus blinded himself and went into exile. The psychiatrist Sigmund Freud invented the term *Oedipus complex* to mean a sexual desire that a child normally feels toward the parent of the opposite sex, along with jealous feelings toward the parent of the same sex. In Freud's theory (not accepted by everyone today), lingering oedipal feelings are an essential source of adult personality disorder, and can result in choosing a spouse who closely resembles your father or mother.

ostracize \\'äs-trə-ˌsīz\\ To exclude someone from a group by common consent.

- Back in the 1950s she had been ostracized by her fellow country-club members for her radical political beliefs.

In the ancient democracy of Athens, citizens were permitted to vote once a year to exile anyone who they thought might pose a problem to the city-state. The man with the most votes was banished for ten years, even if no one had ever made a single charge against him. Voting was done on *ostraka*—bits of broken pottery, the Greek equivalent of scrap paper—and the process was known as *ostrakizein*. Today the most common kind of *ostracism* is exclusion from a social group. It can be especially painful in school: no more sleepovers, no more party invitations, just lots of whispering behind your back.

paean \\'pē-ən\\ (1) A song of joy, praise, tribute, or triumph. (2) A work that praises or honors its subject.

• At his retirement party, the beloved president was treated to paeans from friends and employees to his years at the head of the company.

Originally in ancient Greece, a *paian* was a choral hymn to Apollo as the god of healing. More generally, it could be a hymn of thanksgiving, as when, in Homer's *Iliad*, the followers of Achilles sing a paean on the death of his enemy Hector. Paeans could be sung at banquets, at public funerals, to armies departing for battle and fleets leaving the harbor, and in celebrations of military victories.

philippic \\fə-'li-pik\\ A speech full of bitter condemnation; a tirade.

• Every few days he launches another philippic against teenagers: their ridiculous clothes, their abominable manners, their ghastly music.

In 351–350 B.C., the great Greek orator Demosthenes delivered a series of speeches against King Philip II of Macedon, the so-called *philippikoi logoi* ("speeches regarding Philip"). Three centuries later, in 44–43 B.C., the great Roman orator Cicero delivered a series of speeches against Mark Antony, which soon became known as the *philippica* or *orationes philippicae*, since they were modeled on Demosthenes' attacks. Splendid though both men's speeches were, Demosthenes was eventually exiled by the Macedonians, and Cicero was executed at Mark Antony's orders.

satyr \\'sā-tər\\ A man with a strong desire for many women.

• Still drinking and womanizing at the age of 70, he likes to think of himself as a satyr rather than an old goat.

Satyrs, the minor forest gods of Greek mythology, had the face, torso, and arms of a man, the ears and tail of a goat, and two goatlike legs. Fond of the pleasures associated with Dionysus (or Bacchus), the god of wine, they were full of playful and sometimes violent energies, and spent much of their time chasing the beautiful nature spirits known as nymphs. Satyrs show up over and over in ancient art. The Greek god Pan, with his reed pipes and mischievous delight in life, had the appearance and character of a satyr but greater powers. Notice how *satyr* is pronounced; it's quite different from *satire*.

zealot \\'ze-lət\\ A fanatical supporter.

• My girlfriend's father is a religious zealot, so I always find excuses not to have dinner at their house.

In the 1st century A.D., a fanatical sect arose in Judaea to oppose the Roman domination of Palestine. Known as the Zealots, they fought their most famous battle at the great fortress of Masada, where 1,000 defenders took their own lives just as the Romans were about to storm the fort. Over the years, *zealot* came to mean anyone who is passionately devoted to a cause. The adjective *zealous* may describe someone who's merely dedicated and energetic ("a zealous investigator," "zealous about combating inflation," etc.). But *zealot* (like its synonym *fanatic*) and *zealotry* (like its synonym *fanaticism*) are used disapprovingly—even while Jews everywhere still honor the memory of those who died at Masada.

Quiz

Fill in each blank with the correct letter:

a. paean   e. satyr
b. philippic   f. zealot
c. halcyon   g. oedipal
d. meander   h. ostracize

1. In those _____ summers, he and his cousins spent every day sailing and swimming in the blue Wisconsin lakes.
2. His most famous speech was a _____ on the Vietnam War delivered on the floor of the Senate in 1967.
3. At her 40th birthday party, her best friend delivered a glowing _____ that left her in tears.
4. Meeting him again after five years, she was dismayed to discover that he'd become a religious _____ who could talk about no other subject.

5. Though he hasn't been convicted of anything yet, it's obvious that the community is going to _____ him.

6. She describes her uncle as a _____, who behaves outrageously around every young woman he meets at a party.

7. The paths _____ through the lovely woods, curving back on themselves in long loops.

8. When psychologists refer to _____ behavior, they may think of a four-year-old boy competing with his father for his mother's attention.

Review Quizzes

A. Choose the closest definition:

1. cadaver   a. patient   b. skeleton   c. zombie   d. corpse

2. longueur   a. couch   b. distance   c. boring section   d. length

3. retribution   a. gift   b. revenge   c. response   d. duplication

4. pyrotechnic   a. dazzling   b. fire-starting   c. boiling   d. passionate

5. elongate   a. continue   b. smooth over   c. close off   d. lengthen

6. distended   a. overturned   b. expired   c. swollen   d. finished

7. tenuous   a. weak   b. sturdy   c. contained   d. stubborn

8. zealot   a. spokesman   b. leader   c. joker   d. fanatic

9. neurotoxin   a. brain wave   b. nerve poison   c. brain virus   d. antidepressant

10. aerate   a. fly   b. inflate   c. supply with oxygen   d. glide

B. Fill in each blank with the correct letter:

a. technophobe   f. idiom
b. idiopathic   g. anaerobic
c. cadence   h. extenuating
d. oedipal   i. decadent
e. technocrat   j. attenuated

1. The _____ virus should be incapable of actually causing disease.
2. A piece of music that doesn't end with a firm _____ leaves most audiences tense and unsatisfied.
3. When you use an _____ like "losing your edge" or "dressed to kill" in class, your foreign students are just going to be puzzled.
4. She does a lot of _____ muscle training, but just running for the bus will leave her panting.
5. Getting a _____ like him to start using a cell phone would be a major achievement.
6. The patient's account of her symptoms was so sketchy that for now her condition is just being called _____.
7. His fiancée looks just like his mother, and we joke with him that he's never gotten through his _____ period.
8. The mayor is a _____ who thinks all the city's problems can be fixed by technology and rational management.
9. The scene in the hip downtown nightclubs just seemed _____ and unhealthy to her.
10. If you're caught stealing a flat-screen TV, the fact that you can't afford to buy one doesn't count as an _____ circumstance.

C. Indicate whether the following pairs have the same or different meanings:

1. cadenza / solo section   same ___ / different ___
2. idiosyncrasy / oddity   same ___ / different ___
3. halcyon / delightful   same ___ / different ___
4. toxin / vitamin   same ___ / different ___
5. tribute / praise   same ___ / different ___
6. ostracize / shun   same ___ / different ___
7. meander / wind   same ___ / different ___
8. aerial / lively   same ___ / different ___
9. toxicity / poisonousness   same ___ / different ___
10. technophile / apparatus   same ___ / different ___

ANSWERS

UNIT 1

p. 4
A 1. c 2. c 3. a 4. b 5. c 6. a
   7. a 8. b
B 1. d 2. c 3. b 4. b 5. d 6. d
   7. d 8. a

p. 8
A 1. d 2. g 3. f 4. c 5. h 6. e
   7. b 8. a
B 1. e 2. a 3. f 4. d 5. c 6. h
   7. b 8. g

p. 12
A 1. S 2. D 3. D 4. D 5. D 6. S
   7. S 8. D
B 1. e 2. a 3. b 4. f 5. d 6. h
   7. g 8. c

p. 16
A 1. d 2. f 3. c 4. h 5. b 6. a
   7. e 8. g
B 1. f 2. a 3. g 4. b 5. c 6. h
   7. d 8. e

p. 19
1. d 2. b 3. a 4. c 5. b 6. d
   7. a 8. c

p. 20
A 1. e 2. d 3. k 4. b 5. h 6. l
   7. f 8. j 9. a 10. c 11. n 12. g
   13. m 14. i
B 1. d 2. a 3. c 4. c 5. b 6. b
   7. d 8. b 9. c 10. c 11. c 12. a

C 1. f 2. c 3. e 4. d 5. h 6. g
   7. j 8. a 9. b 10. i

UNIT 2

p. 26
A 1. d 2. a 3. e 4. f 5. b 6. c
   7. g 8. h
B 1. f 2. g 3. h 4. b 5. a 6. c
   7. e 8. d

p. 30
A 1. h 2. g 3. d 4. a 5. b 6. f
   7. e 8. c
B 1. f 2. d 3. b 4. g 5. h 6. c
   7. e 8. a

p. 34
A 1. d 2. c 3. d 4. d 5. d 6. c
   7. b 8. a
B 1. d 2. e 3. h 4. f 5. g 6. a
   7. c 8. b

p. 38
A 1. b 2. c 3. e 4. a 5. g 6. h
   7. d 8. f
B 1. h 2. d 3. a 4. f 5. e 6. b
   7. g 8. c

p. 42
1. a, c 2. d, b 3. b, a 4. c, b
   5. c, a 6. a, b 7. c, a 8. d, a

p. 42
A 1. b 2. b 3. b 4. d 5. d 6. c
   7. c 8. c 9. a 10. d

B 1. c 2. f 3. e 4. a 5. i 6. d 7. b
8. g 9. j 10. h
C 1. f 2. h 3. c 4. i 5. d 6. e 7. j
8. b 9. g 10. a

UNIT 3

p. 48
A 1. b 2. c 3. f 4. d 5. e 6. a
7. g 8. h
B 1. c 2. f 3. e 4. h 5. a 6. d
7. b 8. g

p. 53
A 1. b 2. d 3. b 4. b 5. d 6. c
7. b 8. a
B 1. D 2. D 3. S 4. D 5. D 6. S
7. D 8. D

p. 57
A 1. a 2. g 3. f 4. d 5. c 6. b 7.
h 8. e
B 1. D 2. S 3. S 4. D 5. S 6. D
7. S 8. S

p. 62
A 1. d 2. b 3. b 4. d 5. c 6. d
7. a 8. d
B 1. d 2. g 3. h 4. a 5. f 6. e
7. b 8. c

p. 65
1. c 2. b 3. a 4. c 5. a 6. a
7. b 8. d

p. 66
A 1. b 2. b 3. a 4. d 5. d 6. d
7. b 8. d
B 1. m 2. j 3. c 4. l 5. f 6. i 7. e
8. g 9. d 10. k 11. b 12. n 13. h
14. a 15. o
C 1. S 2. D 3. S 4. S 5. D 6. S
7. S 8. D 9. D 10. D 11. D
12. D 13. D 14. S 15. D

UNIT 4

p. 72
A 1. S 2. D 3. S 4. S 5. D 6. S
7. D 8. S
B 1. f 2. g 3. b 4. h 5. e 6. c
7. d 8. a

p. 76
A 1. h 2. b 3. a 4. c 5. g 6. e
7. f 8. d
B 1. a 2. c 3. h 4. g 5. f 6. b
7. e 8. d

p. 80
A 1. c 2. b 3. e 4. f 5. g 6. h
7. a 8. d
B 1. h 2. a 3. c 4. b 5. g 6. f
7. d 8. e

p. 84
A 1. c 2. b 3. b 4. c 5. d 6. b
7. a 8. a
B 1. b 2. d 3. c 4. a 5. d 6. d
7. a 8. d

p. 88
1. b 2. c 3. f 4. a 5. d 6. e 7. h
8. g

p. 89
A 1. b 2. b 3. d 4. d 5. b 6. a
7. c 8. b 9. b 10. c
B 1. D 2. D 3. S 4. S 5. S 6. D
7. S 8. D 9. S 10. S
C 1. b 2. d 3. d 4. a 5. a 6. c
7. c 8. b

UNIT 5

p. 94
A 1. a 2. c 3. c 4. b 5. d 6. c
7. b 8. d
B 1. D 2. D 3. S 4. S 5. S 6. D
7. S 8. D

p. 98
A 1. d 2. g 3. c 4. b 5. a 6. e
7. h 8. f

B 1. f 2. e 3. d 4. a 5. h 6. g
7. b 8. c

p. 102
A 1. c 2. b 3. d 4. c 5. d 6. b 7.
c 8. a
B 1. D 2. S 3. D 4. D 5. D 6. S
7. S 8. D

p. 106
A 1. a 2. g 3. c 4. e 5. f 6. d
7. h 8. b
B 1. c 2. e 3. f 4. g 5. a 6. h
7. b 8. d

p. 110
1. h 2. f 3. d 4. e 5. b 6. g 7. a
8. c

p. 110
A 1. d 2. b 3. c 4. b 5. c 6. d
7. b 8. a 9. a 10. d
B 1. g 2. i 3. a 4. o 5. b 6. n
7. m 8. k 9. c 10. c 11. f 12. d
13. h 14. j 15. l
C 1. S 2. S 3. S 4. S 5. D 6. D
7. D 8. S 9. D 10. D 11. D
12. D 13. S 14. D 15. D

UNIT 6

p. 116
A 1. D 2. D 3. S 4. D 5. D 6. S
7. D 8. D
B 1. g 2. b 3. c 4. a 5. e 6. f
7. d 8. h

p. 120
A 1. d 2. f 3. h 4. b 5. e 6. a
7. g 8. c
B 1. b 2. c 3. d 4. a 5. b 6. a
7. d 8. b

p. 124
A 1. S 2. D 3. S 4. S 5. S 6. D
7. D 8. S
B 1. b 2. e 3. c 4. h 5. g 6. a
7. f 8. d

p. 127
A 1. c 2. b 3. d 4. c 5. d 6. a
7. c 8. b
B 1. f 2. c 3. e 4. b 5. d 6. a
7. h 8. g

p. 131
1. c 2. c 3. b 4. a 5. a 6. b 7. c
8. a

p. 132
A 1. g 2. a 3. j 4. c 5. i 6. b
7. d 8. e 9. h 10. f
B 1. a 2. b 3. b 4. c 5. a 6. d
7. d 8. e 9. h 10. f
C 1. e 2. j 3. a 4. i 5. f 6. h 7. c
8. b 9. d 10. g

UNIT 7

p. 137
A 1. b 2. d 3. g 4. f 5. c 6. h
7. a 8. e
B 1. c 2. e 3. f 4. b 5. a 6. g
7. d 8. h

p. 141
A 1. c 2. a 3. a 4. b 5. a 6. a
7. d 8. b
B 1. D 2. D 3. D 4. S 5. D 6. S
7. D 8. D

p. 145
A 1. a 2. e 3. b 4. f 5. c 6. g
7. d 8. h
B 1. d 2. c 3. c 4. a 5. b 6. b
7. d 8. a

p. 150
A 1. S 2. D 3. D 4. D 5. D 6. S
7. D 8. D
B 1. c 2. f 3. d 4. a 5. e 6. g
7. h 8. b

p. 153
1. a 2. d 3. c 4. h 5. f 6. g 7. b
8. e

p. 154
A 1. d, a 2. d, b 3. a, b 4. b, c
 5. c, a 6. a, b 7. d, c 8. c, a 9. d,
 a 10. a, c 11. c, d 12. b, c
B 1. c 2. a 3. b 4. b 5. c 6. a
 7. c 8. a 9. d 10. a 11. b 12. b
 13. c 14. a 15. c
C 1. i 2. f 3. c 4. h 5. e 6. j 7. g
 8. a 9. b 10. d

UNIT 8

p. 161
A 1. d 2. b 3. d 4. a 5. c 6. d
 7. b 8. c
B 1. f 2. b 3. e 4. a 5. g 6. c
 7. h 8. d

p. 165
A 1. a 2. g 3. b 4. h 5. e 6. c
 7. d 8. f
B 1. D 2. S 3. D 4. S 5. S 6. D
 7. S 8. D

p. 169
A 1. d 2. a 3. c 4. f 5. g 6. b
 7. e 8. h
B 1. b 2. f 3. d 4. c 5. g 6. h
 7. a 8. e

p. 174
A 1. d 2. a 3. b 4. d 5. c 6. b
 7. d 8. b
B 1. e 2. d 3. g 4. h 5. c 6. f
 7. a 8. b

p. 178
1. g 2. f 3. e 4. d 5. a 6. h 7. b
8. c

p. 179
A 1. j 2. e 3. c 4. f 5. h 6. b
 7. a 8. d 9. g 10. i
B. 1. D 2. S 3. S 4. D 5. S 6. S
 7. D 8. S 9. S 10. D 11. D
 12. D 13. S 14. S 15. D 16. D
 17. D 18. S 19. D 20. S
C 1. h 2. g 3. i 4. b 5. a 6. f
 7. d 8. j 9. c 10. e

UNIT 9

p. 184
A 1. a 2. g 3. f 4. b 5. c 6. e
 7. h 8. d
B 1. a 2. b 3. c 4. d 5. d 6. b
 7. d 8. b

p. 188
A 1. b 2. b 3. b 4. a 5. b 6. b
 7. a 8. d
B 1. d 2. c 3. e 4. f 5. g 6. h
 7. a 8. b

p. 192
A 1. b 2. a 3. b 4. a 5. a 6. c
 7. b 8. c
B 1. S 2. D 3. S 4. D 5. S 6. D
 7. S 8. D

p. 196
A 1. h 2. c 3. g 4. d 5. e 6. b
 7. f 8. a
B 1. g 2. f 3. b 4. c 5. h 6. a
 7. e 8. d

p. 200
1. c 2. b 3. b 4. b 5. c 6. d 7. b
8. c

p. 200
A 1. a 2. d 3. c 4. b 5. a 6. d
 7. c 8. a 9. a 10. c
B 1. d 2. g 3. a 4. b 5. j 6. e
 7. c 8. i 9. h 10. f
C 1. a 2. h 3. i 4. b 5. e 6. d
 7. g 8. c 9. j 10. f

UNIT 10

p. 205
A 1. S 2. S 3. D 4. D 5. S 6. D
 7. D 8. D
B 1. d 2. c 3. d 4. b 5. a 6. b
 7. d 8. d

p. 209
A 1. c 2. c 3. d 4. c 5. b 6. a
 7. b 8. d

B 1. f 2. h 3. g 4. e 5. d 6. a
7. c 8. b

p. 213
A 1. a 2. g 3. c 4. f 5. b 6. h
7. e 8. d
B 1. c 2. a 3. d 4. c 5. b 6. c
7. a 8. b

p. 217
A 1. d 2. d 3. a 4. a 5. d 6. b
7. a 8. d
B 1. c 2. d 3. h 4. a 5. b 6. e
7. g 8. f

p. 221
1. e 2. b 3. d 4. c 5. g 6. f 7. a
8. h

p. 222
A 1. D 2. S 3. D 4. S 5. D 6. D
7. S 8. D 9. S 10. D 11. S 12. D
13. S 14. S 15. D 16. D 17. S
18. D 19. D 20. S
B 1. d 2. a 3. d 4. b 5. a 6. a
7. d 8. a 9. d 10. a
C 1. c 2. e 3. a 4. d 5. f 6. b
7. h 8. g

UNIT 11

p. 227
A 1. b 2. a 3. a 4. b 5. c 6. b
7. a 8. d
B 1. D 2. D 3. D 4. D 5. D
6. D 7. D 8. D

p. 231
A 1. a 2. g 3. b 4. h 5. e 6. c
7. d 8. f
B 1. c 2. d 3. b 4. c 5. a 6. a
7. b 8. d

p. 235
A 1. d 2. b 3. a 4. d 5. c 6. a
7. c 8. a
B 1. b 2. e 3. h 4. a 5. f 6. g
7. d 8. c

p. 238
A 1. a 2. d 3. e 4. b 5. h 6. c
7. f 8. g
B 1. S 2. D 3. S 4. S 5. D 6. S
7. D 8. D

p. 242
1. a 2. g 3. f 4. d 5. c 6. e 7. b
8. h

p. 243
A 1. d 2. a 3. c 4. d 5. d 6. b
7. d 8. d 9. a 10. b 11. c 12. c
13. a 14. c 15. d
B 1. D 2. D 3. D 4. S 5. D 6. S
7. S 8. S 9. D 10. S
C 1. f 2. b 3. e 4. g 5. i 6. j 7. l
8. h 9. a 10. d 11. k 12. c

UNIT 12

p. 248
A 1. f 2. c 3. g 4. d 5. e 6. a
7. b 8. h
B 1. f 2. h 3. g 4. c 5. b 6. e
7. a 8. d

p. 253
A 1. a 2. g 3. c 4. b 5. f 6. d
7. e 8. h
B 1. c 2. f 3. h 4. e 5. d 6. g
7. a 8. b

p. 258
A 1. b 2. b 3. c 4. b 5. c 6. d
7. a 8. d
B 1. a 2. f 3. d 4. b 5. g 6. c
7. h 8. e

p. 262
A 1. b 2. c 3. a 4. b 5. c 6. b
7. d 8. c
B 1. S 2. D 3. S 4. D 5. D 6. S
7. D 8. D

p. 266
1. a 2. f 3. b 4. g 5. e 6. h 7. d
8. c

p. 266
A 1. b 2. b 3. d 4. a 5. c 6. a
   7. d 8. a 9. d 10. c 11. b 12. d
   13. b 14. d 15. a 16. b
B 1. f 2. b 3. g 4. j 5. d 6. e 7. i
   8. a 9. h 10. c
C 1. h 2. j 3. g 4. a 5. i 6. c 7. d
   8. f 9. e 10. b

UNIT 13

p. 272
A 1. b 2. d 3. c 4. b 5. c 6. c
   7. b 8. a
B 1. g 2. h 3. b 4. f 5. a 6. e
   7. d 8. c

p. 276
A 1. c 2. b 3. f 4. g 5. a 6. h
   7. e 8. d
B 1. D 2. D 3. D 4. S 5. D 6. S
   7. S 8. S

p. 280
A 1. g 2. b 3. a 4. c 5. e 6. h
   7. d 8. f
B 1. e 2. f 3. a 4. c 5. b 6. g
   7. h 8. d

p. 284
A 1. e 2. a 3. b 4. g 5. c 6. h
   7. f 8. d
B 1. a 2. b 3. d 4. d 5. b 6. c
   7. a 8. b

p. 288
1. D 2. S 3. D 4. D 5. D 6. S
   7. D 8. S

p. 288
A 1. g 2. h 3. c 4. m 5. j 6. e
   7. k 8. i 9. a 10. b 11. n 12. f
   13. d 14. l 15. o
B 1. c 2. a 3. d 4. a 5. b 6. c
   7. d 8. a 9. d 10. b
C 1. c 2. b 3. d 4. d 5. a 6. c
   7. b 8. c 9. b 10. d

UNIT 14

p. 294
A 1. d 2. g 3. a 4. e 5. f 6. b
   7. h 8. c
B 1. g 2. a 3. d 4. c 5. h 6. f
   7. e 8. b

p. 299
A 1. S 2. D 3. S 4. D 5. D 6. D
   7. S 8. S
B 1. d 2. a 3. f 4. c 5. e 6. h
   7. g 8. b

p. 303
A 1. f 2. g 3. b 4. a 5. d 6. e
   7. h 8. c
B 1. c 2. b 3. h 4. g 5. d 6. f
   7. a 8. e

p. 307
A 1. a 2. a 3. c 4. c 5. d 6. c
   7. b 8. b
B 1. D 2. S 3. S 4. D 5. D 6. D
   7. D 8. S

p. 311
1. b 2. h 3. g 4. c 5. e 6. a 7. f
   8. d

p. 312
A 1. a 2. c 3. b 4. d 5. d 6. b
   7. b 8. d 9. c 10. b 11. a 12. d
B 1. a 2. b 3. h 4. i 5. d 6. e
   7. f 8. c 9. g 10. j
C 1. D 2. S 3. D 4. D 5. S 6. S
   7. S 8. S 9. S 10. S

UNIT 15

p. 317
A 1. b 2. d 3. d 4. b 5. b 6. a
   7. b 8. b
B 1. h 2. c 3. f 4. b 5. e 6. a
   7. d 8. g

p. 322
A 1. d 2. e 3. h 4. a 5. c 6. b
   7. f 8. g

B   1. d 2. g 3. f 4. e 5. a 6. h
    7. b 8. c

p. 326
A   1. S 2. D 3. S 4. S 5. S 6. S
    7. S 8. D
B   1. d 2. f 3. e 4. h 5. c 6. g
    7. a 8. b

p. 330
A   1. c 2. b 3. c 4. c 5. b 6. a
    7. c 8. b
B   1. c 2. e 3. f 4. g 5. h 6. d
    7. b 8. a

p. 334
1. h 2. e 3. a 4. d 5. f 6. g 7. b
8. c

p. 335
A   1. q 2. f 3. h 4. o 5. m 6. k
    7. d 8. n 9. r 10. l 11. p 12. c
    13. e 14. s 15. b 16. a 17. i 18. t
    19. g 20. j
B   1. d, c 2. b, c 3. b, d 4. b, a
    5. b, c 6. a, d 7. d, a 8. c, d
    9. c, a 10. b, a
C   1. a 2. b 3. a 4. b 5. c 6. a
    7. d 8. b 9. d 10. c

UNIT 16

p. 341
A   1. c 2. e 3. h 4. b 5. g 6. f
    7. d 8. a
B   1. e 2. d 3. f 4. b 5. h 6. g
    7. c 8. a

p. 345
A   1. b 2. a 3. d 4. b 5. b 6. c
    7. c 8. b
B   1. c 2. d 3. c 4. b 5. d 6. a
    7. c 8. a

p. 350
A   1. a 2. e 3. c 4. b 5. f 6. g
    7. h 8. d
B   1. f 2. c 3. e 4. h 5. d 6. g
    7. b 8. a

p. 354
A   1. b 2. d 3. c 4. a 5. b 6. c
    7. d 8. a
B   1. c 2. g 3. h 4. f 5. d 6. e
    7. b 8. a

p. 358
1. b 2. c 3. c 4. c 5. b 6. c 7. d
8. b

p. 359
A   1. j 2. g 3. i 4. d 5. o 6. a
    7. h 8. m 9. n 10. e 11. c 12. l
    13. k 14. b 15. f
B   1. c 2. c 3. b 4. c 5. b 6. b
    7. c 8. d 9. d 10. a
C   1. i 2. d 3. f 4. j 5. g 6. b 7. h
    8. a 9. e 10. c

UNIT 17

p. 364
A   1. a 2. g 3. f 4. e 5. b 6. c
    7. h 8. d
B   1. D 2. S 3. D 4. D 5. D 6. S
    7. D 8. S

p. 368
A   1. c 2. b 3. c 4. b 5. d 6. b
    7. a 8. c
B   1. c 2. d 3. f 4. e 5. g 6. h
    7. b 8. a

p. 372
A   1. f 2. c 3. b 4. h 5. d 6. a
    7. e 8. g
B   1. D 2. S 3. D 4. D 5. S 6. D
    7. D 8. S

p. 376
A   1. b 2. a 3. c 4. d 5. c 6. b
    7. d 8. a
B   1. c 2. e 3. f 4. a 5. d 6. g
    7. h 8. b

p. 379
1. f 2. g 3. e 4. b 5. a 6. c 7. h
8. d

p. 380
A 1. a, c 2. d, b 3. b, d 4. d, a
 5. c, a 6. d, b 7. b, c 8. b, c
 9. d, b 10. c, a
B 1. c 2. i 3. k 4. o 5. a 6. t 7. s
 8. l 9. n 10. j 11. f 12. g 13. b
 14. e 15. h 16. d 17. m 18. r
 19. p 20. q
C 1. g 2. i 3. d 4. a 5. c 6. f
 7. b 8. h 9. j 10. e

UNIT 18

p. 386
A 1. d 2. f 3. b 4. h 5. g 6. a
 7. e 8. c
B 1. d 2. e 3. a 4. g 5. h 6. f
 7. c 8. b

p. 391
A 1. a 2. c 3. b 4. a 5. c 6. a
 7. d 8. b
B 1. D 2. S 3. D 4. D 5. D 6. S
 7. D 8. D

p. 395
A 1. b 2. c 3. d 4. b 5. c 6. b
 7. d 8. a
B 1. h 2. b 3. f 4. g 5. c 6. e
 7. a 8. d

p. 399
A 1. S 2. D 3. S 4. D 5. D 6. S
 7. S 8. S
B 1. f 2. e 3. h 4. b 5. c 6. d
 7. a 8. g

p. 403
1. f 2. g 3. d 4. e 5. a 6. h 7. c
 8. b

p. 404
A 1. d 2. b 3. d 4. c 5. d 6. c
 7. b 8. c 9. c 10. a
B 1. k 2. d 3. i 4. f 5. l 6. e 7. o
 8. b 9. m 10. a 11. h 12. c 13. j
 14. g 15. n

C 1. c 2. a 3. d 4. c 5. c 6. a
 7. c 8. d 9. c 10. b 11. d 12. a
 13. a 14. d 15. b

UNIT 19

p. 410
A 1. f 2. g 3. c 4. d 5. e 6. b
 7. h 8. a
B 1. S 2. D 3. S 4. S 5. S 6. S
 7. D 8. D

p. 415
A 1. a 2. b 3. a 4. d 5. c 6. a
 7. b 8. d
B 1. a 2. b 3. c 4. b 5. c 6. d
 7. b 8. b

p. 419
A 1. d 2. f 3. b 4. a 5. g 6. h
 7. e 8. c
B 1. c 2. d 3. g 4. a 5. f 6. b
 7. h 8. e

p. 423
A 1. c 2. a 3. d 4. b 5. a 6. c
 7. d 8. b
B 1. S 2. D 3. D 4. D 5. S 6. D
 7. D 8. S

p. 428
1. d 2. e 3. h 4. g 5. c 6. b 7. a
 8. f

p. 428
A 1. a 2. a 3. d 4. c 5. d 6. d
 7. c 8. d 9. a 10. d
B 1. f 2. k 3. d 4. l 5. g 6. n 7. i
 8. m 9. b 10. j 11. h 12. c 13. o
 14. e 15. a
C 1. D 2. S 3. D 4. D 5. D 6. D
 7. S 8. S 9. D 10. S

UNIT 20

p. 435
A 1. d 2. f 3. b 4. a 5. e 6. c
 7. g 8. h

B 1. c 2. e 3. d 4. a 5. h 6. g
7. f 8. b

p. 439
A 1. b 2. c 3. c 4. b 5. d 6. a
7. b 8. c
B 1. h 2. g 3. c 4. e 5. f 6. d
7. a 8. b

p. 443
A 1. a 2. b 3. b 4. b 5. c 6. a
7. d 8. c
B 1. D 2. S 3. D 4. S 5. S 6. D
7. S 8. S

p. 447
A 1. e 2. f 3. g 4. a 5. b 6. c
7. d 8. h
B 1. h 2. g 3. f 4. e 5. d 6. c
7. b 8. a

p. 451
1. f 2. b 3. h 4. d 5. a 6. g 7. c
8. e

p. 452
A 1. b 2. d 3. c 4. d 5. d 6. c
7. c 8. d 9. a 10. d
B 1. b 2. b 3. c 4. a 5. c 6. c
7. a 8. d 9. b 10. c 11. c 12. b
13. b 14. d 15. d
C 1. k 2. l 3. g 4. o 5. m 6. h
7. d 8. a 9. j 10. e 11. i 12. f
13. n 14. b 15. c

UNIT 21

p. 459
A 1. d 2. h 3. g 4. f 5. e 6. c
7. b 8. a
B 1. f 2. g 3. a 4. e 5. h 6. b
7. c 8. d

p. 463
A 1. b 2. a 3. d 4. d 5. c 6. b
7. b 8. c
B 1. a 2. c 3. e 4. f 5. b 6. d
7. g 8. h

p. 468
A 1. h 2. b 3. a 4. g 5. f 6. e
7. c 8. d
B 1. d 2. e 3. c 4. f 5. h 6. a
7. b 8. g

p. 472
A 1. c 2. d 3. b 4. b 5. d 6. c
7. c 8. c
B 1. S 2. S 3. D 4. D 5. S 6. D
7. S 8. D

p. 476
1. f 2. c 3. b 4. a 5. e 6. h 7. d
8. g

p. 476
A 1. d 2. b 3. c 4. b 5. c 6. a
7. d 8. c 9. c 10. d
B 1. g 2. a 3. b 4. o 5. m 6. i
7. c 8. j 9. k 10. e 11. f 12. d
13. n 14. h 15. l
C 1. a 2. a 3. d 4. a 5. b 6. c
7. b 8. d 9. a 10. c 11. a 12. a
13. d 14. d 15. c

UNIT 22

p. 482
A 1. S 2. D 3. D 4. S 5. D 6. S
7. D 8. D
B 1. h 2. a 3. g 4. e 5. d 6. b
7. c 8. f

p. 487
A 1. d 2. c 3. c 4. d 5. a 6. b
7. b 8. d
B 1. D 2. S 3. S 4. S 5. D 6. D
7. S 8. D

p. 491
A 1. f 2. g 3. h 4. a 5. b 6. d
7. c 8. e
B 1. c 2. a 3. b 4. b 5. b 6. b
7. a 8. d

p. 495
A 1. c 2. c 3. b 4. d 5. d 6. b
7. c 8. c

B 1. D 2. D 3. S 4. S 5. S 6. S
7. S 8. S

p. 499
1. h 2. f 3. b 4. g 5. e 6. c 7. d
8. a

p. 499
A 1. a 2. c 3. d 4. d 5. d 6. d
7. b 8. b 9. c 10. a
B 1. h 2. i 3. j 4. g 5. f 6. e 7. o
8. n 9. m 10. l 11. k 12. a 13. b
14. c 15. d
C 1. d 2. a 3. b 4. b 5. b 6. c
7. b 8. c 9. c 10. b 11. c 12. b
13. c 14. c 15. d

UNIT 23

p. 505
A 1. d 2. f 3. g 4. c 5. e 6. a
7. b 8. h
B 1. d 2. e 3. f 4. a 5. h 6. c
7. b 8. g

p. 509
A 1. b 2. c 3. c 4. a 5. c 6. d
7. d 8. b
B 1. S 2. S 3. D 4. D 5. S 6. S
7. D 8. D

p. 513
A 1. f 2. g 3. h 4. b 5. c 6. e
7. a 8. d
B 1. f 2. e 3. g 4. h 5. a 6. d
7. c 8. b

p. 517
A 1. b 2. c 3. a 4. d 5. b 6. b
7. c 8. d
B 1. D 2. D 3. S 4. S 5. D 6. S
7. D 8. D

p. 521
1. f 2. b 3. h 4. c 5. e 6. g 7. a
8. d

p. 522
A 1. c 2. d 3. b 4. d 5. a 6. d
7. a 8. d

B 1. g 2. l 3. d 4. i 5. b 6. m
7. j 8. c 9. a 10. f 11. o 12. e
13. k 14. h 15. n
C 1. a 2. b 3. d 4. b 5. d 6. b
7. a 8. d 9. c 10. d 11. b 12. b
13. c 14. d 15. c

UNIT 24

p. 528
A 1. h 2. b 3. c 4. g 5. a 6. e
7. f 8. d
B 1. d 2. g 3. e 4. c 5. h 6. a
7. b 8. f

p. 532
A 1. d 2. b 3. a 4. a 5. c 6. d
7. c 8. d
B 1. D 2. D 3. S 4. D 5. D 6. S
7. S 8. D

p. 536
A 1. d 2. f 3. b 4. g 5. a 6. h
7. c 8. e
B 1. f 2. d 3. e 4. b 5. a 6. g
7. h 8. c

p. 540
A 1. b 2. c 3. d 4. a 5. b 6. c
7. c 8. b
B 1. S 2. D 3. D 4. D 5. S 6. D
7. D 8. D

p. 544
1. c 2. f 3. g 4. d 5. e 6. h 7. b
8. a

p. 545
A 1. d 2. d 3. c 4. d 5. c 6. b
7. b 8. a 9. b 10. a 11. b 12. c
13. c 14. a 15. c
B 1. m 2. k 3. o 4. c 5. a 6. f
7. h 8. n 9. e 10. b 11. i 12. d
13. j 14. g 15. l
C 1. g 2. h 3. e 4. f 5. c 6. a 7. i
8. b 9. j 10. d

UNIT 25

p. 551
A 1. d 2. h 3. g 4. a 5. c 6. e
7. b 8. f
B 1. c 2. b 3. d 4. a 5. a 6. d
7. b 8. c

p. 556
A 1. c 2. d 3. a 4. b 5. a 6. c
7. a 8. a
B 1. e 2. b 3. c 4. g 5. d 6. h
7. a 8. f

p. 560
A 1. f 2. g 3. c 4. d 5. a 6. h
7. b 8. e
B 1. b 2. a 3. d 4. h 5. e 6. f
7. g 8. c

p. 564
A 1. a 2. c 3. b 4. b 5. c 6. d
7. a 8. c
B 1. D 2. S 3. S 4. S 5. D 6. D
7. D 8. S

p. 568
1. h 2. f 3. g 4. b 5. c 6. a 7. d
8. e

p. 569
A 1. d 2. a 3. c 4. d 5. d 6. a
7. d 8. b 9. d 10. b
B 1. b 2. k 3. f 4. d 5. o 6. j
7. h 8. g 9. e 10. m 11. n 12. a
13. c 14. i 15. l
C 1. o 2. l 3. n 4. d 5. g 6. i 7. f
8. h 9. e 10. j 11. a 12. c 13. k
14. b 15. m

UNIT 26

p. 575
A 1. c 2. d 3. b 4. a 5. f 6. h
7. g 8. e
B 1. f 2. b 3. a 4. g 5. c 6. d
7. e 8. h

p. 580
A 1. c 2. d 3. b 4. g 5. f 6. e
7. h 8. a
B 1. f 2. c 3. e 4. a 5. d 6. b
7. h 8. g

p. 584
A 1. b 2. c 3. d 4. f 5. h 6. g
7. e 8. a
B 1. b 2. c 3. d 4. b 5. c 6. c
7. b 8. d

p. 588
A 1. h 2. g 3. c 4. d 5. e 6. f
7. a 8. b
B 1. h 2. g 3. a 4. c 5. d 6. f
7. b 8. e

p. 593
1. e 2. b 3. a 4. h 5. c 6. g 7. f
8. d

p. 594
A 1. c 2. d 3. a 4. h 5. i 6. j 7. f
8. g 9. e 10. b
B 1. h 2. j 3. i 4. e 5. f 6. g 7. a
8. b 9. d 10. c
C 1. D 2. S 3. D 4. S 5. S 6. D
7. S 8. D 9. D 10. D

UNIT 27

p. 600
A 1. D 2. D 3. S 4. D 5. S 6. D
7. S 8. D
B 1. g 2. d 3. a 4. c 5. f 6. h
7. e 8. b

p. 604
A 1. g 2. b 3. f 4. d 5. c 6. a
7. h 8. e
B 1. f 2. e 3. c 4. g 5. h 6. a
7. b 8. d

p. 608
A 1. b 2. e 3. f 4. h 5. g 6. d
7. a 8. c
B 1. S 2. D 3. D 4. D 5. D 6. S
7. S 8. D

p. 613
A 1. d 2. b 3. a 4. e 5. f 6. g
7. h 8. c
B 1. S 2. S 3. D 4. D 5. S 6. D
7. D 8. D

p. 617
1. d 2. a 3. e 4. b 5. f 6. g 7. h
8. c

p. 618
A 1. d 2. h 3. g 4. b 5. a 6. f
7. i 8. e 9. j 10. c
B 1. d 2. c 3. j 4. a 5. f 6. i 7. g
8. e 9. h 10. b
C 1. S 2. D 3. D 4. S 5. S 6. D
7. S 8. S 9. S 10. D

UNIT 28

p. 623
A 1. f 2. h 3. c 4. a 5. b 6. g
7. d 8. e
B 1. D 2. S 3. S 4. S 5. S 6. D
7. D 8. D

p. 628
A 1. S 2. S 3. D 4. D 5. S 6. D
7. S 8. S
B 1. b 2. c 3. d 4. e 5. h 6. a
7. f 8. g

p. 633
A 1. c 2. a 3. d 4. b 5. f 6. h
7. e 8. g
B 1. a 2. g 3. c 4. b 5. f 6. e
7. h 8. d

p. 637
A 1. c 2. a 3. h 4. g 5. b 6. e
7. f 8. d
B 1. S 2. S 3. S 4. D 5. D 6. D
7. S 8. D

p. 641
1. d 2. f 3. g 4. b 5. e 6. h 7. a
8. c

p. 642
A 1. d 2. i 3. a 4. b 5. f 6. g 7. j
8. h 9. c 10. e
B 1. j 2. c 3. g 4. f 5. a 6. h 7. i
8. d 9. b 10. e
C 1. D 2. D 3. S 4. S 5. S 6. D
7. S 8. S 9. S 10. S

UNIT 29

p. 648
A 1. b 2. e 3. f 4. d 5. h 6. a
7. g 8. c
B 1. D 2. S 3. D 4. S 5. S 6. S
7. S 8. S

p. 652
A 1. h 2. b 3. c 4. f 5. g 6. d
7. e 8. a
B 1. e 2. g 3. a 4. d 5. c 6. h
7. f 8. b

p. 657
A 1. d 2. a 3. c 4. e 5. f 6. b
7. g 8. h
B 1. b 2. f 3. c 4. g 5. h 6. a
7. e 8. d

p. 662
A 1. f 2. b 3. e 4. a 5. h 6. d
7. g 8. c
B 1. D 2. S 3. S 4. D 5. S 6. S
7. S 8. S

p. 666
1. e 2. g 3. b 4. a 5. h 6. f 7. d
8. c

p. 666
A 1. c 2. b 3. c 4. a 5. d 6. c
7. a 8. b 9. b 10. d
B 1. c 2. d 3. b 4. a 5. f 6. e 7. i
8. j 9. g 10. h
C 1. D 2. D 3. D 4. D 5. D 6. S
7. S 8. D 9. D 10. S

UNIT 30

p. 673
A 1. b 2. c 3. a 4. e 5. f 6. d
   7. g 8. h
B 1. f 2. g 3. h 4. b 5. e 6. a
   7. c 8. d

p. 677
A 1. D 2. S 3. S 4. D 5. D 6. S
   7. D 8. D
B 1. d 2. b 3. c 4. g 5. e 6. a
   7. h 8. f

p. 682
A 1. a 2. g 3. d 4. b 5. e 6. f
   7. c 8. h
B 1. S 2. S 3. D 4. S 5. D 6. S
   7. D 8. S

p. 686
A 1. S 2. D 3. S 4. D 5. D 6. S
   7. D 8. S
B 1. c 2. b 3. h 4. a 5. d 6. g
   7. f 8. e

p. 690
1. c 2. b 3. a 4. f 5. h 6. e 7. d
8. g

p. 691
A 1. d 2. c 3. b 4. a 5. d 6. c
   7. a 8. d 9. b 10. c
B 1. j 2. c 3. f 4. g 5. a 6. b
   7. d 8. e 9. i 10. h
C 1. S 2. S 3. S 4. D 5. S 6. S
   7. S 8. D 9. S 10. D

INDEX

AB/ABS, 293
aberrant, 125
abjure, 398
abnegation, 422
abscond, 293
absolution, 561
abstemious, 293
abstraction, 293
abstruse, 294
accede, 126
acclamation, 511
accord, 269
accretion, 537
acculturation, 256
ACER/ACR, 479
acerbic, 479
Achilles' heel, 150
acme, 496
acquisitive, 115
acrid, 479
acrimony, 480
acrophobic, 587
acropolis, 574
acupuncture, 515
adequacy, 113
adherent, 181
ad hoc, 62
ad hominem, 63
adjunct, 189
Adonis, 663
adumbrate, 245
advocate, 139
aegis, 565
aeolian harp, 175
AER/AERO, 680
aerate, 680
aerial, 680
aerobic, 681
aerodynamics, 390
affidavit, 75
affluence, 440
a fortiori, 107
aggravate, 14
aggregate, 437

agnostic, 274
agoraphobia, 587
alleviate, 14
alphanumeric, 577
alter ego, 63
AM, 3
amazon, 663
AMBI, 45
ambient, 45
ambiguous, 45
ambit, 46
ambivalent, 46
ambrosia, 518
amicable, 3
amorous, 3
amorphous, 323
amortize, 171
anachronism, 353
anaerobic, 681
Anglophile, 421
ANIM, 361
animated, 361
animosity, 362
ANN/ENN, 365
annuity, 365
annulment, 604
ANT/ANTI, 469
antagonist, 469
ANTE, 96
antebellum, 5
antecedent, 97
antechamber, 97
antedate, 97
anterior, 98
ANTHROP, 384
anthropoid, 385
anthropology, 385
anthropomorphic, 323
antigen, 469
antipathy, 470
antithesis, 470
antonym, 554
apathetic, 210

apiary, 285
Apollonian, 39
apologia, 541
a posteriori, 107
apotheosis, 249
append, 159
appendage, 160
appendectomy, 614
apprehend, 441
approbation, 10
appropriate, 486
a priori, 107
AQU, 215
aquaculture, 216
aquamarine, 208
aquanaut, 216
aqueduct, 216
aquifer, 217
aquiline, 263
arachnid, 197
arachnophobia, 588
arcadia, 151
aristocrat, 512
ARM, 605
armistice, 605
armada, 605
armory, 606
ART, 278
artful, 278
arthroscopic, 625
artifact, 279
artifice, 279
artisan, 279
ascendancy, 553
asinine, 263
aspect, 136
assimilate, 550
atheistic, 250
atrium, 541
atrophy, 172
attenuated, 671
attribute, 684
AUD, 121
audition, 121

auditor, 121
auditory, 121
Augean stable, 128
AUT/AUTO, 506
autism, 507
autocratic, 512
autoimmune, 507
automaton, 506
autonomy, 507
aver, 230
avert, 321
bacchanalian, 39
bariatric, 616
BELL, 5
bellicose, 5
belligerence, 6
BENE, 1
benediction, 1
benefactor, 1
beneficiary, 2
benevolence, 2
BI/BIN, 333
biennial, 333
bilateral, 612
binary, 333
BIO, 407
biodegradable, 408
bioluminescent, 238
bionic, 407
biopsy, 407
biosphere, 319
bipartisan, 333
bipartite, 190
bipolar, 334
bona fide, 108
bon vivant, 489
bovine, 263
British thermal
  unit, 52
bronchitis, 592
bureaucrat, 512
bursitis, 591
cacophony, 141
CAD, 683

cadaver, 683
cadence, 683
cadenza, 684
calligraphy, 277
calliope, 197
calypso, 85
canine, 264
CANT, 224
cantata, 224
cantilever, 15
cantor, 225
caper, 285
CAPIT, 383
capitalism, 383
capitulate, 384
carcinogenic, 410
cardiology, 205
CARN, 70
carnage, 71
carnal, 71
carnivorous, 69
carpe diem, 108
Cassandra, 151
CATA, 92
cataclysm, 92
catacomb, 93
catalyst, 93
catatonic, 94
catharsis, 496
caveat emptor, 108
CED, 126
cede, 126
CENT, 426
centenary, 426
centigrade, 426
centimeter, 427
CENTR/CENTER,
  339
centrifugal, 182
centurion, 427
CEPT, 27
cereal, 218
charisma, 565
chimera, 663
choreography, 277
CHRON, 352
chronic, 352
chronology, 353
cicerone, 17
CIRCU/CIRCUM,
  649
circuitous, 649
circumference, 649
circumscribe, 557
circumspect, 650
circumvent, 650
CIS, 283
CLAM/CLAIM,
  510
clamor, 510

CLUS, 493
CO, 658
coalesce, 658
codependency, 659
codex, 373
CODI/CODE, 373
codicil, 373
codify, 373
coeval, 366
cogeneration, 658
cognitive, 274
cohere, 181
cohesion, 659
collateral, 612
colloquial, 532
colloquium, 531
colossus, 496
commandeer, 526
commute, 413
compel, 194
complement, 117
comport, 158
comprehend, 442
compunction, 515
concede, 126
concise, 283
concord, 269
concurrent, 77
condescend, 553
conducive, 35
configuration, 363
confine, 29
confluence, 440
conform, 325
congregation, 437
conjecture, 32
conjunct, 190
conscientious, 187
conscription, 557
consequential, 37
constrict, 481
construe, 484
contemporary, 351
context, 502
contort, 488
CONTRA, 470
contraband, 470
contraindication,
  471
contrarian, 471
contravene, 471
converter, 320
convoluted, 234
CORD, 269
cordial, 270
cornucopia, 664
CORP, 369
corporal, 369
corporeal, 369
corpulent, 369

corpus delicti, 109
COSM, 185
cosmology, 185
cosmopolitan, 186
cosmos, 185
counterinsurgent,
  607
CRAC/CRAT, 512
CRE/CRET, 537
CRED, 73
credence, 73
credible, 73
credo, 74
credulity, 74
crescent, 537
CRIM, 9
criminology, 9
CRIT, 396
criterion, 396
critique, 396
Croesus, 129
cross-cultural, 256
CRYPT, 291
crypt, 291
cryptic, 292
cryptography, 292
CULP, 270
culpable, 270
CULT, 255
CUR, 142
curative, 142
curator, 142
CURR/CURS, 77
curriculum vitae,
  109
cursory, 77
cyclopean, 151
cynosure, 175
DE, 601
debase, 601
DEC, 424
decadent, 683
decalogue, 424
decapitate, 384
decathlon, 425
decibel, 425
decimate, 425
declaim, 511
decode, 374
deconstruction, 483
decriminalize, 9
deduction, 35
de facto, 63
defamation, 601
definitive, 29
deflect, 81
defunct, 412
degenerative, 601
degrade, 392
dehydrate, 563

dejection, 602
de jure, 398
delegation, 436
delphic, 39
deltoid, 622
DEM/DEMO, 259
demagogue, 260
demographic, 259
demotic, 260
dendroid, 623
deplete, 118
deportment, 158
DERM, 638
dermal, 638
dermatitis, 639
descant, 225
descendant, 553
desensitize, 147
detritus, 497
devolve, 233
DI/DUP, 331
dichotomy, 331
DICT, 272
diction, 273
dictum, 274
diffident, 75
diminutive, 652
dimorphic, 332
Dionysian, 40
dipsomaniac, 23
directive, 102
DIS, 60
disarming, 606
discordant, 270
discredit, 61
discursive, 77
disjunction, 190
dislodge, 61
disorient, 60
disparity, 586
dispiriting, 228
disrepute, 202
dissolution, 562
dissonant, 122
dissuade, 60
distemper, 445
distended, 672
divert, 320
divest, 246
DOC/DOCT, 327
docent, 327
doctrinaire, 328
doctrine, 327
dogma, 518
DOM, 342
domination, 343
domineering, 343
dominion, 342
draconian, 152
dragon's teeth, 129

dryad, 197
DUC/DUCT, 35
duplex, 332
duplicity, 332
DYNAM, 389
dynamic, 389
dynamo, 389
DYS, 104
dysfunctional, 412
dyslexia, 105
dyspeptic, 105
dysplasia, 106
dystopia, 104
dystrophy, 173
eccentric, 340
ectopic, 338
edict, 273
effigy, 363
effluent, 440
effusive, 539
ego, 566
egocentric, 340
egomaniac, 24
egregious, 438
elevation, 14
elongate, 676
elucidate, 168
Elysium, 664
emissary, 193
empathy, 210
enamored, 3
encomium, 542
encrypt, 291
encyclopedic, 296
endemic, 259
ENDO, 639
endocrine, 639
endodontic, 640
endogenous, 640
endorphin, 641
endoscope, 624
entropy, 297
enumerate, 577
envisage, 135
EPI, 46
epicenter, 340
epicure, 665
epidermis, 638
epilogue, 47
epiphyte, 47
epitaph, 47
epithet, 48
eponymous, 554
EQU, 113
equable, 113
equestrian, 286
equilateral, 612
equilibrium, 114
equinox, 114
equivalent, 535

equivocate, 138
ERR, 124
errant, 125
erratic, 125
erroneous, 126
ethnocentric, 341
ethos, 566
EU, 103
eugenic, 103
eulogy, 104
euphemism, 103
euphoria, 104
eureka, 519
eutrophication, 173
EV, 366
evolution, 234
ex post facto, 64
exacerbate, 480
excise, 283
exclusive, 494
excrescence, 538
exculpate, 271
exodus, 665
expatriate, 434
expel, 195
expropriate, 486
expurgate, 445
extemporaneous,
  352
extenuating, 672
extort, 488
EXTRA, 163
extradite, 163
extramural, 573
extraneous, 165
extrapolate, 164
extrasensory, 147
extrovert, 164
exurban, 254
FAC, 235
facile, 236
facilitate, 236
factor, 236
factotum, 236
FALL, 558
fallacious, 559
fallacy, 558
fallibility, 559
fauna, 198
feline, 264
FID, 74
fiduciary, 75
FIG, 362
figment, 363
figurative, 362
FIN, 29
finite, 30
FLECT, 81
flora, 198
FLU, 440

FORM, 324
formality, 325
format, 324
formative, 326
FORT, 281
forte, 282
fortification, 281
fortify, 281
fortitude, 282
FRACT, 416
fractal, 416
fractious, 416
FUG, 182
fugue, 183
FUNCT, 411
functionary, 411
FUS, 538
gastrectomy, 614
GEN, 409
generator, 409
genesis, 409
genre, 409
genuflect, 81
GEO, 315
geocentric, 316
geophysics, 316
geostationary, 316
geothermal, 317
geriatric, 616
GNI/GNO, 274
gorgon, 665
GRAD, 392
gradation, 392
gradient, 392
GRAPH, 277
GRAT, 508
gratify, 508
gratis, 519
gratuitous, 509
gratuity, 508
GRAV, 13
grave, 13
gravitas, 13
gravitate, 13
GREG, 437
habeas corpus, 474
Hades, 129
hagiography, 277
halcyon, 687
hector, 17
hedonism, 17
heliotrope, 298
HEM/HEMO, 589
hematocrit, 397
hematology, 590
HEMI/SEMI, 449
hemiplegia, 450
hemisphere, 319
hemoglobin, 591
hemophilia, 590

hemorrhage, 589
hepatitis, 592
HER, 181
herbivorous, 69
herculean, 198
hoi polloi, 497
HOL/HOLO, 346
holistic, 346
holocaust, 347
Holocene, 347
hologram, 347
HOM/HOMO, 58
homogeneous, 59
homogenize, 60
homologous, 59
homonym, 59
horticulture, 256
hubris, 567
humanoid, 623
HYDR, 562
hydraulic, 562
hydrodynamic, 390
hydroelectric, 563
hydroponics, 563
HYP/HYPO, 49
HYPER 457
hyperactive, 457
hyperbole, 457
hypercritical, 397
hyperkinetic, 387
hypertension, 457
hypertext, 503
hypertrophy, 172
hyperventilate, 458
hypochondriac, 49
hypoglycemia, 50
hypothermia, 50
hypothetical, 50
IATR, 615
iatrogenic, 616
ICON, 251
icon, 251
iconic, 251
iconoclast, 252
iconography, 252
id, 567
ideology, 204
IDIO, 678
idiom, 678
idiomatic, 678
idiopathic, 679
idiosyncrasy, 679
ignominious, 432
immure, 573
immutable, 413
impartial, 191
impediment, 79
impel, 195
impetus, 520
implacable, 505

impose, 304
impotent, 516
impunity, 212
impute, 203
in memoriam, 473
inanimate, 362
inaudible, 122
incantation, 224
incarnate, 71
incisive, 283
incognito, 275
incoherent, 182
incorporate, 370
increment, 538
incriminate, 10
inculpate, 271
indeterminate, 314
indoctrinate, 328
induce, 36
infallible, 559
infinitesimal, 30
inflection, 82
infraction, 416
infrastructure, 484
ingratiate, 509
inherent, 182
innovation, 302
inquisition, 114
inscription, 557
insectivorous, 70
insignia, 374
instrumental, 484
insuperable, 598
insurgency, 607
intemperate, 444
INTER, 653
intercede, 653
intercept, 28
interdict, 654
interject, 31
intermediary, 621
interminable, 315
interpolate, 654
interregnum, 393
interstice, 654
interurban, 255
intractable, 34
intramural, 572
intuition, 329
inundate, 527
investiture, 247
iridescent, 239
irrevocable, 138
ITIS, 591
JECT, 31
jovial, 40
JUNCT, 189
juncture, 189
Junoesque, 218
JUR, 397

jurisdiction, 273
jurisprudence, 397
juxtapose, 304
KILO, 578
kilobyte, 578
kilogram, 579
kilohertz, 579
kilometer, 578
KINE, 387
kinescope, 388
kinesiology, 387
kleptomania, 23
kudos, 497
laconic, 175
laparoscopy, 625
LATER, 611
lateral, 611
LEGA, 436
legacy, 436
legate, 436
leonine, 264
lethargic, 130
LEV, 14
levity, 15
libido, 567
LINGU, 225
lingua franca, 226
linguine, 227
linguistics, 225
lithograph, 278
LOG, 203
LONG, 675
longevity, 367
longitude, 676
longueur, 676
LOQU, 531
loquacious, 532
LUC, 168
lucid, 168
lucubration, 168
LUM, 237
lumen, 237
luminary, 238
luminous, 237
lupine, 286
lycanthropy, 386
magnanimous, 361
magnum opus, 473
MAL, 92
malevolent, 92
malfunction, 412
malicious, 92
malign, 93
malnourished, 92
MAND, 525
mandate, 525
mandatory, 525
MANIA, 23
MAR, 208
marina, 208

mariner, 208
maritime, 209
martial, 219
mastectomy, 615
maternity, 214
MATR/MATER,
  214
matriarch, 214
matrilineal, 215
matrix, 215
mausoleum, 240
mea culpa, 271
meander, 687
MEDI, 620
median, 620
mediate, 621
medieval, 367
mediocrity, 621
megalomaniac, 24
megalopolis, 575
mellifluous, 441
memento mori, 473
mentor, 240
mercurial, 41
META, 464
metadata, 464
metamorphosis, 323
metaphorical, 464
metaphysics, 465
meter, 119
methodology, 204
metonymy, 465
METR/METER,
  118
metric, 118
MICRO, 581
microbe, 581
microbiologist, 581
microbrew, 581
microclimate, 582
microcosm, 186
Midas touch, 130
MILL, 448
millefleur, 448
millenarianism, 448
millennium, 366
millipede, 449
millisecond, 449
MINI/MINU, 650
minimalism, 651
minuscule, 651
minutiae, 651
MIS, 193
misanthropic, 385
misnomer, 432
mission, 193
missionary, 193
mnemonic, 176
modus operandi, 64
modus vivendi, 65

MONO, 308
monoculture, 308
monogamous, 308
monolithic, 309
monotheism, 309
MOR/MORT, 170
moribund, 171
MORPH, 323
morphology, 324
mortality, 170
mortify, 171
MULTI, 582
multicellular, 582
multidisciplinary,
  583
multifarious, 583
multilateral, 583
multilingual, 226
MUR, 572
muralist, 572
muse, 239
MUT, 413
myrmidon, 152
NANO, 596
nanoparticle, 597
nanosecond, 597
nanostructure, 597
nanotechnology,
  596
narcissism, 240
NECRO, 644
necromancer, 644
necropolis, 645
necropsy, 645
necrosis, 644
NEG, 422
negligent, 422
negligible, 422
nemesis, 152
NEO, 299
neoclassic, 299
neoconservative,
  300
Neolithic, 300
neonatal, 301
nescience, 187
nestor, 18
neurosis, 542
neurotoxin, 671
NOM, 431
nomenclature, 431
nominal, 431
nonpareil, 586
non sequitur, 37
NOV, 301
novel, 302
novice, 301
NUL/NULL, 602
null, 602
nullify, 603

nullity, 603
NUMER, 576
numerology, 576
oblong, 677
occlusion, 493
odometer, 119
odyssey, 85
oedipal, 688
oenophile, 420
OID, 622
oligarchy, 541
Olympian, 41
OMNI, 344
omnibus, 344
omnipotent, 344
omniscient, 345
omnivore, 344
onus, 498
ONYM, 554
opprobrium, 543
opus, 520
ornithologist, 287
ORTHO, 99
orthodontics, 99
orthodox, 100
orthography, 100
orthopedics, 100
oscilloscope, 626
ostracize, 688
ovine, 286
PAC, 6
pace, 7
pacifist, 7
pacify, 6
pact, 7
paean, 689
PALEO, 646
paleography, 646
Paleolithic, 646
paleontology, 647
Paleozoic, 647
palladium, 86
PAN, 162
panacea, 162
pandemonium, 162
Pandora's box, 199
panoply, 163
pantheism, 162
pantheon, 250
PAR, 585
PARA, 461
paralegal, 462
paramedic, 462
paramilitary, 462
paramour, 4
paraphrase, 461
parity, 585
PART, 190
parterre, 206
participle, 191

partisan, 191
PATER/PATR, 433
paternalistic, 434
PATH, 210
pathos, 210
patriarchy, 433
patrician, 433
patronymic, 555
PED, 78
PED, 295
pedagogy, 292
pedant, 296
pedestrian, 79
pediatrician, 296
pedigree, 79
PEL, 194
PEN/PUN, 212
penal, 212
penance, 212
PEND, 159
pendant, 159
Penelope, 86
PENT, 400
pentameter, 401
Pentateuch, 400
pentathlon, 400
Pentecostal, 401
penumbra, 246
per se, 519
PER, 466
perceptible, 28
percolate, 466
perennial, 366
perfidy, 75
perimeter, 143
periodontal, 144
peripatetic, 144
peripheral, 145
perjury, 398
permeate, 467
permutation, 414
perquisite, 115
persevere, 467
perspective, 136
perturb, 232
pervade, 466
PHIL, 420
philanthropy, 421
philatelist, 420
philippic, 689
PHOB, 587
PHON, 139
phonetic, 140
phonics, 140
PHOT, 166
photoelectric, 166
photon, 167
photosynthesis, 167
photovoltaic, 166

physiology, 204
PLAC, 504
placate, 504
placebo, 504
placidity, 504
platonic, 176
PLE/PLEN, 117
plenary, 117
plenipotentiary, 516
plutocracy, 513
podiatrist, 617
POLIS/POLIT, 573
politic, 574
politicize, 574
POLY, 54
polyglot, 54
polygraph, 55
polymer, 55
polyp, 54
polyphonic, 140
POPUL, 260
populace, 261
populist, 261
populous, 261
porcine, 265
PORT, 157
portage, 157
portfolio, 157
POS, 304
POST, 82
posterior, 82
posthumous, 83
postmodern, 83
postmortem, 83
POT, 516
potentate, 517
potential, 516
PRE, 460
precedent, 127
precision, 284
preclude, 460
precocious, 460
precursor, 78
predispose, 460
predominant, 342
PREHEND/
  PREHENS, 441
prehensile, 441
prerequisite, 461
prescient, 187
prevalent, 535
PRIM, 56
primal, 56
primate, 56
primer, 56
primeval, 367
primordial, 57
PRO, 629
PRO, 631
proactive, 629

PROB, 10
probate, 11
probity, 11
pro bono, 630
proclaim, 511
procrustean, 86
procure, 143
pro forma, 630
profusion, 539
prognosis, 275
projection, 32
prologue, 632
Promethean, 219
promulgate, 632
PROP/PROPRI, 485
prophylaxis, 631
proponent, 630
proprietary, 485
propriety, 485
proscribe, 558
prospect, 136
prospectus, 137
PROT/PROTO, 95
protagonist, 95
protean, 87
protocol, 95
protoplasm, 96
prototype, 96
protracted, 34
protrude, 631
proverb, 548
pseudonym, 555
PSYCH, 25
psyche, 25
psychedelic, 25
psychosomatic, 26
psychotherapist, 26
psychotropic, 298
PUNC, 514
punctilious, 514
punctual, 515
punitive, 212
PURG, 445
purgative, 446
purgatory, 446
purge, 445
PUT, 202
putative, 203
pyrotechnic, 675
Pyrrhic victory, 130
QUADR/QUART,
  376
quadrant, 376
quadrille, 377
quadriplegic, 377
quadruped, 78
quartile, 377
quid pro quo, 64
quincentennial, 401
QUINT, 401

quintessential, 402
quintet, 402
quintile, 403
QUIS, 114
RE, 634
RE, 635
rebellion, 6
rebut, 636
recapitulate, 384
reception, 28
reciprocal, 635
recluse, 494
reconcile, 635
recrimination, 10
RECT, 101
rectify, 101
rectilinear, 101
rectitude, 101
redound, 527
redundancy, 528
referendum 543
reflective, 81
refraction, 417
refuge, 183
REG, 393
regalia, 394
regency, 394
regimen, 393
regress, 636
reincarnation, 72
reiterate, 634
rejuvenate, 634
relegate, 437
remand, 526
remorse, 634
renege, 423
repel, 195
replete, 118
reprehensible, 442
reprobate, 11
reputed, 202
requisition, 115
resolute, 562
resonance, 123
respirator, 228
restrictive, 481
resurgent, 608
retract, 33
retribution, 686
RETRO, 348
retroactive, 348
retrofit, 348
retrograde, 393
retrogress, 349
retrospective, 349
revert, 321
revivify, 490
revoke, 636
rhomboid, 622
rigor mortis, 474

sacrosanct, 530
SANCT, 529
sanctimonious, 530
sanction, 529
sanctuary, 530
sapphic, 177
satyr, 689
SCEND, 552
SCI, 186
SCOP, 624
SCRIB/SCRIP, 557
Scylla and
    Charybdis, 199
seclusion, 494
seduction, 36
segregate, 438
semicolon, 450
semiconductor, 450
semitone, 449
SENS, 146
sensor, 146
sensuous, 147
SEQU, 36
sequential, 36
serpentine, 287
SERV, 492
serviceable, 492
servile, 492
servitude, 492
sibyl, 87
SIGN, 374
signatory, 375
signet, 375
signify, 374
simian, 287
SIMIL/SIMUL, 549
simile, 550
simulacrum, 550
simulate, 551
sinecure, 143
sine qua non, 474
siren, 87
Sisyphean, 219
Socratic, 177
solecism, 177
soliloquy, 531
SOLU, 561
soluble, 561
SON, 122
sonic, 122
SOPH, 148
sophisticated, 148
sophistry, 148
sophomoric, 149
spartan, 18
SPECT, 135
SPHER, 318
spherical, 318
SPIR, 228
spirited, 228

stentorian, 18
stigma, 498
stoic, 19
STRAT, 609
stratification, 610
stratocumulus, 610
stratosphere, 319
stratum, 609
STRICT, 480
stricture, 480
STRU/STRUCT,
    483
stygian, 131
SUB, 455
subconscious, 445
subculture, 257
subjugate, 445
subliminal, 456
subpar, 586
subsequent, 37
subservient, 493
substrate, 610
subterfuge, 183
subterranean, 206
subtext, 503
subversion, 456
suffuse, 539
SUPER, 598
superannuated,
    365
superfluous, 598
superimpose, 305
superlative, 599
supernova, 302
supernumerary, 577
supersede, 599
SUR, 655
surcharge, 655
surfeit, 656
SURG, 607
surmount, 655
surreal, 656
susceptible, 28
suspend, 160
sybaritic, 19
symbiosis, 408
SYN, 660
synchronous, 353
syndrome, 661
synergy, 661
syntax, 660
synthesize, 660
tabula rasa, 475
tachometer, 119
tact, 370
tactile, 371
TANG/TACT, 370
tangential, 371
tangible, 371
tantalize, 241

taxidermist, 638
TECHNI/
    TECHNO, 674
technocrat, 674
technophile, 675
technophobe, 674
TELE, 417
telecommute, 418
telegenic, 417
telekinesis, 388
telemetry, 418
teleological, 418
telepathic, 210
TEMPER, 443
temper, 444
temperance, 444
TEMPOR, 351
temporal, 351
temporize, 352
TEN, 305
TEN/TENU, 671
tenable, 306
tenacious, 306
tendinitis, 592
tenet, 307
tenuous, 671
tenure, 306
TERM/TERMIN,
    314
terminal, 314
terminus, 315
TERR, 206
terra incognita, 475
terrarium, 207
terrestrial, 207
TETR, 378
tetracycline, 378
tetrahedron, 378
tetralogy, 379
tetrapod, 379
TEXT, 502
textual, 502
THE/THEO, 249
theocracy, 250
theosophy, 149
THERM/
    THERMO, 51
thermal, 51
thermodynamics, 51
thermonuclear, 52
thesis, 520
thespian, 241
titanic, 220
TOM, 614
tonsillectomy, 615
TOP, 338
topical, 338
topography, 339
TORT, 488
tortuous, 489

TOXI, 669
toxicity, 670
toxicology, 670
toxin, 669
TRACT, 33
traction, 33
trajectory, 32
TRANS, 626
transcend, 552
transcendent, 628
transfiguration, 627
transfusion, 539
transient, 626
translucent, 169
transmission, 194
transmute, 414
transpire, 229
transponder, 627
transpose, 305
transvestite, 247
trauma, 568
travesty, 248
TRI, 355
triad, 355
TRIB, 684
tributary, 684

tribute, 684
triceratops, 356
trident, 356
trilogy, 355
trimester, 356
trinity, 357
triptych, 357
Triton, 220
triumvirate, 533
trivial, 357
Trojan horse, 153
TROP, 296
TROPH, 172
tropism, 297
tuition, 329
TURB, 232
turbid, 232
turbine, 232
turbulent, 233
TUT/TUI, 329
tutelage, 330
tutorial, 329
ultimatum, 543
ultrasonic, 123
umber, 245
UMBR, 245

umbrage, 246
unconscionable, 188
UND, 526
undulant, 527
UNI, 309
unicameral, 309
unilateral, 310
unison, 310
unitarian, 311
upsurge, 607
URB, 254
urbane, 254
urbanization, 255
utopian, 339
VAL, 534
validate, 536
valor, 535
vasoconstrictor, 482
venereal, 41
VER, 229
veracity, 230
VERB, 548
verbatim, 549
verbiage, 549
verbose, 548
verify, 229

verisimilitude, 230
VERT, 320
VEST, 246
VIR, 533
virago, 534
virility, 533
virtuosity, 534
VIS, 134
vis-à-vis, 134
visionary, 135
vista, 134
VIV, 489
vivacious, 489
vivisection, 490
VOC, 138
vociferous, 139
VOLU/VOLV, 233
voluble, 233
VOR, 69
voracious, 70
vox populi, 262
vulcanize, 220
vulpine, 265
xenophobe, 588
zealot, 690
zephyr, 242